John Willis
Theatre World
1987–1988 SEASON

VOLUME 44

CROWN PUBLISHERS, INC.
201 EAST 50TH STREET
NEW YORK, NEW YORK 10022

**TO
BERNADETTE PETERS**

*the adorable, multi-talented actress
who deservedly has earned her recognition and admiration as one
of Broadway's greatest musical stars.*

CONTENTS

EDITOR: JOHN WILLIS
Assistant Editor: Walter Willison
Assistants: Herbert Hayward, Jr., Doug Holmes, Jerry Lacker, Tom Lynch,
Barry Monush, Stanley Reeves, Giovanni Romero, John Sala
Staff Photographers: Bert Andrews, Michael Riordan, Evan Romero, Michael Viade, Van Williams
Designer: Peggy Goddard

Photos opposite page (clockwise from top left): 1967, below: 1970, "Dames at Sea" (1968), "On the Town" (1971), "George M!" (1968), 1971, "Mack and Mabel" (1974), 1979, 1982, "Sunday in the Park with George" (1984), "Song and Dance" (1985), 1987, "Sally and Marsha" (1982), "La Strada" (1969). Photos by Friedman-Abeles, Gerry Goodstein, Martha Swope, Zodiac

Danielle Ferland, Ben Wright, Kim Crosby, Chip Zien, Bernadette Peters in "Into-the-Woods," winner of 1988 "Tonys" for Best Book of a Musical, Best Original Score, and Best Actress in a Musical (Joanna Gleason), and 1988 New York Drama Critics Circle citation, as well as Drama Desk Award for Best Musical (*Martha Swope Photo*)

REVIEW OF THE SEASON
Monday, June 1, 1987–Tuesday, May 31, 1988

Statistics from the League of American Theatres and Producers show an all-time record in boxoffice sales, with a 21% increase over last season. Attendance also showed an increase of 16%, and an increase in the number of playing weeks. There were 32 new productions: 12 musicals, 8 plays, 6 revivals (3 musicals and 3 plays), 5 special attractions, and 1 return (Jackie Mason). There were more musicals than in any of the 3 previous seasons. However, the number of Broadway productions equated the 1984–85 all-time low. There were 24 shows running at both the beginning and the ending of the season, but not all the same productions. The average admission price ($31.10) was up 4% and the top ticket price rose to $50 for some musicals. "The Phantom of the Opera" recorded the largest advance sale in Broadway history, topping last season's "Les Miserables." Current long-running Broadway productions are "A Chorus Line" (#1), "Oh! Calcutta!" (although #1 in number of performances, it is #2 in weeks played), "42nd Street" (#5), "Cats" (#11), and, from last season: "Fences," "Les Miserables," "Me and My Girl," and "Starlight Express". all musicals, except "Fences." Actually, the season was notable for its exceptionally good-quality straight plays and the increased number of new American plays, among them: "Burn This," "Joe Turner's Come and Gone," "M. Butterfly," "Speed-the-Plow," and "A Walk in the Woods." Revivals were "Anything Goes," "Cabaret," "Dreamgirls," "Broadway," "Macbeth," and "A Streetcar Named Desire." Special attractions included Michael Feinstein in Concert, Mort Sahl on Broadway, Rodney Dangerfield, "Oba Oba" (a Brazilian revue), Penn & Teller, and the return of Jackie Mason's "The World According to Me."

Now in its 42nd year, the American Theatre Wing Antoinette Perry Awards ("Tonys") honored "M. Butterfly" for Best Play, Best Featured Actor (B. D. Wong), and Best Direction of a Play. "The Phantom of the Opera" was voted Best Musical, Best Actor (Michael Crawford), Best Featured Actress (Judy Kaye), Best Direction of a Musical (Harold Prince's 16th Tony), Best Scenic Design, Best Costumes, and Best Lighting Design. "Into the Woods" was awarded Best Musical Book, Best Score, and Best Actress in a Musical (Joanna Gleason). Ron Silver was awarded Best Actor in a Play ("Speed-the-Plow"), and Joan Allen the Best Actress in a Play ("Burn This"). Best Featured Actress in a Play was L. Scott Caldwell in "Joe Turner's Come and Gone." "Anything Goes" was voted Best Revival, Best Featured Actor in a Musical (Bill McCutcheon), and Best Choreography. Special Tonys went to the Brooklyn Academy of Music (BAM), and to the South Coast Repertory Theatre in Costa Mesa, Ca. The presentations were televised on Sunday, June 5, 1988, with exemplary direction by Don Mischer for the second year, and with the gracious and elegantly beautiful Angela Lansbury as hostess. With fewer than usual lengthy, boring acceptance speeches, the proceedings were tastefully presented in the Minskoff Theatre; however, TV ratings for the occasion were the lowest on record. The New York Drama Critics Circle chose to honor August Wilson's "Joe Turner's Come and Gone" as Best American Play, Athol Fugard's "The Road to Mecca" as Best Foreign Play, and "Into the Woods" as Best Musical.

RANDOM NOTES during the season: On June 16, 1987, the marquees of all Broadway theatres were dimmed for one minute as a tribute to the deceased actress Geraldine Page, who had been appearing in "Blithe Spirit," and similarly, on Sept. 24th, theatres in Washington, DC, joined Broadway in a tribute to Bob Fosse, who died of a heart attack in Washington—a tremendous loss to the theatre.... Rocco Landesman, one of Broadway's youngest producers, became president of Jujamcyn Theatres, the smallest of the 3 Broadway theatre-owning groups, succeeding Richard G. Wolff.... Andrew Lloyd Webber threatened to cancel the Broadway production of "Phantom" if Actors Equity Association did not allow his wife, Sarah Brightman, to sing the leading female role. AEA contended that she was not an international star, but a compromise was reached.... Helen Hayes put her signature and footprints in concrete in front of the theatre named for her. The slab was immediately stolen, but was quickly replaced.... Broadway musicians accepted a new 3-year contract that allows producers to use synthesizers/replicators and curtails the practice of hiring non-working players in exchange for guaranteed minimums in the size of Broadway theatre orchestras for 6 years, and increases in pay and benefits. Only about ⅓ of their 16,000 membership is annually employed.... Andrew Lloyd Webber and Harold Prince announced the formation of a new company that will produce their future collaborations. Mr. Webber currently has 3 musicals playing on Broadway: "Cats," "Phantom," and "Starlight Express."... Tanya Berezin, a founding member of the prestigious Circle Repertory Theatre, was named its artistic director to succeed Marshall W. Mason who resigned.... The summer of 1987 experienced an increase in tourism.... TKTS (half-price tickets) booths in Duffy Square, Wall Street, and Brooklyn accounted for ¼th of the tickets sold. Musicals account for ¾ths of the boxoffice intake... . A new 4-year contract was signed, giving directors and choreographers of Off-Broadway shows more money and a greater share in profits from these productions.... A dispute over resources and space ended the 24-year partnership of Wynn Handman, who was a cofounder of the American Place Theatre, and associate director Julia Miles who created the Women's Project 9 years ago.... Producers Emanuel Azenberg, Robert Whitehead, and Roger Berlind have joined forces to create theatre that will be accessible and popular to the public. The Shubert Organization is donating the use of its Ethel Barrymore Theatre. Off-Broadway will benefit from this organization as will regional and university theatres.... The future of the 40-year-old 582-member Actors Studio under the artistic direction of Ellen Burstyn was in doubt because of debts, lack of funding, and angry dissidents among the group. Frank Corsaro became its new director.... The stock market's "Black Monday" (10/19/87) made "angels" for productions even more scarce than previously. Plays are a high-risk investment and Broadway's health is tenuous at best. Big musicals keep people from attending good non-musical productions. The rising cost of productions and dwindling investment capital has made Broadway riskier than usual for investors, and corporate gift-giving has declined. There seems to be an insufficient audience to sustain serious plays. There is a need for a larger arts subsidies for producing such worthy dramas.... Off-Broadway Theatres and Producers and AEA negotiated a 3-year contract that increases the earnings of actors and stage managers, and compensates original actors in productions that move to larger houses if they are not offered their roles in subsequent productions.... On 11/10/87 there was a ground-breaking ceremony at Lincoln Center for a 2-tower building that will have 10 floors for cultural groups, including the New York City Ballet and Juilliard students. The Lincoln Center Theater Co. has garnered a generous measure of success with its succession of hit productions. LaGuardia High School of Performing Arts at Lincoln Center, after 4 years in residence, finally opened its multimillion-dollar high-technology stage with Euripides' "Trojan Women".... Broadway's 1987 Christmas-to-New Year's boxoffice receipts broke its 1982 record.... AEA celebrated the first half of its 75th anniversary year.... Lincoln Center's Beaumont Theater began quarterly publication of a new magazine *(The New Theater Review),* coedited by Laura Jones and John Guare, the playwright.... On March 11, 1988, the New York Preservation Committee gave landmark status to several additional theatres, much to the opposition of their owners. Designated theatres now include the Ambassador, Brooks Atkins (formerly Richard Mansfield), Ethel Barrymore, Martin Beck, David Belasco, Biltmore, Booth, Broadhurst, Cort, Embassy, 46th Street, John Golden, Mark Hellinger, Hudson, Imperial, Lyceum, Neil Simon (formerly Alvin), Palace, and Virginia (formerly ANTA)....

BROADWAY PRODUCTIONS

(June 1, 1987 through May 31, 1988)

HAPPY BIRTHDAY, MR. ABBOTT!
or Night of 100 Years

A celebration benefitting The Actors' Fund of America; Produced by Barry Brown; Director, Fritz Holt; Scenery, John Falabella; Costumes, Theoni V. Aldredge; Lighting, Natasha Katz; Musical Direction, Donald Pippin; New Orchestrations, Chris Bankey, Michael Gibson, Jim Tyler; Sound, Peter Fitzgerald; Benefit Coordinator, Barbara Israel Associates; Musical Contractor, John Monaco; Costume Coordinator, Suzy Benzinger; Special Material, Mark Waldrop; Production Coordinator, James Pentecost; Musical Staging, Dennis Callahan; Associate Musical Director, Nicholas Archer; Stage Managers, Amy Pell, Peggy Peterson, Sondra Katz, Lauren Class Schneider, Allan Sobek, Janet Friedman, Michael Passaro, Mary Lawson; Wardrobe, Gayle Patton; Press, Shirley Herz/David Roggensack. Presented at the Palace Theatre for one night only on Monday, June 22, 1987.

CAST

Edie Adams, American Dance Machine, Elizabeth Ashley, Tom Bosley, Joan Caulfield, Carol Channing, Keene Curtis, Nanette Fabray, Jose Ferrer, Arlene Francis, Jack Gilford, Lillian Gish, Kitty Carlisle Hart, June Havoc, Helen Hayes, George S. Irving, Van Johnson, Larry Kert, Hal Linden, Jo Sullivan Loesser, Dorothy Loudon, Peter Marshall, Karen Morrow, Butterfly McQueen, Russell Nype, Janis Paige, Chita Rivera, Arthur Rubin, Donald Saddler, Maureen Stapleton, Elaine Stritch, Gwen Verdon, and the cast of "La Cage aux Folles"

MUSICAL NUMBERS

Overture, The Most Beautiful Girl in the World, Too Good for the Average Man, It's Love, There Once Was a Man, Sing Happy, Papa Won't You Dance with Me?, All My Laughter, You're Just in Love, Something to Dance About, Rodgers and Hart Medley, Little Old New York, Lonely Town, The Name's LaGuardia, My Darling My Darling, New Ashmolean Marching Society and Students Conservatory Band. Once in Love with Amy, Bewitched, Step to the Rear, Heart
   Performed with one intermission.

Martha Swope Photos

Right: George Abbott (left with cane)
and his wife to his left Above: Carol Channing (left), Betty
Comden, Adolph Green Top: Stars honoring Mr. Abbott

George Abbott (with cane) and entertainers
for finale

Nanette Fabray, Donald Saddler

Russell Nype, Elaine Stritch

BROADWAY

By Philip Dunning and George Abbott; Director, George Abbott; Sets, John Ezell; Costumes, Jeanne Button; Lighting, Martin Aronstein; Musical Staging, Donald Saddler; General Management, GRQ Productions/Gene Wolsk/Steven Suskin; Props, Jan Marasek; Wardrobe, Sydney Smith; Musical Supervisor, Zalmen Mlotek; Casting, Pat McCorkle; Assistant Producer, Dick Miller; Associate Manager, Brian Dunbar; Stage Managers, Michael R. Prevulsky, Richard Costabile; Presented by Frank Goodman; Press, Frank Goodman, Catherine L. Leone, Gregory Tarmin, Susan Bloch & Co./Ellen Zeisler, Ken Bloom. The Great Lakes Theater Festival production in celebration of the life, times and artistry of George Abbott on the occasion of his 100th birthday. Opened at the Royale Theatre on Thursday, June 25, 1987*

CAST

Nick Verdis	David Rogers
Pearl	Dorothy Stanley
Roy Lane	Lonny Price
Ruby	Janet Aldrich
Mazie Smith	Jennifer M. Thorsby
Ann	Karen Luschar
Grace	Donna English
Lil Rice	Maureen Sadusk
Katie	K. T. Sullivan
Joe, a waiter	Steve Routman
Billie Moore	Peggy Taphorn
Steve Crandall	Richard Poe
Dolph	Kurt Ziskie
"Porky" Thompson	Eugene J. Anthony
"Scar" Edwards	Hal Robinson
Dan McCorn	Joseph Culliton
Benny	Bruce Adler
Larry	David Ossian
Mike	Christopher Wells

UNDERSTUDIES: Karen Luschar (Ruby/Lil), David Ossian (Scar/Dan), Hal Robinson (Steve/Porky), Steve Routman (Dolph), K. T. Sullivan (Pearl/Mazie), Christopher Wells (Roy), Kurt Ziskie (Nick)

A melodrama in three acts. The action takes place backstage at the Paradise Night Club in New York City, on a spring evening in 1926.

*Closed June 27, 1987 after 4 performances and 3 previews.

Martha Swope Photos

Top: Peggy Taphorn, Lonny Price
(also top right)

David Rogers, Janet Aldrich, Kurt Ziskie,
Jennifer Thorsby, David Ossian

DREAMGIRLS

Book and Lyrics, Tom Eyen; Music, Henry Krieger; Sets, Robin Wagner; Costumes, Theoni V. Aldredge; Lighting, Tharon Musser; Sound, Otts Munderloh; Musical Supervision/Orchestrations, Harold Wheeler; Musical Coordinator, Yolanda Segovia; Musical Director, Marc Falcone; General Manager, Joey Parnes; Vocal Arrangements, Cleavant Derricks; Hairstylist, Ted Azar; Casting, Johnson-Liff; Production Supervisor, Bob Avian; Co-Choreographer, Michael Peters; Director-Choreographer, Michael Bennett; Presented by Marvin A. Krauss and Irving Siders; Company Manager, Allan Williams; Stage Managers, Peter B. Mumford, Thomas A. Bartlett, Robert B. Gould; Technical Coordinator, Arthur Siccardi; Props, Charles Zuckerman, Alan Steiner, Gregory Martin, Joe Schwarz; Wardrobe, Alyce Gilbert, Walter Douglas, Colleen Mazurek; Dance Captain, Brenda Braxton; Press, Fred Nathan, Marc P. Thibodeau, Anne Abrams, Dennis Crowley, Bert Fink, Merle Frimark, Rachel Abrams, Stephanie McCray, Norman Zagier. Opened at the Ambassador Theatre on Sunday, June 28, 1987.*

CAST

The Stepp Sisters	Susan Beaubian, Rhetta Hughes, R. LaChanze Sapp, Lorraine Velez
Charlene	Yvette Louise Cason
Joanne	Lynda McConnell
Marty	Roy L. Jones
Curtis Taylor, Jr.	Weyman Thompson
Deena Jones	Alisa Gyse
The M. C.	Vernon Spencer
Tiny Joe Dixon	Leonard Piggee
Lorrell Robinson	Arnetta Walker
C. C. White	Kevyn Morrow
Effie Melody White	Lillias White/Sharon Brown
Little Albert & the Tru-Tones	Bobby Daye, Robert Clater, Matthew Dickens, Germaine Edwards, Robert Fowler
James Thunder Early	Herbert L. Rawlings, Jr.
Edna Burke	Fuschia Walker
James Early Band	Robert Clater, Bobby Daye, Matthew Dickens, Germaine Edwards, Robert Fowler, David Thome
Wayne	Milton Craig Nealy
Dave & the Sweethearts	Stephen Bourneuf, Shirley Tripp, Lorraine Velez
Frank, a press agent	Tim Cassidy
Dwight, a tv director	David Thome
TV Stage Manager	Stephen Bourneuf
Michelle Morris	Susan Beaubian
Jerry, a nightclub owner	Leonard Piggee
Carl, a piano player	Robert Fowler
The Five Tuxedos	Robert Clater, Bobby Daye, Matthew Dickens, Germaine Edwards, Robert Fowler
Les Style	Yvette Louise Cason, Rhetta Hughes, Lynda McConnell, R. LaChanze Sapp
Film Executives	Matthew Dickens, Robert Fowler, David Thome
Mr. Morgan	Vernon Spencer
Security Guard	Leonard Piggee
Swings	Brenda Braxton, Graciela Simpson, Phillip Gilmore, Darryl Eric Tribble

MUSICAL NUMBERS: I'm Looking for Something, Goin' Downtown, Takin' the Long Way Home, Move, Fake Your Way to the Top, Cadillac Car, Steppin' to the Bad Side, Party Party, I Want You Baby, Family, Dreamgirls, Press Conference, Only the Beginning, Heavy, It's All Over, And I Am Telling You I'm Not Going, Love Love You Baby, I Am Changing, One More Picture Please, When I First Saw You, Got to Be Good Times, Ain't No Party, I Meant You No Harm, Quintette, The Rap, I Miss You Old Friend, One Night Only, I'm Somebody, Faith in Myself, Hard to Say Goodbye

A musical in 2 acts and 20 scenes. The action takes place in the early Sixties and the early Seventies.

*Closed Nov. 29, 1987 after 177 performances and 7 previews. For original production, see THEATRE WORLD Vol. 38. It opened Sunday, Dec. 20, 1981 and played 1521 performances.

Martha Swope Photos

Top Left: Sharon Brown, Alisa Gyse, Arnetia Walker

Susan Beaubian, Alisa Gyse, Sharon Brown, Arnetia Walker Above: Beaubian, Gyse, Walker

Jennie Ventriss
Top Left: Donal Donnelly,
Frank Langella
and below with Pat McNamara

Pat McNamara
Above: Langella, Melinda Mullins

SHERLOCK'S LAST CASE

By Charles Marowitz; Director, A. J. Antoon; Scenery, David Jenkins; Costumes, Robert Morgan; Lighting, Pat Collins; Music, Michael Ward; Hairstylist/Make-up, Steve Atha; Casting, Hughes/Moss; General Manager, Roy A. Somlyo; Presented by Alfie Productions, The Kennedy Center/ANTA, Ray Larsen, The Landmark Entertainment Group; Company Manager, Jodi Moss; Technical Supervisor, Theatrical Services; Props, Patrick Sullivan; Wardrobe, Elonzo Dann; Sound, Otts Munderloh, Barbara Schwartz; Stage Managers, Alan Hall, Ruth E. Rinklin, Betsy Nicholson; Press, Joshua Ellis, Adrian Bryan-Brown, Jackie Green, Leo Stern, Susanne Tighe. Opened in the Nederlander Theatre on Thursday, Aug. 20, 1987.*

CAST

Sherlock Holmes	Frank Langella
Doctor Watson	Donal Donnelly
Mrs. Hudson	Jennie Ventriss
Liza	Melinda Mullins
Inspector Lestrade	Pat McNamara
An Impostor	Morris Yablonsky
Damion	Daniel M. Sillmun

STANDBYS & UNDERSTUDIES: Graeme Malcolm (Sherlock), Jack Davidson (Watson Lestrade), Marcia Kash (Liza), Jeanette Landis (Mrs. Hudson), Mark Ashica (Damion/Impostor)

A mystery drama in 2 acts and 7 scenes. The action takes place in Victorian England in the Baker Street flat, and in a cellar.

Paul B. Goode/Joan Marcus Photos

Frank Langella, Donal Donnelly

ROZA

Book & Lyrics, Julian More; Music, Gilbert Becaud; Based on "La Vie Devant Soi" by Romain Gary; Director, Harold Prince; Musical Staging, Patricia Birch; Costumes, Florence Klotz; Scenery, Alexander Okun; Lighting, Ken Billington; Sound, Otts Munderloh; Musical Direction/Vocal and Dance Arrangements, Louis St. Louis; Orchestrations, Michael Gibson; Executive Producer, Ruth Mitchell; Production Consultant, Mervyn Nelson; Presented by The Producer Circle Co., Mary Lea Johnson, Martin Richards, Sam Crothers, and the Shubert Organization by arrangement with Les Editions Musicales et Artistiques; Associate Producer, Allen M. Shore; General Management, Gatchell & Neufeld; Company Manager, Michael Gill; Associate Conductor, Lawrence Yurman; Technical Supervisor, Theatre Services; Props, Nick Laudano, Robert Bostwick; Wardrobe, Max Hager; Hairstylist, Phyllis Della Illien; Press, Mary Bryant, David Musselman, James Jay Wilson. Opened in the Royale Theatre on Thursday, Oct. 1, 1987.*

CAST

Madame Roza	Georgia Brown
Max	Al DeCristo
Raoul	Ira Hawkins
Madame Bouffa	Michele Mais
Jasmine	Yamil Borges
Hamil	Neal Ben-Ari
Doctor Katz	Jerry Matz
Madame Katz	Marcia Lewis
Michel	David Shoichi Chan
Banania	Mandla Msomi
Salima	Monique Cintron
Young Momo	Max Loving
Lola	Bob Gunton
Young Moise	Stephen Rosenberg
Woman	Thuli Dumakude
Man	Richard Frisch
Moise	Joey McKneely
Momo	Alex Paez
Yussef Kadir	Neal Ben-Ari

STANDBYS & UNDERSTUDIES: Chevi Colton (Roza), Bob Frisch (Lola), Thuli Dumakude (Mme. Bouffa), Richard Frisch (Max/Katz/Hamil/Yussef), Francisco Paler-Large (Young Momo/Young Moise/Michel/Banania), Anny DeGange (Woman/Salima/Jasmine), Raymond del Barrio (Momo/Moise)

MUSICAL NUMBERS: Happiness, Max's Visit, Different, Is Me, Get the Lady Dressed, Hamil's Birthday, Bravo Bravo, Moon Like a Silver Window, Merci, House in Algiers, Yussef's Visit, Life Is Ahead of Me, Sweet 17, Lola's Ceremony, Don't Make Me Laugh, Live a Little, Finale.

A musical in 2 acts. The action takes place in a house in Belleville, an immigrant quarter of Paris, inhabited by many different ethnic groups, during 1970 (Act I) and 1974 (Act II).

*Closed Oct. 11, 1987 after 12 performances and 20 previews.

Jay Thompson/Martha Swope Photos

**Right: Yamil Borges, Alex Paez, Michelle Mais
Above: Mais, Neal Ben-Ari, Bob Gunton, Georgia
Brown, Marcia Lewis, Borges, Ira Hawkins
Top: Bob Gunton, Georgia Brown**

Max Loving, Ira Hawkins, Georgia Brown

Georgia Brown

MORT SAHL ON BROADWAY!

Presented by James L. Nederlander and Arthur Rubin; Executive Producer, Marvin A. Krauss; Lighting, Roger Morgan; General Manager, Peter H. Russell; Stage Manager, Jane Neufeld; Press, Jeffrey Richards, C. George Willard, Ben Morse, Irene Gandy, Susan Chicoine, Patt Dale, Naomi Grabel, Roger Lane, Jillana Devine. Opened in the Neil Simon Theatre on Sunday, October 11, 1987.*

A solo performance without intermission.

*Closed Nov. 1, 1987 after 25 performances and 5 previews.

Left: Mort Sahl

Irvin Arthur Photo

ITALY ON STAGE
October 5–29, 1987
Mark Hellinger Theatre

LA SERVA PADRONA (The Mistress Maid) by Giovanni Battista Pergolesi; Performed by Teatro di San Carlo; Libretto, Gennarantonio Federico; Director, Roberto De Simone; Conductor, Herbert Handt; Set/Costumes, Mauro Carosi; Assistant Conductor, Lucia Tramontano; Assistant Director, Ivo Guerra; Stage Manager, Gennaro Simonetti; Lighting, Pasquale Netti; Props, Aldo Cristini; Press, Hill & Knowlton/Maria Somma, John O'Keefe. CAST: Valeria Baiano (Serpina), Silvano Pagliucca (Uberto), Virgilio Villani (Uberto's Servant), Ugo Ranieri (Young Servant)

PULCINELLA by Manlio Santanelli; From an unpublished text by Roberto Rossellini; Director, Maurizio Scaparro; Performed by Teatro di Roma; Scenery, Roberto Francia; Costumes, Emanuele Luzzati; Original Music, Giancarlo Chiaramello; Masks, Giancarlo Santelli; Lighting, Gino Potini; Stage Manager, Amadeo Frati. CAST: Massimo Ranieri (Pulcinella), Beppe Tosco (Giuseppe), Vittorio Petito (Saverio), Orlando Forioso (Comic), Francesco De Rosa (Humpback), Massimo Tisci (Aniello), Salvatore Chiosi (Renzino), Tommaso Bianco (Andrea Calcese), Anna Walter (Calcese's Sister), Antonella Monetti (Angelica), Mauro Di Domenico (Guitar player), Domenico Maglionico (Flut player), Luigi Uzzo (Palmariello), Amalija Tomassini Barbarossa (Caterina), Aide Aste (Apollina Biancolelli), Giuliano Manetti (Michel Baron), Franco Javarone (Tiberio Fiorilli)

PODRECCA PUPPET THEATRE: The Toy Box, The Love of Three Oranges, World of the Moon, Variety/Classical and Modern

Above: Massimo Ranieri in "Pulcinella"

**Valeria Baiano, Silvano Pagluca
in "La Serva Padrona" (also above)**

BURN THIS

By Lanford Wilson; Director, Marshall W. Mason; The Circle Repertory Company/ Mark Taper Forum Production; Set, John Lee Beatty; Costumes, Laura Crow; Lighting, Dennis Parichy; Presented by James B. Freydberg, Stephen Graham, Susan Quint Gallin, Max Weitzenhoffer; Associate Producers, Maggie Lear, Harold Reed; Fight Direction, Randy Kovitz; Sound, Chuck London Media/Stewart Werner; Original Music, Peter Kater; General Management, Fremont Associates, James B. Freydberg, Dana Sherman; Stage Managers, Mary Michele Miner, Jody Boese; Technical Supervision, Theatrical Services; Wardrobe, Kathleen Gallagher; Hairstylist, Joan Weiss; Press, Shirley Herz, Peter Cromarty, Pete Sanders, Glenna Freedman, David Roggensack, Miller Wright, Sam Rudy. Opened in the Plymouth Theatre on Wednesday, October 14, 1987.*

CAST

Anna Mann .... Joan Allen[†1]
Burton .... Jonathan Hogan
Larry .... Lou Liberatore[†2]
Pale .... John Malkovich[†3]

UNDERSTUDIES: Cotter Smith, Paul Perri (Pale), Lisa Emery, Ann-Sara Matthews, (Anna), Randy Kovitz (Larry)

A play in 2 acts and 7 scenes. The action takes place at the present time in a loft of a converted cast-iron building in lower Manhattan of New York City.

*Closed Oct. 22, 1988 after 437 performances and 7 previews.
†Succeeded by: 1. Lisa Emery, 2. James Krag during vacation, Randy Kovitz, Lonny Price, 3. Eric Roberts, Scott Glen

Jay Thompson/Martha Swope Photos

Left: Jonathan Hogan, Lisa Emery
Top: Joan Allen, John Malkovich

Scott Glenn, Lonny Price, Lisa Emery
Above: Joan Allen, Lou Liberatore

Lisa Emery, Eric Roberts, Lou Liberatore,
Jonathan Hogan

Robert LuPone, and right
with Teresa Tracy

LATE NITE COMIC

Book, Allan Knee; Music & Lyrics, Brian Gari; Director, Philip Rose succeeded by Tony Stevens; Presented by Rory Rosegarten; Choreography, Dennis Dennehy; Scenery, Clarke Dunham; Lighting, Ken Billington; Costumes, Gail Cooper-Hecht; Musical Direction, Gregory J. Dlugos; Orchestrations, Larry Hochman; Vocal/ Dance Arrangements, James Raitt; Sound, Abe Jacob; General Management, Frank Scardino Associates; Stage Managers, Mortimer Halpern, Brian A. Kaufman, Lorna Littleway; Production Associate, Rita Mandel; Casting, Linda Watson; Dance Captain/Assistant Choreographer, Danielle P. Connell; Props, Reggie Carter; Wardrobe, Joel Vig; Hairstylist, Howard Leonard; Press, Henry Luhrman, Terry M. Lilly, Andrew P. Shearer, David J. Gerstan, Brian Drutman. Opened in the Ritz Theatre on Thursday, October 15, 1987.*

CAST

David Ackerman	Robert LuPone
Gabrielle	Teresa Tracy
Susan/Hooker/Ensemble	Pamela Blasetti
Ensemble/Club Owner/Hooker	Kim Freshwater
Ensemble/Jenny/Hooker	Lauren Goler
Cecil/Club Owner/Voice of God/Krazy Korn M.C.	Patrick Hamilton
Ensemble/Hooker	Judine Hawkins
Ensemble/Tanya/Delilah	Aja Major
Club Owner/Mike/Las Vegas M.C.	Michael McAssey
Ensemble/Hooker/Metropolitan Ballerina	Sharon Moore
Nat/Bartender/Alter Ego/Male Dancer	Mason Roberts
Ensemble/Clara/Hooker	Susan Santoro
Ensemble/Clubowner/Bartender/Busboy	Don Stitt

UNDERSTUDIES: Patrick Hamilton (David), Susan Santoro (Gabrielle), Swings: Danielle P. Connell, Barry Finkel
MUSICAL NUMBERS: Gabrielle, The Best in the Business, Clara's Dancing School, This Lady Isn't Right for Me, Having Someone, Stand-Up, Late Nite Comic, It Had to Happen Sometime, When I Am Movin', Think Big, Relax with Me Baby, Dance, It's Such a Different World, Yvonne

A musical in 2 acts and 21 scenes. The action takes place at the present time in New York and Las Vegas.

*Closed Oct. 17, 1987 after 4 performances and 16 previews. Cast album by Original Cast Records Co.

Martha Swope Photos

Robert LuPone and chorus members
(also above)

CABARET

Music, John Kander; Lyrics, Fred Ebb; Book, Joe Masteroff; Based on play by John Van Druten and stories by Christopher Isherwood; Director, Harold Prince; Dances/Cabaret numbers, Ron Field; Presented by Barry and Fran Weissler; Scenery, David Chapman; Costumes, Patricia Zipprodt; Lighting, Marc B. Weiss; Sound, Otts Munderloh; Based on original designs by Boris Aronson; Hairstylist, Phyllis Della Illien; Assistant Director, Ruth Mitchell; Assistant to Mr. Field, Bonnie Walker; Additional Orchestrations, Michael Gibson; Orchestrator, Don Walker; Musical Supervisor, Don Pippin; Musical Director, Donald Chan; Dance Arrangements, Ronald Melrose; Musical Coordinator, John Monaco; Associate Producer, Alecia Parker; In association with Phil Witt; General Manager, Kevmar Productions/Alecia Parker; Company Managers, Robert H. Wallner, Robert Nolan; Technical Supervisor, Theatrical Services/Artie Siccardi; Props, Andrew Acabbo, Kevin Connors; Wardrobe, Frank Green, John Rinaldi; Hair Supervisor, Richard Harper; Production Assistant, Robert V. Thurber; Stage Managers, Scott Faris, Robert Kellogg, Bonnie Walker; Dance Captain, Bonnie Walker; Press, Fred Nathan Co./Bert Fink, Anne Abrams, Merle Frimark, Philip Rinaldi, Marc Thibodeau, Rachel Abroms. Opened in the Imperial Theatre on Thursday, October 29, 1987 and moved to the Minskoff Theatre on Feb. 9, 1988.*

CAST

The M. C.	Joel Grey
Clifford Bradshaw	Gregg Edelman
Ernst Ludwig	David Staller
Customs Officer	David Vosburgh
Fraulein Schneider	Regina Resnik†1
Fraulein Kost	Nora Mae Lyng
Herr Schultz	Werner Klemperer
Telephone Girl	Ruth Gotschall
Sally Bowles	Alyson Reed†2
Girl Orchestra	Sheila Cooper, Barbara Merjan, Panchali Null, Eve Potfora
Two Ladies	Ruth Gottschall, Sharon Lawrence
Maitre D'	David Vosburgh
Max	Jon Vandertholen
Kissing Couple	Mark Dovey, Sharon Lawrence
German Sailors	Jim Wolfe, Mark Dovey, Gregory Schanuel
Kit Kat Girls	Laurie Crochet, Noreen Evans, Caitlin Larsen, Sharon Lawrence, Mary Rotella
First Waiter	Stan Chandler
Bobby	Michelan Sisti
Victor	Lars Rosager

ENSEMBLE: Stan Chandler, Laurie Crochet, Bill Derifield, Mark Dovey, Noreen Evans, Karen Fraction, Laura Franks, Ruth Gotschall, Caitlin Larsen, Sharon Lawrence, Mary Munger, Panchali Null, Steve Potfora, Lars Rosager, Mary Rotella, Gregory Schanuel, Michelan Sisti, Jon Vandertholen, David Vosburgh, Jim Wolfe
STANDBYS & UNDERSTUDIES: Michelan Sisti (M.C.), Mary Munger (Sally), Laurie Franks (Schneider), David Vosburgh (Schultz), Jon Vandertholen (Cliff/Ernst), Caitlin Larsen (Kost), Swings: Candy Cook, Aurelio Padron, Linda Goodrich
MUSICAL NUMBERS: Wilkommen, So What?, Don't Tell Mama, Telephone Song, Perfectly Marvelous, Two Ladies, It Couldn't Please Me More, Tomorrow Belongs to Me, Don't Go (not in original score), The Money Song, Married, Entr'acte, If You Could See Her, What Would You Do?, I Don't Care Much (not in original score), Cabaret, Finale

A musical in two acts.

*Closed June 4, 1988 after 262 performances and 19 previews. The original production opened Nov. 20, 1966 and played 1166 performances with Joel Grey.
†Succeeded by: 1. Peg Murray during Miss Resnik's illness, 2. Mary Munger

Joan Marcus/Bob Marshak Photos

Top Right: Laurie Crochet, Mary Rotella, Joel Grey, Eve Potfora (pianist), Ruth Gottschall, Caitlin Larsen Below: Regina Resnik, Werner Klemperer

Sharon Lawrence, Joel Grey, Ruth Gottschall Above: Gregg Edelman, Alyson Reed

DON'T GET GOD STARTED

Written by Ron Milner; Story and Idea Development, Barry Hankerson, Ron Milner; Music & Lyrics, Marvin Winans; Director, Ron Milner; Presented by Barry Hankerson & Jeffrey Day Sharp; Associate Producers, Reuben Cannon, Bernard Parker; Sound, Scott Marcellus; Assistant Conductor, Anthony Walker; Vocal/Musical Arranger, Ronald Winans; Additional Staging, Conni Marie Brazelton; Scenery, Llewellen Harrison; Lighting, Shirley Prendergast; Costumes, Victoria Shaffer; Artistic Consultant, Woodie King, Jr.; Casting, Reuben Cannon & Associates; General Manager, Marvin A. Krauss Assoc./Gary Gunas, Joey Parnes; Company Manager, Kathryn Frawley; Production Associate, Alan N. Lichtenstein; Wardrobe, Victoria Shaffer; Hairstylist, Michael Robinson; Stage Managers, Keeth Wallace, Louis Mellini; Press, Jeffrey Richards, C. George Willard, Ben Morse, Irene Gandy, Susan Chicoine, Norman Zaiger. Opened in the Longacre Theatre on Thursday, October 29, 1987.*

CAST

Female Lead Vocalist	Vanessa Bell Armstrong
Wise Old Man/The Reverend	Ernie Banks
Claudette/Sister Needlove	Conni Marie Brazelton
Wise Old Woman	Marilyn Coleman
Jack/Silk	Giancarlo Esposito
Sylvia/Barbara Ann	Chip Fields
Male Lead Vocalist	Be Be Winans
Robert/Lawrence/Buzz	Marvin Wright-Bey

CHOIR: Donald Albert, Margaret Bell, Susan Dawn Carson, Victor Trent Cook, Starletta DuPois, Patty Heaton, Keith Laws, Andrea McClurkin, Donnie McClurkin, Nadine Middlebrooks Norwood, Stefone Pet'tis, Sylvia Simmons, Monique Williams, Angie Winans, Debbie Winans, Ronald Wyche.
UNDERSTUDIES & STANDBYS: Margaret Bell (Female Vocalist), Starletta DuPois (Claudette/Sister Needlove/Wise Old Woman/Sylvia/Barbara Ann, Donald Albert (Male Vocalist/Robert/Lawrence/Buzz), Ronald Wyche (Jack/Silk, Wise Old Man/Reverend)
MUSICAL NUMBERS: Cry Loud, Slipping Away from You, After Looking for Love, Change Your Nature, What's Wrong with Our Love, Don't Turn Your Back, Turn Us Again, Abide with Me, Let the Healing Begin, Renew My Mind, Denied Stone, He'll Make It Alright, Can I Build My Home in You, Bring Back the Days of Yea and Nay, Always, Millions, Still in Love with You.

A musical in two acts.

*Closed Jan. 10, 1988 after 86 performances.

Louis Myrie/Level 5 Photos

**Right: Conni Marie Brazelton, Marvin Wright-Bey
Above: Ernie Banks, Conni Marie Brazelton
Top: Be Be Winans, Vanessa Bell**

Chip Fields, Marilyn Coleman

Marilyn Coleman, Ernie Banks

INTO THE WOODS

Music & Lyrics, Stephen Sondheim; Book, James Lapine; Director, James Lapine; Presented by Heidi Landesman, Rocco Landesman, Rick Steiner, M. Anthony Fisher, Frederic H. Mayerson, Jujamcyn Theaters; Associate Producers, Greg C. Mosher, Paula Fisher, David Brode, The Mutual Benefit Companies/Fifth Avenue Productions; Executive Producer, Michael David; Settings, Tony Straiges; Lighting, Richard Nelson; Costumes, Ann Hould-Ward; Magic Consultant, Charles Reynolds; Sound, Alan Stieb, James Brousseau; Hairstylist, Phyllis Della Illien; Costumes based on original concepts by Patricia Zipprodt & Ann Hould-Ward; Orchestrations, Jonathan Tunick; Musical Director, Paul Gemignani; Musical Staging, Lar Lubovitch; Casting, Joanna Merlin; General Management, David Strong Warner Inc./ Michael David, Edward Strong, Sherman Warner; Company Manager, Sandra Carlson; Production Supervisor, Peter Feller, Sr.; Props, Liam Herbert, Michael Fedigan; Wardrobe, Nancy Schaefer; Production Assistant, Chris Felder; Stage Managers, Frank Hartenstein, Johnna Murray, Marianne Cane, James Dawson; Press, Joshua Ellis, Adrian Bryan-Brown, Jackie Green, Leo Stern, Bill Shuttleworth, Susanne Tighe, David Fuhrer, Tim Ray. Opened in the Martin Beck Theatre on Thursday, November 5, 1987.*

CAST

Narrator	Tom Aldredge[1]
Cinderella	Kim Crosby
Jack	Ben Wright[2]
Baker	Chip Zien[3]
Baker's Wife	Joanna Gleason[4]
Cinderella's Stepmother	Joy Franz
Florinda	Kay McClelland[5]
Lucinda	Lauren Mitchell
Jack's Mother	Barbara Bryne
Little Red Ridinghood	Danielle Ferland[6]
Witch	Bernadette Peters[7]
Cinderella's Father	Edmund Lyndeck
Cinderella's Mother/Grandmother/Giant	Merle Louise
Mysterious Man	Tom Aldredge[8]
Wolf/Cinderella's Prince	Robert Westenberg
Rapunzel	Pamela Winslow[9]
Rapunzel's Prince	Chuck Wagner[10]
Steward	Philip Hoffman[11]
Snow White	Jean Kelly[12]
Sleeping Beauty	Maureen Davis

UNDERSTUDIES: Jeff Blumenkrantz/Michael Piontek (Jack/Rapunzel's Prince), Philip Hoffman (Baker/Cinderella's Father), Michael Piontek/Chuck Wagner (Cinderella's Prince/Wolf), Jeff Blumenkrantz (Steward), Lauren Mitchell/Kay McClelland (Baker's Wife), Carolyn Marlow (Stepmother/Jack's Mother/Cinderella's Mother/Grandmother/Giant), Suzzanne Douglas/Pamela Winslow (Cinderella), Pamela Winslow (Lucinda/Florinda), Maureen Davis/Jean Kelly/(Rapunzel/Red Ridinghood), Suzzanne Douglas/Joy Franz (Witch), Suzzanne Douglas (Sleeping Beauty), Maureen Davis (Snow White), Edmund Lyndeck (Narrator)

MUSICAL NUMBERS: Into the Woods, Hello Little Girl, I Guess This Is Goodbye, Maybe They're Magic, I Know Things Now, A Very Nice Prince, Giants in the Sky, Agony, It Takes Two, Stay with Me, On the Steps of the Palace, Ever After, So Happy, Lament, Any Moment, Moments in the Woods, Your Fault, Last Midnight, No More, No One Is Alone, Children Will Listen

A musical in two acts.

*Still playing May 31, 1988. Winner of "Tonys" for Best Book of a Musical, Original Score, Leading Actress in a Musical (Joanna Gleason).
†Succeeded by: 1. Dick Cavett during vacation, 2. Jeff Blumenkrantz during vacation, 3. Philip Hoffman during vacation, 4. Lauren Mitchell, Mary Gordon Murray, Cynthia Sikes, 5. Teresa Burrell, 6. Heather Shulman during vacation, LuAnn Ponce, 7. Betsy Joslyn, Phylicia Rashad, Betsy Joslyn, Mary Gordon Murray, Cynthia Sikes, Nancy Dussault, 8. Edmund Lyndeck during vacation, 9. Marin Mazzie, 10. Dean Butler, 11. Greg Zerkle during vacation, Adam Grupper, 12. Heather Shulman, Cindy Robinson

Lower Left: Lauren Mitchell, Kay McClelland, Edmund Lydeck, Joy Franz, Robert Westenberg, Kim Crosby, Merle Louise, Philip Hoffman **Above:** Barbara Bryne, Ben Wright **Top:** Chip Zien, Robert Westenberg, Joanna Gleason, Tom Aldredge, Bernadette Peters (front)

(clockwise from bottom left) Tom Aldredge, Bernadette Peters, Robert Westenberg, Joanna Gleason, Chip Zien

TEDDY & ALICE

Book, Jerome Alden; Music, John Philip Sousa; Lyrics, Hal Hackady; Adaptations and Original Music, Richard Kapp; Artistic Consultant, Alan Jay Lerner; Director, John Driver; Choreography, Donald Saddler; Additional Musical Staging, D. J. Giagni; Presented by Hinks Shimberg; Associate Producers, Glen Cross, Clarice Swan Fitzgerald, Wilmor Four in association with Jon Cutler; Scenery, Robin Wagner; Costumes, Theoni V. Aldredge; Lighting, Tharon Musser; Sound, Peter Fitzgerald; Hairstylist/Make-up, Robert Diniro, Alan Schubert; Casting, Myers/Teschner; Orchestrations, Jim Tyler; Vocal Arrangements/Music Supervisor, Donald Pippin; Dance Arrangements, Gordon Lowry Harrell; Musical Director, Larry Blank; General Management, Sylrich Management/Richard Seader; Company Manager, G. Warren McClane; Technical Supervisor, Theatrical Services; Props, Jan Marasak, Mark Colvin; Wardrobe, Mario Brera, Alice Testa; Assistant Musical Director, Jim May; Production Assistant, Cheryl Mintz; Stage Managers, Mary Porter Hall, Marc Schlackman, John C. McNamara; Press, Jeffrey Richards, C. George Willard, Ben Morse, Irene Gandy, Susan Chicoine, Jillana Devine, Naomi Grabel, Roger Lane, Carrie Kramer, Gary Kimble. Opened in the Minskoff Theatre on Thursday, November 12, 1987.*

CAST

James Amos	Tony Floyd
Belle Hagner	Karen Ziemba
J. P. Morgan/Admiral Murphy	David Green
Harriman/Samuel Gompers	John Witham
Henry Cabot Lodge	Raymond Thorne
Elihu Root	Gordon Stanley
William Howard Taft	Michael McCarty
Theodore "Teddy" Roosevelt	Len Cariou
Edith Roosevelt	Beth Fowler
Ted Roosevelt, Jr.	Robert D. Cavanaugh
Kermit Roosevelt	Seth Granger
Ethel Roosevelt	Sarah Reynolds
Archie Roosevelt	Richard H. Blake
Quentin Roosevelt	John Daman
Ida Tarbell	Mary Jay
Wheeler	John Remme
Officer O'Malley	Christopher Wells
Alice Roosevelt	Nancy Hume
Eleanor Roosevelt	Nancy Opel
Nick Longworth	Ron Raines
Franklin Roosevelt	Alex Kramarevsky
Elliott Roosevelt	Ken Hilliard
Ghost	Pamela McLernon

SERVANTS, REPORTERS, ETC.: Ellyn Arons, Ruth Bormann, Kathleen Gray, Ken Hilliard, Alex Kramarevsky, Mark Lazore, Keith Locke, Pamela McLernon, Elizabeth Mozer, Keith Savage, Jeff Shade
UNDERSTUDIES: Gordon Stanley (Teddy), Mary Jay (Edith), Karen Ziemba (Alice), Christopher Wells (Longworth), Tom Boyd (Morgan/Harriman/Lodge/Root/Taft/Murphy/Gompers), Ellyn Arons (Ida), Diana Stadlen (Ethel), Seth Granger (Ted, Jr.), Andrew Harrison Leeds (Kermit/Quentin/Archie), Kathleen Gray (Belle), Ruth Bormann (Eleanor), Travis Layne Wright (James Amos), Keith Locke (Wheeler/O'Malley), Swings: Kaylyn Dillehay, Travis Layne Wright
MUSICAL NUMBERS: The Thunderer, This House, But Not Right Now, She's Got to Go, The Fourth of July, Charge, Battlelines, The Coming-Out Party Dance, Leg O' Mutton, Not Love, Her Father's Daughter, Perfect for Each Other, He's Got to Go, Wave the Flag, Nothing to Lose, Election Eve, Can I Let Her Go?, Private Thoughts

A musical in 2 acts and 15 scenes.

*Closed Jan. 17, 1988 after 77 performances and 11 previews.

Peter Cunningham Photos

Top Left: Beth Fowler, Len Cariou
Below: Len Cariou with Sarah Reynolds, Richard
H. Blake, Seth Granger, Robert Cavanaugh, John Daman

Nancy Hume, Ron Raines
Above: Len Cariou (with flag)

Derek Jacobi, Rachel Gurney, Jenny Agutter,
Above: Robert Sean Leonard, Rachel Gurney,
Derek Jacobi Top Right: Jacobi with Michael Gough

BREAKING THE CODE

By Hugh Whitemore; Based on the book "Alan Turing, The Enigma" by Andrew Hodges; Director, Clifford Williams; Presented by Jerome Minskoff, Duncan C. Weldon, James M. Nederlander, The Kennedy Center/A.N.T.A., by arrangement with Triumph Theatre Productions and Michael Redington; Scenery and Costumes, Liz da Costa; Lighting, Natasha Katz; Casting, Julie Hughes/Barry Moss; General Management, Joseph Harris Associates/Steven E. Goldstein, Peter T. Kulok; Company Manager, Steven H. David; Technical Supervisor, Jeremiah J. Harris Associates; Props, Joseph Harris, Jr., Clyde Churchill; Wardrobe, James Michael Kabel; Hairstylist, Howard Leonard; Management Associate, Gerri Higgins; Stage Managers, Susie Cordon, Laura deBuys, Mary-Susan Gregson; Press, Fred Nathan Co./ Merle Frimark, Anne Abrams, Bert Fink, Philip Rinaldi, Marc Thibodeau. Opened in the Neil Simon Theatre on Sunday, November 15, 1987.*

CAST

Mick Ross	Colm Meaney
Alan Turing	Derek Jacobi
Christopher Morcom	Robert Sean Leonard
Sara Turing	Rachel Gurney
Ron Miller	Michael Dolan
John Smith	Richard Clarke
Dillwyn Knox	Michael Gough
Pat Green	Jenny Agutter
Nikos	Andreas Manolikakis

UNDERSTUDIES: David Silber (Alan Turing), Richard Neilson (Mick/John/ Dillwyn), Lucy Martin (Sara/Pat), Michael David Morrison (Christopher/Ron/ Nikos)

A drama in two acts. The action takes place in England from 1929–1954.

*Closed April 9, 1988 after 169 performances and 9 previews.

Joan Marcus Photos

Jenny Agutter, Derek Jacobi
Above: Derek Jacobi, Michael Dolan

SALLY
(in concert)

Music, Jerome Kern; Book & Lyrics, Guy Bolton, Clifford Grey; Ballet Music, Victor Herbert; Direction and Choreography, James Brennan; Musical Direction, Jack Lee; Presented by The New Amsterdam Theatre Company (Bill Tynes, Founding Director); Setting, Roger LaVoie; Lighting, Peter M. Ehrhardt; Sound, Tom Morse; Animals trained by William Berloni; Executive Director, Marjorie E. Hassenfelt; General Manager, Michael A. Ruff; Technical Supervisor, Lee Iwanski; Props, Bob Trelfall; Wardrobe, Curtis Hay; Associate Conductor, Dennis Buck; Production Assistant, Carol Tomlinson; Stage Managers, John Frederick Sullivan, Greta Minsky; Press, Jeffrey Richards, Ben Morse, Irene Gandy, Susan Chicoine, Diane Judge, Naomi Grebel, Roger Lane. Opened in the Academy Theatre on Wednesday, January 20, 1988.*

CAST

Rosaline Rafferty	Louisa Flaningam
Otis Hooper	Alan Sues
Pops	Gabor Morea
Mrs. Ten Brock	Jen Jones
Sally	Christina Saffran
Constantine (Connie)	Jack Dabdoub
Blair Farquar	Don Correia
Custard	Sandy
Richard Farquar	Edwin Bordo

ENSEMBLE: Melinda Buckley, Luther Fontaine, Andrea Goodman, Darrell Hankey, Niki Harris, Barbara Hoon, K. Craig Innes, Heidi Joyce, Carolyn Kirsch, Rosemary Loar, Karen Luschar, Rex Nockengust, William Ryall, John Scherer, Cheryl Spencer, Guy Stroman, Craig Wells, James Young
MUSICAL NUMBERS: In the Night Time, On with the Dance, Joan of Arc, Look for the Silver Lining, Sally, The Social Game, A Wild Wild Rose, The Schnitza Komiski, Whip-Poor-Will, The Lorelei, The Church around the Corner, The Nockerova Ballet, Finale

A musical in two acts. The action takes place during the 1920's in the Elm Tree Alley Inn, the garden of Richard Farquar, and in the Broadway Theatre.

*Closed Jan. 24, 1988 after a limited engagement of 5 performances. The original production opened Dec. 12, 1920 in the Amsterdam Theatre and played 570 performances with Marilyn Miller as its star.

Martha Swope/Carol Rosegg Photos

(front center) Don Correia, Cristina Saffran

PENN & TELLER

Presented by Richard Frankel, Thomas Viertel, Steven Baruch; Director, Art Wolff; Set, John Lee Beatty; Lighting, Dennis Parichy; Sound, Chuck London Media/Stewart Werner; Director of Covert Activities, Marc Garland; General Management, Richard Frankel Productions/Marc Routh, Daniel Kearns; Company Manager, Daniel Kearns; Production Manager, Cathy B. Blaser; Wardrobe, Peter J. FitzGerald; Management Assistant, Felicia Lansbury; Press, Cindy Valk, Cammie Sweeney. Opened in the Ritz Theatre on Tuesday, November 24, 1987.*

CAST

PENN JILLETTE & TELLER

ACT I: Casey at the Bat, A Card Trick, Cups and Balls, Suspension, Domestication of Animals, East Indian Needle Mystery, Quote of the Day
ACT II: Another Card Trick, MOFO the Psychic Gorilla, How We Met, Shadows, 10 in 1

*Closed March 20, 1988 after 130 performances.

Gerry Goodstein Photos

Penn Jillette, Teller

THE PHANTOM OF THE OPERA

Music, Andrew Lloyd Webber; Lyrics, Charles Hart; Additional Lyrics, Richard Stilgoe; Book, Richard Stilgoe, Andrew Lloyd Webber; Director, Harold Prince; Musical Staging/Choreography, Gillian Lynne; Presented by Cameron Mackintosh and The Really Useful Theatre Company; Production Design, Maria Bjornson; Lighting, Andrew Bridge; Sound, Martin Levan; Musical Supervision/Direction, David Caddick; Orchestrations, David Cullen, Andrew Lloyd Webber; Casting, Johnson-Liff & Zerman; Assistant tp Director, Ruth Mitchell; General Management, Alan Wasser, Allan Williams; Technical Production Manager, John H. Paull III; Associate Manager, Thom Mitchell; Dance Captain, Denny Berry; Props, Timothy Abel, Michael Bernstein, Victor Amerling; Wardrobe, Adelaide Laurino, Alan Eskolsky; Associate Conductors, Jack Gaughan, Jeffrey Huard; Production Assistant, Rachel Abroms; Stage Managers, Mitchell Lemsky, Fred Hanson, Bethe Ward; Press, Fred Nathan Co./Philip Rinaldi, Dennis Crowley, Bert Fink, Merle Frimark, Marc Thibodeau, David Alberico, Fifi Schuettich. Opened in the Majestic Theatre on Tuesday, January 26, 1988.*

CAST

The Phantom of the Opera	Michael Crawford†1
Christine Daae	Sarah Brightman†2
(Thursday evenings/Saturday matinees)	Patti Cohenour
Raoul, Vicomte de Chagny	Steve Barton
Carlotta Guidicelli	Judy Kaye
Monsieur Andre	Cris Groenendaal
Monsieur Firmin	Nicholas Wyman
Madame Giry	Leila Martin
Ubaldo Piangi	David Romano
Meg Giry	Elisa Heinsohn
Monsieur Reyer	Peter Kevoian
Auctioneer	Richard Warren Pugh
Porter/Marksman	Jeff Keller
Monsieur Lefevre	Kenneth Waller
Joseph Buquet	Philip Steele
Don Attilio ("Il Muto")/Passarino	George Lee Andrews
Slave Master ("Hannibal")	Luis Perez
Flunky/Stagehand	Barry McNabb
Policeman	Charles Rule
Page ("Don Juan Triumphant")	Olga Talyn
Porter/Fireman	William Scott Brown
Page ("Don Juan Triumphant")	Candace Rogers-Adler
Wardrobe Mistress/Confidante ("Il Muto")	Mary Leigh Stahl
Princess ("Hannibal")	Rebecca Luker
Madame Firmin	Beth McVey
Innkeeper's Wife ("Don Juan Triumphant")	Jan Horvath
Ballet Chorus of the Opera Populaire	Irene Cho, Nicole Fosse, Lisa Lockwood, Lori MacPherson, Dodie Pettit, Catherine Ulissey
Ballet Swing	Denny Berry
Swings	Frank Mastrone, Alba Quezada

UNDERSTUDIES: Jeff Keller (Phantom), Rebecca Luker (Christine), Cris Groenendaal (Raoul), Peter Kevoian, George Lee Andrews (Firmin/Andre), Beth McVey, Jan Horvath (Carlotta), Olga Talyn, Mary Leigh Stahl (Madame Giry), Richard Warren Pugh, William Scott Brown (Piangi), Catherine Ulissey, Dodie Pettit (Meg Giry), Barry McNabb (Slave Master/Solo Dancer).

MUSICAL NUMBERS: Think of Me, Angel of Music, Little Lotte, The Mirror, The Phantom of the Opera, The Music of the Night, I Remember, Stranger Than You Dreamt It, Magical Lasso, Notes, Prima Donna, Poor Fool He Makes Me Laugh, Why Have You Brought Me Here, Raoul I've Been There, All I Ask of You, Masquerade, Why So Silent, Twisted Every Way, Wishing You Were Somehow Here Again, Wandering Child, Bravo Bravo, The Point of No Return, Down Once More, Track Down This Murderer.

A musical in 2 acts and 19 scenes. The action takes place in the Paris Opera House in 1911, and Paris in 1881.

*Still playing May 31, 1988. It had the largest advance sale of any production on record. 1988 "Tonys" were awarded for Best Musical, Leading Actor in a Musical (Michael Crawford), Featured Actress in a Musical (Judy Kaye), Scenic Design, Costume Design, Lighting, Direction of a Musical.

†Succeeded by: 1. Timothy Nolen, 2. Patti Cohenour

Clive Barda/Bob Marshak Photos

Top Left: Sarah Brightman, Michael Crawford

Steve Barton, Patti Cohenour Above: Nicholas Wynn, Judy Kaye, Cris Groenendaal

Steve Barton, Sarah Brightman
Above: David Romano (center)
Top: Michael Crawford, Patti Cohenour

Patti Cohenour Above: Sarah Brightman,
Steve Barton (center) Top: Leila Martin

21

SARAFINA!

Written by Mbongeni Ngema; Music Composed and Arranged by Mbongeni Ngema, Hugh Masekela; Conceived and Directed by Mbongeni Ngema; Presented by Lincoln Center Theater (Gregory Mosher, Director; Bernard Gersten, Executive Producer) in association with Lucille Lortel, The Shubert Organization; Set and Costumes, Sarah Roberts; Lighting, Mannie Manim; Conductor/Additional Choreography, Ndaba Mhlongo; Sound, Tom Sorce; Production Manager, Jeff Hamlin; Company Managers, Lynn Landis, Helen V. Meier; Wardrobe, Ellen Lee; Stage Managers, Bruce A. Hoover, Jerry Cleveland, Monique Martin; Committed Artists Company Manager, Mali Hlatshwayo; Press, Merle Debuskey, Robert W. Larkin. Opened in the Cort Theatre on Thursday, January 28, 1988.*

CAST

Magundane	Ntomb'khona Dlamini
Scabha	Khumbuzile Dlamini
Colgate	Pat Mlaba
Teaspoon	Lindiwe Dlamini
Crocodile	Dumisani Dlamini
Silence	Congo Hadebe
Stimela Sase-Zola	Nhlanhla Ngema
S'Ginci, Police Sergeant	Mhlathi Khuzwayo
Sarafina	Leleti Khumalo
Mistress It's a Pity	Baby Cele
Dumadu	Nonhlanhla Mbambo
China	Linda Mchunu
Lindiwe	Lindiwe Helengwa
Zandile	Zandile Hlengwa
Siboniso	Siboniso Khumalo
Timba	Cosmas Sithole
Priest	Thandani Mavimbela
Charnele	Charnele Dozier Brown
Mubi	Mubi Mofokeng
Nandi	Nandi Ndlovu
Thandekile	Thandekile Nhlanhla
Police Lieutenant	Pumi Shelembe
Kipzane	Kipzane Skweyiya
Regina	Regina Taylor
Thandi	Thandi Zulu

MUSICAL NUMBERS: It's Finally Happening, Do You See What I See?, Sarafina, The Lord's Prayer, Yes Mistress It's a Pity, Give Us Power, What Is the Army Doing in Soweto?, Nkosi Sikeleli'Afrika, Freedom Is Coming Tomorrow, Excuse Me Baby Please, Meeting Tonight, We Are Guerrillas, Uyamemeza Ungoma, We Will Fight for Our Land, Mama, Sechaba, The Nation Is Dying, Goodbye, Kilimanjaro, Africa Burning in the Sun, Stimela Sasezola, It's All Right, Bring Back Nelson Mandela, Wololo!

A musical in two acts.

*Still playing May 31, 1988.

Brigitte Lacombe Photos

Top Right: Leleti Khumalo, Khumbuzile Dlamini, Thandekile Nhlanhla, Siboniso Khumalo

SERIOUS MONEY

By Caryl Churchill; Director, Max Stafford-Clark; Presented by Joseph Papp in association with The Shubert Organization; Associate Producer, Jason Steven Cohen; Scenery/Costumes, Peter Hartwell; Lighting, Rick Fisher; Music and Lyrics, Ian Dury, Micky Gallagher, Chas Jankel; Musical Arranger, Colin Sell; Casting, Rosemarie Tichler/James Mulkin; General Management, Bob Macdonald, Susan Sampliner; Company Manager, Steven H. David; Props, Larry Trezza; Wardrobe, Elonzo Dann; Vocal Supervision, Allan Corduner; Dialect Coach, Elizabeth Himelstein; Stage Managers, James Bernardi, Pat Sosnow; Press, Richard Kornberg, Barbara Carroll, Reva Cooper, Kevin Patterson, Carol Fineman. Opened in the Royale Theatre on Tuesday, February 9, 1988.*

CAST

Scilla Todd, a LIFFE dealer	Melinda Mullins
Jake Todd, Scilla's brother, paper dealer	Michael Wincott
Grimes, a gilts dealer	Alec Baldwin
Zackerman, banker with Klein Merrick	John Pankow
Merrison, banker, co-chief executive Klein Merrick	Wendell Pierce
Durkfeld, trader, co-chief executive Klein Merrick	Allan Corduner
Greville Todd, Jake and Scilla's father, stockbroker	Allan Corduner
Frosby, a jobber	Michael Wincott
T. K., personal assistant to Marylou Baines	Wendell Pierce
Marylou Baines, an American arbitrageur	Kate Nelligan
Jacinta Condor, a Peruvian businesswoman	Cordelia Gonzalez
Nigel Ajibala, importer from Ghana	Wendell Pierce
Billy Corman, corporate raider	Alec Baldwin
Mrs. Etherington, a stockbroker	Kate Nelligan
Duckett, chairman of Albion	Allan Corduner
Ms. Biddulph, a white knight	Melinda Mullins
Dolcie Starr, a PR consultant	Kate Nelligan
Grevett, a DTI inspector	Michael Wincott
Soat, President of Missouri Gumballs	Allan Corduner
Gleason, a cabinet minister	Allan Corduner

LIFFE members and traders: Valerie Bahakel, Christine Dunford, Gregory Jbara, Olivia Negron, Liann Pattison, Stephen Rowe, Michael Rudko, Harold J. Surratt.

UNDERSTUDIES: Christine Dunford (Scilla/Biddulph), Gregory Jbara (Zackerman), Olivia Negron (Jacinta), Liann Pattison (Marylou/Mrs. Etherington/Dolcie), Stephen Rowe (Grimes/Corman), Michael Rudko (Durkfeld/Greville/Duckett/Soat/Gleason/Jake/Frosby/Grevett), Harold J. Surratt (Merrison, T. K., Nigel)

A play in two acts. The action takes place mainly between October 1986 and June 1987 in London and New York.

*Closed Feb. 20, 1988 after 15 performances and 21 previews.

Martha Swope Photos

Top Right: Alec Baldwin

Alec Baldwin, Melinda Mullins

Kate Nelligan, John Pankow
Above: Wendell Pierce, Kate Nelligan

A WALK IN THE WOODS

By Lee Blessing; Director, Des McAnuff; Presented by Lucille Lortel in association with American Playhouse Theatre Productions and Yale Repertory Theatre; Set, Bill Clarke; Costumes, Ellen V. McCartney; Lighting, Richard Riddell; Music, Michael S. Roth; Sound, G. Thomas Clark; Casting, Meg Simon/Fran Kumin; General Manager, Leonard Soloway; Technical Supervision, Theatrical Services/Arthur Siccardi; Company Liaison, Linda Wright; Assistant Director, Beverly Smith-Dawson; Dramaturg, Walter Bilderback; Production Assistant, Regina Lickteig; Props, Jan Marasek; Wardrobe, Karen Lloyd; Stage Manager, Jim Woolley; Press, Jeffrey Richards, Ben Morse, Irene Gandy, Susan Chicoine, Diane Judge, Jillana Devine, Carrie Kramer, Joan Curtis Michael. Opened in the Booth Theatre on Sunday, February 28, 1988.*

CAST

Andrey Botvinnik, a Soviet Diplomat ....Robert Prosky
John Honeyman, an American negotiator ....Sam Waterston

STANDBYS: Frederick Neumann (Botvinnik), Eric Booth (Honeyman)

   A play in two acts. The action takes place at the present time in a pleasant woods on the outskirts of Geneva.

*Closed June 26, 1988 after 136 performances and 22 previews.

Peter Cunningham Photos

Top Left: Sam Waterston, Robert Prosky
Below: Sam Waterston, Robert Prosky

Blythe Danner, Aidan Quinn
Right: Frank Converse, Blythe Danner, and
below with Frances McDormand

A STREETCAR NAMED DESIRE

By Tennessee Williams; Director, Nikos Psacharopoulos; Presented by Circle in the Square Theatre (Theodore Mann, Artistic Director; Paul Libin, Producing Director); Scenery, John Conklin; Costumes, Jess Goldstein; Lighting, Curt Ostermann; Incidental Music, Michael O'Flaherty; Fights, B. H. Barry; Company Manager, Susan Elrod; Casting, Hughes-Moss; Props, Frank Hauser; Wardrobe, Claire Libin; Stage Managers, Michael F. Ritchie, William Hare; Press, Merle Debuskey, William Schelble, Leo Stern. Opened in Circle in the Square Theatre on Thursday, March 10, 1988.*

CAST

Stella Kowalski	Frances McDormand[†1]
Eunice Hubbell	Becky Gelke
Negro Woman	Louise Stubbs
Stanley Kowalski	Aidan Quinn[†2]
Harold Mitchell (Mitch)	Frank Converse[†3]
Blanche Du Bois	Blythe Danner[†4]
Steve Hubbell	Gary Cookson
Pablo Gonzales	Mateo Gomez
Young Collector	Linc Richards
Flower Vendor	Myra Taylor
Doctor	Ken Costigan
Nurse	Kathleen Marsh
Sax Player	Seldon Powell

STANDBYS & UNDERSTUDIES: April Shawhan (Blanche), Kim Coates (Stanley), Jean Hackett (Stella/Eunice), Jonathan Mann (Collector/Pablo), Louise Stubbs (Vendor/Nurse), Myra Taylor (Negro Woman)

A drama in two acts. The action takes place in the Spring, Summer and early Fall in New Orleans.

*Closed May 22, 1988 after 85 performances and 20 previews. Original production opened Dec. 3, 1947 at the Ethel Barrymore Theatre with Jessica Tandy and Marlon Brando in the cast and played 855 performances.
†succeeded by: 1. Jean Hackett, 2. Kim Coates, 3. Kevin Geer, 4. Pamela Payton-Wright

Martha Swope Photos

Kim Coates, Frank Converse, Pamela
Payton-Wright, Jean Hackett

M. BUTTERFLY

By David Henry Hwang; Director, John Dexter; Presented by Stuart Ostrow and David Geffen; Scenery and Costumes, Eiko Ishioka; Lighting, Andy Phillips; Hairstylist, Phyllis Della Illien; Music, Giacomo Puccini, Lucia Hwong; Casting, Meg Simon/Fran Kumin; Peking Opera Consultants, Jamie H. J. Guan, Michele Ehlers; General Management, Joseph Harris Associates/Steven E. Goldstein, Peter T. Kulok, Nancy Simmons; Technical Supervision, Jeremiah J. Harris Associates; Props, Joseph Harris, Jr.; Wardrobe, Barrett Hong; Musical Director, Lucia Hwong; Management Associate, Gerri Higgins; Sound, Peter J. Fitzgerald: Make-up Design, Joe Compayno; Music Coordinator, John Miller; Live Music Arranged by Jason Hwang, Yukio Tsuji; Stage Managers, Bob Borod, Barry Kearsley; Press, John Springer, Gary Springer. Opened in the Eugene O'Neill Theatre on Sunday, March 20, 1988.*

CAST

Kurogo	Alec Mapa, Chris Odo, H. J. Guan
Rene Gallimard	John Lithgow†1
Song Liling	B. D. Wong
Marc/Man2/Consul Sharpless	John Getz†2
Renee/Woman at party/Girl in magazine	Lindsay Frost
Comrade Chin/Suzuki/Shu Fang	Lori Tan Chinn
Helga	Rose Gregorio†3
M. Toulon/Man 1/Judge	George N. Martin

UNDERSTUDIES: Richard Poe (Rene/Marc), Alec Mapa (Song Liling/Comrade Chin), Kathleen Chalfant (Helga), Tom Klunis (M. Toulon), Kathryn Layng (Renee)

A drama in three acts with one intermission. The action takes place in a Paris prison, 1988, and in recall the years 1960–1986 in Beijing and Paris.

*Still playing May 31, 1988. "Tonys" were awarded for Best Play, Best Featured Actor in a Play (B. D. Wong), Best Direction of a Play.

†Succeeded by: 1. David Dukes, 2. Richard Poe, 3. Pamela Payton-Wright

**Top: John Lithgow, and left with
B. D. Wong Below: Alec Mapa,
B. D. Wong, H. J. Guan**

**B. D. Wong, John Lithgow (also
above)**　　　　**John Lithgow**

B. D. Wong, David Dukes, also above with
George N. Martin Top: Dukes, Wong
Below: Rose Gregorio, David Dukes

David Dukes, and above
and top with B. D. Wong

27

THE GOSPEL AT COLONUS

Morgan Freeman

Book and Lyrics, Lee Breuer; Music, Bob Telson; Director, Lee Breuer; Presented by Dodger Productions, Liza Lorwin, Louis Busch Hager, Playhouse Square Center, Fifth Avenue Productions; Production and Set Design, Alison Yerxa; Costumes, Ghretta Hynd; Lighting, Julie Archer; Sound, David Hewill, Ron Lorman; Executive Producers, Michael David, Edward Strong, Sherman Warner; Based on an adaptation of Sophocles' "Oedipus at Colonus" in the version by Robert Fitzgerald and incorporates passages from both Sophocles' "Oedipus Rex" and "Antigone" in the versions by Dudley Fitts and Robert Fitzgerald; Company Manager, Douglas C. Baker; Sound, Daryl Bornstein; Wardrobe, Dianne Hylton; Props, James J. Fedigan; Administrative Associate, Kara Vallow; Stage Managers, Peter Glazer, Susan Green, Dwight R. B. Cook; Press, Joshua Ellis Office/Adrian Bryan-Brown, Jackie Green, Leo Stern, Susanne Tighe. Opened in the Lunt-Fontanne Theatre on Thursday, March 24, 1988.*

CAST

Messenger	Morgan Freeman
Oedipus	Clarence Fountain and the Five Blind Boys of Alabama
Antigone	Isabell Monk
Theseus	Rev. Earl F. Miller
Ismene	Jefetta Steele and the J. D. Steele Singers
Creon	Robert Earl Jones
Polyneices	Kevin Davis
Choragos	Martin Jacox, J. J. Farley and The Soul Stirrers
The Singer	Sam Butler, Jr.
The Choir Soloist	Carolyn Johnson-White
Chorus	The Institutional Radio Choir
Guest Choir Director	J. D. Steele

UNDERSTUDIES: Rev. Earl F. Miller, Jim Craven (Messenger), James Carter (Oedipus), Jim Craven (Theseus/Polyneices), Pamela Poitier (Antigone), Carl Williams, Jr. (Creon), Hayward Gregory (The Singer), Parthea Hill (Choir Soloist/J. D. Steele Singers), Billy Steele (J. D. Steele Singers)

MUSICAL NUMBERS: The Welcome and Quotations, Live Where You Can, Recapitulation, Fair Colonus, Stop! Do Not Go On, Who Is This Man?, How Shall I See You Through My Tears?, Narrative of Ismene, The Rite, A Voice Foretold, No Never, All My Heart's Desire, Numberless Are the World's Wonders, Lift Me Up, Evil, You Break My Heart, Love Unconquerable, Heaven's Height Has Cracked!, Oh Sunlight of No Light, Eternal Sleep, Now Let the Weeping Cease

A musical in two acts.

*Closed May 15, 1988 after 61 performances and 15 previews.

Fred Steele, Jevetta Steele, Janice Steele, J. S. Steele

Martha Swope Photos

Delroy Lindo, Ed Hall, Mel Winkler
Above: Ed Hall, Bo Rucker

JOE TURNER'S COME AND GONE

By August Wilson; Director, Lloyd Richards; Presented by Elliot Martin and Vy Higginsen/Ken Wydro in association with the Yale Repertory Theatre; Associate Producers, Jeffrey Steiner, Kery Davis, Charles Grantham; Scenery, Scott Bradley; Costumes, Pamela Peterson; Lighting, Michael Giannitti; Music Direction, Dwight Andrews; Casting, Meg Simon/Fran Kumin; General Management, Joseph P. Harris/Steven E. Goldstein, Peter T. Kulok; Company Manager, Mitchell Brower; Props, Sal Sciafani; Wardrobe, Cindy Steffens; Hairstylist, Lloyd Kindred; Management Associate, Gerri Higgins; Stage Managers, Karen L. Carpenter, Elliott Woodruff; Press, Jeffrey Richards/Ben Morse, Irene Gandy, Susan Chicoine, Diane Judge, Naomi Grabel, Roger Lane, Jillana Devine, Carrie Kramer. Opened in the Ethel Barrymore Theatre on Sunday, March 27, 1988*

CAST

Seth Holly	Mel Winkler
Bertha Holly	L. Scott Caldwell
Bynum Walker	Ed Hall
Rutherford Selig	Raynor Scheine
Jeremy Furlow	Bo Rucker
Herald Loomis	Delroy Lindo
Zonia Loomis	Jamila Perry
Mattie Campbell	Kimberleigh Aarn
Reuben Mercer	Richard Parnell Habersham
Molly Cunningham	Kimberly Scott
Martha Pentecost	Angela Bassett

STANDBYS: Robinson Frank Adu (Seth/Bynum), Ernestine Jackson (Molly/Martha/Bertha/Mattie), Lanny Flaherty (Rutherford), Chrisse Jackson (Zonia), Kimble Joyner (Reuben)

A drama in two acts. The action takes place in a boardinghouse in Pittsburgh, Pennsylvania during 1911.

*Closed June 26, 1988 after 105 performances and 11 previews. Voted Best Play of season by the New York Drama Critics Circle, and L. Scott Caldwell received a "Tony" for Best Featured Actress in a Play.

Joan Marcus Photos

Top Left: Mel Winkler, Bo Rucker
Below: Raynor Scheine, Ed Hall, Delroy Lindo

Mel Winkler, L. Scott Caldwell

OBA OBA

Franco Fontana's Brazilian Extravaganza; Musical Director, Wilson Mauro; Choreographer, Roberto Abrahao; Assistant Choreographers, Soraya Bastos, Luis Bocanha; Technical Consultant, Mario Ruffa; Co-Producer, Dino Cuzzoni; General Management, Marvin A. Krauss, Irving Siders; Company Manager, Kathryn Frawley; Production Coordinator, Randall Buck; Props, Charles Zuckerman, Gregory Martin; Wardrobe, Gayle Patton; Sound, Peter FitzGerald; Lighting Consultant, Steve Cochrane; Press, Mark Goldstaub/Kevin P. McAnarney, Dan Kellachan, Virginia Gillick, Peter Morris. Opened in the Ambassador Theatre on Tuesday, March 29, 1987*

CAST

Bebeto, Beicola, Borracha, Brecho, Chita, Claudia Jacomo, Claudinho Nascimento, Cobra Mansa, Concheta, Gerson Do Pandeiro, Jose Roberto Ferreira, Ledinha Da Mangueira, Lindete Souza, Lucia Helena Maximo, Luis Bernardo, Luis Bocanha, Marcia Souza, Marcos Negao, Marquinho Da Dona Geralda, Marta Sargentelli, Miguel Do Repinique, Milani Nicolau, Olga Maria, Paulo Xavier, Pedro Pottier, Roberto Silva, Rosemary Silva, Soninha Toda Pura, Soraya Bastos, Tome De Bebedouro, Vivian Machado Soares, Waldir Cavalcanti, Wilmar Vieira, Wilson Mauro, and stars: Eliana Estevao, Nilze Carvalho, Toco Preto, Jaime Santos

ENSEMBLE: Claudio Sargentelli, Cristino Ricardo, Dalto Macedo, Garcia De Aragao, Iole Fernandes, Lucelita Barros, Maria Elza De Jesus, Monica Goncalves, Nino, Ondina Lopes, Vera Lima

PROGRAM

ACT I: Xica Da Silva, Homage to Baiao and Chorinho, Samba De Roda, Homage to the Northeast, Brazil Capela, Homage to the Bossanova and Brazilina Music of the 'Seventies, Tribute to the "Brazilian Bombshell" Carmen Miranda, ACT II: Macumba, Afro-Brazilian Folk Songs and Dances, Rhythm Beaters, Show of Samba Dancers, Grand Carnival

*Closed May 8, 1988 after 53 performances and 11 previews.

MAIL

Book and Lyrics, Jerry Colker; Music, Michael Rupert; Director, Andrew Cadiff; Choreography, Grover Dale; Presented by Michael Frazier, Susan Dietz, Stephen Wells and the Kennedy Center/ANTA; Scenery and Projections, Gerry Hariton, Vicki Baral; Costumes, William Ivey Long; Lighting, Richard Nelson; Sound, Tom Morse; Multi Image Production, Nelson & Sixta; Hairstylist, Phyllis Della Illien; Musical Supervision, Paul Gemignani; Orchestrations, Michael Gibson; Musical Direction/Dance Arrangements, Tom Fay; Casting, Eleanor Albano/Susan Chieco; Associate Producer, Kenneth Biller; Assistant Choreographer, Stephen Jay; General Management, Frank Scardino Associates; Technical Supervisor, Peter Fulbright; Managerial Associate, Jim Brandeberry; Dance Captain, Stephen Jay; Production Assistant, Philip Allen; Props, Dennis Randolph; Wardrobe, Peter J. FitzGerald; Assistant Conductor, Henry Aronson; Stage Managers, Craig Jacobs, Michael F. Wolf, C. C. Cary, Larry Collis; Press, Joshua Ellis/Jim Sapp, Adrian Bryan-Brown, Jackie Green, Tim Ray, Susanne Tighe. Opened in the Music Box Theatre on Thursday, April 14, 1988*

CAST

Alex	Michael Rupert
Dana	Mara Getz
Radio Announcer/Life Exec/Billy Ray Binger/Con Ed Man/Hunter/Stansbury/ Pitchman	Rick Stockwell
Radio Singer/Mama Utility/Brunhilda/Operator/ Lois T. Wertshafter	Mary Bond Davis
Franklin	Brian Mitchell
Sandi	Antonia Ellis
Max	Robert Mandan
Kathy Sue Binger/Democratic Party Delegate/Power Lady/ Candi Suwinski	Michele Pawk
LIFE Exec/Con Ed Man/Boy Scout/Craterface Callahan/Pitchman	Robert Loftin
LIFE Exec/Con Ed Man/I.R.S. Auditor/Takeuchi Fujimoto/Pitchman	Alan Muraoka
Power Lady/Gypsy/Harmony Steinberg	Louise Hickey

STANDBYS: Jerry Colker (Alex), Michele Pawk (Dana/Sandi), Larry Collis (Max), Milton Craig Nealy (Franklin), Swings: Stephen Jay, Rachelle Ottley
MUSICAL NUMBERS: Overture, Monolithic Madness, Gone So Long, Hit the Ground Running, It's Your Life, Cookin' with Steam, It's Just a Question of Technique, It's None of My Business, Crazy World, Ambivalent Rag, It's Your Life II, You Better Get Outta Town, We're Gonna Turn Off Your Juice, The World Set on Fire by a Black and a Jew, Where Are You/Where Am I?, Family Ties, One Lost Weekend, Junk Mail, Disconnected, Helplessness at Midnight, What Have You Been Doing for the Past Ten Years, A Blank Piece of Paper, Sweepstakes, It's Getting Harder to Love, Publish Your Book, Ambivalent Rag II, Pages of My Diary, One Step at a Time, Ambivalent Rag III, Don't Count on It, Friends for Life, 29 Years Ago, Finale

A musical in two acts and a prologue. The action takes place at the present time in a Manhattan apartment one winter morning and four months later.

*Closed May 14, 1988 after 36 performances and 20 previews.

Ron Scherl Photos

Top Right: (seated) Louise Hickey, Brian Mitchell, Antonia Ellis, Michael Rupert, Mara Getz, Robert Mandan (standing) Rick Stockwell, Michele Pawk, Alan Muraoka, Robert Loftin, Mary Bond Davis

Antonia Ellis, Michael Rupert, Mara Getz

Michael Rupert (seated), Brian Mitchell

MICHAEL FEINSTEIN
IN CONCERT

Presented by Ron Delsener; Conceived by Michael Feinstein, Christopher Chadman; Special Material, Bruce Vilanch; Staged by Christopher Chadman; Musical Director, Elliot Finkel; Set, Andrew Jackness; Lighting, Beverly Emmons; Sound, Tom Sorce; General Management, David Strong Warner/Michael David, Ed Strong, Sherman Warner; Associate Producers, Jonathan Scharer, Peter Kapp; Production Manager, Chip Quigley; Stage Manager, Sam Ellis; Press, Barbara McGurn, Solters/Roskin/ Friedman, Sylvia Weiner, Susan DuBow, Keith Sherman. Opened in the Lyceum Theatre on Tuesday, April 19, 1988 and closed there on June 12, 1988 after 57 performances.

Michael Feinstein

THE WORLD ACCORDING TO ME

Created and Written by Jackie Mason; Supervised by Ron Clark; Scenery and Lighting, Neil Peter Jampolis; Sound, Bruce D. Cameron; Presented by Nick Vanoff; Associate Producer, Jyll Rosenfeld; General Management, Joseph Harris, Ira Bernstein, Peter T. Kulok, Steven E. Goldstein; Manager, Nancy Simmons; Associate Manager, Russ Lori Rosensweig; Technical Supervision, Jeremiah J. Harris; Production Assistant, Gerri Higgins; Stage Manager, Don Myers; Props, Joseph Harris, Jr.; Press, Zarem, Inc. Opened in the Brooks Atkinson Theatre on May 3, 1988*

CAST

JACKIE MASON

Presented in two parts, with material selected from U.S. Politics, World Affairs, Hollywood Producers and Celebrities, Dating, Communism, Sex Education, Psychiatry, Hookers, Health Hazards, the Army, the Weather, Gentiles and Jews.

*Still playing May 31, 1988. Mr. Mason had presented his one-man show in the same theatre from Monday, Dec. 22, 1986 to Jan. 2, 1988 for 367 performances and 7 previews, and was the recipient of a 1987 Special "Tony" Award.

Martha Swope Photos

Jackie Mason

MACBETH

By William Shakespeare; Director, Kenneth Frankel; Additional Direction, Zoe Caldwell; Presented by Barry and Fran Weissler and Garth H. Drabinsky; Settings, Daphne Dare; Costumes, Patricia Zipprodt; Lighting, Marc B. Weiss; Sound, Otts Munderloh; Hairstylist, Patrik D. Moreton; Make-up, Brad Scott; Music, William Penn, Louis Applebaum; Casting, Pat McCorkle; Associate Producer, Melinda Howard; General Management, Kevmar Productions/Alecia Parker, Karen E. Etcoff; Company Manager, Michael Gill; Technical Supervisor, Theatre Services/Arthur Siccardi; Props, C. J. Simpson, Al Steiner; Wardrobe, Irene Ferrari; Fight Captain, Thomas Schall; Production Assistants, Allison Rabenau, Bruce Faulk; Stage Managers, James Harker, Amy Pell; Press, Solters/Roskin/Friedman, Susan Lee, Keith Sherman. Opened in the Mark Hellinger Theatre on Thursday, April 21, 1988*

CAST

Three Witches	Jeff Weiss, Tanny McDonald, Annette Helde
Duncan, King of Scotland	Jack Gwillim
Malcolm, son of Duncan	Randle Mell
Caithness, a captain	Bruce Gooch
Lennox	Thomas Hill
Ross	Philip Kerr
Macbeth	Christopher Plummer
Banquo	Paul Shenar
Donalbain, son of Duncan	Conan McCarty
Lady Macbeth	Glenda Jackson
Seyton	Robert Burke
Fleance, son of Banquo	Michael Butler
A Porter	Jeff Weiss
Macduff	Alan Scarfe
Two Murderers	Thomas Schall, Jeff Weiss
Lady Macduff	Cherry Jones
Son of Macduff	Richard H. Blake
A Doctor	Paul Soles
A Gentlewoman attending Lady Macbeth	Tanny McDonald
Siward, Earl of Northumberland	Jeff Weiss
Young Siward, his son	Jack Hannibal
Lords, Soldiers, etc:	Gary Bradford, David DeBesse, Bill Ferrell, Michael Alan Gregory, Jack Hannibal, Todd Jamieson, Gordon Paddison, Paul Soles, Gregory Zaragoza

STANDBYS & UNDERSTUDIES: Sarah-Jane Gwillim (Lady Macbeth), Paul Shenar (Macbeth), Robert Burke (Banquo), Marcell Rosenblatt (Witches/Gentlewoman), Thomas Hill (Duncan), Bruce Gooch (Malcolm/Macduff), Gordon Paddison (Ross/Caithness/Murderer), Edwin J. McDonough (Seyton/Siward/Doctor/Messenger), Paul Soles (Lennox/Porter/Murderer), Jack Hannibal (Donalbain/Fleance/Boy Macduff), Annette Helde (Lady Macduff), Michael Butler (Young Siward)

A tragedy performed with one intermission. The action takes place in Scotland and England.

*Closed June 26, 1988 after 77 performances and 8 previews.

Henry Grossman/Robert C. Ragsdale Photos

**Center Right: Christopher Plummer, Glenda Jackson;
Paul Shenar, Christopher Plummer Top:
Jack Gwillim, Glenda Jackson**

**Christopher
Plummer**

**Glenda
Jackson**

**Bill Ferrell, Christopher Plummer,
Glenda Jackson**

CHESS

Music, Benny Andersson, Bjorn Ulvaeus; Lyrics, Tim Rice; Book, Richard Nelson; Based on an idea by Tim Rice; Director, Trevor Nunn; Dance Staging, Lynne Taylor-Corbett; Presented by The Shubert Organization, 3 Knights Ltd., Robert Fox Ltd.; Scenery, Robin Wagner; Costumes, Theoni V. Aldredge; Lighting, David Hersey; Sound, Andrew Bruce; Musical Director/Supervisor, Paul Bogaev; Orchestrations/Arrangements, Anders Eljas; Executive Producers, General Management, Gatchell & Neufeld Ltd.; Casting, Johnson-Liff & Zerman; Hairstylist, Schubert & DiNiro; Original Cast Album by RCA Victor; General Management Associate, Nina Lannan; Dance Captain, Karen Babcock; Technical Supervisors, Theatre Services/Arthur Siccardi, Peter Feller; Props, George Green, Jr., Robert Bostwick, Nicholas Laudano; Wardrobe, Alyce Gilbert, Daniel Lomax; Stage Managers, Alan Hall, Jake Bell, Zane Weiner, Ruth E. Rinklin; Press, Bill Evans/Sandy Manley, Jim Randolph, Patt Dale; Cast Recording by RCA Victor. Opened in the Imperial Theatre on Thursday, April 28, 1988*

CAST

Gregor Vassey	Neal Ben-Ari
Young Florence	Gina Gallagher
Freddie	Philip Casnoff
Florence	Judy Kuhn
Anatoly	David Carroll
Molokov	Harry Goz
Nickolai	Kurt Johns
Walter	Dennis Parlato
Arbiter	Paul Harman
Svetlana	Marcia Mitzman
Joe & Harold, Embassy Officials	Richard Muenz, Eric Johnson
Swings	Karen Babcock, Craig Wells

ENSEMBLE: John Aller, Neal Ben-Ari, Suzanne Briar, Steve Clemente, Katherine Lynne Condit, Ann Crumb, David Cryer, R. F. Daley, Deborah Geneviere, Kurt Johns, Eric Johnson, Paul Laureano, Rosemary Loar, Judy McLane, Jessica Molaskey, Richard Muenz, Kip Niven, Francis Ruivivar, Alex Santoriello, Wysandria Woolsey

UNDERSTUDIES: Ann Crumb (Florence/Svetlana), Judy McLane (Florence), Richard Muenz (Anatoly), Paul Harman (Anatoly), Kurt Johns (Freddie), David Cryer (Molokov), Kip Niven (Walter), Wysandria Woolsey (Svetlana), Alex Santoriello (Arbiter), Chrystal Pennington (Young Florence)

MUSICAL NUMBERS: The Story of Chess, Press Conference, Where I Want to Be, How Many Women, Merchandisers Song, U.S. versus U.S.S.R., Chess Hymn, A Model of Decorum and Tranquility, You Want to Lose Your Only Friend?, Someone Else's Story, One Night in Bangkok, Terrace Duet, So You Got What You Want, Nobody's Side, Anthem, Arbiter's Song, Hungarian Folk Song, Heaven Help My Heart, No Contest, You and I, A Whole New Board Game, Let's Work Together, I Know Him So Well, Pity the Child, Lullaby, Endgame

A musical in two acts. The action takes place during 1956 in Budapest, Bangkok, and Kennedy Airport in New York.

*Closed June 25, 1988 after 68 performances and 17 previews.

Martha Swope Photos

Top Left: Philip Casnoff (at podium)
Below: Philip Casnoff, Paul Harman,
Judy Kuhn, David Carroll

Judy Kuhn, David Carroll

Judy Kuhn, Harry Goz, Marcia Mitzman,
David Carroll Above: "One Night in Bangkok"

ROMANCE/ROMANCE

Book & Lyrics, Barry Harman; Music, Keith Herrmann; Director, Barry Harman; Choreography, Pamela Sousa; Presented by Dasha Epstein, Harve Brosten, Jay S. Bulmash; Produced in association with George Krynicki, Marvin A. Krauss; Scenery, Steven Rubin; Lighting, Craig Miller; Costumes, Steven Jones; Sound, Peter FitzGerald; Musical Director, Kathy Sommer; Vocal/Dance Arrangements, Keith Herrmann, Kathy Sommer; Orchestrations, Michael Starobin; Casting, Leonard Finger; Assistant Director, Edward Marshall; Production Supervisor, James Pentecost; Additional Orchestrations, Daniel Troob, Joe Gianono; General Management, Marvin A. Krauss, Gary Gunas, Joey Parnes; Company Manager, Steven Suskin; Technical Director, Peter Fulbright; Wardrobe, Sahra Henrickson; Production Assistant, Alexandra Mankiewicz; Stage Managers, James A. Pentecost, Joseph Onorato; Press, Henry Luhrman/Terry M. Lilly, David Lotz, Carl Leech; Cast recording by MCA Classics. Opened in the Helen Hayes Theatre on Sunday, May 1, 1988*

CAST

ACT I: *The Little Comedy* based on the short story by Arthur Schnitzler; Translated by George Edward Reynolds. The action takes place in Vienna at the turn of the century

Alfred von Wilmers ....Scott Bakula†
Josefine Weninger ....Alison Fraser
"Him" ....Robert Hoshour
"Her" ....Deborah Graham

MUSICAL NUMBERS: The Little Comedy, Goodbye Emil, It's Not Too Late, Great News, Oh What a Performance, I'll Always Remember the Song, Happy Happy Happy, Women of Vienna, Yes It's Love, A Rustic Country Inn, The Night It Had to End
ACT II: *Summer Share* based on the play "Pain de Menage" by Jules Renard; Translated by Max Gulack. The action takes place in the Hamptons during August of the current year.

Lenny ....Robert Hoshour
Barb ....Deborah Graham
Sam ....Scott Bakula†
Monica ....Alison Fraser
Standbys: Jana Robbins, Sal Viviano

MUSICAL NUMBERS: Summer Share, Think of the Odds, It's Not Too Late, Plans A & B, Let's Not Talk about It, So Glad I Married Her, Small Craft Warnings, How Did I End Up Here?, Words He Doesn't Say, My Love for You, Moonlight Passing Through a Window, Now, Romantic Notions, Romance! Romance!

*Closed January 15, 1989 after 297 performances and 10 previews. It had opened Friday, Oct. 30, 1987 Off Broadway at Actors Outlet where it played 37 performances and 19 previews before moving to Broadway.

†Succeeded by Sal Viviano, Barry Williams

Martha Swope Photos

**Top: Scott Bakula, Alison Fraser, Robert
Hoshour, Deborah Graham (also top right)
Below: Barry Williams, Alison Fraser**

**Barry Williams,
Alison Fraser**

**Alison Fraser,
Dennis Parlato**

CARRIE

Music, Michael Gore; Lyrics, Dean Pitchford; Book, Lawrence D. Cohen; Based on novel by Stephen King; The Friedrich Kurz/Royal Shakespeare Company Production; Director, Terry Hands; Choreography, Debbie Allen; Set, Ralph Koltai; Costumes, Alexander Reid; Lighting, Terry Hands; Sound, Martin Levan; Assistant Director, Louis W. Scheeder; Casting, Lyons/Isaacson; General Manager, Waissman & Buckley; Orchestrations, Anders Eljas, Harold Wheeler, Michael Starobin; Music Supervisor, Harold Wheeler; Musical Director, Paul Schwartz; Produced in association with Whitecap Productions and Martin Barandes; Production Manager, Simon Opie; Props, David J. Walters; Wardrobe, Irene L. Bunis; Hairstylist, Joe Anthony; Associate Conductor, Gregory Dlugos; Stage Managers, Joe Lorden, Jeremy Sturt, Jack Gianino, Ed Fitzgerald; Press, PMK Public Relations/Jim Baldassare, Leslee Dart, Lisa Kasteler, Catherine Olim, Lisa Hintelmann, Diana Son. Opened in the Virginia Theatre on Thursday, May 12, 1988*

CAST

Margaret White	Betty Buckley
Carrie White	Linzi Hateley
Chris	Charlotte D'Amboise
Tommy	Paul Gyngell
Miss Gardner	Darlene Love
Billy	Gene Anthony Ray
Sue	Sally Ann Triplett

ENSEMBLE: Jamie Beth Chandler (Jamie), Catherine Doffey (Cathy), Michele Du Verney (Michele), Michelle Hodgson (Shelley), Rosemarie Jackson (Rose), Kelly Littlefield (Kelly), Madeleine Loftin (Maddy), Michelle Nelson (Michelle), Mary Ann Oedy (Mary Ann), Suzanne Maria Thomas (Squeezie), Gary Co-Burn (Gary), Kevin Coyne (Kevin), David Danns (David), Matthew Dickens (Matthew), Eric Gilliom (Eric), Kenny Linden (Kenny), Joey McKneely (Joey), Mark Santoro (Mark), Christopher Solari (Chris), Scott Wise (Scott)
STANDBYS/UNDERSTUDIES: Audrey Lavine (Margaret), Lillias White (Miss Gardner), Rosemarie Jackson (Carrie), Catherine Coffey (Sue), Jamie Beth Chandler (Sue), Mary Ann Oedy (Chris), Christopher Solari/David Danns (Billy), Matthew Dickens/Kenny Linden (Tommy), Swing Dancers: Mary Ann Lamb, Darryl Eric Tribble
MUSICAL NUMBERS: In, Dream On, Carrie, Open Your Heart, And Eve Was Weak, Don't Waste the Moon, Evening Prayers, Unsuspecting Hearts, Do Me a Favor, I Remember How Those Boys Could Dance, Out for Blood, It Hurts to Be Strong, I'm Not Alone, When There's No One, Wotta Night, Heaven, Alma Mater, The Destruction

A musical in 2 acts and 12 scenes with a prologue and epilogue. The action takes place at the present time.

*Closed May 15, 1988 after 5 performances and 16 previews.

Peter Cunningham Photos

Right: Charlotte d'Amboise and chorus
Above: (center) Charlotte d'Amboise
Top: Paul Gyngell, Sally Ann Triplett,
Charlotte d'Amboise, Gene Anthony Ray

Linzi Hateley, Betty Buckley

Betty Buckley,
Linzi Hateley

Darlene Love,
Linzi Hateley

BROADWAY PRODUCTIONS FROM PAST SEASONS
THAT PLAYED THROUGH THIS SEASON

BROADWAY BOUND

By Neil Simon; Director, Gene Saks; Presented by Emanuel Azenberg; Scenery, David Mitchell; Costumes, Joseph G. Aulisi; Lighting, Tharon Musser; Sound, Tom Morse; Casting, Simon/Kumin; Hairstylist, J. Roy Helland; Assistant Director, Bill Molley; Technical Supervision, Arthur Siccardi, Pete Feller/Theatrical Services; Props, Jan Marasek; Assistant to Producer/Company Manager, Leslie Butler; Consultant, Jose Vega; Company Liaison, Linda Wright; Production Assistant, Katrina Stevens; Assistant Company Manager, Sammy Ledbetter; Props, John R. Wright; Stage Managers, Henry Velez, Barbara-Mae Phillips, Kurt Deutsch; Press, Bill Evans/Sandra Manley, Jim Randolph. Opened in the Broadhurst Theatre on Thursday, December 4, 1986*

CAST

Kate	Linda Lavin†1
Ben	John Randolph†2
Eugene	Jonathan Silverman†3
Stanley	Jason Alexander†4
Blanche	Phyllis Newman†5
Jack	Philip Sterling†6
Radio Voices:	
Mrs. Pitkin	Marilyn Cooper
Chubby Waters	MacIntyre Dixon
Announcer	Ed Herlihy

STANDBYS: Karen Ludwig (Kate/Blanche), Ben Hammer (Ben/Jack), Murray Rubinstein (Eugene/Stanley), Kurt Deutsch (Eugene)

A comedy in two acts. The action takes place in Brighton Beach, Brooklyn, New York, in February of the late 1940's.

*Closed Sept. 25, 1988 after 756 performances. "Tonys" were awarded Linda Lavin for Best Actress in a Play, and to John Randolph for Best Featured Actor in a Play.

†Succeeded by: 1. Elizabeth Franz, Joan Rivers, 2. Alan Manson, 3. Evan Handler, Adam Philipson, Kurt Deutsch, 4. Mark Nelson, David Nackman, 5. Carol Locatell, Karen Ludwig, 6. Dick Latessa

Martha Swope Photos

Right: Dick Latessa, Elizabeth Franz, Mark Nelson, Alan Manson, Evan Handler Top: (back) Carol Locatell, Dick Latessa, Mark Nelson, (seated) Elizabeth Franz, Evan Handler, Alan Manson

Adam Philipson, Joan Rivers

Evan Handler, Elizabeth Franz, Mark Nelson

CATS

Based on "Old Possum's Book of Practical Cats" by T. S. Eliot; Additional Lyrics, Trevor Nunn, Richard Stilgoe; Music, Andrew Lloyd Webber; Director, Trevor Nunn; Associate Director/Choreographer, Gillian Lynne; Presented by Cameron Macintosh, The Really Useful Company, David Geffen, The Shubert Organization; Executive Producers, R. Tyler Gatchell, Jr., Peter Neufeld; Design, John Napier; Lighting, David Hersey; Sound, Martin Levan; Musical Directors, Stanley Lebowsky, Jack Gaughan, David Caddick; Casting, Johnson-Liff & Zerman; Orchestrations, David Cullen, Andrew Lloyd Webber; Production Supervisor, Jeff Lee; Dance Supervisor, Richard Stafford; Company Manager, James G. Mennen; Make-up, Candace Carell; Assistant Choreographer, Jo-Anne Robinson; Dance Captain, Greg Minahan; Associate Conductor, Bill Grossman; Assistant Conductor, Arthur Greene; Management Associate, J. Anthony Magner; Production Assistant, Nancy Hall; Technical Supervisors, Theatre Services/Arthur Siccardi, Peter Feller; Props, George Green, Jr., Merlyn Davis, George Green III; Wardrobe, Adelaide Laurino, Rachele Bussanich; Hairstylists, Leon Gagliardi, Frank Paul, Beverly Belletiere, Byron Thomas, Michael Wasula; Wigs, Paul Huntley; Stage Managers, Sally J. Jacobs, Sherry Cohen, Don Walters; Press, Fred Nathan/Merle Frimark, Bert Fink, Philip Rinaldi, Marc P. Thibodeau, Fifi Schuettich; Cast Album by Geffen. Opened in the Winter Garden Theatre on Thursday, October 7, 1982*

CAST

Alonzo .... Scott Taylor
Bustopher Jones/Asparagus/Growlinger .... Bill Carmichael†1
Bombalurina .... Marlene Danielle
Cassandra .... Julietta Marcelli
Coricopat .... Johnny Anzalone
Mungojerrie .... Joe Antony Cavise†2
Demeter .... Patricia Ruck
Grizabella .... Laurie Beechman†3
Jellylorum/Griddlebone .... Bonnie Simmons
Jennyanydots .... Anna McNeely
Mistoffelees .... Don Johanson†4
Munkustrap .... Rob Marshall†5
Old Deuteronomy .... Clent Bowers†6
Plato/Macavity/Rumpus Cat .... Jamie Patterson
Pouncival .... Robert Montano†7
Rumpleteazer .... Paige Dana
Rum Tum Tugger .... Steve Yudson†8
Sillabub .... Teresa DeZarn†9
Skimbleshanks .... Robert Burnett
Tantomile .... Sundy Leigh Leake
Tumblebrutus .... Jay Poindexter
Victoria .... Claudia Shell
Cats Chorus .... Michael DeVries, Jay Aubrey Jones,
Susan Powers, Brenda Pressley

STANDBYS & UNDERSTUDIES: Brian Andrews/Jack Magradey/Greg Minahan (Alonzo), Michael DeVries (Bustopher/Asparagus/Growltiger), Karen Curlee/Rebecca Timms (Bombalurina/Cassandra), Lily-Lee Wong (Cassandra), Mark Hunter/Wade Laboissonniere/Jack Magradey/Greg Minahan (Corcopat), Karen Curlee/Susan Santoro/Rebecca Timms (Demeter), Karen Curlee/Brenda Pressley (Grizabella), Susan Powers/Mimi Wyche (Jennyanydots), Johnny Anzalone/John Joseph Festa (Mistoffelees), Brian Andrews/Wade Laboissoniere/Jack Magradey/Greg Minahan (Mungojerrie), Jack Magradey/Greg Minahan/Scott Taylor (Munkustrap), Jay Aubrey Jones (Old Deuteronomy), Susan Santoro/Suzanne Viverito/Lily-Lee Wong (Rumpleteazer), Marc Hunter/Jack Magradey/Greg Minahan/Jamie Patterson/Scott Taylor (Rum Tum Tugger), Karen Curlee/Rebecca Timms/Lily-Lee Wong (Tantomile), Brian Andrews/Wade Laboissonniere/Greg Minahan (Tumblebrutus), Paige Dana/Suzanne Viverito/Lily-Lee Wong (Victoria)

MUSICAL NUMBERS: Jellicle Songs for Jellicle Cats, The Naming of the Cats, The Old Gumbie Cat, The Rum Tum Tugger, Grizabella the Glamour Cat, Bustopher Jones, Mungojerrie and Rumpleteazer, Old Deuteronomy, The Awefull Batt of the Pekes and Pollicles, Marching Songs of the Pollicle Dogs, The Jellicle Ball, Memory, Moments of Happiness, Gus the Theatre Cat, Growltiger's Last Stand, Skimbleshanks, Macavity, Mr. Mistoffelees, Memory, The Journey to the Heaviside Layer, The Ad-Dressing of Cats

A musical in two acts and twelve scenes.

*Still playing May 31, 1988. Winner of 1983 "Tonys" for Best Musical, Book, Score, Direction, Supporting Musical Actress (Betty Buckley as Grizabella), Costumes, and Lighting. For original production, see THEATRE WORLD Vol. 39.

†Succeeded by: 1. Stephen Hanan, 2. Ray Roderick, 3. Loni Ackerman, 4. Kevin Poe, 5. Robert Amirante, 6. Larry Small, 7. John Joseph Festa, 8. Frank Mastrocola, 9. Susan Santoro

Martha Swope Photos

Loni Ackerman, and top with
Larry Small

A CHORUS LINE

Conceived/Choreographed/Directed by Michael Bennett; Book, James Kirkwood, Nicholas Dante; Music, Marvin Hamlisch; Lyrics, Edward Kleban; Co-Choreographer, Bob Avian; A New York Shakespeare Festival production presented by Joseph Papp in association with Plum Productions; Musical Direction/Vocal Arrangements, Don Pippin; Orchestrations, Bill Byers, Hershy Kay, Jonathan Tunick; Setting, Robin Wagner; Costumes, Theoni V. Aldredge; Lighting, Tharon Musser; Sound, Abe Jacob; Music Director, Jerry Goldberg; Music Coordinator, Robert Thomas; Associate Producer, Bernard Gersten; Original Cast Album by Columbia Records; Assistant to Choreographers, Baayork Lee; Company Manager, Robert Reilly; Dance Captain, Troy Garza; Wardrobe, Alyce Gilbert; Stage Managers, Tom Porter, Ronald Stafford, Morris Freed, Fraser Ellis; Press, Merle Debuskey, William Schelble, Richard Kornberg. Opened in the Shubert Theatre on Friday, July 25, 1975*

CAST

Roy	Tommy Re†1
Kristine	Kerry Casserly†2
Sheila	Cynthia Fleming†3
Mike	Mark Bove†4
Val	DeLyse Lively-Mekka†5
Butch	Michael-Pierre Dean
Larry	J. Richard Hart
Maggie	Pam Klinger†6
Richie	Bruce Anthony Davis
Tricia	Robin Lyon
Tom	Frank Kliegel
Zach	Eivund Harum†7
Mark	Andrew Grose
Cassie	Laurie Gamache
Judy	Trish Ramish†8
Lois	Cindi Klinger†9
Don	Michael Danek
Bebe	Tracy Shayne†10
Connie	Sachi Shimizu
Diana	Mercedes Perez†11
Al	Kevin Neil McCready†12
Frank	Fraser Ellis†13
Greg	Bradley Jones
Bobby	Ron Kurowski
Paul	Wayne Meledandri
Vicki	Laureen Valuch Piper†14
Ed	Morris Freed
Jarad	Troy Garza
Linda	Laurie Gamache†15
Douglas	Gary Chryst
Herman	Robert Amirante†16
Hilary	Dorothy Tancredi†17

UNDERSTUDIES: Arminae Azarian (Diane/Maggie/Connie/Bebe), Gary Chryst (Paul/Larry), Michael Danek (Zach), Michael-Pierre Dean (Richie), Fraser Ellis (Mark/Bobby/Don), Cynthia Fleming (Judy/Sheila/Cassie/Kristine), Morris Freed (Mark), Troy Garza (Mike/Greg/Paul/Larry/Al), J. Richard Hart (Zach/Mike), Bradley Jones (Bobby), Frank Kliegel (Don/Zach/Bobby), Robin Lyon (Bebe/Diana/Val/Maggie), Kevin Neil McCreedy (Al/Larry), William Mead (Al/Greg/Mike), Dana Moore (Cassie), Tommy Re (Greg), Wanda Richert (Cassie/Sheila), Julie Tussey (Val/Kristine)

MUSICAL NUMBERS: I Hope I Get It, I Can Do That, And . . . , At the Ballet, Sing!, Hello 12 Hello 13 Hello Love, Nothing, Dance 10 Looks 3, The Music and the Mirror, One, The Tap Combination, What I Did for Love, Finale

A musical performed without intermission. The action takes place in 1975 during an audition in this theatre.

*Still playing May 31, 1988. Cited as Best Musical of 1975 by NY Drama Critics Circle, winner of 1976 Pulitzer Prize, and 1976 "Tonys" for Best Musical, Book, Score, Direction, Lighting, Choreography, Best Actress in a Musical (Donna McKechnie), Best Featured Actor and Actress in a Musical (Sammy Williams, Kelly Bishop), and a Special Theatre World Award was presented to each member of the creative staff and original cast. See THEATRE WORLD Vol. 31. On Thursday, Sept. 29, 1983 it became the longest running show in Broadway history.

†Succeeded by: 1. Dale Stotts, 2. Flynn McMichaels, 3. Dana Moore, 4. Tommy Re, Kelly Patterson, Danny Herman, 5. Wanda Richert, 6. Dorothy Tancredi, 7. Robert LuPone, 8. Cindi Klinger, 9. Julie Tussey, 10. Karen Ziemba, 11. Denise Direnzo, 12. Tommy Re, 13. William Mead, 14. Cindi Klinger, Cynthia Fleming, 15. Dana Moore, Wanda Richert, Niki Harris, 16. Fraser Ellis, 17. Arminae Azarian

Martha Swope Photos

Cast in finale Above: Bruce Anthony Davis Top: Laurie Gamache

FENCES

By August Wilson; Director, Lloyd Richards; Presented by Carole Shorenstein Hays in association with the Yale Repertory Theatre; Set, James D. Sandefur; Costumes, Candice Donnelly; Lighting, Danianne Mizzy; Casting, Meg Simon/Fran Kumin; General Manager, Robert Kamlot; Company Manager, Lisa M. Poyer; Technical Supervision, Theatre Services/Arthur Siccardi, Peter Feller, Sr.; Props, George Wagner; Wardrobe, John A. Guiteras; Stage Managers, Martin Gold, Terrence J. Witter, Robert Gossett; Press, Joshua Ellis/Adrian Bryan-Brown, Leo Stern, Jackie Green, Susanne Tighe, Tim Ray. Opened in the 46th Street Theatre on Thursday, March 26, 1987*

CAST

Troy Maxson .... James Earl Jones†1
Jim Bono, Troy's friend ....Ray Aranha
Rose, Troy's wife .... Mary Alice†2
Lyons, Troy's older son ....Charles Brown†3
Gabriel, Troy's brother ....Frankie R. Faison†4
Cory, Troy and Rose's son ....Courtney B. Vance†5
Raynell, Troy's daughter ....Karima Miller†6

UNDERSTUDIES & STANDBYS: Gilbert Lewis (Troy), Ethel Ayler (Rose), Mike Hodge (Jim/Gabriel), Kevin Jackson (Cory), Robert Gossett (Lyons), Tamara Baker (Raynell)

A drama in 2 acts and 9 scenes. The action takes place from 1957 to 1965 in the backyard of the Maxson house in an urban neighborhood of a North American industrial city.

*Closed June 26, 1988 after 526 performances and 11 previews. Recipient of 1987 Pulitzer Prize for Drama, and adjudged Best Play by the New York Drama Critics Circle, the Outer Critics Circle, and the Drama Desk, and "Tonys" for Best Play, Best Actor (James Earl Jones), Best Featured Actress (Mary Alice), Best Director. It is the only play ever to win all 5 major theatre awards for best play.

†Succeeded by: 1. Billy Dee Williams, 2. Lynne Thigpen, 3. Vince Williams, 4. Roscoe Orman, 5. Byron Keith Minns, 6. Tatyana Ali

Ron Scherl Photos

Ray Aranha, Lynne Thigpen, Billy Dee Williams (front)

Top: (clockwise from top left) Ray Aranha, Vince Williams, Lynne Thigpen, Roscoe Orman, Tatyana Ali, Byron Keith Minns, Billy Dee Williams

42nd STREET

Music, Harry Warren; Lyrics, Al Dubin; Book, Michael Stewart, Mark Bramble; Based on novel by Bradford Ropes; Direction/Choreography, Gower Champion; Scenery, Robin Wagner; Costumes, Theoni V. Aldredge; Presented by David Merrick; Lighting, Tharon Musser; Musical Direction/Dance Arrangements, Donald Johnston; Orchestrations, Philip J. Lang; Vocal Arrangements, John Lesko; Sound, Richard Fitzgerald; Hairstylist, Ted Azar; Casting, Julie Hughes/Barry Moss; Dance Assistants, Karin Baker, Randy Skimmer; General Manager, Leo K. Cohen; Dance Captain, Lizzie Moran; Props, Leo Herbert; Wardrobe, Gene Wilson, Shelly Friedman; Assistant Musical Director, Bernie Leighton; Company Manager, Marcia Goldberg; Stage Managers, Jack Timmers, Harold Goldfaden, Michael Pule, Dennis Angulo; Press, Joshua Ellis/Adrian Bryan-Brown, Jackie Green, Bill Shuttleworth, Susanne Tighe. Opened in the Winter Garden Theatre on Monday, Aug. 25, 1980, moved to the Majestic Theatre on Monday, March 30, 1981, and to the St. James Theatre on Tuesday, Apr. 7, 1987*

CAST

Andy Lee	Danny Carroll
Oscar	Robert Colston
Mac/Doctor	Stan Page
Annie	Beth Leavel
Maggie Jones	Denise Lor†1
Bert Barry	Joseph Bova
Billy Lawlor	Lee Roy Reams†2
Peggy Sawyer	Clare Leach
Lorraine	Neva Leigh
Phyllis	Jeri Kansas
Julian Marsh	Jamie Ross†3
Dorothy Brock	Elizabeth Allen
Abner Dillon	Don Crabtree
Pat Denning	Steve Elmore†3
Thugs	Stan Page, Ron Schwinn

ENSEMBLE: Susan Banks, Carole Banninger, Dennis Batutis, Paula Joy Belis, Kelly Crafton, Ronny DeVito, Rob Draper, Barndt Edward, Judy Ehrlich, David Fredericks, Cathy Greco, Christine Jacobsen, Suzie Jary, Jeri Kansas, Billye Kersey, Neva Leigh, Bobby Longbottom, Chris Lucas, Maureen Mellon, Ken Mitchell, Bill Nabel, Don Percassi, Rosemary Rado, Anne Rutter, Linda Sabatelli, Jeanna Schweppe, David Schwing, Ron Schwinn, Pamela S. Scott, J. Thomas Smith, Karen Sorensen, Susanne Leslie Sullivan, Vickie Taylor, Mary Chris Wall
UNDERSTUDIES: Connie Day (Dorothy/Maggie), Karen Sorensen (Dorothy), Steve Elmore/Stan Page (Julian), Vickie Taylor/Debra Ann Draper (Peggy), Rob Draper/Dennis Angulo (Billy), Bill Nabel/Ron Schwinn (Bert/Mac), Don Percassi/Ron Schwinn (Andy), Stan Page (Abner), Stan Page/Brandt Edwards (Pat), Billye Kersey (Linda Sabatelli (Annie), Bernie Leighton (Oscar), Lizzie Moran/Debra Ann Draper (Phyllis/Lorraine), Ensemble: Debra Ann Draper, Lizzie Moran, Brenda Pipik, Dennis Angulo, John Salvatore
MUSICAL NUMBERS: Audition, Young and Healthy, Shadow Waltz, Go into Your Dance, You're Getting to Be a Habit with Me, Getting Out of Town, Dames, I Know Now, We're in the Money, Sunny Side to Every Situation, Lullaby of Broadway, About a Quarter to Nine, Overture, Shuffle Off to Buffalo, 42nd Street

A musical in 2 acts and 16 scenes. The action takes place during 1933 in New York City and Philadelphia.

*Closed Jan. 8, 1989 after 3485 performances. Recipient of 1981 "Tonys" for Best Musical, and Best Choreography. For original production, see THEATRE WORLD Vol. 37.

†Succeeded by: 1. Bobo Lewis, 2. Jim Walton, 3. Barry Nelson during vacation, 4. Michael Dantuono

Martha Swope Photos

Top Right: Jim Walton and chorus

LES MISERABLES

Music, Claude-Michel Schonberg; Lyrics, Herbert Kretzmer; Book, Alain Boublil, Claude-Michel Schonberg; Based on novel of same name by Victor Hugo; Directed and Adapted by Trevor Nunn, John Caird; Presented by Cameron Mackintosh; Original French text by Alain Boublil, Jean-Marc Natel; Additional Material, James Fenton; Orchestral Score, John Cameron; Musical Supervision/Direction, Robert Billig; Designed by John Napier; Lighting, David Hersey; Costumes, Andreane Neofitou; Sound, Andrew Bruce/Autograph; Executive Producers, Martin McCallum, Richard Jay-Alexander; Conductor, Ted Sperling; Casting, Johnson-Liff & Zerman; General Management, Alan Wasser; Produced in association with the JFK Center for the Performing Arts (Roger L. Stevens, Chairman); Original Cast Album by Geffen Records; Associate Director, Richard Jay-Alexander; Production Supervisor, Sam Stickler; Associate General Manager, Allan Williams; Technical Manager, John H. Paull III; Associate Manager, Beth Riedmann; Lighting Coordinator, Betsy Pool; Associate Sound Designer, Abe Jacob; Dance Captains, Diane Della Piazza, Jordan Leeds; Associate Production Manager, Marie Barrett; Props, Timothy Abel; Wardrobe, Adelaide Laurino; Wigs, Jody Thomas; Stage Managers, Bill Buxton, Marybeth Abel, Susan L. Derwin; Press, Fred Nathan/Marc Thibodeau, Merle Frimark, Bert Fink, Philip Rinaldi, Scott Taylor, Fifi Schuettich. Opened in the Broadway Theatre on Thursday, March 12, 1987*

CAST

Prologue (1815, Digne): Jean Valjean (Colm Wilkinson succeeded by Gary Morris/Tim Shew), Javert (Terrence Mann succeeded by Anthony Crivello), Chain Gang (Tim Shew, Joel Robertson, Stephen Bogardus, John Dewar, Leo Murmeister, Joseph Kolinski, Ray Walker, Bruce Kuhn, Michael Maguire), Farmer (Jesse Corti), Labourer (Bruce Kuhn), Innkeeper's Wife (Susan Goodman), Innkeeper (John Norman), Bishop (Norman Large), Constables (Marcus Lovett, Steve Shocket).
1823 Montreuil-sur-Mer: Fantine (Randy Graff), Foreman (Joel Robertson), Workers (Jesse Corti, John Dewar, Cindy Benson, Marcie Shaw, Jane Bodle, Joanna Glushak), Factory Girl (Ann Crumb succeeded by Janene Lovullo), Sailors (Joseph Kolinski, John Dewar, Tim Shew), Whores (Susan Goodman, Joanna Glushak, Jane Bodle, Kelli James, Janene Lovullo, Lisa Ann Grant, Tracy Shayne, Gretchen Kingsley-Weihe), Old Woman (Cindy Benson), Crone (Marcie Shaw), Pimp (Steve Shocket), Bamatabois (Stephen Bogardus), Fauchelevent (Steve Shocket)
1823 Montfermeil: Young Cosette (Donna Vivino, Amy Beth, Shanelle Workman), Mme. Thenardier (Jennifer Butt), Thenardier (Leo Murmeister), Young Eponine (Shanelle Workman, Amy Beth), Drinker (Jesse Corti), Young Couple (Bruce Kuhn, Gretchen Kingsley-Weihe), Drunk (John Norman), Diners (Norman Large, Joanna Glushak), Other Drinkers (Steve Shocket, Stephen Bogardus, Tim Shew, Janene Lovullo, Susan Goodman, Cindy Benson), Young Man (Joseph Kolinski), Young Girls (Jane Bodle, Lisa Ann Grant), Old Couple (Marcie Shaw, John Dewar), Travelers (Joel Robertson, Marcus Lovett)
1832 Paris: Gavroche (Danny Gerard), Old Beggar Woman (Susan Goodman), Young Prostitute (Janene Lovullo), Pimp (John Norman), Eponine (Frances Ruffelle succeeded by Kelli James), Montparnasse (Bruce Kuhn), Babet (Marcus Lovett), Brujon (Tim Shew), Claquesous (Steve Shocket), Enjolras (Michael Maguire), Marius (Ray Walker), Cosette (Judy Kuhn succeeded by Tracy Shayne), Combeferre (Joel Robertson), Feuilly (Joseph Kolinski), Courfeyrac (Jesse Corti), Joly (John Dewar), Grantaire (Stephen Bogardus), Lesgles (Norman Large), Jean Prouvaire (John Norman)

UNDERSTUDIES: Joel Robertson (Valjean), Stephen Bogardus/Bruce Kuhn/Norman Large (Javert), John Dewar/Bruce Kuhn/Steve Shocket (Bishop), Janene Lovullo/Joanna Glushak (Fantine), Amy Beth/Shanelle Workman (Young Cosette), Cindy Benson/Marcie Shaw (Mme. Thenardier), Norman Large/John Norman/Bruce Kuhn (Thenardier), Amy Beth (Young Eponine), David Burdick (Gavroche), Lisa Ann Grant/Gretchen Kingsley-Weihe (Eponine), Marcus Lovett/Joseph Kolinski (Marius), Gretchen Kingsley-Weihe/Jane Bodle (Cosette), Joseph Kolinski/Jordan Leeds (Enjolras), Swings: Patrick A'Hearn, Anny Degange, Nina Hennessey, Jordan Leeds

MUSICAL NUMBERS: Prologue, Soliloquy, At the End of the Day, I Dreamed a Dream, Lovely Ladies, Who Am I?, Come to Me, Castle on a Cloud, Master of the House, Thenardier Waltz, Look Down, Stars, Red and Black, Do You Hear the People Sing?, In My Life, A Heart Full of Love, One Day More, On My Own, A Little Fall of Rain, Drink with Me to Days Gone By, Bring Him Home, Dog Eats Dog, Turning, Empty Chairs at Empty Tables, Wedding Chorale, Beggars at the Feast, Finale

A dramatic musical in 2 acts and 4 scenes with a prologue.

*Still playing May 31, 1988. Winner of 1987 "Tonys" for Best Musical, Best Musical Book, Best Musical Score, Best Featured Actor and Actress in a Musical (Michael Maguire, Frances Ruffelle), Best Direction of a Musical, Best Scenic Design, Best Lighting Design.

Michael LePoer/Bob Marshak/Joan Marcus Photos

Michael Maguire (center) Above: Gary Morris, Randy Graff

Top Left: Gary Morris, Anthony Crivello
Below: Gary Morris; Kelli James

ME AND MY GIRL

Book and Lyrics, L. Arthur Rose, Douglas Furber; Music, Noel Gay; Book Revision, Stephen Fry; Contributions to revision, Mike Ockrent; Director, Mike Ockrent; Presented by Richard Armitage, Terry Allen Kramer, James M. Nederlander, Stage Promotions Ltd.; Choreography, Gillian Gregory; Sets, Martin Johns; Costumes, Ann Curtis; Lighting, Chris Ellis, Roger Morgan; Musical Direction, Stanley Lebowsky; Sound, Tom Baker; Casting, Howard Feuer; General Manager, Ralph Roseman; Company Manager, Robb Lady; Technical Director, Jeremiah Harris; Props, Joseph Harris, Jr., Ted Wondsel; Wardrobe, Linda Berry, Cissy Obidowski; Dance Captain, Tony Parise; Wigs, Tiv Davenport, Antonio Belo; Make-up, Margaret Sunshine; Hairstylist, Paul Huntley; Associate Music Director, Tom Helm; Stage Managers, Steven Zweigbaum, Arturo E. Porazzi, Tracy Crum; Press, Jeffrey Richards/C. George Willard, Ben Morse, Susan Lee, Marie-Louise Silva, Ken Mandelbaum, Audrey Scheiderman. Opened the new Marquis Theatre on Sunday, August 10, 1986*

CAST

Lady Jacqueline Carstone .... Jane Summerhays†1
Honorable Gerald Bolingbroke ....Nick Ullett†2
Lord Battersby ....Eric Hutson†3
Lady Battersby ....Justine Johnston†4
Stockbrokers .... Cleve Asbury†5, Randy Hills,
                                        Barry McNabb†6
Footman ....Larry Hansen
Herbert Parchester ....Timothy Jerome
Sir Jasper Tring ....Leo Leyden
Maria, Duchess of Dene ....Jane Connell
Sir John Tremayne ....George S. Irving
Charles Heathersett, butler ....Thomas Toner
Bill Snibson ....Robert Lindsay†7
Sally Smith ....Maryann Plunkett†8
Pub Pianist ....John Spalla
Mrs. Worthington-Worthington ....Gloria Hodes
Lady Diss ....Elizabeth Larner†9
Lady Brighton/Lambeth Tart ....Susan Cella†10
Bob Barking ....Kenneth H. Waller†11
Telegraph Boy ....Bill Brassea†12
Constable ....Eric Johnson†13
Mrs. Brown ....Elizabeth Larner†14

ENSEMBLE: J. B. Adams, Marc Agnes, Gail Benedict, Michael Turner Cline, Sheri Cowart, Michael Duran, Larry Hansen, Ann Heinricher, Ida Henry, Nancy Hess, Randy Hills, Gloria Hodes, John Jellison, Kenneth Kantor, Wiley Kidd, Bobby Longbottom, John MacInnis, Donna Monroe, Barbara Moroz, John Spalla, Cynthia Thole, Martin Van Treuren, Dana Walker, John M. Wiltberger
UNDERSTUDIES: Larry Hansen (Gerald), Sheri Cowart (Sally), Justine Johnston (Duchess), Eric Hutson (Sir John), Susan Cella (Jacqueline), John Spalla (Parchester), Kenneth H. Waller (Jasper/Battersby/Heathersett), Elizabeth Larner (Lady Battersby), Donna Monroe (Mrs. Brown), Barbara Moroz (Lady Brighten/Lady Diss), Michael Hayward-Jones (Constable), Jonathan Brody (Barking), Swings: Corinne Melancon, Tony Parise
MUSICAL NUMBERS: A Weekend at Hareford, Thinking of No-One But Me, The Family Solicitor, Me and My Girl, An English Gentleman, You Would If You Could, Hold My Hand, Once You Lose Your Heart, Preparation Fugue, The Lambeth Walk, The Sun Has Got His Hat On, Take It on the Chin, Song of Hareford, Love Makes the World Go Round, Leaning on a Lamppost, Finale

A musical in 2 acts and 9 scenes with a prologue. The action takes place in the late 1930's in and around Hareford Hall, Hampshire, Mayfair and Lambeth.

*Still playing May 31, 1988. "Tonys" were awarded Robert Lindsay and Maryann Plunkett (Best Actor and Actress in a Musical), and Gillian Gregory for Best Choreography.

†Succeeded by: 1. Dee Hoty, 2. Edward Hibbert, Nick Ullett, 3. Herb Foster, Merwin Goldsmith, 4. Eleanor Glockner, 5. Bobby Longbottom, 6. John MacInnis, 7. Jim Dale, James Brennan, 8. Ellen Foley, 9. Donna Monroe, 10. Ann Heinricher, 11. J. B. Adams, 12. Jamie Torcellini, John M. Wiltberger, 13. John Jellison, 14. Eleanor Glockner

Arturo E. Porazzi Photos

Ensemble in "Hold My Hand" Above: Jim Dale, Ellen Foley Top: George S. Irving, Jane Connell, Jim Dale, Ellen Foley

OH! CALCUTTA!

Devised by Kenneth Tynan; Conceived and Directed by Jacques Levy; Presented by Hillard Elkins, Norman Kean; Production Supervisor, Ron Nash; Authors & Composers, Robert Benton, David Newman, Jules Feiffer, Dan Greenburg, Lenore Kandel, John Lennon, Jacques Levy, Leonard Melfi, Sam Shepard, Clovis Trouille, Kenneth Tynan, Sherman Yellen; Music & Lyrics, Robert Dennis, Peter Schickle, Stanley Walden; Conductor, Tim Weil; Scenery/Lighting, Harry Silverglat Darrow; Costumes, Kenneth M. Yount; Sound, Sander Hacker; Assistant to Director, Nancy Tribush; Projections, Gardner Compton; Live Action Film, Ron Merk; Company Manager, Doris J. Buberl; Producer, Norman Kean; Executive Producer, Maria Productions; Production Associates, Karen Nagle, Nancy Arrigo; Assistant General Manager, Tobias Beckwith; Assistant Musical Conductor, Dan Carter; Wardrobe, Mark Bridges; Stage Managers, Maria DiDia, Ron Nash; Press, Les Schecter. Opened at the Eden Theatre on Friday, June 17, 1969 and at the Edison Theatre on Friday, Sept. 24, 1976*

CAST

Cheryl Hartley†	William Thomas
Jodi Johnson	David Heisey
Danielle P. Connell	Louis Silvers
Deborah Robertson	James E. Mosiej

MUSICAL NUMBERS & SKITS: Taking Off the Robe, Will Answer All Sincere Replies, Playing, Jack and Jill, The Paintings of Clovis Trouille, Delicious Indignities, Was It Good for You Too?, Suite for Five Letters, One on One, Rock Garden, Spread Your Love Around, Four in Hand, Coming Together Going Together

*Still playing May 31, 1988. For original production see *THEATRE WORLD* Vol 26.

†During the year the following replacements joined William Thomas to complete the cast: Scott Baker, Jacqueline Fay, Amy Fortgang, Philip Gibson, Peter Lanigan, Katherine Miller, Ann Neville.

Right: David Heisey, Nannette Bevelander, Charles Klausmeyer, Jodi Johnson, Deborah Robertson, Michael A. Clarke, Cheryl Hartley, James E. Mosiej

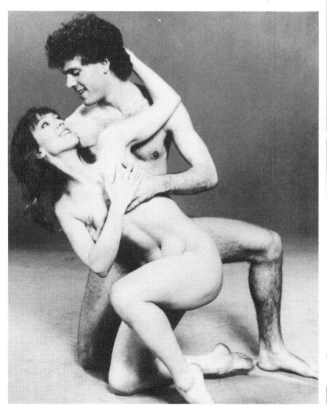

Cheryl Hartley, Michael Clarke

Michael A. Clarke, Cheryl Hartley, James E. Mosiej,
David Heisey, Nannette Bevelander, Deborah Robertson,
Charles Klausmeyer, Jodi Johnson

STARLIGHT EXPRESS

Music, Andrew Lloyd Webber; Lyrics, Richard Stilgoe; Director, Trevor Nunn; Choreography, Arlene Phillips; Designer, John Napier; Presented by Martin Starger and Lord Grade in association with MCA Music Entertainment Group, Stage Promotions (Four) Strada Holdings, Weintraub Entertainment Group; Executive Producer, Gatchell & Neufeld; Production Adviser, Arthur Cantor; Casting, Johnson-Liff; Orchestrations, David Cullen, Andrew Lloyd Webber; Musical Direction/Supervision, David Caddick; Musical Director, Paul Bogaev; Sound, Martin Levan; Lighting, David Hersey; Concept album on MCA Compact Discs, HiQ Cassettes and Records; Company Managers, Roger Gindi, Tom Domenici; Technical Supervisor, Peter Fulbright; Computer Designer, Dan Hoffman; Skating Coach/Consultant, Michal Fraley; Dance Captain, Denny Shearer; Second Director, Dion McHugh; Wardrobe, Adelaide Laurino, David Hemenway; Hairstylists, Leon Gagliardi, Wayne Herndon, David Brian Brown; Make-up, Nanci Powell; Production Assistant, Graham Ingle; Stunt Coordinator, J. P. Romano; Wigs, Paul Huntley; Stage Managers, Perry Cline, Randall Whitescarver, Janet Friedman, Bonnie Panson, Michael J. Passaro, Clayton Phillips; Press, Bill Evans/Sandra Manley, Jim Randolph. Opened in the Gershwin Theatre on Sunday, March 15, 1987*

CAST

Bobo	A. C. Ciulla†1
Espresso	Philip Clayton
Weltschaft	Michael Berglund
Turnov	William Frey†2
Hashamoto	D. Michael Heath†3
Prince of Wales	Sean McDermott
Greaseball	Robert Torti†4
Greaseball's Gang	Todd Lester, Sean Grant, Ronald Garza, Angel Vargas, Joey McNeely†5, Gordon Owens, Marc Villa
Rusty	Greg Mowry
Pearl	Reva Rice
Dinah	Jane Krakowski
Ashley	Andrea McArdle†6
Buffy	Jamie Beth Chandler†7
Rocky I	Frank Mastrocola†8
Rocky II	Sean Grant
Rocky III	Ronald Garza
Rocky IV	Angel Vargas
Dustin	Michael Scott Gregory†9
Flat-Top	Todd Lester†10
Red Caboose	Berry K. Bernal†11
Krupp	Joey McKneely†12
Wrench	Christina Youngman
Joule	Nicole Picard†13
Volta	Mary Ann Lamb†14
Purse	Gordon Owens
Electra	Ken Ard
Poppa	Steve Fowler
Belle	Janet Williams Adderley
Voice of the boy	Braden Danner
Voice of the mother	Melanie Vaughan
Starlight Chorus	Paul Binotto†15, Lon Hoyt, Melanie Vaughan, Mary Windholtz

STANDBYS & UNDERSTUDIES: Ashley (Amelia Prentice, Christina Youngman), Belle (Lola Knox/Janice Lorraine/Amelia Prentice), Bobo (Anthony Galde/D. Michael Heath/Ron Morgan/Dwight Toppin), Buffy (Janice Lorraine/Jennifer Prescott), Dinah (Kimberly Blake/Dorie Herndon/Amelia Prentice/Jennifer Prescott), Dustin (Anthony Galde/D. Michael Heath/Sean McDermott/Ron Morgan), Electra (Michael-Demby Cain/Philip Clayton/Broderick Wilson), Espresso (Anthony Galde/D. Michael Heath/Broderick Wilson), Flat-Top (Anthony Galde/D. Michael Heath), Greaseball (Bryan Batt/Ron DeVito), Joule (Janice Lorraine/Amelia Prentice/Jennifer Prescott), Krupp (Anthony Galde/Ron Morgan/Broderick Wilson), Pearl (Janice Lorraine/Jennifer Prescott), Poppa (Danny Strayhorn/Broderick Wilson) Purse (Michael-Demby Dain/Ron Morgan, Dwight Toppin/Broderick Wilson), Red Caboose (Anthony Galde/Ron Morgan), Rocky I (Michael-Demby Cain/Ron Morgan/Dwight Toppin/Broderick Wilson), Rocky II (Michael-Demby Cain/Ron Morgan/Dwight Toppin/Broderick Wilson), Rocky III (Michael-Demby Cain/Ron Morgan/Dwight Toppin/Broderick Wilson), Rocky IV (Michael-Demby Cain/Sean Grant/Sean McDermott), Turnov (D. Michael Heath/Ron Morgan/Dwight Toppin), Volta (Janice Lorraine/Amelia Prentice/Jennifer Prescott/Christina Youngman), Weltschaft (Anthony Galde D. Michael Heath/Ron Morgan), Wrench (Janice Lorraine/Amelia Prentice/Jennifer Prescott), Swings: Michael-Demby Cain, Anthony Galde, D. Michael Heath, Ron Morgan, Janice Lorraine, Amelia Prentice, Jennifer Prescott, Dwight Toppin, Broderick Wilson

Top Right: Robert Torti (center)
Bottom: Greg Mowry, Reva Rice, Jane Krakowski, Lola Knox, Andrea McArdle

MUSICAL NUMBERS: Overture, Rolling Stock, Engine of Love, Lotta Locomotion, Freight, Pumping Iron, Make Up My Heart, Race One, There's Me, Poppa's Blues, Belle, Race Two, Laughing Stock, Starlight Express, Silver Dollar, U.N.C.O.U.P.L.E.D., Wide Smile High Style That's Me, First Final, Right Place Right Time, I Am the Starlight, Final Selection, One Rock & Roll Too Many, Only You, Light at the End of the Tunnel

A musical in two acts.

*Closed Jan. 8, 1989 after 761 performances and 22 previews. Recipient of 1987 "Tony" for Best Costume Design.

†Succeeded by: 1. Brian Carmack, 2. Ron DeVito, 3. Ken Rose, 4. John Schiappa, 5. Roger Kachel, 6. Stacia Goad, 7. Lola Knox, 8. Bryan Batt, 9. Keith Allen, 10. Marc Villa, 11. Todd Lester, 12. Roger Kachel, 13. Kimberly Blake, 14. Dorie Herndon, 15. Willy Falk

Martha Swope Photos

OFF-BROADWAY PRODUCTIONS

(Samuel Beckett Theatre) Wednesday, June 3, 1987 (closing and number of performances not provided) Quaigh Theatre (Will Lieberson, Artistic Director; Judith Rubin, Executive Producer) presents:
HOLY HEIST by Ann Harson; Director, Patricia Place; Set & Lighting, David Perkins; Costumes, Deanna Majewski; Special Effects, Deedee Bush; Sound, George Jacobs; Stage Managers, Nancy Rutter, Pedro J. Rosado, Jr.; Casting, Timothy Wilson; Press, David Rothenberg, Jeffrey Smith. CAST: Adam Philipson (Boy/Understudy), Michael Twaine (Monsignor), Peter Love (Domenic), Louis Mustillo (Carooch), Rafael Ferrer (Lujohn), Elizabeth Karr (Pompelia), Joseph Rose (Victor), Gene Santarelli (Father Sylvester), Judith Scarpone (Angela), Bill Ferriter (Announcer). A play in 2 acts and 6 scenes. The action takes place in an alcove of St. Joseph's Church at the present time, and in the basement of the Buongiovanni home in Brooklyn in 1939.

(Harold Clurman Theatre) Wednesday, June 3–21, 1987 (24 performances) Stage Three (Artistic Associates, Patty Heaton, James Ryan, Joy Young; Managing Director, Jerry Polner; Administrator, Sarah Horowitz) presents:
THE JOHNSTOWN VINDICATOR by Quincy Long; Director, Evan Yionoulis; Set, Rosario Provenza; Lighting, Donald Holder; Costumes, Candice Donnelly; Dramaturg, Kathleen Dimmick; Technical Director, Peter Barbieri; Casting, Lisa Peterson; Stage Managers, Kathleen Mellor, Judith Scher; Press, Shirley Herz, Peter Cromarty. CAST: James Harper (Vern), Elizabeth Owens (Mother), Matthew Lewis (Howard), Vince Grant (J.J.), Ron Faber (Funk), Tessie Hogan (Janet), David Thornton (Carl), Patty Heaton (Pepper), Paul Geier (Tucci). A play in 3 acts with one intermission. The action takes place at the present time in the city room of a daily newspaper.

(Open Space) Wednesday, June 3–28, 1987 (28 performances) The Open Space Theatre Experiment (Lynn Michaels, Artistic Director) presents:
THE BALD SOPRANO/THE LEADER by Eugene Ionesco; Translated by Donald M. Allen; Director, Joseph Chaiken; Associate Director, Nancy Gabor; Set, Watoku Ueno; Lighting, Beverly Emmons; Costumes, Mary Brecht; Sound, Gary Harris; Dramaturg, Bill Coco; Technical Director, Ken Young; Stage Managers, T. J. Carroll, Lillian Butler; Press, Bruce Cohen, Kathleen von Schmid. CAST: Yolande Bavan, Geoffrey C. Ewing, Judith Cohen, Sam Tsoutsouvas, John Turturro, Jayne Haynes

Elizabeth Owens, James Harper in "Johnstown Vindicator" *(Carol Rosegg Photo)* Top: Peter Love, Elizabeth Karr, Rafael Ferrer in "Holy Heist" *(Adam Newman Photo)*

(Courtyard Playhouse) Wednesday, June 3, 1987, and moved to McGinn/Cazale Theatre before transfer Friday, Oct. 16, 1987 to 47th Street Theatre, and then to the Harold Clurman Theatre where it was still playing May 31, 1988. Presented by Actors Collective in association with the Methuen Company.
PERFECT CRIME by Warren Manzi; Director, Jeffrey Hyatt; Set, Chris Pickart; Lighting, John Sellars; Costumes, Barbara Blackwood; Sound, Phil Lee, Scott G. Miller, Tim Pritchard; Stage Manager, Tim Pritchard; Press, Bruce Cohen/Kathleen von Schmid, Michelle Vincents. CAST: Cathy Russell (Margaret Thorne Brent), Perry Pirkkanen (Inspector James Ascher), Warren Manzi (W. Harrison Brent), John Sellars (Lionel McAuley), W. MacGregor King (David Breuer)
A psychological "thriller" in two acts.

(INTAR Hispanic American Arts Center) Wednesday, June 3,–July 5, 1987 (33 performances). Presented by INTAR (Max Ferra, Artistic Director; Dennis Ferguson-Acosta, Managing Director)
OUR LADY OF THE TORTILLA by Luis Santeiro; Director, Max Ferra; Set, James Sandefur; Lighting, Michael R. Chybowski; Costumes, Arnall Downs; Sound, Gary & Timmy Harris; Casting, Janet L. Murphy; Stage Manager, Jesse Wooden, Jr.; Press, Bruce Cohen/Kathleen von Schmid CAST: Lillian Hurst (Dolores Cantu), Al Septien (Nelson Cruz), Maria Cellario (Dahlia Cruz), Betsy Aidem (Beverly Barnes), Roger Rignack (Eddy Cruz), Beatriz H. Milian (Voice of Valerie Spinetti)
A comedy in two acts. The action takes place at the present time in the living room of a New Jersey town—although it could happen in any Latin neighborhood of the U.S.

(Westside Arts Theatre) Thursday, June 11,–July 25, 1987 (54 performances and 9 previews). Barbara Darwall, Peter von Mayrhauser, Maggie Lear, Janet Robinson, Harold Thau present the Manhattan Class Company (Executive Directors, Robert LuPone, Bernard Telsey) production of:
BEIRUT by Alan Bowne; Director, Jimmy Bohr; Set, Elizabeth Doyle; Costumes, Walker Hicklin; Lighting, John Hastings; Casting, Bernard Telsey; Associate Producers, Robert Courson, Arthur Dinitz; Company Manager, Ken Silverman; Sound, Tom Source; Stage Manager, Laura Kravets; Press, Bill Evans/Sandra Manley, Jim Randolph CAST: Michael David Morrison (Torch), Laura San Giacomo (Blue), Terry Rabine (Guard), Understudies: Jack Gwaitney, Robin Morse. A drama without intermission. The action takes place in the near future on the lower East Side of Manhattan.

Michael David Morrison, Laura SanGiacomo in "Beirut" Above: Cathy Russell, Warren Manzi in "Perfect Crime" *(Martha Swope Photo)*

(John Houseman Theatre) Tuesday, June 16,–July 17, 1987 (23 performances and 2 previews) Eric Krebs and Arthur Shafman Ltd. present: **THE LATE GREAT LADIES OF BLUES AND JAZZ** conceived, written and performed by Sandra Reaves-Phillips; Musical Director, George Butcher; Set, Daniel Proett; Lighting, Shirley Prendergast; Costumes, Michael Hannah; Supervisor, Christopher Dunlop; Wigs/Hairstylist, Gwen Nelson; Additional Costumes, Camille Howard; Staging Consultant, Mike Malone; Additional Staging, Lacy Darryl Phillips; Presented by arrangement with Great Lady Productions; General Management, Whitbell Productions; Wardrobe, Gwen Nelson; Sound, Josette Amato; Associate General Manager, Paul Morer; Press, Shirley Herz Associates/Glenna Freedman, Peter Cromarty, Pete Sanders, David Roggensack, Miller Wright.

A musical in two acts.

(Riverwest Theatre) Wednesday, June 17–20, 1987 (limited 7 performances). Dragonfly Theatre Company (William Lucas Walker, Artistic Director) presents four one-act plays under the title of: **SLIVERS:** Set, William Lucas Walker; Lighting, Karl E. Haas; Sound, Ron Barrett; Production Coordinator, Mary Anne Rubacky; Stage Manager, Leah Schneider *"Nights in Hohokus"* by Jason Milligan; Director, Angelo Tiffe; with Kevin Cristaldi, Max Jaffe. *"The Good Father"* by Roy Cockrum; Director, Tina Ball; with Susanna M. Banks, Navida Stein. *"PxP"* by Scott Shook; Director, James Luse; with Carl Zeliger, Scott Shook. *"Sorry"* by Timothy Mason; Director, Max Jaffe; with Beth Koules, William Lucas Walker

(Perry Street Theatre) Friday, June 19,–July 1, 1987 (11 performances) Upstart Crow (Cheryl Royce, Artistic Director) presents: **UNDER THE SKIN** by Betty Lambert; Director, Anthony Giaimo; Set, Andrew Greenhut; Lighting, Deborah Constantine; Costumes, Jay Stanzel; Sound, Bob Davies; Casting, John Cavoto; Technical Directors, Gerald J. Quimby, John French; Props, Alex Flamberg; Stage Managers, Gerald J. Quimby, Tom Downey; Press, Annette Paparella CAST: Cheryl Lesley Royce (Maggie Benton), Ellen Fiske (Renee Gifford), Robert King (John Gifford)

A drama in two acts and eight scenes. The action takes place at the present time in the Gifford house in a college surburb on the Northwest Coast.

(T.O.M.I. Theatre) Thursday, June 18–30, 1987 (11 performances) Our Workshop East (Lenore Dekoven, Artistic Director) presents: **THE HOUSE OF BERNARDA ALBA** by Fererico Garcia Lorca; Producer/Director, Julia Robinson; Set/Lighting, Ronald Lee Hiatt; Costumes, Beatrix Aruna Pasztor; Sound, David Pastecchi; General Manager, David Conte; Visual Artist, Linda Harvey; Music, Jill Garland, Felix Mendes, Rafael Picorelli, Yamila Constantina; Press, Bruce Cohen, Kathleen von Schmid CAST: Elizabeth Bove, Sarah Melici, Charlotte Fleck, Alexandra Gittes, June Squibb, Luz Castanos, Monica Ziegler, Lally Ross, Victoria Boomsma, Laura Garcia, Barbara Gruen, Kathie Longtin

(Space 603) Thursday, June 23–26, 1987 (4 performances). Staret . . . The Directors Company (Michael Parva, Artistic-Producing Director; Victoria Lanman Chesshire, Artistic-Managing Director) presents: **TALES OF PETE MULDOON—G-MAN!** by John Averill; Director, Jane I. Roth; Set, Clifton Taylor; Costumes, Barbara Wolfe; Lighting, Deborah Ellen Matlack; Sound, L. Allen Scheid; Production Manager, Terry Dudley; Stage Manager, Thais Fitzsimmons; Press, Elizabeth Tooker. CAST: Andrew Watts (Voice of Authority), Allan Havey (Pete Muldoon), David Grant Munnell (Layflat), Joseph Reed (Berryman), Liz Trepel (Maryanne/Claire), Carol McCann (Natasha)

A play in 2 acts and 11 scenes. The action takes place sometime in the 1940's in the United States with a quick trip to Buenos Aires.

(Space 603) Thursday, July 7–10, 1987 (4 performances) Staret . . . The Directors Company (Artistic/Producing Director, Michael Parva; Artistic/Managing Director, Victoria Lanman Chesshire) presents: **THE MAGIC MAN** by Jeanne Marshall; Director, James Dawson; Set/Lighting, Sean Murphy; Sound, Bruce D. Cameron; Associate Producer, Nelson Taxel; Production Manager, Terry Dudley; Stage Manager, Adam Kushner; Press, Elizabeth Tooker. CAST: Kymberly Dakin (Audrey), Russ Jolly (Winston), Paul Urbanski (Mitchell), Herb (Himself)

A play in 2 acts and 12 scenes. The action takes place at the present time in a loft on the lower east side of Manhattan.

(Lucille Lortel Theatre) Friday, June 19, 1987–and still playing May 31, 1988. Kyle Renick by special arrangement with Lucille Lortel presents the WPA Theatre production of:
STEEL MAGNOLIAS by Robert Harling; Director, Pamela Berlin; Setting, Edward T. Gianfrancesco; Lighting, Craig Evans; Costumes, Don Newcomb; Hairstylist, Bobby H. Grayson; Sound, Aural Fixation; Stage Manager, Karen Moore, Bryan Burch; General Manager, Albert Poland; Company Manager, Marion Finkler; Wardrobe, Brionna McMahon; Press, Jeffrey Richards Associates CAST: Margo Martindale succeeded by Susan Mansur (Truvy), Constance Shulman (Annelle), Kate Wilkinson succeeded by Betty Moore (Clairee), Betsy Aidem (Shelby) succeeded by Stacy Ray, Rosemary Prinz (M'Lynn), Mary Fogarty succeeded by Anna Minot, Anne Pitoniak (Ouiser). Understudies: Stacy Ray (Annelle/Shelby), Ginger Prince (M'Lynn/Truvy), Anna Minot (Ouiser/Clairee)

A play in 2 acts and 4 scenes. The action takes place at the present time in Chinquapin, Louisiana.

(Players Theatre) Tuesday, July 7, 1987–May 15, 1988 (344 performances and 16 previews). Theatre in Limbo, Kenneth Elliott and Gerald A. Davis present:
PSYCHO BEACH PARTY by Charles Busch; Director, Kenneth Elliott; Set, B. T. Whitehill; Costumes, John Glaser; Lighting, Vivien Leone; Choreography, Jeff Veazey; Original Music, Tom Kochan; Associate Producer, Julie Halston; Company Manager, Terry Byrne; Assistant Producer, Mario Andriolo; Production Assistant, David Anthony Bahrt; Wardrobe, Bob Locke; Props/Technical Director, Brandon Doemling; Stage Managers, Elizabeth Katherine Carr, Mike Leitheed; Press, Shirley Herz/Pete Sanders, Peter Cromarty, Glenna Freedman, David Roggensack, Miller Wright. CAST: Michael Belanger (Marvel Ann), Ralph Buckley (The Great Kanaka), Charles Busch (Chicklet), Robert Carey (YoYo), Andy Halliday (Provoloney), Judith Hansen (DeeDee), Arnie Kolodner (Star Cat), Mike Leitheed (Nicky), Becky London (Berdine), Theresa Marlowe (Bettina Barnes), Meghan Robinson (Mrs. Forrest), Understudies: Judith Hansen, Laurence Overmire

Performed without an intermission. The action takes place in 1962 on and around a beach in Malibu.

(Skylight Lounge/Hamburger Harry's) Wednesday, July 8, 1987– The Skylight Lounge presents:
THE WORLD OF WALLOWITCH with Music and Lyrics by John Wallowitch; Director, Charles Maryan; Musical Director, Ken Lundie; Press, David Rothenberg CAST: Ken Lundie succeeded by John Wallowitch, Melissa Eddy, Betsy Ann Leadbetter

A musical revue performed without intermission.

(Interart Theatre) Friday, July 10–26, 1987 (16 performances) Interart Theatre (Margot Lewitin, Artistic Director/Marie Girard, Managing Director) and Acorn Productions present:
BEDROOM FARCE by Alan Ayckbourn; Director, Caymichael Patten; Set, Wendy Ponte; Lighting, Larry G. Decle; Costumes, Ildane Meltzer; Supervising Producer, Susan Waring Morris; Technical Director, Will Barker; Stage Managers, Cynthia S. Baker, Madeleine Ali-Elancry; Press, Francine L. Trevens CAST: Mary Doyle (Delia), Michael Tolan (Ernest), Jane Myers (Jan), David Bulasky (Nick), Michael Wilding (Malcolm), Brooke Palance (Kate), Mac Crowell (Trevor), Pamela Moller (Susannah)

A comedy in two acts. The action takes place during the winter of 1977 in a middle-class neighborhood of London.

(Space 603) Thursday, July 14–17, 1987 (4 performances) Staret . . . The Directors Company (Michael Parva, Artistic/Producing Director; Victoria Lanman Chesshire, Artistic/Managing Director) presents:
HITTING TOWN by Stephen Poliakoff; Direction and Design, Rosey Hay; Lighting, Sean Murphy; Scenic Artist, Anne Lishner; Production Manager, Terry Dudley; Stage Managers, Darsell B. Brittingham, Valerie J. Roux CAST: John Bjostad (Voice of Leonard Brazil/DJ), Rudy Caporaso (Ralph), Colleen Flynn-Lawson (Clare), Susan Stover (Nicola)

A play in 7 scenes performed without intermission. The action takes place at the present time in a city in the Midlands of England.

(American Theatre of Actors) Wednesday, July 15–18, 1987 (4 performances limited). Pegasus Productions presents:
RUFFLES FIRST LAY! by Wayne Maxwell; Director, M. David Samples; Set/Lighting, Steven Hart; Sound, George Jacobs; Jeffrey L. Pearl, Mark Corum. CAST: Flora Mae Elkins (Cynthia), John McIlveen (Ron), Estelle Ritchie (Mattie), J. J. Quinn (Stephen), Ella Gerber (Sylvia)

The action takes place at the present time at a dog run in Riverside Park in Manhattan, New York.

Top Right: Rosemary Prinz, Anne Pitoniak,
Stacy Ray, Constance Shulman, Susan Mansur,
Betty Moore in "Steel Magnolias" *(Martha Swope Photo)*
Below: Becky London, Charles Busch, Michael Belanger
in "Psycho Beach Party" *(Adam Newman Photo)*

Michael Wilding, Brooke Palance in "Bedroom Farce"
(Anita Feldman-Shevett Photo) Above: John Wallowitch,
Betsy Ann Leadbetter, Ken Lundie, Melissa Eddy
(Bert Andrews Photo)

(Stage Arts Theatre) Thursday, July 16–August 9, 1987 (16 performances). Two Sergeants Production Company presents:
NOTHING TO REPORT by Sam Ciccone; Director, John Augustine; Executive Producer, Charles H. Cochrane, Jr. Set, Anna Louizos; Lighting, Christopher Kondek; Props, Grisha, Larry Kirwin; Costumes, Chris Serluco; Producer, Sam Ciccone; Stage Manager, Jenny Peek; Press, David Rothenberg. CAST: Don Striano (Christopher Corvello), Mark Shannon (Kelly O'Brien), Richard Willis (John Corvello), Lou Spirito (Anthony Corvello), Arthur Salmon (Peter Corvello)
A comedy in 2 acts and 4 scenes. The action takes place at the present time.

(Samuel Beckett Theatre) Thursday, July 16,–August 9, 1987 (16 performances). Presented by Richmond Shepard in association with Actors and Directors Lab.
NOTHING BUT BUKOWSKI two one-act plays by John Ford Noonan; "The Raunchy Dame in the Chinese Raincoat" directed by Richmond Shepard; with Larry Fleischman (Gino), Michael E. Cooke (Harry), Kate Redway (Marla). "The Heterosexual Temperature in West Hollywood" directed by Robert Fuhrmann; with Ann Parr Corley (Dink), Robert Silver (Arno), Elizabeth Hess (Liza). Both plays take place in Hollywood, California, at the present time.

(CSC Theatre) Thursday, July 16–   Presented by People's Playhouse.
THE INVASION OF ARATOOGA by Peter Bach; Director, Katharine Fehl; Set, Matthew Radford; Lighting, Lausanne Davis; Sound, H. E. Jones; Music, Twist & Pappy Corsicato. CAST: Lara Harris (Sue), Robert Katims (Colonel), Roma Maffia (Ava), Daryl Marsh (Al), Bill Schroeder (David)
A play in two acts.

(Space 603) Thursday, July 21–24, 1987 (4 performances) Staret . . . The Directors Company (Michael Parva, Artistic/Producing Director; Victoria Lanman Chesshire, Artistic/Managing Director) presents:
NEW ANATOMIES by Timberlake Wertenbaker; Director, Jennifer McDowall; Set/Lighting, Ron Kidd; Costumes, Hilarie Blumenthal; Musical Director, David Gaines; Sound, Allen Scheid; Production Manager, Terry Dudley; Associate Producer, Nelson Taxel; Assistant Director, Gary Dunnington; Combat Director, Benny Cartwright; Casting, David Munnell; Production Assistant, Jonathan Wagner Carmel; Wardrobe, Sabado Lam; Stage Manager, Susan "Q" Gutmann; Press, Elizabeth Tooker CAST: Caroline Beck (Natalie), Alex Bond (Verda Miles), Arden Lewis (Isabelle Eberhardt), Louise Roberts (Jenny), Carla-Maria Sorey (Severine)
A play in 2 acts and 12 scenes. The action takes place at the turn of the century in Europe and Algeria.

(Perry Street Theatre) Thursday, July 23,–Aug. 30, 1987 (28 performances). Reopened Friday, Sept. 4, 1987 in the 47th Street Playhouse and closed Oct. 11, 1987 after 45 additional performances. The Glines (John Glines, Artistic Director; Lawrence Lane, Managing Director) presents:
WILD BLUE a collection of short plays by Joseph Pintauro; Director, Robert Fuhrmann; Sets/Lighting, Jeffrey Schissler; Costumes, Charlie Catanese; Music/Sound, Donald Lovelace; Stage Manager, William Castleman; Assistant Producer, Casey Wayne; Props, Laurie Rae Waugh, Steven E. Thornburg; Press, Maya Associates/Penny M. Landau. CASTS: "Men Without" with Richard M. Hughes (Boomer), Dana Bate (Pop); "Uncle Chick" with Richard M. Hughes (Uncle Chick), Tom Calabro (Nickey); "Pony Ride" with Tom Calabro (Zeke), Dana Bate (Wendell), Park Overall (Ellie); "Five Dollar Drinks" with Richard M. Hughes (Bert), Tom Calabro (The Star); "Seymour in the Very Heart of Winter" with Tom Calabro (Tony), Dana Bate (Victor); "Rex" with Richard M. Hughes (Eric), Tom Calabro (John); "The Real Dark Night of the Soul" with Richard M. Hughes (Sal), Dana Bate (Farnsworth), Park Overall (Celeste), Tom Calabro (The Caller); "Rosen's Son" with Dana Bate (Rosen), Richard M. Hughes (Eddie), Tom Calabro (Harrison); "Lenten Puddings" with Dana Bate (Uncle Wayne), Park Overall (Megan). Richard M. Hughes was succeeded by Ken Kliban

(John Houseman Theatre) Friday, July 24, 1987 and still playing May 31, 1988. The Daisy Company in association with Playwrights Horizons* presents:
DRIVING MISS DAISY by Alfred Uhry; Director, Ron Lagomarsino; Set, Thomas Lynch; Costumes, Michael Krass; Lighting, Arden Fingerhut; Sound, Joshua Starbuck; Incidental Music, Robert Waldman; General Management, Richard Frankel/Marc Routh; Company Manager, Marshall B. Purdy; Production Associate, Kate Clark; Technical Director, Albert W. Webster; Props, Barbara Lee; Wardrobe, Cathy Lee Cawley; Casting, Pat McCorkle; Hair, Randy Mercer; Stage Managers, Franklin Keysar, Daniel S. Lewin; Press, David Powers. *The play was the 1988 recipient of the Pulitzer Prize for Drama.* CAST: Dana Ivey succeeded by Frances Sternhagen (Daisy Werthan), Ray Gill (Boolie Werthan), Morgan Freeman succeeded by Earle Hyman (Hoke Coleburn), Standbys: Rochelle Oliver, Arthur French, Anderson Matthews
Performed without intermission. The action takes place in Atlanta, Georgia, from 1948 to 1973.
*Playwrights Horizons presented this play originally in their theatre for 80 performances, from March 31,–June 7, 1987.

Park Overall, Dana Bate in "Wild Blue"
(Ken Howard Photo) **Top: Sam Ciccone (front),**
Mark Shannon, Don Striano, Richard Willis,
Arthur Salmon, Lou Spiritos *(Adam Newman Photo)*

Morgan Freeman, Ray Gill, Dana Ivey
in "Driving Miss Daisy" *(Bob Marshak Photo)*
Above: Frances Sternhagen, Earle Hyman
in "Driving Miss Daisy" *(Carol Rosegg Photo)*

49

(Astor Place Theatre) Tuesday, Aug. 4,–Dec. 13, 1987 (152 performances). The Moms Company in association with Paul B. Berkowsky presents:
MOMS by Ben Caldwell; Based on a concept by Clarice Taylor; Director, Walter Dallas; Music and Lyrics/Musical Supervision, Grenoldo Frazier; Set, Rosario Provenza; Costumes, Judy Dearing; Lighting, Robert Wierzel; Sound, Aural Fixation; Associate Producer, James Pulliam; General Manager, Paul B. Berkowsky; Company Manager, Joey Loggia; Technical Director, Ted Wallace; Props, Janet Smith; Wardrobe, Sarah Phillips; Stage Managers, John O'Neill, Kenny Brauner; Press, Jeffrey Richards Associates. The production was originally presented for 36 performances at the Hudson Guild Theatre. CAST: Grenoldo Frazier (Luther/Pianist/Others), Carol Dennis (Anna Mae/Dresser/Sister), Clarice Taylor (Jackie "Moms" Mabley), Understudies: Kenny Brawner, Eleanore Mills
Presented in two acts. The action takes place in 1970 . . . before and after.

(Theatre Four) Wednesday, Aug. 5,–Oct. 11, 1987 (80 performances). The Negro Ensemble Company (Douglas Turner Ward, Artistic Director; Leon B. Denmark, Managing Director) presents:
TWO CAN PLAY by Trevor Rhone; Director, Clinton Turner Davis; Set, Llewellyn Harrison; Lighting, Sylvester Weaver; Sound, Bernard Hall; Costumes, Julian Asion; Design Adaptations, Artie Reese; General Manager, Larry K. Walden; Press, Howard Atlee CAST: Hazel J. Medina (Gloria), Sullivan H. Walker (Jim)
A comedy in 2 acts and 9 scenes. The action takes place during the late 1970's in the home of Jim and Glori Thomas in Kingston, Jamaica, West Indies.

(Pelican Studio) Friday, August 7–22, 1987 (12 performances, and 5 additional performances Oct. 2–5, 1987) The New Rude Mechanicals (Co-Artistic Directors, Robert Hall, John Pynchon Holms) presents:
THE MISANTHROPE by Moliere; Adapted by Robert Hall, Lorraine Ross Hall; Director, Robert Hall; Set, Daniel Proett; Lighting, Keith Hutchings; Costumes, Nancy Konrardy; Stage Manager, Denise Laffer CAST: Mitch Tebo (Alceste), Eric Kramer (Philinte), Robert K. Watson (Oronte), Julia Glander (Celimene), David Cleaver (Basque), Constance McCord (Eliante), Rainard Rachele (Clitandre), Ronald Brice (Acaste), John Pynchon Holms succeeded by Tim McGillicuddy (Officer), Maggie Hawthorne (Arsinoe), David Cleaver (DuBois)
A comedy performed with one intermission and five scenes. The action takes place in Celimene's loft on the Left Bank, south of Tribeca.

**Rainard Rachele, Julia Glander, Ron Brice
in "The Misanthrope"** *(Lis Lewis Photo)*
**Top: Grenoldo Frazier, Clarice Taylor, Carol Dennis
in "Moms"** *(Bert Andrews Photo)*

(Don't Tell Mama) Saturdays, August 22 & 29, 1987 (2 performances)
SALLY-JANE HEIT STARTS IN THE MIDDLE with Music & Lyrics by Shirley Grossman, Marion and Uel Wade; Book, Sally-Jane Heit; Lighting, Shawn Moninger; Press, Francine L. Trevens, Sandra Lord. CAST: Sally-Jane Heit

(Samuel Beckett Theatre) Thursday, Aug. 27,–Oct. 25, 1987 (68 performances). The Harold Clurman Theatre (Jack Garfein, Artistic Director) and Foxrock Productions present:
HAPPY DAYS by Samuel Beckett; Director, Shivaun O'Casey; Set/Costumes, Shivaun O'Casey; Lighting, John Hastings; Technical Director, Christopher Smith; Stage Manager, Robert Vandergriff; General Management, Darwall Associates; Press, Joe Wolhandler CAST: Aideen O'Kelly (Winnie), John Leighton (Willie)
A play with one intermission.

(13th Street Theatre) Tuesday, Sept. 1,–Dec. 29, 1987 (18 performances)
MY ALAMO FAMILY written and performed by Jerry Strickler

(Mazur Theatre) Thursday, September 10–26, 1987 (9 performances). The Blue Heron Theatre (Ardelle Striker, Artistic Director) presents:
ON THE TIGHTROPE or The Ballad of the Phantom Train by Fernando Arrabal; Translated by Ardelle Striker; Director, W. A. Finlay; Set/Costumes, Irineu Chamiso, Jr.; Lighting, Sean Dolan; Sound, Rob Salafia; Stage Manager, Deborah A. Edwards CAST: Thomas Bruno (Duke DeGaza), Nelson Camp (Tharsis), J. C. Hoyt (Wichita)
A play in two acts. The action takes place in April of 1974 in Madrid, New Mexico.

**John Leighton, Aideen O'Kelly in "Happy Days"
Above: Sally-Jane Heit, Jerry Strickler**

Dan Gerrity, Gerrit Graham, Anthony M. LaPaglia,
Adrian Paul in "Bouncers" *(Ron Link Photo)* **Right**
Center: Brenda Denmark, Verneice Turner, June
Duell in "From the Mississippi Delta"

(Harry DeJur Playhouse/Henry Street Settlement) Thursday, September 24,–October 25, 1987 (30 performances). The New Federal Theatre (Woodie King, Jr., Producer) presents:
FROM THE MISSISSIPPI DELTA by Dr. Endesha Ida Mae Holland; Director, Edward G. Smith; Set, Steven Perry; Costumes, Judy Dearing; Lighting, William H. Grant III; Sound, Jacqui Casto; Choreographer, Dianne McIntyre; Company Manager, Linda Herring; Technical Director, Richard Arnold; Wardrobe/Props, Harriet D. Foy; Stage Manager, Jesse Wooden, Jr.; Press, Max Eisen CAST: Verneice Turner (Woman One), Brenda Denmark (Woman Two), June Duell (Woman Three)

Performed without intermission. The action takes place from the early 1950's through the mid-1980's.

(TOMI Theatre) Thursday, September 24–October 4, 1987 (10 performances). The New York Hotel and Motel Trades Council presents:
THE ACTORS' GYM: *Car Tunes* by Duane LaDage; Director, Daniel Jordano; with Eric McGill (Wagoneer), Ted McElroy (Larry), Swayne Foster (Charlie), Caroline Cornell (Nova), Ruben Pla (Escort). *Half Deserted Streets* by Robert Moresco; Director, Albert Sinkys; with Daniel Jodano (Bug), Michael C. Mahon (Frankie). *Mickey's Fifty-Third Birthday* by Marvin Chernoff; Director, Brian Tarantina; with Caroline Cornell (Minnie), Ruben Pla (Mickey), Eric McGill (Cameraperson), Daniel Austin Butler (Announcer). *The Plumber* by Robert Moresco; Director, Don Billet; with Karen Burbach (Woman), Avi Fisher (Plumber). *Heather McKay* by Marilyn Roberts; Director, Vincent Gugleotti; with Dwayne Foster, Ted McElroy, Arvelio Lopez, Marilyn Roberts (McKay). *Prep Work* written & directed by Bruce Gelfand; with Michael C. Mahon (Robert), Daniel Austin Butler (Raymond), Donna Vilella; Artistic Director, Robert Moresco; Stage Managers, Kim Snyder, Madeleine Janover; Associate Producer, Paul Rosenbaum; Sets, Naj Wikoff; Costumes, Susan Branch; Sound, Shawnee Perryman; Lighting, Chis Keegan

An evening of 6 one-act plays.

(Riverwest Theatre) Friday, September 25,–October 17, 1987 (19 performances). CHS Productions and Playful Productions in association with Riverwest Theatre present:
THE PALEONTOLOGIST by Jon Garon; Director, Jerry Neuman; Set, James Bacon; Lighting, Mardie Bixler; Costumes, Goran Sparrman; Sound, David Lawson; Stage Managers, Paul A. Kochman, Carol Venezia; Press, FLT/Francine L. Trevens CAST: Bob Adrian (Cleo), Nancy Groff (Adea), Christine McElroy (Breal), John Bianchi (Ted), James Deschenes (Edric), William F. X. Klan (Matic)

A drama in two acts.

(Minetta Lane Theatre) Thursday, Sept. 10,–Oct. 24, 1987 (44 performances and 7 previews). Lou Adler and Michael White present:
BOUNCERS by John Godber; Director, Ron Link; Choreography, Jeff Calhoun; Set, Cliff Kaulkner; Lighting, Peter Maradudin; Music/Sound, Nathan Wang; Music for Rap, Jim Klein, Jeff Calhoun, Nathan Wang; Casting, Joe Abaldo, Kimba Hill; Associate Producer, Michael Buckley; General Management/Co-Producer, M Square Entertainment; Company Manager, Margay Whitlock; Wardrobe, Julianne Hoffenberg; Stage Manager, J. Barry Lewis; Press, Judy Jacksina Co./Marcy Granata, Julianne Waldhelm, Melody Morgan and Joe Wolhandler/Emily Cohen CAST: Anthony M. LaPaglia (Les), Adrian Paul (Ralph), Gerrit Graham (Lucky Eric), Dan Gerrity (Judd), Anthony Alda (Understudy)

Performed without intermission.

(Perry Street Theatre) September 11, 1987–   American Theatre Alliance (Aaron Levin, Robert J. Weston, Artistic Directors) present:
PHILISTINES by Maxim Gorky; Adapted by H. A. Levitoff; Director, Aaron Levin; Set, Campbell Baird; Costumes, Richard Hornung; Lighting, Natasha Katz; Sound, Thomas Hawk; Wigs/Hairstylist, Cydney Cornell; Stage Manager, Evan A. Georges CAST: Margaret Dulaney (Tatyana), Lynn Chausow (Polya), Tony Carlin (Pyotr), Jack Betts (Bessemenov), June Prud'homme (Akulina), Kaye Kingston (Stepanida), Will Hare (Perchikhin), Ron Orbach (Teterev), Sandra LaVallee (Yelena), John Hutton (Nil), Erica Stevens (Isvetaeva), Jack Kenny (Shishkin), Gregory Chase (Doctor)

A drama in two acts.

(Palsson's) Tuesday, September 15–November 15, 1987 (46 performances). Moon Pie Productions presents:
HENRY THE 8th AT THE GRAND OLE OPRY written and directed by Alan Bailey; Musical Director, Lawrence W. Hill; Costumes, Patricia Sloane; Lighting, Nadine Charlsen; Stage Manager, David Schaap; Press, Chris Boneau, Becky Flora; Crown Designer, Addison Pettit; Velvet Henry Artist, Elinor Pettit CAST: Trey Kay (Red Sawyer), William Mesnik (Henry the 8th), Diana Georger (Katharine of Aragon), Jennifer Smith (Anne Boleyn), Linda Miles (Jane Seymour), Linda Kerns succeeded by Deborah Unger (Anne of Cleves), Laura Carney (Catherine Howard), Blair Ross (Catherine Parr), Lawrence W. Hill (Piano), Billy Dan Zam succeeded by Russell Warne (Bass Guitar)

A musical comedy revue "chronicling the life of the Tudor king through country music."

John Bianchi, Nancy Groff in
"The Paleontologist"
(Rebecca Zilenziger Photo)

51

(Cubiculo) Wednesday, September 30–October 10, 1987 (12 performances and 2 previews). Goodwater Theatre Company presents:

NEW WORKS 1987 produced by Chris Boneau; Lighting, Debra J. Kletter; Projections, Teresa Bell; Sound, Lawrence S. White; Costumes, Cathy Geiger; Stage Managers, Michael Griffith, Judith Sostek; Company Manager, Carol Luigs; Press, Chris Boneau

BILL #1: *Not to Mention Her Love* written & directed by Jim Luigs; with Allen Evans (Buddy Fuller), Mary B. Ward (Younger Eleanor Udden), Tracey Moore (Wilma Hines), Craig Derrick (James Johnson), Lee Chamberlin (Wilma Hines Johnson), Monica Moran (Eleanor Udden). *If He Hollers Let Him Go* written & directed by Jim Luigs; with Eric Schrode (Frank Reed), David Toney (Russell Fuller), George Gerdes (Darrell June). *Starry Road to the Ice Machine* by William Robert Nave; Director, Janet L. Murphy; with Colleen Davenport (Azalea), Bob Fennell (Pie), Nancy Sullivan (Medorah), Aimee Gautreau (Fay).

BILL #2: *Neverland* by Tim Powers; Director, Melia Bensussen; with Bob Fennell (Peter), Illeana Douglas (Wendy), Allen Evans (Ben). *Cowboy Moment* by Jim Luigs; Director, George Gerdes; with Paul Mougey (Cowboy). *Hyphenated Women* written & directed by Jim Luigs; with Cathy Geiger (Celia), Aimee Gautreau (Edie), Illeana Douglas (Minx). *About Food* by William Robert Nave; Director, David Nelson; with Paul Mougey (Michael), Colleen Davenport (Mamaw), Kevin Read (Papaw). *Devil Talk* by Jim Powers; Director, Melia Bensussen; with Kevin Read (Bud), Cathy Geiger (Brenda), Nancy Sullivan (Betty Silver), Eric Schrode (Bobby Hammer). *Dream House* written & directed by Jim Luigs; with Colleen Davenport (Taylor), Paul Mougey (Alex), Cathy Geiger (Paige), Allen Evans (Max), Nancy Sullivan (Leigh), Aimee Gautreau (Dee), Illeana Douglas (Lynn), Eric Schrode (Stuart), Bob Fennell (Mel), Kevin Read (Gary). *Somewhere Where Your Head Still Be a Crown* by Eric Schrode; Director, Joel Bishoff; with Perri Gaffney (Momma/Alberta Turner), L. B. Williams (King/Luther Turner), Frank Guy (Hit Man/Xavier Turner), Darryl Robinson (Gitar/Emmet Turner)

An evening of one-act plays.

(Westbeth Theatre Center) Wednesday, September 30–October 25, 1987 (18 performances). Dark Angel Productions presents:

SHERLOCK HOLMES AND THE HANDS OF OTHELLO by Alexander Simmons; Director, Greg Freelon; Set, Charles McClennahan; Costumes, Myrna Colley-Lee; Lighting, Shirley Prendergast; Sound, Todd Hemleb; Fight Director, Ralph H. Anderson; Production Coordinator, D. M. Lee; Title Theme Music, Alex Simmons; Additional Music, John Mahoney, Steve Postel; Technical Director, Steve Peloquin; Stage Managers, D. C. Rosenberg, Arlene Mantek; Assistant to Director, Kass Thomas; Wardrobe, Shari Carpenter; Props, Maureen Heffernan; Press Consultant, David Lotz CAST: Sherlock Holmes (Time Winters), Mizan Nunes (Amanda Aldridge), Robert Blumenfeld (Ninsky/Lestrade/Piker), Nicolas Sandys (Phillipe Moreau), Eric Coleman (Thomas Kane), Ron Dortch (Elisha Carver), Stephanie Correa (Countess Alexandria Tambov), Ward Asquith (Sir Lawrence Pritchard)

A play in 2 acts and 10 scenes. The action takes place in London, during December, 1886.

(West Bank Downstairs Theatre Bar) Thursday, October 1–7, 1987 (5 performances/limited engagement). The West Bank Downstairs Theatre Bar presents:

THE HOODED EYE: A Trilogy by Katharine Houghton; Director, Rand Foerster; Costumes, David Toser; Stage Managers, Judy Avioli, Katharyn Pinder; Photography, Len Tavares; CASTS: *Buddah*—Act I: Katharine Houghton (Phoebe), Joseph Daly (Fred Bishop). *On the Shady Side*—Act II: Schuyler Grant (Nome), Katharine Houghton (Alice). *The Right Number*—Act III: Rand Foerster (Edmund), Katharine Houghton (Fuzz-Buzz).

An evening of 3 one-act plays.

(Madison Square Garden) Friday, October 2–4, 1987 (6 performance limited engagement). Lorimar presents a Steven Goldberg Production of:

THUNDERCATS LIVE! written, directed, and choreographed by Nancy Gregory; Associate Producer, Randolph Gale; Set, Jeremy Railton; Costumes, Phillip Dennis; Soundtrack Supervisor; Lighting, Kirk Bookman; Music Supervisor, Earl Manky; Assistant to Producer, Bianka Lunecke-Branstner; Production Manager/Coordinator, Jimmy Lewis; Wardrobe, Frieda M. Paras, Kari Ann Messina; Dance Captain, Evel; Rollerskating Captain, Billy Richardson; Assistant to Director, Randy Doney; Flying, Flying by Foy; Press, John Urban, Nancy Moon, Steve Rosen CAST: Marty Almaraz, Chris Bethards, Jeff Biggs, Greg Carrillo, Christy Curtis, Derek J. K. Delanoza, Marcie Dinardo, Evel, Vernon David Gallegos, Gregory Gonzales, Tracy Ann Guaderrama, Enrique Hernandez, Michael Jefferson Judy Kathleen, Peter Lajos, Chuck Merrell, Michelle Miracle, Jane Phillips, Billy Richardson, Allison Spinella, Michael Spinella, Kimberly Talbert, Gavin Van, Deanna Wilshire

A musical in 2 acts featuring a cast of cartoon superstars come-to-life.

Schuyler Grant, Katharine Houghton in "The Hooded Eye" *(Len Tavares Photo)*

Time Winters, Ron Dortch in "Sherlock Holmes. . . ." *(Rebecca Lesher Photo)* Top: Lee Chamberlin, Monica Moran in "New Works" *(Rebecca Lesher Photo)*

(Promenade Theatre) Friday, October 2–November 15 (24 performances and 29 previews). John A. McQuiggan presents:
BIRDS OF PARADISE with Book by Winnie Holzman & David Evans; Music, David Evans; Lyrics, Winnie Holzman; Director, Arthur Laurents; Sets, Philipp Jung; Costumes, David Murin; Lighting, Jules Fisher; Musical Staging, Linda Haberman; Musical Director, Frederick Weldy; Orchestrations, Michael Starobin; Production Manager, Laura Heller; Production Stage Manager, James Harker; Co-Producer, Ruth Rosenberg; Casting, Stuart Howard Associates; Executive Producer, Douglas M. Lawson; General Management, New Roads Productions; Press, Henry Luhrman Associates/Terry M. Lilly, Andrew P. Shearer; Stage Manager, Jill Larmett; Sound, T. Richard Fitzgerald; Associate Lighting Designer, Peggy Eisenhauer; Casting Associate, Amy Schecter; Technical Director, Steve Small; Wardrobe, Nancy Lawson; Props, Betsy Kelleher CAST: Barbara Walsh (Stella), Mary Beth Piel (Marjorie), Andrew Hill Newman (Dave), J. K. Simmons (Andy), Donna Murphy (Hope), Todd Graff (Homer), John Cunningham (Lawrence Wood), Crista Moore (Julia)

A musical in 2 acts. The action takes place in the Meeting Hall of the oldest church on Harbor island, a small fictional island somewhere on the eastern seaboard, at the present.

(BACA Downtown) Friday, October 2–10, 1987 (4 performances). BACA/The Brooklyn Arts Council in association with Primary Stages Company presents:
ANGEL FACE by Laura Harrington; Director, Liz Diamond; Music, Roger Ames; Set, Richard Hoover; Lighting, Pat Dignan; Costumes, Janna Gjesdal; Production Manager, Douglas M. Green; Associate Set Designer, Anne Elias; Associate Lighting Designer, Karen Williams; Co-Producer, Casey Childs CAST: Teres Unsoelo (Lil), Tom Wright (Gabriel)

A play in 1 act.

(Raft Theatre) Tuesday, October 6–22, 1987. The Raft Theatre (Terry D. Kester, Producing Director) presents:
AS THE WIND ROCKS by Amy Warner; Director, Michael Haney. No other credits provided. CAST: Amy Warner

A one-woman show about four pioneer women crossing the Continental United States in covered wagons in the 1800's.

(Westside Arts Theatre Upstairs) Tuesday, October 6–18, 1987 (5 performances and 7 previews). Aaron Zaitman presents The Tide Theatre Company's production of:
ISLE OF SWANS by Daniel Keene; Director, Rhonda Wilson; Scenic Supervision, Ray Recht; Production Designers, Rhonda Wilson, Daniel Keene; Lighting, Marshal S. Spiller; Music, Allan Zavod; Executive Producer/General Manager, Paul B. Berkowsky; Press, Shirley Herz, David Roggensack, Peter Cromarty, Glenna Freedman, Pete Sanders, Miller Wright; Production Stage Manager, Wm. Hare; Company Manager, Jean Rocco; Management Associates, Sheala N. Berkosky, Joey Loggia; Costume Consultant, Judy Dearing; Sound Consultant, Tom Gould; Props/Wardrobe, Charlie Eisenberg CAST: Rosemary Hochschild (Alexandra), Lindzee Smith (Tom), Rhonda Wilson (Isabelle)

A play performed without intermission. The action takes place on a small island just off the coast of Australia, circa 1900.

Rhonda Wilson, Lindzee Smith in "Isle of Swans"
(Adam Newton Photo) Top: Todd Graff, John Cunningham,
Mary Beth Peil in "Birds of Paradise"
(Martha Swope Photo)

(Unitarian Church of All Souls) Friday, October 16–November 1, 1987 (14 performances). All Souls Players presents:
BAREFOOT IN THE PARK by Neil Simon; Director, David McNitt; Set, Norb Joerder; Costumes, Judy Kahn; Lighting, David Bean; Sound, Hal Schuler; Production Stage Manager, Dale Shields; Producer, Tran Wm. Rhodes; Stage Managers, Robert Coppola, Jim Bumgardner; Props/Wardrobe, Michelle Collier; Assistant to Producer, Cathy Tague CAST: Amy Greenhill (Corrie Bratter), Furley Lumpkin (Telephone Repair Man), Dale Shields (Delivery Man), Richard Ross (Paul Bratter), Constance Kane (Mrs. Banks), Wallace Capobianco (Victor Velasco)

A comedy in 3 acts. The action takes place over a five day period in an apartment on the top floor of a brownstone on East 48th Street, New York City.

(Susan Bloch Theatre) October 21,–December 6, 1987 (54 performances and 6 previews). Cress Darwin and Randal Martin for Darwin/Howe/Martin Productions present:
CIRCUMSTANCES by Louis Mustillo; Director, Janis Powell; Set, Diann Duthie; Lighting, Deborah Constantine; Press, Mitchell Uscher Associates/Mitchell Uscher, Michael D. Thompson; Stage Manager; Rich Johnson. CAST: Louis Mustillo

A solo performance without intermission.

Louis Mustillo
in "Circumstances"
(Peter Ligeti Photo)

Tom Wright, Terres Unsoeld
in "Angel Face" *(Douglas Green
Photo)*

A SHAYNA MAIDEL

By Barbara Lebow; Presented by K&D Productions, Margery Klain and Robert G. Donnalley, Jr.; Director, Mary B. Robinson; Set, William Barclay; Costumes, Mimi Maxmen; Lighting, Dennis Parichy; Sound, Aural Fixation; Associate Producer, Susan Urban Horsey; Casting, David Tochterman; General Manager, Darwell Associates; Press, Jeffrey Richards Associates/C. George Willard, Ben Morse, Irene Gandy, Francine Trevens, Susan Chicoine, Naomi Grabel, Roger Lane, Jillana Devine; Company Manager, Ken Silverman; Stage Managers, Crystal Huntington, Susan Cameron; Sound Assistant, John C. Wise; Hair, Vito Mastragiovanni; Wardrobe, Anne Delano; Casting Associate, Julie Mossberg; Casting Assistant, Michelle Ortlip; Opened at Westside Arts Theatre, Friday October 16, 1987.*

CAST

Rose Weiss	Melissa Gilbert†1
Mordechai Weiss	Paul Sparer†2
Luisa Weiss Pechenik	Gordana Rashovich†3
Duvid Pechenik	Jon Tenney†4
Hanna	Cordelia Richards†5
Mama	Joan MacIntosh

A play in 2 acts. The action takes place in a small Polish village, 1976, and in Rose Weiss' apartment on New York City's West Side; early Spring, 1946.

*Closed Jan. 8, 1989 after 501 performances and 14 previews.

†Succeeded by 1. Ava Daddad, 2. Stephen Pearlman, 3. Tandy Cronin, Gordana Rashovich, 4. Bruce Nozick, 5. Katherine Hiler, 6. Suzanne Toren

Melissa Gilbert in "A Shayna Maidel"

Gordana Rashovich, Katherine Kamhi in "A Shayna Maidel"
(Linda Alaniz Photo)

(Cathedral of Saint John the Divine) Wednesday, October 21–31, 1987 (9 performances). The Cathedral of Saint John the Divine and The Mettawee River Company presents:
THE WILDMAN conceived and Directed by Ralph Lee; Music, Paul Haley; Lyrics, Martin Edmunds; Text, Dave Hunsaker; Choreography, Don Redlich; Musical Director/Arrangements, Jody Kruskal; Costumes, Casey Compton; Production Coordinator, Bruce Fifer; Production Design/Masks, Ralph Lee; Stage Manager, Lenny Bart; Maskmaking Assistants, Anne Ellsworth, Steven Kaplan, Becky Kravetz, Merrill Rauch. CAST: David Amarel, Lenny Bart, Bruce Edward Barton, Pamela Dharamsey, Martha Gilpin, Tom Marion, Debra Piver, Elliott Scott. *Musicians:* Dan Erkkila, Karen Lundquist, Jody Kruskal, Thomas Calabro, John Loose, Jill Fogel; *Sopranos:* Alexandra Ivanoff, Alimo Russell
MUSICAL NUMBERS: Pilgrims' Song, Song of the Forest, Lullaby, Sailor's Song, Magdalen's Meditations, Maidens' Song, Madrigal
A performance piece incorporating masks, puppets and visual effects, inspired by the comprehensive exhibit on the wildman of the Middle Ages at the Cloisters in 1980, and the book *The Wild Man* by Timothy Husband.

(The New Theatre of Brooklyn/TNT) Thursday, Oct. 22,–Nov. 15, 1987 (16 performances). The New Theatre of Brooklyn/TNT (Deborah J. Pope, Steve Settler, Artistic Directors) presents:
CONVERSATIONS IN EXILE by Bertolt Brecht; Adapted by Howard Brenton; Translated by David Dollenmayer; Director, Clinton Turner Davis; Set, Daniel Conway; Lighting, John Gisondi; Costumes, C. Jane Epperson; Sound, Tom Gould; Production Manager, Mathew Williams; Technical Director, Richard Morganelli; Stage Managers, Debora E. Kingston, Devra Cohen; Press, Clare Cotugno. CAST: Helmar Augustus Cooper (Ziffel), Ruben Santiago-Hudson (Kalle)
Performed without intermission.

(Riverwest Theatre) Friday, October 23–November 14, 1987 (17 performances). CHS Productions & Riverwest Theatre presents:
ONE WAY TO ULAN BATOR by Elliott Caplin; Director, Jerry Heymann; Set, James Bacon; Costumes, Goran Sparrman; Lighting, Matt Ehlert; Sound, David Lawson; Stage Managers, Paul A. Kochman, Carol Venezia CAST: Kerry Beck, Barbara Erwin, Alice Haining, Richard Michael Hughes, Louise Roberts, Ron Seibert

(Actors' Playhouse) Sunday, October 25–November 29, 1987 (53 performances and 20 previews). Stephen W. Nebgen and M. Ricque Williams in association with Carl Jaynes present:
FORTUNE AND MEN'S EYES by John Herbert; Director, Edward Ormond; General Manager, Stephen W. Nebgen; Press, David Rothenberg; Stage Manager, Frank Macri; Press Assistant, Jeffrey Smith; Makeup, Perry Scott CAST: Edward Ormond (Queenie), Will Scheffer (Mona), Jon Pavlovsky succeeded by Carl Jaynes (Rocky), Thom Politico (Guard), Drew Murphy (Smitty)
A drama in 2 acts. The action takes place in a boys' reformatory on a mid-October evening, three weeks later, and on Christmas Eve.

Drew Murphy, Jon Pavolovsky in "Fortune and Men's Eyes" *(Adam Newman Photo)*
Above: Kerry Beck, Ron Siebert in "One Way. . . ."
(Rebecca Zilenziger Photo)

Top Left: Helmar Augustus Cooper, Ruben S. Hudson in "Conversations"
(Jessica Katz Photo)

Mary Soreanu, Joanne Borts, Bruce Adler
in "On Second Avenue" *(Martha Swope Photo)*

(Norman Thomas Theatre) Sunday, October 25, 1987–January 10, 1988 (Closed after 54 performances to tour nationally.) Raymond Ariel, Moishe Rosenfeld, and Lawrence Toppall present:

ON SECOND AVENUE created by Zalmen Mlotek & Moishe Rosenfeld; Songs by Moyshe Oysher, Abe Ellstein, Zalmen Mlotek, Moishe Rosenfeld, Michl Gordon, Abraham Goldfaden, Chana Mlotek, Solomon Small (Smulevitz), Z. Kornbluth, Joseph Brady, L. Friedsell, Z. Kornbluth, Joseph Brody, Aaron Lebedeff, Herman Wohl, Sholom Aleichem, Joseph Cherniavsky, Moses Milner, A. L. Wolfson, Alexander Olshanetsky, Jack Rechtselt, Jacob Jacobs, Avrom Shevach, I. Tsigaler, Nochum Stuchkoff, Joseph Rumshinsky, E. Ostroff, Illa Trilling, Moishe Oysher, Jennie Goldstein, Morris Rand, Sholem Secunda, Hyman Prizant, Abe Schwartz, Anshel Schorr, Louis Gilrod, Reuben Osofky, Abe Ellstein, Isidore Lilian, Molly Picon, Itsik Manger, Jacob Kalich, Fischel Kanopoff, Bella Meisell, Chayim Tauber; Scenes adapted from works by Abraham Goldfaden, Jacob Gordin, Joseph Lateiner, Mark Slobin, M. Nudelman, Sholom Aleichem; Director, Isiah Sheffer; Choreography, Derek Wolshonak; Musical Director/Arrangements, Zalmen Mlotek; Set, Brian Kelly; Costumes, Barbara Blackwood; Lighting, Victor En Yu Tan; Sound, Tyrone Sanders; Orchestrations, Peter Sokolow; Stage Manager, Michael Chudinsky; Press, Max Eisen, Madelon Rosen; Dance Captain, Carolyn Goor; Assistant to Musical Director-Arranger, Michael Larsen; Technical Director-Scenery, Michael Schutte; Wardrobe, Abigail Roland; Sound, Donna Gallers; Technical Consultant, Ray Crawly. CAST: Mary Soreanu, Bruce Adler, Robert Abelson, Joanne Borts, Seymour Rexsite, Carolyn Goor, Nicole Flender, Gary John Larosa, Andre Noujaim, Elise Ariel, and *The Second Avenue Klezmer Orchestra:* Zalman Mlotek, Michael Larsen, Sandra Schipior, Howard Leshaw, Edward Kalny, Paul Bernardi, Greg Maker, Don Mulvaney. *Understudies:* Stewart Figa, Joanne Borts, Nicole Flender

A new Yiddish-English musical revue in 2 acts and 21 scenes.

(Jan Hus Theatre) Sunday, October 25–November 24, 1987 (15 performances). **MY FOUR MOTHERS** by Ward Morehouse III; Director, Nancy Panzarella; Set, Morrie Breyer; Lighting, Marc Weiss; Stage Managers, Chris Kelly, Lionel Van Duyne; Press, Phil Leshin; Production Coordinator, Frank Melfo CAST: Peggy Huntley Winter (Cynthia Exline), Nelson Winter (William Gurr), Dixie Dee Winter (Andrea Lauren Herz), Julia Winter Clark (Eleanora Kaye), Miriam Winter McKenna (Evelyn Solann)

A play in 2 acts and 4 scenes. The action takes place in the apartment of the late Broadway producer William Winter and at a memorial service, over three days in the Spring of 1987.

(New York Actors' Institute) Monday, October 26–28, 1987 (3 performance limited engagement).

OSCAR REMEMBERED by Maxim Mazumdar CAST: James Beaman (Bosie Douglas)

A one-character play in 2 acts. No other credits submitted.

(Nat Horne Theatre) Tuesday, October 27–November 14, 1987 (18 performances and 3 previews). Peter Samelson and Ted Killmer, in association with The Nat Horne Musical Theatre, Inc., present:

PAPERWORK conceived by Peter Samelson; Written & Produced by Peter Samelson, Ted Killmer; Music, Michael Canick; Additional Music, Mundaka Lee, Randy Wanlas; Set/Puppet, Joe Silke; Lighting, Nadine Charlsen; Videomation, Albert Reyes; Costumes, Natalie Caron; Production Manager, Christopher C. Dunlop; Technical Director, Josette Amato; Props/Illusions, Steve Pitella; Assistants, Bob Ferreri, Mike Buscemi; Press, Ted Killmer; Creative Consultants, Robert Baxt, Harry Levine, Max Maven, Jamy Swiss; Management, Arthur Shafman International CAST: Peter Samelson

An entertainment in 2 acts: *Ideas Committed to Paper:* The History of Paper, Professor Papier, Money as Object, The Return of Mr. Papier, Object as Money, May I See Your Papers?, and *Paper Committed to Ideas:* The Color Red, The Bride, Sort of Damocles, Encore Mr. Papier, Getting Absorbed in the Sunday Times, Paradise, The Snowstorm

(Kaufman Theater) Wednesday, October 28–November 29, 1987 (40 performances and 3 previews). Martin R. Kaufman presents:

JULIE WILSON: FROM WEILL TO SONDHEIM—A CONCERT featuring the Songs of Kurt Weill and Stephen Sondheim; Musical Director, William Roy; Production Manager/Lighting, Nadine Charlsen; General Management, Marshall B. Purdy; Press, Henry Luhrman Associates/Terry M. Lilly, Andrew P. Shearer, Brian Brutman, David Gersten; Company Manager, Ron Drummond; Gowns, Lenore Smith; Make-up, Steven Herrald CAST: Julie Wilson, William Roy

A Concert. *Act One* features the songs of Kurt Weill, *Act Two* features the songs of Stephen Sondheim.

(Don't Tell Mama) Thursday October 29–November 28, 1987 (16 performances). **JIMMY JAMES SHOW** by Jimmy James. CAST: Jimmy James (Marilyn Monroe, Eartha Kitt, Cher, Diana Ross, Judy Garland, Barbra Streisand and others)

A solo performance in 2 acts, with vocal impressions of famous female stars.

Peter Samuelson
in "Paperwork"

Jimmy James

Above: William Roy, Julie Wilson

(Westbeth Theatre Center) Wednesday, October 28–December 20, 1987 (47 performances). INTAR Hispanic American Arts Center (Max Ferra, Artistic Director/Dennis Ferguson-Acosta, Managing Director) presents:
TANGO APASIONADO based upon the works of Jorge Luis Borges; Music, Astor Piazolla; Lyrics, William Finn; Adaptation, Graciela Daniele, Jim Lewis; Conceived/Choreographed/Directed by Graciela Daniele; Set/Costumes, Santo Loquasto; Lighting, Peggy Eisenhauer; Fights, B. H. Barry; Music Direction/Vocal-Dance Arrangements, Pablo Zinger; Casting, Jordan Thaler; General Manager, Darren Lee Cole; Associate Producer, Kathryn Ballou; Stage Manager, Robert Mark Kalfin; Associate to Ms. Daniele, Tina Paul; Dance Captain, Luis Perez; Fight Captain, Robert Mark Kalfin; Technical Director, Robert L. Anderson; Production Assistant, Paula Gray; Wardrobe, Ewa Swensson; Sound Consultant, Otts Munderloh; Speech Coach, Cindia Huppeler CAST: Leonardo Cimino (The Writer), Tina Paul (His Mother/Juliana), John Mineo (Cristian), Gregory Mitchell (Eduardo), Camille Saviola (Leonor) Luis Perez (Rosendo), Valarie Pettiford (La Lujanera), Nicholas Gunn (Luis/Francisco Real), Rene Ceballos (Casilda), Denise Faye (Rosita), Norbeto Carlos Simonian (Antonio), Mercedes Acosta (Pilar), Mark Maxwell, Lisa Rinehart (Understudies), Pablo Zinger, Rodolfo Alchourron, Jorge Alfano, Osvaldo Ciancio, Carel Kraayendof (Musicians)

A new dance-music-theatre collaboration, performed without intermission. The action takes place in Buenos Aires just after the turn-of-the-century.

(45th Street Theatre) Thursday, October 29–November 22, 1987 (15 performances and 1 preview). Primary Stages Company, Inc. and Dina and Alexander E. Racolin present:
STOPPING THE DESERT by Glen Merzer; Director, Casey Childs; Assistant Director, Sara Maxwell; Production Stage Manager, Sara Gormley Plass; Set, Joel Reynolds; Costumes, Bruce H. Goodrich; Lighting, John Bickerton; Sound, Paul Garrity; Dialect Coach, John Sperry; Electrical Design, Curtis Ardourel; Assistant Stage manager, Ardina Cerra; CAST: Robert Michael Tomlinson (Walter), John Wesley Shipp (Rick), Sally Dunn (Nina), Marilyn McIntyre (Lauren), Jason Parris Fitz-Gerald (Malik), Victoria Boothby (Cat), Wyman Pendleton (Reed)

A play in 2 acts. The action takes place in the San Francisco Bay area, 1973 to 1984.

(Raft Theatre) Thursday, October 29–November 1, 1987 (5 performances limited engagement). Fountainhead Theatre Co. presents:
IN THE BOOM BOOM ROOM by David Rabe; Director, L. R. Hults; Stage Manager, Tracy Becker; Set, Jim Crocker; Lighting, Beau Kennedy; Props, Bill Hooper; Sound, Winston Bostwick; Dance Consultant, Mary Lilygren; Costume Consultant, Susan Theaume; Fountainhead Theatre Co.: Artistic Director, Charles Anderson/Managing Director, Frank J. Simpson/Technical Director, Harold Simpson/Dramaturg, Jill Mackavey CAST: Jill Mackavey (Chrissy), Bill Corsair (Harold), Edie Avioli (Susan), Susan Ross (Vikki), Mary Lilygren (Melissa), Rachel White (Sally), Casey Jones (Irene), Frank J. Simpson (Eric), Harold Simpson (Al), Scott Sears (Ralphie), Charles Anderson (Guy), Janis Corsair (Helen), Jim Crocker (Janitor), Gregory Vaughan Ward (Man)

A play in 2 acts. The action takes place during the turn of a decade: the cusp of the seventies, in Philadelphia: the go-go bars, streets, apartments and neighborhoods of Chrissy's life.

(Folksbiene Playhouse) Sunday, November 1, 1987–March 27, 1988 (45 performances). The Folksbiene Playhouse presents:
RIVERSIDE DRIVE by Leon Kobrin; Adaptation, Miriam Kressyn; Director, Roger Sullivan; Music, Ed Linderman; Arrangements, Barry Levitt; Lighting, Nicholas Vizzini; Costumes, Evelyn Green; Set, Barry Axtel; Set Construction, Brian Kelly, Michael Schute; English Narration, Dr. Saul Lifson; Stage Managers, Beth Lord, Harriet Gold; Folksbiene Manager, Ben Schechter; Chairman, Morris Adler CAST: Norman Kruger (Dr. Schlesinger), Diane Cypkin (Gertrude), Elayne Wilks (Frances), Rebecca Varon (Adele), Jacob Mirer (Mortimer), Richard Silver (Teddy), Richard Carlow (David), I. W. Firestone (Herman), Zypora Spaisman (Rivke Jaffe), Leon Liebgold (Shlomo Jaffe)

A play with music in 2 acts. The action takes place in the apartment of Herman and Gertrude Jaffe on New York's Riverside Drive, on a Saturday evening and seven weeks later, in the 1920's. Presented in Yiddish with simultaneous live English translation.

**Diane Cypkin, Zipora Spaisman
in "Riverside Drive"**

(Village Gate Downstairs) Tuesday, November 3, 1987–January 3, 1988 (71 performances and 11 previews). Art D'Lugoff, Burt D'Lugoff, Lipper Productions, Inc., and Gerald Wexler Presents, Inc. present:
SING HALLELUJAH! conceived by Worth Gardner & Donald Lawrence; Songs by Donald Lawrence, Walter Hawkins, Richard Smallwood, Andre Crouch, Michael Terry, Dorothy Love Coates, and traditional hymns; Staged & Directed by Worth Gardner; Musical Director, Donald Lawrence; Production Consultant, Pepsi Bethel; Lighting, Kirk Bookman; Set, Joseph P. Tilford; Sound, Otts Munderloh; Costumes, Rebecca Senske; General Manager, Albert Poland/Peter Bogyo; Press, Milly Schoenbaum; Company Manager, Barbara Carrelias; Stage Managers, Duane Mazey, Kenneth Hanson; Sound, Geoffrey D. Fishburn; Wardrobe, Bobby Pearce CAST: Curtis Blake, Rose Clyburn, Patricia Ann Eveson, Ann Nesby, Clarence Snow (Vocalists), Craig Harris, Richard Odom, Victor Ross, Michael Terry (Instrumentalists)
MUSICAL NUMBERS: Sing Hallelujah!, Everybody Ought to Know, Good News, We Can't Go on This Way, Safe in His Arms, Right Now, Bright Side Somewhere, New World, Didn't It Rain, Hollywood Scene, I'm Just Holdin' On, Anyway You Bless, Shut de' Do', Can't Nobody Do Me Like Jesus, Oh Happy Day, Couldn't Hear Nobody Pray; Oh Mary Don't You Weep, The Question Is, No Ways Tired, Runnin' for Jesus.

An all-singing, all-dancing gospel musical in 2 acts.

(Circle in the Square Theatre) Tuesday, November 3, 1987 (11 previews and still running as of June 1, 1988). Lois Deutchman, Mary T. Nealon and David Musselman present:

OIL CITY SYMPHONY by and with Mike Craver, Mark Hardwick, Debra Monk, Mary Murfitt; Director, Larry Forde; Set, Jeffrey Schissler; Sound, Otts Munderloh; Lighting, Natasha Katz; Associate Producers, Thomas DeWolfe, George Gordon; General Management, Mary T. Nealon, David Musselman; Press, Joshua Ellis Office/Adrian Bryan-Brown, Jackie Green, Leo Stern, Bill Shuttleworth, Susanne Tighe; Assistant Manager, James Jay Wilson; Casting Consultant, Jay Binder; Songs by Mark Hardwick, Debra Monk, Mike Craver, Rev. Johnson Oatman & E. Q. Excell, Doug Ingle, Frank Loesser, John Philip Sousa, Zez Confrey, Oscar Hammerstein/Richard Rodgers, Sylvia Dee, Arthur Kent, S. F. Bennett/J. P. Webster, Charles E. Pat Boone/Ernest Gold CAST: Mike Craver (Synthesizers & Vocals), Mark Hardwick (Piano, Accordion & Vocals), Debra Monk (Drums & Vocals), Mary Murfitt (Violin, Flute, Saxophone & Vocals)

MUSICAL NUMBERS: Count Your Blessings, Czardas, Musical Moments, A Classical Selection, A Popular Selection, Ohio Afternoon, Baby-It's Cold Outside, Beaver Ball at the Bug Club, Beehive Polka, Musical Memories A Patriotic Fantasy, Dueling Pianos/Dizzy Fingers, Introductions, Iris, The End of the World, A Tribute, Coaxing the Ivories, Bus Ride, In the Sweet By and By, My Old Kentucky Rock and Roll Home

Oil City Symphony in recital in 2 acts with refreshments afterward.

(Charles Ludlam Theatre) Wednesday, November 4, 1987–December 13, 1987 (33 performances and 27 previews). The Ridiculous Theatrical Company in:

MEDEA *A Tragedy* by Charles Ludlam; Freely adapted from the play by Euripides; Director, Lawrence Kornfeld; Set, Jack Kelly; Costumes, Everett Quinton; Lighting, Richard Currie; Music, Peter Golub; Managing Director, Steven Samuels; Stage Manager, Angelique Kenney; Technical Director, Douglas Gerlach; Technical Coordinator, Mike Taylor; Electrician/Props, Daphne Groos; Scenic Artist, Alex Garvin; Costume Assistant, Daniel Boike; Sound, Edward McGowan CAST: Black-Eyed Susan or Everett Quinton (Medea or Nurse), John D. Brockmeyer (Kreon), Jud Lawrence (Jason), Bill Vehr (Aegeus), Katy Dierlam, Vicky Raab, Eureka (Chorus of Korinthian Women), Kathy Fink, Leslie Ford, Bruce Wang, Sunita Stanislav, Peter Golub (Musicians).

Performed without intermission. The action takes place in front of Medea's house in Korinth.

(Billie Holiday Theatre) Wednesday, November 4, 1987–May 29, 1988. Billie Holiday Theatre (Marjorie Moon, Producer) presents two plays in repertory:

COME AND GET THESE MEMORIES by Pearl Cleage; (75 performances). Director, Mikell Pinkney; Set/Costumes, Felix E. Cochren; Lighting, Tim Phillips; Production Coordinator, Trudy Burris; Props, Trudy Burris, Gwen Frost, Armando Colon; Wardrobe, Ardis Johnson; Technical Director, Roger Smiley; Stage Manager, Avan; Press, Howard Atlee. CAST: Mikell Pinkney (Jay Poole), Gwendolyn Roberts-Frost (Ann Poole), Denise Burse-Mickelbury (Tida Jameson), David Roberson (Lance Johnson), Maurice Carlton (Woody Andrews), Melissa Fonts (Monique LeBeau). A comedy in two acts. The action takes place in early summer in a rented country house at a mountain resort a few hours drive from New York City.

REUNION IN BARTERSVILLE by Celeste Walker; (69 performances). CAST: Denise Burse-Mickelbury (Janie Mae Hopper), Maurice Carlton (Cous Pickett), Gwendolyn Roberts-Frost (Pollina Davis), David Roberson (Ronnie Davis), Chuck Patterson (Perry Rousell), Melissa Fonts (Liz Rousell), William Williams (A. J. Hamm). A play in two acts. The action takes place during late Spring 1985 in the livingroom of Janie Mae Hopper's home in a tiny Southeast Texas town.

(Ensemble Studio Theatre) Saturday, November 4–29, 1987 (13 performances and 4 previews). The Ensemble Studio Theatre (Curt Dempster, Artistic Director/Dorothy Chansky, Managing Director) presents:

HOUSE ARREST by Bill Bozzone; Director, Risa Bramon; Set, Kevin Joseph Roach; Lighting, Greg MacPherson; Costumes, Deborah Shaw; Sound, Bruce Ellman; Music, Susan Feingold, Michael Bramon, Turnstyle Productions; Production Stage Manager, Denise Laffer; Producing Director, John McCormack; Production Manager/Technical Director, David M. Mead; Production Coordinator, Dean Gray; Stage Managers, Jane Sanders, Diane Ward; Props, Shannon Graves; Wardrobe, Maria Tirabassi; Hairstylist, Michael Kriston. CAST: Suzanne Shepherd (Marie Yolango), Dominic Chianese (Duke Yolango), Kevin Geer (Lt. Scales), Brian Tarantina (Lonnie Yolango), Crystal Field (Stella Monte), Ann Talman (Denise Monte), Patrick John Hurley (Father Dooley), Ira Belgrade, Bruce Diker (TV Voices)

A new comedy in 2 acts. The action takes place during the present June, on Staten Island, New York.

(Triangle Theatre) Thursday, November 5–29, 1987 (16 performances). Triangle Theatre Company presents:

THE EMPEROR CHARLES by Spencer Vibbert; Director, Michael Ramach; Sets, Bob Phillips; Lighting, Danianne Mizzy; Costumes, Amanda J. Klein; Production Stage Manager, Anne M. Cantler; Press, Bruce Cohen, Kathleen von Schmid CAST: Jasper McGruder (Slim), Charles Dumas (Charles Gilpin), Chet Carlin (Jig Cook), Gerry Paone (Micky James), Midge Montgomery (Eleanor "Fritzi" O'Brien), Caitlin Hart (Edna Kenton), Joel Parkes (Eugene O'Neill), Robyn Hatcher (Alice Gilpin), George McGrath (Ken MacGowen), Gerry Paone (Jacob Weiss), Anne Cantler (Blonde)

A play in 2 acts. The action takes place in New York in the early 1920's.

Mike Craver, Mary Murfitt, Mark Hardwick, Debra Monk in "Oil City Symphony" *(Peter Cunningham Photo)* Below: Black-Eyed Susan, Everett Quinton in "Medea" *(Anita & Steve Shevett Photo)*

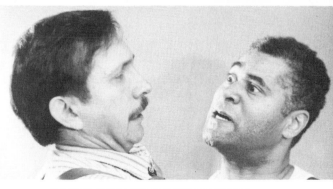

Joel Parks, Charles d'Umas in "Emperor Charles" Above: Denise Burse-Mickelbury, Melissa Fonts, Gwen Roberts-Frost in "Come and Get These Memories" *(Jessica Katz Photo)*

57

(Playhouse 46) Thursday, November 5–22, 1987 (12 performances). Merely Players (Brian Hargrove, President/Monica Hayes, President-Elect) and Women in Theater Network, Inc. (Susan Gitenstein, Executive Director/Lois F. Alexander, Associate Director), in association with Women's Interart Center Annex presents:
THE WOMEN IN THE FAMILY by Susan Kipp; Director, Marnie Andrews; Set/Lighting/Sound, Chris McHale; Stage Manager, Nancy Hornecker; On-Line Producer, Eric Farber; Press, Patricia Barrett; Costume Consultant, Stacy Chaikin CAST: Estelle Kemler (Alma), Alan Leach (Ed Baxter), Deborah Strang (Jenny), Lois Raebeck (Emma), Rachel Stephens (Aggie), Monica M. Hayes (Katie)

A play in 2 acts. The action takes place in and around an old farmhouse on the edge of a medium-sized Iowa town, at the present.

(Samuel Beckett Theater) Thursday, November 5, 1987– Quentin Vidor presents: **SCOONCAT** by Eve Ensler; Director, Toni Kotite; Set, Peter Harrison; Costumes, Grace Williams; Lighting, Nancy Collings; Music, Tom Kochan; Sound, J. Bloomrosen; Props, Joanne Basinger; Slide Design, John Chimples CAST: Dylan McDermott (Scooncat), Jill Larson (Mother), Alexandra Gersten (Nancy), Edmond Genest (Father), Judson Camp (Priest/Dr. Cock/Newscaster/Space-Place Salesman), Stivi Paskoski (Bernie)
A play in 2 acts.

Dennis Boutsikaris, Josh Mostel, Joe Grifasi, William Jay, Joe Urla in "Boys Next Door"
(Peter Cunningham Photo)

(Theatre at Saint Peter's Church) Tuesday, November 17, 1987–January 17, 1988 (55 performances and 17 previews). Jane Hunt Mayer, Lynne H. Lyons, Jessica Levy, Lee Minskoff, Lawrence Goossen present:
REAL ESTATE by Louise Page; Director, Brian Murray; Set, Desmond Heeley; Costumes, Muriel Stockdale; Lighting, John Michael Deegan; General Management, Kingwill & Goossen/Larry Goosen; Press, David Powers, Robert Ganshaw; Production Stage Manager, Wm. Hare; Assistant Stage Manager, Alan Murley; Production Assistant, Joseph Travers; Wardrobe, Barbara Welsley; Assistants, Luke Yankee, Barbara Sorensen, Peter Villapolo, Stephen Olson, Donna Langman CAST: Sada Thompson (Gwen), Roberta Maxwell (Jenny), Charles Cioffi (Dick), Lewis Arlt (Eric)
A play in 2 acts. The action takes place in Gwen's house and office, on the outskirts of London. The time is the present.

Above: Charles Cioffi, Sada Thompson, Lewis Arlt, Roberta Maxwell in "Real Estate"
(Martha Swope Photo)

(Space 603) Saturday, November 7–24, 1987 (13 performances) Staret . . . The Directors Company (Artistic/Producing Director, Michael Parva; Artistic/Managing Director, Victoria Lanman Chesshire) presents:
SOHO, THEY CALL IT by Kipp Osborne; Director, Terry Dudley; Set/Lighting, Ron Kidd; Costumes, Anne Kenney; Light Choreography, Ralph H. Anderson; Technical Director, Scott Palmer; Props, Deborah Sarria; Wardrobe, Anne Kenney; Stage Manager, Lynne Harris; Press, Elizabeth Tooker CAST: Florence Anglin (Margret), Alice Barrett (Ann), William Esper (Sal), Paul Goodman (George), Don Peoples (Tony), Howard Spiegel (Bono)
A play in 2 acts and 5 scenes with an epilogue. The action takes place during the early 1980's in a small family-run live poultry market in New York City.

(Lamb's Theatre) Monday, November 9, 1987–April 17, 1988 (168 performances and 16 previews). Jay H. Fuchs, A. Joseph Tandet, in association with Sports Entertainment Group & Little Prince Productions present:
THE BOYS NEXT DOOR by Tom Griffin; Director, Josephine R. Abady; Set, David Potts; Costumes, C. L. Hundley; Lighting, Michael Chybowzki; Sound, Lia Vollack; Hairstylist, Marcia Ann Ames; Casting, Pat McCorkle; Associate Producer, Robin Benson Fuchs; General Management, Gatchell & Neufeld/R. Tyler Gatchell, Jr., Peter Neufeld; Company Managers, Donald Joslyn, Kearen Anderson; Assistant to Director, Paul Brown; Production Assistant, Connie Womack; Movement, Nora Kasarda; Technical Director, Ted Wallace; Props, David Fletcher, Jill Cordle; Wardrobe/Hair, Lena Barry; Stage Managers, Peggy Peterson, Robin Anne Joseph; Press, Fred Nathan Co./Marc P. Thibodeau, Anne Abrams, Bert Fink, Merle Frimark, Philip Rinaldi, Rachel Abroms, David Alberico. CAST: Joe Grifasi succeeded by Michael Jeter (Arnold), William Jay (Lucien P. Smith), Dennis Boutsikaris succeeded by Arthur Hanket, Woody Harrelson (Jack), Josh Mostel succeeded by Adam LeFevre (Norman Bulansky), Joe Urla succeeded by John Short (Barry Klemper), John Wylie (Mr. Hedges/Mr. Corbin/Sen. Clarke), Laurinda Barrett (Mrs. Fremus/Mrs. Warren/Clara), Christine Estabrook succeeded by Innes-Fergus McDade (Sheila), Ed Setrakian (Mr. Klemper), Innes-Fergus McDade, Victor Raider-Wexler, John Shepard, Robert Trebor, Ellis E. Williams (Standbys).
A comedy in two acts. The action takes place in an apartment located in New England during the present summer.

(TOMI Theatre) Wednesday, November 11–December 6, 1987 (18 performances). The Metropolitan Theatre Alliance (Paul Leavin, Artistic Director), in association with the Eureka Theatre presents:
ABOUT FACE by Dario Fo; English Translation, Ron Jenkins; Director, Richard Seyd; Set, Peggy Snider; Lighting/Associate Set Designer, Robert Alan Harper; Costumes, P. Chelsea Harriman; Production Stage Manager, Wendy Kaufman; General Manager, Kate Harper; Production Consultants, George Krevsky, Vincent Procida; Props, Alice Forrester; Music, Steven Le Grande, Eric Feldman CAST: Joe Bellan (Antonio Berardi/Gianni Agnelli), Lisa Meryll (Lucia Rismondi), Joseph Siravo (Chief Surgeon/Spy), Sharon Lockwood (Rosa Berardi), Pierre Epstein (Inspector), Philip Abrams (Prosecutor/Intern/Spy), Brian Hargrove (Constable/Intern/Stagehand), Warren Keith (Group Leader/Intern), Paul Kerry (Washing Machine Man/Intern)
A comedy in 2 acts.

(Baldwin Theatre) Thursday, November 12–December 6, 1987 (13 performances and 3 previews). The Baldwin Theatre (Anita Sorel, Artistic Director) presents:
LIFE ON THE THIRD RAIL by Mitchell Uscher; Director, B. Matthew Stuart; Set, Barry Axtell; Lighting, Deborah Constantine; Costumes, Anita Sorel; Sound, Jeffrey H. Allgeier; Stage Manager, Page P. Billingham; Assistant Stage Manager, Jason A. Cina; Press, Michael D. Thompson; Technical Director, Scott Sorrels; CAST: Timothy Charles (Jim Manfredi), Florence Hayle (Mrs. Dix/Miriam Donnelly/Bank Teller), David Brand (Tap Dancer/Newscaster/Bruce/Taxi Driver), Karen Lynn Gorney (Chi-Chi), Craig Stepp (Kenny Baxter), Jessie K. Jones (Sandra Donnelly), Charles Herrick Cragin (Gallery Director/Jacques/Harold Donnelly/Man in Subway)
A play in 2 acts. The action takes place on a spring evening at various locations around New York City.

(Theater for the New City) Thursday, November 12–December 6, 1987 Theatre for the New City presents:
THE THREE LIVES OF LUCIE CABROL from the novella by John Berger; Adaptation/Director, Paul Zimet; Music, Ellen Maddow, Harry Mann; Choreography, Rocky Bornstein; Set/Puppet Design, Janie Geiser; Lighting, Arden Fingerhut; Costumes, Gabriel Berry; Stage Manager, Jane Grey; Sound Recording, Phil Lee; Full House; Press, Jim Baldassare CAST: *The Talking Band:* Roger Babb (Marius Cabrol/Henri Cabrol/Percussion), William Badgett (Cheesemaker/Saint-Just/Trombone/Guitar), Ellen Maddow (Emile Cabrol/Resistance Fighter/Saxophone/Electric Keyboard), Harry Mann (Edmond Cabrol/Mille a Lapraz/Clarinet/Piano), Tina Shepard (Lucie Cabrol), Paul Zimet (Jean)
A play in 2 acts. The action takes place in the Village of Brine, France; *Part I:* 1900–1944, *Part II:* September 1967, and *Part III:* Fall, 1967 - Summer, 1968.

(Second Avenue Theatre) Sunday, November 15, 1987–January 10, 1988 (6 performances and 52 previews). M Square Entertainment, Inc., Mitchell Maxwell, Alan J. Schuster, Marvin R. Meit, and Robert de Rothschild in association with Edie and Ely Landau present:

THE CHOSEN with Book by Chaim Potok; Music, Philip Springer; Lyrics, Mitchell Bernard; Based on the novel *The Chosen* by Chaim Potok; Director, Mitchell Maxwell; Choreography, Richard Levi; Musical Director, Eric Stern; Musical Consultation/Orchestrations, Samuel Matlovsky; Music Coordinator, John Monaco; Associate Producer, Warren Trepp; Sets, Ben Edwards; Costumes, Ruth Morley; Lighting, Thomas R. Skelton; Sound, Abe Jacob; Production Stage Manager, Jake Bell; Hair Design, Howard Leonard; Casting, Pat McCorkle, C.S.A. and Richard Cole; Assistant to the Director, Richard Holland; Production Associates, Kathleen Conforti, Fred H. Krones, Victoria Maxwell; Assistant Choreographer, Patricia Wilcox; General Management, M Square Entertainment, Inc.; Press, Joe Wolhandler Associates/Emily Cohen; Associate General Manager, Malcolm Allen; Additional Dance & Vocal Arrangements/Assistant Conductor, Patrick S. Brady; Stage Managers, Frank DiFilia, Robert Montano; Assistant Company Manager, Joshua Rosenblum; Assistants, Beth Kunin, Pat Woodbridge, John Heretz, Melissa Binder, Duncan R. Edwards; Hairdresser, Joe Anthony; Technical Supervisor, Michael S. Egna; Sound, Duncan R. Edwards; Props, Deb Clelland, Jill Merzon, Matt Silver; Wardrobe, Craig Aspen, Janna M. Notick; Casting Assistant, Richard Cole; Production Assistant, Marnie Waxman; Special Consultant, Albert Poland CAST: Richard Cray (Danny Saunders), George Hearn (Reb Saunders), Gerald Hiken (David Malter), Michael Ingram (Coach Galanter), Caryn Kaplan (Miriam), Daniel Marcus (Davey Cantor), Rob Morrow (Reuven Malter), Lynnette Perry (Hindie Saunders), Patricia Ben Peterson (Esther), Tia Riebling (Rachel), Joey Rigol (Levi Saunders), Mimi Turque (Mrs. Saunders), Patricia Alexander, Lawrence Asher, Zelie Daniels, Anny DeGange, Paul Dobie, Jack Drummond, Michael Edwin, Jeff Gardner, Jonathan Gold, Matthew Grant, Michael Greenwood, Joe Gustern, Eileen Hawkins, Linda Hess, Tracy Katz, Kevin Ligon, Gary Schwartz, Christopher Scott, Elaine Wright (Ensemble), Paul Haber (Standby for Reuven), Zelie Daniels, Michael Greenwood, Gary Schwartz, Michael Edwin, Jonathan Gold (Understudies), Robert Montano (Swing), Patricia Wilcox (Dance Captain/Swing)

MUSICAL NUMBERS: Play to Win, Words, Soon You'll Be Here in My Arms, Holy Little World, Ribbono, Processional, Ladder to the Lord, The Prince and Me, A Woman of Valor (After Proverbs), Wake Us with Your Song, Our New Jerusalem, The Chosen, Tune in My Heart, Danny's Plea, Silence, Finale

A musical drama in 2 acts and 14 scenes. The action takes place in Williamsburg, Brooklyn, between 1944 and 1948.

Right: Bob Morrow, Richard Cray, Mimi Turque, Lynnette Perry in "The Chosen" Below: Veanne Cox, Peter Frechette in "Flora, the Red Menace"
(Carol Rosegg Photo)

(Vineyard Theatre) Friday, November 20, 1987–January 23, 1988 (46 performances). Vineyard Theatre (Barbara Zinn Krieger, Executive Director; Gary P. Steuer, Managing Director; Susan Wilder, Production Manager; Mary Virginia Brooks, General Manager; Douglas Aibel, Artistic Director; Press, Bruce Cohen/Kathleen von Schmid) presents:

FLORA, THE RED MENACE with Book by David Thompson; Based on novel "Love Is Just Around the Corner" by Lester Atwell; Originally Adapted by George Abbott; Music, John Kander; Lyrics, Fred Ebb; Director, Scott Ellis; Choreography, Susan Stroman; Set, Michael J. Hotopp; Lighting, Phil Monat; Costumes, Lindsay W. Davis; Musical Direction, David Pogue; Production Coordinator, Susan Wilder; Stage Manager, Mary Fran Loftus. CAST: Veanne Cox (Flora Meszaros), Ray DeMattis (Mr. Weiss), Peter Frechette (Harry Toukarian), Maggi Corrill (Maggie), Lyn Greene (Charlotte) B. J. Jefferson (Elsa), Eddie Korbich (Willy), Dirk Lumbard (Kenny), David Ossian (M. Stanley).

MUSICAL NUMBERS: Unafraid, The Kid Herself, All I Need Is One Good Break, Not Every Day of the Week, Sign Here, A Quiet Thing, The Flame, Dear Love, Keepin' It Hot, Express Yourself, Where Did Everybody Go?, You Are You, The Joke, Sing Happy

A musical in two acts. The action takes place in 1935 in New York City.

(The Cubiculo) Friday, November 20–December 13, 1987. Practical Cats Theatre Company presents:

OKLAHOMA SAMOVAR by Alice Eve Cohen; Director, Lou Rackoff; Set, Gary Dartt; Costumes, Madeline Cohen; Lighting, Todd Lichtenstein; Doll Design, Marcia Whitney; Production Stage Manager, Kay Foster; Technical Director, Dave Morkal; Lighting Operator, Walter Mantani; Assistant Costume Designer, Marcia Whitney; Musical Director, Alice Eve Cohen; Press, Bruce Cohen/Kathleen von Schmid; Recording Engineers, Brad Keimach, Phil Lee, Walter Mantini; Violinist, Peter Winnograd; CAST: Anna Berger (Sylvia/Mrs. Ginventer), Tara Hugo (Alice/Maxine), Mary Baird (Hattie's Mother), Jacob Harran (Jake), Michele Seyler (Hattie), Ben Gotlieb (Max/Charlie), Patricia Norcia (Rose), Marisa Zahler (Louise)

A drama in 2 acts. The action takes place over 100 years in the lives of five generations in a Jewish family, and their journey from a shtetl in Europe to the Oklahoma Land Rush of 1889.

(Harry DeJur Henry Street Settlement Playhouse) Sunday, November 22,–December 20, 1987 (30 performances). Henry Street Settlement's New Federal Theatre (Woodie King Jr., Producer) presents:

TRINITY by Edgar White; Director, Oz Scott; Set, Scott Bradley; Costumes, C. Jane Epperson; Lighting, Victor En Yu Tan; Sound, Carmen Whiip; Production Stage Manager, Lisa L. Watson; Executive Director, Daniel Kronenfeld; Director, Arts for Living Center, Barbara Tate; Company Manager, Linda Herring; Assistant to Producer, Pawnee Sills; Press, Max Eisen, Madelon Rosen; Technical Director, Richard Arnold; Scenic Artist, Scott Bradley; Wardrobe, Harriet D. Foy; Props, Ileana Peyron CAST: *Man and Soul:* Cortez Nance, Jr. (Faigan), Lanyard Williams (Ikuru), Paul C. Harris (Policeman). *The Case of Dr. Kola:* Al Freeman, Jr. (Dr. Kola), Vondie Curtis-Hall (Sgt. Kay). *That Generation:* Paul Benjamin (Wallace), Madge Sinclair (Phyllis), Regina Taylor (Carol).

3 one act plays: *Man and Soul* takes place in a detention cell in London, in late August during the Notting Hill Carnival. *The Case of Dr. Kola* takes place in a cell somewhere in Africa. *That Generation* is set in a furnished room in Shepherds Bush, London.

(Alice Tully Hall) Monday, November 23, 1987 (1 performance)

MAGDALENA by Heitor Villa-Lobos; Lyrics/Adaptation, Robert Wright, George Forrest; Original Book, Frederick Hazlitt Brennan, Homer Curran; Concert Adaptation, Evans Haile, Dona D. Vaughn; Stage Direction, Dona D. Vaughn; Presented by Evans Haile; General Manager, David Cash; Conductor, Evans Haile. CAST: Charles Damsel (Padre Jose), Faith Esham (Maria), Kevin Gray (Pedro), Keith Curran (Major Blanco), Charles Repole (Zoggie), George Rose (General Carabana), Judy Kaye (Teresa), John Raitt (Tribal Elder), Simon Jones (Narrator), Orchestra of New England, Connecticut Choral Artists

(South Street Theater) Wednesday, November 25, 1987–January 3, 1988 (38 performances). Metropolitan Theatre Alliance (Paul Leavin, Artistic Director) presents:

WORDS FROM THE MOON by Tom Ross; Director, Bill Herndon; Sets, Jack Chandler; Lighting, Spencer Mosse; Costumes, Arnall Downs; Sound, Tom Gould; Associate Producers, Suzanne Arden, Vincent Perocida; Press, Bruce Cohen/Kathleen von Schmid CAST: Amy Wright, Drew Snyder, Janni Brenn, Sally Gracie, Molly Langmuir, Brad Lowry, James Goodwin Rice, Colter Rule, Tim Van Pelt

A comedy in 2 acts. The action takes place in the house and yard of a family in Haw River, North Carolina, near a polluting power plant.

(Noho Theatre) Friday, November 27–December 20, 1987 (16 performances). The Village Theatre Company presents:

THE ENCLAVE by Arthur Laurents; Director, Julia McLaughlin; Set, George Grier; Sound/Music, Jimmy Flynn; Assistant Director/Production Stage Manager, Lisa Grey Beeson; Costumes, Marjorie Feenan; Lighting, Alan Baron CAST: Marjorie Feenan (Elanor), Howard Thoresen (Bruno), Susan Farwell (Cassie), Keith Michl (Donnie), Randy Kelly (Ben), David McConnell (Wyman), Scott C. Krohn (Oliver), Jesse N. Holmes (Roy Lee), Barbara Berque (Janet)

A play in 2 acts and 7 scenes. The action takes place in New York City at Elanor and Bruno's, Ben's, and Cassie and Donnie's on a Thursday thru Saturday evening in 1973.

**Rebecca Renfroe, William McClary, Dan Delafield
in "The Gifts of the Magi"** *(Carol Rosegg Photo)*

(The Raft Theatre) Wednesday December 2–19, 1987 (16 performances). The Raft Theatre and the Phoenix Ensemble present:
CAFE TOULOUSE by James Edward Luczak; Director, Terry D. Kester; Set, Martin Zurla; Costumes, Paul Ravich; Lighting/Sound, Terry D. Kester; Stage Manager, Phyllis Malanka CAST: Harold Dean James (Claudia), Reenie Upchurch (Amanda), Carter Inskeep (Obadiah), Shelley Crandall (Hazel), Diane Reynolds (Valerie)
A play in 2 acts and 6 scenes. The action takes place in the alley, kitchen and waitress station of the Cafe Toulouse, New Orleans, 1965.

(Home for Contemporary Theatre and Art) Wednesday, December 2–19, 1987 (12 performances and 2 previews). Mutual Artists Productions presents:
THE SCHOOL OF JOLLY DOGS Directed by Randy Rollison; Musical Arrangements, Leslie Steinweiss; Choreography, Kenneth Tosti; Original Material, Denise Lanctot; Set, Mark Beard; Lighting, M. L. Geiger CAST: Becky Borczon, Kate Fuglei, Mary Gilbert, Denise Lanctot, Kevin G. McMillan, Randy Rollison, Stuart Sherman, Leslie Steinweiss, Parsley Steinweiss, Kenneth Tosti, Lissy Walker, Paul Walker
MUSICAL NUMBERS: Prehistoric Man, Champagne Charlie, Bang! Went the Chance of a Lifetime, Polly Perkins of Paddington Green and other popular songs from 1856–1908 (complete list not provided)
A new revue of classic songs from the English music hall.

(Park Avenue Armory) Wednesday, December 2, 1987 and still playing as of June 1, 1988. Moses Znaimer in association with Lawrence N. Dykun and Barrie Wexler presents:
TAMARA by John Krizanc; Director, Richard Rose; Executive Producer, Moses Znaimer; Associate Producers, Lawrence N. Dykun, Barrie Wexler; Conceived by Richard Rose, John Krizanc; Associate Director, Phil Killian; Design, Robert Checchi; Music, William Schallert; Choreography/Fight Direction, Gary Mascaro; Costumes, Gianfranco Ferre; Assistant Director, George Rondo; Casting, Johnson-Liff/Zerman; Lighting, Brian Bailey; Hairstylist, Bobby H. Grason; General Management, Maple Interactive Entertainment Ltd.; Company Managers, Melinda P. Bloom, L. Glenn Poppleton III; Technical Director, David Kennedy; Props, Tom Swift, Douglas Kane, Nancy Greensten; Wardrobe, Briona McMahon, Mary Lou Rios; Dance/Fight Captain, Norb Joerder; Dialect Coach, Sam Chwat; Stage Managers, Bruce Kagel, Cosmo P. Hanson; Press, Jeffrey Richards/Irene Gandy, Ben Morse, Susan Chicione, C. George Willard, Diane Judge, Roger Lane, Naomi Grabel, Jillana Devine CAST: Sara Botsford succeeded by Anna Katarina, Christine Dunford (Tamara de Lempicka), Lally Cadeau succeeded by Laura Esterman (Luisa Baccara), Cynthia Dale succeeded by Terry Hawkes, Lyn Vaux (Carlotta Barra), Roma Downey succeeded by Sue Giosa (Emilie Pavese), Patrick Horgan succeeded by Sam Tsoutsouvas (Gian Francesco de Spiga), Marilyn Lightstone (Aelis Mazoyer), Leland Murray (Dante Fenzo), Frederick Rolf succeeded by Ted Sorel (Gabriele d'Annunzio), August Schellenberg succeeded by Thom Christopher (Aldo Finzi), Jack Wetherall (Mario Pagnutti)
A melodrama in two acts with dinner served at intermission. The action takes place on 2 successive days of 1927 in Il Vittoriale, the country retreat of Gabriele d'Annunzio.

(Lamb's Little Theatre) November 27, 1987–January 2, 1988 (40 performance limited engagement). Lamb's Theatre Company (Carolyn Rossi Copeland, Producing Director/Joel K. Ruark, General Manager) presents:
THE GIFTS OF THE MAGI with Book & Lyrics by Mark St. Germain; Music & Lyrics, Randy Courts; Based on the classic O'Henry stories; Director, Stephen A. Zorthian; Set, Michael C. Smith; Costumes, Hope Hanafin; Lighting, Heather Carson; Choreography, Carol Conway; Musical Director, Alkiviades Sterioopoulos; Production Stage Manager, Melissa L. Burdick; Originally Staged by Christopher Catt; Incidental Music, Steven M. Alper; Press, G. Theodore Killmer; Stage Managers, Melissa L. Burdick, Tara Greenway; Production Manager, David Pilot; Technical Assistant, Thomas H. Tuttle; Consulting Carpenter, Jim Murphy; Carpenter, Paul Grigoridis. CAST: Dan Delafield (Him), Rebecca Renfroe (Her), Martin Moran (Willy), John David Westfall (Jim), Jessica Beltz (Della), William McClary (Soapy)
MUSICAL NUMBERS: Star of the Night, The Gifts of the Magi, Jim and Della, Christmas Is to Blame, How Much to Buy My Dream, The Restaurant, Once More, Bum Luck, Greed, Pockets, The Same Girl, The Gift of Christmas
A musical performed without intermission. The action takes place in New York City, December 23 thru 25, 1905.

(Nat Horne Theatre) Friday, November 27–December 8, 1987 (12 performances).
THREE IN TIME by Dan Blue; Director, Celia Braxton; Production Stage Manager, Connie Drew; Set, Bonny Ann Whitehouse; Lighting, Boban Pantic; Costumes, Susan DeMasi; Sound, Paul Garrity; Assistant Stage Manager, Peter W. Kilsch; Set Assistant, Geraldine Whitehouse; Light Assistant, Jeffrey Sanchez; Crew, Kathleen Boatswain; Hair, Neil Dickson CAST: Katherine Brecka (Karen), Daryn Kent-Duncan (Carla), David Sitler (Mark)
A play in 2 acts. The action takes place in the 1980's, in an anti-room in an apartment on upper 5th Avenue.

(Sanford Meisner Theatre) Tuesday, December 1–20, 1987 (13 performances, 3 previews limited engagment). Dragonfly Theatre Company presents:
LANFORD WILSON'S HALL OF NORTH AMERICAN FORESTS by Lanford Wilson: *The Bottle Harp* Directed by William Lucas Walker/*Say de Kooning* Directed by Max Jaffe/*A Betrothal* Directed by Claris Nelson; Artistic Director, William Lucas Walker; Sets, Paul C. Weimer; Lighting, Tracy Dedrickson; Costumes, Deborah Rooney; Sound, Chuck London Media/Stewart Werner; Music, Norman Noll; Production Stage Manager, Sanja Kabalin; Technical Director, Harry E. Lee; Production Coordinator, Robin Rogers CASTS: *The Bottle Harp:* Beth Koules (Dorry), Stefanie Milligan (Pat), Kevin Cristaldi (Bobby). *Say de Kooning:* Timothy Wahrer (Don), Mimi Bensinger (Willie), Susanna M. Banks (Mandy). *A Betrothal:* Maggie Burke (Ms. J. H. Joslyn), Tom Celli (Mr. Kermit Wasserman)
Three one-act plays. *The Bottle Harp* takes place in early summer, 1964, in a kitchenette apartment on Central Park West. *Say de Kooning* takes place in an old house near the beach on the East End of Long Island during Labor Day Weekend, 1980. *A Betrothal* takes place in the end of a large tent in Putnam County, New York, on an afternoon in mid-May.

Marilyn Lightstone, Frederick Rolf in "Tamara"
(Martha Swope Photo)

60

(Westside Arts Theatre) Friday, December 4, 1987–still playing May 31, 1988. Steven Baruch, Thomas Viertel, Richard Frankel, Jujamcyn Theaters/Margo Lion present the Manhattan Theatre Club production of:
FRANKIE AND JOHNNY IN THE CLAIR DE LUNE by Terrence McNally; Director, Paul Benedict; Set, James Noone; Costumes, David Woolard; Lighting, David Noling; Sound, John Gromada; General Management, Richard Frankel/Marc Routh; Company Manager, Jean Rocco; Technical Director, Thomas Shilhanek; Wardrobe, Anne Marie Paolucci; Stage Managers, Pamela Singer, Craig Palanker; Press, Fred Nathan Co./Marc Thibodeau. CAST: Kathie Bates succeeded by Carol Kane, Debra Jo Rupp, Bonnie Franklin (Frankie), Kenneth Welsh succeeded by Bruce Weitz, James Harper, Tony Musante (Johnny), Dominic Cuskern (Voice of Radio Announcer).

A play in two acts. The action takes place at the present time in Frankie's one-room apartment in a walk-up tenement in the West 50's in Manhattan.

(Theatre Off Park) Wednesday, December 9, 1987–January 17, 1988 (28 performances and 12 previews). Theatre Off Park presents:
MADEMOISELLE COLOMBE with Music by Michael Valenti; Lyrics, Edwin Dulchin; Book, Edwin Dulchin, Albert Harris, Michael Valenti; Based on a play by Jean Anouilh; From the English Adaptation by Louis J. Kronenberger; Director, Albert Harris; Choreographer, William Fleet Lively; Set, Philipp Jung; Costumes, Lindsay Davis; Lighting, Donald Holder; Musical Director, Rod Derefinko; Casting, Warren Pincus; Orchestrations, Greg Smith; General Management, Whitbell Productions, Inc.; Production Stage Manager, Susan D. Greenbaum; Hair Design, Robert W. Cybula, Carmel Vargyas; Press, Henry Luhrman Assoc./Terry M. Lilly, David J. Gersten, Andrew P. Shearer, Brian Drutman; Stage Managers, John M. Atherlay, Laura Gewurz; Dance Captain, Richard Stegman; Assistants, John M. Atherlay, Peter Harrison, Pat McGillicuddy, Chelsea Harriman, Laura Drawbaugh; Wardrobe/Wigs, John Baroucas; Scenic Artist, Elizabeth Linn; Props/Scenic Artist, Betsy Kelleher; Props, Neil Jacob CAST: Tammy Grimes (Mme. Alexandra), Joaquin Romaguera (Robinet), David Cryer (Gaulois), Michael Tartel (Deschamps), Dick Decareau (Gourette), Georgia Creighton (Mme. Georges) Robert Cooner (Stagehand), Judith McLane (Judith), Richard Stegman (Hairdresser), Lisa Vroman (Lisa/Colombe Understudy), Elizabeth Walsh (Manicurist), Campbell Martin (Chiropodist), Victoria Brasser (Colombe), Keith Buterbaugh (Julien), Tom Galantich (Édouard)
MUSICAL NUMBERS: Prologue, The Goddess of Love, Two against the World, What's the Mail?, Only So Much I Can Give, Yes Alexandra-No Alexandra, Perfect, Moon Dear, This Bright Morning, More Than One Man in Her Life, After Rehearsal, And If I Tell You That I Want You, She's an Actress, The Color Red, Folies Bergeres, Why Did It Have to be You, The Realm of Passion (or The Soldier's Wife), Years From Now, Georgie and I, From This Day

A new musical in 2 acts and 5 scenes. The action takes place in a Paris Theater, around 1900.

(Nat Horne Theatre) Thursday, December 10–20, 1987 (12 performances). PSM Productions presents:
MERRY CHRISTMAS, MISS MOLLY by Paul Surace; Director, Seth Gordon; Set, J. C. Sasportas; Lighting, Ian Stoval; Stage Manager, Fayton Hollington; Press, Marion S. Marcovitz CAST: Paul Surace (Joseph Aiello), Marion Covit (Molly Hawkins), Greg Natale (Chester), Albert Michael Goudy (Luther), George Anthony Rae (Raphael), Richard Welch (Madman)

A comedy performed without intermission. The action takes place on Christmas Eve, 1987, in a deserted back alley in New York City.

**Michael Tartel, Dick Decareau, Jaoquin Romaguera,
Tammy Grimes, Tom Galantich, Georgia Creighton
in "Mlle. Colombe"** *(Martha Swope Photo)*

**Bruce Weitz, Carol Kane in "Frankie and
Johnny in the Clair de Lune"** *(Peter Cunningham)*

(Actors' Playhouse) Saturday, December 12, 1987–January 7, 1988 (1 performance and 21 previews). Anne Productions present:
S.O.S. by Burt Young; Dramaturgist, Elaine Aiken; Production Coordinator, Chris A. Kelly; Contributing Editor, Sidney Sparrow; Set, Peter R. Feuche; Lighting, Bruce R. Kahle; Sound/Music, Tom Kocha; Personal Manager, Andrew Giovingo; General Manager, Anne Productions; Press, Jeffrey Richards Assoc./Diane Judge, Francine Trevens; Production Coordinator, Chris A. Kelly; Company Manager, Temmie Rosenthal; Assistant Press Agent, Naomi Grable; Sound Technician, J. Bloomrosen; Lighting Technician, Mr. Morris; Technical Director, Trevor Brown; Scenic Artist, Stav CAST: Burt Young (as six characters, including Amelia Earhart)

A solo performance of a surrealistic contemporary drama.

(Harold Clurman Theater) Wednesday December 16, 1987–January 19, 1988 (15 performances and 1 preview). Paul Morer in association with Levin Theater Company at Rutgers University, presents:
A MOST SECRET WAR by Kevin Patterson; Director, John Battenbender; Sets, Joseph F. Miklokjcik, Jr.; Costumes, Kathryn Wagner; Lighting, Andrew Segaloff; Casting, Joseph Abaldo; Sound, Rob Gorton; Production Stage Manager, Doug Hosney; Press, Shirley Herz Associates/Glenna Freedman, David Roggensack, Peter Cromarty, Pete Sanders, Miller Wright; Casting Associate, Bob Hoffman; Props, David McMurtrie, Justine Angelis; Wardrobe, Valerie Warick CAST: Steven Dennis (Alan Turning), Susan Verducci (Alice Hill), Mary Loughran (Sara Turing/Eliza Clayton), Gary Glor (Barrister/Senhouse), Ron Wisniski (Judge/Duncan/Donnell), Brian Dykstra (Charles Bird/Perkins/Detective), Tony Carlin (John Turning/Hargove/MacKendrick/Hodges, etc.), Eddie Grossman (Bob Augenfeld)

The present action of the play is set in 1954, the other events take place between 1927 and 1954, in England.

(Nat Horne Theatre) Friday, January 1, 1988–The Sidewalks Theatre presents:
THE SEARCHING SATYRS by Sophocles; Adapted by Gary Beck; Director, Gary Beck; Choreographer, Loretta Thomas; Costumes, Arnold Levine; Set, Neil Johnson; Lighting, Alan Baron; Press, Bruce Cohen, Kathleen von Schmid. CAST: Nancy Guarino (Kyllene), Mark R. Hunt (Hermes), T. J. Harvin (Apollo), Autry Davis (Silenus), Clay Dickinson (1st Satyr), Satyrs: Roisin Baldwin, Corrine Francois, Jonathan Russo, Perry Glenn Thomas, Glenn Thompson

(Church of the Holy Trinity) Thursday, January 7–February 6, 1988 (18 performances). Triangle Theatre Company presents:
THE LAST RESORT by Tom Ziegler; Director, Will Cantler; Stage Manager, Anne M. Cantler; Costumes, Amanda J. Klein; Sets, Bob Phillips; Lighting, Danianne Mizzy; Technical Director, Edmond Ramage; Sound, Mike Whalen; Press, Bruce Cohen/Kathleen Von Schmid CAST: Rob Donohoe (Steven Kendrick), Meg Mundy (Marjorie Kendrick), Anne Stone (Mary Dillard), Albert S. Bennett (Abe Fishman), Fred Burrell (Henry Downs), Gerri Beckham (Rose Ferguson), Kathryn Eames (Isabel Lowery), Marjorie Lovett (Dottie Bartel)

A play in 2 acts. The action takes place in the recreation room and outdoor patio of the Sunset Nursing Home, somewhere on Long Island.

(The Producers Club) Thursday, January 7–31, 1988 (16 performances). Nightcap Productions presents:
THE LIGHTS ON WALDEN COURT by Bill Ervolino; Director, Thomas M. Ratzin; Design Consultant, Arnold Peer Hruska; Stage Manager, Steve Purnick; Assistant Stage Manager, Matt Gitkin; Press, Maya Associates/Penny M. Landau

A play in 2 acts. The action takes place in a ranch house in Farmingdale, L.I., two days before Christmas and through the evening of Christmas day.

(Promenade Theatre) Wednesday, January 13–31, 1988 (22 performances and 22 previews). William P. Suter and Donald V. Thompson present:
THE RIVER with Music & Lyrics by Peter Link; Staged & Choreographed by Michael Shawn; Set, William Barclay; Lighting, Phil Monat; Costumes, David Dille; Sound, Jeremy Harris; Vocal Arranger, Danny Madden; Musical Director, Ronald P. Metcalf; Assistant Choreographer, Paul Nunes; Executive Producer, William Spencer Reilly; Associate Producer, Douglas A. Love; General Manager, Leonard A. Mulhern; Production Stage Manager, Anita Ross; Press, Shirley Herz Associates Miller Wright; Associate General Manager, James Hannah; Stage Manager, Donald Christy; Dance Captain, Lawrence Hamilton; Sound, Jeremy Harris, Cathy Kavat; Wardrobe, Elizabeth Strader, Peter Le Maitre; Props, Louanne Gilleland; Casting, Johnson-Liff and Zerman CAST: Jenny Burton (Woman #2), Carol Dennis (Woman #1), Valerie K. Eley (Woman #3), Lawrence Hamilton (Man #1), Stephanie Renee James (Woman #4), Danny Madden (High Priest/Man #3), Ray Stephens (Man #2), Jerry Dixon, Val Scott, Jeffery Hairston-Smith (Acolytes) Jenny Dawn Douglas, Val Scott, Jeffery Hairston-Smith, Jerry Dixon (Understudies)
MUSICAL NUMBERS: Genesis, Mandala, Didn't It Rain, Put the Fire Out, Interlude I: One Drop Alone, Wanderin' in the Wilderness, A Still Small Voice, Interlude II: The Stream, Lead Me to the Water, Don't It Feel Good, Interlude III: The River's in Me, The River, Interlude IV: The Waterfall, All Around the World, Run River Run, Over the Edge, Interlude V: Wallowing in the Mire, Burnin' Up, This Is All I Ask, Carnival, Love Runs Deeper Than Pride, Interlude VI: Into the Sea, Revelation, Take Me Up
A "Musical Revelation" in 2 acts.

(Actors Outlet Theatre) Thursday, January 14–February 7, 1988 (16 performances). MRM Productions, James Rooney and Kevin McLoughlin in association with Actors Outlet Inc. presents:
HALF DESERTED STREETS by Robert Moresco; Director, Richard Compton; Set, Naj Wilkoff; Lighting, Alan Moyer; Sound, Ty Sanders; Associate Producers, Kim Snyder, John Moresco; Costumes, G. D. Turner; Stage Manager, Madeleine Janover; Props, Sylvia Aviles CAST: Michael Imperoili succeeded by Daniel Jordan (Frankie), Victor Colicchio (Bugs), Dan Grimaldi (Joe), Maria Cellario (Rose), Grace Miglio (Kate), Billy Cameron (Tony), Ralph A. Waite (Patty), P. R. Paul (Chuck), Kathleen Brant, Daniel Jordan (Understudies)
A play in 2 acts. The action takes place over a period of three days in a hot September in Hell's Kitchen in Manhattan; on the Street, in the Kitchen, and on the Roof.

(Town Hall) Friday, January 22–February 12, 1988 (7 performance limited engagement). Reuben Hoppenstein presents the International 20th Anniversary production of:
JACQUES BREL IS ALIVE AND WELL AND LIVING IN PARIS with English Lyrics & Conception by Eric Blau & Mort Shuman; Director, Elly Stone; Set/ Costumes, Don Jensen; Choreography, Susan Osberg; Lighting, Steve Helliker; Conductor, Jonathan Irving; Musicians, Bobby Grillo, Scott Kuney, Eddie Caccavale; General Manager, Lily Turner; Press, M. J. Boyer; Production Stage Manager, Bill McComb; Sound, David Smith/Triton Sound CAST: Karen Akers, Shelle Ackerman, Elmore James, Kenny Morris, Aileen Savage, Adam Bryant
MUSICAL NUMBERS: My Childhood, Overture, Marathon, Alone, Madeleine, I Loved, Mathilde, Bachelor's Dance, Timid Frieda, My Death, Girls and Dogs, Jackie, Statue, The Desperate Ones, Sons Of, Amsterdam, The Bulls, Old Folks, Marieke, Brussels, Fanette, Funeral Tango, Middle Class, No Love, You're Not Alone, Next, Carousel, If We Only Have Love
A musical revue in 2 acts.

(Perry Street Theatre) Saturday, January 23–February 13, 1988. The Spuyten Duyvil Theatre Company, Inc. presents:
BROTHERHOOD by John D. Richardson; Directed by Denni Delaney; Set, Ron Kadri; Lighting, Christopher S. Gorzelnik; Fight Director, Rick Sordelet; Set Construction, Charles Golden; Press, Carol Brooks; Costume Consultant, Margaret Benson; Stage Manager, Russell Owen; Company Producers, Isabel Glasser, Maureen MacDougall CAST: Michael Krauss (Digger), Howard Kuttner (Chuck), Frederick Wessler (Charles), Robert Poletick (Jack), Mark Shannon (Jackson)
A play in 2 acts. The action takes place on the porch and backyard of a house somewhere in suburban America just after twilight on a summer night in 1969, and a summer night sixteen years later.

(Puerto Rican Traveling Theatre) Thursday, January 28,–February 28, 1988 (42 performances). The Puerto Rican Traveling Theatre (Founder/Artistic Director/ Producer, Miriam Colon; Managing Director, Patricia Baldwin; Technical Director, Ed Bartosik; Props, Amy Meisner, Melvin Vasquez; Press, Max Eisen, Madelon Rosen) presents:
ARIANO by Richard V. Irizarry; Director, Vicente Castro; Spanish Translation, Margarita Lopez Chiclana; Set, James Sandefur; Lighting, Rachel Budin; Costumes, Toni-Leslie James; Sound, Gary and Timmy Harris; Stage Manager, Sandra M. Bloom. CAST: Rafael Baez/Eddie Trucco (Ariano), Graciela Lecube (Dona Aida), David Medina (Soldier), Georgina Corbo (Dolores), Jimmy Borbon (Serafin), Elizabeth Ruiz (Clara), Candace Brecker (Crystal)
A play in 2 acts and 7 scenes. The action takes place at the present time.

Carol Dennis, Ray Stephens, Stephanie Renee James, Lawrence Hamilton, Valerie K. Eley, Danny Madden, Jenny Burton in "The River" *(Martha Swope Photo)*

(Actors' Playhouse) Tuesday, February 2–June 5, 1988 (135 performances and 9 previews). Gary Bowen and Greg Spagna present the American Premiere of a Quaigh Theatre Production produced by Ruth Preven:
THE GOOD AND FAITHFUL SERVANT by Joe Orton; Director, Will Lieberson; Designer, Donald L. Brooks; Sound, George Jacobs; Production Stage Manager, Winifred H. Powers; Press, FLT/Francine L. Trevens; Manager, Ruth Preven; Assistant Stage Managers, Valentina Fratti, Robert Mahnkem; Press Assistants, Bernice Harrison, Robert Weston. CAST: Terry Ashe-Croft (Edith), Michael Allinson (Buchanan), Lezlie Dalton (Mrs. Vealtoy), Laura Lane (Debbie), William Carrigan (Raymond), Gene A. Morra (Old Man), Eddie Lane (Worker)
A play performed without intermission. The action takes place in a small English factory town.

(Theatre at St. Marks Church In–the Bowery) Thursday, February 4–14, 1988 (8 performances). 2nd Story Theatre Project presents:
A DELICATE HEART by Jean Reynolds; Directors, Alan Wynroth, Bo Walker; Designer, Daniel R. Peterson-Snyder; Design Assistant, Michael Pellegrino; Sound, Jonathan Sherry; Stage Manager, Catherine Gradnigo CAST: Monica Lundry (Dorothea Hoyt), Bob Jordan (James Hoyt), Jean Anderson (Margaret Dunreath), Dan Rubinate (Harry Loveland), Tim Ashford (Turner)
A play in 1 act. The action takes place around 1950 in Slingerlands, a small town near Albany, New York. presented with:
EMILY AND EMILIA, AND BOB by William Russell; Director, William Russell; Co-Director, John Anthony; same technical credits as above CAST: Jean Reynolds (Emily), Lola Michael (Emilia), William Russell (Bob)
A play in 1 act. The action takes place in the present, in Emilia's East Village storefront boutique and in her apartment.

(New Federal Theatre) Thursday, February 11–March 13, 1988 (30 performances). Henry Street Settlement's New Federal Theatre (Woodie King, Jr., Producer), with the Second Generation of Brooklyn presents:
AFTER CRYSTAL NIGHT by John Herman Shaner; Director, Max Mayer; Henry Street Settlement Executive Director, Daniel Kronefeld; Director Arts for Living Center, Barbara Tate; Set, Scott Bradley; Lighting, Michael Chybowski; Costumes, Judy Dearing; Sound, Kathy Chaffe; Production Stage Manager, Ruth Kreshka; Company Manager, Linda Herring; Press, Max Eisen, Madelon Rosen; Casting, Samantha Eden; Technical Director, Michael Schaefer; Wardrobe, Vicki Platt; Props, Ilena Peyron CAST: Anthony Call (Jerry Gardner/Jacob Goldstein), Stephen Giese (Keith Goldstein), Barbara eda-Young (Joyce Goldstein), Steve Franken (Seymour Goldstein), Michael Marcus (Uncle Morris), Michael Ornstein (Joe), Ben Mittleman (Doug), Lily Watkins (Susanna), Warren Pincus (Herbert Cohen)
A play in 2 acts and 3 scenes. The action takes place in the livingroom of the Goldstein Home in Beverly Hills, California.

Terry Ashe-Croft, Michael Allinson in "Good and Faithful Servant"
(Anita & Steve Shevett Photo)

(The Triplex) Saturday, February 6, 1988. Moved, after a fire, May 5, to 890 Broadway, and closed March 26, 1988 (48 performances). Theatre for a New Audience (Jeffrey Horowitz, Artistic-Producing Director; Deirdre Moyniha, Managing Director; Bill Reichblum, Associate Artistic Director), in association with North Shore Music Theatre (Joe Kimbell, Executive Producer) presents:

THE TAMING OF THE SHREW by William Shakespeare; Director, Julie Taymor; Music, Elliot Goldenthal; Set, G. W. Mercier; Costumes, Catherine Zuber; Lighting, Beverly Emmons; Voice & Text Consultant, Robert N. Williams; Casting, Ellen Novack; Musical Director, Jody Kruskal; Musicians, Jody Kruskal, John Loose, Tom Zajac; Production Stage Manager, Lee Bloomrosen; Production Manager, Tim Raphael; Assistant Director, Joel Bishoff; Stage Manager, Steven H. Wildern; Technical Director, Tim Lea; Props, Paul Ferrara; Production Assistant, Shannon Graves; Wardrobe, Michael McKinney; Abridged by Jeffrey Horowitz and Julie Taymor CAST: Frank Licato (Christopher Sly), Nancy-Elizabeth Kammer (Hostess/Widow), Curt Karibalis (Lord/Vincentio), Kelly Walters (Huntsman/Grumio), Ray Virta (Huntsman/Hortensio), Jack Kenny (Huntsman/Tranio), Joel Miller (Huntsman/Biodello), Paul Kandel (Huntsman/Pedant/Tailor), Scott Sowers (Page/Cutis), Brian Cousins (Lucentio), Graham Brown (Baptista/Minola), William Preston (Gremio), Sheila Dabney (Katherina), Wendy Makkena (Bianca), Sam Tsoutsouvas (Petrucio), Shelley Wyant (Servant), Jody Kruskal (Servant/Officer)

A play in 2 acts. The action takes place in Warwickshire, Padua, and near Verona.

(Washington Square Church/Carmelita's) Saturday, February 6, 1988 (still playing as of June 1, 1988). Joseph Corcoran, Daniel Corcoran, Mark Campbell present:

TONY 'N' TINA'S WEDDING by Artificial Intelligence; Director, Larry Pelligrini; Conception, Nancy Cassaro; Choreography, Hal Simons; Costumes/Hair/Make-Up, Juan DeArmas; Cake Design & Construction, Randal Thropp; Executive Producers, Joseph Corcoran, Daniel Corcoran; Producer, Mark Campbell; Press, David Rothenberg, Terence Womble, Todd Lundgren; Artistic Director, Nancy Cassaro; Artificial Intelligence Core Group, James Altuner, Mark Campbell, Chris Fracchiolla, Jack Fris, Larry Pellegrini CAST: Nancy Cassaro (Valentina Lynne Vitale Nunzio), Mark Nassar (Anthony Angelo Nunzio), Moira Wilson (Connie Mocogni), Mark Campbell (Barry Wheeler), Elizabeth Dennehy (Donna Marsala), James Altuner (Dominick Fabrizzi), Patricia Cregan (Marina Gulino), Eli Ganias (Johnny Nunzio), Susan Varon (Josephine Vitale), Thomas Michael Allen (Joseph Vitale), Jacob Harran (Luigi Domenico), Jennifer Heftler (Rose Domenico), Elizabeth Herring (Sister Albert Maria), Chris Fracchiolla (Anthony Angelo Nunzio, Sr.), Jeannie Moreau (Madeline Monroe), Denise Moses (Grandma Nunzio), Jack Fris (Michael Just), Phil Rosenthal (Father Mark), Kevin A. Leonidas (Vinnie Black), Joanna Cocca (Loretta Black), Mickey Abbate (Mick Black), Tom Hogan (Timmy Sullivan), Vincent Floriani (Sal Antonucci), Michael Winther (Donny Dulce), Kia Colton (Celeste Romano), Charlie Terrat (Carlo Cannoli), Towner Gallaher (Rocco Caruso), Judy Sheehan, Carolyn Scott, Judy Sheehan (Understudies)

An environmental theatre play. The action takes place at Tony and Tina's wedding.

(Nat Horne Theatre) Wednesday, February 10,–March 5, 1988 (16 performances). CAVU Productions presents:

SHIRLEY BASIN by Jack Gilhooley; Director, Liz Wright; Set, Mark Haack; Lighting, David Tasso; Costumes, Julie Ratcliffe; Associate Producer/Production Stage Manager, Laura Gallagher; Artistic Adviser, Ed Stern; General Management, Gail Bell/Whitbell; Press, Bruce Cohen/Kathleen von Schmid, Musical Consultant, Jack O'Hara; Sound, Kenn Doval, Carie Dobie Kramer; Props, Betty Berkowitz; Lighting, Bob Katz, Thom Mangan, Doug Rogers, Tyler Learnade; Music, The Sawmill Creek Band, Jack Gilhooley CAST: Norma Jean Giffin (Phyllis), Rita Gardner (Mary), Mary Portser (Darla), Susan Harney (Sarah), June Daniel White (Ruby), Helen-Jean Arthur (Marge), Timothy Woodward (Buddy)

A play in 2 acts. The action takes place sometime in the 1980's in Shirley Basin, Wyoming.

(Unitarian Church of All Souls) Friday, February 12–March 6, 1988 (19 performances). All Souls Players present:

COMPANY with Book by George Furth; Music & Lyrics, Stephen Sondheim; Director, Jeffery K. Neill; Musical Director, Brian Russell; Set, Robert Edmonds; Costumes, Judy Kahn; Lighting, Tran Wm. Rhodes; Fight Choreographer, M. Leah Schneider; Assistant to Director, Cindy Stroud; Production Stage Manager, Mary Tiefenbrunn; Producers, Marie and Walter Landa & Harry Blum; Stage Manager, Nick Xenos; Assistant Stage Manager, Peter Levine; Props, Kevin Lewis; Sound Effects, Peter Sauerbrey; Dance Captain, Cindy Stroud; Wardrobe, Judy Baird, Robin Alice Delp, Nancy D. Fell CAST: Kevin Daly (Robert), P. J. Nelson (Sarah), Woody Howard (Harry), Elizabeth Williams (Susan), Christopher Regan (Peter), Jennifer Dorr White (Jenny), David McKeown (David), Janet Metz (Amy), Scott Logsdon (Paul), Lorraine Serabian (Joanne), William Walters (Larry), Eadie Cohen (Martha), Cindy Stroud (Kathy), Christina Britton (April), Judy Baird, Nick Xenos (Understudies)

MUSICAL NUMBERS: Overture, Company, The Little Things You Do Together, Sorry-Grateful, You Could Drive a Person Crazy, Have I Got a Girl for You, Someone Is Waiting, Another Hundred People, Getting Married Today, Entr'acte, Side by Side, What Would We Do without You, Poor Baby, Tick Tock, Barcelona, The Ladies Who Lunch, Being Alive, Finale

A musical in 2 acts. The action takes place in New York City.

**Top Right: Mark Nassar, Nancy Cassaro
in "Tony 'n' Tina's Wedding"
(*Bruce Schwarz Photo*)
Below: Liliane Montevecchi**

(Theatre Four) Thursday, February 11–28, 1988 (20 performances). American Folk Theater, Inc. (Dick Gaffield, Producer) presents:

ANCHORMAN Written & Directed by Paul Carter Harrison; Music, Julius Hemphill; Set/Costumes, Oliver Jackson; Lighting, Sylvester Weaver, Jr.; Sound, Steven Menasche; Musical Director/Arrangements, Howard Kilik; Production Stage Manager, Lisa L. Watson; Company Manager, Didi Shapiro; Press, G. Theodore Killmer; Technical Director, Artie Reese; Costume Consultant, Natalie B. Walter; Set Design Consultants, Artie Reese, Lisa L. Watson; Assistant Stage Manager, Daniel Carlton; Sound Technician, John Cherry; Production Assistant, Rebecca Hoffman CAST: Giancarlo Esposito (Ignatius), Peter DeMaio (Coach Smalls), Al Freeman, Jr. (Red Rooster), Micki Grant (Delta), Michael Shelle (Nemesis), Craig Kelly (Peter), Daniel Carlton (Ignatius Understudy)

A "blues operetta" in 2 acts. The action takes place on the west coast, USA, in the recent past.

(Kaufman Theater) Friday, February 12–April 22, 1988 (64 performances and 7 previews). Martin R. Kaufman in association with Jean-Claude Baker presents:

LILIANE MONTEVECCHI ON THE BOULEVARD with Production Supervised by Tommy Tune; Musical Director, Joel Silberman; Set, Dain Marcus; Costumes, Michael Katz; Lighting, Nadine Charlsen; Violinist, Eric Schaberg; General Manager, Marshall B. Purdy; Press, Henry Luhrman Associates/Terry M. Lilly, Andrew P. Shearer, David J. Gersten; Prouction Manager, Nadine Charlsen CAST: Liliane Montevecchi, Joel Silberman, Eric Schaberg

MUSICAL NUMBERS: *Act One: A La Carte:* Paris Canaill, Sweet Beginnings, Bruxelles, Le Dernier Pierrot, Le Temps, I Never Do Anything Twice, Let's Call the Whole Thing Off, Tico Tico, It Might As Well Be Spring, Autumn Leaves, I've Got You Under My Skin, La Vie En Rose, My Man, You Don't Know Paree, I Love Paris, Ballet Barre; *Act Two: On the Boulevard:* Je Cherche Un Millionaire, Formidable, Just a Gigolo, The Boulevard of Broken Dreams, Bridge of Caulaincourt, Hey Jacque, Irma La Douce, New Fangled Tango, But Beautiful, Ne Me Quitte Pas, I Don't Want to Know, Folies Bergere, Bon Soir

A musical evening in 2 acts.

(Samuel Beckett Theatre) Friday, February 12–March 6, 1988 (18 performances and 2 previews). Shakespeare Stage Company, Ltd. presents:

TWELFTH NIGHT (or What You Will) by William Shakespeare; Director, Anthony Naylor; Musical Director, Shawn Norton; Costumes, Renee Sykes; Set, George Alexander Allison; Lighting, Laura Perlman; Production Coordinator, Marc Battista; Production Stage Manager, Vic DiMonda CAST: Sean Hopkins (Orsino), Clifton Bolton (Curio), Joseph Gardner (Valentine/First Officer), Lisa Griffith (Viola), John Schmerling (Sea Captain), Charles Michael Howard (Sir Toby Belch), Ann Schlumberger (Maria), Russ Billingsly (Sir Andrew Aguecheek), Robert Perillo (Feste), Nancy McDonald (Olivia), Edward Griffith (Malvolio), Ron Piretti (Sebastian), Craig Purinton (Antonio), Marc Wolf (Fabian), Virginia Kaycoff, Robert Jackson, Sandi Leibowitz (Musicians)

Performed with one intermission.

(Riverwest Theatre) Thursday, February 12–March 5, 1988 (2 performances). CHS Productions in association with Riverwest Theatre presents:
THE LAST MUSICAL COMEDY with Book & Lyrics by Tony Lang; Music, Arthur Siegel; Director/Choreographer, Pamela Hunt; Musical Director/ Arrangements, Bob McDowell; Set, Alan Kimmel; Costumes, Robert deMora; Lighting, Matt Ehlert; Production Stage Manager, Lori Lundquist; Production Coordinator, Paul A. Kochman; Stage Manager, Carol Venezia; Assistant to Director, John Geurts; Technical Director, Patrick Eagleton; Press, Chris Boneau; Producers, Nat Habib, June Sumems, Joe Cahalan; Props, Carol Venezia; Wardrobe, Latricia Neal; Musicians, John Howard, Jonathan Kemper CAST: Donna English (Betty), Eddie Korbich (Chip), Beth Blatt (Gladys), Laura Streets (Bambi), Mark Esposito (Buzz), Michael DeVries (Bill), Suzanne Dawson (Rita), Jonathan Bal (Charlie) MUSICAL NUMBERS: The Last Overture, The Last Opening, The Last Home Town Song, The Last Soubrette Song, The Last Love Duet, The Last Hate Song, The Last Soft Shoe, The Last Production Number, The Last Waltz, The Last Dream Ballet, The Last Jazz Specialty, The Last Torch Song, The Last Tap Dance, The Last Seduction Song, The Last Soliloquy, The Last Eleven O'Clock Number, The Last Finale

A musical comedy in 2 acts. The action takes place in the offices of AP&J, and various locations in New York City, roughly thirty years before "Cats."

(Baldwin Theatre) Wednesday, February 17–28, 1988 (10 performances). The Baldwin Theatre presents:
TOMORROW'S BROADWAY (*A Look Back*) with Music by David Bruen, Jeff Loden, Laurence Dresner, Neil Wolf, Earl Rose, Jim Moses, Mark Gabriel, Madeline Stone, Vince Morton; Lyrics, David Bruen, Tony Tanner, Nelson Jewell, George P. Choma, Susan Zelouf, Mantell, Frank Evans, Ingrid Russell, Vince Morton, Ron Troutman, Neil Wolf; Conceived by Leslie Welles & Robert Carson; Directed by David Bruen; Musical Director, Vince Morton; Choreography, David Hedrick; Dialogue, Shirlee Strother; Announcer, Sean Reynolds; A Carson-Welles Production CAST: Robert Carson, Mark Guerette, Sharlene Hartman, Richmond Johnson, Tracey Phelps, Leslie Welles

A musical revue in 2 acts. The action takes place at the 1999 Tony Awards Show and is a retrospective view of "the last ten years of Broadway" (1989–1999).

(The New Theatre of Brooklyn/TNT) Thursday, February 18,–March 13, 1988 (16 performances). TNT/The New Theatre of Brooklyn (Deborah J. Pope, Steve Stettler, Artistic Directors) presents:
NORA adapted by Ingmar Bergman from Henrik Ibsen's "A Doll's House"; Translated by Frederick J. Marker, Lise-Lone Marker; Director, Steve Stettler; Set, Sarah Edkins; Costumes, Arnall Downs; Lighting, Victor En Yu Tan; Sound, Tom Gould; Assistant Director, Devra Cohen; Dance Consultant, Virginia Freeman; Production Manager/Technical Director, Richard Morganelli; Wardrobe, Evelyn Green; Props, Gary Miller; Stage Managers, Debora E. Kingston, Gary Miller, Christopher Eigeman; Press, Clare Cotugno. CAST: Joyce Fideor (Nora Helmer), Michael French (Torvald Helmer), Dana Smith (Mrs. Christine Linde), John Tyrrell (Nils Krogstad), Arthur Strimling (Dr. Rank).

A drama in two acts.

(The Shakespeare Center) Friday, February 19–March 13, 1988 (17 performances). The Classic Theatre (Executive Director, Nicholas John Stathis/Artistic Director, Maurice Edwards) and The Armenian General Benevolent Union presents:
GRANDMA, PRAY FOR ME by Nishan Parlakian; Director, Joseph S. King; Producer, Nicholas John Stathis; Set, Daniel Proett; Costumes, Natalie Walker; Lighting, Bernadette Englert; Sound, George Jacobs; Assistant to Director, Terence Keenan; Technicians, Jimmy Schwatzman, Kimlee Jenkins; Production Stage Manager, James Whelan; Associate Producer, Adda D. Gogoris; Press, Francine L. Trevens CAST: Joseph Forbrich (Mickey), Eileen Prince Burns (Grandma), Elizabeth Bove (Diamond), Terri Galvin (Pearl), Janet Aspinwall (Agate), Krikor Satamian (Deacon), Alan Dolderer (Virgil), Warren Kliewer (Dr. Cyclops), Larry Swansen (Dr. Achilles), Jeff Robins (Doctor), Alan Dolderer, James Whelan (Attendants)

A play in 2 acts about an Armenian Family in America. The action takes place at the present, in the downstairs living room and yard of a two family house.

(Westbeth Theatre Center) Thursday, February 25–March 13, 1988 (13 performances and 1 preview). Westbeth Theatre Center (Arnold Engelman, Producing Director; Granville Burgess, Roger T. Danforth, Jule Selbo, Juda Youngstrom, Creative Directors) presents:
GUADELOUPE by Mindi Dickstein; Director, Christopher Catt; Sets, Venustiano Borromeo; Costumes, Joanie Canon; Lighting, Julia T. Anthony; Sound, Aural Fixation; Production Manager, Kathryn Ballou; Stage Manager, Kathryn Adisman; Press, David Lotz, Arnold Engelman CAST: Betsy Howie (Marie), Jean Tafler (Janie), James Lally (Emile), Roma Maffia (Virginie Tom), Michael Patrick King (Inspector Debenier), Kim Weston Moran (Adele G), Ralph E. Friar (Prefect)

A play in 2 acts. The action takes place at the present time, in a hotel bungalow on Guadeloupe beach.

(Avery Fisher Hall) Sunday, February 21, 1988 (1 performance/limited engagement). The New York Conference of the United Methodist Church presents:
ALDERSGATE '88 *A Musical Celebration* with Book by Lynette Bennett; Music & Lyrics, Paul Trueblood; Lyrics, Jarlath Barsanti-Jacobs; Additional Lyrics, Don Dunn; Director, Jack Eddleman; Producer, Dr. Warren L. Danskin; Musical Director, Eric Stern; Stage Manager, Rebecca Green; Lighting, Lisa Grossman; Costume Co-ordinator, Pam Penenber; Staff, Beth Hurt, Norman Brown; Instrumentalists, Bruce Doctor, Ray Kilday, Joel Mofsenson; Special Assistant to the Director, Stephanie Hall CAST: June Angela, Lynette Bennett, Earl Grandison, Patty Holley, Salome Martinez, Jorge Padulles, Guy Stroman, Walter Willison
MUSICAL NUMBERS: I Want to Make a Diff'rence, The Aldersgate Connection, Let the Ladies Do It, Hymns of Wonder Anthems of Praise, Ev'rything Was Heaven to Their Eyes, The Quintessential Methodist, Don't Be a Stranger, There Is One, *Aldersgate Scene:* Why Couldn't I See?, It Happens, Duet, Baby Boomers, The Sound of Drums, And Peace Begins

An inspirational musical revue in one act.

Preceded by a one act concert: Earl Wrightson in *Songs of the Spirit* with Paul Trueblood and James Stenborg on piano.

(500 Greenwich Street) Tuesday, March 1–26, 1988 (18 performances). En Garde Arts presents:
THREE PIECES FOR A WAREHOUSE: *Hidden Voices: A Building in Transition* A sound installation piece by Matthew Goodheart/*Dirty Work* by Quincy Long; Director, William Foeller/*Hunger* Written & Directed by Maria Irene Fornes; Set, Phillip Baldwin; Costumes, Candice Donnelly (*Dirty Work*), Gabriel Berry (*Hunger*); Producer, Anne Hamburger; Lighting, Clay Shirkey; Sound, Matthew Goodheart; Production Stage Manager, Gail A. Burns; Production Manager, Richard Sasson; Casting, Jeffery Passero; Assistant Stage Manager, Chris Orbach; Press, G. Theodore Killmer CAST: *Hidden Voices: A Building in Transition:* Rip Hayman, Matthew Goodhear Goodheart, Jimmy Swaggart (Voices)/*Dirty Work:* Allen Payne (Helper), Kenneth Ryan (Worker), Emily Zacharias (Real Estate Developer), Claire Daly (Musician)/*Hunger:* Marilyn Dodds Frank (Reba), Joe Pichette (Ray), Meghan Robinson (Bea), Joe Sharkey (Charley), Amy McLellan (Angel)

Three one-act plays developed to be performed in three different spaces of the warehouse building, in an effort to explore and develop the relationship of theatre to architecture and its surroundings.

(Lindenbaum Center) Wednesday, March 2–27, 1988 (19 Performances and 4 previews). The Open Eye/New Stagings (Amie Brockway, Artistic Director) presents:
A CIRCLE ON THE CROSS by Thomas Cadwaleder Jones; Director, Amie Brockway; Set, Adrienne J. Brockway; Costumes, David Kay Mickelsen; Lighting, Spencer Mosse; Stage Manager, Pamela Edington; Sound, Aural Fixation; Assistant Director, Kim Sharp; Fights, Steven Earl-Edwards; Press, Becky Flora CAST: Al Mohrmann (James Monroe Good), Steven Earl-Edwards (Billy McKinley Good), Debbie McLeod (Jo Ann Good), Jim Winston (Chester Arthur Good)

A play in 2 acts. The action takes place during the late 1980's in Northwest Arkansas.

(45th St Theatre) Thursday, March 3–19, 1988 (14 performances). Primary Stages Co. (Casey Childs, Artistic Director; Janet Reed, Associate Director) and Dina & Alexander E. Racolin presents:
THE WEDDING OF THE SIAMESE TWINS by Burton Cohen; Director, Scott M. Rubsam; Set, Andrew Greenhut; Lighting, William Simmons; Costumes, Bruce Goodrich; Puppets, Agnes Anderson; Sound, Graham Slater/Enefvi Prod.; Music, Frank Canino; Production Manager, Herbert H. O'Dell; Production Stage Manager, Amy Huggans; General Manager, Sheila Mathews; Casting, Marilyn McIntyre; Public Relations, Anne Einhorn; Press, Shirley Herz/Miller Wright CAST: Marvin Einhorn (Announcer, et al . . .), Matt Nikko (Eng Bunker), Kevin John Gee (Chang Bunker), Lauren Thompson (Sally Yates), Elaine Rinehart (Adelaide Yate)

A play in 2 acts. The action takes place between 1838 and 1843 in North Carolina, and after the Civil War.

(Harold Clurman Theatre) Thursday, March 3, 1988– Michael J. Holland presents:
CAUGHT IN THE MIDDLE WITH NO WAY OUT . . . written and directed by Michael J. Holland; Sets, J. C. Happersberger, Dario Del Core; Lighting, Alice Blue; Choreography, John Russell; Press, Jeffrey Richards/Naomi Grabel, Robert Ganshaw. CAST: Karen Bankhead, Doris B. Bennett, John Russell, Eugene Twyman Berry, Jacqueline Shonk, Frank Aragon, Bill Robertson

A drama in 2 acts. The action takes place in New York City in 1966.

Top of next page: Michael Devries, Donna English
in "The Last Musical Comedy" *(Paul Yuen)* **Below:**
Al Mohrmann, Jim Winston in "Circle on the Cross"
(Ken Howard Photo)

(Samuel Beckett Theatre) Thursday, March 3–27, 1988 (21 performances and 3 previews). Spencer Benedict Productions presents:

STEALING HEAVEN written and directed by Stephen Romagnoli; Associate Producer, Sirob Gonoturk; Assistant Producer, Donna DeSomma; Stage Manager, Wendy Herrick; Assistant Director, Jim Richards; Company Managers, Maureen Dillon, Rosemary Quigley; Set, David Wynne; Lighting/Technical Director, John French; Music, Billy Ruyle; Choreography, Errol Grimes; Costumes, Denise Hudson; Production Assistants, Rita Buscanics, Ken Valente, Dalia Algava. CAST: James M. Armstrong (Marty Prindle), Josefa Mulaire (Mink Prindle), Anthony J. DiMurro (Sal Schiano), Boris Krutonog (Jeslow Flowers), Gina Bonati (Nickel/Lina), James Farrell, Lucille Weston, Laura Delano (Understudies)

A play in 3 acts and 17 scenes. The action takes place in the present, over a two week period, and also in the distant past.

(Apollo Theatre) Saturday, March 5–May 26, 1988 (20 performances limited engagement). Rev. John Howard, Frank Oaman (Executive Producers), Robin Peterson (Associate Producer), Atlantic City Fellowship of Churches and Vicinity (Rev. I. S. Cole, President) present:

YES, GOD IS REAL by James M. Brown; Director, Al (Suavae) Mitchell; Musical Director, Thomas Jennings; Arrangements & Orchestrations, Thomas Jennings, Rev. Charles Lyles; Special Choreography/Make Up, Lydia Abarca Mitchell; Drums, Kevin Holmes; Organist, William "Butch" Oatman; Bass, Ben Graves; Technical Director, Ronald Sommerville; Costumes, Lydia Abarca Mitchell, Robin Peterson and Company; Set, Ronald Sommerville; Technical Staff, Robert Foster, Steve Garrett; Additional Songs, George Bernard, Rev. James Cleveland, Stuart K. Hine, Thomas Dorsey, Arland Gilliam, Billy Lee, War; Press, Dolph Browning CAST: Betty Graves Scott (Mama Jones), Rev. Charles Lyls (Bobby Lewis), Wendy Mason (Wanda Brown), Bill Greene (JoJo)

MUSICAL NUMBERS: Down by the River, How Great Thou Art, Old Time Religion, Happy Birthday, Old Rugged Cross, Holy Matrimony, Precious Lord Take My Hand, She's Gone Away, Please Don't Follow the Pain, Come to the Casino, Somebody Said, Taking Jesus to the Street, World Is a Ghetto, Yes God is Real

A musical in 2 acts. The action takes place in Casino City, 1985, over a period of three weeks.

(Stage Arts Theatre) Saturday, March 5–26, 1988 (16 performances and 4 previews). Stage Arts Theatre Company, Inc. and Acorn Productions, Inc. present:

BETWEEN DAYLIGHT AND BOONEVILLE by Matt Williams; Director, Fred Kareman; Set, Chris Pickart; Lighting, Robert Bessoir; Sound, Timothy Pritchard; Costumes, Edward Nashen; Stage Manager, Alison Coles; Press, FLT/Francine L. Trevens CAST: Jessica Zoel (Stacey), Pamela Moller (Carla), Atticus Brady (Jimmy), Gregg Glick (Bobby), John David Westfall (Cyril), Brooke Palance (Marlene), Jennie Ventriss (Lorette), Jane Myers (Wanda), John Mayo ("Radio Announcer")

A play in 2 acts. The action takes place in a trailer court in the strip mining country of Southern Indiana, otherwise known as the "Valley of Opportunity", on an August day in 1980.

(Minetta Lane Theatre) Tuesday, March 8–27, 1988 (6 performances and 17 previews) Jennifer Manocherian Productions Ltd. presents:

THE PALACE OF AMATEURS by John PiRoman; Director, Norman Rene; Scenery, Andrew Jackness; Costumes, Walker Hicklin; Lighting, Debra J. Kletter; Sound, Bruce D. Cameron; Musical Staging, Theodore Pappas; Company Manager, Sally Campbell; Production Stage Manager, M. A. Howard; Press, David Roggensack. CAST: Laura Dern (Charlene Loody), Thomas Mills Wood (Alvin Coolidge), David Schramm (Slim O'Rourke), Kristine Nielsen (Kitty O'Rourke), Carmen Decker (Rosemary), Ed Zang (Billy Dix), Kyle MacLachlan (Terrence Beebe), Alice Haining, Gus Kaikkonen, Robert Duncan McNeill (Understudies)

A comedy in two acts.

(Opera Ensemble Of New York) Wednesday, March 9–27, 1988 (9 performances). Opera Ensemble Of New York presents:

A LITTLE NIGHT MUSIC with Music and Lyrics by Stephen Sondheim; Book by Hugh Wheeler; Director, John J. D. Sheehan; Music Director, Richard Parrinello; Sets, Dain Marcus; Choreography, William Whitener; Costumes, Hope Hanafin; Lighting, Clifton Taylor; Production Stage Manager, Stan Schwartz; Production Executive, Howard R. McBride; Production Manager, Darren Cole; Stage Manager, Steven Petrillo; Assistant Stage Manager, Alison Ross; Technical Director, Keith Tatum CAST: Kelly Hogan (Mrs. Nordstrom), Julia Davidson (Mrs. Segstrom), Jacqueline Marx (Mrs. Anderssen), Craig Collins (Mr. Erlanson), Gregg Lauterbach (Mr. Lindquist), Cady McClain (Fredrika), Lucille Patton (Mme. Armfeldt), Matthew McClanahan (Frid), Colby Thomas (Anne Egerman), Franc D'Ambrosio (Henrik Egerman), Ron Raines (Fredrik Egerman), Kate Egan (Petra), Mary Beth Peil (Desiree Armfeldt), David Trombley (Count Carl-Magnus Malcolm), Rebecca Mercer-White (Countess Charlotte Malcolm)

MUSICAL NUMBERS: Overture, Night Waltz, Now/Later/Soon, The Glamorous Life, Remember?, You Must Meet My Wife, Liaisons, In Praise of Women, Every Day a Little Death, A Weekend in the Country, The Sun Won't Set, It Would Have Been Wonderful, Perpetual Anticipation, Silly People, Send in the Clowns, The Miller's Son, Finale

A musical in 2 acts. The action takes place at the turn of the century in Sweden. For original production see *Theatre World, Vol. 29.*

Carmen Decker, Thomas Mills Wood, Laura Dern, Kristine Nielsen, David Schramm in "Palace of Amateurs" *(Martha Swope Photo)* Above: Bill Greene, Charles Lyles, Betty Graves Scott in "Yes, God Is Real" *(Bert Andrews)*

Anita Gillette, Peter Hedges
in "Class 1 Acts" *(Carol Rosegg Photo)*

(Puerto Rican Traveling Theatre) Wednesday, March 16,–May 1, 1988 (42 performances). The Puerto Rican Traveling Theatre (Miriam Colon, Founder/Artistic Director/Producer) presents:
SENORA CARRAR'S RIFLES by Bertolt Brecht; English Translation, Wolfgang Sauerlander; Spanish Translation, Oscar Ferrigno; Director, Alejandro Quintana; Original Music, Jose Raul Bernardo; Set, Robert Klingelhoefer; Lighting, Rick Butler; Costumes, Laura Drawbaugh; Sound, Kenn Dovel; Song Lyrics, Federico Garcia Lorca and Jose Raul Bernardo; Stage Manager, Beth Lord. CAST: Miriam Colon (Mother), Jorge Tort (Her Son), Jorge Luis Ramos (The Worker), Carlos Linares (Wounded Man), Georgina Corbo (Young Girl), Norberto Kerner (Priest), Theodora Castellanos (Neighbor)
A drama performed without intermission. The action takes place in a fisherman's cottage in Andalusia on a night in April of 1937.

(Theatre Four) Wednesday, March 16–April 24, 1988 (48 performances) The Negro Ensemble Company presents:
LIKE THEM THAT DREAM by Edgar White; Director, Samuel P. Barton; Sound, Samuel P. Barton, Phil Lee; Set, Daniel Proett; Costumes, Karen Perry; Lighting, Victor En Yu Tan; General Manager, Larry Kevin Walden; Stage Manager, Sandra L. Ross; Press, Howard Atlee; Producing Director, Leon B. Denmark; President, Douglas Turner Ward. CAST: Lanyard A. Williams (Sparrow), Lorey Hayes (Sharon), Lilene Mansell (Miss Derris), Chet London (Van Muellin).
A drama in two acts. The action takes place at the present time in New York City (Greenwich Village, Riverside Drive).

(Theatre Upstairs) Thursday, March 17–April 3, 1988 (16 performances) Theatre Upstairs presents:
TRAPS by Caryl Churchill; Director John Stix; Sets, Derek McLane; Lighting, David Noling; Costumes, Ticia Blackburn; Sound, Aural Fixation; Fight Director, B. H. Barry; Production Stage Manager, D. C. Rosenberg; Press, Peter Cromarty CAST: Eric D. Conger, Shelly Conger, Daniel Houlihan, Ken Kliban, Derek Smith, Mary M. Stein
New York premiere of a play about commune living in the early 1970s.

(Westbeth Theatre Center) Thursday March 17–April 10, 1988 (18 performances) Westbeth Theatre Center (Arnold Engelman, Producing Director), Granville Burgess, Roger T. Danforth, Jule Selbo, Juda Youngstrom, present:
ISOLATE by Jule Selbo; Director, Allan Carlsen; Sets, Ray Recht; Costumes, Pamela Scofield; Lighting, Phil Monat; Sound, Maxim Townsend Surla; Choreography, Ricarda O'Conner; Fight Moves, Richard Raether; Production Stage Manager, Kate Riddle; Assistant Stage Manager, Lillian Butler; Technical Director, Michael J. Kondrat; Assistant Tech, Richard Wojnowski; Scenic Artists, Bo Davis, Greg O'Gara; Press, David Lotz CAST: Jacqueline Schultz (Janet), Marnie Andrews (Mimi), Mary Kaye Swedish (Viv), Michael Guido (Frank), Jordan Roberts (George)
The action takes place during the dark season at the Antarctic.

(Nat Horne Theatre) Tuesday, March 13–April 9, 1988 (24 performances and 8 previews). Manhattan Class Company (Robert LuPone/Bernard Telsey, Exective Directors) presents:
CLASS1ACTS produced by W. D. Cantler & Bernard Telsey; Associate Producers, Rona Carr, Christopher A. Smith; Sets, Dan Conway; Lighting, Mary Louise Geiger; Costumes, Diane Finn-Chapman; Sound, Michael Whalen; Production Manager, Laura Kravets; Casting, Laurel Smith, Bernard Telsey; Press, G. Theodore Killmer; Assistant Production Manager, Jill Cordle; Associate Designer/Scenic Artist, Gregory Mercurio; Associate Sound, Jordan Pankin; Assistant Stage Managers, Jenny Seaquist, Jennifer E. Boggs, Lori Culhane.
EVENING A: *Fast Eddie* by Edward Louis Gold; Director, Ellen Nickles; Stage Manager, Eva C. Schegulla; with Patrick Breen (Fast Eddie), Ken Marks (Scott), Constance Ray (Val). *Chatham Songs* by Mark Hymen; Director, Christopher A. Smith; Musical Director, Linda Greenberg; Stage Manager, Jodi Feldman; with Kevin Dwyer (Paul), Jon Ehrlich (Jerome), Jaclyn Ross (Alicia). *Code 34 (A One-act Pineapple)* by James Bosley; Director, Bruce Kronenberg; Stage Manager, Michael Soule; with James Doerr (First Man), Kent Adams (Second Man). *June 8, 1968* by Anna Theresa Cascio; Director, Jimmy Bohr; Stage Manager, Michael Griffith; with Thomas Gibson (Cookie), Anne Marie Bobby (Bedra), James Doerr (Twitchell).
EVENING B: *Everything We've Ever Wanted* by Jennifer Houlton; Director, Laurel Smith; Stage Manager, Ira Mont; with Karen Braga (Ellie), John Conley (Ed), Ted Neustadt (Jon T. Shimer). *Unoccupied Territory* by Edward Louis Gold; Director, Michael Warren Powell; Stage Manager, Cheryl Zoldowski with Robin Morse (Vickie), William Fichtner (Robert), Margaret Klenck (Maxx). *A Perfect Act of Contrition* by Stephen Willems; Director, Brian Mertes; Stage Manager, Cheryl Zoldowski; with Keith Szarabajka (Thomas). *Just Horrible* by Nicholas Kazan; Director, W. D. Cantler; Stage Manager, Betsy Boesel; Sound, Chris Kowanko; with Anita Gillette (Frannie), Larry Bryggman (Bill), Peter Hedges (Clarence), Bridget Fonda (Sissy)

(Triplex/Manhattan Community College) Tuesday, March 15–27, 1988 (14 performances). The Triplex, The Allied Irish Bank and The Abbey Theatre (The National Theatre Of Ireland) present:
THE GREAT HUNGER by Tom MacIntyre; Director, Patrick Mason; Based on the poem by Patrick Kavanagh; Sets & Costumes, Bronwen Casson; Lighting, Tony Wakefield; Artistic Director, Vincent Dowling; General Manager, Martin Fahy; Tour Manager, John Costigan; Press Attache, Tomas Hardiman; Press, David Rothenberg Associates CAST: Tom Hickey (Maguire), Vincent O'Neill (Priest), Brid Ni Neachtain (Mary Anne), Michele Forbes (Schoolgirl), Joan Sheehy (Agnes), Conal Kearney (Tom Malone), Dermod Moore (Packy), Anthony Coleman, Hillary Fannin (Understudies)
A play in 2 acts, which examines life on the small farms of Ireland in the early 1940's.

Lanyard A. Williams, Lorey Hayes in "Like Them That Dream" *(Bert Andrews)* **Above: Jorge Luis Ramos, Miriam Colon, Jorge Tort, Norberto Kerner in "Senora Carrar's Rifles"** *(Peter Krupenye)*

**Ed Dixon, Scott Waara, Donna Kane
in "Johnny Pye. . . ."** *(Carol Rosegg)*

**Miller Lide, Jeffrey C. Woodman, Marcus Powell,
Julia Brooks in "Doctor's Dilemma"**

(Promenade Theatre) Tuesday, March 29,–September 11, 1988 (172 performances and 16 previews). Stephen Graham, Jujamcyn Theatres, Jonathan Farkas, Norma and David Langworthy, Maurice Rosenfield and Lois F. Rosenfield in association with James B. Freydberg and Max Weitzenhoffer present:
THE ROAD TO MECCA by Athol Fugard; Directed by Mr. Fugard; Set, John Lee Beatty; Costumes, Susan Hilferty; Lighting, Dennis Parichy; Casting, Meg Simon/Fran Kumin; Associate Producers, Robin Ullman, Stuart Thompson; General Management, Fremont Associates/Dana Sherman; Company Manager, Sara Hedgepeth Braun; Wardrobe, Eileen Miller; Props, Robert G. Johnson; Press, Shirley Herz/Pete Sanders, Glenna Freedman, David Roggensack, Miller Wright.

CAST

Miss Helen	Yvonne Bryceland
Elsa Barlow	Amy Irving†
Marius Byleveld	Athol Fugard

A drama in two acts. The action takes place in the small Karoo village of New Bethesda, South Africa.
†Succeeded by Kathy Bates. The play was cited as Best Foreign Play of the 1987–88 season by the New York Drama Critics Circle.

(Lambs Little Theatre) Tuesday, March 22–April 2, 1988 (14 performances) Lambs Theatre Company (Carolyn Rossi Copeland, Producing Director; Joel K. Ruark, General Manager) presents:
JOHNNY PYE AND THE FOOLKILLER; Music and Lyrics, Randy Courts; Book and Lyrics, Mark St. Germain; Director, Paul Lazarus; Based on short story by Stephen Vincent Benet; Musical Director, Steven M. Alper; Sets, William Barclay; Costumes, Mary Hayes; Lighting, Phil Monat; Assistant Musical Director, Doug Besterman; Incidental and Piano Arrangements, Alper & Besterman; Production Stage Manager; Tom Clewell; Choreography, Patrice Soriero; Casting, McCorkle Casting, Richard Cole; Assistant Stage Manager, Tara Greenway; Press, G. Theodore Killmer CAST: Bob Bejan (Wilber/Mr. Wilberforce), Barbara Broughton (Mrs. Miller/Scholor/Waitress), Ed Dixon (Foolkiller), Frank Hankey (Bob/Banker/Congressman), Donna Kane (Suzy/Mrs. Marsh), Devon Michaels (Young Johnny/John Jr./Little Boy), Stacey Moseley (Young Suzy/Young Girl), Ron Lee Savin (Barber/Preacher/Mr. Wilde/Reverend/President), Gordon Stanley (Bill/Mayor/Captain/Minister), Scott Waara (Johnny Pye)
MUSICAL NUMBERS: John's Prologue, The Fool, Shower of Sparks, I Can See Him, Goodbye Johnny, Opportunity Knocks, The Weasel, Thinkin' of Suzy, I Can See Him, Second Chance, Challenge to Love, One Good Reason, Barbershop, Married with Children, Land Where There Is No Death, Time Passes, Never Felt Better, John's Epilogue
A work in progress that takes place 1870–1950 in Martinsville, USA.

(Shandol Theatre) Tuesday, March 22–April 3, 1988 (12 performances) Tarquin Jay Bromley in association with The Village Theatre Company presents:
TWO ONE ACT PLAYS: F.M./ROSALINE; Sets, Robert Lopez; Costumes, Marj Feenan; Lighting, John-Paul Szczepanski; Original Music, Jimmy Flynn. "F.M." by Romulus Linney; Director, William Royce with Barbara Berque, Marj Feenan, Kit Jones, Randy Kelly "Rosaline" by Michael Hill; Director, Henry Fonte with Susan Farwell, Patrick Turner

(Heritage Theatre) Wednesday, March 23,–April 2, 1988 (10 performances) The Heritage Theatre presents:
THE DOCTOR'S DILEMMA by George Bernard Shaw; Director/Producer, Thomas Luce Summa; Sets, Peter Page; Lighting, Julia T. Anthony; Art Consultant, Alexandra Worme; Stage Manager, Michael Huber CAST: Louisa Horton (Emmy), Tod Engle (Redpenny), Miller Lide (Sir Colenso Ridgeon), David Landon (Leo Schutzmacher), John Messenger (Sir Patrick Cullen), Kevin Bailey (Cutler Walpole), Marcus Powell (Sir Ralph Bloomfield Bonington), Dale Engle (Dr. Blenkinsop), Julia Brooks (Jennifer Dubedat), Jeffrey Clarke Woodman (Louis Dubedat), Dori Freeman (Minnie Tinwell), Tod Engle (Newspaper Man), Michael Huber (Mr. Danby)
Performed in three acts. The action takes place in 1903 in and around Bond Street.

(Henry Street Settlement New Federal Theatre) Thursday, March 24–April 24, 1988 (30 performances). New Federal Theatre (Producer, Woodie King, Jr.) presents:
MR. UNIVERSE by Jim Grimsley; Director, Steven Kent; Set, Steven Perry; Lighting, Linda Essig; Costumes, Stephanie Kaskel; Sound/Music, Michael Keck; Production Stage Manager/Technical Director, Michael W. Schaefer; Company Manager, Linda Herring; Press, Max Eisen; Executive Director, Daniel Kronefeld; Director/Arts for Living Center, Barbara Tate CAST: Nao Takeuchi (The Saxaphone Player), Shami Chaikin (Juel Laurie), Vicki Hirsch (The Police Woman), Del Hamilton (Vick), Peter Toran (Judy), Charles Mandracchia (The Muscle Man), Donna Biscoe (Katy Jume)
A play in 2 acts and 5 scenes. The action takes place in the French Quarter of New Orleans in 1979.

**Kathy Bates, Yvonne Bryceland
in "The Road to Mecca"**

Athol Fugard
(Brian Astbury Photos)

(45th St Theatre) Thursday, March 31–April 17, 1988 (16 Performances) Cynthia LePosa and Evan Salton present:
SADNESS OF A FADED DREAM by Eddie Kegley; Director, William Gaynor Dovey; Scenery, Pepper Ross; Costumes, Shirley Busby; Lighting, Anthony Hume; Production Stage Manager, Donna Rimple; Press, Max Eisen, Madelon Rosen CAST: Mel Silverman (Billy/Virgil), Vita Lucia (Suzanne/Cherie), William Gaynor Dovey (Bobby/Jay/Bo), Robin Meloy (Happy, Marsha)

A new play in two acts. The action takes place at the present time in NYC and New England.

(Orpheum Theatre) Thursday, March 31–October 2, 1988 (214 Performances and 9 Previews). M.C.E.G. Presents:
SANDRA BERNHARD: WITHOUT YOU I'M NOTHING by Sandra Bernhard with John Boskovich; Director, John Boskovich; Producer, Jonathan D. Krane; Executive Producer, Terry Danuser; Production Design, Leni Schwendinger; Sound, Bruce D. Cameron; Associate Producers, Leah Palco, Rachel Langsam; Musical Director, Mitch Kaplan; Company Manager, David Cash; Production Stage Manager, M. Cherese Campo; Production Assistant, John Malatesta; Press, Burnham-Callaghan Associates/Jill Larkin CAST: Sandra Bernhard with Musicians: Mitch Kaplan, Denise Fraser, Ivan Julian, Spyder Mittleman

A solo performance of comedy and songs.

Sandra Bernhard
(Matthew Rolston Photo)

(L) Vondie Curtis-Hall, Tenney Walsh   **(R) Adam Storke, Annette Hunt in "White Rose of Memphis"** *(Carol Rosegg Photos)*

(Double Image Theatre/St. Peters) Friday April 1–24, 1988 (21 Performances) Double Image (Helen Waren Mayer, Founder/Artistic Director) presents:
A WHITE ROSE OF MEMPHIS by David J. Hill; Director, Susann Brinkley; Sets, David Birn; Lighting, Susan Chute; Costumes, Denise Hudson; Sound, Michael Schmalz; Dramaturg, Christopher Breyer; Casting, Brian Chevanne; Press, Gerald Siegal, Aimee Gautreau, Chris Boneau CAST: Annette Hunt (Dorothy Van Landingham), Adam Storke (Lucian Van Landingham), Tenney Walsh (Rachel Van Landingham), Vondie Curtis-Hall (Roger Thomas), Louise Roberts (Suzanne Van Landingham)

A comic tragedy in two acts. The action takes place in the summer and fall of 1987.

(Hartley House Theatre) Saturday, April 2–May 8, 1988 (20 Performances) On Stage Productions presents:
MERMAIDS with Book by Robert J. Gardner & Monica Hayes; Lyrics, Robert J. Gardner; Music, Robert J. Gardner & Terry Bovin; Director, Monica Hayes; Choreographer, Rhonda Hayes; Musical Director, Terry Bovin; Sets, Bob Briggs; Lighting, Farid Kebour; Puppet/Costume Design, Robert J. Gardner; Stage Manager, Nancy Hornecker; Costume Coordinator, Judi Jasinski; Artistic Director, Lee Frank; Managing Director, Dinah Gravel; Press, Lee Frank, Robert J. Gardner CAST: Les Zeiders (Sailor/Crab), Kimberley Campell (Little Mermaid), Melanie Kimball (Queen Mother), Michael J. Schultz (Seymour Seahorse), William Neish (Cecil Seahorse), Catherine Dyer (Miranda), Kathleen R. Delaney (Sabrina/Princess), Dennis Figueroa (Prince), Carol Cornicelli (Sea Witch), Kip Rathke (Puppets), Vienna Hagen (Other Creatures)
MUSICAL NUMBERS: Mermaid Jubilee, Someday, Prince's Jubilee, Sailor Boy, So Unaware, Seahorse Song, Briny Bubbles, Dark & Briny Ocean, Are You Willing?, Mysterious Maiden, Diddle Dee, Finale

A musical based on the Hans Christian Anderson story "The Little Mermaid".

(Apple Corps Theatre) Wednesday, April 6–24, 1988 (23 Performances) The Women's Project & Productions, Inc. (Julia Miles, Artistic Director) with The Los Angeles Theatre Center (Bill Bushnell, Artistic Producing Director) present:
ETTA JENKS by Marlane Meyer; Director, Roberta Levitow; Sets, Rosario Provenza; Lighting, Robert Wierzel; Costumes, Ray C. Naylor; Sound, Jon Gottlieb; Stage Manager, Joan Toggenburger; Dramaturg, Mame Hunt; Technical Director, Tom Carroll; Press, Fred Nathan Co./Meryl Frimark CAST: Sheila Dabney (Sheri), Abdul Salaam El Razzac (Clyde, Spencer), Carmine Iannoccone (Dwight/Alec/Director's Voice), John Nesci (Ben), Deidre O'Connell (Etta), John Pappas (James), Ebbe Roe Smith (Burt/Sherman/Max), Dendrie Taylor (Kitty/Shelly/Audition Woman), Ching Valdes/Aran (Dolly)

Performed without intermission. The time is the present, the place is L.A.

(Susan Bloch Theatre) Wednesday April 13–June 5, 1988 (78 Performances). Moved and re-opened at Actor's Playhouse June 7, 1988 and still playing at press time; Susan Bloch Theatre presents:
TEN PERCENT REVUE with Words and Music by Tom Wilson Weinberg; Director, Scott Green; Producer, Laura Green; Choreography, Tee Scatuorchio; Costumes, Kevin-Robert; Backdrop, Edwin Perez-Carrion; Musical Director, Lisa Bernstein; Assistant Director, John Corker; Musical Arrangements, Tom Wilson Weinberg, Lisa Bernstein; Lighting, Joshua Starbuck; Stage Manager, Jeff King; Conceived by & dedicated to Joey Brandon; Press, Peter Cromarty CAST: Lisa Bernstein, Robert Tate, Timothy Williams succeeded by James Humphrey, Trish Kane succeeded by Rainie Cole, Valerie Hill succeeded by Helena Snow, Cathleen Riddley
MUSICAL NUMBERS: Flaunting It, Best Years of My Life, Threesome, Wedding Song, If I Were/I'd Like to Be, Gay Name Game, Home, Not Allowed, Personals, Safe Sex Slut, Homo Haven Fight Song, Turkey Baster Baby, High Risk for Afraids, Obituary, And The Supremes, Before Stonewall, Write A Letter, We're Everywhere.

A gay musical revue in two acts.

(clockwise from top) Lisa Bernstein, Robert Tate, Timothy Williams, Trish Kane, Valerie Hill in "Ten Percent Revue" *(Carol Rosegg Photo)*

(The Baldwin Theatre) Wednesday, April 13–May 8, 1988 (18 performances and 2 previews). The Baldwin Theatre (Anita Sorel, Artistic Director/Michael Thompson, Managing Director/Harry Roff, Youth Theatre Co-ordinator) presents:
COUNTER SERVICE written and directed by Tony Tanner; Set, Barry Axtell; Lighting, Deborah Constantine; Costumes, Clifford Capone; Technical Director, Scott Sorrels; Lighting Operator, Alex Grablewski; Stage Managers, John C. Wall, Victor Araque, Steven Thompson, James Rubin; Press, Mitchell Uscher CAST: Joe Duquette (Harry), Jeffrey Hayenga (Drew), Judith A. Hansen (Sandy), Anita Sorel (Dinah), Charles Redell (Skip), Tracey Phelps (Mother)
A play in two acts. The action takes place in the present, at a roadside diner in Greenhill, North Carolina

(Panache Encore) Wednesday, April 13–May 25, 1988 (12 performances and 1 preview).
STAGES with Music by Elaine Chelton; Based on an original concept by Ms. Chelton; Lyrics, Elaine Chelton, Tony Michael Pann; Additional Music, Leslie Harnley; Director/Staging/Music Director, Jim Coleman; Stage Managers, Jim L'Ecuyer, Marie Lane, Carolyn Ledwith; Press, Dolph Browning CAST: Tony Michael Pann (Anthony Damon), Ann Brown (Missy Welch), Barry Burns (Roger Ashburton), Susan J. Jacks (Judy Ann Butts), Brooks Almy, Elly Barbour (Brittany Edwards), Paul Guzzone (Bassist), Jim L'Ecuyer, Lorrie Harrison, Christine Pedi, Ryan Hilliard (Standbys)
MUSICAL NUMBERS: Showtime Tonight, One More Ride on the Merry-Go-Round, What Could Go Wrong?, Queen of the Bus and Trucks, Tonight I Get That Chance Again, My Magnificent Career, My Nerves Are Shot to Hell, In the Footlights, The Trouble with Men, Blue Violets, My Old Friend, The Intermission Song, Center Stage, I'm Coming Back Again, One More Beat of the Drum, Common Ordinary Kind of People (The Reviews Blues), Where Did The Magic Go?
A new cabaret musical performed without intermission.

Judith Hansen, Anita Sorel
in "Counter Service"
(Scott Sorrels Photo)

Mark Lotito, Porfirio Figueroa
in "Studio"

(Hartley House Theatre) Friday, April 22–May 15, 1988 (13 performances). Playwrights Preview Productions (Frances Hill, Artistic Director) presents:
GOOD NIGHT, TEXAS by Terry Dodd; Director, Ann Brebner; Producers, Youssif Kamal, Joe McGranaghan, Thais Fitzsimmons; Set, Reagan Cook; Lighting, Pat Dignan; Costumes, Mary Tetreault; Press, Ellen T. White CAST: Nancy Rothman (Coleen), Jayne Chamberlin (Kristin), Peter Ratray (Alec), Roderick Aird (Brad), Brendan Harris (Guy)
A contemporary comedy. The action takes place on a pivotal day in Dallas, Texas

(The West Bank) Tuesday, April 26–30, 1988 (4 performances).
THE MARRY MONTH OF MAY with Book by Katharine Houghton; Music & Lyrics, Peter Ekstrom; Director, Charlotte Moore; Music Director, Frank Schiro; Lighting, Judy Avioli; Costumes, David Toser; Stage Managers, Katharyn Piuder, Sarah Houghton CAST: Jerome Dempsey, Carla Falcone, Ciaran O'Reilly, Rose Roffman
A one act musical.

(Vineyard Theatre) Wednesday, April 27,–June 5, 1988 (38 performances). The Vineyard (Doug Aibel, Artistic Director; Barbara Zinn Kreiger, Executive Director; Gary P. Steuer, Managing Director) presents:
THE GRANDMA PLAYS by Todd Graff; Director, Steve Gomer; Set, William Barclay; Lighting, Phil Monat; Costumes, Jennifer von Mayrhauser; Sound, Phil Lee; Stage Manager, Carol Fishman. CAST: Jane Hoffman (Pearl), Taina Elg (Rutanya), Alma Cuervo (Bibby), Francine Beers (Becky), Tony Carlin (Voice of Arthur)
A comedy in three acts. The action takes place in Pearl Berman's kitchen in Brooklyn, in 1942, 1968 and 1984.

(The Cubiculo) Thursday, April 14,–May 7, 1988 (16 performances). The Classic Theatre (Nicholas John Stathis, Executive Director) in association with The National Shakespeare Company (Elaine Sulka, Artistic Director) presents:
LUCKY PEHR by August Strindberg; Director/Designer, Raymond David Marsiniak; Producer, Nicholas John Stathis; Associate Producer, Adda C. Gogoris; Press, Audrey Ross CAST: Paul Bolger (Petitioner/Shoemaker/Mullah), Daniel Bunten (Lawyer/1st Friend/Relative/Poet), Mike Finesilver (Tax Collector/Pillory/Wagon-Maker/Amir), Michael Lengel (Pehr), Deborah McDowell (Lise), Julie Pasqual (The Woman/Chiropodist/Bride), Craig Purinton (Butler/Statue/Street Paver/Grand Vizier/Death/Wise Man), Jeff Robins (Constable/2nd Friend/Burgomaster/Chamberlain)
The saga of a man from birth to old age, performed without intermission.

(Duo Theatre) Thursday, April 14–May 7, 1988 (12 Performances) Duo Theatre (Manuel Martin, Jr., Artistic Director; Michael Alasa, Managing Director) presents:
STUDIO with Book & Lyrics by Michael Alasa; Music by David Welch; Director and Designer, Michael Alasa; Choreographer, Mario Nugara; Costumes, Natalie Barth Walker; Musical Director, David Welch; Stage Manager/Assistant Director, Mary Lisa Kinney; House Manager/Sound, Hektor Muñoz CAST: Blanca Camacho, Porfirio Figueroa, Susan Groeschel, Jody Walker-Lichtig, Catherine Lippencott, Mark Lotito, Tony Loudon, Jon Spano, Luciano Valerio
A musical based on the life of Serge Diaghilev.

Alma Cuerva, Jane Hoffman
in "The Grandma Plays"
(Carol Rosegg)

69

(The New Theatre of Brooklyn/TNT) Thursday, April 28,–May 22, 1988 (16 performances). TNT/The New Theatre of Brooklyn (Deborah J. Pope, Steve Stettler, Artistic Directors) present:
THE DISPUTE by Pierre Marivaux; Translated by Daniel Gerould; Director, Liz Diamond; Set, Stephen Quinn; Costumes, Sally J. Lesser; Lighting, Pat Dignan; Sound, John Kilgore; Production Manager/Technical Director, Richard Morganelli; Wardrobe, Deb Phelan; Props, Abby Feder; Stage Managers, Casandra Scott, Abby Feder; Prologue assembled by Liz Diamond and Daniel Gerould from texts by Diderot, Crebillon fils, Marivaux, translated by Jacques Barzun and Daniel Gerould. CAST: Edward Baran (Prince), Adam Biesk (Azor), Lionel Chute (Meslis), Monique Cintron (Egle), Charles Halden (Mesrou), Shauna Hicks (Adine), Mia Katigbak (Carise), Maggie Rush (Dina), Raymond Anthony Thomas (Mesrin), Shelley Wyant (Hermiane).
   Presented with one intermission.

(Community Center) Sunday, May 1–2, 1988 (2 performances/limited engagement). The Community Center presents:
HOT COFFEE by Herbert Hayward; Director, John Wall; Lighting, Joe Pazillo. CAST: Andrew Addams (Bubba), Eddie Cobb (Rodney), Rod C. Hayes III (Dixon), Jared Matesky (Big Daddy), John Wuchte (Virgil)
   A comedy in two acts. The action takes place in Hot Coffee, Mississippi.

Adam Biesk, Monique Cintron
in "The Dispute" *(Jessica Katz)*

(The Women's Interart Annex) Wednesday, April 27–May 1, 1988 (5 performances). Lace Productions and W.I.T. in association with Women's Interart present:
SWEET STUFF by Juan Shamsul Alam; Director, Imani; Stage Manager, Beverly Jenkins; Set/Lighting, Jean Claude Canceddas; Fights, Ron Piretti CAST: Doreen Pica (Santana, Ace), Alonia King (C. O. Jackson), Diane Acciavatti (Rosa, The Roe), Karen Malina White (Simmons, T-Bone), Noemi Soulet (Cruz, The Hoe), Bobbi Berger (Carson, The Flea), Francine Mancini (Marie "Sweet Stuff" Tousand), Veronica Brown, Manera Smith (Understudies)
   A drama in 2 acts. The action takes place in the dayroom of a women's prison.

Left: Francine Mancini, Diane Acciavatti
in "Sweet Stuff"

(Lamb's Theatre) Thursday, April 28–May 21, 1988 (24 performances and 5 previews). The Lamb's Theatre Company, Ltd. (Carolyn Rossi Copeland, Producing Director/Joel K. Ruark, General Manager) presents:
ST. HUGO OF CENTRAL PARK by Jeffrey Kindley; Director, Robert Bridges; Music, Randy Courts; Set, Carl Baldasso; Costumes, Barbara A. Bell; Lighting, Rachel Budin; Sound, Ed Fitzgerald; Production Stage Manager, Allison Rabenau; Technical Director, Paul Grigoridis; Press, G. Theodore Killmer CAST: Jeff Garret (Hugo DePew), Judith Tillman (Emily DePew), Mace Barrett (Edgar DePew/Hawker), Roger Chapman (Mr. Muncy/Elroy/Reporter/Mr. Pinckney/Ron Blodgett), Marilyn Caskey (Dr. Kitchener/Judy/Reporter/Nurse Noble), Anna Holbrook (Susie/Martha/Jili Gerard), Ian D. Shupeck (John/Reporter/Dr. Petricoff), James Hartman (Policeman/Reporter/Harley Goodrich/Perry Porter)
   A play in 2 acts. The action takes place in New York City, 1959 to 1968

Judith Tillman, Jeff Garrett, Mace Barrett
in "St. Hugo of Central Park" *(Carol Rosegg)*

(The Cubiculo) Tuesday, May 3–22, 1988 (22 Performances) Theatre for a New Audience (Jeffrey Horowitz, Artistic/Producing Director; Deirdre M. Moynihan, Managing Director; Bill Reichblum, Associate Artistic Director) presents:
EVENING STAR by Milcha Sanchez-Scott; Director, Paul Zimet; Sets/Costumes, G. W. Mercier; Lighting, Mary Louise Geiger; Music, Ellen Maddow; Casting, Janet L. Murphy; Production Stage Manager, Max Storch; Press, George Ashley CAST: Cara Buono (Olivia Pena), Eddie Sambucci (Junior Rodriguez), Roland F. Sanchez (Vendor), Marisa Tomei (Lilly Rodrigues), Virginia Arrea (Tina Pena), Carlos Rafart (Juan Pena), Carmen Rosario (Mrs. Rodrigues)
   Performed without intermission. The action takes place in a barrio in the U.S. in spring.

(Don't Tell Mama) Friday, May 6–June 30, 1988 (16 performances).
OUR LADY OF THE HARBOR BAR & GRILL by Bruce Hopkins; Poetry and Psycho-metaphysical material by Teller Thomas; Songs, Monty Python, Henry Krieger/Tom Eyen, Arthur Kirson, Gus Kahn/Walter Donaldson, Cy Coleman/Barbara Freid and others; Musical Director, Paul Greenwood; Lighting, Tony De-Cicco; Set, Jeff Ide; Costumes, Gerry McCarthy CAST: Bruce Hopkins
MUSICAL NUMBERS: The Universe Song, And I Am Telling You, Lilacs, Show-Tune Medley, My Buddy, The Way I See It
   A performance piece without intermission.

(The Triplex) Sunday May 8, 1988 (One performance only) The Triplex presents a benefit for Childrensfare, the Triplex's International Children's Theatre Festival: **WAITIN' IN THE WINGS: THE NIGHT THE UNDERSTUDIES TAKE CENTERSTAGE;** with great moments from A Chorus Line, Anything Goes, Cabaret, Carrie, Cats, Chess, Into The Woods, Les Miserables, Me and My Girl, No Frills Revue, Starlight Express, The Phantom of the Opera and The River; Evening written by Charles Leighton and Peter Link; Director, Peter Link; Musical Director/Arranger, Sariva Goetz; Lighting, Stuart Duke; Sound, Jeremy Harris; Costume Coordinator, Heidi Hollmann; Production Stage Manager, Carol Cleveland; Conceived and Produced by William Spencer Reilly; Chairman, Edward J. Ross; Chairwoman, Augusta Souza Kappner; Press, Becky Flora. CAST: Hosted by Vincent Sardi; Special Guests; Sarah Brightman, Geraldine Fitzgerald, Anne Jackson, Richard Kiley, Judy Kuhn, Dorothy Loudon, Phylicia Rashad, Donna Vivino, Eli Wallach; Starring Mana Allen, Robert Ashford, Arminae Azarian, Jeff Blumenkrantz, James Brennan, Jenny Burton, Larry Cahn, Candy Cook, Nick Corley, Sheri Cowart, Ann Crumb, Karen Curlee, Michael Demby-Cain, Jerry Dixon, Cynthia Fleming, Dan Fletcher, Jeffery Hairston-Smith, Linda Hart, Rosemarie Jackson, Stephanie Renee James, Kurt Johns, Jeff Keller, Janene Lovullo, Robin Lyon, Judy McLane, Amy O'Brien, Michelle O'Steen, Val Scott, Michelan Sisti, Danny Strayhorn, Bonnie Walker, Lillias White, Wysandria Woolsey, Greg Zerkle

Benefit featuring this season's understudies included original song "Waitin' In the Wings" by Peter Link.

(Astor Place Theatre) Wednesday, May 11,–July 24, 1988 (96 performances) Marlyn Tsai and John Bard Manulis in association with New Writers at the Westside present: **THREE WAYS HOME** by Casey Kurtti; Director, Chris Silva; Setting, Donald Eastman; Lighting, Anne Militello; Costumes, April Curtis; Sound, Daniel Moses Schreier; Production Stage Manager, Peter C. Cook; Associate Producer, Raymond L. Gaspard; Executive Producer, Marc Routh; Company Manager, Daniel Kearns; Press, Fred Nathan/Marc Thibodeau/Philip Rinaldi CAST: Mary McDonnell (Sharon), S. Epatha Merkerson (Dawn), Malcolm-Jamal Warner (Frankie), Monte Russell (Standby for Frankie)

A comedy-drama in two acts. The action takes place at the present time in New York City.

(Apple Corps Theatre) Wednesday, May 11–29, 1988 (7 performances and 7 previews) Theatre Ararat (Louise Simone, Executive Producer) presents: **THE YELLOW DOG CONTRACT** by Ed Setrakian; Director, Joseph Ragno; Set Design, E. F. Morrill; Costume Design, MaryAnn D. Smith; Lighting Design, Robert W. Rosentel; Sound Design/Original Music, Richard Reiter; Associate Producer, Terri Owen; Press, Peter Cromarty and Co. CAST: Paul Villani (Price/Alfredo), Christopher James Wright (Davis/Clyde/Informer/Aide), Tom Kubiak (Stanley), Mark Hofmaier (Jimmy McCoy/Aide), Martha Senseney (Sally), David Parker (Phillip/Walter Thorne), Martin Shakar (Vahan Bagdasarian), Christopher Rodrigues (Aram Bagdasarian), Jill Giles (Priscilla/Informer's Wife/Aide), Larry Block (Cecil), Dunsten J. McCormick (Patrick/Reporter/Gardener), Stuart Rudin (Preacher Ross), Janet Ward (Sister Alice), Vasek Simek (Avedis)

A play in two acts. The action takes place in the spring and summer of 1920 in and around a town in southern West Virginia.

(Kaufman Theatre) Wednesday May 11–June 12, 1988 (28 performances and 6 previews) Martin R. Kaufman presents: **KAYE BALLARD: WORKING 42ND ST. AT LAST!;** Creative Consultant, Ben Bagley; Sets/Lighting, Jeffrey Schissler; Music/Lyrics, Barry Kleinbort, Cy Coleman, Carolyn Leigh, Arthur Siegel, Suzanne Buhrer, Leslie Eberhard, David Levy, Nancy Hamilton, Morgan Lewis, Jerome Kern, Dorothy Fields, Gordon Connell, Suzanne Buhrer, Harold Arlen, Yip Harburg, Fred Silver, Irving Berlin, Charlotte Kent, Martha Caples, Michael Brown, June Carroll, Cole Porter, Norman Martin, John LaTouche, Jerome Moross, Charles Strouse, Philip Springer, Mary McCarty, Buddy Pepper, Kaye Ballard; Stage Manager, Elizabeth Heeden; Technical Director, David Bornstein; Costumes, Clovis Ruffin, Grace Costumes, Reuben Panis; Production Assistant, Dian Roche; General Manager, Marshall B. Purdy; Press, Henry Luhrman Associates, Terry M. Lilly, David Lotz CAST: Kaye Ballard, Arthur Siegel, Miss Faun

MUSICAL NUMBERS: Don't Ask the Lady What the Lady Did Before, Sondheim Song, My Son, Burger Beguine, The Old Soft Shoe, Remind Me, Folk Song, Country Song, Is That All There Is?, Wizard of Oz medley, I Just Found Out, Irving Berlin medley, I Gotta Make My Own Music, I Hate Spring, Lizzie Borden, Love Is a Simple Thing, When, Tale of the Oyster, Paramount Capitol and the Strand, After Forty, Yellow Flower, I Just Kissed My Nose Goodnight, My City/You Can Be a New Yorker Too, Lady Lyricists medley, Time You Old Gypsy Man

A musical entertainment in two acts.

Top Right: Mary McDonnell, S. Epatha Merkerson,
Malcolm-Jamal Warner in "Three Ways Home"
(Carol Rosegg Photo) Below: Martin Shakar,
Janet Ward in "Yellow Dog Contract"
(Linda Alaniz Photo)

Miss Faun, Kaye Ballard, Arthur Siegel
in "Working 42nd. . . ."

(45th St Theatre) Thursday, May 12–28, 1988 (15 Performances) Primary Stages Company (Casey Childs, Artistic Director) presents:
FOUR NEW COMEDIES: Production Stage Manager, Kevin Lambert; Lighting, William Simmons; Production Manager, Herbert H. O'Dell; Casting, Marilyn McIntyre, Cindy Storm Segal; Stage Manager, Tony Luna; Scenic Artist, Sandy Allison; Sound, Paul Garrity, Curtis Ardurel; Production Assistant, Amy Huggans; Technical Director, William Simmons; Press, Anne Einhorn; THE TIME I DIED by Ron Carlson; Director, Gregory Lehane; CAST: Janet Reed (Linda). MADAME ZELENA FINALLY COMES CLEAN by Ron Carlson; Director, Casey Childs; CAST: Scotty Bloch (Madame Zelena). LONE DEER by Donald Wollner; Director, Gregory Lehane; CAST: Marilyn McIntyre (Gloria), Tony Campisi (Cole Durham). SPLITSVILLE by Richard Dresser; Director, Gloria Muzio; CAST: Dave Florek (Roy), J. Smith-Cameron (Wendy), Luke Sickle (Gary), Phyllis Somerville (Jill), Lilene Mansell (Betty), James Gleason (Chuck).

Phyllis Somerville, Luke Sickle
in "Splitsville" *(Lori Bank)*

(Theatre Four) Friday, May 13,–July 31, 1988. (42 performances) The Negro Ensemble Company (Douglas Turner Ward, President/Founder) presents the Crossroads Theatre Company (Rick Khan, Producing Artistic Director; Kenneth Johnson, Associate Producer; Elizabeth Bullock, General Manager) production of:
WEST MEMPHIS MOJO by Martin Jones; Director, Rick Khan; Set, Charles McClennahan; Lighting, Shirley Prendergast; Costumes, Judy Dearing; Sound, Rob Gorton; Company Manager, Wayne Elbert; Production Assistant, Wendy Turner; Stage Manager, Kenneth R. Saltzman; Press, Howard Atlee. CAST: Richard Gant (Teddy), Tico Wells (Elroi), Tucker Smallwood (Frank), Kate Redway (Maxine).
A comedy-drama in two acts. The action takes place in Teddy's Barbershop & Records, West Memphis, Arkansas, in November of 1955.

(Intar Stage 2) Friday, May 13–May 29, 1988 (17 performances) The Working Theatre (Bill Mitchelson, Artistic Director) presents:
WORKING ONE-ACTS 1988; Production Manager, Louis D. Pietig; Associate Producers, Nelson Simon, Larry Beers; Settings, Shelly Barelay; Lighting, Spencer Mosse; Sound, Ed Costa, Tom Gould; Costumes, Leslie Anne McGovern; Stage Managers, Gregg Fletcher, Rona Bern; Press, Bruce Cohen, Kathleen von Schmid THE ROAD TO RUIN by Richard Dresser; Director, John Pynchon Holms CAST: Victor Bevine (Cliff), Cedering Fox (Connie), Nelson Simon (Fred), Robert Arcaro (Jimbo)
The action takes place during the middle of a rainy night at Jimbo's Garage in Jersey City.
HARVEST SUN by John Olive; Director, Kent Paul CAST: Ralph Bell (Henry Pearson), Robin Polk (Meg), Janet Aspers (Rebecca)
The action takes place September 1968 on a deserted farm near Maple Lake, Minn.
NO TIME by Laurence Klavan; Director, Paul Dorman CAST: Murray Rubinstein (Randolph Hackmeat), Jay Devlin (Dad), Susan Blommaert (Secretary), Suzanne Marshall (Suze), Paul O'Brien (Brother/Lawyer/Cop/Messenger/Butler/Investment Counselor/Thug), Jordan Lund (Psychiatrist/Employee), Pam Cuming (Miranda), Johnny Kline, Robert Arcaro (Understudies)
The action takes place at present in a mid-Manhattan office.
THE LAST TEMPTATION OF JOE HILL by Willy Holtzman; Director, Robert Owens Scott CAST: Johnny Kline (Joe Hill), Brad Greenquist (Joe 2), Thomas Kopache (Smith), Bill Mitchelson (Wobbly 1), Mary Daciuk (Wobbly 2), Honour Molloy (Wobbly 3), Herb Downer (Wobbly 4)

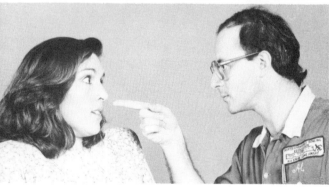

Cedering Fox, Nelson Simon in "Road to Ruin"
(Carol Rosegg Photo) **Above: Tucker Smallwood,**
Tico Wells, Richard Gant in "West Memphis Mojo"

(Riverwest Theatre) Friday, May 13–June 4, 1988 (11 performances and 9 previews) CHS Productions and Dina & Alexander E. Racolin in association with Riverwest Theatre presents:
MONSIEUR AMILCAR by Yves Jamiaque; English adaptation by George Gonneau and Norman Rose; Director, Loukas Skipitaris; Stage Managers, Carol Venezia, Paul A. Kochman, Manny Fernandez; Sets, Brian Kelly; Lighting, Norman Coates; Costumes, Susan DeMasi; Sound; Lou Piccirillo; Original Music composed, performed and recorded by Jacob Stern, Howard Salat; Press, Cromarty & Co./Peter Cromarty CAST: Peter Pagan (Alexander Amilcar), Ron Randell (Machou), Bonnie J. Debouter (Virginia), Billie Anita Stewart (Eleanor), Albert Insinnia (Nicky), Sheila Smith (Melie)
The action takes place in Paris in "the present."

Ron Randell, Bonnie DeBauter, Peter Pagan
in "M. Amilcar" *(Carol Rosegg Photo)*

(City Center Theater) Wednesday, May 14–22, 1988 (5 performances, limited engagement). City Center 55th Street Theater Foundation, Inc. in association with Bill Irwin & Friends presents:
LARGELY/NEW YORK *(The Further Adventures of a Post-Modern Hoofer)* Created by Bill Irwin; Ensemble Choreography & Direction, Kimi Okada; On Stage Video, Dennis Diamond, Video D Studios; Original Video Design, Skip Sweeney with Bill Irwin; Lighting, Jan Kroeze; Costumes, Cynthia Flynt; Sound, Bob Bielecki; Original Sound Design, Steve Klein; Specialty Props, David Logan; Stage Managers, Nancy Harrington, Joseph S. Kubala; General Manager, Susan West; Music, Run DMN, Ice T & The Glove, Charlie Barnet, Wayne Horvitz, Vincent Youmans & Irving Ceasar CAST: Bill Irwin (The Post-Modern Hoofer), Leon Chesney, John Christian (The Poppers), Meg Eginton (Soloist), Dennis Diamond (Videographer), Michael P. Hesse, Harold James (Video Assistants), Jeff Gordon (Dean), Jonathan Brandt, Gabrielle Brite, Hilary Chaplain, Peg Evans, Jeanne Feeney, Jenny Klion, Elan Koszuk, Carol Kuchler, Johnnie Moore, Meredith Ponte, Caroline Ryburn, Jack Scott, Toni Wisty (Academics and Ensemble)

A performance piece in one act, with music, dance, and mime. The action takes place in New York City.

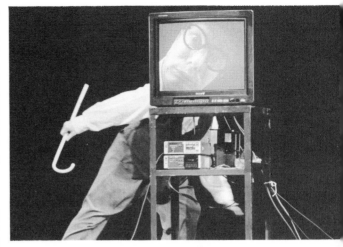
Bill Irwin in "Largely/New York"

(Palsson's Supper Club) Monday, May 16–June 12, 1988 (42 performances)
BITTERSUITE–ONE MORE TIME with Music by Elliot Weiss; Lyrics/Director, Michael Champagne; Executive Producer, Bittersuite Company; Production Stage Manager, Ann Chitwood; Musical Director, Elliot Weiss; Associate Musical Director, Andrew Wilder; Press, Peter Cromarty; Associate Producers, Daniel Glassman, Lee Roth, Dr. Norton Scherer, Oscar Trepel, Alan Wang; Lighting, Eric Cornwell; Sound, Gayle Jeffery. CAST: David Edwards, Suellen Estey, Roger Neil, Barbara Scanlon. MUSICAL NUMBERS: The Bittersuite, The Life That Jack Built, Try a Little Harder, Lonely Man Lonely Woman, Rank and File, The Recipe, Ice Cream, Soap Opera, I'll Make a Place, Win and Lose, Fathers and Sons, Mama Don't Cry, Snap Back, The Cliche Waltz, I've Got to Be Famous, Money Is Honey, Narcissism Rag, Dungeons and Dragons, Twentieth Reunion, I'll Be There, I'm Going to Live Forever, One More Time.

A musical revue in two acts.

Right: Roger Neil, Barbara Scanlon, SuEllen Estey, David Edwards in "Bittersuite. . . ."
(Carol Rosegg Photo)

(Upstairs Theatre/St. Mark's On-the-Bowery) Thursday, May 19–June 5, 1988 (15 performances) Heavy Manners presents:
BEAT THE AIR by Katt Lissard; Director, Gregor Paslawsky; Set/Paintings, Nikolai Klein; Lighting, Susan Chute; Costumes, Betty LaRoe; Stage Manager, Ghislaine Rump; Props, Jacqueline Reinbold, Jim Gaines, Marivie Davis; Publicity, Edward Ratliff. CAST: Wendy Brennan (Old Woman/Peasant), Anna Brown (Court Apprentice/Military/Crowd), Connie Childs (Friend/Peasant), James Encinas (Bar Tender/Peasant), Adam Gavzer (Juggler/Military/Crowd), Gordon Gray (Attorney/Inquisitor), Bruce Grossberg (Judge/Pope), Gillian Hemstead (Little Girl/Peasant), Harriet Hendlin (Young Woman/Peasant), Marceline Hugot (Bar Fly/Peasant), Betty LaRoe (Court Stenographer/Military), Jesse Levy (Lawyer/Advocate), Michael Nordstrom (Cameraman), Lisa Perkins (Military/Crowd), Julieanne Rumsey (Announcer/T.V. Director/Peasant), Alison Shanks (Bailiff/Military), Richard Skipper (Announcer/Defendant/Peasant/Crowd), Jon David Weigand (Announcer/Military/Defendant/Crowd).

(Nat Horne Theatre) Thursday May 19–22, 1988 (4 performances). Manhattan Class Company presents:
DASH by John Thorburn Hall; Director, Novella Nelson; Associate Producer, Rona Carr; Dramaturg, Janet Herzenberg; Stage Manager, Michael Soule; Press, G. Theodore Killmer CAST: Pat McNamara (Fred Connors), Richard Bekins (Phil Collier), Scott Bryce (Nick Pagorus), Christopher Randolph (Lother Von Lutz), Madison Arnold (Harry Abrams), Lee Roy Giles (Awahla), Dean Badarou (Doctor), Yvette Hawkins (Mrs. Noragbin).

A work in progress in two acts. The action takes place in April of 1976 in a hotel room in Lagos, Nigeria.

(Samuel Beckett Theater) Sunday, May 22–June 5, 1988 (13 performances and 11 previews) Vietnam Veterans Ensemble Theatre Company presents:
WALKING POINT: A VIETNAM VOYAGE by Thomas Bird; Director, John Pynchon Holms; Producer, Marty Kovach; Stage Manager, Anne Marie Hobson; Lighting, Matt Berman; Sound, Tom Gould; Assistant Director, Cedering Fox; Press, Bruce Campbell.

A monologue by Mr. Bird performed without intermission.

Thomas Bird in "Walking Point"
(Susan Cook Photo)

Left: Jason Gedrick, Judith Ivey
in "Mrs. Dally Has a Lover"
(Carol Rosegg Photo)

(Top of the Gate) Wednesday, May 25–June 12, 1988 (23 performances and 17 previews) Russ Thacker and Dwight Frye present:
THE WONDER YEARS with Music and Lyrics by David Levy; Book, David Levy, Steve Liebman, David Holdgrive, Terry LaBolt; Based on an idea by Leslie Eberhart; Director/Choreographer, David Holdgrive; Set, Nancy Thun; Costumes, Kenneth M. Yount; Lighting, Ken Billington; Musical Director/Orchestrations/Additional Vocal Arrangements, Keith Thompson; Musical & Vocal Arrangements, Terry LaBolt; General Management, Maria Productions/Maria Di Dia; Production Stage Manager, David Flasck; Assistant to Mr. Holdgrive, Susan Orem Lipko; Press, Shirley Herz Associates; Advertising, Attisano Levine, Inc.; Sound, Lewis Mead. CAST: Alan Osburn (Ken), Louisa Flaningam (Carol), Adam Bryant (Scott), Meghan Duffy (Lynnie), Kathy Morath (Patti), Lenny Wolpe (Skippy), Ann Brown, James Hindman (Understudies). MUSICAL NUMBERS: Baby Boom Babies, Thru You, Another Elementary School, First Love, Monarch Notes, Teach Me How to Fast Dance, Skippy A-Go-Go, The Wonder Years, Flowers from the Sixties, The Me Suite, Pushing Thirty, Takin' Him Home to Meet Mom, The Girl Most Likely.
A musical revue in two acts.

(Westbeth Theater Center) Tuesday, May 24–June 19, 1988 (24 performances) WTC American Playwright Program Performance Series presents:
MRS. DALLY HAS A LOVER by William Hanley; Director, Brian Murray; Set, Bob Phillips; Costumes, Walker Hicklin; Lighting, Michael Chybowski; Sound/Music, Deena Kaye; Production Stage Manager, Signe Helmen; Assistant Stage Managers, Mark Opshinsky, Linda Stewart. CAST: Judith Ivey (Evalyn Dally), Jason Gedrick (Frankie), Ron Orbach (Sam Dally).
A play in three acts. The action takes place in a railroad apartment in Manhattan in 1962.

Tower on Wheels/Cirque du Soleil
(Barry King Photo)

(Battery Park City Tent) Wednesday, May 25–June 10, 1988
CIRQUE DU SOLEIL; Artistic Director, Guy Caron; Stage Director, Franco Dragone; Composer, René Dupéré, Choreographer, Debra Brown; Costumes, Michel Crête; Lighting, Luc Lafortune; Stage Designer, André Caron; Assistant Directors, Claude Lemay, Lorraine Desmarais; Artistic Production Coordinators, Sylvie Arbour, Benoît Jodoin; Mask Design, André Soucy, Danielle Ethier; Make-Up, Richard Lacroix, Dany Cournoyer; Touring Assistant, Lou Arteau; Tour Production, Carole Baribeau; Sound, Robert Bilodeau; Massage, Pietro Biondo; Publicist, Lucie Bourassa; Administrative Tour Assistant, Carole Gagnon; Wardrobe, Marcelle Gravel; Media, Jean Héon; Accountant, Louis Landry; Head Usher, Pierre Méthot, Tour Manager, Yves Neveu; Tour Coordinator, Danny Pelchat; Teacher, Serge Robert; Technical Director, Richard Bouthillier, Assistant Technical, Jean-Pierre Pelletier; Site Manager, Lucie Tremblay; President, Guy Laliberté; Press, Susan Bloch & Co.
THE COMPANY: Michel Barette, Daniel Chrétien, Amélie Demay, Marie-Eve Dumais, Nicolas Dupéré, Alan Gauthier, Louise-Hélene Lacasse, Denis Lacombe, Angela Laurier, Tonatiuh Morales, Daniel Ouimet, Corinne Pierre, Faon River-Shane-Bélanger, André Saint-Jean, Luc Tremblay, Éric Varelas, Andrew Watson, Jacqueline Williams, Luc Dagenais, Noémie Gélinas
MUSICIANS: Lucie Cauchon, Benoit Jutras, Yvan Payeur, Stephen Poulin, Claude Vendette
An unconventional circus.

(clockwise from center) Louise Flaningam,
Kathy Morath, Adam Bryant, Lenny Wolpe, Alan
Osburn, Meghan Duffy in "The Wonder Years"
(David Holdgrive Photo)

(The Ohio Theatre) Thursday, May 26–June 12, 1988 (15 performances) Terese Hayden presents:

HOME SWEET HOME/CRACK by Charles Cissel; Director, Terese Hayden; Stage Managers, Ed Clements, Julie Swenson, Mitchell Florer, Diego Taborda; Production Designer, Fred Kolo; Press, Max Eisen. CAST: Jacqueline Brookes (Mom), Patricia Fochtman (Maggie), Raymond Haigler (Duffy), Ken Baldwin (Billy), James Stevenson (Dad), Roger Kovary (Phi), Victoria Polone (Heely), Douglass Cheek (Rev. Tiller), Hannah Cheek (Caitlin).

A comedy-drama in two acts. The action takes place in the family's house in a large mid-western town in 1972 and 1978, and in an off-campus house in an eastern college in 1978.

Left: (L) Victoria Polone, Raymond Haigler
(R) Jacqueline Brookes in "Home Sweet Home"
(Tom Palumbo Photo)

(Lambs Theatre) Tuesday May 31–Dec. 31, 1988 (225 performances and 15 previews). The Lambs Theatre Company (Carolyn Rossi Copeland, Producing Director) presents:

GODSPELL with Music and "new" lyrics by Stephen Schwartz; Conceived by John-Michael Tebelak; Director, Don Scardino; Scenery, Allison Campbell; Costumes, David C. Woolard; Lighting, Phil Monat; Sound; T. Richard Fitzgerald; Casting, Pat McCorkle, CSA/Richard Cole; Musical Director, Steven M. Alper; Musical Consultant, Paul Shaffer; Production Stage Manager, Fredric H. Orner; General Management, Gordon G. Forbes; Additional Orchestrations, Steven M. Alper, Douglas Besterman; Original Orchestration, Stephen Schwartz; Press, Ted Killmer; CAST: Trini Alvarado, Anne Bobby, Bill Damaschke, Laura Dean, Angel Jemmott, Eddie Korbich, Mia Korf, Robert McNeill, Harold Perrineau, Jr, Jeffrey Steefel, Marietta De Prima (understudy)

MUSICAL NUMBERS: Tower of Babble, Prepare Ye the Way of the Lord, Save The People, Day by Day, Learn Your Lessons Well, Bless The Lord, All For The Best, All Good Gifts, Light of the World, Turn Back O Man, Alas For You, By My Side (Music, Peggy Gordon Lyric, Jay Hamburger), We Beseech Thee, On The Willows, Finale

A revival of the musical based on St Matthew's Gospel. Original Production opened May, 17, 1971. (See THEATRE WORLD Volume 27)

(L) Jeffrey Steefel, Mia Korf and cast of "Godspell"
Right Center: Jeffrey Steefel, Robert McNeil
(Carol Rosegg Photos)

THE FANTASTICKS

Book & Lyrics, Tom Jones; Music, Harvey Schmidt; Suggested by Edmund Rostand's play "Les Romanesques"; Presented by Lore Noto; Director, Word Baker; Original Musical Direction/Arrangements, Julian Stein; Production Design, Ed Wittstein; Co-Producer, Don Thompson; Associate Producers, Sheldon Baron, Dorothy Olim, Jules Field; Assistant Producer, Michael Yarborough; Production Assistant, John Krug; Original Stage Manager, Geoffrey Brown; Stage Managers, Kim Moore, Steven Michael Daley; Press, Tony Noto. Opened in the Sullivan Street Playhouse on Tuesday, May 3, 1960*

CAST

The Narrator/El Gallo	Michael Licata†1
The Girl	Lorrie Harrison†2
The Boy	Kim Moore†3
The Boy's Father	Ron Lee Savin†4
The Girl's Father	William Tost
The Old Actor	Bryan Hull
The Man Who Dies/Indian	John Thomas Waite†5
The Mute	Jim Charles†6
At the piano	Dorothy Martin
At the harp	Elizabeth Etters†7

UNDERSTUDIES: Lorrie Harrison (The Girl), Steven Michael Daley (The Boy), William Tost (The Boy's Father), Neil Nash (The Narrator/El Gallo)
MUSICAL NUMBERS: Overture, Try to Remember, Much More, Metaphor, Never Say No, It Depends on What You Pay, Soon It's Gonna Rain, Rape Ballet, Happy Ending, This Plum Is Too Ripe, I Can See It, Plant a Radish, Round and Round, They Were You

*The world's longest running musical was still playing May 31, 1988. Performed in two acts.

†Succeeded by: 1. George Lee Andrews, Robert Vincent, 2. Glory Crampton, Anne Fisher, Kate Suber, 3. Paul Blankenship, Neil Nash, 4. Dale O'Brien, Ron Kidd, 5. Earl Aaron Levine, 6. Kim Moore, Neil Nash, Matthew Bennett, Steven Michael Daley, 7. Joy Plaisted

Van Williams, Martha Swope Photos

**Right: (front) John T. Waite, Lorrie Harrison,
Bill Perlach, Bryan Hull, (back) William Tost,
George Lee Andrews, Kim Moore, Ron Lee Savin
Above: (L) Glory Crampton, Neil Nash, (R) Robert
Vincent, Glory Crampton** (*Charlyn Zlotnik Photos*)

Bryan Hull

Dale O'Brien, William Tost

NUNSENSE

Written and Directed by Dan Goggin; Musical Staging/Choreography, Felton Smith; Presented by the Nunsense Theatrical Company in association with Joseph Hoesl, Bill Crowder, Jay Cardwell; Scenery, Barry Axtell; Lighting, Susan A. White; Musical Direction, Ethyl Will; Casting, Joseph Abaldo; Musical Arrangements, Michael Rice; General Management, Roger Alan Gindi; Company Manager, Jim Singlar; Technical Supervisor, Ted Kent Wallace; Stage Managers, Mary E. Lawson, Paul Botchis; Cast album on DRG Records; Press, Shirley Herz/Pete Sanders, Peter Cromarty, Glenna Freedman, David Roggensack, Miller Wright. Opened in the Cherry Lane Theatre on Tuesday, Dec. 3, 1985; moved Monday, Feb. 27, 1986 to the Circle Repertory Theatre, and to the Douglas Fairbanks Theatre on Monday, Sept. 8, 1986*

CAST

Sister Mary Regina ....Marilyn Farina[†1]
Sister Mary Hubert ....Vickie Belmonte[†2]
Sister Robert Anne .... Christine Anderson[†3]
Sister Mary Amnesia .... Semina DeLaurentis[†4]
Sister Mary Leo ....Suzi Winson

UNDERSTUDIES: Ann Kittredge, Carolyn Droscoski
MUSICAL NUMBERS: Nunsense Is Habit Forming, A Difficult Transition, Benedicite, The Biggest Ain't the Best, Playing Second Fiddle, So You Want to Be a Nun, Turn Up the Spotlight, Lilacs Bring Back Memories, Tackle That Temptation with a Time Step, Growing Up Catholic, We've Got to Clean Out the Freezer, Just a Coupl'a Sisters, Soup's On, I Just Want to Be a Star, The Drive In, I Could've Gone to Nashville, Gloria in Excelsis Deo, Holier Than Thou

A musical comedy in two acts. The action takes place at the present time in Mt. Saint Helen's School auditorium in Hoboken, NJ.

*Still playing May 31, 1988.

†Succeeded by: 1. Travis Hudson, Mary-Pat Green, Julie J. Hafner, 2. Edwina Lewis, Nancy Johnston, 3. Helen Baldassare, 4. Nancy Johnston, Susan Gordon-Clark

Martha Swope Photos

Carole Monferdini, Matt Bradford Sullivan
Above: A. J. Vincent, David Drake, Monica Horan
(T. L. Boston Photos)

Susan Gordon-Clark, Mary-Pat Green,
Julie J. Hafner in "Nunsense"
(Linda Alaniz Photos)

VAMPIRE LESBIANS OF SODOM
with SLEEPING BEAUTY or COMA

By Charles Busch; Director, Kenneth Elliott; Presented by Theatre in Limbo, Kenneth Elliott and Gerald A. Davis; Choreography, Jeff Veazey; Set, B. T. Whitehill; Costumes, John Glaser; Lighting, Vivien Leone; Casting, Stuart Howard; Wigs, Elizabeth Katherine Carr; Company Manager, Richard Biederman; Wardrobe, Alee Ralph; Production Assistant, Loretta Grande; Stage Managers, Jim Griffith, Jeff Barneson; Press, Shirley Herz/Pete Sanders, Glenna Freedman, David Roggensack, Miller Wright. Opened in the Provincetown Playhouse on Wednesday, June 19, 1985*

CAST

"Sleeping Beauty" or "Coma"
Miss Thick .... Chuck Brown[†1]
Enid Wetwhistle .... Becky London[†2]
Sebastian Lore .... Ralph Buckley[†3]
Fauna Alexander ....David Drake
Ian McKenzie .... Wilder Gutterson[†4]
Anthea Arlo .... Theresa Marlowe[†5]
Barry Posner .... Robert Carey[†6]
Craig Prince .... Ed Wintle[†7]

The action takes place in and around London in the 1960's.

"Vampire Lesbians of Sodom"
Ali, a guard/P.J. a chorus boy .... Robert Carey[†6]
Hujar, a guard/Zack a chorus boy .... Arnie Kolodner[†7]
A Virgin Sacrifice/Madeleine Astarte an actress ....David Drake
The Succubus/LaCondesa, a silent screen vamp .... Becky London[†2]
King Carlisle, movie idol .... Ralph Buckley[†4]
Etienne, butler/Danny a chorus boy .... Chuck Brown[†1]
Renee Vain, starlet/Tracy a singer .... Beata Baker
Oatsie Carewe, a gossip columnist .... Wilder Gutterson[†3]

UNDERSTUDIES: Monica Horan, Mark Hamilton

Performed with three scenes: Sodom in days of old, Hollywood in 1920 in La Condesa's mansion, and in a Las Vegas rehearsal hall today.

*Still playing May 31, 1988.

†Succeeded by: 1. Paul Kassel, Chuck Brown, 2. Carole Monferdini, 3. Brick Hartney, 4. Nick Kaledin, 5. Beata Baker, 6. Jeff Barneson, 7. A. J. Vincent

OFF-BROADWAY SERIES

AMAS REPERTORY THEATRE

Nineteenth Season

Founder/Artistic Director, Rosetta LeNoire; Administrator/Business Manager, Gary Halcott; Administrator, Eric M. Schussel; Chairman of the Board, Don Ellwood; Development, Arnold Falleder; Press, Fred Nathan Co./Merle Frimark

Thursday, October 15,–November 8, 1987 (16 performances)
CONRACK with Music by Lee Pockriss; Lyrics, Anne Croswell; Book, Granville Burgess, Anne Croswell, Lee Pockriss; Based on novel "The Water Is Wide" by Pat Conroy; Director, Stuart Ross; Choreographer, Sheila D. Barker; Musical Director/Arranger, James Followell; Set, Dick Block; Costumes, Debra Stein; Lighting, Donald Holder; Technical Director, Paul Reynolds; Stage Managers, Jay McManigal, Seth Gordon. CAST: Donald Acree (Top Cat), Peggy Alston (Mrs. Brown), Lisa Boggs (Cindy Lou), Harold Cromer (Quick Fella), J. P. Dougherty (Dr. Henry Piedmont), Ellia English (Edna Graves), Birdie M. Hale (Kate), Steven F. Hall (Pat Conroy), Pamela Isaacs (Dr. Jackie Brooks), Herb Lovelle (Sam), Jamila Perry (Anna), Victoria Platt (Mary), Kobie Powell (Prophet), Tarik Winston (Richard)
MUSICAL NUMBERS: Find Me a Body, He Gon' Stay, Bye Bye Conrack, The Water Is Wide, Hey I'm Talkin' to You Beethoven!, Southern Charm, White Liberal to the Rescue, Tune in Tomorrow, Our Night to Howl, The 1920 Agricultural Exposition, A Regular Family, Hopes an' Dreams, City Lights, I'm a Teacher

A new musical in 2 acts and 17 scenes. The action takes place on the island of Yamacraw, and in Beaufort, S.C., in 1969.

Thursday, February 11,–March 6, 1988 (16 performances)
STRUTTIN' with Book, Music, Lyrics and Direction by Lee Chamberlin; Arrangements/Musical Direction, Neal Tate; Choreography, Bernard M. Walsh; Set, Jeffrey Miller; Costumes, Bernard Johnson; Lighting, Shirley Pendergast; Sound, Phil Lee; Hairstylist, Glenn Wiehl; Wardrobe, Migdalia Luzula; Stage Managers, Jay McManigal, Bernita Robinson. CAST: Harriett D. Foy (Nan), Jillian C. Hamilton (Ida Mae), Casey McClellan (Jack), William Newhall (Donald), Roumel Reaux (Jim), Ensemble: Angelo Adkins, Jeff Bates, Josei Conte, Richard Costa, Dexter Jones, Shari Krikorian, David Lowenstein, Valerie Macklin, Chiquita Ross
MUSICAL NUMBERS: Struttin', Fly Away, Apricot Stockings, Seventeen and Sassy, Elite Feet, I've Met You Before, Someone to Guide Me, Hit the Number, Not My Season, Move Over Mr Hoover, Better Times, Truckin' from Harlem, Raggedy Ramble, Chanson Francaise, Paris High, Not My Season, Two Aspirine, You Got Me Wrong, Changes, Finale

A musical in 2 acts and 21 scenes.

Thursday, April 14,–May 8, 1988 (16 performances)
ROBIN'S BAND with Book by Jerome Eskow, Anthony Abeson; Music/Lyrics, Maija Kupris; Director, Anthony Abeson; Musical Direction/Arrangements, David Wolfson; Choreography, Rodney Nugent; Set, Jeffrey Miller; Costumes, David Mickelsen; Lighting, Kathy Kaufmann; Consultant to playwrights/Composer, Mason Bendewald; Technical Director, Gordon Brown; Wardrobe, Migdalia Luzula; Stage Managers, Jay McManigal, Bernita Robinson, Matthew Seiden. CAST: Peg Boas (Keyboards), Melissa DeSousa (Carla), Jeffrey Harmon (Hi-My-Name-Is), Carl H. Jaynes (Dispossessed Man), Experience Robinson (Karina), Kecia Lewis-Evans (Bobbie Bills), Liz Amberly (Sup), Vince Morton (Joe), John McCurry (Big Willie), Herb Lovelle (Lupin), Wayne Gordy (Councilman Minor), Gregory Harvey (Chelsea), Al Rodriguez (McDonald Meld), Jill Romero (Marion), Kelly Hinman (Robin)
MUSICAL NUMBERS: Symphony in Technophilia, There's Got to Be a Place, Shuffle Boogie, We Won't Let Them Take It Away, I Don't Have a Clue, You've Got to Pay the Price, Robin's Song, Get It Before It Comes Out, Something New, Give It to Me Now, In Sherwood, Little Boy Blue, Melophonia, Don't It Feel Right, Where We Want to Be

A musical in 2 acts and 10 scenes. The action takes place in the near future when the developers have taken over.

Top Right: Steven F. Hall (center)
and children in "Conrack" Below: William Newhall,
Casey McClellan, Jillian C. Hamilton in "Struttin' "
(Gilbert Johnson Photos)

"Robin's Band" company

AMERICAN JEWISH THEATRE

Thirteenth Season

Artistic Director, Stanley Brechner; Associate Artistic Director, Jan Hartman; Dramaturg, Ari Roth; General Manager, David Lawlor; Special Programs, Evanne Christian; Development, Robyn L. Stern; Press, David Rothenberg, Peter Cromarty (Theatre Guinevere) Saturday, October 17,–November 15, 1987 (16 performances)
TWO FRIDAYS two one-act plays: "Today a Little Extra" by Michael Kassin; Director, Gene Lasko; Set, Paul Wonsek; Lighting, Susan A. White; Costumes, Arnold S. Levine; Technical Director, Gregory Erbach; Sound Hal Schuler; Managing Coordinator, Julia Hansen; Stage Manager, Bruce Ostler. CAST: Norman Golden (Zalman Abrams), Michael Ornstein (Mark Levine), Frances Chaney (Esther Finkelstein) "The Irish Hebrew Lesson" by Wolf Mankowitz; Director, Gene Lasko. CAST: Nicholas Kepros (The Jew), Michael Ornstein (The Man), Norman Golden (Black and Tan), Gregory Erbach (Black and Tan)
Saturday, January 9,–February 6, 1988 (16 performances)
K (The Mind and Imagination of Franz Kafka) by Jan Hartman; Director, John Pynchon Holms; Set, Tim Saternow; Lighting, Michael Chybowski; Sound, Genji Ito; Costumes, Ellen V. McCartney; Technical Director, Gregory Erbach; Assistant Director, Cedering Fox; Stage Manager, Uriel Menson. CAST: Graeme Malcolm as Franz Kafka
Saturday, March 5,–April 3, 1988 (30 performances)
TEMPLE by Robert Greenfield; Director, Ethan D. Silverman; Set, Keith Ian Raywood; Lighting, Natasha Katz; Costumes, Karen Hummel; Sound, Tony Meola; Assistant Director, Michael Blowney; Casting, Deborah Brown; Stage Manager, Julie Swenson; Press, Peter Cromarty & Company. CAST: Robert Blumenfeld (Rabbi Simeon Hakveldt), Tibor Feldman (Schissel/Marvin), Sol Frieder (Mendel), Michael Marcus (Nat Weiss), Judd Nelson (Paulie), Ron Rifkin (Morty), Alice Spivak (Esther)
A play in two acts. The action takes place on Yom Kippur of 1969 in Morty's apartment and in and around Ahavath Mizrach.
Saturday, May 14,–June 12, 1988 (30 performances)
LAST OF THE RED HOT LOVERS by Neil Simon; Director, John Driver; Set, Randy Benjamin; Costumes, Arnold S. Levine; Lighting, Susan A. White; Sound, Hal Schuler; Stage Manager, Debora E. Kingston; Press, Peter Cromarty. CAST: Ethan Phillips (Barney Cashman), Becky London (Elaine Navasio), Tovah Feldshuh (Bobbi Michele), Marcia Jean Kurtz (Jeanette Fisher)
A comedy in three acts. The action takes place in an apartment in New York City's East Thirties during 1969.

Right: Judd Nelson, Sol Frieder in "Temple"
Top: Nicholas Kepros, Michael Ornstein in
"Two Fridays" (Larry Racioppo Photo)
Carol Rosegg Photos

Tovah Feldshuh, Ethan Phillips, Becky London, Marcia Jean Kurtz
in "Last of the Red Hot Lovers"

AMERICAN PLACE THEATRE

Twenty-fourth Season

Director, Wynn Handman; Associate Director, Julia Miles; Manager, Mickey Rolfe; Business Manager, Joanna Vedder; Literary Manager, Chris Breyer; Press, Fred Nathan/Marc Thibodeau

Wednesday, June 10,–21, 1987 (21 performances) Jubilee! A theatre festival celebrating the Black experience.

HER TALKING DRUM conceived by Vinie Burrows; Adapted for the stage by Vinie Burrows, Lenwood O. Sloan; Director, Lenwood O. Sloan; Music created and performed by Madeleine Yayodele Nelson; Set, Brian Martin; Lighting, Steven R. Jones; Costumes, Judy Dearing; Sound, Bill Turley/The Edge; Technical Director, Anthony Hume; Casting, Paul Garten; Dialect Coach, McKinley Winston; Stage Manager, Casandra Scott CAST: Vinie Burrows, Madeleine Yayodele Nelson, Kim Staunton, Hattie Winston

"Portraits of Black women echoing couplets of gold to crease the ground" and performed without intermission.

Tuesday, June 2–

JAMES THURBER KINTYPES a solo performance by John Valentine of James Thurber's works and life; Director, Wynn Handman; Set/Lighting, Marc D. Malamud; Stage Manager, Mary Fran Loftus.

Wednesday, Oct. 7,–25, 1987 (21 performances) The Women's Project and Productions (Julia Miles, Director) presents:

ABINGDON SQUARE by Maria Irene Fornes; Director, Ms. Fornes; Sets, Donald Eastman; Lighting, Anne Militello; Costumes, Sam Fleming; Casting, Myers/Teschner; Technical Director, Mark Bagnall; Assistant to Director/Musical Director, Beatriz Cordoba; General Manager, William Hopkins; Wardrobe, Deborah Jeanne Culpin; Stage Managers, Rebecca Green, Harvey Vincent CAST: Madeleine Potter (Marion), John David Cullum (Michael), John Seitz (Juster), Myra Carter (Minnie), Anna Levine (Mary), Michael Cerveris (Frank), Mark Bagnall (Glazier). A play in two acts. The action takes place in New York from 1908–1913, 1915–1917.

Thursday, November 12,–December 6, 1987 (23 performances)

THAT SERIOUS HE-MAN BALL by Alonzo D. Lamont, Jr.; Director, Clinton Turner Davis; Set, Charles McClennahan; Lighting, William H. Grant III; Costume Consultant, Julian Asion; Technical Director, Richard Tattersall; Stage Manager, Casandra Scott CAST: Tom Wright (Jello), Roger Guenveur Smith (Sky), Walter Allen Bennett, Jr. (Twin). A play in two acts. The action takes place at the present time at a suburban playground during the summer.

Friday, January 1,–February 7, 1988 (13 performances) American Humorists' Series.

ROY BLOUNT'S HAPPY HOUR AND A HALF written and performed by Roy Blount, Jr.; Designed by Marc D. Malamud

Tuesday, February 9, 1988–

AT THE BACK OF MY HEAD written and performed by Stephanie Silverman, and joined in repertory on Friday, February 19, 1988–

THE BOOB STORY written and performed by Jane Gennaro; Director, Wynn Handman; Designed by Marc D. Malamud; Stage Manager, Carl Zutz.

Wednesday, March 16–April 3, 1988 (22 performances)

TALLULAH TONIGHT! by Tony Lang; Director, Wynn Handman; Pianist, Paul Greenwood; Original Music, Bruce W. Coyle; Original Lyrics, Tony Lang; Lighting, Brian MacDevitt; Stage Manager, Rebecca Green. A solo performance by Helen Gallagher without intermission. MUSICAL NUMBERS: Today I Love Ev'rybody, Eugenia, Crack Wise, Most Gentlemen Don't Like Love, Roundabout, They Knew Tallulah, I'm Throwing a Ball Tonight, A Little Something Different, Everything I've Got, I've Seen That Face, I'll Be Seeing You.

Friday, April 15,–May 8, 1988 (26 performances) Jubilee! A theatre festival celebrating the Black experience presents:

SPLENDID MUMMER by Lonne Elder III; Director, Woodie King, Jr.; Set, Charles McClennahan; Lighting, Brian MacDevitt; Costumes, Edi Giguere; Sound, Terry Van Richardson; Stage Manager, 'Femi Sarah Heggie. a solo performance by Charles S. Dutton as Ira Aldridge in two acts. The action takes place at the present and circa 1807 through 1867 in New York City, England, and various countries in Europe where Mr. Aldridge starred on stage.

Martha Holmes Photos

**Left: John David Cullum, Madeleine Potter,
Anna Levine in "Abingdon Square" Above: (L) Charles S.
Dutton in "Splendid Mummer" (R) Helen Gallagher in
"Tallulah Tonight!" Top: Vinie Burrows, Madeleine Yayodele
Nelson, Kim Staunton, Hattie Winston in "Her Talking Drum"**
(Martha Holmes Photos)

Roy Blount   **Jane Gennaro**

AMERICAN THEATER EXCHANGE

Second Season

(Joyce Theater) Monday, June 8–27, 1987 (21 performances) The Joyce Theater Foundation (Cora Cahan, Vice President) presents the Long Wharf Theatre production of:

SELF DEFENSE by Joe Cacaci; Director, Arvin Brown; Scenery, Marjorie Bradley Kellogg; Costumes, Bill Walker; Lighting, Ronald Wallace; Stage Manager, Anne Keefe; Press, Ellen Jacobs CAST: Steven Marcus (Ronnie Gordon, a client), Michael Wikes (Mickey Reisman, a public defense attorney), Lewis Black (Eddie Reisman, his brother), Kevin O'Rourke (Edgar Lewis, a client), Charles Cioffi (Phil Lehman, a District Attorney), Kevin Nova Davis (Mark Robbins, a law student), Julia Newton (Deborah James, Assistant District Attorney), Paul Austin (Gerald McMahon, a public defense attorney), Jose Santana (Julio Lopez, a client)

A drama in two acts. The action takes place in and around the Bronx during three weeks in the winter of 1986.

(Theatre 890) Monday, June 29,–July 25, 1987 (32 performances) The Joyce Theater Foundation presents the Berkeley Repertory Theatre (Sharon Ott, Artistic Director; Mitzi Sales, Managing Director) production of:

HARD TIMES by Charles Dickens; Adapted by Stephen Jeffreys; Director, Richard E. T. White; Scenery, John Bonard Wilson; Costumes, Cathleen Edwards; Lighting, Derek Duarte; Music composed and performed by Jeffrey Bihr; Company Manager, Kevin Shea; Stage Manager, Kimberly Mark Webb; Press, Ellen Jacobs CAST: Laurence Ballard (Bitzer, Mr. Sleary, Josiah Bounderby, Slackbridge, Station Master, Waiter, Ensemble), Jeffrey Bihr (Young Tom, Rescuer, Ensemble), Kathleen Chalfant (Sissy Jupe, Mrs. Gradgrind, Mrs. Sparsit, Rachael, Mary Stokes, Ensemble), Patricia Hodges (Louisa, Emma Gordon, Mrs. Blackpool, Mrs. Pegler, Chairwoman, Ensemble), Jarion Monroe (Thomas Gradgrind, Stephen Blackpool, James Harthouse, Ensemble)

A play in three acts. The action takes place in Coketown, an industrial town in Lancashire, England, in the 1840's.

(Joyce Theater) Monday, July 13,–August 1, 1987 (23 performances). The Joyce Theater Foundation present the Wilma Theater (Artistic/Producing Directors, Blanka Zizka, Jiri Zizka) production of:

1984 by George Orwell; Adapted by Pavel Kohout; Director, Jiri Zizka; Set, Phillip Graneto; Projections, Jeffrey S. Brown; Costumes/Makeup, Pamela Keech; Cinematography, Michael Bailey; Lighting, James Leitner; Translation, Jiri Zizka, Michael Ladenson; Sound, Adam Wernick, Charles Cohen; Original Music, Adam Wernick; Dramaturgy/Additional Lyrics, Michael Ladenson; Casting, Myers/Teschner; Stage Manager, Ken Wesler; Press, Ellen Jacobs Co. CAST: Sky Ashley Berdahl (John Parsons), Susanna Clemm (Arresting Officer), Deanna DuClos (Evelyn Parsons), George Feaster (Oceania Citizen), Frances Fisher (Julia), Leata Galloway (Washerwoman), James Hurdle (Dr. Charrington), Jodie Lynne McClintock (Mrs. Parsons), Daniel J. O'Shea (Oceania Citizen), Lucille Patton (Prostitute/Citizen), Oliver Platt (Syme), Jenny Psaki (Citizen/Police), Roger Serbagi (Tom Parsons), John Shepard (Winston Smith), Charles Techman (Old Man/Martin), Evan Thompson (O'Brien)

(Theatre 890) Monday, August 3–29, 1987 (29 performances) The Joyce Theater Foundation presents the San Diego Repertory Theatre (Sam Woodhouse, Producing Director; Douglas Jacobs, Artistic Director) production of:

HOLY GHOSTS by Romulus Linney; Director, Douglas Jacobs; Scenery/Lighting, D. Martyn Bookwalter; Costumes, Ray C. Naylor; Music Direction, Victor P. Zupanc, Linda Vickerman; Sound, Victor P. Zupanc; Stage Manager, Shirley Stary; Press, Ellen Jacobs CAST: Diana Castle (Nancy Shedman), Bradley Fisher (Coleman Shedman), W. Dennis Hunt (Rogers Canfield), Dana Hart (Obediah Buckhorn, Jr.), Michael Lewis (Virgil Tides), Bill Dunnam (Orin Hart), Ric Barr (Howard Rudd), Barbara Murray (Lorena Cosburg), Priscilla Allen (Mrs. Wall), Cynthia Ann Williams (Muriel Boggs), Jim Mooney (Billy Boggs), Ollie Nash (Rev. Obediah Buckhorn, Sr.), Don R. McManus (Carl Specter), Terry Eaton (Bonnie Bridge), Tavis Ross (Cancer man)

A drama in two acts. The action takes place at the present time in the rural South on an early summer evening.

**Left: John Shepard in "1984" Above: Laurence
Ballard, Jarion Monroe, Patricia Hodges in
"Hard Times"** *(Fred Speiser Photo)* **Top: Michael
Wikes, Julia Newton in "Self Defense"** *(T. Charles Erickson)*

Cast of "Holy Ghosts"
(Ken Jacques Photo)

BROOKLYN ACADEMY OF MUSIC

President/Executive Producer, Harvey Lichtenstein; Director Next Wave Festival, Joseph V. Melillo; General Manager, Michael O'Rand; Press, Peter B. Carzasty, Karen Goldman, Amy Budinger, Michael McGovern, Robert Boyd
(BAM Majestic Theater) Tuesday, October 13, 1987–January 3, 1988 (26 complete cycles). BAM, Centre International de Creations Theatrales, and the Royal Shakespeare Theatre present:
THE MAHABHARATA by Jean-Claude Carriere; Adapted into English and Directed by Peter Brook; Set/Costumes, Chloe Obolensky; Producers, Micheline Rozan, William Wilkinson; Technical Directors, Philippe Mulon, Jean-Guy Lecat; Production Coordinator, Marie-Helene Estienne; Assistant to Director/Fight Arranger, Alain Maratrat; Lighting, Jean Kalman; Language Coach, Clifford DeSpenser. CAST: Urs Bihler (Dushassana), Ryszard Cieslak (Dhritarashira), Georges Corraface (Duryodhana), Mamadou Dioume (Bhima), Richard Fallon (Djayadratha/Salva), Miriam Goldschmidt (Kunti), Nolan Hemmings (Abhimanyu/Ekalavya/Uttara), Ciaran Hinds (Nakula/Aswattaman), Corinne Jaber (Gandhari's Servant/Subhadra), Jeffery Kissoon (Karna), Sotigui Kouyate (Bhishma/Parashurama), Tuncel Kurtiz (King of Fishermen/Shakuni/Virata/Sandjaya/Adiratha), Robert Langdon Lloyd (Vyasa) Mireille Maalouf (Gandhari/Ganga/Gudeshna), Mavuso Mavuso (The Sun/Sisupala/Ghatotkatcha), Vittorio Mezzogiorno (Arjuna), Bruce Myers (Ganesha/Krishna), Yoshi Oida (Drona/Kitchaka), Helene Patarot (Amba), Mallika Sarabhai (Draupadi/Satyavati), Andrzej Seweryn (Yudishthira), Tam Sir (Madri/Hidimbi/Urvasi), Antonin Stahly-Viswanadhan (Child), Tapa Sudana (Pandu/Siva/Salya/Maya), Musicians: Djamchid Chemirani, Kudsi Erguner, Kim Menzer, Mahmoud Tabrizi-Zadeh, Toshi Tsuchitori.
  Performed in three parts (The Game of Dice, Exile in the Forest, The War) for nine hours.
(BAM/Carey Playhouse) Tuesday, October 20,–November 1, 1987 (15 performances)
SWING conceived and directed by Elizabeth Swados; Music, Elizabeth Swados, Andrew Julian Meyers, Preston Fulwood, Jr., David Levitt, Connie Alexander; Choreography, Mama Lu Parks; Scenery/Lighting, Mitchell Bogard; Costumes, Sharon Sobel; Assistant to Director, Margaret Schultz; Associate Producer, Diane J. Malecki; Additional Arrangements/Musical Director, Jeff Waxman; Assistant General Manager, Peter G. Tumbelston; Production Manager, Paul E. King; Company Manager, Elsa Jacobson; Stage Manager, Steven M. Coleman. CAST: Connie Alexander, Anne Cavallo Brienza, Tony Brienza, Craig Chang, Yasmeen Coaxum, Albert Delatorre III, Thomas Freund, Preston Fulwood, Jr., Elizabeth Grad, Delva M. Haynes, Selena Higgs, Ashanti Isabell, Tremaine Jackson, Roslyn Jarrell, Frank Kero, David Levitt, Maribel Lizardo, Belinda Lee Lucatorto, Julissa Marquez, Crystal Mayo, Andrew Julian Meyers, Steven W. Moses, Robert Lovick Pearson, Lori Puglia, Myim Rose, Amit Shamir, Alfred Shepherd, Curtis Thomas, Harry W. Thompson III.
  Performed without intermission.
(BAM/Lepercq Space) Tuesday, November 17,–December 6, 1987 (23 performances)
ZANGEZI: A Supersaga in Twenty Planes by Velimir Khlebnikov; English Text, Paul Schmidt; Director, Peter Sellars; Set/Costumes, George Tsypin; Lighting, James F. Ingalls; Sound, Stephen Cellum; Music composed and performed by Jon Hassell; Assistant General Manager, Jeffrey R. Costello; Production Manager, Paul E. King; Company Manager, Martha David; Coordinator, L. Bayly Ledes; Stage Managers, John Beven, Steven M. Coleman. CAST: David Warrilow, Ruth Maleczech, Ben Halley, Jr.
  Performed without intermission.

Right: Natasha Parry, Erland Josephson
Above: Natasha Parry, Brian Dennehy
in "The Cherry Orchard" Top: Andrezej
Seweryn, Mallika Saraghai, Miriam Goldschmidt,
Mamadou Dioume in "The Mahabharata"
(Martha Swope Photos)

(BAM/Carey Playhouse) Tuesday, December 1–6, 1987 (7 performances). BAM Next Wave Festival presents the Squat Theatre production of:
"L" TRAIN TO ELDORADO by Stephan Balint; Director, Mr. Balint; Film Cinematography, Bobby Bukowski; Music, Peter Scherer, Arto Lindsay; Art/Stage Design, Eva Buchmuller; Lighting, Anne Militello; Sound, Connie Kieltyka; Creative Consultants, Mark Boone, Jr., Peter Berg, Jan Gontarczyk, Klara Palotai; Music Coordinator, Exzter Balint; Coordinator, Kate Mennone; Pyrotechnical Effects, Fred Buchholz; General Management, International Production Associates. CAST: Mark Boone, Jr., Peter Berg, Eszter Balint, Jennifer Stein, Susan Williams (film), Vit Horejs, Rebecca Major, Klara Palotai, Jan Gontarczyk, Stephan Balint, Alexandra Auder (film), Jon Vorhees (film)
  Performed without intermission.
(BAM/Majestic Theater) Monday, January 18,–April 10, 1988 (96 performances)
THE CHERRY ORCHARD by Anton Chekhov; English Translation, Elisaveta Lavrova; Director, Peter Brook. Set/Costumes, Chloe Obolensky; Lighting, Jean Kalman; Incidental Music Composed by Marius Constant; Casting, Risa Bramon/Billy Hopkins, Lisa Peterson, Marie-Helene Estienne; Company Manager, Ellen Dennis; Assistant to Director, Nina Soufy; Hair/Makeup, Vito Mastrogiavanni; Stage Managers, Andrew Feigin, Caty Laignel. CAST: Roberts Blossom (Firs), Brian Dennehy (Lopakhin), Howard Hensel (Passerby/Understudy), Linda Hunt (Charlotta), Zeljko Ivanek (Trofimov), Erland Josephson (Gaev), Kate Miller (Dunyasha), Chris McNally (Stationmaster/Understudy), Rebecca Miller (Anya), Mike Nussbaum (Pishchik/Understudy), Natasha Parry (Lyubov), David Pierce (Yasha), Stephanie Roth (Varya), Jan Triska (Yepikhodov), Ludmilla Bokievsky (Understudy), Caty Laignel (Understudy)
  A drama in four acts, performed without intermission.

CIRCLE REPERTORY THEATRE

Nineteenth Season

Artistic Director, Tanya Berezin; Managing Director, Tim Hawkins; Associate Artistic Director, B. Rodney Marriot; Lab Director, Michael Warren Powell; Artistic Associate, Mark Ramont; Associate Literary Manager, Adrienne Hiegel; Business Manager, Paul R. Tetreault; Marketing, Loretta Scheer; Production Manager, James B. Simpson; Assistant Production Manager, Shannon Curran; Technical Director, Brian Aldous; Props, Brook Sigal, John Viscardi; Wardrobe, Jannie Wolff; Sound, Chuck London Media/Stewart Werner; Sets, David Potts; Lighting, Dennis Parichy; Costumes, Jennifer von Mayrhauser; Stage Manager, Fred Reinglas; Press, Gary Murphy.

(Circle Repertory Theatre) Wednesday, September 23,–November 8, 1987 (54 performances)

EL SALVADOR by Rafael Lima; Director, John Bishop; Assistant Stage Manager, Jordan Mott. CAST: Bruce McCarty (Skee), John Spencer (Fletcher), John Dossett (McCutcheon), Michael Ayr (Fuller), Zane Lasky (Larry), Cotter Smith (Pinder), Lorraine Morin-Torre (Rosita), Understudies: Joel Anderson (Fletcher/Pinder), Renee Sicignano (Rosita), Richard Craine (Larry), Jordan Mott (Skee), John Viscardi (McCutcheon/Fuller)

A drama performed without intermission. The action takes place in a television news bureau in El Salvador on an early evening in January of 1981.

Wednesday, November 25, 1987–January 3, 1988 (43 performances)

ONLY YOU by Timothy Mason; Director, Ron Lagomarsino; Set, John Lee Beatty; Costumes, Ann Emonts; Stage Managers, Denise Yaney, Catherine Parrinello. CAST: Greg Germann (Leo), Julie Boyd (Miriam), Park Overall (Heather), Bruce McCarty (Eddie), Rob Gomes (Bo), Richard Seff (Big Voice)

A comedy in two acts.

Wednesday, January 27,–March 6, 1988 (46 performances)

CAVE LIFE by David Steven Rappoport; Director, Paul Lazarus; Set, William Barclay, Lighting, Phil Monat; Costumes, Nancy Konrardy; Sound, Jan Nebozenko; Choreography, Patrice Soriero; Assistant Stage Manager, Richard Craine; Technical Director, Larry Springer. CAST: Robin Bartlett (Charleston), Tom Celli (Doctor and more), Bruce McCarty (Enki), Mark Blum (Frank), Jeffrey Kearney (Augie/Benjamin/Others), Randy Danson (Sophronia/Others), Jo Henderson (Irene/Others), John Viscardi (Policeman/Others), Renee Sicignano (Nurse/Tina/Others)

A comedy in two acts. The action takes place at the present time in New York City.

Wednesday, March 23,–May 8, 1988 (55 performances)

BORDERLINES by John Bishop; Director, Robert Bailey; Set, John Lee Beatty; Assistant Stage Manager, Richard Courtney. CAST: "Borderline": Brenda Denmark (Lecturer), Cotter Smith (Charles Graham), Edward Seamon (Detective), Susan Bruce (Susan), Bruce McCarty (Dan), Sharon Schlarth (Karen), Colleen Quinn (Lee), Charles Brown (Kearney), John Viscardi (Eddie). "Keepin' an Eye on Louie" with Bruce McCarty (Dave), Charles Brown (Frank), Colleen Quinn (Angie), Joe Maruzzo (Joey), Sharon Schlarth (Judy), Cotter Smith (Psychiatrist), Brenda Denmark (Ruth), John Viscardi (Bobby Detroit), Edward Seamon (Louie)

Wednesday, May 25,–July 3, 1988 (46 performances)

V & V ONLY by Jim Leonard; Director, Marshall W. Mason; Set, John Lee Beatty; Lighting, Dennis Parichy; Costumes, Susan Denison Geller; Stage Managers, Denise Yaney, Forrest Williams; Presented in association with South Coast Repertory (David Emmes/Martin Benson, Artistic Directors). CAST: Dick Boccelli (Vito), Robert Minicucci (Tommy), Brian Tarantina (Donny), Erich Anderson (Nick), Allan Arbus (Antonio), Tresa Hughes (Raffiella), Roxann Biggs (Janey), Jordan Mott (Customer), Ben Siegler (Steinway), Understudies: Edward Seamon (Vito/Antonio), John Viscardi (Donny/Nick), Jordan Mott (Tommy/Steinway), Catherine Parrinello (Janey), Forrest Williams (Customer)

A play in two acts. The action takes place at the present time in a coffee shop in Little Italy/SoHo, New York City.

Right: Renee Sicignano, Randy Danson, Robin Bartlett, Jeffrey Kearney, Bruce McCarty, Tom Celli, Jo Henderson in "Cave Life" Above: Richard Seff, Greg Germann, Julie Boyd, Bob Gomes, Park Overall in "Only You" Top: John Dossett, Cotter Smith in "El Salvador" *(Gerry Goodstein Photos)*

Sharon Schlarth, Cotter Smith, Bruce McCarty in "Borderlines"

CLASSIC STAGE COMPANY
CSC REPERTORY, LTD.

Artistic Director, Carey Perloff; Producing Director, Carol Ostrow; Associate Artistic Director, Todd London; General Manager, Elizabeth Versalie; Production Manager, Jeffrey Berzon; Administrative Assistant, Dominique J. Cook; Casting, Ellen Novack; Press, Liz Versalie, Gary Murphy
(CSC Theatre) Monday, November 1–28, 1987 (32 performances)
ELEKTRA by Ezra Pound; In collaboration with Rudd Fleming; Based on "Elektra" by Sophocles; Director, Carey Perloff; Set, Donald Eastman; Costumes, Candice Donnelly; Lighting, Frances Aronson; Composer/Sound Design, Wayne Horvitz; Assistant to Director, Marima Kotzamani; Assistant Composer, Robin Holcomb; Musician, Marty Erlich; Stage Managers, Dara Hershman, Dominique J. Cook. CAST: Veronica Cartwright (Chrysothemis), William Duff-Griffin (Tutor), Nancy Marchand (Klytemnestra), Isabell Monk (Chorus), Joe Morton (Orestes), Lola Pashalinski (Chorus), Pamela Reed (Elektra), Jaime Sanchez (Aegisthus), Attendants: Christina Flint, Jillian Miller, Nia Lourekas, Mary Ethel Schmidt, Don Egan, Stephanie Lane, Leslie Brett Daniels, Understudies: John Aaron Bell (Orestes), Leslie Brett Daniels (Chrysothemis), Nia Lourekas (Klytemnestra), Mary Ethel Schmidt (Elektra), Mary Micari, Susan Walker (Chorus)
 Performed without intermission.
 Wednesday, December 9, 1987–January 3, 1988 (20 performances)
UNCLE VANYA by Anton Chekhov; Revised and Directed by Maria Irene Fornes; From a translation by Marian Fell; Set, Donald Eastman; Costumes, Gabriel Berry; Lighting, Jennifer Tipton; Sound, Daniel Moses Schreier; Stage Manager, Nancy Harrington. CAST: Margaret Barker (Marina), Michael O'Keefe (Astroff), Austin Pendleton (Voitski), Bill Moor (Serebrakoff), Patricia Mattick (Sonia), Alma Cuervo (Yelena), Ralph Williams (Telegin), Jen Jones (Mme. Voitskaya), Don Egan (Workman), Keith Overton (Watchman), Peasants: Christina Flint, Jillian Miller, Susan Walker
 Tuesday, April 12, 1987–
THE BIRTHDAY PARTY by Harold Pinter; Director, Carey Perloff; Set, Loy Arcenas; Costumes, Gabriel Berry; Lighting, Beverly Emmons; Sound, Daniel Moses Schreier; Dialect Coach, Nadia Venesse; Technical Director, David von Salis; Assistant to Director, Michael Sexton; Props/Wardrobe, Dominique J. Cook; Stage Managers, Maude Brickner, Bill Blank. CAST: Robert Gerringer (Petey), Georgine Hall (Meg), David Strathairn (Stanley), Wendy Makkena (Lulu), Peter Riegert (Goldberg), Richard Riehle (McCann)
 A drama in 3 acts. The action takes place in the living room of a house in an English seaside town.

(Pamela Court, Michael Tighe Photos)
**Left: David Strathairn, Peter
Riegert, Wendy Makkena in "The
Birthday Party" Top Left: Pamela
Reed, Nancy Marchand in "Ezra
Pound's Elektra"**

**Peter Riegert, David Strathairn in
"The Birthday Party"**

Pamela Reed, Joe Morton in "Elektra"

HUDSON GUILD THEATRE

Thirteenth Season

Producing Director, Geoffrey Sherman; Associate Director, James Abar; Literary Manager, Steve Ramay; Production Manager/Technical Director, John D. Tees III; Business Manager, Paul K. Hutchison; Press, Jeffrey Richards Associates/Ben Morse, Susan Chicoine, Irene Gandy, Naomi Grabel

(Hudson Guild Theatre) Wednesday, October 7,–November 1, 1987 (15 performances and 13 previews).

YEAR OF THE DUCK by Israel Horovitz; Based on Henrik Ibsen's "The Wild Duck"; Director, Fredrick Hahn; Costumes, Mimi Maxmen; Set/Lighting, Paul Wonsek; Production Assistants, Eric Winzenreid, Debbie Bedford; Props, Mimi Cohen; Stage Manager, Fredrick Hahn; Presented in association with Portland Stage Company (Barbara Rosoff, Artistic Director; Mark Somers, Managing Director) and Gloucester Stage Company (Israel Horovitz, Artistic Director). CAST: Katherine Hiler (Sophie Budd), James Huston (Harry Budd), Ann-Sara Matthews (Margaret Budd), Bernie Passeltiner (Nathan Budd), Paul O'Brien (John Sharp), Kathryn Rossetter (Rosie Norris)

A drama in 2 acts and 5 scenes. The action takes place at the present time in the Budd Family's home in Gloucester, Massachusetts.

Thursday, December 10, 1987–January 10, 1988 (29 performances and 13 previews)

THE SIGNAL SEASON OF DUMMY HOY by Allen Meyer and Michael Nowak; Director, James Abar; Set, Ron Gottschalk; Light, Paul Wonsek; Costumes, Karen Hummel; Sound, Aural Fixation; Assistant Director, John Daines; Props, Catherine Policella; Production Assistants, Debbie Bedford, Eric Winzenried; Sign Language/Deaf Culture Consultant, Alan R. Barwiolek; Stage Manager, Fredrick Hahn. CAST: Cleto Augusto (Mutt), Larry Bazzell (Dummy Hoy), Rick Carter (Tyler), Gregory Chase (Selee), Katherine Diamond (Speaker Hoy), Francois Giroday (Woodrow), James Gleason (Dooley), David Mogentale (Press), Dan Monahan (Tommy), Matthew Penn (D. S.), Ben Thomas (Judge), Nancy Travis (A. C.)

A play in two acts. The action takes place in Wisconsin in 1886.

Wednesday, February 17,–March 20, 1988 (21 performances and 6 previews)

TAPMAN by Karen Jones-Meadows; Director, Samuel P. Barton; Lighting, Paul Wonsek; Sound, Aural Fixation; Costumes, Marianne Powell-Parker; Original Incidental Music, Guy Davis; Props, Catherine Policella; Wardrobe/Props, Rider McCoy; Stage Managers, Fredrick Hahn, John P. Rice. CAST: Moses Gunn (Tapman), Seret Scott (Sherry), Merlin Santana (Keith), Dean Irby (Roscoe), Kim Hamilton (Thelma), Helmar Augustus Cooper (Flipit), Guy Davis (Lonnie), John P. Rice (Alvin/Dennis Pearson)

A drama in 2 acts and 8 scenes. The action takes place in Tapman's house in Chattanooga, Tennessee.

Wednesday, April 20,–May 15, 1988 (28 performances)

THE LOVE TALKER by Deborah Pryor; Director, Steven Ramay; Set/Lights, Paul Wonsek; Costumes, Stephanie Handler; Sound, Aural Fixation; Fight Coordinator, John Curless; Assistant Director, Nicola Sheara; Props, Michael Chudinski; Production Assistant, Elisa Rubin; Stage Manager, Fredrick Hahn. CAST: Vicki Lewis (The Red Head), Jill Tasker (Gowdie Blackmun), Laura San Giacomo (Bun Blackmun), Mark Wilson (The Love Talker)

A play without intermission. The action takes place at the present time in an old house in the Clinch Mountains of Virginia, on the longest day of the year.

Left: Moses Gunn, Seret Scott, Merlin Santana
in "Tapman" *(Bob Marshak)* Above: Larry Bazzell,
Gregory Chase, Rick Carter in "The Signal Season
of Dummy Hoy" *(Bert Andrews)* Top: James Huston,
Katherine Hiler in "Year of the Duck"
(Adam Newman Photo)

Mark Wilson, Jill Tasker, Laura San Giacomo,
Vicki Lewis in "The Love Talker" *(Bob Marshak)*

EQUITY LIBRARY THEATRE

Forty-fifth Season

Producing Director, George Wojtasik; Business Manager, Helen S. Burton; Development, Lisa Salomon; Assistant to Producing Director, Paul Gerard Wiley; Technical Director, Steven Sitler; Wardrobe, Carole Cuming; Press, Lewis Harmon (Master Theatre) Thursday, October 1,–18, 1988 (22 performances)

THE TAVERN by George M. Cohan; Suggested by Cora Dick Gantt's play "The Choice of a Super-Man"; Director, Terence Lamude; Set, Michael E. Daughtry; Costumes, Barbara Forbes; Lighting, Dennis Blaine; Sound, Tom Gould; Props, Judy Deylin; Stage Managers, Meryl S. Jacobs, Dwayne B. Perryman, Carol Lynn Tomlinson. CAST: John Abajian (Vagabond), Richard Bowden (Stevens), Charles Edward Hall (Ezra), Brian Hotaling (Tony/Movement Consultant), Patricia Hunter (Violet), Art Kempf (Freeman), Lori Ann Mahl (Sally), Robert Lee Martini (Tom Allen), Leslie Lynn Meeker (Virginia), Nicholas Saunders (Gv. Lamson), Mary Sharmat (Mrs. Lamson), David Sherrick (Sheriff), Michael Sollenberger (Willum), Don Stephenson (Zach), Alexander Webb (Joshua)

A comedy in two acts. The action takes place in Freeman's Tavern.

Thursday, October 29,–November 22, 1987 (32 performances)

KISMET with Music & Lyrics by Robert Wright, George Forrest; Based on themes of A. Borodin; Book, Charles Lederer, Luther Davis; Based on play by Edward Knoblock; Set, Jeff Modereger; Director, Russell Treyz; Choreographer, Ricarda O'Conner; Musical Director, Jeffrey Buchsbaum; Lighting, S. D. Garner; Costumes, Sue Ellen Rohrer; Dance Captain, Amelia Marshall; Wardrobe, Maureen Frey; Stage Managers, JoAnn Minsker, Michael Abbott, Brendan Smith, Kim McNutt. CAST: Philip Anderson (Silk Merchant), Rebecca Baxter (Slave Girl), Peggy Bayer (Zubbediya), Jeanne Bennett (Marriage Arranger), Matthew Chellis (Bangle Man), Andrew Cuk (Imam/Hassan-Ben), Franc D'Ambrosio (Caliph), Stephen Foster (Wazir), Tom Freeman (Fig Seller), Nancy Hughes (1st Princess of Ababu), Kenneth Kantor (Poet), Jay Keymin (Silk/Orange Merchant), Tony Lawson (Beggar/Prosecutor), Jeff Littiere (Pearl Merchant), Christine A. Maglione (2nd Princess), Amelia Marshall (Samahris), Salome Martinez (Widow Yussef), Steve Mattar (Beggar/Slave Merchant), Leilani Mickey (Lalume), Marina Mikelian (3rd Princess), Munir Nuriddin (Dancing Guard), Mark Peters (Police Chief), Alex Robeson (Omar/Jawan) Rebecca Spencer (Marsinah)

MUSICAL NUMBERS: On the Sands of Time, Rhymes Have I, Fate, Bazaar of the Caravans, Abadu Dance, Not Since Ninevah, Baubles Bangles and Beads, Stranger in Paradise, Gesticulate, Fate, Night of My Nights, Was I a Wazir?, The Olive Tree, Rahadklum, and This Is My Beloved, Zubbediya/Samahris Dance, Finale

A musical in 2 acts and 9 scenes.

Thursday, December 3–20, 1987 (22 performances)

THE GINGERBREAD LADY by Neil Simon; Director, Geoffrey C. Shlaes; Set, Shelley Barclay; Costumes, Stephen L. Bornstein; Lighting, Hakan Backstrom; Sound, Hal Schuler; Props, Karen Lee Kahn; Stage Managers, Jane Rothman, Darsell Beatrice Brittingham, Karen Lyons, Shellie Jackson. CAST: Tony Aylward (Jimmy Perry), Eric Hansen (Lou Tanner), Philip Hernandez (Manuel), Shauna Hicks (Polly), Susan Jeffries (Toby Landeau), Peggy Schoditsch (Evy)

A play in three acts. The action takes palce in a brownstone apartment in the west 70's during November of 1970.

Thursday, January 7,–31, 1988 (32 performances)

SIDE BY SIDE BY SONDHEIM a musical entertainment with Music and Lyrics by Stephen Sondheim; Director, Andrew Glant-Linden; Choreography, Karen Luschar, Andrew Glant-Linden; Musical Director, Paul L. Johnson; Continuity, Ned Sherrin; Additional Music, Leonard Bernstein, Mary Rodgers, Jule Styne; Set, Bob Phillips; Lighting, Rita Ann Kogler; Costumes, Judy Kahn; Stage Managers, Sandra M. Franck, Meryl S. Jacobs, Susan Torres. CAST: Roger Middleton (Narrator), Ann Brown, Marnie Carmichael, Paul Jackel, Alan Osburn, Jessica Sheridan, Ray Wills, At the pianos: Paul Johnson, D. J. Maloney

MUSICAL NUMBERS: Opening, You Must Meet My Wife, The Little Things You Do Together, Getting Married Today, I Remember, Can That Boy Foxtrot, I Never Do Anything Twice, Company, Another Hundred People, Barcelona, Marry Me a Little, You Could Drive a Person Crazy, Beautiful Girls, Ah Paree, Buddy's Blues, Broadway Baby, Everybody Says Don't, Anyone Can Whistle, Send in the Clowns, The Boy from . . ., A Boy Like That, We're Gonna Be All Right, If Momma Was Married, You Gotta Get a Gimmick, Pretty Lady, Losing My Mind, Could I Leave You?, I'm Still Here, Conversation Piece

Performed with one intermission.

Top Right: Robert Lee Martini, Leslie Lynn Meeker, Mary Sharmat, Nicholas Saunders, John Abajian, Art Kempf in "The Tavern" Below: "Kismet"
(Ned Snyder Photos)

Alan Osburn, Ann Brown, Ray Wills, Marnie Carmichael, Jessica Sheridan, Paul Jackel in "Side by Side. . . ." Above: Shauna Hicks, Tony Aylward, Peggy Schoditsch, Susan Jeffries in "The Gingerbread Lady"

Thursday, February 11–28, 1988 (22 performances)
THE ELEPHANT MAN by Bernard Pomerance; Director, Robert M. Nigro; Set, John Kenny; Costumes, Bruce Goodrich; Lighting, A. C. Hickox; Props, Brendan Smith; Stage Managers, Douglas Matranga, Deborah A. Niezgoda, Kim Kremer, Kathleen Williams, Yolanda McClain. CAST: Jonathan Courie (John Goodhue), Dai Kornberg (Bishop Walsham How/Belgian Policeman), Bill McElhiney (Lord John/Snork/Belgian Policeman), Allyson Meric (Cellist), Brian O'Sullivan (Ross), Verna Pierce (Mrs. Kendal), Kathleen Pirkl (Princess Alexandria/Pinhead), Jane Sanders (Miss Sandwich/Pinhead/Duchess), Mitchell Sugarman (Frederick Treves), G. Tom Swift (Pinhead Manager/Will/London Policeman/Count), Ronald Willoughby (Carr Gomm/Conductor).

A drama in two acts. The action takes place 1884–1890 in London and Belgium.

Thursday, March 10,–April 3, 1988 (32 performances)
LEAVE IT TO ME with Music and Lyrics by Cole Porter; Book, Bella and Samuel Spewack; Director, Howard Rossen; Choreography, David Storey; Musical Direction/Vocal & Dance Arrangements, James Followell; Set, David Harnish; Lighting, Alan Baron; Costumes, Claudia Stephens; Sound, Hector Milia; Props, Justine Angelis; Wardrobe, Maureen Frey, Efuru Cottle; Assistant to Director, Andrea Naler; Associate Tap Choreographer, Mary Brienza; Stage Managers, Ellen Sontag, Gerard Mawn, Diane Dolphy. CAST: Mary Ellen Ashley (Leora Goodhue), Mary Brienza (Shirley Goodhue), Gerry Burkhardt (Sozanoff), Chuck Burks (Italian Ambassador), Carrie Quinn Dolin (Decorator), Richard Farwick (Jerry Grainger), Doug Friedman (Foreign Minister), Mary-Kathleen Gordon (Ethel Goodhue), Daniel Timothy Johnson (Alonzo P. Goodhue), Robert Kerr (Prince Alexi), Caitlin Larsen (Colette), Denise LeDonne (Ruth Goodhue), Lori Lynch (Vera Goodhue), Michelle Meade (Dolly Winslow), Michael Scott (Buckley Joyce Thomas), Evan Thompson (Brody/Stalin), Glenn Trickel (German Ambassador), Vera Wagman (Graustein), Laurie Beach, Michael David Winter, Laura Zam (Scene Movers)
MUSICAL NUMBERS: We Drink to You J. H. Brody, Taking the Steps to Russia, I Want to Go Home, Get Out of Town, Most Gentlemen Don't Like Love, From Now On, From the U.S.A. to the U.S.S.R., When All Is Said and Done, Comrade Alonzo, My Heart Belongs to Daddy, The Goodhue Doctrine, Tomorrow, Far Away

A musical in 2 acts and 13 scenes, with a prologue. The action takes place in Paris and Russia.

Thursday, April 14,–May 1, 1988 (22 performances)
MUCH ADO ABOUT NOTHING by William Shakespeare; Director, Elowyn Castle; Set, Dick Block; Lighting, Stephen Petrilli; Costumes, Ben Gutierrez-Soto; Sound/Original Music, Deena Kaye; Props, Justine Angelis; Stage Managers, Rachel S. Levine, Gregg Fletcher, Yolanda McClain. CAST: Michelle Beshaw (Beatrice), Diane Ciesla (Margaret), Robert Edmonds (Conrade), Jim Fitzpatrick (Sexton), Mark Hirschfield (Don Pedro), Ken Lambert (Verges), Raye Lankford (Hero), Michael Lasswell (Claudio), Robert McFarland (Antonio), Michael McKay (Borachio), Tom Morgan (Watch), Suzen Murakoshi (Ursula), David Omar (Don John), Greg Pake (Balthazar), Herbert Mark Parker (Friar Francis), Herman Petras (Leonato), Paul Schoeffler (Benedick), Andrew Thain (Watch), Patrick Turner (Dogberry)

Performed with one intermission. The action takes place in Messina.

Thursday, May 12,–June 5, 1988 (32 performances)
NO, NO, NANETTE with Book by Otto Harbach, Frank Mandel; Music, Vincent Youmans; Lyrics, Irving Caesar, Otto Harbach; Director, Margaret Denithorne; Choreographer, Niki Harris; Musical Director, Annie Lebeaux, Set, John Shimrock; Lighting, Deborah Constantine; Costumes, Lillian Glasser; Stage Managers, Mimi Moyer, Robert Lemieux, Robin Lawford, Ben Kaplan, Craig Rhyne, Efuru Cottle CAST: Denise Ashlynd (Ensemble), Richard Blair (Jimmy Smith), Bob Bucci (Ensemble), Danette Cuming (Flora), Debra Dominiak (Winnie), Anthony Inneo (Billy Early), Diana Laurenson (Ensemble), Nicholas Leone (Ensemble), Cynthia Martells (Betty), Lisa Merrill McCord (Ensemble), Jeannine Moore (Sue Smith), Patty O'Brien (Pauline), Greg Phelps (Ensemble), Eleanor Reissa (Lucille), Jennifer Fymer (Ensemble), D. J. Salisbury (Ensemble), Dick Scanlan (Ensemble), Christopher Scott (Tom), Peggy Taphorn (Nanette), Angela Warren (Bernice)
MUSICAL NUMBERS: Too Many Rings around Rosie, I've Confessed to the Breeze, Call of the Sea, I Want to Be Happy, No No Nanette, Peach on the Beach, The Three Happies, Tea for Two, Love Me Lulu, You Can Dance with Any Girl, Telephone Girlie, Where-Has-My-Hubby-Gone Blues, Waiting for You, Take a Little One-Step, Finale

A musical in 2 acts and 3 scenes. The action takes place in 1925 in the Smith's livingroom, and in Chickadee Cottage in Atlantic City, NJ.

Top Right: "The Elephant Man" Below: Doug Friedman,
Caitlin Larsen, Robert Kerr, Chuck Burks
in "Leave It to Me"

"No, No, Nanette!" Above: Robert McFarland,
Herman Petras, Michael Lasswell in "Much Ado. . . ."

JEWISH REPERTORY THEATRE

Fourteenth Season

Artistic Director, Ran Avni; Associate Director, Edward M. Cohen; Casting, Stephanie Klapper; Press, Shirley Herz Associates/Pete Sanders, Peter Cromarty, David Roggensack, Glenna Freedman, Miller Wright

Tuesday, June 23,–July 12, 1987 (27 performances)

HALF A WORLD AWAY based on stories by Sholom Aleichem; Book, Murray Horwitz; Music, Raphael Crystal; Lyrics, Richard Engquist; Director, Ran Avni; Set, Ray Recht; Costumes, Edi Giguere; Lighting, Donald Holder; Choreography, Julie Arenal; Musical Director, Raphael Crystal; Stage Manager, D. C. Rosenberg CAST: Ivy Austin (Rochel/Beryl/Others), Susan Friedman (Reyle/Chasha/Others), Adam Heller (Heshie/Reb/Others), Michael McCormick (Herschel/Others), Kenny Morris (Moishe/Meyer/Others), Lawrence John Moss (Sholom Aleichem), Neva Small (Nemi-Rose/Others)

Saturday, Oct. 17,–Nov. 22, 1987 (20 performances)

SOPHIE with Book and Lyrics by Rose Leiman Goldemberg; Music, Debra Barsha; Director, Louis O. Erdmann; Choreography, Eugenia V. Erdmann; Set, Christian Tucker; Costumes, Marcy Froehlich; Lighting, David Weller; Sets & Props, James E. Mayo; Arrangements, Debra Barsha; Musical Director, Annie LeBeaux; Production Assistant, Wendall Hinkle; Wardrobe, Nicole Hill, Molly Davis; Stage Managers, Geraldine Teagarden, John Barilla CAST: Judith Cohen (Sophie), John Barilla (Phil/Flink), Deborah Filler (Mama/Queen), Lorraine Goodman (Anna), Adam Heller (Papa/Ziegfeld), Ernestine Jackson (Mollie), Daniel Neiden (Louie/Son), Stephen Parr (Morris Williams), Steve Sterner (Fink/Hart), Shelley Wald (Ada/Star), Rick Zieff (Ieving/Gurman/Larry/George)

MUSICAL NUMBERS: Soup, Work, Nice Girls Don't Do That, Gonna Be Somebody, Keep Movin', De Bluebells, My Man, Don't Forget Your Mama, Pushcart Sellers, Black Up, My Terms, We Still Love Her, She'll Thank Me, Playing the Part of the Maid, Sophie's Love Song, You Think It's Easy to Love Her, She's Comin' to Town, How Many, The Looka Song, Sophie's Waltz, What Do Women Want?, Baby Pictures, One Night Stands, Mollie's Song

A musical in two acts, loosely based on the life of Sophie Tucker.

Thursday, Dec. 17, 1987–Jan. 10, 1988 (20 performances)

COME BLOW YOUR HORN by Neil Simon; Director, Charles Maryan; Set, Atkin Pace; Costumes, Barbara Bush; Lighting, Brian Nason; Sound, Aaron Winslow; Production Assistant, Nancy Goodstein; Technical Director, Michael Kondrat; Stage Managers, Catherine Heusel, Arlene Mantek CAST: Mark Sawyer (Alan Baker), Susan Batten (Peggy Evans), Lonny Price (Buddy Baker), Stephen Pearlman (Mr. Baker), Julia Mueller (Connie Dayton), Chevi Colton (Mrs. Baker), Arlene Mantek (A Visitor)

A comedy in three acts. The action takes place in 1959 in Alan's bachelor apartment in the East 60's in New York City.

Thursday, Feb. 11,–March 20, 1988 (20 performances)

YARD SALE two one-act plays by Arnold Wesker; Director, Edward M. Cohen; Set, Ray Recht; Costumes, Karen Hummel; Lighting, Dan Kinsley; Sound, Laura Lampel; Wig/Hairstylist, Joe Dal Corso; Production Assistant, Paul Greenberg; Technical Director, Michael J. Kondrat; Stage Managers, D. C. Rosenberg, Geraldine Teagarden CAST: "Yard Sale" performed by Marilyn Chris. The action takes place at the present time in Brooklyn. "Whatever Happened to Betty Lemon?" performed by Marilyn Chris. The action takes place at the present time in London

Saturday, April 9,–May 8, 1988 (20 performances)

WASHINGTON HEIGHTS by Larry Cohen; Director, David Saint; Set, Chris Pickart; Costumes, Edi Giguere; Lighting, Douglas O'Flaherty; Props, Paul Carter; Stage Managers, Catherine A. Heusel, Arlene Mantek CAST: Robert Hitt (Dan), Zachariah Overton (Danny), Jeff Brooks (Al), Leah Doyle (Marcia), Martha Greenehouse (Grandma)

A comedy in two acts. The action takes place in Washington Heights, New York City, during 1940.

Martha Swope Photos

Left: Marilyn Chris in "Yard Sale" *(Carol Rosegg)*
Above: Lonny Price, Susan Batten in "Come Blow
Your Horn" *(Rebecca Lesher)* **Top: Ernestine Jackson,**
Judith Cohen in "Sophie" *(Adam Newman)*

Martha Greenhouse, Zachariah Overton
in "Washington Heights" *(Carol Rosegg)*

LIGHT OPERA OF MANHATTAN (L.O.O.M.)

Founder, William Mount-Burke; Artistic Directors, Raymond Allen, Jerry Gotham; Managing Director, Steven M. Levy; Music Director, Todd Ellison; President/Board Chairman, Jean Dalrymple; Choreographer, Jerry Gotham; Musical Consultant, Alfred Simon; Press, Jean Dalrymple, Ward Morehouse, Jack Raymond (Playhouse 91) Wednesday, June 10,–November 15, 1987 (175 performances)
GIVE MY REGARDS TO BROADWAY freely adapted from George M. Cohan's musical "Little Johnny Jones" by Raymond Allen, Todd Ellison, Jerry Gotham; Directors, Raymond Allen, Jerry Gotham; Scenery, Mina Albergo; Costumes, Christina Giannini; Lighting, Frank Meissner, Jr.; Wardrobe, Eugene Lauze, Beth Cullinane; Technical Director, Ron Hiatt; Stage Managers, Michael Dean Smith, Robert Conkling; Assistant Conductor, Brian Molloy. CAST: Raymond Allen (Mr. Wilson), Louis Baldonieri (Inspector), Mayer Bishop (Guide), Fehr Bradley (Florabelle Fly), Robert Conkling (Bell Captain/Track Announcer/Capt. Squirvy), Stephen Fleming (Sing Song), Peder Hansen (Timothy D. McGee), Mark Henderson (Officer), Susan Davis Holmes (Mary Dugan), Bruce MacKillip (Anthony Anstey), Millie Petroski (Mrs. Annette Kenworth), Brian Quinn (Johnny Jones), Kristopher Shaw (Henry Hapgood), Ensemble: Louis Baldonieri, Mayer Bishop, Sheila Clark, Deena Felice, Trisha Gorman, Lucy H. Hallock, Mark Henderson, Joanne McHugh, Elisabeth Miller, Michael Novin, Len Pfluger, Paul Phinney, Swings: Eugene Lauze, Paula Marie Seniors, Helmut Steibl, Gwendolyn Thorne
MUSICAL NUMBERS: The Cecil in London Town, They're All My Friends, I Want You, I'm Just a Mademoiselle, 'Op in Me 'Ansom, New Yorkers, Here at the Derby, Yankee Doodle Dandy, All Aboard, Captain of a Ten Day Boat, Goodbye Flo, Trio, Life's a Funny Proposition, A Girl I Know, Give My Regards to Broadway, Why Is There a Sunrise, Mary, Finale
A musical in 2 acts and 4 scenes. The action takes place in London and New York.
Wednesday, Nob. 25, 1987–Jan. 3, 1988 (45 performances)
BABES IN TOYLAND by Victor Herbert; Cast and credits not submitted.
Wednesday, Jan. 6,–Feb. 14, 1988 (42 performances)
THE MERRY WIDOW by Franz Lehar; Lyrics, Alice Hammerstein Mathias; Directors, Raymond Allen, Jerry Gotham; Scenery, Elouise Meyer; Costumes, George Stinson; Lighting/Technical Director, Ellen Kurrelmeyer; Wardrobe, Eugene Lauze, Stacey Ursta. CAST: Raymond Allen (Baron Popoff), Marla Cahan (Zozo), Paul Chisolm (Marquis de Cascada), Bob Cuccioli (Count Danilo), Mark Henderson (Waiter), Susan Davis Holmes (Natalie Popoff), Penny Jay (Olga), Russ Jones (Raoul de Saint Brioche), Jeff Kozel (Khadja), Igor Milich (Nova Kovitch), William Monnen (Camille de Jolidon), Liz Nolan (Mme. Khajda), Bill Partlow (Nish), Kathryn Radcliffe (Sonia), Ensemble: Carla Ardito, Mark Henderson, Jeff Kozel, Dorothy Kubiak, Stephanie Lynn Lubroth, Rob Marrone, Igor Milich, Andrew Moore, Liz Nolan, Len Pfluger, Barbara Rotter, Kerri Anne Spellman, Swings: Fehr Bradley, Lucy Hallock, Elisabeth Miller, Tom Sinibaldi, Richard Schwartz, Chuck Bricker
An operetta in three acts.
Wednesday, February 17,–March 13, 1988 (28 performances)
THE MIKADO by W. S. Gilbert (Book) and Arthur Sullivan (Music); Directors, Raymond Allen, Jerry Gotham; Musical Director, Todd Ellison; Costumes, George Stinson; Wardrobe, Deborah Anderko, Stacey Ursta; Stage Managers, Chris A. Kelly, David G. O'Connell. CAST: Joel Saeks (Mikado), David Thomas Hampson (Nanki-Poo), John Bonk (Ko-Ko), Bill Partlow (Pooh-Bah), Steve Rove (Pish-Tush), Margaret Astrup (Yum-Yum), Anne Jacobsen (Pitti-Sing), Stephanie Lynn Lubroth (Peep-Bo), Antonia Garza (Katisha), Ensemble: Carla Ardito, Paul Chisolm, Shawn Davis, Russ Jones, Jeff Kozel, Robert Marrone, Igor Milich, Liz Nolan, Len Pfluger, Barbara Rotter, Richard Schwartz, Kerrianne Spellman, Janet Wurst, Swings: Hamilton Fong, Penny Jay, Elisabeth Miller, Andrew Moore
An operetta in two acts.
Wednesday, March 16,–April 10, 1988 (28 performances)
THE DESERT SONG by Sigmund Romberg (Music); Book and Lyrics, Otto Harbach, Oscar Hammerstein II, Frank Mandel; Directors, Raymond Allen, Jerry Gotham; Sets, Elouise Meyer; Lighting, Peggy Clark; Costumes, James Nadeau; Stage Managers, Chrs A. Kelly, David G. O'Connell. CAST: David Thomas Hampson (Sid El Kar), Joe Saeks (Mindar), Jeff Kozel (Hassi), Hans Tester (Pierre Birabeau/The Red Shadow), John J. Bonk (Benjamin Kidd), Jon Brothers (Capt. Paul Fontaine), Richard Schwartz (Lt. La Vergne), Raymond Allen (Gen. Birabeau), Richard Bellazin (Ali Ben Ali), Marla Cahan (Azuri), Siobhan Marshall (Susan), Kathryn Radcliffe (Margot Bonvalet), Ensemble: Scott Britton, Alison Byrne, Paul Chisolm, Jeff Constan, Shawn Davis, Hamilton Fong, Kathryn Haggard, Stephanie Lynn Lubroth, Elisabeth Miller, Steve Mulch, Barbara Rotter, Catherine Ruivivar, Janet Wurst, Swings: Carla Ardito, Carl Cavalier, Penny Jay, Steven Levy, Rob Marrone, Barbara Rouse
An operetta in 2 acts and 7 scenes.

Wednesday, April 13,–May 1, 1988 (21 performances)
H.M.S. PINAFORE by W. S. Gilbert (Lyrics) and Arthur Sullivan (Music); Directors, Raymond Allen, Jerry Gotham; Set, Daniel Aronson; Lighting, Mary Edith Jamison; Men's Costumes, Bradford Wood; Women's Costumes, Deborah Anderko; Hats, Mari O'Connor; Stage Managers, Chris A. Kelly, David G. O'Connell. CAST: Irma Rogers (Buttercup), Eric Armstrong (Boatswain), Richard Bellazzin (Dick Deadeye), Bobby Harris (Ralph Rackstraw), Walter Hook (Capt. Corcoran), Mary Setrakian (Josephine), Raymond Allen (Rt. Hon. Sir Joseph Porter), Liz Nolan Hebe), Chorus: Barry Austin, Carl Cavalier, Jeff Constan, Shawn Davis, Stephen Field, Catherine Haggard, Penny Jay, Jennifer A. Jordan, Jeff Kozel, Marvin J. Kugler, Stephen Lynn Lubroth, Robert V. Marrone, Elana Polin, Barbara Rotter, Bruce Tilley, Jamet Wurst, Swings: Hamilton Fong, Elisabeth Miller, Steve Mulch, Barbara Rouse, Richard Schwartz
An operetta in two acts.
Wednesday, May 4,–May 29, 1988 (28 performances)
NAUGHTY MARIETTA by Victor Herbert. Cast and credits not submitted.

Top Right: Liz Nolan, Bill Partlow
in "Babes in Toyland" *(Michael F. Donadio)*
Below: "Babes in Toyland"

Above: Kathryn Radcliffe, Hans Tester
in "The Desert Song"

89

LINCOLN CENTER THEATER

Third Season

Director, Gregory Mosher; Executive Producer, Bernard Gersten; General Manager, Steven C. Callahan; Company Manager, Lynn Landis; Resident Director, Jerry Zaks; Special Projects, Laura Jones; Casting, Risa Bramon/Billy Hopkins; Casting Director, Lisa Peterson; Assistant to Mr. Mosher, Becky Browder; Production Manager, Jeff Hamlin; Assistant to Executive Producer, Carol Ochs; Wardrobe, Helen Toth; Press, Merle Debuskey, Robert W. Larkin, William Schelble, Bruce Sherwood, Leo Stern

(Mitzi E. Newhouse Theater) Friday, July 10,–August 9, 1987 (34 performances)

THE REGARD OF FLIGHT
and
The Clown Bagatelles

Written by Bill Irwin in collaboration with The Company and Nancy Harrington; Original Music, Doug Skinner; Set, Douglas O. Stein; Lighting, Robert W. Rosentel; Stage Managers, Nancy Harrington, Scott Allison

CAST

Bill Irwin
M. C. O'Connor
Doug Skinner

An "entertainment" performed without intermission.
(Mitzi E. Newhouse Theater) Friday, Sept. 25, 1987–Jan. 3, 1988 (81 performances and 36 previews) Moved Tuesday, Jan. 19, 1988 to the Cort Theatre, and still playing there on May 31, 1988.

Bill Irwin (also left center)

(Mitzi E. Newhouse) Saturday, December 26, 1987–January 3, 1988 (10 performances/limited engagement). Lincoln Center Theater (Gregory Mosher, Director/Bernard Gersten, Executive Producer) and The National Theater of the Deaf (David Hays, Artistic Director) presents:
A CHILD'S CHRISTMAS IN WALES: *Introduction* by the Company; Director, Adrian Blue/*Three Poems* by E. E. Cummings; Director, David Hays/*The Night the Bed Fell* by James Thurber; Director, Ed Waterstreet/*Ghost Story* by the Company; Director, Chuck Baird/*A Child's Christmas in Wales* by Dylan Thomas; Director, Ed Waterstreet/*Your Game* improvisation by the Company; Director, Betty Beekman; Costumes, Fred Boelpel; Set, David Hays; Stage Manager, Fred Noel
CAST: Adrian Blue, Elena Blue, Lewis Merkin, Edward Porter, Chaz Struppmann
    A theatrical collage of poems and sketches.

"A Child's Christmas in Wales"

SARAFINA!

Conceived, Written and Directed by Mbongeni Ngema; Music Composed and Arranged by Mbongeni Ngema, Hugh Masekela; Set/Costumes, Sarah Roberts; Lighting, Mannie Manim; Sound, Tom Sorce; Conductor/Additional Choreography, Ndaba Mhlongo; Production Assistant, Monique Martin; Company Manager, Mali Hlatshwayo; Production Consultant, Duma Ndlovu; Stage Managers, Melanie Dobbs, Bruce Hoover, Jerry Cleveland

CAST

Pat Mlaba (Colgate), Lindiwe Dlamini (Teaspoon), Dumisani Dlamini (Crocodile), Congo Hadebe (Silence), Nhlanhla Ngema (Stimela Sase-Zola), Nhlathi Khuzwayo (S'Ginci), Leleti Khumalo (Sarafina), Baby Cele (Mistress It's a Pity), Other Students: Khumbuzile Dlamini, Ntomb'Khona Dlamini, Lindiwe Hlengwa, Zandile Hlengwa, Sibiniso Khumalo, Cosmas Mahlaba, Thandani Mavimbela, Nonhlanhla Mbambo, Linda Mchunu, Mubi Mofokeng, Nandi Ndlovu, Thandekile Nhlanhla, Pumi Shelembe, Kipizane Skweyiya, Thandi Zulu and Musicians: Amos Mathibe, Eddie Nathibe (Keyboards), Makate Peter Mofolo, Ray Molefe (Trumpets), Douglas Mnisi (Lead Guitar), Bruce Mwandla (Drums), S'Manga Nhlebela (Bass)
MUSICAL NUMBERS: Overture, It's Finally Happening, Do You See What I See?, Sarafina, The Lord's Prayer, Yes! Mistress It's a Pity, Give Us Power, What Is the Army Doing in Soweto?, Nkosi Sikeleli'Afrika, Freedom Is Coming Tomorrow, Excuse Me Baby Please If You Don't Mind Baby Thank You, Talking about Love, Meeting Tonight, We Are Guerrillas, Uyamemeza Ungoma, We Will Fight for Our Land, Mama, Sechaba, The Nation Is Dying, Kilimanjaro, Africa Burning in the Sun, Stimela Sasezola, It's All Right, Bring Back Nelson Mandela, Wololo!
   A South African musical in two acts.
(Mitzi E. Newhouse Theater) Monday, February 29,–May 29, 1988 (103 performances and 28 previews) The Atlantic Theater Company production of:
BOYS' LIFE by Howard Korder; Director, W. H. Macy; Set, James Wolk; Costumes, Donna Zakowska; Lighting, Steve Lawnick; Sound, Aural Fixation; Original Music, David Yazbek; Production Manager, Jeff Hamlin; General Manager, Steve C. Callahan; Assistant Director, Kristen Johnson; Props, Kate Conklin; Stage Manager, Thomas A. Kelly CAST: Jordan Lage (Don), Steven Goldstein (Phil), Clark Gregg (Jack), Mary McCann (Karen), Todd Weeks (Man), Felicity Huffman (Maggie), Melissa Bruder (Lisa), Robin Spielberg (Girl), Theo Cohan (Carla)
   A comedy in two acts. The action takes place in a large city at the present time over the course of a year.
(Royale Theatre) Opened Tuesday, May 3, 1988*

LINCOLN CENTER THEATER

ANYTHING GOES

Music & Lyrics, Cole Porter; Original Book, Guy Bolton, P. G. Wodehouse, Howard Lindsay, Russell Crouse; New Book, Timothy Crouse, John Weidman; Settings & Costumes, Tony Walton; Lighting, Paul Gallo; Musical Director, Edward Strauss; Orchestrations, Michael Gibson; Dance Arrangements, Tom Fay; Sound, Tony Meola; Choreography, Michael Smuin; Assistant, Kirk Peterson; Production Manager, Jeff Hamlin; General Manager, Steven C. Callahan; Company Manager, Lynn Landis; Assistant Director, Lori Steinberg; Props, C. J. Simpson, Richard Harty, Joseph Loglisci, William Muller, Edward Rausenberger; Wardrobe, Joseph Busheme, Don Brassington; Associate Conductor, Joshua Rosenblum; Cast Album by RCA; Hairstylist, David H. Lawrence; Wigs, Paul Huntley; Stage Managers, George Darveris, Chet Leaming, Leslie Loeb; Dance Captain, Alice Anne Oakes. Opened in the Vivian Beaumont Theater on Monday, Oct. 19, 1987.*

CAST

Louie	Eric Y. L. Chan
Elisha Whitney	Rex Everhart
Fred/Quartet	Steve Steiner
Billy Crocker	Howard McGillin
Reno Sweeney	Patti LuPone†
Young Girl	Michele Pigliavento
Sailor	Alec Timmerman
Captain	David Pursley
Purser	Gerry Vichi
Reporter #1	Robert Kellett
Photographer	Gerry McIntyre
Reporter #2/Quartet	Larry Cahn
Purity	Daryl Richardson
Chastity	Barbara Yeager
Charity	Maryellen Scilla
Virtue	Jane Lanier
Minister	Richard Korthaze
Luke	Stanford Egi
John	Toshi Toda
Hope Harcourt	Kathleen Mahony-Bennett
Mrs. Evangeline Harcourt	Anne Francine
Lord Evelyn Oakleigh	Anthony Heald
G-Man #1/Quartet	Dale Hensley
G-Man #2/Quartet	Leslie Feagan
Erma	Linda Hart
Moonface Martin	Bill McCutcheon
Woman in bathchair	Jane Seaman
Her Niece	Alice Anne Oakes
Countess	Pat Gorman
Thuggish Sailors	Mark Chmiel, Dan Fletcher, Lacy Darryl Phillips, Lloyd Culbreath

MUSICAL NUMBERS: I Get a Kick Out of You, No Cure Like Travel, Bon Voyage, You're the Top, Easy to Love, I Want to Row on the Crew, Sailors' Chantey, Friendship, It's Delovely, Anything Goes, Public Enemy #1, Blow Gabriel Blow, Goodbye Little Dream Goodbye, Be Like the Bluebird, All through the Night, The Gypsy in Me, Buddie Beware

A musical in 2 acts and 13 scenes. The action takes place on board a passenger ship in the Atlantic Ocean.

*Still playing May 31, 1988. "Tonys" were awarded for Best Revival, Choreography, and Featured Actor in a Musical (Bill McCutcheon)

†Linda Hart during vacation for Miss LuPone.

Brigitte Lacombe Photos

**Top Right: Bill McCutcheon, Linda Hart, Kathleen
Mahony-Bennett, Howard McGillin, Patti LuPone,
Anthony Heald, Anne Francine, Rex Everhart in finale
Below: Kathleen Mahony-Bennett, Howard McGillin**

**Anthony Heald, Bill McCutcheon, Patti LuPone
Above: Bill McCutcheon, Linda Hart**

(MITZI E. NEWHOUSE THEATRE) Friday, February 5–May 29, 1988 (28 previews and 103 performances).
BOYS' LIFE by Howard Korder; Director, W. H. Macy; Sets, James Wolk; Costumes, Donna Zakowska; Lighting, Steve Lawnick; Sound, Aural Fixation; Music, David Yazbek; Production Manager, Jeff Hamlin; General Manager, Steve C. Callahan; Press, Merle Debuskey; Stage Manager, Thomas A. Kelly. CAST: Jordan Lage (Don), Steve Goldstein (Phil), Clark Gregg (Jack), Mary McCann (Karen), Todd Weeks (Man), Felicity Huffman (Maggie), Melissa Bruder (Lisa), Robin Spielberg (Girl), Theo Cohan (Carla). *Understudies:* Robert Bella, Karen Kohlhaas, Robert S. Ostrovsky, Neil Pepe

A play in 2 acts. The action takes place in the present, at various intervals over the course of a year.

Jordan Lage, Clark Gregg, Steven Goldstein

Clark Gregg, Steven Goldstein, Jordan Lage, Melissa Bruder in "Boys' Life"

SPEED-THE-PLOW

By David Mamet; Director, Gregory Mosher; Presented by Lincoln Center Theater (Gregory Mosher, Director; Bernard Gersten, Executive Producer); Set, Michael Merritt; Costumes, Nan Cibula; Lighting, Kevin Rigdon; Production Manager, Jeff Hamlin; General Manager, Steven C. Callahan; Company Managers, Helen V. Meier, Lynn Landis, Edward Nelson; Wardrobe, Mark Burchard; Props, Kate Conklin; Hairstylist, Debi Mazar; Production Assistant, William Wrubel; Stage Managers, Thomas A. Kelly, Charles Kindl. Opened in the Royale Theatre on Tuesday, May 3, 1988.*

CAST

Bobby Gould	....	Joe Mantegna[†1]
Charlie Fox	....	Ron Silver[†2]
Karen	....	Madonna[†3]

Understudies: David Berman, Farryl Lovett

A play in three acts with one intermission. The action takes place at the present time in Gould's office, and his home in Los Angeles, California.

*Closed Dec. 31, 1988 after 278 performances and 24 previews. Ron Silver received a "Tony" for Leading Actor in a Play.

†Succeeded by: 1. David Rasche. 2. Bob Balaban. 3. Felicity Huffman

Brigitte Lacombe Photos

Joe Mantegna, Madonna, Ron Silver
(also above)

MANHATTAN PUNCH LINE

Nineth Season

Artistic Director, Steve Kaplan; Executive Director, Craig Bowley; Associate Artistic Director, Elizabeth Margid; Development, Kristine Niven; Production Manager, Karla Rawicz-Morley; Press, Chris Boneau; Casting, David Tochterman.

(Judith Anderson Theatre) Friday, November 6,–December 6, 1987 (16 performances and 8 previews)

FUN by Howard Korder; Director, W. H. Macy; Set, James Wolk; Lighting, Steve Lawnick; Costumes, Michael S. Schler; Sound Aural Fixation; Original Music, David Yazbek; Assistant Director, Robert Bella; Props, H. Shep Pamplin; Production Assistant, Kate Haggerty; Stage Managers, John F. Sullivan, Jamie Martin. CAST: Act I-Fun: Tim Ransom (Denny), Rick Lawless (Casper), Andrew Winkler (Guard), Eden Alair (Waitress), Clark Gregg (Matthew), Jim McDonnell (Larry), David Jaffe (Workman) Act II-Nobody: John Christopher Jones (Carl), Frank Hamilton (Walter), Beth McDonald (Cathy), Michael Hume (Ted), Sophie Hayden (Jeanette), Tim Ransom (Denny), Vasili Bogazianos (Jim/Worker), David Jaffe (Bobby/Psychiatrist), Jim McDonnell (Salesman), Joseph Jamrog (Supervisor/Bartender)

A comedy in two acts. The action takes place in and around Roberson City, an Industrial town in the Northeastern United States.

Friday, February 5,–March 20, 1988 (48 performances)

FESTIVAL OF ONE ACT PLAYS: two programs of original plays/Fourth Annual Festival. Technical Director, James Manning; Scenery, Stanley A. Meyer; Lighting, Joseph R. Morley; Costumes, Don Newcomb (Program A), Michael S. Schler (Program B); Sound, Robert Passaretti; Casting, Jay Binder; Fight Choreography, Rick Sordelet; Stage Managers, Barbara Moore (A), Sandra Franck (B). CAST: *Program A:* "The Everafters" by Kenn Adams; Music, Douglas J. Cohen; Director, Robert Jess Roth; Stage Manager, Barbara Lynn Rice; with Laura McDuffie (Happy), Guy Paul (Cheerful), Mary Testa (Rhonda), Veanne Cox (Cynthia), Vicki Lewis (Millie), Kevin Seal (Danny). "Perfect" by Mary Gallagher; Director, Melia Bensussen; Stage Manager, Eileen H. Kim; with Janet Zarish (Tina), Keith Langsdale (Dan), Mary Testa (Kitty). "Johnny Business" by Mark O'Donnell; Director, Laurence Maslon; Music Director, Kathrin King Segal; with Ed Barrett (Johnny), Jack Wallace (Storyteller), James O'Hare (Miner), Marceline Hugot (Ma Bell), Kathrin King Segal, Nancy Giles (Agents). "Oh Baby Oh Baby" by Terri Wagener; Director, Peter Wallace; Stage Manager, Lisa Contadino; with Marita Geraghty (She), Guy Paul (He). "Art for Art's Sake" by David Misch; Director, Steve Kaplan; Assistant Director, Alexa Junge; with Keith Langsdale (Guy), Jack Wallace (Blake), Alan Pottinger (Steve), Veanne Cox (Maggie), William Mooney (Art), Marita Geraghty (Julie), Kathrin King Segal (Jane). *Program B:* "Sure Thing" by David Ives; Director, Jason Buzas; Stage Manager, Carl Gonzalez; with Nancy Opal (Betty), Robert Stanton (Bill). "Where She Went, What She Did" by Laura Cunningham; Director, Elizabeth Margid; Assistant Director, Tim Cantrell; Stage Manager, Richard Allen; with Donna Murphy (Celia), George Curley (Mack), David Chandler (Doleman), Tony Shalhoub (Citrone). "Women and Football" by Bill Bozzone; Director, Robin Saex; Stage Manager, Edwin Figueroa; Assistant Director, Roland Menchell; with Phoebe Cates (Rosaria), Lisa Maurer (Kiki), Thomas Calabro (Vinnie). "Best Half Foot Forward" by Peter Tolan; Director, Charles Karchmer; Stage Manager, Deborah Natoli; with Robert Stanton (Patrick), Dan Butler (Peter), Tim Carhart (Martin), Michael Heintzman (Dave)

Saturday, April 23,–May 22, 1988 (24 performances)

TERRY BY TERRY by Mark Leib; Director, Mark Brokaw; Set, Derek McLane; Lighting, David Noling; Costumes, Michael S. Schler; Sound, Michael Cohen; Production Manager, Cheryl Rave; Props, Karen S. Friedman; Technical Director, Tom Shilhanek; Wardrobe, Kate Haggerty; Casting, Jeffery Passero; Stage Manager, Lisa Buxbaum. CAST: "Terry Won't Talk" with Tamara Jenkins (Suzy), Stephen Rowe (Chester), Leslie Lyles (Mrs. Blade), Richard Grusin (Mr. Blade), Michael Kelly Boone (Terry), Tessie Hogan (Mrs. Monus/Mrs. Proxy), Emily Houpt (Kathy), John Lynch (George), Ead Daniels (Siggy), Terrence Caza (Principal), Act II "Terry Rex" with Tracey Ellis (Kathy), Miles Chapin (Terry), Mary Gordon Murray (Adrienne), Michael Wetmore (Wheeler)

Top Left: Tim Ransom, John Christopher Jones in "Fun" *(Carol Rosegg)*

Miles Chapin in "Terry by Terry"
(Carol Rosegg Photo)

MOSAIC THEATRE

First Season

Artistic Director, Michael Posnick; Managing Director, Melissa Davis; Operations Coordinator, Evanne Marie Christian; Technical Director, Mark Lorenzen; Development, Norman Golden; Literary Manager, Jayme Koszyn; Administrative Assistant, Arlene Appel Kleinberg; Press, Fred Nathan Co./Marc Thibodeau

(92nd Street Y Theatre) Saturday, October 17,–November 22, 1987 (32 performances). Mosaic Theatre presents A Traveling Jewish Theatre in:

BERLIN, JERUSALEM AND THE MOON created and performed by Corey Fischer, Albert Louis Greenberg, Naomi Newman; Director, Michael Posnick; Lighting/Set, David Brune; Masks and Puppets, Corey Fischer; Costumes, Eliza Chugg; Dramaturg, Susan Griffin; Percussionist, Christopher F. Nappi.

Performed without intermission.

Saturday, December 12, 1987–January 18, 1988 (32 performances)

ACTS OF FAITH by Marilyn Felt; Director, William Foeller; Set/Costumes, Ray Kluga; Lighting, Dave Feldman; Sound, Craig Van Tassel; Casting, Ellen Novack; Stage Manager, Linda Carol Young. CAST: Patricia Norcia (Barbara), Mark Zeisler (Ahmed), Andre Noujaim (Offstage Voice)

A play in two acts. The action takes place at the present time in the upstairs passenger cabin of a 747.

Saturday, February 13,–March 27, 1988 (39 performances)

ESTHER: A VAUDEVILLE MEGILLAH written, composed and directed by Liz Swados; Narration based on Elie Wiesel's Purim lecture "Beauty and Commitment"; Set, Ray Kluga; Costumes, Edi Giguere; Lighting, Jeffrey McRoberts; Magic, Charles Reynolds; Musical Director, Jonny Bowden; Percussion, Jim LeBlanc; Stage Managers, Greg Johnson, Linda Carol Young. CAST: Robert Ott Boyle (King Ahashuerus), Peter Herber (Mordechai), Louis Padilla (Haman), Laura Patinkin (Esther), Nancy Ringham (Narrator/Ethyl), Frederique S. Walker (Narrator/Lucy)

Performed without intermission. The action takes place at Purim.

Saturday, April 9,–May 16, 1988 (32 performances)

ROSENFELD'S WAR by Gus Weill; Director, Terry Knickerbocker; Dramaturg, Leon Katz; Original Music, Peter Golub; Set/Projection Design, Ray Kluga; Costumes, Deborah Rooney; Lighting, Dave Feldman; Sound, Aural Fixation; Production Assistant, Jill Cordle; Wardrobe, John James Hickey; Props, Jessica Goodman; Stage Manager, Linda Carol Young. CAST: Chris Baskous (Congressman Allen/Herman Goering), Maggie Burke (Helen Hayes/Eleanor Roosevelt), Helmar Augustus Cooper (Fiorello LaGuardia/Quentin Reynolds), Cynthia Hanson (Narrator/Mrs. Agnes Waters), Frank Licato (Franklin D. Roosevelt/Father Coughlin), Michael Ornstein (Frances H. Kennicut/Dr. Benno Cohen), Gary Swanson (Fritz Rosenfelder/Joe E. Brown), Richard Thomsen (Narrator/Capt. Schroeder)

A play performed without intermission. The action takes place in the United States of America during 1939.

Lower Left: Albert Greenberg, Corey Fischer, Naomi Newman, and above: Naomi Newman, Corey Fischer in "Berlin, Jerusalem and the Moon" *(Chris Fesler)*
Top: Peter Herber, Nancy Ringham, Louis Padilla, Frederique S. Walker, Robert Ott Boyle, Laura Patinkin in "Esther: A Vaudeville Megillah"
(Peter Cunningham Photos)

Mark Zeisler, Sofia Landon in "Acts of Faith"

Richard Thomsen (Left) in "Rosenfeld's War"

MANHATTAN THEATRE CLUB

Sixteenth Season

Artistic Director, Lynne Meadow; Managing Director, Barry Grove; Series Director Stage II, Jonathan Alper; General Manager, Victoria Bailey; Artistic Associates, Jonathan Alper, Michael Bush; Design Associate, John Lee Beatty; Literary Associate, Tom Szentgyorgyi; Casting, Lyons/Isaacson, Randy Carrig; Production Manager, Michael R. Moody; Technical Director, Betsy Tanner; Costumer, MaryAnn D. Smith; Props, Shelley Barclay; Press, Helene Davis, Leisha H. DeHart, Linda Feinberg

(City Center Stage (II) Tuesday, October 6–25, 1987 (24 performances)
TEA by Velina Hasu Houston; director, Julianne Boyd; Set, Wing Lee; Costumes, C. L. Hundley; Lighting, Greg MacPherson; Sound, Bruce Ellman; Stage Manager, Renee F. Lutz. CAST: Patti Yasutake (Himiko Hamilton), Takayo Fischer (Setsuko Banks), Lily Mariye (Teruko Machelli), Natsuko Ohama (Atsuko Yamamoto), Jeanne Mori (Chizuye Juarez)

Performed in 5 scenes and a prelude without intermission. The action takes place in 1968 in the home of Himiko Hamilton in Junction City, Kansas, and an obscure netherworld in which time moves at will.

(City Center Stage I) Wednesday, October 14,–November 29, 1987 (48 performances)
FRANKIE AND JOHNNY IN THE CLAIR DE LUNE by Terrence McNally; Director, Paul Benedict; Set, James Noone; Costumes, David Woolard; Lighting, David Noling; Sound, John Gromada; Stage Managers, Pamela Singer, Craig Palanker; Wardrobe, Sonia D'Angelo; Production Assistant, Sarah Faler CAST: Kathy Bates (Frankie), Kenneth Welsh (Johnny)

A play in two acts. The action takes place at the present time in frankie's one-room apartment in a walk-up tenement in the West 50's.

(City Center Stage II) Tuesday, November 10–29, 1987 (24 performances)
ONE TWO THREE FOUR FIVE a musical work-in-progress; Book, Larry Gelbart; Music and Lyrics, Maury Yeston; Director, Gerald Gutierrez; Musical Direction, Tom Fay; Choreography Consultant, Jerry Mitchell; Design Consultant, James D. Sandefur; Lighting, Michael R. Moody; Wardrobe, Deanna Majewski; Production Assistant, David Tager; Stage Managers, Ed Fitzgerald, Donna A. Drake CAST: Neal Ben-Ari, Liz Callaway, Mary Chesterman, Jon Ehrlich, Davis Gaines, Jonathan Hadary, Ann Harada, James Judy, Linda Kerns, Vicki Lewis, Mary Gordon Murray, Alice Playten, Lewis J. Stadlen, Beatrice Winde, William Youmans

(City Center Stage I) Tuesday, Dec. 8, 1987–Jan. 17, 1988 (48 performances)
THE DAY ROOM by Don DeLillo; Director, Micheal Blakemore; Set/Costumes, Hayden Griffin; Lighting, Natasha Katz; Sound, Jan Nebozenko; Props, Lisa Davies; Wardrobe, Teresa Purcell; Stage Managers, Trey Hunt, Liz Sherman. CAST: Mason Adams (Budge/Arno Klein), Timothy Carhart (Dr. Phelps/Gary), Martha Gehman (Orderly/Maid), Mary Beth Hurt (Nurse Walker/Lynette), John Christopher Jones (TV/Wyatt), Michele Shay (Nurse Baker/Jolene), John Spencer (Grass/Freddie), Eric Swanson (Orderly/Desk Clerk), J. T. Walsh (Dr. Bazelon/Manville). Understudies: Martha Gehman (Lynette), Michael M. Thompson (Budge/Arno/Freddie/Clerk), Beverly Mickins (Nurse Baker/Maid/Orderly), James Harper (Wyatt/Manville)

A comedy in two acts.

(City Center Stage I) Tuesday, February 2,–March 20, 1988 (56 performances)
WOMAN IN MIND by Alan Ayckbourn; Director, Lynne Meadow; Set, John Lee Beatty; Costumes, Ann Roth; Lighting, Pat Collins; Sound, John Gromada; Assistant to Director, Christopher Ashley; Dialect Coach, Tim Monich; Props, Denise Waggoner; Wardrobe, Teresa Purcell; Production Assistant, Tim Lile; Stage Managers, Ed Fitzgerald, Tom Capps. CAST: Stockard Channing (Susan), Patricia Conolly (Muriel), Michael Countryman (Tony), John David Cullum (Rick), Daniel Gerroll (Andy), Simon Jones (Bill), Tracy Pollan (Lucy), Remak Ramsay (Gerald)

A play in 2 acts and 4 scenes. The action takes place within 48 hours in Susan's garden and beyond.

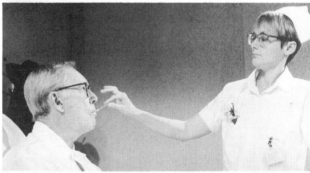

Right lower center: Mason Adams, Mary Beth Hurt in "The Day Room" Above: Kathy Bates, Kenneth Welsh in "Frankie and Johnny in the Clair de Lune" Top: Takayo Fischer, Patti Yasutake in "Tea"
(Gerry Goodstein Photos)

Daniel Gerroll, Stockard Channing, Michael Countryman, Tracy Pollan in "Woman in Mind"

(City Center Stage II) Tuesday, March 15,–April 3, 1988 (24 performances)
APRIL SNOW by Romulus Linney; Director, David Esbjornson; Set, Hugh Landwehr; Costumes, C. L. Hundley; Lighting, Greg MacPherson; Sound, Lia Vollack; Fight Consultant, Glynn Borders; Wardrobe, Peter Mannion; Production Assistant, Mary Hartman; Stage Managers, Renee F. Lutz, Richard Hester CAST: Sloane Shelton (Grady Gunn), Kent Broadhurst (Lucien Field), Linda Atkinson (Claire Dryer), Eddie Jones (Gordon Tate), Cordelia Richards (Selma Perch/Millicent Beck), Brendan Corbalis (Tony Beck/Bill Jones)

A play in two acts. The action takes place on a Saturday in April of 1980's in two lofts in SoHo in New York City.

(City Center Stage I) Tuesday, March 29,–May 8, 1988 (47 performances)
EMILY by Stephen Metcalfe; Director, Gerald Gutierrez; Set, Heidi Landesman; Costumes, Ann HouldWard; Lighting, Pat Collins; Sound, Scott Lehrer; Hairstylist, Phyllis Della; Assistant to Director, Marlene Hodgden; Props, Denise Waggoner; Wardrobe, Deanna Majewski; Production Assistant, Rachel Evans; Stage Managers, Dianne Trulock, Donna A. Drake. CAST: Lisa Banes (Emily), James Eckhouse (Jason/Stein/Others), Patricia Englund (Dierdre/Others), Dave Florek (Sean/McCarthy/Others), Jack Kenny (Fields/Others), Heather MacRae (Hallie/Others), Donald May (Hugh/Others), Robert Stanton (Hill/Others), Standby: Pat Nesbit (Emily)

A play in two acts.

(City Center Stage II) Tuesday, April 26,–May 15, 1988 (24 performances)
THE DEBUTANTE BALL by Beth Henley; Director, Norman Rene; Set, Loy Arcenas; Costumes, Walker Hicklin; Lighting, Debra Kletter; Sound, Joshua Starbuck; Fight Consultant, Glynn Gorders; Props, Wendy Cross; Wardrobe, Peter Mannion; Stage Managers, Mary Fran Loftus, Laura Gewurz. CAST: Carol Kane (Bliss White), Bruce Norris (Brighton Parker), Kellie Overbey (Teddy), Adina Porter (Violet Moone), Mary C. Vreeland (Frances Walker), Ann Wedgeworth (Jen Dugan Parker), Trey Wilson (Hank Turner)

A play in two acts. The action takes place in Hattiesburg, Mississippi, in the autumn.

(City Center Stage I) Wednesday, May 18,–June 26, 1988 (48 performances)
URBAN BLIGHT based on an idea by John Tillinger; Scenes contributed by John Augustine, John Bishop, Christopher Durang, Jules Feiffer, Charles Fuller, Janusz Glowacki, A. R. Gurney, Jr., Tina Howe, E. Katherine Kerr, David Mamet, Terrence McNally, Arthur Miller, Reinaldo Povod, Jonathan Reynolds, Shel Silverstein, Ted Tally, Wendy Wasserstein, Richard Wesley, August Wilson, George C. Wolfe; Music, David Shire; Lyrics, Richard Maltby, Jr.; Additional Song, Edward Kleban; Directors, John Tillinger, Richard Maltby, Jr.; Sets, Heidi Landesman; Costumes, C. L. Hundley; Lighting, Natasha Katz; Musical Supervision, Joel Silberman; Conductor, Michael Skloff; Musical Staging, Charles Randolph-Wright; Sound, Daryl Bornstein; Props, Garfield Mignott; Wardrobe, Theresa Purcell, Denise Waggoner; Stage Managers, Ed Fitzgerald, Daniel Bauer. CAST: Larry Fishburne, Nancy Giles, E. Katherine Kerr, Oliver Platt, Faith Prince, Rex Robbins, John Rubinstein

Understudies: Darlene Bel Grayson, Roxie Lucas, Kenneth L. Marks, Thomas Young

SCENES: Subway Panhandlers, Lonely Bohunks, Cardinal O'Connor, DMV Tyrant, Woman Stand-Up, Rope-A-Dope, Eliot's Coming, Laid Back, White Walls, Teeth, Transfiguration of Gerome, Where Were You When It Went Down, Andre's Mother, Street Talk, Speech to the Neighborhood Watch Committee, Things to Do Today, Lines Composed a Few Miles above Tintern Abbey Part II or If You Like What He Did with the New York Post Wait Till You See Channel 5, Feeding the Baby, Taxi from Hell, Smart Women/Brilliant Choices, Bernard's Lament, Over There, SONGS: Aerobic Cantata, Bill of Fare, Don't Fall for the Lights, Life Story, Loved Over, Miss Byrd, One of the Good Guys, Self-Portrait, The Party Next Door, There There

A revue performed with one intermission.

Right lower center: John Rubinstein,
Larry Fishburne in "Urban Blight"
Above: Brian Kerwin, Lisa Banes in "Emily"
Top: Brendan Corbalis, Kent Broadhurst
in "April Snow"
(Gerry Goodstein Photos)

Remak Ramsay, Stockard Channing
in "Woman in Mind"

MUSICAL THEATRE WORKS

Fifth Season

Artistic Director, Anthony J. Stimac; Associate Artistic Director, Mark Herko; Business Manager, Marilyn Stimac; General Manager, Ruthann Curry; Operations Manager, Denys Baker

(CSC Theatre) Tuesday, September 15,–October 3, 1987 (20 performances) **HAMLET** by William Shakespeare; Director, Anthony J. Stimac; Producer, Del Tenney; Original Music, Michael Valenti; Set, Evelyn Sakash; Lighting, Clarke W. Thornton; Costumes, Amanda J. Klein; Fight Director, B. H. Barry; Special Effects, Bran Ferren; Stage Manager, Sandra M. Franck. CAST: Leonard Auclair (Marcellus/Player/1st Grave Digger), Peter Bartlett (Osric), Dirk Benedict (Hamlet), Jerry Bradley (Gentleman/Player), R. Bruce Connelly (Guildenstern/Francisco/2nd Grave Digger), Rita Gam (Gertrude), Toni Hudson (Ophelia), Bjorn Johnson (Laertes), Richmond Johnson (Player King/Priest), Patrick Kearney (Sailor/Player), William Landis (Polonius), Ty McConnell (Rosencrantz), Kevin McGuire (Horatio), William Metzo (Ghost of Hamlet's Father), William Schenker (Bernardo/Lucianus/Messenger), Douglass Watson (Claudius)

Performed with two intermissions.

Thursday, October 8–25, 1987 (16 performances) It re-opened in the Cherry Lane Theatre on November 25, 1987 and closed there May 22, 1988 after 207 additional performances.

NO FRILLS REVUE conceived and directed by Martin Charnin; Choreography, Frank Ventura; Sketches, Music and Lyrics mostly by Michael Abbott, Marshall Brickman, Martin Charnin, Howard Danziger, Ronny Graham, Marvin Hamlisch, Brian Lasser, Michael Leeds, Thomas Meehan, Ron Melrose, Kirk Nurock, Archie T. Tridmorten, Bill Weeden, David Finkle, Sally Fay; Dialogue and Segues, Martin Charnin, Thomas Meehan, Archie T. Tridmorten; Set, Evelyn Sakash; Costumes, Amanda J. Klein; Lighting, Clarke W. Thornton; Men and Women's Clothing, Perry Ellis; Musical Direction, David Gaines; Orchestrations, Steven M. Alper; Casting, Mark S. Herko; Production Assistant, James Kampf; Wardrobe, Rose Camacho; Stage Manager, Robin Gray; Press, Bruce Cohen, Kathleen von Schmid. CAST: Adinah Alexander, Sasha Charnin, Clare Fields, Stephani Hardy, Sarah Knapp, Eddie Korbich, Andre Montgomery, Lynn Paynter, Justin Ross, Bob Stillman

PROGRAM Stools, The Group, Yma Dream, Being with Me, A Brand New Hammer, My Reunion Prayer, Small Things Come in Small Packages, I Know Where the Bodies are Buried, Pax de Don't, A Vicious Cycle, We Know Why You're Here, Bud, Lou and Who?, I Luv You, Runnin' with the Brat Pack, In the Quiet of Your Arms, Yes We Have the Manuscripts!, It Hasn't Been Easy

Performed with one intermission.

Thursday, January 14–31, 1988 (20 performances) **A WALK ON THE WILD SIDE** based on the novel by Nelson Algren; Book, Music, Lyrics by Will Holt; Direction/Choreography, Pat Birch; Musical Director, Larry Yurman; Fight Director, B. H. Barry; Music Supervisor, Louis St. Louis; Set, Michael Keith; Costumes, Amanda J. Klein; Lighting, Clarke W. Thornton; Production Manager, David Schaap; Production Assistant, Scott Fried; Props/Wardrobe, Karen Kahn; Stage Manager, Deborah Torres. CAST: Mana Allen (Gladys), Brigid Brady (Kitty), David Brand (Schmidt), Jeb Brown (Dove), Rhonda Coullet (Hallie), Connie Fredericks (Lucille), Taylor Jenkins (Flora Lee), Irma Estel LaGuerre (Terasina), John Minneo (Finnerty), Kathi Moss (Reba), Catherine Newman (Frenchy), Gordon J. Weiss (Byron), K. C. Wilson (Fort)

MUSICAL NUMBERS: Stay Way from Waycross, Shut Out the Night, That Old Piano Roll, Don't Put Me Down for the Common Kind, The Life We Lead, The Rex Cafe, Ingenuity, When It Gets Right Down to Evening, Cawfee Man, Turtle Song, A Walk on the Wild Side, Loew's State & Orpheum, Little Darling, Night Time Women, Strongman's Song, Since the Night I Stood in the Dancehall Door, The Way Home, That Boy Can Read, Heaviest Fight in New Orleans, We Been in Love, So Long

A musical in two acts. The action takes place during the Spring and summer of 1931 in East Texas and New Orleans.

Thursday, February 4–14, 1988 (12 performances) **.... AFTER THESE MESSAGES** with Book and Lyrics by Alice Whitfield, David Curtis, James Hammerstein; Music, Ralph Affoumado; Choreography, Tina Paul; Director, John Driver; Musical Direction, Eric Barnes; Set, Michael Keith; Costumes, Amanda J. Klein; Lighting, Clarke W. Thornton. CAST: Charles Boyer, Jeffrey Harmon, Liz Larsen, Jan Neuberger, Bob Sevra, Deanna Wells

Lower Right: Denise Lor, Kurt Peterson, Dick Decareau in "Alias Jimmy Valentine" *(Carol Rosegg)* Above: Sarah Knapp, Stephani Hardy, Justin Ross, Bob Stillman, Clare Fields, Andre Montgomery, Eddie Korbich, Lynn Paynter, Adinah Alexander, Sasha Charnin (center) in "No Frills Revue" *(Linda Alaniz)* Top: Richmond Johnson, Leonard Auclair, R. Bruce Connelly, Dirk Benedict in "Hamlet"

Thursday, February 25,–March 13, 1988 (8 performances and 8 previews) **ALIAS JIMMY VALENTINE** based on the O. Henry short story "A Retrieved Reformation"; Book, Jack Wrangler; Music, Bob Haber; Lyrics, Hal Hackady; Director, Charles Repole; Choreography, Sam Viverito; Musical Supervisor, Nick Cerrato; Musical Arrangements, Hubert "Tex" Arnold; Musical Direction, Arnold Gross; Scenery, Michael Keith; Lighting, Clarke W. Thornton; Costumes, Stephen L. Bornstein; Production Manager, David Schaap; Technical Director, David von Salis; Wardrobe, Karen Lee Kahn; Production Assistants, Kim McNutt, James Horvath, Steve Rose; Stage Manager, Ruth E. Kramer; Press, Henry Luhrman/Terry M. Lilly, Andrew P. Shearer, David Gersten. CAST: Bill Buell (Bowery Boy/Mr. Thompson), Katharine Buffaloe (Ellen Longstreth), Shelly Burch (Beatrice), Dick Decareau (Dink), Lillian Graff (Valerie/Viola), Billy Hipkins (Murk/Gambler), Denise Lor (Hattie), Robert McCormick (Det. Price), Kurt Peterson (Jimmy Valentine), Faith Prince (Lillian Deluxe), Thomas Ruisinger (Longstreth), Keith Savage (Rufus/John Chase)

MUSICAL NUMBERS: Winner Take All, Jimmy's Comin' Back, What's Your Hurry?, I'm Free, Flim-Flam, You're So Good John, Miss Invisible, She'll Get You Yet, That Girl, Dink's Lament, Leave It to Me, Today Is on Me, Love Is a Four-Letter Word, Small Town, I'm Gettin' Off Here, I Love You Jimmy Valentine

A musical in two acts. The action takes place during the Spring of 1912 in New York City's Bowery, and in Willow Run, Idaho.

MUSIC-THEATRE GROUP

Thirteenth Season

Producing Director, Lyn Austin; Associate Producing Directors, Diane Wondisford, Mark Jones; Managing Director, Diane Wondisford; Production Manager, Steve Ehrenberg; Press, Monina von Opel

(St. Clement's Church Theatre) Thursday, November 19–28, 1987 (9 performances)

PRISON-MADE TUXEDOS by George Trow; Conceived by Frank Morgan, George Trow; Director, David Warren; Set, John Arnone; Costumes, David C. Woolard; Lighting, Debra Dumas; Production Assistant, Elizabeth Valsing; Props, Liz Sherman, Nina Mankin; Stage Manager, Shari Melde. CAST: Frank Morgan (Frank), Laura Innes (Deb), Kevin Ramsey (Jailor), Howie Seago (Howie), Henry Stram (Henry), Quartet: Frank Morgan (Saxophone), Ronnie Mathews (Piano), Walter Booker (Bass), Victor Lewis (Drums).

Performed without intermission.

Tuesday, December 15–26, 1987 (13 performances)

HADDOCKS' EYES by David Warren from the diaries and letters of Lewis Carroll; Conceived and Directed by Mr. Warren; Set, John Arnone; Lighting, Debra Dumas; Projections, Wendall K. Harrington, Bo G. Ericksson; Costumes, David C. Woolard; Conductor, Steven Mercurio; Music, David Del Tredici; Sound, John Kilgore; Production Assistants, Elizabeth Valsing, Beth Greenberg; Stage Manager, Shari Melde. CAST: Tom Hulce (Lewis Carroll), Noemi Nadelmann/Susan Narucki (Alice), Jamie Mills (Young Alice).

Performed without intermission.

Wednesday, January 13,–February 5, 1988 (20 performances)

CINDERELLA/CENDRILLON based on an opera by Jules Massenet; Co-conceived/Directed by Anne Bogart; Co-conceived/Musical Adaptation, Jeff Halpern; Text, Eve Ensler; Set, Victoria Petrovich; Lighting, Carol Mullins; Costumes, Gregg Barnes; Associate Costume Designer, Ann Enno; Wardrobe, Jeannie Hill; Stage Managers, Michele Steckler, Elizabeth Valsing. CAST: Joyce Castle (Mme. de la Haltiere), Allison DeSalvo (Noemie), Joan Elizabeth (Lucette), Lauren Flanigan (Cinderella), Theresa McCarthy (Dorothee), Jeffrey Reynolds (Le Prince), Henry Stram (Pandolfe), Elisabeth Van Ingen (Fairy Godmother)

A musical in nine scenes. Sung in French, Text in English.

Friday, March 4–23, 1988 (23 performances)

JUAN DARIEN by Julie Taymor, Elliot Goldenthal; Inspired by Horacio Quiroga's story; Composed by Mr. Goldenthal; Direction/Puppetry/Masks, Julie Taymor; Text chosen and arranged by Mr. Goldenthal; Music Direction, Richard Cordova; Set/Costumes, G. W. Mercier, Julie Taymor; Lighting, Richard Nelson; Synthesizer Sound, Richard Martinez; Stage Managers, Neil Ann Stephens, Elizabeth Valsing. CAST: Ariel Ashwell, Renee Banks, Willie C. Barnes, Thuli Dumakude, Nicholas Gunn, Andrea Kane, Stephen Kaplin, Lawrence A. Neals, Jr., Lenard Petit, Barbara Pollitt, Irene Wiley

Right: Noemi Nadelmann, Tom Hulce
in "Haddock's Eyes" *(Rebecca Lesher)*
Top: Joan Elizabeth, Lauren Flanigan
in "Cinderella/Cendrillon" *(Jennifer Kotter)*

George Trow (Top), Frank Morgan
in "Prison-Made Tuxedos" *(Carol Rosegg)*

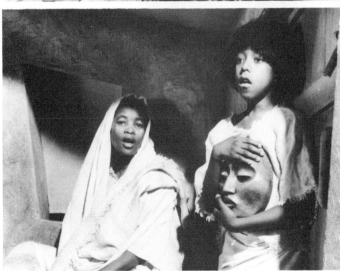

Thuli Dumakude, Lawrence Neals
in "Juan Darien" *(Elliot Goldenthal)*

NEW YORK CITY OPERA

American Musical Theatre Season

THE STUDENT PRINCE

Music, Sigmund Romberg; Book and Lyrics, Dorothy Donnelly; Book Adaptation, Hugh Wheeler; Conductor, Jim Coleman; Director, Jack Hofsiss; Stage Director, Christian Smith; Choreographer, Donald Saddler; Sets, David Jenkins; Costumes, Patten Campbell; Lighting, Gilbert Helmsley, Jr.; Chorus Master, Joseph Colaneri; Assistant Stage Director, David Pfeiffer; Choreography Re-staging, Jessica Redel; Press, Susan Woelzl, Joan McDonald. Opened in the New York State Theater on Saturday, July 11, 1987*

CAST

Dr. Engel (Brian Steele/Chester Ludgin), Count von Mark (David Dae Smith), Secretaries (Glenn Rowen/Jonathan Guss), Prince Karl Franz (John Stewart/Jon Garrison), Lutz (James Billings/Jack Harrold), Gretchen (Susanne Marsee), Ruder (Joseph McKee), Nicholas (Douglas James Hamilton), Toni (Jack Harrold/James Billings), Hubert (William Ledbetter), Detlef (Stanley Cornett), von Asterberg (Robert Brubaker), Lucas (Robert Ferrier), Freshman (Louis Perry), Kathie (Claudette Peterson/Leigh Munro), Grand Duchess Anastasia (Muriel Costa-Greenspon), Princess Margaret (Lisbeth Lloyd/Cynthia Rose), Captain Tarnitz (Cris Groenendaal), Countess Leyden (Rebecca Russell), Lackeys/Huzzars (Edward Zimmerman, Louis Perry, George Wyman, Neil Eddinger, Glen Rowen/Gregory Moore), Girls/Friends of the Huzzars (Madeleine Mines, Paula Hostetter, Beth Pensiero, Jill Bosworth)

MUSICAL NUMBERS: By Our Bearing So Sedate, Golden Days, Garlands Bright with Glowing Flowers, To the Inn We're Marching, Drink Drink Drink, Come Boys Let's All Be Gay, Heidelberg Beloved Vision of My Heart, Gaudeamus Igitur, Deep in My Heart, Come Sir Join Our Noble Saxon Corps, Overhead the Moon Is Beaming, When the Spring Wakens Everything, Student Life, Thoughts Will Come to Me, Ballet, Just We Two, What Memories, Finale

An operetta in 3 acts and 4 scenes. The action takes place in Karlsberg, Germany in "the Golden Years."

*Closed Nov. 8, 1987 after 14 performances in repertory.

Top Right: Leigh Munro, Jon Garrison
in "The Student Prince"

SWEENEY TODD
The Demon Barber of Fleet Street

Music and Lyrics, Stephen Sondheim; Book, Hugh Wheeler; Director, Harold Prince; Orchestrations, Jonathan Tunick; Conductor, Paul Gemignani; Stage Director, Arthur Masell; Set, Eugene Lee; Costumes, Franne Lee; Lighting, Ken Billington; Choreographer, Larry Fuller; Chorus Master, Joseph Colaneri; Assistant Stage Directors, Raymond Menard, Albert Sherman; Musical Preparation, Douglas Stanton; Choreography Re-Created by William Kirk; Press, Susan Woelzl, Joan McDonald. Opened in the New York State Theater on Wednesday, July 29, 1987*

CAST

Anthony Hope (Cris Groenendaal), Sweeney Todd (Stanley Wexler/Timothy Nolen), Beggar Woman (Brooks Almy/Ivy Austin), Mrs. Lovett (Marcia Mitzman/Joyce Castle), Judge Turpin (Joseph McKee/Will Roy), The Beadle (John Lankston), Johanna (Susan Powell/Leigh Munro), Tobias Ragg (Robert Johanson), Pirelli (Jerold Siena), Jonas Fogg (William Ledbetter)

MUSICAL NUMBERS: The Ballad of Sweeney Todd, No Place Like London, The Worst Pies in London, Poor Thing, My Friends, Green Finch and Linnet Bird, Ah Miss, Johanna, Pirelli's Miracle Elixir, The Contest, Wait, Kiss Me, Ladies in Their Sensitivities, Pretty Women, Epiphany, A Little Priest, God That's Good!, By the Sea, Not While I'm Around, Parlor Songs, City on Fire!, Finale

A musical drama in two acts. The action takes place during the nineteenth century in London, Fleet Street and environs.

*Closed Oct. 4, 1987 after 11 performances in repertory.

Martha Swope Photos

Marcia Mitzman, Stanley Wexler, and Above:
Robert Johanson (second from left), Jerold
Siena, Timothy Nolen in "Sweeney Todd"

THE DESERT SONG

Music, Sigmund Romberg; Book and Lyrics, Otto Harbach, Oscar Hammerstein 2nd, Frank Mandel; New Adaptation of Book and Lyrics, Robert Johanson; Conductor, Jim Coleman; Director/Choreographer, Robert Johanson; Co-Choreographer, Sharon Halley; Set, Michael Anania; Costumes, Suzanne Mess; Lighting, Mark W. Stanley; Chorus Master, Joseph Colaneri; Assistant Stage Director, David Pfeiffer; Musical Preparation, John Beeson; Press, Susan Woelzl, Joan McDonald. Opened in the New York State Theater on Tuesday, August 25, 1987*

CAST

Sid El Kar (Michael Cousins/John Stewart), Hassi (Kenneth Kantor), Hadji (William Ledbetter), Neri (Joyce Campana), Benjamin Kidd (Philip William McKinley), Azuri (Louise Hickey), Capt. Paul Fontaine (Theodore Baerg/Cris Groenendaal), Sgt. LaVergne (David Frye), Susan (Lillian Graff), Edith (Paula Hostetter), Margot Bonvalet (Linda Michele/Jane Thorngren), General Birabeau (David Rae Smith), Ali Ben Ali (Raymond Bazemore), Clementina (Joyce Campana), Nogi (Robert Brubaker)

An operetta in 2 acts and 7 scenes. The action takes place during the 1930's in Morocco.

*Closed Sept. 6, 1987 after 16 performances in repertory.

Top Right: William Parcher, Jane Thorngren
Below: Richard White, Raymond Bazemore
in "The Desert Song"

THE MUSIC MAN

Book, Music and Lyrics, Meredith Willson; Story, Meredith Willson, Franklin Lacey; Conductor, Donald Pippin; Director, Arthur Masella; Set, David Jenkins; Costumes, Andrew Marlay; Lighting, Duane Schuler; Choreographer, Marcia Milgrom Dodge; Chorus Master, Joseph Colaneri; Assistant Stage Director, Claudia Zahn; Musical Preparation, Susan Caldwell, John Beeson; Press, Susan Woelzl, Joan McDonald. Opened Friday, February 26, 1988*

CAST

Traveling Salesmen (William Ledbetter, James Clark, Robert Brubaker, Stanley Wexler, Jonathan Green), Newspaper Readers (Louis Perry, Neil Eddinger), Charlie Cowell (Rex Hays), Conductor (Ralph Bassett/John Henry Thomas), Harold Hill (Bob Gunton), Mayor Shinn (Richard McKee), Eulalie Mackecknie Shinn (Muriel Costa-Greenspon), Zaneeta Shinn (Jill Powell), Gracie Shinn (Alexandra Steinberg), Alma Hix (Bridget Ramos), Ethel Toffelmier (Ivy Austin), Maud Dunlop (Lee Bellaver), Mrs. Squires (Rita Metzger), Jacey Squires (Jonathan Green), Marcellus Washburn (James Billings), Ewart Dunlop (James Clark), Oliver Hix (Robert Brubaker), Olin Britt (Don Yule), Marian Paroo (Leigh Munro), Mrs. Paroo (Brooks Almy), Amaryllis (Allegra Victoria Forste), Winthrop Paroo (Joel Chaiken), Tommy Djilas (Steven M. Schultz), Constable Locke (William Ledbetter)

MUSICAL NUMBERS: Overture, Rock Island, Iowa Stubborn, Ya Got Trouble, Piano Lesson, If You Don't Mind My Saying So, Goodnight My Someone, Columbia the Gem of the Ocean, 76 Trombones, Sincere, The Sadder but Wiser Girl, Pick-a-Little Talk-a-Little, Goodnight Ladies, Marian the Librarian, My White Knight, The Wells Fargo Wagon, It's You, Shipoopi, Lida Rose, Will I Ever Tell You?, Gary Indiana, Till There Was You, Minuet in G, Finale

A musical in 2 acts and 17 scenes. The action takes place in July of 1912 in River City, Iowa.

*Closed Apr. 10, 1988 after 51 performances. For original Broadway production, see THEATRE WORLD Vol. 14.

Martha Swope Photos

Leigh Munro, Bob Gunton
in "The Music Man"

NEW YORK SHAKESPEARE FESTIVAL

Twenty-first Season

Producer, Joseph Papp; Associate Producer, Jason Steven Cohen; General Managers, Laurel Ann Wilson, Bob MacDonald; Associate, Susan Sampliner; Plays and Musicals Development, Gail Merrifield; Casting, Rosemarie Tichler; Executive Assistant to Mr. Papp, Barbara Carroll; Production Manager, Andrew Mihok; Technical Director, Mervyn Haines, Jr.; Audio M aster, Gene Ricciardi; Props, James Gill, J. L. Marshall; Art Director, Paul Davis; Press, Richard Kornberg, Kevin Patterson, Reva Cooper, Carol Fineman, Warren Anker.

(Delacorte Theater/Central Park) Friday, June 6,–July 19, 1987 (21 performances)

KING RICHARD II by William Shakespeare; Director, Joseph Papp; Set, Loren Sherman; Costumes, Theoni V. Aldredge; Lighting, Jules Fisher; Music, Peter Golub; presented with the cooperation of the City of New York (Edward I. Koch, Mayor; Diane M. Coffey, Commissioner of Cultural Affairs; Henry J. Stern, Commissioner of Parks) in association with New York Telephone Co.; Production Assistants, Christie Wagner, Victoria Leacock; Technical Director, Tim Lea; Props, Frances Smith; Wardrobe, Carol Gant; Wigs, James Herrera; Stage Managers, James Bernardi, Ellen Raphael

CAST: Tom Aldredge (John of Gaunt), Peter Appel (Herald), Denis Arndt (Northumberland), Oliver Barreiro (Monk), Ron Bottitta (Servant), Graham Brown (Bishop of Carlisle), Rocky Carroll (Green), John Henry Cox (Lord Marshal/ Salisbury), Robert Dorfman (Bushy), David Gianopoulos (Lord Stanley), Tim Guinee (Henry Percy), Thomas Hill (Duke of York), Richard Michael Hughes (Ross), Pauline Lepor (Attendant), John Bedford-Lloyd (Bolingbroke), Victor Love (Aumerle), Geoffrey Lower (Company), Chris McNally (Monk), Peter MacNicol (Richard II), Judith Malina (Duchess of York), Stephen Markle (Mowbray/Berkeley/ Surrey), David Marks (Herald), Devon Michaels (Young Richard II), Donald Newall (Young Bolingbroke), Michael O'Shea (Company), Geoffrey Owens (Lord Fitzwater), James Puig (Gardener/Groom), David Rainey (Company), Michael Rudko (Monk), Kenneth Ryan (Pierce/Welsh Captain), Marco St. John (Willoughby), Marian Seldes (Duchess of Gloucester), Tony Shalhoub (Bagot), Freda Foh Shen (Queen), Beatrice Winde (Queen's Attendant), Edward Zang (Scroop/Abbott)

Performed with one intermission.

(Delacorte Theater/Central Park) Friday, July 24,–August 16, 1987 (21 performances)

TWO GENTLEMEN OF VERONA by William Shakespeare; Director, Stuart Vaughan; Scenery, Bob Shaw; Costumes, Lindsay W. Davis; Lighting, Peggy Eisenhauer; Music, Lee Hoiby; Fights, B. H. Barry; Dances, John DeLuca; Animal Trainer, William Berloni; Production Assistants, Elizabeth Cohen, Emily Fisher; Technical Director, Tim Lea; Props, Susan Prime Kappel; Wardrobe, Carol Grant; Wigs, James Herrera; Stage Managers, Karen Armstrong, Buzz Cohen

CAST: Irwin Appel (Ensemble/Fencing Master), Laura Attis (Ensemble), Greg Babb (Ensemble), Dylan Baker (Launce), Larry Block (Antonio), Jerome Dempsey (Duke), Christine Dunford (Ensemble), Becky Gelke (Lucetta), Thomas Gibson (Proteus), James M. Goodwin (Valentine), Fanni Green (Ensemble), Jamie Hanes (Guitarist/Ensemble), Kimberly Hundley (Ensemble), Mia Korf (Ensemble), James Lally (Eglamour), Jerry Mayer (Outlaw/Host), Elizabeth McGovern (Julia), Christopher McHale (Panthino/Outlaw), John Pankow (Speed), Wendell Pierce (Outlaw), Deborah Rush (Silvia), Daniel Spector (Ensemble), Mark Vietor (Ensemble), Richard Ziman (Thurio), Roxanne (Crab)

Performed with one intermission.

(Delacorte Theater/Central Park) Friday, August 21,–September 13, 1987 (21 performances)

KING HENRY IV PART I by William Shakespeare; Director, Joseph Papp; Set, David Mitchell; Costumes, Theoni V. Aldredge; Lighting, Jules Fisher; Fights, Malcolm Ranson; Music, Peter Golub; Production Assistants, Lloyd Davis, Victoria Leacock, Christine Wagner; Fight Captain, Patrick Mulcahy; Technical Director, Tim Lea; Props, Frances Smith; Wardrobe, Carol Gant, Tony Powell; Stage Managers, James Bernardi, Pat Sosnow, Tony Papp

CAST: Peter Appel (Sheriff/Carrier), Angela Bassett (Lady Percy), Ron Bottitta (Ensemble/Messenger), Rocky Carroll (Walter Blunt), John Henry Cox (Westmoreland/Northumberland), Timothy Davis-Reed (Tavern Fighter/ Messenger), David Gianopoulos (Sir Michael), Fanni Green (Ensemble), Deirdre Lovejoy (Ensemble), Tom Mardirosian (Bardolph), Stephen Markle (Gadshill/ Douglas), Conan McCarty (Hotspur), Chris McNally (Peto), Theresa Merritt (Mistress Quickly), Donald Moffat (Falstaff), Patrick Mulcahy (Servant/Messenger), Michael O'Shea (Traveler/Ensemble), James Puig (Francis/Ostler), David Rainey (Prince John/Carrier), Alan Scarfe (Worcester), Peter Schmitz (Traveler/Ensemble), Tony Shalhoub (Poins/Vernon), Tony Soper (Prince Hal), Edward Zang (Archbishop/Chamberlain), Michael Zaslow (King Henry IV)

Presented with one intermission.

(Public/Shiva Theater) Tuesday, October 27,–December 6, 1987 (32 performances and 15 previews)

OLD BUSINESS written and directed by Joe Cacaci; Scenery/Lighting, Richard Meyer; Costumes, Bill Walker; Presented in association with East Coast Arts at Wildcliff (Artistic Director, Joe Cacaci); Lighting, Debra S. Post; Props, Mark McMahon; Wardrobe, Bruce Brumage; Hair, Paul Huntley; Stage Manager, Buzz Cohen

CAST: Joe Silver (Abe Fleischer), Michael Wikes (David Fleischer)

A play in 3 acts and 6 scenes. The action takes place at the present time in the executive office of the Fleischer Corporation in New York City.

(Martha Swope Photos)

Joe Silver, Michael Wikes in "Old Business"
Above: Donald Moffat, Tony Soper in "Henry IV Part I"
Top: Victor Love, Peter MacNicol, Thomas Hill
in "Richard II" Below: Deborah Rush, James Goodwin,
Thomas Gibson, Elizabeth McGovern in "Two Gentlemen. . . ."

(Public Theater/LuEsther Hall) Tuesday, November 3,–December 20, 1987 (30 performances and 25 previews)

LA PUTA VIDA TRILOGY (This Bitch of a Life) by Reinaldo Povod; Director, Bill Hart; Set, Donald Eastman; Costumes, Gabriel Berry; Lighting, Anne Militello; Sound/Composer, Daniel Moses Schreier; Wardrobe, Odell Perry; Props, Evan Canary; Stage Managers, James Bernardi, Stacey Fleischer
CAST: *"Prologue"* with Michael Carmine (Papo); *"South of Tomorrow"* with Rafael Baez (Lookout), John Leguizamo (Alley Boy), Michael Guess (Randy); *"Nijinsky Choked His Chicken"* with Miguel Correa (Raisin), John Turturro (Chino); *"Poppa Dio!"* with John Turturro (Angelo), Rosana DeSoto (Mafia); *"Epilogue"* with Michael Carmine. Understudies: Rafael Baez (Michael Carmine/John Leguizamo), Rahshan Orange (Miguel Correa). Performed with two intermissions.

(Public/Newman Theater) Sunday, Nov. 22,–Dec. 27, 1987 (28 performances and 9 previews) The Royal Court Theatre (London) production of:
SERIOUS MONEY by Caryl Churchill; Director, Max Stafford-Clark; Music and Lyrics, Ian Dury, Micky Gallagher, Chas Jankel; Scenery and Costumes, Peter Hartwell; Lighting, Rick Fisher; Musical Arranger, Colin Sell; Assistant Director, Hettie MacDonald; Production Assistant, Chris Sinclair; Dialect Coach, Elizabeth Himelstein; Props, Frances Smith, Anne Doherty, Colin Gregory, Jean Paradis; Wardrobe, Ira Rosenbaum; Computer Screens, Dave Satin; Stage Managers, Neil O'Malley, Jack Doulin
CAST: Linda Bassett (Marylou Baines/Mrs. Etherington/Dolcie Starr), Burt Caesar (Merrison/T.K./Nigel), Scott Cherry (Jake Todd/Frosby/Grevett), Allan Corduner (Durkfeld/Freville Todd/Duckett/Soat/Gleason), Paul Moriarty (Zackerman), Joanne Pearce (Scilla Todd/Ms. Biddulph), Meera Syal (Jacinta Condor), Daniel Webb (Grimes/Billy Corman), Valerie Bahakel (Jill), Christine Dunford (Mary), Gregory Jbara (John), Neal Lerner (Sam), Louise Lewis (Annie), Julianne Moore (Mandy), Cameron Ross (Pete), Michael Rudko (Dick)
A play in two acts. The action takes place mainly between October 1986 and June 1987 in London and New York.

(Public/Anspacher Theater) Monday, Dec. 7, 1987–March 27, 1988 (81 performances and 39 previews
A MIDSUMMER NIGHT'S DREAM by William Shakespeare; Director, A. J. Antoon; Choreographer, Garth Fagan; Scenery, Andrew Jackness; Costumes, Frank Krenz; Lighting, Peter Kaczorowski; Music Composed/Directed by Michael Ward; Props, Sandra Doyle, Jean Pierre Demorcy; Wardrobe, Tony Powell; Stage Managers, Alan R. Traynor, Karen Armstrong, Christie Wagner
CAST: F. Murray Abraham (Bottom), Peter Appel (Snug), Erick Avari (Egeus), David Calloway, Ron Dortch, Byron Easley (Followers), Sara Erde (Mustardseed), Julia Gibson (Hermia), Steve Hofvendahl (Robin Starveling/Moonshine), Patty Holley (Hippolyta), Rob Knepper (Lysander), Carl W. Lumbly (Oberon), Elizabeth McGovern (Helena), Bruce Norris (Demetrius), Geoffrey Owens (Puck), Tim Perez (Francis Flute/Thisby), Richard Riehle (Peter Quince), Jack Ryland (Theseus), Gwendolyn J. Shepherd (Peaseblossom), Lorraine Toussaint (Titania), Torri Whitehead (Cobweb), Joe Zaloom (Tom Snout/Wall), Mandla Msomi/Kennan Scott (Changeling), Kim Yancey, Mark Lewis, Deidre Lovejoy, Christopher McHale, Raymond Thomas
Performed in two acts. The action is set in Bahia at the turn of the century.

(Public/Susan Stein Shiva Theater) Tuesday, Feb. 2,–March 13, 1988 (30 performances and 18 previews)
AMERICAN NOTES by Len Jenkin; Director, Joanne Akalaitis; Set, John Arnone; Costumes, David C. Woolard; Lighting, Frances Aronson; Props, Evan Canary; Props, Anne Doherty, Colin Gregory, Jean Paradis; Stage Managers, Mireya Hepner, Lauren Class Schneider
CAST: George Bartenieff (Professor), Jesse Borrego (Tim), Andrew Davis (Reporter), Thomas Ikeda (Pitchman), Laura Innes (Linda), Olek Krupa (Chuckles), Rodney Scott Hudson (Mayor), Stephen McHattie (Faber), Mercedes Ruehl (Karen), Lauren Tom (Pauline)
The action takes place at the present time in America.

(Public/Martinson Hall) Friday, Feb. 12,–Apr. 17, 1988 (54 performances and 23 previews)
WENCESLAS SQUARE by Larry Shue; Director, Jerry Zaks; Set, Loren Sherman; Costumes, William Ivey Long; Lighting, Paul Gallo; Wardrobe, Angela Wendt; Props, Frances Smith, Randy Harris; Dialect Coach, Tim Monich; Stage Managers, Steven Beckler, Clifford Schwartz
CAST: Victor Garber (The Men), Jonathan Hadary (Vince Corey), Bruce Norris (Dooley), Dana Ivey (The Women)
A play in two acts.

Top Right: Miguel Correa, John Turturro
in "La Puta Vida" Below: Daniel Webb, Linda
Bassett in "Serious Money" *(John Haynes)*
Lower Right Center: Julia Gibson, Rob Knepper,
Elizabeth McGovern, Bruce Norris in "A Midsummer
Night's Dream" *(Martha Swope Photos)*

Victor Garber, Jonathan Hadary, Bruce Norris,
Dana Ivey in "Wenceslas Square"

NEW YORK SHAKESPEARE FESTIVAL

(Public/Newman Theater) Tuesday, Feb. 16,–Apr. 3, 1988 (15 performances and 40 previews)

JULIUS CAESAR by William Shakespeare; Director, Stuart Vaughan; Set, Bob Shaw; Costumes, Lindsay W. Davis; Lighting, Arden Fingerhut; Music, Lee Hoiby; Production Assistants, Lisa Buxbaum, Westley Cammon, Jr.; Wardrobe, Tony Powell; Props, Sandra Doyle; Stage Managers, Karen Armstrong, Buzz Cohen; CAST: Scott Allegrucci (1st Soldier), Dion Anderson (Metellus Cimber), Madison Arnold (Trebonius), Gregory Babb (Soldier), Victor Bevine (Claudius), Joseph Costa (Caius Ligarius/Lepidus), Sheridan Crist (Dardanius), Joseph Culliton (Servant/Citizen/Messala), Robert Curtis-Brown (Octavius Caesar), John Fitzgibbon (Cinna/Cinna the Poet/Varro), Walter Flanagan (Publius), James M. Goodwin (Marullus/Strato), Harriet Harris (Calpurnia), Edward Herrmann (Cassius), Damien Leake (Soothsayer/Pindarus), Mark Lewis (Servant/Clitus), Joan MacIntosh (Portia), Jerry Mayer (Citizen/Soldier), Christopher McHale (Artemidorus/Lucilius), Roderick McLachlan (Servant/Volumnius), John McMartin (Julius Caesar), Robert Murch (Decius Brutus), Al Pacino (Marcus Antonius), Joseph Palmas (3rd Soldier), David Rainey (Soldier 4), Martin Sheen (Brutus), Jack Stehlin (Flavius/Titinius), John Madden Towey (Popilius Lena), Tyrone Wilson (Citizen/Messenger/Soldier), Richard Ziman (Casca).

A drama performed in two acts. The action takes place in Rome, near Sardis, and near Philippi.

(Public/LuEsther Hall) Saturday, April 16,–June 5, 1988 (42 performances)

ZERO POSITIVE by Harry Kondoleon; Director, Mark Linn-Baker succeeded by Kenneth Elliott; Set, Adrianne Lobel; Costumes, Susan Hilferty; Lighting, Natasha Katz; Wardrobe, Bruce Brumage; Props, Jean-Pierre Demorcy, Thomas Gordon; Stage Managers, Ruth Kreshka, Lisa Ledwich

CAST: Edward Atienza (Jacob Blank), Beth Austin (Debbie Fine), Reed Birney Succeeded by David Pierce (Himmer), Frances Conroy (Samantha), Richard McMillan (Prentice), Tony Shalhoub (Patrick)

A play in 2 acts and 5 scenes. The action takes place in August 1987 in New York City.

(Public/Anspacher Theater) Tuesday, April 19,–June 5, 1988 (55 performances) Shakespeare Marathon #3.

ROMEO AND JULIET by William Shakespeare; Director, Les Waters; Set, Heidi Landesman; Costumes, Ann Hould-Ward; Lighting, Peter Kaczorowski; Music, Peter Golub; Choreography, Tina Paul; Fights, B. H. Barry; Production Assistants, Frances Smith, Chris Sinclair; Props, Mark McMahon, Liz Heeden; Wardrobe, Carol Grant; Wigs and Hair, Manuela LaPorte; Stage Managers, Stephen McCorkle, Robert Mark Kalfin

CAST: Scott Allegrucci (Balthasar), Jannie Brenn (Lady Montague), W. B. Brydon (Lord Capulet), Maury Cooper (Apothecary/Capulet Cousin), Dan Cordle (Gregory/3rd Witch), Michael Cumpsty (Prince Escalus), Randy Danson (Lady Capulet), Peter Francis James (Benvolio), Rob Knepper (Tybalt), Peter MacNicol (Romeo), Rusty Magee (2nd Citizen/2nd Watch), Anne Meara (Nurse), Patrick Mulcahy (Abram), Cynthia Nixon (Juliet), Milo O'Shea (Friar Lawrence), Angela Pietropinto (Gentlewoman), James Puig (Peter), Christopher Shaw (Page to Paris), Jack Stehlin (Sampson/1st Watch), Harold J. Surratt (Chorus/Friar John), Adrienne Thompson (2nd Gentlewoman), Courtney B. Vance (Mercutio), Neil Vipond (Lord Montague), Bradley Whitford (Paris)

Performed with one intermission.

Martha Swope Photos

(Public Theater) Saturday, August 1–23, 1987

FESTIVAL LATINO (Directors, Oscar Ciccone, Cecilia Vega; Associate Producer, Jason Steven Cohen; Press, Reva Cooper, Julio Marzan) including theatre (most with simultaneous translation), music, dance, film and television programs. The theatrical productions included Argentina's *"The Senorita of Tacna"* by Mario Vargas Llosa, starring Norma Aleandro. Spain's La Cuadra de Sevilla performing *"Las Bacantes,"* an adaptation of Euripides' "The Bacchae," featuring Manuela Vargas. NYSF's production of Carlos Morton's *"Pancho Diablo"* performed in English and featuring Fernando Allende from Mexico. Venezuela's Rajatabla Company under the direction of Carlos Gimenez in *"The Tragi-Comedy of Calixto and Malibea"*, an adaptation of "La Celestina" by Fernando de Rojas. *"The Cockpit"* by Argentina's company, La Comedia Cordobesa; Chile's Taller Teatro Dos in *"The Clowns of Hope,"* and Puerto Rico's Las Bohemias in *"Concerto in Hi-Fi."*

(Public/Shiva Theater) Thursday, April 28,–May 22, 1988 (16 performances). Joseph Papp presents the New York Art Theatre Institute production of:

OLD NEW YORK: NEW YEAR'S DAY from the novel by Edith Wharton; Adapted/Directed by Donald T. Sanders; Set/Lighting/Costumes, Vanessa James; Assistant to Director, Christina Roessler; Props, Stuart Perelson; Wardrobe, Shane Farrell; Stage Managers, Catherine Del Tuffo, Karen Crumley.

CAST: Guy Custis (Henry Prest/Guest), Rosemarie Engle (Mamma/Susan/Mrs. Struthers/Mrs. Mant/Nurse), Kate Farrell (Lizzie Hazeldean), Peter Lane (Narrator), Bianka Langner (Young Lady), Arthur McGuire (Sillerton Jackson/Guest), Janet Scurria (Edith Wharton/Sabina Wesson), John White (Charles Hazeldean/Hubert Wesson/Guest).

Performed without intermission. The action takes place in New York City between 1870 and 1910.

Top Right: Al Pacino, John McMartin, Edward Herrmann, Martin Sheen in "Julius Caesar"
Below: Richard McMillan, Frances Conroy, David Pierce in "Zero Positive" *(Martha Swope Photos)*

104

Norma Aleandro in "La Senorita de Tacna"
Above: Cynthia Nixon, Milo O'Shea, Peter MacNicol in "Romeo and Juliet"

NEW YORK THEATRE WORKSHOP

New Directors Series

Artistic Director, James C. Nicola; Associate Artistic Director, Tony Kushner; Artistic Associate, Maria Gillen; Artistic Assistant, Judy Langford; Managing Director, Nancy Kassak Kiekmann; Development, Patrick Herold; Production Manager, David Feight; Technical Director, Tony Gerber; Sound, Noelle Kalom; Production Assistants, Derrick McQueen, Robyn C. Hardy; Props, Ann Davis; Press, Millie Schoenbaum, Gary Murphy

(Perry Street Theatre) Thursday, October 29,–November 21, 1987 (10 performances)

STELLA by J. W. von Goethe; Translated by Robert M. Browning; Director, Ulli Stephan; Set, Peter Eastman; Lighting, Steven Rosen; Costumes, Barbara Bush; Casting, Joan Fishman/Alan Amtzis; Stage Manager, William H. Lang. CAST: Gabrielle Carteris (Postmistress), Steve Coats (Steward), Francois Giroday (Fernando), Laura Innes (Stella), Michael Lewis (Carl), Camryn Manheim (Post-mistress), Experience Robinson (Annie), April Shawhan (Cecilia)

A play in two acts.

Thursday, November 12–21, 1987 (10 performances)

BLOOD SPORTS by David Edgar; Director, Judy Dennis; Set, Peter Eastman; Lighting, Steven Rosen; Costumes, Barbara Bush; Sound, Richard Einhorn. CAST: Patrick Breen, Larry Bryggman, Michael Cerveris, Don R. McManus, John Gould Rubin. An anthology of short sketches using various English sporting events for commentary on the battle between classes in England.

Friday, November 27,–December 5, 1987 (9 performances)

COYOTE UGLY by Lynn Siefert; Director, Lenora Champagne; Set, Elizabeth Doyle; Lighting, Mary Lou Geiger; Costumes, Jeffrey Ullman; Stage Managers, Richard Hester, Ken Simmons; Adviser, Emily Mann. CAST: Elizabeth Berridge (Scarlet), Pamela Dunlap (Andreas), Bill Buell (Red), Michel R. Gill (Dowd), Louise Smith (Penny)

A comedy in two acts.

Thursday, December 10–19, 1987 (10 performances)

THE LOVE SUICIDES AT AMIJIMA by Chikamatsu; Director, Jorge Cacheiro; Set, Nobert Kolb; Lighting, Mary Louise Geiger; Costumes, Jim Buff; Sound, Matthew Wiener; Stage Manager, Cheryl Mintz. CAST: Natsuko Ohama (Narrator/Osan), Elizabeth Fon Sung (Koharu/Osan), Allan Tung (Jihei), Jeanne Mori (Prostitute), Cathy Foy (Proprietress/Aunt), James Jenner (Tahei), Dalton B. Leong (Samurai/Magoemon), Peter Yoshida (Gozaemon)

The masterpiece of Japan's greatest dramatist.

Wednesday, March 16,–April 9, 1988 (22 performances)

THE BIG LOVE based on book by Florence Aadland, Tedd Thomey; By Brooke Allen; Director, John Tillinger; Set, David Mitchell; Costumes, Jane Greenwood; Lighting, Dennis Parichy; Sound, John Gromada; Production Manager, Darren Lee Cole; Stage Manager, William H. Lang. CAST: Marsha Mason (Florence Aadland)

Performed without intermission. The action takes place in 1961 in Hollywood, California.

Wednesday, April 20,–May 8, 1988 (17 performances)

DOMINO by Robert Litz; Director, David Esbjornson; Set, Elizabeth Doyle; Costumes, Marianne Powell-Parker; Lighting, Greg MacPherson; Sound, Lia Vollack; Stage Manager, Dan M. Weir. CAST: Dan Butler (Langley), Carlos Cestero (Cadre), Christopher McHale (Mahan), Jay Patterson (Rogers), Raoul N. Rizik (Man), Jaime Sanchez (Nueva), Socorro Santiago (Woman)

A comedy in two acts. The action takes place at the present time in an unnamed country of Central America.

Marsha Mason in "The Big Love"
(Bob Marshak)
Above: April Shawhan, Francois Giroday, Laura Innes,
Gabrielle Carteris in "Stella"
(Martha Swope)

PAN ASIAN REPERTORY THEATRE

Eleventh Season

Artistic/Producing Director, Tisa Chang; Managing Director, Bonnie Hyslop; Marketing Director, Maggie Browne; Development Director, Ed Schmidt; Production Manager, Patrick Heydenburg; Sound, Joseph Tornabene; Press, G. Theodore Killmer

(Playhouse 46) Tuesday, June 2–20, 1987 (18 performances)

LIFE OF THE LAND by Edward Sakamoto; Director, Kati Kuroda; Set, Bob Phillips; Lighting, Richard Dorfman; Costumes, Eiko Yamaguchi; Stage Managers, Patrice Thomas, Sue Jane Stoker CAST: Ron Nakahara (Spencer Kamiya), Lily Sakata (Laura Taniguchi), Jeffrey Akaka (Toku Taniguchi), Lori Tanaka (Debbie), Carol A. Honda (Fumiko), Mel Duane Gionson (Aki Kamiya), Eric Miji (Nobu Kamiya), Barbara Pohlman (Susan Kamiya), Ken Baldwin (Daniel Kamiya), Norris M. Shimabuku (Maxwell Lam)

A play in 2 acts and 4 scenes.

Tuesday, Oct. 13,–Nov. 7, 1987 (24 performances)

ROSIE'S CAFE by R. A. Shiomi; Director, Raul Aranas; Set, Bob Phillips; Lighting, Victor En Yu Tan; Costumes, Eiko Yamaguchi; Stage Manager, Arthur Catricala CAST: Carol A. Honda (Rosie Ohara), Keenan Shimizu (Kenji Kadota), Donald Li (Sam Shikaze), Dalton Leong (Michio Tanaka), Steve Park (Johnny Wada), John Quincy Lee (Jimmy Joe Jackson), Mary Lee-Aranas (Kimiko Wada), Ann M. Tsuji (Mayumi), Michael Arkin (Jonathan Webster)

A play in two acts. The action takes place during 1951 in Vancouver, Canada.

Friday, Apr. 22,–May 21, 1988 (24 performances)

MADAME DE SADE by Yukio Mishima; Translated by Donald Keene; Director, Ron Nakahara; Set, Alex Polner; Lighting, Victor En Yu Tan; Costumes, Eiko Yamaguchi; Dramaturg, Anne Deneys; Stage Manager, Patrice Thomas CAST: Jeanne Mori (Comtesse de Saint-Fond), Ann M. Tsuji (Baroness de Simiane), Midori Nakamura (Charlotte), Tina Chen (Mme. de Montreuil, Renee's Mother), Natsuko Ohama (Renee, Mme. de Sade), Lauren Tom (Anne, Renee's younger sister)

A play in three acts. The action takes place in the salon in Mme. de Montreuil's house in 1772, 1778 and 1790.

**Dalton Leong,
Carol A. Honda
in "Rosie's Cafe"**

**Natsuko Ohama,
Tina Chen in
"Mme. de Sade"**

Martha Swope/Carol Rosegg Photos

105

PEARL THEATRE COMPANY

Fifth Season

Artistic Director, Shepard Sobel; General Manager, Mary Hurd; Artistic Associate, Joanne Camp; Dramaturge, Dale Ramsey; Producing Consultant, Tarquin Jay Bromley; Press, Elizabeth L. Henry

Friday, October 9,–November 7, 1987 (20 performances)
MACBETH by William Shakespeare; Director, Shepard Sobel; Set, Robert Joel Schwartz; Lighting, Stephen Petrilli; Costumes, Murrey Nelson; Sound, Tarquin Jay Bromley; Fight Choreographer, Richard Raether; Movement, Alice Teirstein; Stage Managers, Gigi Rivkin, Joanne Schmoll. CAST: Robin Leslie Brown (1st Witch), Frank Geraci (2nd Witch), Kenton Benedict (3rd Witch), Adrien Peyroux (Duncan/Seyward), David Brazda (Malcolm), Tim O'Hare (Lennox), James Nugent (Ross), Stuart Lerch (Macbeth), Joel Swetow (Banquo/Menteth), Donnah Welby (Lady Macbeth), Sky Ashley Berdahl (Fleance/Child Macduff), Pinkney Mikell (Macduff), Michael John McGuinness (Donalbain/Young Seward), Ken Harpster (Murderer/Doctor), Robin Westphal (Lady Macduff)

Friday, November 13,–December 12, 1987 (20 performances)
THE IMAGINARY INVALID by Moliere; New translation by Earle Edgerton; Director, Henry Fonte; Set, Robert Joel Schwartz; Lighting, Douglas O'Flaherty; Costumes, Julie Abels Chevan; Original Music/Sound, Kenn Dovel; Stage Managers, Eva C. Schegulla, Gigi Rivkin. CAST: Frank Geraci (Argan), Laura Margolis (Toinette), Laura Rathgeb (Angelique), Rose Stockton (Beline), James Nugent (M. Bonnefoi/Beralde), David Brazda (Cleante), Stuart Lerch (Diafoirus/Purgon), Michael John McGuinness (Thomas Diafoirus/Fleurant)

Performed with one intermission. The action takes place in Paris in 1775.

Friday, December 12, 1987–January 16, 1988 (20 performances)
CANDIDA by George Bernard Shaw; Director, David Schechter; Set, Robert Joe Schwartz; Lighting, Douglas O'Flaherty; Costumes, Barbara A. Bell; Assissant Director, Daniel S. Lewin; Stage Managers, Sue Jane Stoker, Gigi Rivkin. CAST: Laura Margolis (Miss Proserpine Garnett), Daniel Region (Rev. James Morell), Stuart Lerch (Lexie Mill), Frank Geraci (Mr. Burgess), Rose Stockton (Candida Morell), Michael John McGuinness (Marchbanks)

Friday, January 22,–February 20, 1988 (20 performances)
ELECTRA by Sophocles; Translated by Theodore Howard Banks; Director, Emanuele Pagani; Set, Robert Joel Schwartz; Lighting, Douglas O'Flaherty; Costumes, Ambra Dancon; Sound, Kenn Dovel; Choral Director, Rosemary Murphy; Choreographer, Alice Teirstein; Stage Managers, Eva C. Schegulla, Jennifer Boggs. CAST: Ken Harpster (Pedagogus), David Brazda (Orestes), Robin Leslie Brown (Electra), Joanne Camp (Choragos), Laura Rathgeb (Chrysothemis), Donnah Welby (Clytemnestra), Laurence Gleason (Aegisthus)

Friday, February 26,–March 26, 1988 (20 performances)
UNCLE VANYA by Anton Chekhov; Translated by Earle Edgerton; Director, Shepard Sobel; Assistant Director, Tarquin Jay Bromley; Stage Managers, Gigi Rivkin, Bruce Harpster. CAST: Sylvia Davis (Marina), Daniel Region (Astrov), James Nugent (Voinitsky), Joseph Warren (Serebryakov), Frank Geraci (Telyegin), Robin Westphal (Sonya), Joanne Camp (Elena), Bonnie Horan (Voinitskaya), Stuart Lerch (Yefim)

**Right: Daniel Region, Rose Stockton, Michael
John McGuinness in "Candida" Above: Rose Stockton,
Laura Rathgeb, Laura Margolis in "Imaginary
Invalid" Top: Donnah Welby, Stuart Lerch in
"Macbeth"** *(Carol Rosegg/Martha Swope Photos)*

**James Nugent, Joanne Camp
in "Uncle Vanya"**

**Donnah Welby, Robin Leslie Brown
in "Electra"**

PLAYWRIGHTS HORIZONS

Seventeenth Season

Artistic Director, Andre Bishop; Executive Director, Paul S. Daniels; Production Manager, Carl Mulert; Casting, Daniel Swee; Business Manager, Donna M. Gearhardt; Literary Manager, Tim Sanford; Administrative Director, Susan Forney Hughes; Development Director, Ruth Cohen; Technical Director, Albert Webster; Costumer, Virginia Patton; Props, Carol Silverman; Press, Bob Ullman

Tuesday, September 15,–October 11, 1987 (32 performances). Playwrights Horizons presents the Foundation of the Dramatists Guild' sixth annual Young Playwrights Festival (Nancy Quinn, Producing Director); Sets, Derek McLane; Costumes, Michael Krass; Lighting, Nancy Schertler; Sound, Lia Vollack; Production Manager, Carl Mulert

TINY MOMMY by Juliet Garson (age 18); Director, Amy Saltz; Stage Manager, Roy Harris. CAST: Michael Patrick Boatman (Joe), Nancy Giles (Joanne Jones/Christena), Susan Greenhill (Miss Roddenberg/Chani-Glick/Dr. Ruth), Sylvia Kauders (Chana), Eva Lopez (Millie), French Napier (Buddy/Young Father), Cynthia Nixon (Sharon), Sally Prager (Jennifer), Tonia Rowe (Woman with baby/Lashelle/Gloria), Jill Tasker (Marilyn Zuckerman), Mary Testa (Subway Orator/Cousin Elizabeth/Shalamis), Jose Soto (Angel), Ming-Na Wen (Lam/Young Man with Ghetto Blaster). The action takes place at the present time in New York City.

SPARKS IN THE PARK by Noble Mason Smith (age 18); Director, Gary Pearle; Fights Staged by Bjorn Johnson; Original Music, John McKinney; Stage Manager, Mary Fran Loftus. CAST: Nancy Giles (Janice English/Barry's Mom), Susan Greenhill (Dr. Renee Schmeer), Doug Hutchison (Ben Eckert), Stephen Mellor (Agent 4-h/Dr. Rudolph Schmeer/Craig Strongman/Guy Richmont), Todd Merrill (Barry Daniels), Cynthia Nixon (Stephanie Eckert), Oliver Platt (Indian Waiter/Buddy Hollister/French Waiter/Bart), John Vennema (Louis Reynolds/Chuck Hollister).

Sunday, October 4–8, 1987 (4 performances). Staged readings of the three runners-up:
EBONY by Pamela Mshana (age 16); Director, Sheldon Epps. **CHILDREN** by Debra Neff (16); Director, Charles Karchmer. **SERENDIPITY AND SERENITY** by Jonathan Marc Sherman (17); Director, Thomas Babe

Friday, October 23,–November 29, 1987 (22 performances)
LAUGHING WILD by Christopher Durang; Director, Ron Lagomarsino; Set, Thomas Lynch; Costumes, William Ivey Long; Lighting, Arden Fingerhut; Sound, Stan Metelits); Stage Manager, M. A. Howard CAST: E. Katherine Kerr (Woman), Christopher Durang (Man)

A play in three parts (Laughing Wild, Seeking Wild, Dreaming Wild) performed with one intermission.

Tuesday, Dec. 29, 1987–February 7, 1988 (48 performances)
ANOTHER ANTIGONE by A. R. Gurney, Jr.; Director, John Tillinger; Set/Costumes, Steven Rubin; Lighting, Kent Dorsey; Sound, John Gromada; Stage Manager, Neal Ann Stephens. CAST: George Grizzard (Henry Harper, Professor of Classics), Marissa Chibas (Judy Miller, a student), Debra Mooney (Diana Eberhart, Dean of Humane Studies), Steven Flynn (David Appleton, a student).

Performed without intermission. The action takes place at the present time during the latter part of the spring term in a Boston university.

Wednesday, January 27,–February 7, 1988 (13 performances)
COLD SWEAT by Neal Bell; Director, John Henry Davis; Set, Randy Benjamin; Costume Design, Donna Zakowska; Lighting, F. Mitchell Dana; Sound, Lia Vollack; Stage Manager, Roy Harris. CAST: Amy Aquino (Fay), Kent Broadhurst (Hanson/Ray), Tony Maggio (Jamie), Reggie Montgomery (Gordon), Rosemary Murphy (Bess), Ellen Parker (Alice), James Rebhorn (Leon), Brad Sullivan (Court), Grace Zabriskie (Emma)

A play in two acts. The action begins in Vietnam, then shifts to the United States from 1971–76.

Friday, April 1,–May 8, 1988 (15 performances and 27 previews)
LUCKY STIFF a musical based on "The Man Who Broke the Bank at Monte Carlo" by Michael Butterworth; Book and Lyrics, Lynn Ahrens; Music, Stephen Flaherty; Director, Thommie Walsh; Set, Bob Shaw; Costumes, Michael Krass; Lighting, Beverly Emmons; Sound, Lia Vollack; Musical Direction, Jeffrey Saver; Orchestrations, Michael Abbott; Musical Theatre Program Director, Ira Weitzman; Stage Managers, Robin Rumpf, Jeffery A. Alspaugh; Production Assistant, James Fitzsimmons. CAST: Ron Faber (Uncle Anthony), Patty Holley (Dominique du Monaco/Ensemble), Paul Kandel (Luigi Gaudi), Michael McCarty succeeded by Erick Devine (Solicitor/Emcee/Ensemble), Barbara Rosenblatt (Mrs. Markham/Drunken Maid/Ensemble), Stephen Stout (Harry), Mary Testa (Rita), Julie White (Annabel), Stuart Zagnit (Vinnie), Frank Zagottis (Bellhop/Ensemble). MUSICAL NUMBERS: Something Funny's Going On, Mr. Witherspoon's Friday Night, Rita's Confession, Good to Be Alive, Lucky, Dogs Versus You, The Phone Call, A Day around Town Dance, Monte Carlo!, Speaking French, Times Like This, Fancy Meeting You Here

A musical in 2 acts and 10 scenes. The action takes place in England, New Jersey, and Monte Carlo at the present time.

Wednesday, April 13–24, 1988 (13 performances)
GUS AND AL by Albert Innaurato; Director, David Warren; Set, Jim Youmans; Costumes, David C. Woolard; Lighting, Robert Jared; Sound, John Gromada; Musical Arrangements, Ted Sperling; Stage Manager, Allison Sommers. CAST: Mark Blum (Al), David Brisbin (Kafka/Sigmund Freud), Helen Hanft (Mrs. Briggs), Christina Moore (Justine Mahler), Lois Smith (Natalie Bauer Lechner), Daniel Nathan Spector (Camillo), Sam Tsoutsouvas (Gustav Mahler), Jennifer Van Dyck (Alma Schindler)

A play in two acts. The action starts in Manhattan in 1988, and shifts to Vienna in 1900.

Friday, May 27,–June 26, 1988 (6 performances and 29 previews)
RIGHT BEHIND THE FLAG by Kevin Heelan; Director, R. J. Cutler; Set, Loy Arcenas; Costumes, Candice Donnelly; Lighting, Debra J. Kletter; Sound Lia Vollack; Stage Manager, Suzanne Fry. CAST: Amy Aquino (Catherine), Joe Bellan (Vinnie), W. T. Martin (Frankie), Paul McCrane (Timmerman/Bartender), Richard Riehle (Cop), Herbert Rubens (Joe), Kevin Spacey (Bernie)

A play in 2 acts and 11 scenes. The action takes place in New York City during the mid-1980's

RIVERSIDE SHAKESPEARE COMPANY

Artistic Director, Timothy W. Oman; Executive Director, Mary Ann Hansen; Associate Artistic Director, Eric Hoffmann; Company Manager, Kathleen Bishop
 (New York City Parks) Wednesday, July 8–26, 1987 (15 performances)
A MIDSUMMER NIGHT'S DREAM by William Shakespeare; Director, John Basil; Set, Peter R. Feuche; Costumes, Vicki Davis; Music, Aural Fixation; Choreography, Tim Zimmermann; Manager, Harry Lee; Technical Directors, Peter Brassard, Fiach MacConghail; Wardrobe, Karen Sullivan; Stage Managers, John Basil, Maureen McSherry, Phil Curry; Assistant to Director, Richard Fay. CAST: Jeff Shoemaker (Theseus/Oberon), Lisa Bansavage (Hippolyta/Titania), Richard Fay (Demetrius), Skip Lundby (Lysander), Liz Trepel (Helena), Freda Kavanagh (Hermia), Joel Friedman (Egeus/Starveling/Moonshine), Christopher J. Markle (Philostrate/Snug/Lion), Charles Michael Wright (Puck), Katherine Cloutier (1st Fairy/Peaseblossom/Cobweb), Polly O'Malley (2nd Fairy/Moth/Mustardseed), Christian Kauffmann (Peter Quince/Prologue), Eric Hoffmann (Nick Bottom/Pyramus), Paul Walker (Francis Flute/Thisbe), Oliva Le'Auanae (Tom Snout/Wall)
 (Soldier and Sailor's Monument) Sunday, June 14,–August 23, 1987 (6 performances)
SUNDAYS IN THE PARK WITH SHAKESPEARE: TWELFTH NIGHT directed by Howard Thoresen; JULIUS CAESAR directed by Doug Mosten; TWO GENTLEMEN OF VERONA directed by Daniel T. Johnson; OTHELLO directed by Linda Masson, and featuring F. Murray Abraham; AS YOU LIKE IT directed by Stefan Rudnick; HAMLET directed by Stephen Lloyd Helper, and featuring Terrence Mann
 (Shakespeare Center) Saturday, October 31,–November 7, 1987
BARD-A-THON I: Harvest Bard Part I: The first of the planned readings of Shakespeare's complete works, featuring Comedy of Errors, Macbeth, Hamlet, The Tempest, Coriolanus, Titus Andronicus, The Merry Wives of Windsor, Richard III, Cymbeling, Julius Caesar, A Midsummer Night's Dream. This project ultimately employed the talents of over 20 companies, 30 directors, and 600 actors.
 Friday, December 4–6, 1987
SIREN TEARS (The History of Shakespeare's Sonnets) developed in workshop by members of the company; Director, Daniel T. Johnson; Lighting, Sam Scripps; Stage Manager, Andrea Yoson. CAST: Buck Hobbs (Sir William Harvey), Peter Jack Thatch (Will Shakespeare), Mark Spenser (Henry Wriothsley, 3rd Earl of Southampton), Jane Moffat (His Mother, Lady Mary Wriothsley), Emilia Bassano Lanier (Constance Boardman)
 Thursday, January 7–10, 1988 (5 performances)
ALL'S WELL THAT ENDS WELL by William Shakespeare; Director, Kathleen Bishop; Set, Peter R. Feuche; Lights, Stephen Petrilli; Set/Board Operator, James Schwatzman; Stage Managers, Mindy Pfeffer, Jack Smith. CAST: Charles Halden (Lord H, aide to Bertram), Kirby Wahl (Bertram, Count Roussillion), Margot Stevenson (The Countess Roussillion, his mother), Margot Avery (Helena), Bob J. Mitchell (Lord LaFew), Claude Albert Saucier (Parolles), William Beckwith (King of France), Robert Tekampe (Lord G), Timothy Davis-Reed (Lord E), Tony Mandel (Gentleman Astringer/Lord M), William Brooks (Lord B, Son to Duke of Florence), Woody Sempliner (Interpreter/Lord S), Jack Smith (Rinaldo/Lord J), Gus Demos (Lavache), David Manchester (Duke of Florence), Paula Eschweiler (Widow), Lori Bezahler (Diana), Mindy Pfeffer (Mariana)
 Thursday, January 28–31, 1988 (3 performances)
BRAM by Don Rifkin; Director, Doug Moston; Lighting, Stephen Petrilli; Set, Peter R. Feuche; Sound, Stephen H. Sterns; Audio, William B. Porter; Stage Managers, Heather Garland, Shawn Kane. CAST: Elizabeth W. Forsyth (Jessica Reilly), Jim Lefebvre (Jack Rosen)
 A play in two acts. The action takes place during the early 1980's in Manhattan.
 Friday, February 5–14, 1988 (14 performances)
BARD-A-THON II VALENTINE BARD: Staged readings of Much Ado about Nothing, All's Well That Ends Well, Henry V, Troilus and Cressida, Romeo and Juliet, Twelfth Night, Henry VIII, Two Gentlemen of Verona, Pericles, Othello, Taming of the Shrew, Antony and Cleopatra, Love's Labour's Lost.
 Thursday, March 17–20, 1988 (4 performances)
TITUS ANDRONICUS by William Shakespeare; Director, Timothy W. Oman; Set, Peter R. Feuche; Costumes, David Pearson; Lighting, Stephen Petrilli; Props, Mary Meadsmith; Stage Manager, Heather T. Garland. CAST: Bruce Hobbs (Saturninus), Will Osborne (Bassianus), Herman Petras (Titus Andronicus), William Beckwith (Marcus Andronicus), Gregory Linus Weiss (Lucius), Jim Pratzon (Quintus), Austin Butler (Martius), David Goodman (Mucius), Gary Brownlee (Young Lucius), Rick Gianasi (Publius), Michael Graves (Aemilius), Jimmy Blackman (Alarbus/Clown), James Davies (Demetrius), Jens Krummel (Chiron), Eric McGill (Aaron), Steve Deighan (Captain), John Banta (Caius), David Levine (Valentine), Gerard Cerini (Sempronius), Kathleen Bishop (Tamora), Lisa Nicholas (Lavinia), Elizabeth Teal (Nurse)

Thursday, March 24–27, 1988 (4 performances)
CYMBELINE by William Shakespeare; Director, Eric Hoffmann; Music, Steve Barkhimer; Stage Manager, P. J. Laurel; Fight Choreographer, Lawrence H. Lustberg; Props, Mary Meade-Smith; Sound, Karen St. Pierre. CAST: Geraldine Abbate (Wife to Cymbeline), Grace Bentley (Cornelius), Richard Bowden (Cymbeline), Andy Buckley (Frenchman), Quinton Cockrell (Soothsayer), James Coromel (Lord), Christopher Durham (Iachimo), Jonathan Epstein (Guiderius), Jim Lillie (Arviragus), Thomas Grube (Philario), Christine Linkie (Helen), Frank Lowe (Belarius), David Matthews (Gentleman), Bob J. Mitchell (Caius Lucius), Tony Rust (Cloten), Malcolm Stephenson (Pisanio), Eloise Watt (Imogen), David Wheeler (Posthumus Leonatus)
 Friday, April 22,–May 2, 1988 (14 performances)
BARD-A-THON III BIRTHDAY BARD: staged readings of Merchant of Venice, Henry IV Parts 1 & 2, Measure for Measure, King John, Richard II, A Winter's Tale, Timon of Athens, King Lear, Henry VI Parts 1, 2, 3, As You Like It.
 Tuesday, May 12,–June 4, 1988
TITUS ANDRONICUS by William Shakespeare; Director, Timothy W. Oman; Lighting, Bernadette Englert; Props, Kelly Moorehead; Producers, Kathleen Bishop, Buck Hobbs; Stage Manager, Timothy D. Kelin. CAST: William Beckwith (Marcus), Georg Bishop (Captain), Kathleen Bishop (Tamora), Jimmy Blackman (Alarbus/Clown), Austin Butler (Martius), Robert Emmet (Lucius), Robert Freitas (Valemtine), Rick Gianasi (Publius), David Goodman (Mutius/Goth Captain), Buck Hobbs (Saturninus), Jens Krummel (Chiron), Eric McGill (Aaron), Patrick McGuinness (Martius), Kam Metcalf (Young Lucius), Lisa Nicholas (Lavinia), Albert Owens (Quimtus), Herman Petras (Titus Andronicus), Jim Pratzon (Quintus/Goth), Tony Rust (Chiron), Daniel Dean Scott (Demetrius), Woody Sempliner (Aemilius), Jack Smith (Caius), Malcolm Stephenson (Bassianus), Steven Zorowitz (Sempronius), Elizabeth Teal (Nurse)

ROUNDABOUT THEATRE

Twenty-second Season

Artistic Director, Gene Feist; Executive Director, Todd Haimes; General Manager, Ellen Richard; Literary Manager/Artistic Associate, Eileen Cowel; Assistant Executive Director, Margaret L. Wolff; Technical Director, John Kincaid; Casting, David Tochterman; Hairstylists, Tomo 'n' Tomo, Linda Wager; Production Manager, Ray Swagerty; Costume Director, Cecelia Eller; Wardrobe, Tad Webb; Sound/Music Director, Philip Campanella; Stage Managers, Kathy J. Faul, Matthew T. Mundinger; Press, Joshua Ellis Office/Adrian Bryan-Brown, Jackie Green, Leo Stern, Susanne Tighe, Tim Ray

Friday, July 17,–September 6, 1987 (24 performances and 24 previews)
BUNKER REVERIES by David Shaber; Director, Allen Carlsen; Set, David Jenkins; Costumes, Carol Oditz; Lighting, F. Mitchell Dana; Wigs, Diane Swanson; Props, Betsy Kelleher CAST: Ralph Waite (Jack Packard), Patricia Elliott (Margaret), Kristin Griffith (Patty), Richard Backus (Alan), Sheila MacRae (Annabelle), Robert Stattel (William Skinner), Debra Cole (Andy)

A drama in two acts. The action takes place at the present time in a small hotel of little note in Washington, D.C., on a particular night in November.

Wednesday, October 7,–December 6, 1987 (54 performances and 16 previews)
OF MICE AND MEN by John Steinbeck; Director, Arthur Storch; Set, Victor A. Becker; Costumes, Cecelia Eller; Lighting, Judy Rasmuson; Sound, Scott David Sanders; Fight Director, Patrick Mulcahy; Props, Keith Michl; Assistant to Director, Rob Brownstein; Stage Managers, Kathy J. Faul, Scott Rodabaugh CAST: John Savage (George), Jay Patterson (Lennie), Edward Seamon (Candy), Joseph Warren (Boss), Clifford Fetters (Curley), Jane Fleiss (Curley's Wife), Mark Metcalf (Slim), Matthew Locricchio (Carlson), Ron Perkins (Whit), Roger Robinson (Crooks) succeeded by Daryl Edwards, Sundae (Dog)

A drama in 2 acts and 6 scenes. The action takes place during 1937 in an agricultural valley in Northern California.

Wednesday, December 16, 1987–February 14, 1988 (45 performances and 24 previews)
MAN AND SUPERMAN by George Bernard Shaw; Director, William Woodman; Set, Bob Shaw; Costumes, Andrew B. Marlay; Lighting, F. Mitchell Dana; Production Assistant, Joanne Meynard; Props, Daniel P. Donnelly; Stage Managers, Roy W. Backes, Kathy J. Faul CAST: I. M. Hobson (Roebuck Ramsden), Michael Cumpsty (Octavius Robinson), David Birney (John Tanner), Frances Conroy (Ann Whitefield), Kim Hunter (Mrs. Whitefield), Harriet Harris (Violet Robinson), Anthony Fusco (Henry Straker), Jonathan Walker (Hector Malone), John Carpenter (Mr. Malone), David Barbee, John Boyle (Footmen)

A comedy in three acts. The action takes place during 1905 in Roebuck Ramsden's Study/Portland Place in London, in the courtyard of the Whitefield residence near Richmond, and on the terrace of a hotel in Granada, Spain.

Wednesday, March 2,–April 24, 1988 (59 performances)
RASHOMON by Fay and Michael Kanin; Based on stories by Ryunosuke Akutagawa and Akira Kurosawa's film "Rashomon"; Director, Robert Kalfin; Set, Mina Albergo; Lighting, F. Mitchell Dana; Fight Direction/Movement, David Leong; Assistant to Director, Gail Garrison; Production Assistant, Kenneth Herbert; Props, Patricia Hoffman; Japanese Consultant, Ako; Stage Managers, Kathy J. Faul, Roy W. Backes CAST: Thom Sesma (Priest), Peter Yoshida (Woodcutter), Norris M. Shimabuku (Wigmaker), Allan Tung (Deputy), James Saito (Bandit), Philip Moon (Husband), Kiya Ann Joyce (Wife), Kati Kuroda (Mother), Allan Tung (Medium)

A drama in two acts. The action takes place in and near Kyoto, Japan, about 1000 years ago at the Rashomon Gate, at a magistrate's court, and in a forest.

Wednesday, May 11–June 5, 1988
DANDY DICK by Arthur Wing Pinero; Director, Jimmy Bohr; Set, Daniel Proett; Costumes, Andrew B. Marlay; Lighting, John Hastings; Sound, Philip Campanella; Stage Manager, Kathy J. Faul, Roy W. Backes; Casting, Jay Binder CAST: Gordon Chater (The Very Rev. Augustin Jedd, D.D.), Kathryn Meisle (Salome), Monique Fowler (Sheba), Jan Miner (Georgiana Tidman), Frank Hamilton (Blore), Denis Holmes (Sir Tristram Mardon), Joshua Worby (Hatcham), John C. Vennema (Major Traver), Edward Hibbert (Mr. Darby), J. K. Simmons (Noah Topping), Cynthia Darlow (Hannah Topping)

A play in three acts.

Martha Swope Photos

Lower Right Center: Kim Hunter, David Birney in "Man and Superman"; Denis Holmes, Jan Miner in "Dandy Dick" Above: John Savage, Jane Fleiss, Jay Patterson, Roger Robinson, Edward Seamon in "Of Mice and Men" Top: Kristin Griffith, Richard Backus, Ralph Waite, Robert Stattel, Patricia Elliott in "Bunker Reveries"

James Saito, Kiya Ann Joyce, Philip Moon in "Rashomon"

SECOND STAGE

Ninth Year

Artistic Directors, Robyn Goodman, Carole Rothman; Managing Director, Rosa I. Vega; Marketing, Carol Bixler; Development, John Thew; Business Manager, Jerry Polner; Dramaturg, Anne Cattaneo; Casting, Simon & Kumin; Sound, Gary Harris; Production Supervisor, Alfred Miller; Press, Richard Kornberg

Monday, June 15,–July 18, 1987 (21 performances and 19 previews)

THE REDTHROATS written and performed by David Cale in four parts: his early rural English background, his coming of age in London, and his journey to America.

Wednesday, November 18,–December 27, 1987 (21 performances and 19 previews)

MOONCHILDREN by Michael Weller; Director, Mary B. Robinson; Set, Charles H. McClennahan; Lighting, Mal Sturchio; Costumes, Mimi Maxmen; Hairstylist, Antonio Soddu; Props, Melissa L. Stephenson; Wardrobe, Jenny Peek; Stage Managers, Roy Harris, Carol Fishman CAST: Kevin Anderson (Bob), Larry Block (Willis), Dan Desmond (Lucky), Dave Florek (Bream/Cootie's Father), Jim Fyfe (Dick), Paul McCrane (Norman), Penelope Ann Miller (Ruth), Geoffrey Nauffts (Ralph/Effing), Cynthia Nixon (Kathy), Sam Robards (Cootie), Alan Ruck (Mike), Paul Soles (Murray/Milkman), Kathleen Wilhotte (Shelly)

A play in two acts. The action takes place in a student apartment in an American university town during 1965–1966.

Wednesday, January 27,–February 28, 1988 (19 performances and 13 previews)

LOOSE ENDS by Michael Weller; Director, Irene Lewis; Set, Kevin Rupnik; Lighting, Peter Kaczorowski; Costumes, Candice Donnelly; Sound, Gary and Timmy Harris; Props, Catherine Pollicella; Wardrobe, Christina Heath; Stage Managers, Fredric H. Orner, Jenny Peek CAST: Richard Eng (Balinese Fisherman), Larry Fishburne (Doug), Alexandra Gersten (Janice), Paul Guilfoyle (Ben), Jane Kaczmarek (Susan), Terry Kinney (Paul), Bill Kux (Russell), Jeanne Mori (Selina), Park Overall (Maraya), Joseph R. Sicari (Lawrence), Stephen Stout (Phil)

A play in 2 acts and 8 scenes. The Action takes place in Bali (1970), Upstate New York (1971), Boston (1973–77), New York City (1975–78), New Hampshire (1979)

Friday, April 22,–June 26, 1988 (40 performances and 24 previews)

SPOILS OF WAR by Michael Weller; Director, Austin Pendleton; Set, Kevin Rupnik; Lighting, Betsy Adams; Costumes, Ruth Morley; Choreography, Ronald Young; Wardrobe, Christina Heath; Technical Director, Patrick Heydenburg; Props, Janet E. Smith; Stage Managers, Pamela Edington, Camille Calman CAST: Annette Bening (Penny), Larry Bryggman (Andrew), Christopher Collet (Martin), Kate Nelligan (Elise), Kevin O'Rourke (Lew), Alice Playten (Emma)

A play in two acts. The action takes place in New York City in the 1950's.

**Left: Terry Kinney, Jane Kaczmarek
in "Loose Ends" Top: Penelope Ann Miller,
Alan Ruck, Jim Fyfe, Kevin Anderson, Paul
McCrane, Kathleen Wilhoite, Sam Robards,
Larry Block in "Moonchildren"**
(Susan Cook Photos)

Kate Nelligan, Alice Playten, Kevin
O'Rourke in "Spoils of War"

**Christopher Collet, Kate Nelligan
in "Spoils of War"**

SOHO REPERTORY THEATRE

Thirteenth Season

Artistic Directors, Jerry Engelback, Marlene Swartz; Business Manager, Daniel W. Thompson; Dramaturg, Victor Gluck; Production Assistant, Matthew Sheehan; Press, Bruce Cohen, Kathleen von Schmid; Casting, Brian Chavanne

(Greenwich House) Friday, November 20,–December 13, 1987 (16 performances) **THE RACKET** by Bartlett Cormack; Director, Michael Bloom; Set, Phillip Baldwin; Costumes, Claudia Stephens; Lighting, Robert W. Rosentel; Props, Rose Sennett; Assistant Director, Barbara Nicoll; Technical Director, Harry E. Lee; Stage Managers, Lawrence Berrick, Mimi Cohen. CAST: Sam Guncler (Pratt), Mitchell McGuire (Miller), Jordan Lund (Sgt. Sullivan), Michael Swain (Patrolman Clark), David Reinhardsen (Lt. Gill), Mark Hofmaier (Attorney Welch), James A. Pyduck (Turck/Alderman Kublacek), Dustin R. Evans (Det. Sgt. Delaney), Peter G. Morse (Patrolman Johnson), Brian Evers (Capt. McQuigg), Ted Marcoux (Dave Ames), Robert Cicchini (Joe/Glick), Tracy Kolis (Irene Hayes), Richard Gray (Sgt. Schmidt), Howard Samuelson (Sam Meyer), Matthew Gottlieb (Nick Scarsi)

A melodrama in three acts. The action takes place in the central room of a police station outside Chicago, and in the captain's office.

Friday, January 29,–February 21, 1988 (16 performances) **THE GIRL OF THE GOLDEN WEST** by David Belasco; Director, Julian Webber; Music, Chris and Rachel Turner; Set, Jeffrey David McDonald; Costumes, Patricia Adshead; Lighting, Nancy Collings; Props, Georgia Accola; Assistant Director, Michael Sexton; Technical Director, Rick Lucero; Scenic Artist, David Blankenship; Stage Manager, Alice Perlmutter. CAST: Joseph McKenna (Sonora Slim), Ray Collins (Sidney Duck), Michael Earl Reid (Trinidad Joe), Jason Fitz-Gerald (Nick), David Bates (Happy Halliday), Michael M. Swain (Handsome Charlie), George Emilio Sanchez (Billy Jackrabbit), Andy McCutcheon (Jim Larkens/Jose Castro/Bucking Billy), John Nielsen (Man from the Ridge/Sheriff), Richard Gray (Man from the Ridge/Pony Express Drive/Miner), Chris Turner (Jake Wallace/Musician), Michael Wetmore (Jack Rance), Steven Dennis (Ashby), Monique Fowler (The Girl), Peter Webster (Johnson), Lisa Goodman (Wowkle), Rachel Turner (Musician)

A melodrama in four acts. The action takes place in Cloudy Mountain, Calif., mining camp during the 1849–50 gold rush.

Friday, March 25,–April 17, 1988 (17 performances) **A CUP OF COFFEE** by Preston Sturges; Director, Larry Carpenter; Set, Mark Wendland; Costumes, Martha Hally; Lighting, Stuart Duke; Props, Michael Chudinski; Sound, Philip Campanella; Stage Managers, David Waggett, George A. Tyger, Nick Erickson. CAST: Willie Carpenter (Julius Snaith), Robin Chadwick (Lomax Whortleberry), Nesbitt Blaisdell (J. Bloodgood Baxter), Richard L. Bowne (Oliver Baxter), Ellen Mareneck (Tulip Jones), Gwyllum Evans (Ephraim Baxter), Michael Heintzman (James MacDonald), William McClary succeeded by Tom Bloom (Postman. Sign Painter/Rasmussen), George A. Tyger (Youth)

World premiere of a 1931 comedy in three acts. The action takes place in the Baxter Coffee Warehouse in New York City during May of 1931.

Left: Monique Fowler, Jason Fitzgerald, Joseph McKenna, George Emilio Sanchez, Michael Earl Reid, and Above: Peter Webster, Monique Fowler in "Girl of the Golden West"
Top: Brian Evers, Matthew Gottlieb, Tracy P. Kolis in "The Racket" *(Gerry Goodstein Photos)*

Ellen Mareneck, Michael Heintzman, Nesbitt Blaisdell in "A Cup of Coffee"

Michael Heintzman, Gwyllum Evans, Ellen Mareneck in "A Cup of Coffee"

WPA THEATRE

Eleventh Season

Workshop of the Players Art Foundation; Artistic Director, Kyle Renick; Managing Director, Wendy Bustard; Resident Designer, Edward T, Gianfrancesco; Lighting, Craig Evans; Casting/Literary Advisor, Patricia Hoag; Production Manager/Technical Director, Gordon W. Brown; Press, Jeffrey Richards, C. George Willard, Ben Morse, Ken Mandelbaum, Irene Gandy, Susan Lee, Jim Casey

Wednesday, June 3–June 28, 1987 (15 performances and 13 previews)
COPPERHEAD by Erik Brogger; Director, Mary B. Robinson; Costumes, Mimi Maxmen; Sound, Aural Fixation; Props, Janet Smith; Stage Manager, Crystal Huntington CAST: Dave Florek (Oliver Wright), Kathleen Nolan (Lucille), Campbell Scott (Parker Smith), William Cain (Rev. Paul Raeder), William Wise (Calvin)

A drama in 2 acts and 8 scenes. The action takes place at the present time in Central Pennsylvania.

Wednesday, Nov. 4,–Dec. 27, 1987. (33 performances and 20 previews)
THE MILK TRAIN DOESN'T STOP HERE ANYMORE by Tennessee Williams; Director, Kevin Conway; Costumes, Candice Donnelly; Stage Manager, Henry White; Wardrobe, Christina Heath; Hair, Raymond Granados; Production Assistant, David Scott CAST: Elizabeth Ashley (Flora Goforth), Amanda Plummer (Frances Black), Luis Ramos (Giullo), Ava Haddad (Angelina), Stephen McHattie (Christopher Glander), Marian Seldes (Vera Ridgeway Condotti)

A drama in 2 acts. The action takes place in the present with occasional forays into the supernatural.

Tuesday, Feb. 16,–March 20, 1988. (13 performances and 14 previews)
A SUBJECT OF CHILDHOOD by Loren-Paul Caplin; Director, Bill Castellino; Costumes, Don Newcomb; Stage Manager, Marybeth Ward CAST: Kelle Kerr (Dusty), Gregory Salata (Richard), Novella Nelson (Counselor)

A psychological drama in 2 acts. The action takes place at the present time in Brooklyn, NY.

Tuesday, April 19,–May 24, 1988 (7 performances and 15 previews)
NO TIME FLAT by Larry Ketron; Director, Peter Maloney; Stage Manager, Greta Minsky CAST: Daniel Ahearn (Calter), Linda Cook (Sue), Paul Geier (Irwin), Sandra Bullock (Carolina)

A play in two acts. The action takes place during June of the present and takes place "all over the place."

Martha Swope Photos

Lower Right Center: Daniel Ahearn, Sandra Bullock, Paul Geier in "No Time Flat" Above: Gregg Salata, Novella Nelson, Kelle Kerr in "A Subject of Childhood" Top: Kathleen Nolan, Campbell Scott in "Copperhead"

Elizabeth Ashley, Amanda Plummer in "The Milk Train Doesn't Stop Here Anymore"

Marian Seldes, Amanda Plummer, Elizabeth Ashley in "The Milk Train Doesn't Stop Here Anymore"

YORK THEATRE COMPANY

Nineteenth Season

Producing Director, Janet Hayes Walker; Managing Director, Molly Pickering Grose; Artistic Advisers, John Newton, James Morgan; Production Manager, Sally Smith; Sets, James Morgan; Lighting, Mary Jo Dondlinger; Business Manager, Charles Dodsley Walker; Literary Manager, Ralph David Westfall; Press, Keith Sherman

(Church of the Heavenly Rest) Friday, October 23,–November 14, 1987 (20 performances)

COMPANY with Music and Lyrics by Stephen Sondheim; Book, George Furth; Director, Susan H. Schulman; Costumes, Michael Krass; Technical Director, Serge Hunkins; Choreography, Michael Lichtefeld; Musical Direction, David Krane; Props, Deborah Scott; Wardrobe, Robert Swasey; Stage Managers, Susan Whelan, Shannon Graves. CAST: Barbara Andres (Joanne), Robert Michael Baker (Paul), Judith Blazer (Amy), David Carroll (Robert), John P. Connolly (David), Debra Dickinson (Susan), Michael Elich (Peter), Donna English (April), Louise Hickey (Kathy), Liz Larsen (Marta), Jeanne Lehman (Jenny), Kip Niven (Larry), Susan Elizabeth Scott (Sarah), Lenny Wolpe (Harry)

MUSICAL NUMBERS: Company, The Little Things You Do Together, Sorry-Grateful, You Could Drive a Person Crazy, Have I Got a Girl for You, Someone Is Waiting, Another Hundred People, Getting Married Today, Side by Side by Side, What Would We Do Without You, Poor Baby, Love Dance, Barcelona, The Ladies Who Lunch, Being Alive

A musical in two acts.

Saturday, January 16–31, 1988 (16 performances)

THE VINEGAR TREE by Paul Osborn; Director, Kent Paul; Set, Jane Clark; Costumes, Gene Lakin; Casting, Joseph Abaldo; Props, Deborah Scott; Wardrobe, Robert Swasey; Stage Managers, James D'Asaro, Nicole Rosen. CAST: Joseph Daly (Augustus Merrick), John Horton (Max Lawrence), April Shawhan (Winifred Mansfield), J. Frank Lucas (Louis), Frances Cuka (Laura Merrick), Donna Kane (Leone Merrick), Michael Lasswell (Geoffrey Cole)

A comedy in three acts. The action takes place in the living room of the Merricks' country house in 1930.

Friday, March 25,–April 17, 1988 (16 performances)

LOST IN THE STARS with Musica by Kurt Weill; Words, Maxwell Anderson; Based on Alan Paton's "Cry, the Beloved Country'; Director, Alex Dmitriev; Musical Direction, Lawrence W. Hill; Costumes, Holly Hynes; Production Manager, Herbert H. O'Dell; Stage Managers, William J. Buckley III, Nicole Rosen. CAST: Ruth Adams (Mrs. Mkize/Rose), Fred Anderson (Matthew), April Armstrong (Irina), Sean Ashby (Alex), John Babcock (Edward), Evan Bell (John Kumalo), Dalton Russell Dearborn (James Jarvis), Lothair Eaton (Paulus), Karen Eubanks (Grace), Connie Fredericks (Linda), Steve Harper (Absalom), Tim Johnson (Johannes Pafuri), Rebecca Judd (Ensemble), Rachel Lemanski (Ensemble), Lee Lobenhofer (Arthur Jarvis), George Merritt (Stephen Kamalo), David Ossian (Eland/Judge), Laura Pearson (Laura), Ken Prymus (Leader/William), Desiree Scott (Nita), David Tislow (Burton)

A musical tragedy in two acts. The action takes place in the village of Ndotsheni and the City of Johannesburg, South Africa, from August to November of 1949.

Tuesday, May 24,–June 5, 1988 (12 performances)

TAMMY GRIMES: A CONCERT IN WORDS AND MUSIC; Musical Director, Richard Jameson Bell; Costumes, Clovis Ruffin; Lighting, Jack Jacobs; Technical Directors, Herbert H. O'Dell, Sally Smith; Hair Stylist, Dante; Stage Manager, William J. Buckley III. CAST: Tammy Grimes

MUSICAL NUMBERS: The Rainbow Connection, Ring Them Bells, Could I Have This Dance?, The Snake, Martha (Thomas), Where or When?, More Than One Man in Her Life, A Quarter 'Til Nine, What Will I Do?, If Love Were All, Moritat, Pirate Jenny, Songs from W. B. Yeats, Something So Right, Brother Can You Spare a Dime?, Dreaming My Dreams, It Never Was You, Medley from 'The Unsinkable Molly Brown,' He Went to Paris

Performed with one intermission.

Top: David Carroll, Barbara Andres in "Company"
(Anita & Steve Shevette) **Below: Donna Kane,**
Frances Cuka in "The Vinegar Tree"
(Carol Rosegg/Martha Swope Photos)

Tammy Grimes

Ken Prymus (top), April Armstrong, Steve Harper in "Lost in the Stars"

NATIONAL TOURING COMPANIES

THE ACTING COMPANY

Producing Artistic Director, John Houseman; Executive Producer, Margot Harley; Artistic Director, Michael Kahn; Associate Artistic Director, Gerald Gutierrez; Artistic Associates, David Ogden Stiers, Kevin Kline; General Manager, Mary Beth Carroll; Voice and Speech Consultant, Elizabeth Smith; Staff Repertory, Jennifer McCray; Production Stage Manager, C. A. Clark; Stage Manager, Michael Trent; Promotions Coordinator, Jerry Hasard; Booking Director, Michael C. E. Goodell. The 1987–88 Tour opened Friday August 7, 1987 in Boone, NC and toured 85 cities from coast to coast closing May 28, 1988 in Washington, D.C.
COMPANY: Irwin Appel, Oliver Barreiro, Spencer Beckwith, Constance Crawford, Paul Hebron, Mark Kincaid, Douglas Krizner, Rene Laigo, Oni Faida Lampley, Peter Lewis, Alison Stair Neet, Jonathan Nichols, Laura Perrotta, Ralph Zito.
PRODUCTIONS: FIVE BY TENN; short plays by Tennessee Williams; Director, Michael Kahn; Sets, Derek McLane; Costumes, Ann Hould-Ward; Lighting, Dennis Parichy
MUCH ADO ABOUT NOTHING by William Shakespeare; Director Gerald Gutierrez; Sets, Douglas Stein; Costumes, Ann Hould-Ward; Lighting, Pat Collins
KABUKI MACBETH by Karen Sunde; Director, Shozo Sato; Sets & Costumes, Shozo Sato; Lighting, Dennis Parichy. This was a world premiere which opened in Davis, CA on January 7, 1988.

Right: Oni Faida Lampley, Oliver Barreiro
in "Five by Tenn" *(Bob Marshak)* **Top:**
"Kabuki Macbeth" *(Marty Sohl)*

Oni Faida Lampley, Laura Perrotta,
Alison Stair Neet (below) in "Much
Ado about Nothing" *(Adam Newman)*

Laura Perrotta, Jonathan Nichols
in "Five by Tenn" *(Bob Marshak)*

BIG RIVER

Book, William Hauptman; Adapted from the novel "The Adventures of Huckleberry Finn" by Mark Twain; Music and Lyrics, Roger Miller; Director, Michael Greig; Choreographer, Janet Watson; Stage Movement and Fights, B. H. Barry; Scenery, Heidi Landesman; Costumes, Patricia McGourty; Lighting, Richard Riddell; Sound, Otts Munderloh; Musical Supervisor, Danny Troob; Orchestrations, Steven Margoshes, Danny Troob; Dance and Incidental Music, John Richard Lewis; Musical Director, Michael Rafter; Casting, Soble/La Padura C.S.A.; Production Stage Manager, Charles Collins; Sound Effects, John Kilgore; Hair, Angela Gari; Presented by Tom Mallow, Arthur M. Katz, William H. Kessler, Jr. by arrangement with Rocco Landesman, Heidi Landesman, Rick Steiner, M. Anthony Fisher and Dodger Productions. Opened at the Playhouse Square Center State Theatre, Cleveland, Ohio, on Saturday, July 11, 1987. For original Broadway production, see *THEATRE WORLD* Vol. 41.

CAST

Mark Twain/Counselor Robinson/Doctor	Kevin Cooney[1]
Huckleberry Finn	Romain Fruge
Widow Douglas/Sally Phelps	Frances Ford
Miss Watson/Woman in Shanty/Harmonia Player	Lucinda Hitchcock Cone
Jim	Michael Edward-Stevens
Tom Sawyer	Barry Lee
Ben Rogers/Hank/Hired Hand	Robert Lambert
Jo Harper/Joanna Wilkes	Beth Musiker
Simon/Dick/Young Fool	Thom Cagle
Pap Finn/Andy/Sheriff Bell/Hired Hand	Dale Radunz
Judge Thatcher/Harvey Wilkes/Silas Phelps	Bruce Vernon Bradley
The King	Walker Joyce
The Duke	Michael Calkins
Lafe/Man in Crowd/Hired Hand	Fred Sanders
Mary Jane Wilkes	Carolee Carmello[2]
Susan Wilkes	Heidi Karol Johnson
Bill, a Servant	Ivan Thomas[3]
Alice, a slave	Gwendolyn L. Stewart
Alice's Daughter	Angela Hall
Man on Skiff	Steven Riddle
St. Pete Boy	Lawrence Patrick

[†]Succeeded by 1. Jordan Bowers, 2. Jessie Janet Richards, 3. Brian Everet Chandler

Top Right: Michael Edward-Stevens, Romain Fruge
(Martha Swope Photos)

**Walker Joyce, Michael Edward-Stevens,
Romain Fruge, Michael Calkins**

BROADWAY BOUND

By Neil Simon; Director, Gene Saks; Scenery, David Mitchell; Costumes, Joseph G. Aulisi; Lighting, Tharon Musser; Sound, Tom Morse; Production Supervisor, Peter Lawrence; Casting, Simon & Kumin; Presented by Emanuel Azenberg; General Manager, Leonard Soloway; General Press Representatives, Bill Evans & Associates, Sandy Manley, Jim Randolph; Technical Supervision, Theatrical Services, Inc., Arthur Siccardi, Pete Feller; Company Manager, Brian Dunbar; Consultant, Jose Vega; National Press Representative, Harry Davies; Production Stage Manager, John Brigleb; Stage Manager, Steven Shaw. Opened at the Shubert Theater in New Haven, CT on Tuesday, October 20, 1987. For original Broadway production, see *THEATRE WORLD* Vol. 43.

CAST

Kate	Carole Shelley
Ben	Salem Ludwig
Eugene	William Ragsdale
Stanley	Nathan Lane
Blanche	Bernice Massi
Jack	David Margulies
Radio Voices:	
Mrs. Pitkin	Marilyn Cooper
Chubby Waters	MacIntyre Dixon
Announcer	Ed Herlihy

Left: William Ragsdale, Nathan Lane, Carole Shelley
Top: David Margulies, Carole Shelley, Nathan Lane,
Salem Ludwig, William Ragsdale
(Martha Swope/Carol Rosegg Photos)

Carole Shelley, William Ragsdale

Carole Shelley, William Ragsdale

CAN-CAN

Book, Abe Burrows; Music & Lyrics, Cole Porter; Produced for the Broadway Stage by Feuer & Martin; Director, Dallett Norris; Choreographer, Alan Johnson; Scenery, James Fouchard; Costumes, Dean Brown; Lighting, Brian MacDevitt; Sound, Craig Cassidy; Orchestral Arrangements, David Siegel, Daniel Troob, Hampton F. King, Jr.; Musical Director, Hampton F. King, Jr.; Dances Arranged by Mark Hummel; Conductor, Mark Lipman; Production Stage Manager, Dale Kaufman; Presented by Nicholas Howey, Kenneth H. Gentry, Dallett Norris, The Troika Company Inc., in association with Columbia Artists Theatricals Corp.; General Manager, Stephen B. Kane; Production Manager, Bradford Watkins; Company Manager, Steven Schnepp; Production Stage Manager, Dale Kaufman; Stage Manager, David John O'Brien; Press, Devin Keudell. For original Broadway production, see *THEATRE WORLD* Vol. 9.

CAST

La Mome Pistache	Chita Rivera
Claudine	Erica L. Paulson
The Model	Jacquey Maltby
Laundresses	(The Rockettes):

Stephanie Chase, Lynn Sterling†1, Dominique Decaudain, Vicki Hickerson, Ginny Hounsell, Alyson Lang, Jacquey Maltby, Lori McMacken, Mary McNamara, Nancy Lyn Miller, Kerri Pearsall, Terry Spano, Maureen Stevens

Boris (A Sculptor)	Larry Raiken
Theophile (A Painter)	Don Stitt
Etienne (A Poet)	David Ames
Hercule (An Architect)	Mark Basile
Hillaire Jussac	Michael Connolly
Aristide Forestier	Ron Holgate
President Judge	J. Lee Flynn
Paul Barriere	Mark Basile
1st Policeman	Bill Burns
2nd Policeman	Cris Herrera
Doctor	J. Lee Flynn
Waiter	Cris Herrera
The Second	Bill Burns

STANDBYS & UNDERSTUDIES: Jacquey Maltby (Pistache), Kyle Whyte (Male Swing), Terry Spano (Female Swing), J. Lee Flynn (Aristide), Mark Basile (Boris), Kyle Whyte (Hercule), David Ames (Theophile), Mark Basile (Hilaire), Kyle Whyte (Étienne), Vicki Hickerson (Claudine), Kyle Whyte (Paul Barriere), Stephanie Chase (The Model)

†Succeeded by: 1. Lillian Colon

(Bob Marshak/Joan Marcus Photos)

Chita Rivera, also top

117

CATS

For original creative credits and musical numbers, see Broadway Calendar; Musical Director, Janet Glazener Roma; Executive Producers, Tyler Gatchell, Jr. Peter Neufield; Casting, Johnson-Liff and Zerman; Orchestrations, Stanley Lebowsky; Choreography reproduced by T. Michael Reed, Richard Stafford; Direction reproduced by David Taylor; Associate Production Musical Director, Jack Gaughan; Company Managers, Abbie Strassler, Michael Sanfilippo; Dance Captain, Leigh Webster; Associate Musical Director, Michael Huffman; Stage Managers, B. J. Allen, Scott Faris, L. A. Lavin, Michael McEowen; Press, Fred Nathan Co./Philip Rinaldi, Anne Abrams, Dennis Crowley, Bert Fink, Merle Frimark, Marc Thibodeau. Opened in the Shubert Theatre in Los Angeles, CA. For original Broadway production see *THEATRE WORLD* Vol. 39.

CAST

Alonzo/Rumpus Cat	General McArthur Hambrick
Bustopher Jones/Asparagus/Growltiger	Jeffrey Clonts
Bombalurina	Wendy Walter†1
Cassandra	Paula-Marie Benedetti†2
Demeter	Patricia Everett†3
Grizabella	Donna Lee Marshall
Jellyorum/Griddlebone	Lindsay Dyett
Jennyanydots	Robin Boudreau
Mistoffelees	Eddie Buffum
Mungojerrie	Jack Noseworthy
Munkustrap	Dan McCoy
Old Deuteronomy	Richard Nickol
Plato/Macavity	Davud Reitman†4
Pouncival	Marc C. Oka
Rumpleteazer	Nancy Melius
Rum Tum Tugger	Steven Bland†5
Sillabub	Leslie Trayer†6
Skimbleshanks	Kevin Winkler†7
Tumblebrutus	Robert Torres†8
Victoria	J. Kathleen Lamb†9
The Cats Chorus	Richard Bigelow, Jean Kauffman†10
	Bryan John Landrine, Terry Mason

STANDBYS & UNDERSTUDIES: Alonzo (Paul Clausen/Randy B. Wojcik), Bustopher/Asparagus/Growltiger (Richard Bigelow/Bryan John Landrine), Bombalurina (Felicia Farone/Carol Schuberg), Cassandra (Carol Schuberg/Leigh Webster), Mungojerrie (Michael Fritzke/Charles H. Lubeck), Demeter (Michelle Murlin-Gardner/Carol Schuberg), Rumpleteazer (Felicia Farone/Michelle Murlin-Gardner), Grizabella (Robin Boudreau/Terry Mason), Jellyorum/Griddlebone (Jean Kauffman/Michelle Murlin-Gardner), Jennyanydots (Jean Kauffman/Terry Mason), Mistoffelees (Marc C. Oka/Michael Fritzke), Munkustrap (Paul Clausen), Old Deuteronomy (Richard Bigelow/Bryan John Landrine), Plato/Macavity/Rumpus Cat (Charles H. Lubeck/Randy B. Wojcik), Pouncival (Michael Fritzke/Charles H. Lubeck), Rum Tum Tugger (Paul Clausen/General McArthur Hambrick), Sillabub (Felicia Farone/Michelle Murlin-Gardner), Skimbleshanks (Paul Clausen/Charles H. Lubeck). Tumblebrutus (Michael Fritzke/Randy B. Wojcik), Victoria (Felicia Farone/Carol Schuberg).

†Succeeded by: 1. Helen Frank, 2. Darlene Wilson, 3. Felicia Farone, 4. T. Michael Dalton, Randy B. Wojcik, 5. Bradford Minkoff, 6. Amelia Marshall, 7. John Scherer, 8. Leon Taylor, 9. Natasha Davison, 10. Linda Leonard.

Top Right: Donna Lee Marshall

Bill Nolte, Heidi Stallings

CATS

For original creative credits and musical numbers see Broadway Calendar; Musical Director, Jay Alger; Dance Supervisor, Richard Stafford; Production Musical Director, David Caddick; Company Manager, Brian Liddicoat; Assistant, Jeffrey Capitola; Dance Captain, James Walski; Associate Musical Director, Edward G. Robinson; Production Assistant, Gregg Victor; Props, George Green Jr., Alan Price, Joseph Poc; Wardrobe, Adelaide Laurino, Robert Daily, Jose Tellez Ponce; Hairstylists, Raul Arzola, Charmaine Henninger; Stage Manager, Scott Gleen, William Kirk, Nancy Ann Adler; Press, Fred Nathan Co./Jim Kerber, Anne Abrams, Dennis Crowley, Bert Fink, Merle Frimark, Marc Thibodeau. Opened Thursday. August 7, 1986 in the West Point (NY) Theatre. For original Broadway production, see *THEATRE WORLD* Vol. 39.

CAST

Alonzo/Rumpus Cat	Jeff Siebert
Bustopher Jones/Asparagus/Growltiger	Richard Poole
Bombalurina	Adrea Gibbs Muldoon
Cassandra	Aimee Turner†1
Demeter	Deborah Geneviere†2
Grizabella	Leslie Ellis†3
Jellylorum/Griddlebone	Joanna Beck
Jennyanydots	Cathy Susan Pyles
Mistoffelees	Randy Slovacek
Mungojerrie	Michael O'Steen†4
Munkustrap	Randy Clements
Old Deuteronomy	Larry Small†5
Plato/Macavity	David Roberts
Pouncival	Matt Zarley†6
Rumpleteazer	Beth Swearingen†7
Rum Tum Tugger	Andy Spangler†8
Sillabub	Nikki Rene†9
Skimbleshanks	Jonathan Cerullo
Tumblebrutus	Anthony Bova†10
Victoria	Joann M. Hunter†11
Cats Chorus	Arminae Azarian†12, Austin Jetton Peter Marinos†13, Jacqueline Reilly

Succeeded by 1. Spence Ford, Kim Noor. 2. Jennifer Smith. 3. Heidi Stallings. 4. Bill Brassea, Robert Barry Fleming. 5. Bill Nolte. 6. Robert Bianca. 7. Donna M. Pompei. 8. Brian B. K. Kennelly. 9. Beth Swearingen, Christine Toy. 10. Fred Tallaksen. 11. Michele Humphrey. 12. Julie Waldman. 13. Ken Ward.

STANDBYS & UNDERSTUDIES: Alonzo (Urban Sanchez/Jay Tramel/Alan Sherfield), Bombalurina (Lisa Dawn Cave/Jill B. Gounder/Rachelle Rak), Bustopher/Asparagus/Growltiger (Brian B. K. Kennelly/Brian Lynch/Peter Marinos), Cassandra (Lisa Dawn Cave/Jill B. Gounder), Demeter (Lisa Dawn Cave/Rachelle Rak), Grizabella (Rachelle Rak/Julie Waldman), Jellylorum (Jacqueline Reilly/Julie Waldman), Jennyanydots (Jacqueline Reilly/Julie Waldman), Mistoffelees (Marty Benn/Robert Bianca/Robert Barry Fleming), Mungojerrie (Urban Sanchez/Marty Benn), Munkustrap (Brian Lynch/Jay Tramel/Alan Sherfield), Old Deuteronomy (Austin Jetton), Plato/Macavity (Brian Lynch/Jay Tramel/Alan Sherfield), Pouncival (Marty Benn/Jay Tramel), Rum Tum Tugger (Brian Lynch/Urban Sanchez), Rumpleteazer (Lisa Dawn Cave/Jill B. Gounder), Skimbleshanks (Marty Benn/Urban Sanchez/Randy Slovacek), Sillabub (Rachelle Rak/Donna M. Pompei), Tumblebrutus (Marty Benn/Jay Tramel/Alan Sherfield), Victoria (Lisa Dawn Cave/Jill B. Gounder/Donna M. Pompei)

Top Right: (clockwise from top) Brian B. K. Kennelly, Heidi Stallings, Bill Nolte, Andrea Gibbs Muldoon

Richard Poole, Joanna Beck

DROOD!

Title shortened during Broadway season from "The Mystery of Edwin Drood"; Book/Music/Lyrics/Orchestrations, Rupert Holmes; Director, Edward M. Greenberg; Set, Bob Shaw; Costumes, Lindsay W. Davis, Vicki Davis; Lighting, John McLain; Musical Director, Raymond Allen; Choreographers, Rob Marshall, Kathleen Marshall; Casting, Sherie L. Seff; General Manager, John Rainwater; Company Manager, Ted Stevens; Props, Nick Rouse; Wardrobe, Jean Evans; Hairstylist, Robert Melton; Dance Captain, Kathleen Marshall; Assistant Conductor, Sheilah Walker; Production Assistants, Kelli Kahn, Samuel Finkelstein; Stage Managers, Mark S. Krause, Elisabeth Farwell, Tony Bevinetto; Press, Michael Praver/Karen Hatchett, Tiki Davies; Presented by The Kennedy Center, Atlanta Theater of the Stars (Christopher B. Manos, Producer), in association with Normand Kurtz; Coordinated by National Alliance of Musical Theatre Producers; Tour Director, Columbia Artists Theatricals. Opened in the JFK Center for the Performing Arts (Roger L. Stevens, Chairman/Marta Istomin, Artistic Director) on Tuesday, April 5, 1988 and closed in Wilmington, Del., October 2, 1988. For original Broadway production, see *Theatre World* Vol. 42.

CAST

William Cartwright/Your Chairman	George Rose succeeded by Clive Revill
James Throttle/Stage Manager	Newton Gilchrist
John Jasper/Clive Paget	Mark Jacoby
Edwin Drood/Alice Nutting	Paige O'Hara
Rosa Bud/Deirdre Peregrine	Teresa DeZarn
Wendy/Isabel Yearsley	Rebecca Baxter
Beatrice/Violet Balfour	Jeanne Bennett
Helena Landless/Janet Conover	Jana Schneider
Neville Landless/Victor Grinstead	John DeLuca
Rev. Crisparkle/Cedric Mondrieffe	William McClary
Princess Puffer/Angela Prysock	Jean Stapleton
Durdles/Nick Cricker	Tony Azito
Deputy/Master Nick Cricker	Michael Nostrand
Flo/Florence Gill	Shelley Wald
Christopher Lyon	Troy Myers
Montague Pruitt	Donald Ives
Harry Sayle	Chandler Holland
Alan Eliot	David Mallard
Image of Rosa/Gwendolen Pynn	Kathleen Marshall
Sarah Cook	Jane Matera
Felicity Reed	Betsy Chang
Florence Gill	Shelley Wald
Bazzard/Phillip Bax	Ronn Carroll
Horace/Nicholas Michael	Robert R. McCormick
Julian/Medford Moss	Tony Bevinetto
Dick Datchery	?????????????
Swings	Tony Lillo, Lee Sasfai

MUSICAL NUMBERS: There You Are, Two Kinsmen, Moonfall, The Wages of Sin, Jasper's Vision, A British Subject, Both Sides of the Coin, Never the Luck, Off to the Races, A Private Investigation, The Name of Love, Don't Quit While You're Ahead, The Garden Path to Hell, The Solution.

A musical in 2 acts and 10 scenes, with a prologue and a solution. The action takes place in 1892 in the Music Hall Royale in London.

Cathy Blavis, Joan Marcus Photos

Top Left: George Rose, Jean Stapleton
Below: George Rose and chorus girls
(Cathy Blavis Photos)

Jean Stapleton, Paige O'Hara

42ND STREET

Music, Harry Warren; Lyrics, Al Dubin; Book, Michael Stewart, Mark Bramble; Based on the novel by Bradford Ropes; Gower Champion's original direction and dances adapted and staged by Jon Engstrom; Scenery, Robin Wagner; Costumes, Theoni V. Aldredge; Lighting, Tharon Musser; Musical Director, Michael Duff; Vocal Arrangements, John Lesko; Dance Arrangements, Donald Johnson; Orchestrations, Philip J. Lang; Producer, Tom Mallow; General Management, American Theatre Productions, Inc.; General Press Representative, Max Eisen; Press Representative, Barbara Glenn; Company Manager, John Pasinato; Stage Managers, Dan Langhofer, Cindy Tannenbaum, Jim Carey; Presented by David Merrick. For original Broadway production, see *THEATRE WORLD* Vol. 37.

CAST

Julian Marsh	David Brummel
Dorothy Brock	Judith Thiergaard
Maggie Jones	Elizabeth French
Bert Berry	Richard Blair
Billy Lawler	Doug Okerson
Abner	Tom Elrod
Annie	Linda Griffin
Peggy Sawyer	Gina Trano
Gladys	Becky Lynn Adams
Phyllis	Kristin Dahl
Lorraine	Gail Lohla
Andy Lee	David Lowenstein
Pat Denning	David J. V. Meenan
Mac	Lawrence Motall
Thief	Marc Robin

ENSEMBLE: Scott Fowler, Trudi Green, Gail Cook Howell, Kenny Ingram, Susan A. Johnson, Victoria Kent, Scott Lane, Tonia Lynn, Heidi Anne Meyer, Sara Meyer, Casey Nicholaw, Stephen Reed, Luke Stallings, Annette Thurman, Jani-k Walsh
SWINGS: Marcella Betz, Jim Carey

Left: Gina Trano, Doug Okerson
Above: Gina Trano, David Brummel
Top: Gina Trano
(Jennifer Girard Photos)

Elizabeth French (center)

Doug Okerson and chorus

GROVER'S CORNERS

Book & Lyrics, Tom Jones; Music, Harvey Schmidt; Based upon the play *Our Town* by Thornton Wilder; Director, Dominic Missimi; Musical Director/Vocal Arrangements, Kevin Stites; Orchestrations, David Siegel; Set/Lighting, John & Diane Williams; Costumes, Nancy Missimi; Sound, Randy Allen Johns; Props, Kathy Klaisner; Assistant Director, Fred Klaisner; Assistant-Musical Press, Peter R. Grigsby; Stage Manager, Michael Hendricks; Wigs/Hairstyle Design, Steven Horak; Staging, Charles Misovye; Presented by Kary M. Walker, Dyanne K. Early, Peter R. Grigsby; Produced in Association with the National Alliance of Musical Theatre Producers; *World Premiere* Wednesday July 22, 1987 in Marriott's Lincolnshire Theater and closed November 11, 1987.

CAST

Pianist	Harvey Schmidt
Stage Manager	Tom Jones
Emily Webb	Deanna Wells
Mr. Webb	Richard Henzel
Mrs. Webb	Linda Stephens
Wally Webb	Todd Schmarak
George Gibbs	Michael Bartsch
Doctor Gibbs	Les Hinderyckx
Mrs. Gibbs	Sharon Carlson
Rebecca Gibbs	Randi Beth Stavins
Joe Crowell, Jr.	Rick Boynton
Howie Newsome	Ron Keaton
Simon Stimson	James Harms
Miss Soames	Renee Matthews
Lois Hershey	Kathy Santen
Martha Cartwright	Jeanne Croft
Amos McCarthy	Phil Courington
Mrs. Corcoran	Marilynn Bogetich

UNDERSTUDIES: Kathy Stanton (Emily), Rick Boynton (George), Phil Courington (Doctor Gibbs, Editor Webb)

MUSICAL NUMBERS: Our Town, A Hearty Breakfast, Someplace, Maybe, Evening, Day after Day, It Isn't Hard to Get Married, I Noticed You, I Only Want Somebody to Love Me, Snapshots/Photographs, Time Goes By, Do Not Hold On, Birthday Girl, A Star Is Mighty Good Company, Goodbye World, Conclusion.

A musical in 2 acts divided into three segments: *Daily Life, Marriage,* and *Death,* portraying the life cycles of two neighboring families in the small American town of Grovers Corners.

Top Right: the company
(Tom Maday Photos)

Deanna Wells, Michael Bartsch

Deanna Wells, Tom Jones,
Michael Bartsch

122

HEMINGWAY: ON THE EDGE

Written by Ed Metzger & Willard Manus; Director, Lonny Chapman; Producer, Laya Gelff; *World Premiere* December 1987, closed April 1988.

CAST

Ernest Hemingway .... Ed Metzger

A solo performance portraying the life story of Ernest Hemingway, in two acts. The play takes place in Havana, Cuba, and Ketchum, Idaho.

Right: Ed Metzger as Hemingway

H.M.S. PINAFORE

Lyrics, W. S. Gilbert; Music, Arthur Sullivan; Director/Choreographer, Brian MacDonald; Musical Director/Additional Musical Arrangements, Berthold Carriere; Production Designer/Costumes, Susan Benson; Lighting, Michael J. Whitfield; Additional Lyrics, Jim Betts; Assistant Director/Assistant Choreographer, Madeline Paul; Assistant Musical Directors, Laura Burton, Marilyn Dallman; Company Manager, Lynn McKay; Production Management, Kent McKay and Associates; Presented by Ed and David Mirvish in association with Brian MacDonald Productions. Opened at the Royal Alexandra Theatre, Toronto, Ontario, on Tuesday, November 3, 1987, and closed at the Golden Gate Theater, San Francisco, CA., on April 3, 1988.

CAST

The Rt. Hon. Sir Joseph Porter, K.C.B. .... Ron Moody
Captain Corcoran .... David Dunbar
Ralph Rackstraw .... Michael Brian
Dick Deadeye .... Ted Pearson
Bill Bobstay .... Paul Massel
Bob Becket .... Stephen Beamish
Josephine .... Meg Bussert
Cousin Hebe .... Ruth Croson
Little Buttercup .... Arlene Meadows

ENSEMBLE: Kristine Anderson, Scott Coppola, Allan Craik, Timothy Cruickshank, Susan Cuthbert, Barbara Dunn Prosser, Paul Gatchell, Allison Grant, Larry Herbert, Brian Hill (swing), Kymberley Huffman (swing), Debora Joy, Walter Quigley, David Rogers, Stephen Simms, Joy Thompson-Allen, Scott Weber, Jim White, Karen Wood, Marianne Woods, Joseph Zuccala
UNDERSTUDIES: Stephen Beamish (Sir Joseph), Paul Massel (Captain Corcoran), Stephen Simms (Ralph), Timothy Cruickshank (Deadeye), David Rogers (Bill), Scott Weber (Bob), Susan Cuthbert (Josephine), Debora Joy (Hebe), Kristine Anderson (Buttercup)

**Right: Michael Brian, Ruth Croson (standing),
Meg Bussert in "H.M.S. Pinafore"**

JONATHAN FRID'S FOOLS & FRIENDS

Created and Developed by Jonathan Frid; written by Richard Hughes, William F. Nolan, Saki, Ogden Nash, Edgar Allan Poe, Eve Merrimam, Manuel Deren, Stephen King, Irwin Shaw, John Collier, and Fredric Brown; Co-Producer, Mary O'Leary; Presented by David Oakland in association with Neverending Battle, Inc.; Opened at the Little Theatre, Cleveland on June 15, 1988 and still touring.

CAST

Jonathan Frid as himself in
an evening of short stories.

Jonathan Frid
(Nora Feller Photo)

LA CAGE AUX FOLLES

Book, Harvey Fierstein; Music & Lyrics, Jerry Herman; Based on the play by Jean Poiret; Director, Arthur Laurents; Choreographer, Scott Salmon; Assistant Directors, Fritz Holt, James Pentecost; Scenery, David Mitchell; Costumes, Theoni V. Aldredge; Lighting, Jules Fisher; Sound, Peter J. Fitzgerald; Vocal Arranger, Donald Pippin; Musical Director, Randy Booth; Orchestrations, Jim Tyler; Dance Music Arrangements, Gordon Harrell; Assistant Choreographer, Richard Balestrino; Hair Styles and Make-up, Charles La France; Casting, Stuart Howard Assoc.; Production Stage Manager, Mark S. Krause; General Management, American Theatre Productions, Inc.; General Press Representative, Max Eisen; Company Manager, Daryl T. Dodson; Stage Manager, Elisabeth Farwell; Presented by Tom Mallow and James Janek by special arrangement with Allan Carr and Barry Brown, Fritz Holt, Marvin A. Krauss. Opened at the Music Hall in Dallas, Tx., on Tuesday, August 4, 1987. For original Broadway production, see THEATRE WORLD Vol. 40.

CAST

Georges	Larry Kert
Les Cagelles:	
Chantal	Keith Keen
Hanna	Reece Holland
Phaedra	Carmen Yurich
Angelique	Kerry Finn
Monique	Frank J. Maio
Nicole	Jim Kirby
Bitelle	Joyce Dara
Dermah	Kevin Backstrom
Francis	Wade Collings
Jacob	Kent Gash
Albin	Harvey Evans
Jean-Michel	Dan O'Grady
Anne	Wendy Oliver
Jacqueline	Sheila Smith
M. Renaud	Bob Carroll
St. Tropez Townspeople:	
Mme. Renaud	Robin Manning
Paulette	Diana Lynne Drew
Hercule	Peter Gunther
Etienne	Scott Sigler
Colette	Melodie Wolford
Pepe	Earl Dwayne Minfield
Edouard Dindon	Bob Carroll
Mme. Dindon	Patricia Arnell
Swing Performers	Carol Ann Baxter, John Clonts, Daniel May

UNDERSTUDIES: Bob Carroll (Georges), Keith Keen (Albin), Melodie Wolford (Anne), Diana Lynne Drew (Jacqueline), Robin Manning (Mme. Dindon), Peter Gunther (Jean-Michel), Scott Sigler (Renaud/Dindon), Earl Dwayne Minfield (Jacob), Daniel May (Francis)

Top Left: Larry Kert, Harvey Evans
Below: Cagelles
(Smith/Garza Photos)

Bob Carroll, Patricia Arnell, Harvey Evans, Kent Gash

Harvey Evans

LES MISERABLES

For original creative credits and musical numbers, see Broadway calendar. Opened Tuesday December 15, 1987 in the Shubert Theatre, Boston and still touring as of May 31, 1988. For original Broadway production, see *THEATRE WORLD* Vol. 43.

CAST

Prologue: 1815 Digne: Jean Valjean (William Solo[1]) Javert (Herndon Lackey) Chain Gang (J. Mark McVey, Michael McCormick[2], Scott Elliot, Andy Gale, Tom Robbins, Hugh Panaro, Bjorn Johnson, Joe Locarro) Farmer (Michael Babin) Labourer (Bjorn Johnson) Innkeeper's Wife (Deborah Bradshaw) Innkeeper (Willy Falk) Bishop (Kevin McGuire) Constables (Rick Sparks, Gary Harger). 1823, Montreuil-Sur-Mer: Fantine (Diane Fratantoni) Foreman (Robert DuSold) Workers (Michael Babin, Scott Elliott) Women (Rosalyn Rahn, Olga Merediz, Carolee Carmello, Bertilla Baker) Factory Girl (Kirsti Carnahan) Sailors (J. Mark Mcvey, Andy Gale, Gary Harger) Whores (Deborah Bradshaw, Bertilla Baker, Carolee Carmello, Jennifer Naimo, Kirsti Carnahan, Renee Veneziale, Tamara Jenkins, Betsy True) Old Woman (Rosalyn Rahn) Crone (Olga Merediz) Pimp (Scott Elliott) Bamatabois (Michael McCormick[2]) Fauchelevent (Scott Elliott). 1823, Montfermeil: Young Cosette (Christina Marie DeAngelis, Christa Larson, Sara Nelson) Madame Thenardier (Victoria Clark) Thenardier Tom Robbins)[3] Young Eponine (Christina Marie DeAngelis, Christa Larson, Sara Nelson) Drinker (Michael Babin) Young Couple (Bjorn Johnson, Betsy True) Drunk (Willy Falk) Diners (Kevin McGuire, Bertilla Baker) Drinkers (Gary Harger, Michael McCormick[2], J. Mark McVey, Kirsti Carnahan, Deborah Bradshaw, Rosalyn Rahn) Young Man (Andy Gale) Young Girls (Carolee Carmello, Jennifer Naimo) Old Couple (Olga Merediz, Scott Elliott) Travelers (Robert DuSold, Rick Sparks). 1832 Paris: Gavroche (Lantz Landry, Sam Brent Riegel) Old Beggar Woman (Rosalyn Rahn) Young Prostitute (Kirsti Carnahan) Pimp (Willy Falk) Eponine (Renee Veneziale) Thenardiers Gang (Bjorn Johnson, Rick Sparks, J. Mark McVey, Gary Harger) Enjolras (John Herrera)[4] Marius (Hugh Panaro) Cosette (Tamara Jenkins) Combeferre (Robert DuSold) Feuilly (Andy Gale) Courfeyrac (Michael Babin) Joly (Scott Elliott) Grantaire (Michael McCormick)[2] Lesgles (Kevin McGuire) Jean Prouvaire (Willy Falk)

[†]Succeeded by 1. Craig Schulman 2. Al DeCristo 3. Michael McCormick 4. Joe Locarro

Left: Craig Schulman, Diane Frantantoni
(also at top)
(Bob Marshak Photos)

Herndon Lackey

Hugh Panaro, Joe Locarro

125

ME AND MY GIRL

Book & Lyrics, L. Arthur Rose, Douglas Furber; Music, Noel Gay; Book revisions, Stephen Fry; Director/Contributions to revisions, Mike Ockrent; Choreographer, Gillian Gregory; Scenery, Martin Johns; Costumes, Ann Curtis; Lighting, Roger Morgan, Chris Ellis; Sound, Tom Morse; Musical Supervisor, Thomas Helm; Musical Director, Robert Fisher; Orchestrations & Dance Arrangements, Chris Walker; General Manager, Ralph Roseman; Associate Director, Steven Zweigbaum; Choreographic Assistant, Tony Parise; Casting, Johnson-Liff & Zerman; Production Stage Manager, George Martin; General Press Representatives, Jeffrey Richards Associates/Norman Zagier, Ben Morse, Irene Grandy, Susan Chicoine, Diane Judge; Technical Director, Jeremiah Harris; Producers, The Noel Gay Organisation, Ltd., Terry Allen Kramer, James M. Nederlander, Strada Entertainment. For original Broadway production, see *THEATRE WORLD* Vol. 43.

CAST

Lady Jacqueline Carstone	Susan Cella
Hon. Gerald Bolingbroke	Nick Ullett
Stockbrokers	Cleve Asbury, John Salvatore, Roger Preston Smith
Lord Battersby	Ralph Farnworth
Lady Battersby	Evelyn Page
Herbert Parchester	Walter Charles
Sir Jasper Tring	Gordon Connell
Maria, Duchess of Dene	Ursula Smith
Sir John Tremayne	Barrie Ingham
Charles Hethersett	Keith Perry
Bill Snibson	Tim Curry
Sally Smith	Donna Bullock
Pub Pianist	Brad Moranz
Mrs. Worthington-Worthington	Melody Jones
Lady Diss	Lou Williford
Lady Brighton	Mary Stout
Bob Barking	Peter J. Saputo
Telegraph Boy	Jamie Torcellini
Mrs. Brown	Evelyn Page
Constable	Michael Hayward-Jones
Swing Performers	Kimberly Kalember, Leigh Catlett, William Alan Coats

ENSEMBLE: Cleve Asbury, Gary Barker, Stanley Bojarski, Dani Brownlee, Leigh Catlett, William Alan Coats, Anne-Marie Gerard, Michael Hayward-Jones, Melody Jones, Kimberly Kalember, Gregg Kirsopp, Connie Kunkle, Dan Mojica, Brad Moranz, Ann Neiman, Donald Norris, Tina Parise, Barbara Passolt, Linda Paul, John Salvatore, Peter J. Saputo, Roger Preston Smith, Roger Spivy, Mary Stout, Jamie Torcellini, Lou Williford

UNDERSTUDIES: Jamie Tocellini (Bill Snibson), Connie Kunkle (Sally Smith), Keith Perry (Sir John), Barbara Passolt (Jacqueline), Evelyn Page (Maria), Michael Hayward-Jones (Gerald), Peter J. Saputo (Parchester), Michael Hayward-Jones (Hethersett), Donald Norris (Sir Jasper), Lou Williford (Lady Battersby), Gary Barker (Lord Battersby), Lou Williford (Mrs. Brown), Gregg Kirsopp (Pub Pianist), Dani Brownlee (Lady Brighton), Gregg Kirsopp (Bob Barking), Stanley Bojarski (Constable)

Top Right: Tim Curry, Donna Bullock *(Chris Fesler)*
Below: (center) Tim Curry, Ursula Smith
(Ron Scherl Photos)

Tim Curry, Susan Cella

NATIONAL SHAKESPEARE COMPANY

Artistic Director, Elaine Sulka; Director, Anthony Naylor; Sets and Props, Wade Battley, David R. Zyla, Vaughn Patterson; Costumes, Renee Sykes, Don Mangone; Music, Jeremy Beck; Lighting, Rick Lucero, Blu; Sound, Walter Montani; Company and Production Manager, Felton Richards; Tour Director, William Weir; Administrative Assistant, Kimberly Campbell; Business Manager, Kathleen Stern; Transportation, Dan Shannon (O.D. Anderson Transportation).

COMPANY: Matthew Blomquist, Kay Bourbiel, Amy Brentano, Alison Lani Broda, Pierre Brulatour, Michael Cooper, Anthony W. Ejarque, Leone Fogel, Thomas Grenon, Glyde Hart, Robert G. Johnson, James Karcher, Mark Edward Lang, Bernard J. Lunon, Steve Mehmert, Karen A. Murphy, Paul Parente, Thomas Rice, Elizabeth Slaby, Dan Snow, Timothy D. Stickney, Barbara Wiechmann.
PRODUCTIONS: A Midsummer Night's Dream directed by Elaine Sulka, Julius Caesar directed by Anthony Naylor, The Importance of Being Earnest (by Oscar Wilde) directed by June Pyskacek

Below: Dan Snow, Anthony Ejarque, Robert
Johnson in "Midsummer Night's Dream"
Top Right: "Midsummer Night's Dream"

Elizabeth McGuire, Rik Montgomery
in "The Importance of Being Earnest"

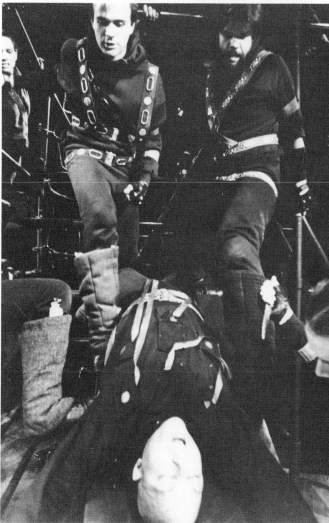

The assassination of
"Julius Caesar"

NUNSENSE

Written and Directed by Dan Goggin; Musical Staging/Choreography, Felton Smith; Scenery, Barry Axtell; Lighting, Susan A. White; Musical Director, Maggie Torre; Press Representative, Violet Welles; Production Stage Manager, David L. Coffman; Producers, Charles Duggan, Drew Dennett, Shirley Herz, Amy Nederlander, Pete Sanders, in association with Jay Cardwell; General Management, Robinwood Enterprises; Stage Manager/Original Choreography recreated by/Dance Captain, Paul Botchis; Production Supervisor, Joel R. Watson. For original New York production, see THEATRE WORLD Vol. 42.

CAST

Sister Robert Anne	Lin Tucci
Sister Mary Leo	Merilee Magnuson
Sister Mary Amnesia	Nancy Hillner
Sister Mary Regina	Phyllis Diller
Sister Mary Hubert	Nancy Johnston

UNDERSTUDY: Mary Jo Connell

Left: Nancy Johnston, Phyllis Diller

A RAISIN IN THE SUN

By Lorraine Hansberry; Director, Harold Scott; Presented by Roundabout Theatre Company, Inc. (Gene Feist/Todd Haimes) and Robert Nemiroff; Set, Thomas Cariello; Costumes, Judy Dearing; Lighting, Shirley Prendergast; Sound, Rick Menke, Philip Campanella; Production Stage Manager, Scott Rodabaugh; Casting, David Tochterman; General Manager, Ellen Richard; Press, The Joshua Ellis Office; Stage Manager, Maxine Krasowski-Bertone. For original Broadway production, see *THEATRE WORLD* Vol. 15.

CAST

Ruth Younger	Starletta DuPois
Travis Younger	Michael Summerlin
Walter Lee Younger (Brother)	Robert Gossett
Beneatha Younger	Kim Yancey
Lena Younger (Mama)	Esther Rolle
Joseph Asagai	Lou Ferguson
George Murchison	Joseph C. Phillips
Bobo	Stephen Henderson
Karl Linder	Richmond Hoxie
Moving Man No. 1	Ron O.J. Parson
Moving Man No. 2	Charles Watts

UNDERSTUDIES: Louise Mike (Mama), Ron O.J. Parson (Walter Lee/Bobo), Carolyn Oldham (Ruth/Beneatha), Charles Watts (Joseph Asagai/George Murchison), Devron Young (Travis)

Left: Esther Rolle, Kim Yancey

SHEAR MADNESS

By Paul Portner; Adapted by Bruce Jordan, Produced and Directed by Bruce Jordan and Marilyn Abrams. Opened January 29, 1980 in Boston's Charles Playhouse Stage II and still playing. Subsequent productions followed in Philadelphia, Chicago, Washington D.C.

This comedy, featuring audience participation, has become the longest running play in U.S. theatre history with over 3,225 performances (Nov 16, 1987) in Boston.

No cast and credit information provided.

Eugene Fleming
Top Left: Bruce Falco

SONG AND DANCE

Music, Andrew Lloyd Webber; Lyrics, Don Black; American Adaptation, Additional Lyrics, Direction by Richard Maltby, Jr.; Choreography, Peter Martins; Recreated by Cynthia Onrubia; Orchestrations, Andrew Lloyd Webber, David Cullen; Musical Advisor, David Caddick; Musical Supervision, David Friedman; Musical Direction, Jerry Sternbach; Presented by Tom Mallow, James B. Freydberg, Max Weitzenhoffer; Executive Producer, Fremont Associates; Associate Tap Choreographer, Gregg Burge; Casting, Joe Abaldo; Sound, Martin Levan; Settings, Robin Wagner; Costumes, Willa Kim; Lighting, Jules Fisher; Original Cast Album by RCA; Company Manager, Patricia Berry; General Management, Fremont Associates; Props, Roger George, Paul Mallick; Wardrobe, Barbara Oleszczuk; Stage Managers, Joel Tropper, Tom Bartlett; Press, Shirley Herz/Peter Cromarty, Pete Sanders, Glenna Freedman, David Roggensack, Miller Wright; Opened in Dallas on June 23, 1987 and closed Dec. 13, 1987 in Tampa, Fla. For original Broadway production, see *THEATRE WORLD* Vol. 42.

CAST

Emma ....Melissa Manchester
Joe ....Bruce Falco†
The Women ....Mindy Cooper, Cynthia Onrubia,
                                                        Deborah Roshe, Valerie C. Wright
The Men .... Eugene Fleming, Danny Herman,
                                                        Herman W. Sebek, Scott Wise
Swings .... Harrison Beal, Kiel Junius,
                                                        Joe Konicki, Lynne Savage

MUSICAL NUMBERS: Take That Look Off Your Face, Let Me Finish, So Much to Do in New York, First Letter Home, English Girls, Capped Teeth and Caesar Salad, You Made Me Think You Were in Love, Second Letter Home, Unexpected Song, Come Back with the Same Look in Your Eyes, Tell Me on a Sunday, I Love New York, Married Man, Third Letter Home, What Have I Done?, Finale

A musical in two acts. The action takes place at the present time in New York and Los Angeles.

†Succeeded by: Victor Barbee, Christopher d'Amboise, John Meehan

Martha Swope Photos

Melissa Manchester

129

**Jack Wagner, Lauri Landry
in "West Side Story"**

SWEET CHARITY

Book, Neil Simon; Music, Cy Coleman; Lyrics, Dorothy Fields; Original and current production conceived, staged and choreographed by Bob Fosse; Based on screenplay by Federico Fellini, Tullio Pinelli, Ennio Flaiano; Sets/Lighting, Robert Randolph; Costumes, Patricia Zipprodt; Conductor, Wayne Green; Orchestrations, Ralph Burns; Sound, Peter Fitzgerald; Hairstylist, Phyllis Della; Casting, Howard Feuer; Presented by Jerome Minskoff, James M. Nederlander, Arthur Rubin, Joseph Harris, Ed & David Mirvish, and the Centrestage Company; Company Manager, Kathleen Lowe; Dance Captains, Mimi Quillin, Chet Walker; Assistant Conductor, Philip Reno; Props, Dennis L. Randolph, Roger Snyder; Wardrobe, Barrett Hong; Assistant to Mr. Fosse, Gwen Verdon; General Management, Joseph Harris Associates/Peter T. Kulok, Steven B. Goldstein; Stage Managers, Craig Jacobs, Pat Trott, Tom Capps; Press, Jeffrey Richards Associates/C. George Willard, Ben Morse, Susan Lee, Ken Mandelbaum, Irene Gandy, Francine L. Trevens, Jillana Devine, Roger Lane. Opened Sunday, July 5, 1987 in the Royal Alexandra Theatre, Toronto, Canada, and closed in Boston, Ma., Nov. 7, 1987.

CAST

Charity	Donna McKechnie
Oscar	Ken Land
Nickie	Lenora Nemetz
Helene	Stephanie Pope
Vittorio Vidal	Mark Jacoby
Herman	Michael Cone
Ursula	Christine Colby
Woman with hat/Receptionist/Good Fairy	Celia Tackaberry
Daddy Johann Sebastian Brubeck	James Stovall
Cop/Brother Harold	Lloyd Culbreath
Mimi	Mimi Quillin
Doorman/Waiter	Tom Wierney
Lead Frug Dancer/Rosie	Alice Everett Cox
Manfred	Fred C. Mann III
Old Maid	Patricia Ben Peterson
Brother Ray	Stanley Wesley Perryman

ENSEMBLE: Quin Baird, Melinda Buckley, Alice Everett Cox, Lloyd Culbreath, Joanne DiMauro, Mamie Duncan-Gibbs, Bill Hastings, Mark Hoebee, Jan Horvath, Michael Licata, Fred C. Mann III, Allison Renee Manson, Kelly Patterson, Stanley Wesley Perryman, Diane Peterson, Patricia Ben-Peterson, Mimi Quillin, Nick Rafello, Cilda Shaur, Lynn Sterling, Tom Wierney, Alternates: Lisa Embs, Diana Laurenson, Raymond C. Harris, Chet Walker
MUSICAL NUMBERS: You Should See Yourself, The Rescue, Big Spender, Rich Man's Frug, If My Friends Could See Me Now, Too Many Tomorrows, There's Gotta Be Something Better Than This, I'm the Bravest Individual, Rhythm of Life, Baby Dream Your Dreams, Sweet Charity, Where Am I Going, I'm a Brass Band, I Love to Cry at Weddings.

For original Broadway production, see THEATRE WORLD Vol. 22.

WEST SIDE STORY

Book, Arthur Laurents; Music, Leonard Bernstein; Lyrics, Stephen Sondheim; Director/Choreography reproduced by Alan Johnson; Entire original production directed and choreographed by Jerome Robbins; Executive Producer, Zev Guber; A Guber/Gross and Young Productions presentation; Scenery, Alan Kimmel; Costumes, Gail Cooper-Hecht; Lighting, Marc B. Weiss; Sound, Abe Jacob; Casting, Jeffrey Dunn; National Public Relations, Mark Goldstaub; General Manager, Robert V. Straus; Associate Choreographers, George Russell, Pamela Khoury; Production Stage Manager, Clifford Schwartz; Musical Director, Milton Rosenstock; Associate Musical Director/Conductor, Michael Biagi; Producers, Lee Guber, Shelly Gross, Robert L. Young Jr. Opened in the O'Keefe Center, Toronto, Canada, on Tuesday, August 4, 1987 and closed Sept. 13, 1987 in the JFK Center, Washington, DC. For original Broadway production, see THEATRE WORLD Vol. 14.

CAST

The Jets:

Riff	John Schiappa
Tony	Jack Wagner
Action	Mark Bove
A-Rab	Rocky Santo
Baby John	Matthew Grant
Snowboy	Troy A. Burgess
Big Deal	George Russell
Diesel	Brian Sutherland
Gee-Tar	Brian Henry
Their Girls:	
Garaziella	Donna DiMeo
Velma	Lisa Lee
Minnie	Barbara Hoon
Clarice	Colleen Durham
Anybodys	Lisa Leguillou

The Sharks:

Bernardo	Rick Negron
Maria	Lauri Landry
Anita	Valarie Pettiford
Chino	Raymond del Barrio
Pepe	Marcial Gonzalez
Indio	Allen Hidalgo
Luis	Marvin Engran
Anxiou	Steven Scionti
Nibbles	Richard Amaro
Their Girls:	
Rosalia	Ruthanna Graves
Consuelo	Joan Henry
Teresita	Robin Kersey
Francisca	Caryn Elizabeth Kaplan
Estella	Colleen Durham

The Adults:

Doc	Carl Don
Schrank	Daniel P. Hannafin
Krupke	Glenn Dube
Gladhand	Don Howard

UNDERSTUDIES: Brian Sutherland (Tony/Riff), Caryn Elizabeth Kaplan (Maria), Ruthanna Graves (Anita), Mark Bove (Bernardo), Don Howard (Doc/Schrank/Krupke), Caryn Elizabeth Kaplan (Rosalia), Allen Hidalgo (Chino), Troy A. Burgess (Action), Brian Henry (Baby John), Barbara Hoon (Anybodys/Velma), George Russell (Gladhand), Troy A. Burgess (Big Deal), Brian Henry (A-Rab), Angelo H. Franboni (Male Swing/Snowboy), Lisa Lee (Graziella)

**(center) Donna McKechnie
in "Sweet Charity"** *(Martha Swope)*

PROFESSIONAL REGIONAL THEATRES

ACT/A CONTEMPORARY THEATRE

Seattle, Washington
Twenty-third Season

Founding Director, Gregory A. Falls; Interim Artistic Director, Jeff Steitzer; Producing Director, Phil Schermer; Managing Director, Susan Trapnell Moritz; Development, Polly Conley; Marketing, Polly Conley; Press, Michael Sande

PRODUCTIONS & CASTS
MARCH OF THE FALSETTOS with Music and Lyrics by William Finn; Director, Jeff Steitzer; Music Director, Todd Moeller; Sets, Scott Weldin; Costumes, Sarah Campbell; Lighting, Rick Paulsen; Orchestrations, Michael Starobin; Stage Manager, Mike Wise. CAST: Christopher Bloch, Gary Jackson, David Hunter Koch, David Armitage, Kristina Sanborn
A LIE OF THE MIND by Sam Shepard; Director, Gregory A. Falls; Sets, Karen Gjelsteen; Costumes, Saly Richardson; Lighting, James Verdery; Sound, Bruce Wynn; Stage Manager, Mary Sigvardt. CAST: Frank Corrado, Tim Streeter, Suzanne Bochard, Randy Hoffmeyer, Cristine McMurdo-Wallis, Katie Forgette, Rick Tutor, Dee Maaske
THE DIARY OF A SCOUNDREL by Alexander Ostrovsky; Adaptation, Erik Brogger; Director, Jeff Steitzer; Assistant Director, Julia Garnett; Sets, Scott Weldin; Costumes, Michael Olich; Lighting, Rick Paulsen; Music, Lev Liberman; Stage Manager, Mike Wise. CAST: John Procaccino, Dee Maaske, Daniel Daily, Marianne Owen, Peter Silbert, R. Hamilton Wright, Jeanne Paulsen, Suzanne Irving, Randy Hoffmeyer, David Pichette, Peggy Platt, Susan Finque, Peggy Poage, David ira Goldstein
THE MARRIAGE OF BETTE AND BOO by Christopher Durang; Director, Anne-Denise Ford; Set, Robert Gardiner; Costumes, Sally Richardson; Lighting, Jennifer Lupton; Sound, David Hunter Koch; Stage Manager, Craig Weindling. CAST: Jan Maxwell, Dee Maaske, Bill Dore, Jeanne Paulsen, Dianne Benjamin-Hill, John Procaccino, Rick Tutor, Priscilla Hake Lauris, John Aylward, Larry Paulsen

Dee Maaske, Rick Tutor, Suzanne Bouchard, Randy Hoffmeyer, Tim Streeter in "A Lie of the Mind"
(Chris Bennion Photo)

Jonathan Fuller, Adale O'Brien in "Whereabouts Unknown" Above: Susan Wands, Richard McWilliams in "Camille" *(David S. Talbot/Richard Trigg)*

ACTORS THEATRE OF LOUISVILLE

Louisville, Kentucky
Twenty-fourth Season

Producing Director, Jon Jory; Administrative Director, Alexander Speer; Associate Director, Marilee Hebert-Slater; Development, Rhea H. Lehman; Press, James Seacat; Sets, Paul Owen; Set Assistant, Robet T. Odorisio; Costumes, Lewis D. Rampino; Costumes Assistant, Kevin R. McLeod; Lighting, Ralph Dressler; Sound, Mark Hendren; Props, Ron Riall; Production Manager, Frazier W. Marsh; Stage Manager, Debra Acquavella; Stage Manager/Assistant to Producing Director, Zan Sawyer-Dailey; Technical Director, S. W. Patteson; Casting Assistance, Elissa Myers, Mark Teschner/Paul Fouquet, Associate; Wardrobe Supervisor, Denise Campion

RESIDENT COMPANY: Jonathan Bolt, Bob Burns, Ray Fry, Jody Gelb, Barbara Gulan, David Manis, William McNulty, Adale O'Brien, Mark Sawyer-Dailey
GUEST ARTISTS: Stage Directors, Michael Maggio, William Roudebush; Director/Writer, Barbara Damashek
PRODUCTIONS: *Camille* by Alexander Dumas fils, adapted by Barbara Field, *Ring Around the Moon* by Jean Anouilh, *The Real Thing* by Tom Stoppard, *Tom Foolery* with Words, Music & Lyrics by Tom Lehrer, adapted by Cameron Mackintosh and Robin Ray, *Taking Steps* by Alan Syckbourn, *The Rocky Horrow Show* by Richard O'Brien, *Caprices of Marianne* by Alfred de Musset, *Faith Healer* by Brian Friel, *Wanderers* compiled by Felicia Londre, *A Christmas Carol* adapted by Barbara Field, *The Gift of the Magi* adapted by Peter Ekstrom
PREMIERES: *Channels* by Judith Fein, *Metaphor* by Murphy Guyer, *The Queen of the Leaky Roof Circuit* by Jimmy Breslin, *Whereabouts Unknown* by Barbara Damashek, *Alone at the Beach* by Richard Dresser, *Lloyd's Prayer* by Kevin Kling, *Sarah and Abraham* by Marsha Norman, *Rock 'N' Roles from William Shakespeare* by Jim Luigs

131

ACTORS THEATRE OF ST. PAUL

St. Paul, Minnesota

Artistic Director, Michael Andrew Miner; Managing Director, Martha Sloca Richards; Marketing Director, Lori Anne Williams; Production Stage Manager, Jeff Couture; Assistant Stage Managers, Tree O'Halloran, Janet L. Hall; Resident Designer, Nayna Ramey; Technical Director, David Radtke; Costumes, Rich Hamson; Artistic Associate, Louis Schaefer; Arts Education Director, D. Scott Glasser; Composers, Randall Davidson, Eric Peltoniemi, Eric Stokes; Playwrights, Steven Dietz, Marilyn Seven, Karen Sunde; Stage Directors, James Cada, D. Scott Glasser, David M. Kwiat, Michael Andrew Miner, Louis Schaefer

RESIDENT COMPANY: James Cada, Annie Enneking, Norma Fire, D. Scott Glasse, Terry Heck, Emil Herrera, David M. Kwiat, David Lenthall, Louis Schaefer, John Seibert
GUEST ARTISTS: Directors, Steven Dietz, Rod Marriott; Lighting, Todd Hensley, Doug Pipan; Sets, Chris Johnson, Dick Leerhoff, Lori Sullivan; Costumes, Sandra Nei Schulte; Actors, Leslie Ball, Dianne Benjamin-Hill, Bruce Bohne, David Anthony Brinkley, Tim Danz, Hassan El-Amin, Stephen Gee, James Harris, Allan Hickle-Edwards, Prudence Johnson, Ruth MacKenzie, Courtney Kjos, Rod Kleiss, John Pasha, Rod Pierce, Sally Ramirez, Don Wellen, Claudia Wilkens, Saly Wingert; Musicians: William Mask, Eric Peltoniemi, Jeffrey Willkomm
PRODUCTIONS: *Breakfast With Strangers* by Vladlen Dozortsev, Translated by Elise Thoron. (World Premiere) *Ten November* written and directed by Steven Dietz, Music & Lyrics by Eric Peltoniemi, *The Second Shepherds' Play* (Traditional) *Why the Lord Come to Sand Mountain* by Romulus Linney, *Joe Egg* by Peter Nichols, *Blue Window* by Craig Lucas
THE MINNESOTA ONE ACT PLAY FESTIVAL: *Mickey's Teeth* by Amlin Gray (World Premiere), *The Zoo Story* by Edward Albee, *Fire in the Basement* by Pavel Kohout, Translated by Peter Stenberg and Marketa Goetz-Stankiewicz, *Hughie* by Eugene O'Neill, *A Betrothal* by Lanford Wilson, *The Business at Hand* by Martha Boesing (World Premiere), *Gurley and the Finn* by David Brunet, *Elsie's Kitchen* by Rick Foster (World Premiere), *The Lost Colony* by Wendy MacLeod

Terry Heck, Norma Fire in "Elsie's Kitchen"
(R) Tim Danz, Leslie Ball in "Ten November"
(Kerry Jorgensen Photos)

ALASKA REPERTORY THEATRE

Anchorage, Alaska

Artistic Director, Andrew J. Traister; Managing Director, Alice Chebba Walsh; Production Manager, Dennis Gill Booth; Press/Development, Jill McGuire; Assistant to the Directors, Suzanne Launer; Production Stage Manager, Robert H. Satterlee; Stage Managers, William R. Ferrara, Sarah Wilkinson; Sets, Connie Lutz, Everett Chase; Costumes, Jennifer Svenson; Lighting, Lauren Miller; Sound, Tony M. Vaillancourt; Props, Paul Stone; Technical Director, Darryl S. Waskow

RESIDENT COMPANY: Ed Bourgeois, Mitchell Edmonds, David Ellenstein, Peter Ellenstein, Robert Ellenstein, Lynnda Ferguson, Robert Hackman, James H. Hotchkiss, Judith Jordan, Priscilla Hake Lauris, Christine McMurdo-Walis, James Morrison, Gary Pannullo, Susan Ronn, Kamella Tate, John Walcutt
GUEST ARTISTS: Directors, James Edmonson, Molly Smith; Costumes, Frances Kenny
PRODUCTIONS: *Cat on a Hot Tin Roof* by Tennessee Williams, Director, Andrew J. Traister; *The Importance of Being Ernest* by Oscar Wilde, Director, James Edmonson; *Bus Stop* by William Inge, Director, Molly Smith; *Broadway Bound* by Neil Simon, Director, Andrew J. Traister

Chris Arend Photos

**Top Left: Mitchell Edmonds, James Morrison
in "Cat on a Hot Tin Roof"**

**Lynnda Ferguson, Kamella Tate in
"The Importance of Being Earnest"**

THE ALLEY THEATRE

Houston, Texas
Forty-first Season

Artistic/Executive Director, Pat Brown; Managing Director, Michael Tiknis; Marketing, Carl Davis; Press, Julie Devane.

PRODUCTIONS & CASTS

HENCEFORWARD written & directed by Alan Ayckbourn *(American Premiere)*; Set, Charles D. Kading; Lighting, James Sale; with George Segal, Judy Geeson, Brenda Daly, Adam LeFevre
STEPPING OUT by Richard Harris; Choreographer, Chesley Ann Santoro; Music Supervisor, Rob Landes; Arrangements, Peter Howard; with Bonnie Gallup, Chesley Ann Santoro, Patricia Kilgarriff, Laurel Anne White, Jackie Teamer
THE MIRACLE WORKER by William Gibson; with James Pritchett, Catherine Fleming, Ella E. Garner, Kraig Oliver, Robin Moseley, Amanda Goyen
THE LUCKY SPOT by Beth Henley; Choreographer, Brandon Smith, Dance Consultant, Chesley Santoro; Set, Charels S. Kading; with Terres Unsoeld, Jennie Welch, Harold Suggs
A CLASS "C" TRIAL IN YOKOHAMA by Roger Cornish; Director, Burry Fredrik; Set, Charles S. Kading; Lighting, James Sale; with John Newton, Doug Yasuda, Anne Marbella, Dalton Leong, Valerie Lau-Kee, Tom Matsusaka, Keenan Shimizu, Ako
THE NERD by Larry Shue; with Alan Brooks, Parker Esse
THE LAST FLAPPER by William Luce *(American Premiere)*; Director, Charles Nelson Reilly; Costumes, Noel Taylor; Sound, Timothy John Helgeson; Set/Lighting, Patrick Hughes, Christopher Mandich; Musical Design, Stan Freeman; Choreographer, Robert Fitch
SELF DEFENSE by Joe Cacaci; Lighting, James Sale; with David Gregory, David Berman, Kelvin R. Shepard, Ambrosio Guerra
HUNTING COCKROACHES by Janusz Glowacki; Director, Joan Vail Thorne; Dialect Coach, Maria Tittel; with Zach Grenier
SHARON & BILLY by Alan Bowne; with Susan Welby, Joey Hartdegen
A SHAYNA MAIDEL by Barbara Lebow; Dialect Coach, Paula Spiegel; with Bonnie Black, Philip Fisher, Katie C. Sparer, Bill Roberts, Susan Welby, Bonnie Gallup

Carl Davis Photos

Right: James Black, Joey Hartdegen, Susan Welby, Charlene Bigham in "Sharon & Billy"
Top: James Michael Reilly, Annalee Jefferies, Zach Grenier in "Hunting Cockroaches"

Judy Geeson, George Segal in "Henceforward. . . ."

Marietta Marich, Chesley Ann Santoro in "Stepping Out"

133

THE AMERICAN STAGE COMPANY

Fairleigh-Dickinson University
Teaneck, New Jersey
Third Season

Artistic Director, Paul Sorvino; Executive Producer, Theodore Rawlins; Executive Director, James R. Singer; Associate Producer, Jamie Milestone; Business Manager, Robert A. Lusko; Press, Nikki Brown; Director of Conservatory, Roberta Simon; Technical Director, Garrit Lydecker; Stage Directors, David Schramm, Morton DaCosta, Stephen Rosenfield, George Rondo, Sheldon Epps; Sets, Garrit Lydecker, James Morgan, John Falabella; Costumes, Barbara A. Bell, Joan V. Evans, Barbara Forbes, John Falabella; Lighting, Jon Terry, Mal Sturchio, Stuart Duke; Stage Managers, Diane C. Hartdagen, John W. Calder III, Gerald A. Carter, Mary Ellen Allison; Sound, Ivan Julian

PRODUCTIONS & CASTS
THE PRICE by Arthur Miller; Director, David Schramm. CAST: Donald May, Kathleen Noone, Michael M. Ryan, Martin Rudy
POSSESSED *(World Premiere)* with Book by Robert Marasco and Jason Darrow; Music, Carter Cathcart; Lyrics, Jason Darrow; Director, Morton DaCosta. CAST: Robert Michael Baker, Katherine Buffaloe, Penny Fekany, Florence Fox, Jeannie Hudak, Richard Kinter, Lee Lobenhofer, James Hillgartner, Chris Quartana, Barbara Reierson, Ted Scheffler, Paul Schoeffler, Steven Wishnoff, Michael Zaslow
FAST GIRLS *(World Premiere)* by Diana Amsterdam; Director, Stephen Rosenfiel. CAST: Carol Hanpeter, Michael C. Mahon, Kate Redway, Elizabeth Perry, David H. Sterry
WHISPERS *(World Premiere)* by James Elward; Director, George Rondo. CAST: Malachy Cleary, Steven Crossley, Pauline Lepor, Sylvia Short, Gretchen Walther
THE VOICE OF THE PRAIRIE by John Olive; Director, Sheldon Epps. CAST: Tony Carlin, David Chandler, Sarah Fleming

Emmet Francois Photos

**Left: Michael Zaslow, Katherine Buffaloe
in "Possessed" Top: Michael Miller, Kathleen
Noone in "The Price"**

Steven Crossley, Gretchen Walther, Pauline Lepor
in "Whispers" Above: Kate Redway, Elizabeth Perry,
Carol Hanpeter in "Fast Girls"

Tony Carlin, David Chandler, and Above: Tony
Carlin, Sarah Fleming in "Voice of the Prairie"

Tony Todd, Evelyn Thomas in "Les-Blancs"
Top Right: Mitchell Greenberg, Charles Janasz,
Stephen Mellor, Ralph Cosham in "The Cocoanuts"
Below: Shirley Knight, Tana Hicken, Rebecca
Ellens in "The Cherry Orchard"

ARENA STAGE

Washington, D.C.
Thirty-seventh Season

Directors, Lloyd Richards, Douglas C. Wager, James C. Nicola; Zelda Fichandler, Mel Shapiro, Harold Scott, Paul Walker, Woodie King, Jr., Lucian Pintilie; Musical Directors, Dwight Andrews, Mark Novak, Robert Fisher; Sets, Scott Bradley, Douglas Stein, Michael Franklin-White, Andrew Jackness, Karl Eigsti, David Glenn, Thomas Lynch, Radu Boruzescu; Costumes, Pamela Peterson, Marjorie Slaiman, Noel Borden, Martin Pakledinaz Miruna Boruzescu; Lighting, Michael Gianitti, Allen Lee Hughes, Nancy Schertler, Beverly Emmons; Stage Managers, Karen L. Carpenter, Maxine Krasowski Bertone, Pat Cochran, Jessica Evans, Martha Knight, Wendy Streeter

RESIDENT COMPANY: Stanley Anderson, Richard Bauer, Marissa Copeland, Ralph Cosham, Terrence Currier, Mark Hammer, Tom Hewitt, Tana Hicken, Bob Kirsh, John Leonard, David Marks, Cary Anne Spear, Henry Strozier, Halo Wines
GUEST ARTISTS: Kimberleigh Aarn, Jorge Abreu, Haimanot Alemu, Ian C. Armstrong, Judith Bardi, Angela Bassett, Francine Beers, Kevin Berdini, Kim Bey, Richard Beymer, Casey Biggs, Susan Bofinger, Candy Buckley, L. Scott Caldwell, Karma Camp, Kevin Campbell, Brigid Cleary, Brian Cousins, Kevin Crawford, Ruby Dee, Darren Dooley, Tony Duncanson, Stanley Noel Dunn, Beverly Edwards, Rebecca Ellens, Robbie Farer, Lou Ferguson, Lili Flandes, Al Freeman, Jr., Gale Garnett, Kathleen Goldpaugh, Martin Goldsmith, Mitchell Grenberg, Richard Grusin, Ed Hall, Kippen Hay, Terry Hinz, Emily Holtz, John Hoshko, David Ingram, David Inloes, Gisele Jackson, Charles Janasz, James Johns, Keith Johnson, Tom W. Jones, II, Shirley Knight, Jane Labanz, Mikel Sarah Lambert, Clayton LeBouef, Kaiulani Lee, Delroy Lindo, Joey Lutz, Walt MacPherson, Frank Maraden, Anderson Matthews, Stephen Mellor, Sharrone Mitchell, Lex Monson, Mary Naden, LaFontaine Oliver, Anton Perkins, Stephanie Preston, Vincent Prevost, Zelda Rubinstein, Bo Rucker, Eric Ruffin, Raynor Scheine, Scott Schofield, Kimberly Scott, Joshus Shirlen, Lilia Skala, Henry Stram, Victor Strengaru, Fred Strother, Carolyn Swift, Evelyn Thomas, Barbara Tobias, Tony Todd, Katrina Van Duyn, Elizabeth Van Dyke, Paul Walker, Basil Wallace, Deanna Wells, Michael Wells, Steven Major West, Isiah Whitlock, Jr., Barnett Williams, Kellie S. Williams, Mel Winkler, Jeffrey Wright
PRODUCTIONS: Joe Turner's Come and Gone, All the King's Men, Light Up the Sky, Enrico IV, Les Blancs, Checkmates, The Cocoanuts, The Cherry Orchard
WORLD PREMIERES: From Off the Streets of Cleveland Comes . . . American Splendor based on the comic books by Harvey Pekar, Adapted for the stage by Lloyd Rose; The Rivers and Ravines by Heather McDonald

(Joan Marcus Photos)

Stanley Anderson, Henry Strozier in "Enrico IV"
Above: Richard Bauer, Tana Hicken in "Light Up the Sky"

135

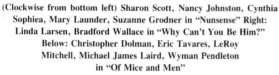

(Clockwise from bottom left) Sharon Scott, Nancy Johnston, Cynthia
Sophiea, Mary Launder, Suzanne Grodner in "Nunsense" Right:
Linda Larsen, Bradford Wallace in "Why Can't You Be Him?"
Below: Christopher Dolman, Eric Tavares, LeRoy
Mitchell, Michael James Laird, Wyman Pendleton
in "Of Mice and Men"

ASOLO STATE THEATER

Sarasota, Florida
Twenty-ninth Season

Executive Director, Lee H. Warner; Associate Executive Director, Donald P.
Creason; Artistic Director, John Ulmer; Stage Director, Robert G. Miller; Sets,
Jeffrey Dean, Keven Lock; Costumes, Ainslie G. Bruneau; Lighting, Martin Petlock;
Production Stage Manager, Marian Wallace; Stage Managers, Stephanie Moss,
Juanita Munford, Barbara Burton; Production Coordinator, Victor Meyrich

COMPANY: Lydia Bruce, Stephen Daly, Mary Doyle, Suzanne Grodner, Nancy
Johnston, Michael James Laird, Mary E. Launder, Kathleen Masterson, Michael
Mckenzie, Wyman Pendleton, Karl Redcoff, Sharon E. Scott, Leon B. Stevens,
Parry B. Stewart, Cynthia Sophiea, Eric Tavares, Peter Gregory Thomson, Bradford
Walace, Jane Welch, Joyce Wosley Robert Michael Baker, Dan Cronin, Rory Kelly,
Michael James Laird, Carolyn Michel, Lauren Mufson, Lou Myers, Cynthia
Sophiea, Eric Tavares, Bradford Wallace, John DiPinto, Preston Boyd, Mary E.
Launder, Carol McCann, Luke Nelson, Scott Wakefield
GUEST ARTISTS: Guest Directors, Jamie Brown, Tony Tanner; Sets, Bennett
Averyt, Holmes Easley, John Ezell; Playwright in Residence, John Ford Noonan;
Musical Director, David Brunetti; Choreographers, Judith Haskell, Rob Marshall
PRODUCTIONS: *Nunsense* by Dan Goggin, *Philadelphia, Here I Come!* by Brian
Friel, *The Heiress* by Ruth and Augustus Goetz, *Of Mice and Men* by John Steinbeck,
Ladies in Retirement by Edward Percy and Reginald Denham, *Pump Boys and
Dinettes* by John Foley, Mark Hardwick, Debra Monk, Cass Morgan, John Schim-
mel, and Jim Wann, *I'm Not Rappaport* by Herb Gardner, *Berlin to Broadway* with
Music by Kurt Weill, Text by Gene Lerner; *First Time Anywhere!* by Leo B. Meyer,
Mass Appeal by Bill C. Davis
WORLD PREMIERE: *Why Can't You Be Him?* by John Ford Noonan

Gary W. Sweetman Photos

Luke Nelson, Scott Wakefield, Preston Boyd,
Mary Launder, Carol McCann in "Pump Boys. . . ."

BARTER THEATRE

Abingdon, Virginia
Fifty-fifth Season

Artistic Director/Producer, Rex Partington; Business Manager, Pearl Hayter; Directors, Ken Costigan, John Foley, Frank Lowe, Allen Schoer, William Van Keyser; Costumes, M. Lynne Allen, Karen Brewster, Barbara Forbes, Doothy Marshall, Lisa Micheels; Sets, M. Lynne Allen, Daniel Ettiner, Jim Stauder; Lighting, Al Oster; Stage Managers, Champe Leary, William Stuart Snyder, Marjorie Terry, James Wood; Marketing, Pamela E. Martin; Technical Director, Jim Stauder; Props, Kevin Hoffman

COMPANY: William Addy, Nick Andrews, Douglas Balfour, Dorita Beh, Ross Bickell, Ron Brice, Tom Cannold, Rodney Clark, Rebecca Colness, Schery Collins, Jason Edwards, T. Cat Ford, Stephen Gabis, Charles Geyer, Jack Kelly Gooden, William Gore, Mary Gutzi, Richard A. Hinz, Cleo Holladay, Mark Johannes, Richard Kinter, Jim Kirk, Dane Knell, Miller Lide, Aaron Lustig, Christopher James Wright, Kim McIntyre, Elise Melrood, Sally Mercer, Barbara Niles, Sean O'Sullivan, Rex Partington, Tony Partington, Robert Putnam, Paula Redinger, Mitchell Rund, Stephen Rust, Wesley Stevens, Michael M. Thompson, Peter Van Schyndel, Diane Warren, June Daniel White, Shelley Williams, Dan Wright
PRODUCTIONS: *The Odyssey* by Gregory A. Falls & Kurt Beattie, *My Fat Friend* by Charles Laurence, *See How They Run* by Philip King, *Children* by A.R. Gurney, Jr., *Pump Boys and Dinettes* by John Foley, Mark Hardwick, Debra Monk, Cass Morgan, John Schimmel, & Jim Wann, *The Rainmaker* by N. Richard Nash, *Relatively Speaking* by Alan Ayckbourn, *Angel Street* (tour) by Patrick Hamilton, *Beyond the Fringe* by Allen Bennett, Peter Cook, Jonathan Miller, & Dudley Moore, *Village Wooing and Others* by George Bernard Shaw, *Oh, Coward!* devised by Roderick Cook

Mike Kaylor Photos

Stephen Rust, Douglas Balfour, Jason Edwards,
Dan Wright in "Pump Boys. . . ." Above: Cleo Holladay,
Diane Warren, Christopher James Wright in "Children"

BEEF AND BOARDS DINNER THEATRE

Indianapolis, Indiana
Fifteenth Season

Artistic Director, Douglas E. Stark; Managing Director, Robert Zehr; Musical Director, Richard Laughlin; Stage Manager, Ed Stockman; Sets/Lighting, Michael Layton; Costumes, Livingston; Assistant to Producers, Peggy Zehr; Press, Mayla Alexander, Amy Jo Stark; Set Construction, Sean Brown; Choreographers, Stephen Essner, Kathleen Conry; Stage Directors, Robert Zehr, Douglas E. Stark

PRODUCTIONS & CASTS
OKLAHOMA! with Music by Richard Rodgers; Book and Lyrics, Oscar Hammerstein 2nd.; Assistant to Director, Michael Worcel; CAST: Walter Willison (Curly McLaine), Laura Clay (Laurey Williams), Doug Holmes (Ali Hakim), Laurie Walton (Ado Annie), Elenor Glockner (Aunt Eller), Brian Horton (Will Parker), Ty Stover (Jud Fry), Bonnie Swanson (Gertie Cummings), Geb Johnson (Andrew Carnes), Douglas King (Slim), Richard Rebilas (Cord Elam)
SOPHISTICATED LADIES with Music by Duke Ellington; CAST: Myron E. El, Stephen Essner, Kim Nazarian, Shirese Hursey, Keith Stewart, Anita L. Walker
MAME with Book by Jerome Lawrence and Robert E. Lee; Music & Lyrics, Jerry Herman; CAST: Cynthia Meryl (Mame), Jay Clator, J. Gregory Davis, Doug Holmes, Brian Horton, Diane Houghton, Judy Johnson, Kim Johnson, Mark Korres, Garrett Lutz, Jill Patton, Richard Rebilas, Bonnie Swanson
ANNIE with Music and Lyrics by Charles Strouse; Book, Thomas Meehan; CAST: Richard Pruitt (Oliver Warbucks), Adrienne Doucette (Miss Hannigan), Monica Lynn Ramey (Annie), Kathleen Conry (Grace Farrell), Doug Holmes (Franklin Delano Roosevelt), Carol Worcel (Lily), Brian Horton (Rooster), Jana Lugar (Molly), Jennifer Decker (Pepper), Kori McOmber (Duffy), Stephanie Chalmers (July), Tara Holland (Tessie), Brandy Stultz (Kate), Michael D. Cupp (Bundles/Drake/Harold Ickes), Greg Davis (Dog Catcher/Bert Healy/Cordell Hull), Garrett Lutz (Lt. Ward/Louis Howe), Judy Johnson (Mrs. Greer/Bonnie Boylan), Jill Patton (Cecille/Bonnie Boylan/Francis Perkins), Bonnie Swanson (Mrs. Pugh/Conni Boylan)
THE TWELVE DAYS OF CHRISTMAS; a musical revue with Suzanne Stark, Sharon Zehr, Brian Horton, Andy Cosentino
SINGIN' IN THE RAIN with Book by Betty Comden, Adolph Green; Songs, Nacio Herb Brown, Arthur Freed; CAST: Stephen W. Essner (Don Lockwood), Jill Patton (Kathy Selden), Brian Horton (Cosmo Brown), Doug Holmes (Roscoe Dexter), Debby Shively (Lina Lamont), Geb Johnson (R. F. Simpson), Tracey Edwards (Zelda Zanders), Judy Johnson, Garrett Lutz, Glenn Leslie, Michael Worcell, Doug King, Kimberly Rheam, Sherrill McCracken, Christine Hull
BEST OF BURLESQUE; CAST: Sandy O'Hara, Bob Moak, Riki Dunn, Michael Chirrick, Teddy King, Lee Bredenbeck, Debra Gregory, Roxanne D'Ascenzo, Amanda Linhares, Elizabeth Campbell, Robin Long

D. Todd Moore Photos

Stephen Essner, Debby Shively, Doug Holmes
in "Singin' in the Rain" Above: Walter Willison,
Laura Clay in "Oklahoma!"

137

Edward Earle, Dana Bate in "Knock Knock"
Top: (left) Ching Valdes/Aran, Calvin Jung
in "The Good Earth" (right) Joanne Bradley,
Brendan Mulvey in "Gifts of the Magi"
(Photos by Klein)

BRISTOL RIVERSIDE THEATRE

Bristol, Pennsylvania

Artistic Director, Susan D. Atkinson; Managing Director, Robert K. O'Neill; Technical Director, Russell Wadbrook; Marketing, Linda Lee; Press, Betty Cichy; Assistant to Managing Director, Gina L. Girotti; Secretary to Managing Director, Josephine Lalli; Assistant to Artistic Director, Judith Lehrhaupt; Assistant Technical Director, Charles Scott; Stage Manager, Ben Janney; Interns, Marty Joyce, Allison Froyd, Christine Mundy.

PRODUCTIONS & CASTS
PEARL S. BUCK'S "THE GOOD EARTH" adapted by Owen Davis and Donald Davis; Director, Susan D. Atkinson; Sets/Lighting, Wolfgang Roth; Costumes, Michael Sharp. CAST: Norris M. Shimabuku (Narrator/Gatekeeper/Speaker/Yi Ling), Calvin Jung (Wang Lung), Kim Chan (Father), Leticia Ferrer (Cuckoo), Beth Browde (Ancient Lady/Beggar/Lotus), Ching Valdes/Aran (Olan), Michael G. Chin (Peach Vendor/Ching/Beggar), Clifford Arashi (Uncle), Lily Froehlich (Aunt), Karen Lee (Beggar/Slave Girl/Maid), Prudence Lo (Fool Child), Kevin Vertucio (Middle Son), Jason Vertucio (Youngest Son), JoJo Gonzales (Eldest Son/Beggar), Richard E. Joyce (Fat Lord/Doctor).
O. HENRY'S "GIFTS OF THE MAGI" adapted by Mark St. Germain & Randy Courts; Director, Susan D. Atkinson; Set, Nels Anderson; Lighting, G. Todd Vaules; Costumes, Helen Clark; Choreography, Lisa Sagolla; Piano, Joe Nappi. CAST: Brendan Mulvey (The City/Him), Joanne Bradley (The City/Her), James Goode (Willy Porter), Sarah Rice (Della Dillingham), Garrett States (Jim Dillingham), Sel Vitella (Soapy Smith).
THE MIDDLE PASSAGE by Dan Rustin *(World Premiere);* Director, Susan D. Atkinson; Set, George Black; Lighting, Dan Gitomer; Costumes, Helen Clark. CAST: Kyra Hider (Desdemonia/Younger Phillis), Stephanie Berry (Phillis), Cyrus Newitt (John), Alla Nedoresow (Susannah), Geneva Wiggin (India), Gregory Simmons (Prince), Lee Golden (Rev. Sewell), Kathleen Butler (Madam Traver), Churchill Clark (Gen. George Washington).
KNOCK KNOCK by Jules Feiffer; Director, Michael Ladenson; Set, Geroge Black; Lighting, Jerold R. Forsyth; Costumes, Michelle Vogt. CAST: Edward Earle (Abe), Dana Bate (Cohn), Sophia Maletsky (Joan), Robert Lee Martini (Wiseman/Joan's Voices).
THE ROBBER BRIDEGROOM with Book & Lyrics by Alfred Uhry; Music, Robert Waldman; Director, Peter Webb; Set, Joseph A. Varga; Lighting, Scott Pinkney; Costumes, Debra Stein; Musical Director, James Stenborg; Choreographer, Derek Wolshonak. CAST: Brad Little (Jamie Lockhart), Alan Gilbert (Clement Musgrove), Verna Pierce (Salome), Barbara McCulloh (Rosamund), Alex Corcoran (Little Harp), Barry E. Moore (Big Harp), Scott Macdonald (Goat), Tracy Lee Bell (Airie), Janice Baldwin Moule (Goat's Mother), Shannon McGough (Raven), Robert Osborne (Caller), Mark Guerette (Innkeeper) Jeannie Dobie (Innkeeper's Wife), Barry Hillman (Preacher), Mimi Barbra Schultz (Queenie Sue Stevens), Frank Berry (Captain).

CALDWELL THEATRE COMPANY

Boca Raton, Florida

Artistic Director/Managing Director, Michael Hall; Sets, Frank Bennett; Lighting, Mary Jo Dondlinger; Costumes, Bridget R. Bartlett; Graphics, James Morgan; Press, Joe Gillie, Paul Perone; Company Manager, Patricia Burdett; Marketing, Kethy Walton; Theatre Education, Nancy Yohe; Production Coordinator, Chip Latimer; Technical Director, David Heath; Stage Manager, Bob Carter; Musical Directors, Michael Allen Harrison, Chris Salerno

PRODUCTIONS & CASTS
CANDIDA by George Bernard Shaw, with Barbara Bradshaw; Conan McCarty, Peter Haig, Don Spalding, Max Gulack, Glynis Bell
THE CHOPIN PLAYOFFS by Israel Horovitz; with Jim Tabakin, Joy Johnson, Max Gulack, Samuel D. Cohen, Mona Jones, Frank Andeson, Marilyn Whitehead, Gary Nathanson
SOMETHING'S AFOOT by James McDonald, David Vos & Robert Gerlach, additional Music by Ed Linderman; with Heidi White, Don Spalding, Mandy Beason, Bick Ferguson, Kim Cozort, Joe Gillie, Gary Goodson, Mark Hardy, Jackalyn Carpenter, Michael O. Smith
LOOK HOMEWARD, ANGEL adapted by Ketti Frings from the novel by Thomas Wolfe; with June Prud'homme, David Burke Chrisman, Art Kempf, Joy Johnson, David McDonald, Barbara Bradshaw, Gary Goodson, Heidi White, Don Spalding, Kay Brady, Frances Mansfield, Jackalyn Carpenter, Amy McDonald, Richard Liberty, Peter Haig, Tom Disney, Bick Ferguson
LADY DAY AT EMERSON'S BAR AND GRILL by Lanie Robertson; with Jackie Lowe, William Foster McDaniel
23 SKIDOO (Cabaret) with Kay Brady, Joe Gillie, Susan Hatfield, Jean Bolduc, Chris Salerno, Rupert Ziawinski

Joyce Brock Photos

Conan McCarty, Barbara Bradshaw
in "Candida"

CAPITAL REPERTORY COMPANY

Albany, New York

Producing Directors, Bruce Bouchard, Peter H. Clough; Administrative Operations, Peter M. Kindlon; Development, Christopher Lino, Julie Galloway; Business Operations, Maureen Salkin; Marketing, Hilde Schuster, Vauna Bernstein; Literary Manager, Robert Meiksins; Outreach, Jennifer Greenfield; Sets, Dale F. Jordan, Ray Recht, Robert Thayer, Rick Dennis; Lighting, Dale F. Jordan, Jackie Manassee, John Ambrosone, Dan Kinsley, David Yergan; Costumes, Lynda L. Salsbury, Martha Haly, David Woolard; Production Stage Manager, Paricia Frey; Stage Manager, Julie Fife; Technical Director, Laurence S. Clark.

PRODUCTIONS & CASTS
THE SEARCH FOR SIGNS OF INTELLIGENT LIFE IN THE UNIVERSE by Jane Wagner; Directors, Bruce Bouchard, Peter H. Clough; Sets/Lighting, Dale F. Jordan; Costumes, Lynda L. Salsbury; with Cynthia Darlow, Mary Catherine Wright, Valorie Armstrong, Roma Maffia, Diane Kagan.
LIKE THEM THAT DREAM by Edgar White; Director, Basil Wallace; Sets, Ray Recht; Costumes, Martha Hally; Lighting Jackie Manassee; with Lou Ferguson, Gail Grate, Lilene Mansell, Chet London.
MRS. CALIFORNIA by Doris Baizley; Director, Peter H. Clough; Sets, Robert Thayer; Lighting, John Ambrosone; Costumes, Lynda L. Salsbury; with Kate Kelly, Maureen Garrett, Mark Hofmaier, Pamela Nyberg, Dorothy Cantwell, Pat Dougan, Marc Duncan, Anne Aiken, Maria Memole, Richard Parent.
THURSDAY'S CHILD by Julie Jensen *(World Premiere);* Director, Gordon Edelstein; Set, Ray Recht; Lighting, Dan Kinsley; Costumes, David Woolard; with Marylouise Burke, Sally Ann Cohen, Trish Gray, Tho Fields, Burke Pearson, Cheryl E. Andrews.
THE BIG KNIFE by Clifford Odetr; Director, Bruce Bouchard; Set, Rick Dennis; Lighting, Jackie Manassee; Costumes, Lynda L. Salsbury; with Hugh L. Hurd, Frank Muller, William Leone, Barbara Perry, Nicole Orth-Pallavicini, William Newman, Burke Pearson, Frank Biancamano, Heather Rattray, James DeMarse, Carol Wade.
THE NERD by Larry Shue; Director, Michael J. Hume; Set, Dale F. Jordan; Lighting, David Yergan; Costumes, Martha Hally; with Jayne Bentzen, Robertson Dean, Jack Laufer, Christopher Wynkoop, Patty Dworkin, Joshua Stedman Rozett, Brad Bellamy.

CALIFORNIA MUSIC THEATRE

Pasadena, California
First Season

Artistic Director/Stage Director, Gary Davis; Managing Director, Lars Hansen; Production Manager, Thomas E. Ware; Marketing, Jerry Robin; Administration, Melanie Peterson; Development, Kathryn Laird-Johnson, Jodi Gilbert; Press, Richard T. Spittel; Musical Director, Jeff Rizzo; Lighting, Ward Carlisle; Sets, Charles Ketter; Stage Manager, Danny Michaels; Choreography, Patty Columbo

PRODUCTIONS & CASTS
THE DESERT SONG with Music & Lyrics by Sigmund Romberg; Book, Otto Harbach, Oscar Hammerstein, II, & Frank Mandel; Musical Directors, Stephen Gothold, Jeff Rizzo; Sets, Peter Wolfe; Costumes, Pamela Johnson-Gill; CAST: Laurence Guittard (The Red Shadow/Pierre), Dale Kristien (Margot Bonvalet), David Ruprecht (Benjamin Kidd), Marsha Kramer (Susan), Dan Tullis, Jr. (Ali Ben Ali), Jack Ritschel (Gen. Birabeau), Richard Riffel (Sid El Kar), Lewis Landau (Mindar), Mark Miller (Neri), Carl Packard (Hassi), Rachell Ottley (Azuri), Steven Davis (Capt. Paul Fontaine), James Whitson (Lt. LaVergne), Rieka Wallach (Edith), Roberta B. Wall (Clementina), Marilynn Avery, Karen Benjamin, Catherine Cravens, Gina Ehren, Rebecca Eichenberger, Kathie Freeman, Carolyn Kimball, Linda Milliken, Grace Sagara, Leslie Tinnaro, Roberta B. Wall, Phil Chaffin, Tom Flynn, Jeffrey Gerstein, Richard Hilton, Lewis Landau, Christian Nova, LaRue Palmer, Don Rey, Harry Schlager
SHE LOVES ME with Book by Joe Masteroff; Music, Jerry Bock; Lyrics, Sheldon Harnick; Additional Staging, Rob Barron; Costumes, Garland Riddle. CAST: Susan Watson (Amalia Balash), Gary Beach (Georg Nowak), Beth Howland (Ilona Ritter), Steeve Arlen (Steven Kodaly), Tom Hatten (Ladislav Sipos), Sandy Kenyon (Mr. Maraczek), Randy Brenner (Arpad), Von Schauer (Keller), Ace Mask (Headwaiter), Kevin Pariseau (Busboy), Rion Garrison (Victor), Jeff Austin (Ferencz), Josie Dapar (Violinist), Karen Benjamin, Ann Winkowski, Brenda Runyan, Kathie Cole Freeman, Nicolette Abernathy, Susan Mieras (Customers)
DROOD! by Rupert Holmes; Sets, Bob Shaw; Costumes, Garland Riddle. CAST: George Rose (Mr. William Cartwright), Karen Morrow (Princess Puffer), Terry Lester (John Jasper), Lisa Robinson (Edwin Drood), Stacy Sullivan (Rosa Bud), Lorella Brina (Helena Landless), James Dybas (Neville Landless), Ray Stewart (Rev. Crisparkle), Patrick Richwood (Deputy), Robert Machray (Durdles), Paul Ainsley (James Throttle), Diana Kavilis (Wendy/Succubae), Leslie Woodies (Beatrice), Richard Byron, Malcolm Perry, Reggie Phoenix (Puffer's Clients), Reggie Phoenix (Shade of Drood), Jim Ruttman (Shade of Jasper), Nora Frank (Image of Rosa), Natasha Kautsky, Renee Stork, Leslie Woodies, (Succubae), Whitney Rydbeck (Waiter), Whitney Rydbeck (Bazzard), ??????? (Dick Datchery), Joe Foronda, Nora Frank, Dan Haggard, Nanette Hofer, Stephanie Huffman, Lena Marie, Kevin Pariseau, Alan Rosenbaum (Music Hall Patrons)

Craig Shwartz Photos

Top Left: Laurence Guittard, Steven Davis, Dale Kristien in "The Desert Song" Below: George Rose, Patrick Richwood, Robert Machray in "Drood"

Maureen Garrett, Mark Hofmaier in "Mrs. California" *(Skip Dickstein)*

CENTER STAGE

Baltimore, Maryland

Artistic Director, Stan Wojewodski, Jr.; Managing Director, Peter W. Culman; Management Assistant, Fori C. Daniel; Marketing/Press, Barbara Kaplan, Betsy Junzelman, JoCarol Sachs; Development, Mary E. Howell, Terry H. Morgenthaler, M. Nancy Pinto; Artistic Administrator, Del W. Risberg; Dramaturgs, Rick Davis, Walter Bilderback, Scott T. Cummings, Brian Johnson, Michael Zelanak; Production Manager, Katharyn Davies; Stage Managers, Keri Muir, Janet E. Roos, Meryl Lind Shaw, Julie Thompson; Technical Director, Tom Rupp; Costumer, F. T. Brown; Wardrobe, Kendal E. Hullihen; Props, Julie Jordan Harrington; Sound, L. R. Smith; Young People's Theatre Playwrights, Jim Cary, Ann G. Sjoerdsma.

PRODUCTIONS & CASTS

HAMLET by William Shakespeare; Director, Stan Wojewodski, Jr.; Set, Hugh Landwehr; Costumes, Robert Wojewodski; Lighting, Pat Collins; Fight Director, David S. Leong; Music, Kim D. Sherman; Speech Consultant, Timothy Monich; CAST: Boyd Gaines (Hamlet), Thomas Barbour (Polonius), Barry Boys (Ghost/Gravedigger), Roland Bull (Player King), Michael Buster (Barnardo/Osric), Larry Clarke (Francisco/2nd Gravedigger/Lord), Alan Coates/John Hutton (Claudius), Tony Cummings (Laertes), Denise Diggs (Player Queen), Anthony Fusco (Guildenstern), Dennis Green (Rosencrantz), Christina Haag (Ophelia), Jennifer Harmon (Gertrude), David B. Hunt (Horatio), Edward Luther (Fortinbras), Philip Moon (Marcellus/Ambassador), Ramon Ramos (Cornelius)

AUNT DAN & LEMON by Wallace Shawn; Director, Irene Lewis; Set, John Conklin; Costumes, Catherine Zuber; Lighting, Pat Collins; Speech Consultant, Timothy Monich; Stage Violence Coordinator, David S. Leong. CAST: Larry Clarke (Jasper), Brian Cousins (Andy/Marty), Denise Diggs (June), Cara Duff-MacCormick (Mother/Flora), Susan Gibney (Mindy), Margaret Gibson (Aunt Dan), Mart Hulswit (Father/Freddie), Lily Knight (Lemon), Ramon Ramos (Raimondo)

THE COLORED MUSEUM by George C. Wolfe; Director, L. Kenneth Richardson; Music/Co-Arranger, Kysia Bostic; Musical Director/Co-Arranger, Daryl Waters; Choreography, Hope Clarke; Set, Brian Martin; Costumes, Nancy L. Konrardy; Lighting, Victor En Y Tan; Sound, Rob Gorton; Slide Design, Anton Nelessen. CAST: Reg E. Cathey (Model/Miss Roj/Walter Lee/The Man), Ellia English (Aunt Ethel/Janine/Mama/Admonia/Topsy Washington), Sharita Hunt (Miss Pat/The Woman/Medea Jones/Normal Jean Reynolds), Michele Mais (Model/La Wanda/Lady in Plaid/Lala), Tico Wells (Junie Robinson/Waiter/Narrator/The Kid/Flo'rance), Lauren Battle/Ashleigh Hicks (Little Girl), Darrell Taylor (Percussionist)

PARADISE LOST by Clifford Odets; Director, Michael Engler; Set, Loren Sherman; Costumes, Robert Wojewodski; Lighting, Jennifer Tipton; Speech Consultant, Lilene Mansell. CAST: Anna Berger (Clara Gordon), Donald Berman (Felix), Larry Clarke (Schnabel/Post/Williams/Cop), Denise Diggs (Lucy), Charles Dumas (Mr. Pike), Amy Griscom Epstein (Pearl Gordon), Brian Evers (Phil Foley), Rudy Goldschmidt (Julie Gordon), Charles Graham (Milton), Michelle Kronin (Libby Michaels), Stan Lachow (Leo Gordon), Grace Roberts (Bertha Katz), Martin Rudy (Gus Michaels), Armand Schultz (Kewpie), Jim Shanklin (Mr. May), Tony Soper (Ben Gordon), Daniel Szelag (Det./Rogo/Camera Man/Paul), Irwin Ziff (Sam Katz)

THE LADY FROM THE SEA by Henrik Ibsen; Director, Stan Wojewodski, Jr.; Set, Christopher Barreca; Costumes, Catherine Zuber; Lighting, Stephn Strawbridge. CAST: Kia Heath (Hilda), Warren Keith (Arnholm), Nicholas Kepros (Dr. Wangel), Patrick Kerr (Ballested), Peter Mackenzie (Lyngstrand), Laila Robins (Ellida Wangel), Amy Ryan (Bolette), Armand Schultz (Stranger)

IN PERPETUITY THROUGHOUT THE UNIVERSE by Eric Overmyer *(World Premiere);* Director, Stan Wojewodski, Jr.; Set, Christopher Barreca; Costumes, Robert Wojewodski; Lighting, Stephen Strawbridge; Sound, Janet Kalas. CAST: Troy Evans (Mr. Ampersand Qwerty/Oscar Rang), Arthur Hanket (Lyle Vial), Jennifer Harmon (Maria Montage/Claire Silver), Laura Innes (Buster/Miss Peterson/Joculatrix), Tzi Ma (Dennis Wu/Tai-Tung Tranh), Carolyn McCormick (Christine Penderecki)

A TEMPORARY PLACE by Frederick Gaines *(World Premiere);* Director, Irene Lewis; Set, Christopher Barreca; Costumes, Robert Wojewodski; Lighting, Stephen Strawbridge; Sound, Janet Kalas; Media Design, Kirby Malone. CAST: Roger Anderson (Noah Wiley), Amelia Campbell (Ane Lindstrom), Marissa Chibas (Kate Mertz), William Foeller (Merle Lindstrom), Neal Jones (Daryl Reimers), June Squibb (Myrna Lindstrom), Victor Steinbach (Mikhail Ozols), Jennifer Sternberg (Nell Waters), Alex Wipf (Tom Mertz)

JUDGEMENT DAY by Odon von Horvath; Translation, Martin and Renata Esslin *(World Premiere);* Director, Jackson Phippin; Set, Christopher Barreca; Costumes, Robert Wojewodski; Lighting, Stephen Strawbridge; Sound, Janet Kalas; Media Design, Kirby Malone. CAST: Roger Anderson (Kohut), Amelia K. Campbell (Child), Marissa Chibas (Anna), Troy Evans (Alfons), William Foeller (Policeman), Arthur Hanket (Det./Forestry Worker/Guest), Jennifer Harmon (Prosecutor), John Hutton (Thomas Hudetz), Neal Jones (Ferdinand), Tzi Ma (Inspector/Railway Worker), Carolyn McCormic (Leni), June Squibb (Mrs. Leimgruber), Victor Steinbach (Salesman/Pokorny), Jennifer Sternberg (Mrs. Hudetz), Alex Wipf (Landlord)

Richard Anderson Photos

Tzi Ma, Laura Innes Above: Tzi Ma,
Troy Evans in "In Perpetuity. . . ." Top: Boyd Gaines as Hamlet

CENTER THEATRE GROUP
AHMANSON THEATRE

Los Angeles, California
Twenty-first Season

PRODUCTIONS & CASTS

THE BEST MAN by Gore Vidal; Director, Jose Ferrer; Sets, Douglas W. Schmidt; Costumes, Madeline Ann Graneto; Lighting, Martin Aronstein; Production Stage Manager, Joe Cappelli; Stage Manager, Arthur Gaffin. CAST: Mel Ferrer (William Russell), Don Murray (Joseph Cantwell), Hope Lang (Alice Russell), Buddy Ebsen (Arthur Hockstader), Lois Chiles (Mabel Cantwell), Lynne Thigpen (Mrs. Gamadge), Christopher Murry (Don Blades), Paul Tulley (Dick Jensen), Fredric Cook (Sheldon Marcus), Charles McDaniel (Sen. Carlin), Ryan MacDonald (Dr. Artinian), Brian Avery, Michael Fox, Luise Heath, Paul Laramore, Jack Manning, Kerry Slattery, Edson Stroll

I NEVER SANG FOR MY FATHER by Robert Anderson; Director, Josephine Abady; Sets, David Potts; Costumes, Linda Fisher; Lighting, Jeff Davis; Sound, Scott Lehrer; Company Manager, Martin Cohen; Production Stage Manager, Amy Pell; Stage Manager, Robert S. Garber; A Berkshire Theatre Festival production; Presented by Jay Fuchs, The Kennedy Center/ANTA, and PACE Theatrical Group in association with Sports Entertainment Group, Inc. CAST: Daniel J. Travanti (Gene Garrison), Harold Gould (Tom Garrison), Dorothy McGuire (Margaret Garrison), Margo Skinner (Alice), William Cain (Dr. Mayberry), Scott Kanoff (Porter/Waiter), Sonja Lanzener (Mary), Edward Penn (Marvin Scott), Jeni Royer (Nurse), Richard Thomsen (Rev. Pell), Alfred Karl, Sally Parrish

SUMMER AND SMOKE by Tennessee Williams; Director, Marshall W. Mason; Sets, John Lee Beatty; Costumes, Laura Crow; Lighting, Dennis Parichy; Hair Design, Jeffrey Sacino; Music, Peter Kater; Production Stage Manager, Frank Marino; Stage Manager, Joe Cappelli. CAST: Christopher Reeve (John Buchanan, Jr.), Christine Lahti/Carol Potter Eastman (Alma Winemiller), Carol Barbee (Nellie), Michael Chieffo (Roger Doremus), Lois De Banzie (Mrs. Winemiller), Wanda de Jesus (Rosa Gonzales), Russel Lunday (Dr. John Buchanan, Sr.), Richard Seff (Rev. Winemiller), Leo Carranza (Dusty), Jacque Lynn Colton/Beth Grant (Mrs. Bassett), Beau Gravitte (Archie Kramer), Joaquin Martinez (Gonzales), Rand Mitchell (Vernon), Kristina Oster (Rosemary), Gary Berner, Beth Grant, Paul Laramore, Bel Sandre, Kerry Slattery

BROADWAY BOUND by Neil Simon; Director, Gene Saks; Set, David Mitchell; Costumes, Joseph G. Aulisi; Lighting, Tharon Musser; Sound, Tom Morse; Production Supervisor, Peter Lawrence; Company Managers, Brian Dunbar, Jody Moss; Production Stage Manager, John Brigleb; Stage Manager, Steven Shaw; Producer, Emmanuel Azenberg. CAST: Carole Shelley (Kate), William Ragsdale (Eugene), Nathan Lane/Brian Drillinger (Stanley), Salem Ludwig (Ben), David Margulies (Jack), Bernice Massi (Blanche)

(Jay Thompson Photos)
**Left: Harold Gould, Daniel J. Travanti in "I Never
Sang. . . ." Above: Buddy Ebsen, Don Murray in "The Best Man"
Top: Don Murray, Christopher Murry, Hope Lange
in "The Best Man"**

**Daniel J. Travanti, Dorothy McGuire
in "I Never Sang for My Father"**

**Christine Lahti, Christopher Reeve
in "Summer and Smoke"**

THE CLEVELAND PLAY HOUSE

Cleveland, Ohio
Seventy-second Season

Artistic Director, William Rhys; Managing Director Dean R. Gladden; Associate Artistic Director, Evie McClroy; Musical Director/Composer/Consulant, David Gooding; Company Manager, Angela Pohlman; Production Manager, Kathleen Christian; Technical Director of Special Effects, Deborah Malcolm; Sound, Steve Shapiro; Props, James A. Guy, Denis C. Mullaney, Mark Hare; Scenic Artist, Charles F. Morgan, Susan Kowalski; Costume Supervisor/Designer, Dawna L. Gregory; Wardrobe, M. K. Steeves; Stage Managers, Michael Stanley, Deborah A. Gosney, Allen Leatherman, Jan Wolf, Carlyle Owens, Kathleen Higgens; Stage Directors, Evie McElroy, William Rhys, Kenneth Albers, Jack Eddleman, George Ferencz, Sue Lawless, Nicholas Pennell, Dudley Swetland; Sets, Richard Gould, Keith Henery; Costumes, Estelle Painter; Designers, Charles Berliner, Beverly Emmons, Marc Kehoe, Dawna L. Gregory, Paul Mathiesen, Charles Dramaturg, Wayne S. Turney, F. Morgan, Bill Stabile; Sound Design, Vox; Acting Fellows, Stephanie Erb, Phoebe McBride, Rebecca Manning, Paul Sandberg, Greg Steres; Assistant to Managing Director, Louise Slusser; Development, David Hagar; Marketing/Press, Nancy E. Depke, Gayle Waxman

PRODUCTIONS & CASTS

TAKING STEPS by Alan Ayckbourn; Director, Sue Lawless. CAST: Catherine Albers (Elizabeth), John Buck, Jr. (Mark), Andrew May (Tristram), Richard Halverson (Roland), Wayne S. Turney (Leslie), Sharon Bicknell (Kitty), Rebecca Manning, Stephanie Erb, Greg Steres (Understudies)

K2 by Patrick Meyers; Director, Evie McElroy. CAST: William Rhys (Taylor), Morgan Lund (Harold), Paul Sandberg (Understudy)

THE FANTASTICKS with Book & Lyrics by Tom Jones; Music, Harvey Schmidt; Director, Jack Eddleman; Assistant Director, Stephanie Hall. CAST: Walter Willison (El Gallo), Marcy DeGonge (Luisa), Buddy Crutchfield (Matt), David O. Frazier (Hucklebee), John Buck, Jr. (Bellomy), Richard Halverson (Henry), Buddy Butler (Mortimer), Jeffrey Guyton (Mute), Phoebe McBride, Greg Steres (The Other Mutes/Understudies)

CHARLES DICKENS' A CHRISTMAS CAROL adapted by Dois Baizley; Director, William Rhys. CAST: Wayne S. Turney (Stage Manager/Scrooge), Morgan Lund (Director/Marley's Ghost), Stephanie Erb (Ingenue/Belle), Andrew May (Leading Man/Fred), Catherine Albers (Leading Lady/Mrs. Cratchit/Christmas Past), James Richards (Leading Man/Bob Cratchit), Rebecca Manning (Prop Girl/Tiny Tim), Evie McElroy (Wardrobe Mistress/Mrs. Fezziwig), Allen Leatherman (Old Clown/Fezziwig), Robert C. Rhys (Arlecchino/Christmas Present), Chuck Richie (Clown/Christmas Present), Paul Sandberg (Clown/Christmas Future), Christine Malik, Carlyle Owens, Yvette (Clowns/Ensemble)

DEATHRAFT by Harald Mueller; Translation, Roger Downey; Director, George Ferencz. CAST: Raul Aranas (Cheka), William Rhys (Itai), Roger Robinson/Wayne S. Turney (Cuckoo), Mary Lee-Aranas

Other productions during the season were *Much Ado About Nothing* by William Shakespeare, *Exit the King* by Eugene Ionesco, *The Common Pursuit* by Simon Grey, and *The Immigrant* by Mark Harelik. Casts and credits were not submitted

QUINTESSENCE SERIES: Ian McKellen in *Acting Shakespeare;* Jack Eddleman in *A Perfectly Weill Evening* with Music by Kurt Weill & Lyrics by Bertold Brecht, Marc Blitzstein, Alan Jay Lerner, Ogden Nash, Maxwell Anderson, Arnold Sundgaard, Ira Gershwin, & Langston Hughes, Staged by Stephanie Hall; Karen Akers in *And Now, Karen Akers—A Theatrical Concert;* Nanette Fabray in *Yes, Yes Nanette!;* Barbara Rush in *A Woman of Independent Means* by Elizabeth Forsythe Hailey; Michael Fienstein in *The Sophisticated Sound of a Steinway*

Top Right: (left) Walter Willison, Buddy Crutchfield, Marcy DeGonge in "The Fantasticks" (right) Sharon Bicknell, Andrew May in "The Immigrant" Below: Will Rhys, Raul Aranas in "Deathraft"
(Benjamin Margalit Photos)

**Carol Schultz, Andrew May
in "Much Ado about Nothing"**

**Andrew Vasnick, Mary Lee-Aranas
in "Exit the King"**

COCONUT GROVE PLAYHOUSE

Coconut Grove, Florida

Producing Artistic Director, Arnold Mittelman; Associate producer, Lynne Peyser; General Manager, Jordan Bock; Production Stage Manager, Rafael Blanco; Stage Managers, David Flasck, Heather D. MacKenzie; Sets, Wade Stuart Foy; Costumes, Ellis Tillman; Sound, Richard Camuso, Allen Zipper; Props, Steven Lambert; Production Manager, Lee Zimmerman.
RESIDENT COMPANY: Names not submitted
GUEST ARTISTS: Eli Wallach, Eileen Heckart, Lanie Kazan, Marilyn Sokol, Ron Orbach, Rene Enriquez, Liz Torres, Robert Reed, Janis Paige, Desi Arnaz, Jr., Roz Ryan; Russ Thacker, Marcia King, Martin Vidnovic; Directors, Robert Lewis, Jack Allison, Mel Shapiro, Arnold Mittelman; Authors in Residence: A. E. Hotchner, Cy Coleman, John Guare
PRODUCTIONS: *The Flowering Peach* by Clifford Odets; *Some Enchanted Evenings* with Music by Richard Rodgers & Lyrics by Oscar Hammerstein II; *The Rink* with Music by Fred Ebb & Lyrics by John Kander, Book by Terrance McNally (New Revised Version); *The House of Blue Leaves* by John Guare; *Alone Together* by Lawrence Roman
WORLD PREMIERES: *Let 'Em Rot* by A. E. Hotchner & Cy Coleman; *Boogie Woogie Bugle Girls; Waiting For You*

Luis Castaneda, Deborah Gray Mitchell Photos

Right: Liz Larsen, Martin Vidnovic, Marcia King, Russ Thacker, Ernestine Jackson in "Some Enchanted Evening" **Below:** Liz Torres, Rene Enriquez, Ruben Rabasa, Monica Carr, Judith Delgado in "House of Blue Leaves" **Top:** Tom McBride, Lesly Kahn, Sean Boling, Robert Reed, Janis Paige, Desi Arnaz, Jr. in "Alone Together"

Eileen Heckart, Eli Wallach in "Flowering Peach" **Above:** Julie Prosser, Felecia Rafield, Avery Sommers in "Boogie Woogie Girls"

Roz Ryan in "Waiting for You"

143

CROSSROADS THEATRE COMPANY

New Brunswick, New Jersey
Tenth Season

Producing Artistic Director, Rick Khan; Associate Producer, Kenneth Johnson; Managing Director, Elizabeth Bulluck; Marketing, Delphine Lester; Press, Adam Dyer; Development, Clarence H. Carter, Talvin W. Wilks; Production Manager, Gary Kechely; Technical Director, Gene Kish; Costumes, Henri Ewaskio; Scenic Artist, Tammera Boyle; Props, Neil Jacob; Musical Consultant, Ernie Scott

PRODUCTIONS & CASTS

WEST MEMPHIS MOJO by Martin Jones; Director, Rick Khan; Set, Charles McClennahan; Lighting, Shirley Prendergast; Costumes, Judy Dearing; Sound, Rob Gorton; Stage Manager, Kenneth R. Saltzman; Song by Rick Snyder, Martin Jones. CAST: Richard Gant (Teddy), Tico Wells (Elroi), Tucker Smallwood (Frank), Kate Redway (Maxine)

SPELL #7 by Ntozake Shange; Director, A. Dean Irby; Set, Daniel Proett; Lighting, Victor En Yu Tan; Costumes, Alvin Perry; Sound, Rob Gorton; Choreographer, Dyane Harvey; Stage Manager, Cheri Bogdan-Kechely. CAST: Rick Khan (Lou), Gregory Cole (Alec), Amparo Chigui Santiago (Dahlia), Reginald Veljohnson (Eli), Carla Brothers (Lily), Stephanie Berry (Bettina) Brenda Thomas (Natalie), Gregg Daniel (Ross), Lizan Mitchell (Maxine)

DUKE ELLINGTON'S SOPHISTICATED LADIES Directed and Choreographed by Bernard J. Marsh; Assistant Choreographer, Traci Robinson; Musical Director William Foster McDaniel; Set, Felix E. Cochren; Lighting, Susan A. White; Costumes, Bernard Johnson; Stage Manager, Cheri Bogdan-Kechely. CAST: Franz C. Alderfer, Gina Breedlove, Lawrence Clayton, Cheryl Howard, Janice Lorraine, Richard Mason, Sam Owens, Forest Ray, Traci Robinson, Melodee Savage

Left: Cast of "Spell #7"
Top: Richard Mason, Traci Robinson, Franz C.
Alderfer in "Sophisticated Ladies"
(Eddie Birch Photos)

DALLAS THEATRE CENTER

Dallas, Texas

Artistic Director, Adrian Hall; Executive Managing Director, Peter Donnelly; Designer, Eugene Lee; Associate Artistic Director, Ken Bryant; General Manager, Carl Wittenberg; Press, Patty Hetherwick; Development, Susan Swan; Costumes, Donna Kress; Lighting, Natasha Katz, Linda Blase; Production Stage Manager, David Glynn

RESIDENT COMPANY: Bill Bolender, Candy Buckley, Linda Gehringer, Anne Gerety, Dee Hannigan, Sean Hennigan, Steven Kalstrup, William Larsen, Beverly May, Allen McCala, Randy Moore, John Morrison, Martin Rayner, Nance Williamson, Jack Willis

GUEST ARTIST: Director, Larry Arrick; Director/Performance Artist, Fred Curchack; Repertorio Espanol of New York

PRODUCTIONS: *Through the Leaves* by Franz Xaver Koetz, *The Tempest* by William Shakespeare, *Cat on a Hot Tin Roof* by Tennessee Williams, *A Christmas Carol* by Charles Dickens/Adapted by Adrian Hall & Richard Cumming, *Glengarry Glen Ross* by David Mamet, *Uncle Vanya* by Anton Chekhov, *The House of Blue Leaves* by John Guare, *The Diary of a Scoundrel* by Alexander Ostrovsky/Adapted by Erik Brogger

Richard Bradley, Linda Blase, Susan Kandell Photos

Left Center: Ryland Merkey, Kurt Rhoads,
Willie H. Minor, Martin Rayner, John
Rainone in "The Tempest"

Stephen Kalstrup, Linda Gehringer
in "Cat on a Hot Tin Roof"

DENVER CENTER THEATRE COMPANY

Denver, Colorado
Ninth Season

Artistic Director, Donovan Marley; Executive Director, Sarah Lawless; Conservatory Director, Malcolm Morrison; Producing Director, Barbara E. Sellers; Associate Artistic Directors, Peter Hackett, Richard L. Hay; Casting, Randal Myler; Associate Artistic Director, Laird Williamson; Stage Directors, Andre De Shields, Frank Georgianna, Donovan Marley, Malcolm Morrison, Randal Myler, Bruce K. Sevy, Laird Williamson; Choreographers, Carolyn Dyer, Michael Kane, Leslie Watanabe; Conductor/Musical Director/Musical Arrangements, Larry Delinger; Designers, John Dexter, Pavel M. Dobrusky, Claudia Everett, Ralph Funicello, Richard L. Hay, Charles MacLeod, Peter Maradudin, Janet S. Morris, Daniel L. Murray, Rick Paulsen, Vicki Smith, Greg L. Sullivan, Laird Williamson, Patricia Ann Whitelock, Andrew V. Yelusich; Design Associates, Bruce J. Brisson, Bill Curley, Judith M. Pedeson, David Wallace, Patricia Ann Whitelock; Technical Director, Dan McNeil; Production Stage Manager, Lyle Raper; Assistant to Producing Director, Rodney J. Smith; Assistant to Musical Director, Lee Stametz; Stage Managers, D. Adams, Christopher C. Ewing, Paul Jefferson, Rod A. Lansberry; Props, Jaylene Graham; Costume Director, Janet S. Morris; Wardrobe, Charlene M. White; Sound, John E. Pryor, Thomas James Falgien, Donald P. Johnson, Steve Stevens; Administrative Director, Karen Knudsen; Marketing, Jay Drury.

ACTING COMPANY: Stephen Lee Anderson, Jim Baker, Wayne Ballantyne, Richard Barton, Tamra Benham, John Berrier, Joline K. Black, Kathy Brady Garvin, Richard Bugg, Riette Burdick, Betty K. Bynum, Seraiah Carol, Rocky Carroll, Karen Casteel, David Cleveland, Dina Corsetti, Joe Costanza, James Coyle, Melinda Deane, Craig Diffenderfer, Robert Eustace, Gwyllum Evans, Victor Garron, Frank Georgianna, Ruthanna Graves, Ann Guilbert, Jossie DeGuzman, Roland Hayes, Frantz G. Hall, Barta Heiner, Leslie Hendrix, Chad Henry, Jamie Horton, Leticia Jaramillo, Carol Mayo Jenkins, Brian K. Jennings, Byron Jennings, Kim D. Jensen, Lyle Kanouse, David E. Kazanjian, James Kiberd, Danis Kovanda, David Kudler, Pamela Kwong, Sandra Ellis Lafferty, James J. Lawless, Jim Litten, Peter Lohnes, Eric Lorentz, Trary Maddalone, Sharon Mann, Michael X. Martin, Marin Mazzie, Jeff McCarthy, Michael McClure, Hector Jaime Mercado, Victor A. Morris, Johanna Morrison, James Newcomb, Matthew Nickerson, Caitlin O'Connell, Stack Pierce, Timothy McCuen Piggee, Gregory Poth, Guy Raymond, Mick Regan, Jose Rico, Jamey Roberts, Dean Michael Schafer, Barry Sherman, Bharbara Sinclaire, Archie Smith, Leslie C. Smith, Edward Stevlingson, Albert Valdez, Carmen Vazquez, Laura P. Vega, Barry Wallace, Danny Wheetman, Ronnie J. Whittaker, Vernon Willet, Michael Winters, Taylor Young.

PRODUCTIONS: *World Premiere* of *Koozy's Piece* by Frank X. Hogan; *World Premiere* of *Veterans Day* by Donald Freed; *Guys and Dolls* with Music & Lyrics by Frank Loesser, Book by Joe Swerling & Abe Burrows; *Holiday Memories: A Child's Christmas in Wales* based on a story by Dylan Thomas, Adapted by Jeremy Brooks & Adrian Mitchell/*A Christmas Memory* by Truman Capote; *The Price* by Arthur Miller; *Long Day's Journey Into Night* by Eugene O'Neill; *World Premiere* of *Trophy Hunters* by Kendrew Lascelles; *THE TWO GENTLEMEN OF VERONA* by William Shakespeare; *Table Manners* by Alan Ayckbourn; *The Colored Museum* by George Wolfe; *A Lie of the Mind* by Sam Shpard; *Man of La Mancha* by Dale Wasserman, Music, Mitch Leigh, Lyrics, Joe Darion.

Tad Trainor, T. Charles Erickson Photos

**Top Left: James J. Lawless, Jamie Horton, Johanna
Morrison, Taylor Young in "Table Manners"
Below Right: Betty K. Bynum, Timothy McCuen Piggee
in "The Colored Museum" Left: Guy Raymond
in "The Price"**

**Stack Pierce, Gywllum Evans (seated)
in "Trophy Hunters"**

145

DELAWARE THEATRE COMPANY

Wilmington, Delaware
Ninth Season

Artistic Director, Cleveland Morris; Managing Director, Dennis Luzak; Business Manager, Robert R. Ramirez; Development, Ann G. Schenck; Marketing, Mary L. Haynes; Administrative Assistant, Sara M. Smarr; Assistant to Artistic Director, Danny Peak; Artistic Associate, Melody Owens; Press Celeste Carter; Production Stage Manager, Patricia Christian; Sets, Eric Schaeffer, Lewis Folden, James F. Pyne, Jr.; Costumes, Marla Jurgalanis; Lighting, Bruce K. Morriss; Assistant Stage Manager, Amy Cuomo; Props, Peter J. Knecht; Sound, George Stewart; Costume Assistant, Melody Holton; Lighting Assistant, Lynn Stouffer

PRODUCTIONS & CASTS

BENITO CERENO by Robert Lowell; Director, Cleveland Morris. CAST: Frank Licato (Capt. Amasa Delano), John Elijah Bauman (John Perkins), Barry Mulholland (Don Benito Cereno), William Lucas (Babu), Daryl Roach (Atufal), Keenan Zeno (Francesco), Keith Olivier, Thomas Spence, Jonathan Turner, Andrew Woodruff (American Sailors), Bob Balick, Ben Lipitz, Edwin W. Walters (Spanish Sailors), Dorcia Battin, Michelle Antoninette Brown, William Crosby, Marvin L. Duell, Ruth C. Gooden, Carole Hardin, Bruce R. Harris, Charles Johnson, Susan Laws, Raymond Medley, Cyndy B. Monteiro, Hassan Shabazz, Jerome S. Simpson, Maurice R. Sims, Gregory Steven Small, Charo Taylor (African Slaves)
THE FOREIGNER by Larry Shue; Director, Dorothy Danner. CAST: Robertson Carricart ("Froggy" LeSueur), Roderick McLachlan (Charlie Baker), Susan Willis (Betty Meeks), Stephen McNaughton (Rev. David Marshall Lee), Leslie Hicks (Catherine Simms), Barry Mulholland (Owen Musser), Adam Redfield (Ellard Simms), Bob Balick, Charles Conway, Julie Gross, Sara Smarr, Andrew Woodruff
THREE GUYS NAKED FROM THE WAIST DOWN by Jerry Colker & Michael Rupert; Director/Choreographer, Derek Wolshonak; Musical Director, Judy Brown; Musicians, James Weber, Arthur Marks, Harvey Price. CAST: Gary Lynch (Ted Klausterman), Michael McGrath (Kenny Brewster), David Dollase (Phil Kunin)
CASH FLOW by D. B. Gilles; Director, William Woodman. CAST: Michael M. Ryan (Casey McDermott), Jay E. Raphael (Elliot Gallagher), Sarah Burke (Carolyn McNeil), F. Gregory Tigani (Wyatt Buchman)
BIOGRAPHY by S. N. Behrman; Director, Cleveland Morris. CAST: Silas Cooper (Richard Kurt), Terry Reamer (Minnie), Nick Olcott (Melchior Feydak), Mary Gordon Murray (Marion Froude), Steven F. Hall (Leander Nolan), Gavin Troster (Warwick Wilson), Wil Stutts (Orrin Kinnicott), Nancy Daly (Slade Kinnicott)

Richard C. Carter Photos

Roderick McLachlan, Adam Redfield
in "The Foreigner" Top: Daryl Roach,
Barry Mulholland in "Benito Cereno"

DETROIT REPERTORY THEATRE

Detroit, Michigan
Thirtieth Season

Artistic Director, Bruce E. Millan; Advertising/Marketing Director, Reuben Yabuku; Development, Dino A. Valdez; Outreach, Dee Andrus; Literary manager, Barbara Busby; Costumer, B. J. Essen; Music Director, Kelly Smith; Sets, Bruce Millan, Sharon Yesh; Scenic Artist, John Knox; Stage Managers, William Boswell, John W. Puchalski; Lighting, Kenneth R. Hewitt, Jr., Laura S. Higle; Sound, Reuben Yabuku, Karl Yabuku; Props, Dee Andrus; Graphics, Barbar Weinberg-Barefield

PRODUCTIONS & CASTS

GLENGARRY GLEN ROSS by David Mamet; Director, Barbara Busby. CAST: Frank Washington, William Boswell, John Hardy, Mack Palmer, Gary Stewart-Jones, Reginald McCloud, Booker Hinton
THE COLORED MUSEUM by George C. Wolfe; Director, Reuben Yabuku. CAST: Miche Braden, Catrina Ganey, Michael Joseph, Sid Skipper, Venti Valdez
MORNING'S AT SEVEN by Paul Osborn; Director, Bruce E. Millan. CAST: Ruth Allen, Fran Washington, Mahlon Sharp, Dee Andrus, Darius Dudley, William Boswell, Alma Parks, Jesse Newton, Barbara Busby
INVICTUS by Laurie H. Hutzler; Director, Dee Andrus. CAST: Fran Washington, Sandi Litt, Thomas Galasso, Richard Klautsch, John Puchalski, Jackie Scott, Charles Jackson, Terry Hunt, Darryl Dalton, Tyrone Franklin

Bruce E. Millan Photos

Gary Stewart-Jones, John W. Hardy, Booker T.
Hinton in "Glengarry Glen Ross"

FORD'S THEATRE

Washington, D.C.
Twentieth Season

Executive Producer, Frankie Hewitt; Artistic Director, David H. Bell; General Manager, Nancy Nagel Gibbs; Company Manager, Patricia Humphrey; Press, Erin Dunn

PRODUCTIONS & CASTS

A WOMAN OF INDEPENDENT MEANS by Elizabeth Forsythe Hailey; Director, Norman Cohen; Scenic Consultant, Roy Christopher; Costumes, Garland Riddle; Lighting, Pam Rank; Music, Henry Mancini; Sound, Jon Gottleib; Stage Manager, Carleton Scott Alsop; General Manager, Cheryl L. Fluehr; Production Manager, Joe R. Watson; Presented in Association with Charles H. Dugga. CAST: Barbara Rush
GREATER TUNA by Jaston Williams, Joe Sears, Ed Howard; Director, Ed Howard; Set, Kevin Rupnik; Costumes, Linda Fisher; Lighting, Judy Rasmuson; Stage Manager, Kathy E. Richardson; Production Manager, Joe Watson; General Manager, Cheryl L. Fluehr; Presented in Association with Charles H. Duggan. CAST: Joe Sears, Jaston Williams
AMERICAN INDIAN DANCE THEATRE Directed and Staged by Hanay Geiogamah & Raoul Trujillo; Lighting, Jeffrey McRoberts; Stage Manager, Douglas Drew; Presented in Association with Barbara Schwei, Allen M. Shore, James Bourne. CAST: Candice Anderson, Joy Anderson, Bill Baker, Sidrick Baker, Saunders BearsTail, Jr., Lisa Ewack, Fabian Fontenelle, Troy Fontenelle, Philip Kaiyou, Chester Mahooty, Dorothy Mahooty, Arlie Neskahi, Adam Nordwal, Marty Pinnecoose, Edwin Preston, Charles Tailfeathers, Danell Tailfeathers, Morgan Tosee, Andy Vasquez, Tom Mauchahty Ware, Norwyn Wesley, Stacey Wesley, Jonathan WindyBoy, Lloyd Yellowbird
A CHRISTMAS CAROL by Charles Dickens; Adaptation/Director, David H. Bell; Musical Supervision/Arrangements, Rob Bowman; Sets, Daniel Proett; Costumes, D. Polly Kendrick; Lighting, David Kissell; Stage Manager, Roy Meachum; Assistant Stage Manager, Jeffery A. Alspaugh; Casting, Jilian Childers Hewitt. CAST: Jim Beard (Mr. Fezziwig/Christmas Present), Steven Crossley (Scrooge), Gillian Doyle (Belle/Bess), Meg Durkin (Caroler/Belinda Cratchit), Kevin Ferguson (Tom Watkins/Dick Wilkins/Undertaker), Catherine Flye (Mrs. Cratchit/Party Guest), Gail Pearce Frye, Steve Grad (Marley's Ghost/Schoolmaster/Young Marley/Christmas Yet To Come), Frank Hankey (Bob Cratchit), Helen Hedman (Missy Watkin/Goose Vendor/Martha Cratchit), David Jasper (Fred/Schoolmate), John J. Kaczynski (Carolor/Schoolmate/Topper), Mikel Sarah Lambert (Christmas Past/Peg), Mike Magee (Peter Cratchit/Schoolmate), Paul Anthony Mullin (Town Crier/Young Scrooge/Businessman), Beth Williams (Carolor/Mrs. Dilber/Mrs. Fezziwig), Aaron David Zielski (Tiny Tim)
ELMER GANTRY by John Bishop; Based on the novel by Sinclair Lewis; Music, Mel Marvin; Lyrics, Robert Satuloff, John Bishop; *World Premiere;* Director, David H. Bell; Sets, Marjorie Bradley Kellogg; Costumes, David Murin; Lighting, Pat Collins; Musical Director, Rob Bowman; Orchestrator, Michael Gibson; Casting, Jilian Childers Hewitt; Production Stage Manager, Roy Meachum; Assistant Stage Manager, Eric S. Osbun. CAST: Casey Briggs (Elmer Gantry), Sharon Scruggs (Sharon Falconer), John Almberg (Merle Blanchard), Joe Barrett (Bob/Tom), Ray DeMattis (Art), Queen Esther Marrow (Mary Washington), John Seeman (Shallard/Shartel), Mary Denise Bentley (Epatha Washington), Brigid Brady (Paula), Tony Gilbert (Dave/Wetzel), Tina Johnson (Maude), John-Charles Kelly (Young Man), Laura Kenyon (Shirley/Elderly Woman), Peter Lombard (Stationmaster/Norbert/Rigney/Father), Jacquelyn Piro (Daughter), J. K. Simmons (Ed/Higby), Barry J. Tarallo (Paul/Martin), John Leslie Wolfe (Harry/Faucher/Billy)

Joan Marcus Photos

Barbara Rush in "A Woman of Independent Means"

Sharon Scruggs, Casey Biggs in "Elmer Gantry"

GEORGE STREET PLAYHOUSE

New Brunswick, New Jersey

Producing Director, Gregory S. Hurst; Acting Artistic Director, Maureen Heffernan; General Manager, Geoffrey Merrill Cohen; Production Managers, Carol Andrew, Cynthia Hart; Stage Manager, Crystal K. Craft; Technical Director, John Griffith; Costumer, Beth A. Ribblett; Communications, Margaret V. Sherrer; Press, Heidi W. Hopkins

PRODUCTIONS & CASTS

PRINCESS GRACE AND THE FAZZARIS by Marc Alan Zagoren; Director, Mary G. Guaraldi; Sets, Daniel Proett; Costumes, Jeffrey Ullman, Patricia Sanftner; Lighting, Kirk Bookman; Sound, James Capenos; Stage Manager, Patricia Flynn. CAST: Diane Martella, Colleen Quinn, Vara Lockwood, Lisa Hertz, George Loros, Rose Anna Mineo, Gordon MacDonald
NUNSENSE by Dan Goggin; Director, Maureen Heffernan; Musical Director, Bruce W. Coyle; Choreographer, Schelle Archbold; Sets, Daniel Gray; Costumes, Michael J. Cesario; Lighting, Daniel Stratman; Stage Manager, Crystal K. Craft. CAST: Marsha Bagwell, Betty Ann Grove, Tonia Rowe, Tia Spero, Tricia Witham
LEAR by William Shakespeare; Director, Lee Breuer; Music, Pauline Oilveros; Sound, Bob Bielecki, L. B. Dallas; Scenic Pieces, Alison Yerxa; Costumes, Ghretta Hynd; Lighting, Julie Archer; Stage Managers, Anthony Gerber; Dramaturg, Alisa Solomon. CAST: Joanna Adler, David Brisbin, Karen Evans-Kandel, Honora Fergusson, Clove Galilee, Matthew Hansell, Ruth Maleczech, Ellen McElduff, Greg Mehrten, Isbell Monk, Maya O'Reilly, Lola Pashalinski, Lute Ramblin, Bill Raymond, Kimberly Scott, Ran Vawter
MAX AND MAXIE by James McLure; Director, D. Lynn Meyers; Sets/Costumes, Eduardo Sicangco; Lighting, Kirk Bookman, David Neville; Stage Manager, Crystal K. Craft; Co-produced with Cincinnati Playhouse. CAST: Robin Haynes, John Newton, Sandy Rovetta
TRACES by Vincent Caristi, Richard Chaves, John DiFusco, Eric Emerson, Rick Gallavan, Merlin Marston, & Harry Stephens with Sheldon Lettich; Director, John DiFusco; Sets, John Falabella; Costumes, David Navarro Velasquez; Lighting, Terry Wuthrich; Sound, John DiFusco; Stage Manager; Co-produced with the Whole Theatre Company. CAST: David Adamson, Haskell V. Anderson III, Anthony Chisholm, John DiFusco, Nathan Holland, Sean Michael Rice, Ray Robertson, Jim Tracy
I'M NOT RAPPAPORT by Herb Gardner; Director, Maureen Heffernan; Set, Atkin Pace; Costumes, Patricia Adshead; Lighting, Donald Holder; Sound, Dirk Duyk; Stage Manager, Patricia Flynn; Co-produced with Pennsylvania Stage Company. CAST: Suzanne Grodner, David S. Howard, Mark L. Mikesell, Christopher Mixon, Will Osborne, Corliss Preston, Samuel W. Wright

Suzanne Karp Krebs Photos

David S. Howard, Samuel E. Wright in "I'm Not Rappaport"

Jayne Houdyshell, Donna Snow in "Stepping Out"
**Above: Michael Mauldin, Dan Diggles in
"The Mystery of Irma Vep"**

GeVa THEATRE

Rochester, New York

Producing Director, Howard J. Millman; Managing Director, Thomas Pechar; Assistant to the Directors, Christine Orr Pohlig; Advertising, Diane E. Stoffel; Marketing, Kathryn MacIntyre; Development, Kenneth F. Brant, Judith Anne Yoho; Literary Director, Ann Patrice Carrigan; Press/Marketing, Elizabeth Bilgore, Joy L. Hey; Production Manager, James K. Finsley; Costumer, Dana Harnish Tinsley; Wardrobe, Therese McIntyre; Sound, Nic Minetor, Stephen Farmer; Props, Ruth Watson; Scenic Artist, Ruth Barber; Stage Managers, Catherine Norberg, James K. Tinsley; Casting, Stuart Howard

PRODUCTIONS & CASTS

CHARLEY'S AUNT by Brandon Thomas; Director, Walt Jones; Set, Chris Barreca; Costumes, Pamela Peterson; Lighting, Danianne Mizzy. CAST: Simon Brooking (Jack Chesney), Dillon Evans (Brassett), Gregory Jbara (Charley Wykeham), Adam Redfield (Lord Fancourt Babberly), Holly Felton (Kitty Verdum), Devora Millman (Amy Spettigue), Mart Hulswit (Col. Sir Francis Chesney) Maury Cooper (Stephen Spettigue), Maeve McGuire (Donna Lucia), Margurite Kelly (Ela Delahay)

PRIVATE LIVES by Noel Coward; Director, Walt Jones; Set, Scott Bradley; Costums, Pamela Peterson; Lighting, Danianne Mizzy. CAST: Donna Kane (Sibyl Chase), Geoff Pierson (Elyot Chase), Thomas Schall (Victor Prynne), Randall Edwards (Amanda Prunne), Melissa Weil (Louie)

THE ROSE TATTOO by Tennessee Williams; Music, David Diamond; Director, Howard Millman; Music, David Diamond; Set, Victor Becker; Costumes, Pamela Scofield; Lighting, Phil Monat; Sound, Jan Nebozenko. CAST: Micah Smyth (Salvatore), Alyssa Fico (Vivi), Dominick Morano (Bruno), Sarah Melici (Assunta), Roxanne Biggs (Rosa DelleRose), Isa Thomas (Serafina DelleRose), Jill Wilson (Estelle Hohengarten), Gay Clarke (Strega), Melissa Weil (Giuseppina), Lois Grant (Peppina), Deanna Birrittella (Violetta), Patricia Mangefrida (Mariella), Gerald Richards (Fr. DeLeo), Frank Dwyer (Doctor), Mary Stark (Miss Yorke), Barbara Redmond (Flora), Monique Morgan (Bessie), Peter Bensen (Jack Hunter), Patrick Egan (Salesman), Rudolph Willrich (Alvaro)

A CHRISTMAS CAROL by Charles Dickens; Adaptation/Director, Eberle Thomas; Music, John Franceschina; Set, Bob Barnett; Costumes, Pamela Schofield; Lighting, Nic Minetor; Choreography, Jim Hoskins; Singing Coach, Lou Gritter. CAST: Liza Agban, Cynthia Anderson, John Keene Bolton, Thomas Carson, Vicki Casarett, Robert Colston, Tim Douglas, Frank Dwyer, Patrick Egan, Brad Fullagar, Elaine Good, Mark Hirschfield, Hugh Hodgin, Leonard Kelly-Young, Jennifer McCaffrey, Monique Morgan, Natale Petti, Barbara Redmond, Gerald Richards (Scrooge), Mary Stark, Weesley Stevens, Frankie Michael Storace, Melissa Weil, Christian Zwahlen

STEPPING OUT by Richard Harris; Director, Carl Schurr; Choreography, Pamela Sousa; Set, Michael Miller; Costumes, Maria Marrero; Lighting, Rachel Budin; Music Arranger, Peter Howard; Casting, David Tochterman. CAST: Fran Barnes (Mrs. Fraser), Jan Buttram (Mavis), Susan Duvall (Sylvia), Venida Evans (Rose), Jayne Houdyshell (Maxine), Susanne Marley (Vera), Leslie Nipkow (Lynne), Mary Ed Porter (Dorothy), Donna Snow (Andy), David Young (Geoffrey)

ALFRED STIEGLITZ LOVES O'KEEFE by Lanie Robertson; Director, Allen R. Belknap; Music, Norman L. Berman; Set, William Barclay; Costumes, Mimi Maxmen; Lighting, Richard Winkler. CAST: Judith Ann Roberts (Georgia O'Keeffe), Jeremiah Sullivan (Alfred Stieglitz)

THE MYSTERY OF IRMA VEP by Charles Ludlam; Director, Everet Quinton; Music, Peter Golub; Set, Bob Barnett; Costumes, Everett Quinton; Lighting, Nic Minetor. CAST: Dan Diggles (Jane Twisden/Lord Edgar Hillcrest/Intruder), Michael Mauldin (Nicodemus Underwood/Lady Enid Hillcrest Alcazar)

EQUUS by Peter Shaffer; Director, Allen R. Belknap; Set, David Potts; Costumes, Mimi Maxmen; Lighting, Richard Winkler; Music, Gus Kaikkonen; Dialect Coach, Deborah Hecht. CAST: Charles Antalosky (Martin Dysart), Claire Beckman, Mary Boucher (Hester Salomon), Hewitt Brooks (Frank Strange), Libby George (Dora Strang), Cynthia Hayden (Nurse), Gus Kaikkonen (Horseman/Nugget), Anderson Matthews (Harry Dalton/Horse), Douglas DuBrin, Thomas Hamilton, Alfred Schmitz, Craig Wroe (Horses)

Nic Minetor, Fred Shippey Photos

**Top Left: Marguerite Kelly, Maeve McGuire
in "Charley's Aunt" Below: Geoff Pierson,
Randall Edwards in "Private Lives"**
(Michael Lutzky Photo)

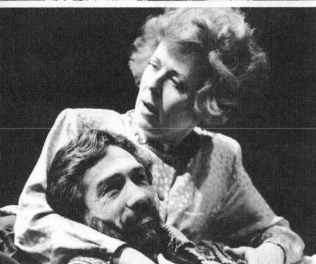

Frank Galati, William J. Norris
in "A Flea in Her Ear"

THE GOODMAN THEATRE

Chicago, Illinois

Producing Director, Roche Schulfer; Artistic Director, Robert Falls; General Manager, Katherine Murphy; Associate Director, Frank Galati; Resident Director, Michael Maggio; Development, Alida Caster, Molly Landgraf; Press, Cindy Bandle; Marketing, Joanna Lohmiller; Operations, Kendall Marlow; Production Manager, Philip Eickhoff; Production Stage Managers, Joseph Drummond, Malcolm Ewen; Lighting, Robert Shristen; Costume Manager, Nancy Missimi; Casting, Jason La Padura, Stanley Soble

PRODUCTIONS & CASTS

RED NOSES by Peter Barnes. CAST: William Brown (Viennet/Herald), Ray Toler (Moncriff/Jacques Boutros), Victoria Zielinski (Evaline/Sabine), Richard Fire (Bonville/Pellico/Vasques), Pat Bowie (Mme. de Bonville/Mother Metz), Michael Tezla (Dr. Antrechau/Lefranc), Ivar Brogger (Father Flote), John Mohrlien (Grez), Sean Baldwin, James Marsters (Flagellants), John Cothran, Jr. (Scarron), Paul Barrosse (Druce), Carl DeSanti (Sonnerie), Bradley Mott (Monselet/Bigod), Peter Silbert (Toulon), Cameron Pfiffner (Attendant), Skipp Sudduth (Mistral/Patris), Richard Riehle (Brodin), B. J. Jones (Rochfort), Susan Osborne-Mott (Marguerite), Tanya White (Camille/Leper), Tami Workentin (Marie/Leper), Tom Towles (LeGrue), Steve Totland (Bembo), Jeffrey Hutchinson (Frapper), Bruce Turk (Alain Boutros), Lawrence McCauley (Pope Clement VI)

A CHRISTMAS CAROL adapted by Larry Sloan, based on Charles Dicken's novel; Music/Musical Director, Larry Schanker; Vocal Consultant, Gillian Lane-Plescia. CAST: William J. Norris (Scrooge), Robert Scogin (Bob Crachit), William Brown (Fred), Bill Bush, Stephen Finch (Businessmen) James Otis (Marley's Ghost/Party Guest/Undertaker), Linda Kimbrough (Christmas Past/Party Guest), John Mohrlein (Schoolmaster/Joe), John Joseph Duda (Boy Scrooge), Nikko Garcia (Fan/Belinda), Terence Gallacher (Young Scrooge/Christmas Yet to Come), Darius De Haas (Dick Wilkins), Dennis Kennedy (Fezziwig/Businessman), Susan Osborne-Mott (Mrs. Fezziwig/Charwoman), Sally Murphy (Belle), David Malcolm Thompson (Fiddler/Party Guest), Ernest Perry, Jr. (Christmas Past), Pat Bowie (Mrs. Cratchit), Crystal R. Walker (Martha), Tony Russell, Jr. (Peter), Erin Creighton (Emily), Kevin Michael Duda (Tim), Anthony Wong (Ignorance/Urchin)

PASSION PLAY by Peter Nichols. CAST: Seana McKenna (Kate), David Darlow (James), Holland Taylor (Eleanor), Ann Stevenson Whitney (Agnes), Stephen Markle (Jim), Janice St. John (Nell), Martin Arons, Henri Boyd, Louise Freistadt, Margaret Ingraham, Jacqueline Kim, Melissa McFarlane, James Noah, Antonio Pulido, Mary Seibel, Brian Terrell, JoAnn Kulesza

LANDSCAPE OF THE BODY by John Guare. CAST: Barbara E. Robertson (Betty), Gary Cole (Capt. Marvin Holahan), Peggy Roeder (Rosalie), Ray Bradford (Raulito), Anthony Rapp (Bert), Jason Moser (Donny), Amy Elizabeth Geis (Joanne), Delfina Robles (Margie), Tom Towles (Masked Man/Dope King/Bank Teller), Chelcie Ross (Durwood Peach), Larry Schanker (Pianist)

A FLEA IN HER EAR by Georges Feydeau. CAST: Ray Chapman (Claude Deboshe), Linda Balgord (Nanette), Timothy Monsion (Perrier), William J. Norris (Dr. Panache), Amy Morton (Lucille), Shannon Cochran (Yvonne), Frank Galati (Victor), Larry Wyatt (Maurice), Ramiro Carillo (Carlos), Sarah Bradley (Babette), Tom Towles (Henri), Laurel Cronin (Olympia), Dennis Kennedy (Benedictine), John Mohrlein (Maher Ravvi), Frank Galati (Goshe), Donna Powers, Carmen Roman, Carlos John Seda, David Sinaiko, Ray Toler

PAL JOEY with Book by John O'Hara; Lyrics, Lorenz Hart; Music, Richard Rodgers. CAST: Kevin Anderson (Joey Evans), Carlin Glynn (Vera Simpson), Katherine Meloche (Linda English), Shannon Cochran (Gladys Bump), Del Close (Ludlow Lowell), Bonnie Sue Arp (Melba Snyder), John Malloy (Capt. O'Brien), Ivory Ocean (Bartender), David Studwell (Santa/Billy), Vill Bisteen (Mike), Dev Kennedy (Doorman), Paul Henry Thompson (Ernest), Karin Berutti, Tina Deleone, Becky Downing, Adam Goldman, Brent Hendon, Gail Lohla, Lori Longstreth, Teri Schultz, Judith T. Smith, John Sterchi, Jack Sullivan, Treva Tegtmeier, Rhae Ann Theriault, Sherry Zunker, Lee Ann Marie

Charles Osgood Photos

Top Left: Barbara E. Robertson, Anthony Rapp
in "Landscape of the Body" Below: David Darlow,
Holland Taylor in "Passion Play"

THE GOODSPEED OPERA HOUSE

East Haddam, Connecticut
Twenty-fifth Season

Executive Director, Michael P. Price; Associate Artistic Director, Dan Siretta; Musical Director, Lynn Crigler; Associate Producer, Sue Frost; Casting Director/New York Representative, Warren Pincus; Press, Kay McGrath, Max Eisen; Development, Laurie Scott-Martin; Marketing, Bill Berloni; Company Manager, Karen Pizzuto; Production Coordinator, Holly Nilsen; Wardrobe, John Riccucci; Props, Betsy Egan

PRODUCTIONS & CASTS

ONE TOUCH OF VENUS with Music by Kurt Weill; Book, S. J. Perelman & Ogden Nash; Lyrics, Ogden Nash; Director, Ben Levit; Choreography, Rodney Griffin; Sets, James Leonard Joy; Costumes, Marjorie Mc Cown; Lighting, Craig Miller; Assistant Musical Director, Mark Mitchell; Technical Director, Daniel Renn; Music Research Consultant, Alfred Simon; Stage Manager, Michael Brunner; Assistant Stage Manager, Dave Harris; Arrangements/Orchestrations, Kurt Weill. CAST: Richard Sabellico (Whitelaw Savory), Semina De Laurentis (Molly Grant), Dale O'Brien (Taxi Black), Nick Corley (Stanley), Michael Piontek (Rodney Hatch), Lynnette Perry (Venus), Genette Lane (Mrs. Moats/Rose), Diana Brownstone (Girl), Kyle Whyte (Free French Sailor), Gerry McIntyre (Bus Starter), Paul Laureano (Sam), Irma Rogers (Mrs. Kramer), Karen Cantor (Gloria Kramer), Gerry McIntyre (Lieutenant), Helen Anne Barcay, Peggy Bayer, Mamie Duncan-Gibbs, Christine Hunter, Paul Laureano, Christopher Nilsson, Daniel Pelzig, Jeff Siebert

LADY, BE GOOD! with Music by George Gershwin; Lyrics, Ira Gershwin; Book, Guy Bolton, Fred Thompson; Director, Thomas Gruenewald; Choreography/Staging, Dan Siretta; Sets, Eduardo Sicangco; Costumes, John Carver Sullivan; Lighting, Curt Ostermann; Technical Director, Daniel Renn; Special Consultant, Alfred Simon; Dramaturg, Tommy Krasker; Stage Manager, Michael Brunner; Dance Arrangements/Russell Warner; Additional Orchestrations, Lynn Crigler, Russell Warner; Assistant Stage Manager, Dave Harris; Assistant Musical Director, Mark Mitchell. CAST: Jim Walton (Dick Trevor), Nikki Sahagen (Susie Trevor), Bobby Clark (Moving Man), Steve Watkins (Jack RobinsoN), Bryan Harris (Policeman), Richard Stillman (Jeff White), Bobby Clark (Delivery Boy), Iris Revson (Daisy Parke), Christopher Seppe (Bertie Bassett), Marlena Lustik (Josephine Vanderwater), Russell Leib (Watty Watkins), Alain Freulon (Waiter), Karen Culliver (Shirley Vernon), Bryan Harris (Rufus Parke/Waiter), Ron Crofoot, Janice Cronkhite, Richard Dodd, Patricia Lockery, David Monzione, Dana Pinchera, Ann-Marie Rogers, Tara Tyrrell

THE LITTLE RASCALS with Music & Lyrics by Joe Raposo; Book, Michael Loman; Director, Robert Nigro; Choreography, Marcia Milgrom Dodge; Sets, James Leonard Joy; Costumes/Producer, Franne Lee; Lighting, Craig Miller; Technical Director, Daniel Renn; Stage Manager, Michael Brunner; Animals, William Berloni; Dance Music, G. Harrell; Orchestrations, Lynn Crigler, Bob Goldstone, G. Harrell, Joe Raposo; Production Consultant, Diana King; Assistant Stage Manager, Dave Harris; Assistant Musical Director, Mark Mitchell. CAST: Kevin Joseph (Alfalfa), Jason Minor (Spanky), Dule Hill (Stymie), Richard Schuh (Scottie), Eric Michael Hailey (Buckwheat), Jake (Pete), Ronn Carroll (Oliver Wendell Ho), Betsy Joslyn (Lily Crabtree), Devon Michaels (Waldo Rogers), Joe Duquette (Joe Hood), Jenna von Oy (Darla Hood), Erick Devine (Walter Rogers), Ken Jennings (Tom Turpin), John Deyle (Harry Remmington), Eugene J. Anthony (Ed Wilson), Jill Powell (Miss Hansetter), Rollie Mayo (Mayor Rhufus J. Crabtree), Michael Mulheren ("Arms" Malone), Lee Mathis ("Scalpel Morrison), Edward Prostak (P. P. White), Anita Flanagan (Mrs. Henrietta Tithill III), Jack Rowles, Jr. (Kenny Clark), James Van Treuren (Man/Rev. J. Walter Peckinworth), Anita Flanagan, Michael Mulheren, Jill Powell, Jane Wasser

Nikki Sahagen, Jim Walton in "Lady, Be Good!"
Top: Ronn Carroll, Jason Minor (right)

GOODSPEED AT THE NORMA TERRIS THEATRE/CHESTER

KALEIDOSCOPE with Book & Lyrics by Mary Bracken Phillips; Music, Jan Mullaney, Mary Bracken Phillips; Director, Munson Hicks; Musical Staging, Terry Riser; Musical Direction/Arrangements, Jeff Waxman; Producer, Sue Frost; Set, Timothy Jozwick; Costumes, Mardi Philips; Lighting, Judy Rasmuson; Technical Director, Daniel Renn; Stage Manager, Ruth Feldman. CAST: Mary Bracken Philips (Paula), P. J. Benjamin (Jonathan), Louise Flaningam (Susan), Gibby Brand (Harding), Patricia Kies, Robert Alton (Standbys)

ABYSSINIA with Music by Ted Kociolek; Lyrics, James Racheff; Book, James Racheff, Ted Kociolek; Based on the novel *Marked By Fire* by Joyce Carol Thomas; Director, Tazewell Thompson; Musical Director/Arrangements, Daryl Waters; Producer, Dan Siretta; Set, James Leonard Joy; Costumes, Amanda J. Klein; Lighting, Allen Lee Hughes; Technical Director, Daniel Renn; Stage Manager, Ruth Feldman. CAST: Jennifer Leigh Warren (Abyssinia Jackson), Tina Fabrique (Mother Vera), Cheryl Freeman (Patience Jackson), LaDonna Mabry (Selma), Darlene Bel Grayson (Corine), Kimberly Harris (Mavis), B. J. Jefferson (Lily Noreen/Mother Samuels), Lehman Beneby (Minister), Jaison Walker (Marcus), Bill Myers (Leon), Allen Gilmore (Jesse), Paul Osborne (Brother Samuels), Karen Jackson (Trembling Sally), Daryl Waters, Jim Carroll, Sal Ranniello

BUTTERFLY with Book by Craig Safan, Mark Mueller; Music, Craig Safan; Lyrics, Mark Mueller; Director, Jack Hofsiss; Choreography, Patrice Soriero; Musical Director, Jeanine Levenson; Producer, Sue Frost; Set, Loy Arcenas; Costumes, Jess Goldstein; Lighting, Allen Lee Hughes; Sound, Tony Meola; Technical Director, Daniel Renn; Musical Supervision/Orchestrations, Keith Levenson; Stage Manager, Ruth Feldman. CAST: Jack Wagner (Pink), Peter Slutsker (Sharp), Elizabeth Reiko Kubota (Butterfly), Brie Howard (Suzy), Erika Honda (Bar Singer), Francis Ruivivar (Bouncer), Joseph Fong, Kevin John Gee, Michael Gee, Cheri Nakamura, Ryoko Sawaishi, Jeanine Levenson, Keith Levenson, Joe Baker, Sal Ranniello

Diane Sobolewski Photos

P. J. Benjamin, Mary B.
Phillips in "Kaleidoscope"

Elizabeth Reiko Kubota, Jack
Wagner in "Butterfly"

THE GUTHRIE THEATER

Minneapolis, Minnesota
Twenty-fifth Season

Artistic Director, Garland Wright; Executive Director, Edward A. Martenson; Directors, JoAnne Akalitis, Liviu Ciulei, Michael Maggio, Richard Ooms, Les Waters, Garland Wright; Sets, Joel Fontaine, John Arnone, Liviu Ciulei, Annie Smart, Jack Barkla, George Tyspin; Costumes, Jack Edwards, Martin Pakledinaz, Patricia Zipprodt, Adelle Lutz, Ann Hould-Ward; Lighting, Peter Maradudin, Frances Aronson, Marcus Dilliard, James F. Ingalls, Jennifer Tipton; Composers, Terry Allen, John McKinney, Hiram Titus, Janika Vandervelde; Fight Director, David Leong; Film, Babette Mangolte; Movement, Maria Cheng, Loyce Houlton, Linda Shapiro; Playwrights & Translators; Albert Bermel, Kenneth Cavander, Barbara Field, Henry J. Scmidt, Timberlake Wertenbaker, Richard Wilbur; Vocal Coach, Elizabeth Smith; Resident Director, Charles Newell; Dramaturg/Literary Manager, Mark Bly; Stage Managers, Janet P. Callahan, Diane DiVita, Russell Johnson, Jill Rendall; Press, Dennis Behl

ACTING COMPANY: Jo Harvey Allen, Eunice Anderson, Amy Aquino, Michelle Barber, Trazana Beverley, Olivia Birkelund, Bruce Bohne, Jesse Borrego, Julie Boyd, David Anthony Brinkley, Jim Cada, Terrence Caza, Don Cheadle, Lynn Cohen, Miriam Colon, Jim Craven, Nesba Crenshaw, Michael Cumpsty, Russell Curry, Stephen D'Ambrose, Pamela Danser, Bob Davis, Daniel Davis, Curzon Dobell, Herb Downer, Paul Drake, Morgan Duncan, Rebecca Ellens, Wayne A. Evenson, Katherine Ferrand, Gina Franz, Randy Fuhrmann, Nathaniel Fuller, June Gibbons, D. Scott Glasser, Brian Grandison, Gail Grate, Michael Grodenchik, Allen Hamilton, Rosemary Hartup, Elaine Hausman, Annette Helde, Richard Hicks, Richard S. Iglewski, Thomas Ikelda, Peter Frances James, Charles Janasz, Byron Jennings, Scott Johnson, Patrick Kerr, Barbara Kingsley, Caroline Lagerfelt, Katherine Leask, John Lewin, Mimi Lieber, Jessica Litwak, John Carroll Lynch, Jeff McCarthy, Christina Moore, Mary O'Brady, Richard Ooms, Stephen Pelinski, Deirdre Peterson, Faye Price, Rajika Puri, Gary Rayppy, Richard Riehle, Lia Rivamonte, Ken Ruta, Socorro Santiago, Louis Schaefer, Kurt Schweikhardt, Buffy Sedlachek, Bernadette Sullivan, Peter Syvertsen, Jill Tanner, Michael Tezla, Peter Thoemke, Adrienne Thompson, Lauren Tom, Lorraine Toussaint, Brenda Wehle, Bradley Whitford, Claudia Wilkens, Sally Wingert, Stephen Yoakam

PRODUCTIONS: *The Misanthrope, The Piggy Bank, The Bacchae, A Christmas Carol, The House of Bernarda Alba, Richard III;*
WORLD PREMIERES: *Leon & Lena (and lenz)* and *Frankenstein—Playing with Fire* (Tour)

Joe Giannetti Photos

**Top Right: Caroline Lagerfelt, Daniel Davis
in "The Misanthrope"**

**Byron Jennings, Bradley Whitford
in "Richard III"**

**Peter Francis James, Michael Cumpsty
in "The Bacchae"**

151

HARTFORD STAGE COMPANY

Hartford, Connecticut
Twenty-fifth Season

Artistic Director, Mark Lamos; Managing Director, David Dawkanson; Resident Playwright/Literary Manager, Constance Congdon; Dramaturg, Greg Leaming; Development, Linda G. Harmon; Marketing, Jeffrey Woodward; Press, Howard Sherman; Business Manager, Karen Price; Production Manager, Candice Chirgotis; Technical Director, Jim Keller; Costumer, Martha Christian; Props, Sandy Struth; Sound, Frank Pavlich; Casting, David Tochterman; Sound, David Budries; Wigs, Paul Huntley

PRODUCTIONS & CAST
HAMLET by William Shakespeare; Director, Mark Lamos; Set/Costumes, John Conklin; Lighting, Pat Collins; Fights, Charles Conwell; Stage Managers, Alice Dewey, Buzz Cohen; Assistant Director, Ron Nakahara. CAST: Richard Thomas (Hamlet), Nick Bakay (Rosencrantz), Jonathan Baker, John Carpenter (First Gravedigger), Catherine Colder, Sheridan Crist (Guildenstern), Ken Festa, Monique Fowler (Ophelia), Robert Gerringer (Polonius), Gary Greenberg, Jeffrey Hayenga (Horatio), Jessica Hecht, Gary Jerolmon, Robert Krakovski, Geoffrey Lower (Osric), David Magee (Fortinbras), Tyrone Murphy, Pamela Payton-Wright (Gertrude), Stephen Pelinski (Laertes), Richard Poe (Claudius), Bobbi Randall, Mark Scavetta, David Squires, Daniel St. Laurent, Ted van Griethuysen (Ghost/First Player)
THE VOICE OF THE PRAIRIE by John Olive (*World Premiere* of expanded version of *"Holy Fools"*); Director, Norman Rene; Set, Alexander Okun; Costumes, Walker Hicklin; Lighting, Debra J. Kletter; Stage Manager, Katherine M. Goodrich. CAST: Michael Countryman (Poppy/David Quinn), Barry Cullison (James/Frankie's Father/Watermelon Man/Jailer), Brenda Currin (Susie/Frances), Alice Haining (Frankie), Knowl Johnson (Davey), David Schramm (Leon Schwab)
HEDDA GABLER by Henrik Ibsen; Translation, Gerry Bamman, Irene B. Berman; Director, Mark Lamos; Set, George Tsypin; Costumes, Jess Goldstein; Lighting, Pat Collins; Sound, David Budries; Stage Manager, Alice Dewey; Assistant Director, Ron Nakahara. CAST: Richard Bekins (Eilert Lovborg), Elizabeth Berridge (Thea Elvsted), Virginia Downing (Berte), William Duff-Griffin (Judge Brack), Mary Layne (Hedda Tesman), Bethel Leslie (Juliane Tesman), Scott Wentworth (Jorgen Tesman)
SERENADING LOUIE by Lanford Wilson; Director, Mary B. Robinson; Set, Marjorie Bradley Kellogg; Costumes, Jess Goldstein; Lighting, Ken Tabachnick; Stage Manager, Katherine M. Goodrich. CAST: William Carden (Alex), Lizbeth Mackay (Mary), Molly Regan (Gabrielle), Tom Stechschulte (Carl)
PRINCIPIA SCRIPTORIAE by Richard Nelson; Director, James Simpson; Set, Andrew Jackness; Costumes, Claudia Brown; Lighting, Stephen Strawbridge; Stage Manager, Alice Dewey. CAST: James Cahill (Hans Einhorn), Christofer De Oni (Man in Prison), Greg Germann (Bill Howell), Mart Hulswit (Norton Quinn), Alan Mixon (Alberto Fava), Rene Moreno (Ernesto Pico), Gregorio Rosenblum (Julio Montero)
THE SCHOOL FOR WIVES by Moliere; English verse translation, Richard Wilbur; Director, Mark Lamos; Set, John Arnone; Costumes, Martin Pakledinaz; Lighting, Peter Kaczorowski; Stage Manager, Katherine M. Goodrich. CAST: Gerry Bamman (Arnolphe), Donald Christopher (Oronte), Darryl Croxton (Chrysalde), Alice Haining (Gabrielle), Barbara Howard (Agnes), Don R. McManus (Alain), Eric Swanson (Horace), Ian Trigger (Notary), Ted van Griethuysen (Enrique)

T. Charles Erickson Photos

**Left: Barbara Howard, Gerry Bamman
in "School for Wives" Top: Richard
Thomas, Monique Fowler in "Hamlet"**

**Michael Countryman, David Schramm
in "Voice of the Prairie"**

**Mary Layne, William Duff-Griffin
in "Hedda Gabler"**

HIPPODROME STATE THEATRE

Gainesville, Florida

Producing Directors, Gregory von Hausch, Mary Hausch; TYA Producing Director, Margaret Bachus; Sets, Carlos Francisco Asse; Costumes, Marilyn Wall-Asse; Lighting, Robert P. Robins; Stage Managers, Kevin Rainsberger, Michael Johnson; Marketing, Joseph P. Buonfiglio

PRODUCTIONS & CASTS
BILOXI BLUES with Scott Tiler, Kevin Rainsberger, Shawn Black, Jon Beshara, Rena Carney, Joseph Cirnick, Stewart Clarke, Stephanie Disandis, Jimmy Jay
HAIR with Malcolm Gets, John-Michael Flate, Scott Isert, Lance Harmeling, Melissa Weinstein, Debbie Laumand, Arline Williams, Ann Leslie Wren, Irene Adjan, Mike Alicia, M. Clark Canine, Sharon Cline, Jennifer Grace, Elizabeth Homan, Joan Taylor Larrick, Andy Pratt, James Randolph II, Bruce Rise, Janet Read Rucker, Stephanie Disandis, Judith Walton, Reeves S. Watson
AS IS with Scott Winters, Reeves S. Watson, Rusty Salling, Malcolm Gets, Robert Browne, Nell Page Sexton, Kevin Rainsberger, Rena Carney
SO LONG ON LONELY STREET with Kevin Rainsberger, Lizan Mitchell, Nell Page Sexton, John Ammerman, Mariah von Hausch, Rusty Salling
RUM & COKE with Mark Sexton, Gregory von Hausch, Gregory R. Jones, Nell Page Sexton, Michel Beistle, Kevin Rainsberger, Dan Jesse, Rusty Salling, Carroll Tolman
PUMP BOYS AND DINETTES with Irene Adjan, Matt Morrison, Randy Glass, Mariah von Hausch, Eddie Gwaltney, Clay Williams

Gary Wolfson Photos

Right: Scene from "Hair"

Kristie Hannum, Cathy Bieber
in "More Fun Than Bowling"

HERITAGE ARTIST LTD.

Cohoes, New York

Producing Director, Robert W. Tolan; General Manager, Maureen Salking; Marketing/Press, Sarah S. Burke; Business Manager, Pat Buckley; Development, Martie Mutsch; Assistants to Producing Director, Andrew McGibbon, William J. Coulter; Sets, Stephen Spoonamore, James M. Youmans; Lighting, Rachel Bickel; Costumes, Mary Marsicano, Lloyd Waiwaiole; Stage Managers, Clifford V. Ammon, Jonathan D. Secor

PRODUCTIONS & CASTS
NUNSENSE with Book, Music & Lyrics by Dan Goggin; Director/Choreographer, David Holdgrive; Musical Director, Caryl Ginsburg Gershman; with Amanda Butterbaugh, Lisa Cartmell, Elaine Grollman, Consuelo Hill, Ellen Margulies, Allison McKay, Kelley Sweeney, Laura Turnbull, Mone Walton, John-Ann Washington, Judi Wilfore
BILLY BISHOP GOES TO WAR by John Gray & Eric Peterson; Director, William S. Morris; with Robin Haynes (Billy Bishop), Jason McAuliffe (Piano Player)

Skip Dickstein, Randall Perry Photos

Top Left: Elaine Grollman, Ellen Margulies
in "Nunsense" *(Randall Perry Photo)*

ILLINOIS THEATRE CENTER

Park Forest, Illinois

Artistic Director, Steve S. Billig; Musical Director, Jonathan Roark; Sets, Archway Scenic; Costumes, Pat Dekker, Henriette Swearingen; Lighting, Richard Peterson, August Ziemann; Technical Director, August Ziemann; Choreographer, Jim Corti

PRODUCTIONS & CASTS
SANTA ANITA '42 by Alan Knee; Director, Jim Coti; with Cheryl Hamada, Tony Mockus, Jr., Quincy Wong, James Sie, Tom C. Ching, Marc Rita, Diane Smith, Chris Morrow, Patrick Trettenaro, Colleen Dougherty
MORE FUN THAN BOWLING by Steven Dietz; Director, Steve S. Billig; with Jim Johnson, Cathy Bieber, Kristie Hannum, Fred Zimmerman, Treva Tegtmeier
THE ROBBER BRIDEGROOM by Alfred Uhry & Robert Waldman; Director/Choreographer, Jim Corti; with Joe Morgan, Roberta Duchak, Jillann Gabrielle, Steve S. Billig, Anthony Cesaretti, Todd Zamarripa, Treva Tegtmeier, Deanna Boyd, Ethel Billig, Leah Stanko, Scott Calcagno, Mark Brandon, Nick Anselmo, Bernard Rice, Janet Rice
HANDY DANDY by William Gibson; Director, David Perkovich; with Etel Billig, Steve S. Billig
YOURS ANNE by Enid Futterman & Michael Cohen; Director, Etel Billig; with Gail Norris, David Perkovich, Marney MacAdam, Iris Lieberman, Burke Fry, Steve S. Billig, Todd Zamarripa, Tina Krimmer
THE SCHOOL FOR SCANDAL by Richard Brinsley Sheridan; Adaptation, William A. Miles; Director, Steve S. Billig; with Claudia Lee Dalton, Richard Rowan, William A. Miles, Robert Taylor, Don McGrew, Shelley Crosby, Valerie Harris, Deborah Stadt, Patrick Bednarczyk, Etel Billig
NICKEL UNDER MY SHOE Conceived & Staged by Steve S. Billig; with Laura Collins, Karen Wheeler, Percy Littleton, Steve S. Billig, Bernard Rice, Etel Billig

Peter LeGrand Photos

HUNTINGTON THEATRE COMPANY

Boston, Massachussetts
Sixth Season

Producing Director, Peter Altman; Managing Director, Michael Maso; Business Manager, Mary Kiely; Company Manager, Jill Kutok; Marketing/Press, Virginia Louloudes; Press, Jennifer Maxwell; Production Manager, Roger Meeker.

PRODUCTIONS & CASTS

REMEMBRANCE by Graham Reid; Director, Munson Hicks; Set, John Falabella; Costumes, Susan Tsu; Lighting, Jackie Manassee. CAST: Emery Battis (Bert Andrews), Ross Bickell (Victor), Monica Merryman (Jenny), Kim Hunter (Theresa Donaghy), Robin Moseley (Deirdre), Susan Pellegrino (Joan)

THE WINTER'S TALE by William Shakespeare; Director, Sharon Ott; Set, Kate Edmunds; Costumes, Jess Goldstein; Lighting, Daniel Kotlowitz. CAST: Donald Christopher (Time/Mariner), John Camera (Archidamus), Munson Hicks (Camillo), David McIlwraith (Polixenes), Stephen Markle (Leontes), Michele Farr (Hermione), Ross Eldridge (Mamillius), James Bodge (Antigonus), Barbara Caruso (Palina), Deborah Thomas (Emilia), John Camera (Jailer), Damien Leake (Cleomenes), Michael Pereira (Dion), John Henry Cox (Court Officer/Steward), William Preston, Gina Leishman (Shepards), Ernest Abuba (Autolycus), Alexander Cima (Florizel), Mia Koft (Perdita), Ellen Harvey (Dorcas), Susanna Burney (Mopsa), Kernan Bell, Nathan Buege, Michael Cicone, Michael Costa, Scott Koh, Allison Moseley

THE PIANO LESSON by August Wilson (*World* Premiere); Director, Lloyd Richards; Set, E. David Cosier, Jr.; Costumes, Constanza Romero; Lighting, Christopher Akerlind. CAST: Carl Gordon (Doaker), Charles S. Dutton (Boy Willie), Rocky Carroll (Lymon), Starletta DuPois (Berneice), Jaye Skinner (Maretha), Tommy Hollis (Avery), Sharon Washington (Grace)

SATURDAY, SUNDAY, MONDAY by Eduardo de Filippo; Director, Jacques Cartier; Set, James Leonard Joy; Costumes, John Falabella; Lighting, Roger L. Meeker. CAST: Mikel Lambert (Rosa), Roger Serbagi (Peppino), Jerome Kilty (Antonio), Chip Bolcik (Rocco), Susan Gabriel (Giulianella), M. H. Rogers (Roberto), Terrence Caza (Federico), Marina Re (Maria), Betty Miller (Meme), Michael Pereira (Attilio), Louis Turenne (Raffaele), Nealla Spano (Virginia), Frank S. Palmer (Michele), Munson Hicks (Luigi Ianniello), Peggy Schoditsch (Elena), James Bodge (Catiello), Neal Lerner (Dr. Cefercola)

ANIMAL CRACKERS by George S. Kaufman & Morrie Syskind; Lyrics, Bert Kalmar, Harry Ruby; Director, Larry Carpenter; Set, James Joy; Costumes, Lindsay Davis; Lighting, Marcia Mdeira. CAST: Joel Blum (Wally Winston), Karen Culliver (Mary Stewart), Frank Ferrante (Spalding), Marian Haraldson (Mrs. Whitehead), Eric Hutson (Hives), Joel Imbody (Jamison), Justine Johnston (Mrs. Rittenhouse), Donna Kane (Arabella), Kurt Knudsen (Chandler) Les Marsden (Professor), Jon Schwartz (M. Doucet), Peter Slutsker (Ravelli), Brian Sutherland (John Parker), Victoria Tabaka (Grace Carpenter), Jack Brenton, Barry Finkel, Deanna Fiscus-Ford, Randall Graham, Ginny King, Karen Lifshey, Mary Frances McCatty, Ken Leigh Rogers, Lise Simms, Michael Watson

Gerry Goodstein Photos

Top Right: "Saturday, Sunday, Monday"
Below: William Preston, David McIlwraith,
Munson Hicks in "The Winter's Tale"

Peter Slutsker, Frank Ferrante, Les Marsden
in "Animal Crackers"

Susan Pellegrino, Kim Hunter
in "Remembrance"

INDIANA REPERTORY THEATRE

Indianapolis, Indiana

Artistic Director, Tom Haas; Managing Director, Victoria Nolan; Artistic Associate, Janet Allen; Stage Managers, Joel Grynheim, Augie Mericola; Press, Sanna Yoder; Sets, Charles McCarry, G. W. Mercier, Bill Clark, Anne Sheffield, Russ Metheny; Costumes, Bobbi Owen, Bill Walker, G. W. Mercier, Connie Singer, Gail Brassard; Lighting, Stuart Duke, Michael Lincoln, Rachel Budin; Cabaret Directors, Ben Cameron, Paul Frellick, Bernadette Galanti, Su Ours, Tom Haas, Barry Keating, Frederick Farrar; Cabaret Musical Directors, Hank Levy, Kyle Latshaw, Nathan Hurwitz; Stage Directors, Paul Moser, Larry Arrick, Tom Haas
RESIDENT COMPANY: Clyde Bassett, Bella Jarrett, Michael Lipton, Frederick Farrar, Matthew Harrington, Hamilton Gillett, Amelia Penland, Ron Seibert, Priscilla Lindsay, Frank Raiter, Jerry Bradley, Bernadette Galanti, Mark Goetzinger, Su Ours
GUESTS ARTISTS: Amy McDonald, Steve Pudenz, Nixon Richman, David Williams, Norman Leger, Anne Wessels, Barbara Garren, Ben Lemon, Ann Sara Matthews, Burke Moses, Susan Wands, Alan Nebelthau, Lindsay Margo Smith, David Neighbors, Bob Hungerford, Richard Kneeland, Maeve McGuire
PRODUCTIONS: Mainstage: *Inherit the Wind, Frankenstein (World Premiere), A Streetcar Named Desire, The Cocktail Party, The Misanthrope, Light Up the Sky;* Cabaret: *My Fair Lyricist: The Music of Lerner and Lowe, Prime Time TV: Beyond the Soaps, Cabaret Christmas, The Baby Boomer's Second Edition: The 70's, Murder in the Cabaret, Murder in Cairo, Annette Saves the 500*

Sid Rust, Michael Heitz, Tod Martens, Photos

Top: (left) Maeve McGuire in "Light Up the Sky"
(right) Mark Goetzinger, Bernadette Galanti
in "Annette Saves the 500"

LONG ISLAND STAGE

Rockville Centre, New York

Artistic Director, Clinton J. Atkinson; Managing Director, Ralph J. Stalter, Jr.; Artistic Associates, Dan Conway, John Hickey, David Navarro Velasquez; Administrative Director, Sally Cohen; Development/Press, Jeffrey E. Ranbom; Technical Production Manager, Chris Davis; Stage Manager, David Wahl

PRODUCTIONS & CASTS
FLIGHTS OF DEVILS by Tom McClary; Director, Clinton J. Atkinson; Set, James Singelis; Costumes, Gail Brassard; Lighting, John Hickey. CAST: Paddy Croft, Bara-Cristin Hansen, Steven Haworth, Jim Hillgartner, J. P. Linton, Jeffrey Spolan
CHILDREN by A. R. Gurney, Jr.; Director, Terence Lamude; Set, Steven Perry; Costumes, Don Newcomb; Lighting, Linda Essig. CAST: Pamela Burrell, Daren Kelly, Julia Meade, Maureen Stillman
BACK ON THE TOWN: A CABARET FOR THE THEATRE; Production Supervisor, Clinton J. Atkinson; Set, Andrew Earl Jones; Lighting, John Hickey. CAST: John Wallowitch, Bertram Ross
MRS. WARREN'S PROFESSION by George Bernard Shaw; Director, Clinton J. Atkinson; Set, Steven Perry; Costumes, Gail Brassard; Lighting, John Hickey. CAST: Robert Blackburn, Catherine Byers, Jim Hillgartner, George Hosmer, Don R. McManus, Abigail Pogrebin
THE OWL AND THE PUSSYCAT by Bill Manhoff; Director, Clinton J. Atkinson; Set, Daniel Conway; Costumes, Don Newcomb; Lighting, John Hickey. CAST: Kimiko Gelman, Jason Graae
GETTING THE GOLD by P. J. Barry *(World Premiere);* Director, Clinton J. Atkinson; Set, Daniel Conway; Costumes, Claudia Stephens; Lighting, John Hickey. CAST: Don Billett, Nancy-Elizabeth Kammer, Marilyn Rockafellow, Amy Ryan, Anne Shropshire

Brian Balweg Photos

Right Center: Jim Hillgartner, Don R. McManus,
Catherine Byers, George Hosmer, Abigail Pogrebin,
Robert Blackburn in "Mrs. Warren's Profession"

Julia Meade, Daren Kelly
in "Children"

JOHN F. KENNEDY CENTER FOR THE PERFORMING ARTS

Washington, D.C.

PRODUCTIONS & CASTS

SHERLOCK'S LAST CASE by Charles Marowitz; Director, A. J. Antoon; Sets, David Jenkins; Costumes, Robert Morgan; Lighting, Pat Collins; General Manager, Roy A. Somlyo; Stage Manager, Alan Hall; Music, Michael Ward; Casting, Hughes/Moss. CAST: Frank Langella (Sherlock Holmes), Donal Donnelly (Dr. Watson), Helena Carroll, Pat McNamara, Melinda Mullins, Daniel M. Sillmun

SHEAR MADNESS by Paul Portner; Director/Designer, Bruce Jordan; Lighting, Daniel MacLean Wagner; Set Design Adapted by Kim Peter Kovac; Sound, John Vengrouskie; Stage Manager, John Gray. CAST: Marilyn Abrams, Robin Baxter, Matt Callahan, Michael Gabel, Bruce Jordan, Steve O'Connor

I NEVER SANG FOR MY FATHER by Robert Anderson; Director, Josephine R. Abady; Sets, David Potts; Costumes, Linda Fisher; Lighting, Jeff Davis; Sound, Scott Lehrer. CAST: Daniel J. Travanti (Gene Garrison), Harold Gould (Tom Garrison), Dorothy McGuire (Margaret Garrison), Caroline Aaron (Alice), William Cain, Scott Kanoff, Sonja Lanzener, Edward Penn, Jeni Royer, John Wylie

BREAKING THE CODE by Hugh Whitemore; Director, Clifford Williams; Set/Costumes, Liz da Costa; Lighting, Natasha Katz; Stage Manager, Susie Cordon; Casting, Julie Hughes, Barry Moss. CAST: Derek Jacobi, Rachel Gurney, Jenny Agutter, Richard Clarke, Colm Meaney, Michael Dolan, Robert Sean Leonard, Andreas Manolikakis, Michael Gough

DROOD! by Rubert Holmes; Director, Edward M. Greenberg; Choreographer, Rob Marshall; Musical Director, Raymond Allen; Set, Bob Shaw; Costumes, Lindsay W. Davis; Lighting, John McLain; Additional Costumes, Vicki Davis; Casting, Sherie L. Seff; Stage Manager, Mark S. Krause; Assistant Choreographer, Kathleen Marshall; presented with Theater of the Stars, Atlanta (Christopher B. Manos, Producer) in association with Norman Kurtz. CAST: George Rose, Jean Stapleton, Paige O'Hara, Jana Schneider, Mark Jacoby, Teresa De Zarn, Ronn Carroll, Tony Azito, John DeLuca, William McClary, Michael Nostrand

Joan Marcus, Mario Ruiz Photos

Left: Derek Jacobi, Jenny Agutter, Michael Gough in "Breaking the Code" Top: Frank Langella in "Sherlock's Last Case"

Harold Gould in "I Never Sang for My Father"

Steve O'Connor, Michael Gabel, Robin Baxter in "Shear Madness"

LONG WHARF THEATRE

New Haven, Connecticut
Twenty-third Season

Artistic Director, Arvin Brown; Executive Director, M. Edgar Rosenblum; Literary Consultant, John Tillinger; Associate Artistic Director, Kenneth Frankel; General Manager, John K. Conte; Assistant to the Directors, Janice Muirhead; Script Development, James Luse; Development, Hart Caparulo, Kathryn Champlin; Stage Managers, Beverly Andreozzi, Ruth Feldman, Anne Keefe, Robin Kevrick; Technical Director, Ted Zuse; Scenic Artist, Keith Hyatte; Props, David Fletcher, Fred Thompson, Benjamin Rayner; Sound, Brent Paul Evans; Wigs, Paul Huntley; Wardrobe, Jean M. Routt; Casting, Deborah Brown; Press, David Mayhew

PRODUCTIONS & CASTS

THE DOWNSIDE by Richard Dresser; Director, Kenneth Frankel; Sets, Loren Sherman; Costumes, Jess Goldstein; Lighting, Judy Rasmuson. CAST: Mark Blum (Ben), Bruce Davison (Jeff), Daniel De Raey (Dave), Paul Guilfoyle (Gary), Eddie Jones (Alan), Kevin O'Rourke (Carl), Lisa Pelikan (Roxanne), J. Smith-Cameron (Diane), Peter Zapp (Stan)

LAUGHING STOCK by Romulus Linney; Director, David Esbjornson; Sets, Hugh Landwehr; Costumes, Dunya Ramicova; Lighting, Ronald Wallace. CAST: Dan Patrick Brady (Intern/Hershel), Kathleen Chalfant (Alice/Suzanne Lachette/Mary), Thomas Kopache (Dr. Bailey/Buford Bullough/Griswold Plankman), Frances Sternhagen (Sarah/Constance Lindell/Old Woman), Sloane Shelton (Edna/May Ford/Neighbor), Richard Topol (Charles/Cardell)

OUR TOWN by Thornton Wilder; Director, Arvin Brown; Sets, Michael H. Yeargan; Costumes, David Murin; Lighting, Ronald Wallace. CAST: Lynn Cohen (Mrs. Soames), Frank Converse (Mr. Webb), Joyce Ebert (Mrs. Gibbs), John Griesemer (Howie Newsome), William Hardy (Constable Warren), Hal Holbrook (Stage Manager), John Leighton (Prof. Willard/Joe Stoddard), Rex Robbins (Dr. Gibbs), Louise Roberts (Emily Webb), Niki Scalera (Rebecca Gibbs), Terrence Sherman (Sam Craig), Ian Stuart (Simon Stimson), Daniel Nathan Spector (George Gibbs), Pamela Payton-Wright (Mrs. Webb)

SCENES FROM AMERICAN LIFE by A. R. Gurney, Jr.; Director, John Tillinger; Sets, Steven Rubin; Costumes, Bill Walker; Lighting, David F. Segal. CAST: Richard Backus, William Braun, Amanda Carlin, Edmond Genest, Jack Gilpin, Cynthia Harris, E. Katherine Kerr, Ann McDonough, Rex Robbins

FATHERS AND SONS by Brian Friel; Director, Austin Pendleton; Sets, John Conklin; Costumes, David Murin; Lighting, Pat Collins. CAST: James Andreassi (Yevgeny Bazarov), Margaret Barker (Princess Olga), Denise Bessette (Dunyasha), Maurice Brenner (Timofeich), Caris Corfman (Anna), Joyce Ebert (Arina), Clement Fowler (Prokofyich), Michel R. Gill (Arkady Kirsanov), Eve Gordon (Fenichka), Gary Greenberg (Fedka), Shelley Love Latham (Katya), Drew McVety (Piotr), George Morfogen (Pavel), William Swetland (Vassily), Ralph Williams (Nikolai Kirsanov)

FIGHTING CHANCE by N. J. Crisp *(American Premiere)*; Director, Kenneth Frankel; Sets, Marjorie Bradley Kellogg; Costumes, Jennifer von Mayrhauser; Lighting, David F. Segal. CAST: John Braden (Douglas), Brendan Burke (Len), Selena Carey-Jones (Speech Therapist-Ann), James Lancaster (Phillip), Cynthia Mace (Physiotherapist-Helen), David Magee (Kevin), Elizabeth Quinn (Kathy), Doug Stender (Tony), Pamela Tucker-White (Nurse-Mary)

REGINA by Marc Blitzstein; Director, Arvin Brown; Musical Director, Murry Sidlin; Additional Staging, David Bell; Sets, Michael H. Yeargan; Costumes, Jess Goldstein; Lighting, Ronald Wallace. CAST: Sean Barker (Horace Giddens), Karla Burns (Addie), Rosalind Elias/Kristen Hurst-Hyde (Regina), Vaughn Fritts (Oscar Hubbard), Harlan Foss/Jerry Lanning (Benjamin Hubbard), Michael Greenwood (Leo Hubbard), Jan Juline Leeds (Alexandra Giddens), Michael Lofton (Cal), Monica Robinson (Birdie Hubbard), Charles Walker (William Marshall)

T. Charles Erickson Photos

Lower Left Center: Edmond Genest, Ann McDonough, Amanda Carlin, Rex Robbins, Richard Backus, Cynthia Harris in "Scenes from American Life" Above: (L) Richard Topol, Kathleen Chalfant, Frances Sternhagen, Daniel Patrick Brady in "Laughing Stock" (R) Daniel Nathan Spector, Hal Holbrook, Louise Roberts in "Our Town" Top: Kevin O'Rourke, Bruce Davison, Eddie Jones, J. Smith-Cameron, Mark Blum, Peter Zapp in "The Downside"

Rosalind Elias, Charles Walker in "Regina"

LOS ANGELES THEATRE CENTER

Los Angeles, California
Fourth Season

Artistic Director, Bill Bushnell; Artistic Producing Director, Diane White; Sets/Lighting/Costumes, Timian Alsaker; Sound, Jon Gottlieb; Playwright in Residence, Marlane Meyer; Associate Director/New Play Development, Mame Hunt; Dramaturg, Halldis Hoaas

PRODUCTIONS & CASTS

MA RAINEY'S BLACK BOTTOM by August Wilson; Director, Claude Purdy; Set, Jesse Hollis; Costumes, Fritha Knudsen; Lighting, Derek Duarte; Musical Director/Arrangements, Dwight D. Andrews. CAST: Abdul Salaam El Razzac (Toledo), Kimberley LaMarque (Dussie Mae), Richard Lawson (Levee), Kent Minault (Irvin), Gordon D. Pinkney (Slow Drag), Larry Radden (Sylvester), Stephen Rockwell (Policeman), Sydney Walker (Sturdyvant), Vernon Washington (Cutler), Ann Weldon (Ma Rainey)

JACQUES AND HIS MASTER by Milan Kundera; Director/Translation, Simon Callow; Lighting, Todd Jared. CAST: Sam Anderson (Chevalier de Saint-Ouen), Mark Arnott (Marquis), Larry Hankin (Jacques), Emily Kuroda (Justine), Michael Morrison (Agathe's Father), David Rasche (Master), Shabaka/Barry Henley (Old Bigre), Madge Sinclair (Innkeeper), Deborah Thalberg (Agathe)

ANTONY AND CLEOPATRA by William Shakespeare; Director, Tony Richardson; Music, John Addison. CAST: Brian Brophy (Thidias), Ron Campbell (Proculeus), Rosalind Cash (Cleopatra), Michael Joseph Cutt (Pompey), Jean-Edward Demery (Eros), J. Edwards (Soothsayer), John Goodman (Enobarbus), Ann Hearn (Octabia), David Kagen (Philo), Patrick Kilpatrick (Menas), Mark Christopher Lawrence (Diomedes), Alan Mandell (Lepidus), George McDaniel (Messenger), Warren Munson (Canidius), CCH Pounder (Chairman), Geof Prysirr (Agrippa), Lance Roberts (Alexas), Mitchell Ryan (Antony), Kyle Secor (Octavius Caesar), Michelle LeSean Simms (Iras), Dan Tullis Jr. (Mardian)

SARCOPHAGUS by Vladimir Gubaryev *(American Premiere);* Director, Bill Bushnell; Make-Up Design, Bob Scribner, Stacey Zimmerman. CAST: Broan Brophy (Dr. Kyle), Jere Burns (Cyclist), E. J. Castillo (Driver), Aled Davies (Investigator), Juanita Jennings (Charity), Alan Mandell (Physicist), Nan Martin (Lydia Stepanovna Plitsyna), Patrice Martinez (Faith), Nobu McCarthy (Klava), John Cameron Mitchell (Fireman), Ben Piazza (Power Plant Director), Daniel Roebuck (Geiger Counter Operator), Tom Rosqui (Fire Marshall), Henry G. Sanders (Control Room Operator), Robert Symonds (Lev Ivanovich Segeyev), Barbara Tarbuck (Anna Petrovna), Gregory Wagrowski (Bessmertny), Erin Creddisa Wilson (Hope)

ELISABETH: ALMOST BY CHANCE A WOMAN by Dario Fo *(West Coast Premiere);* Translation, Ron Jenkins; Director, Arturo Corso; Set/Lighting, Arturo Corso; Costumes, Douglas D. Smith; CAST: Gisela Caldwell (Martha), Larry Cedar (Assassin), Anthony Finetti (Stephen Quadros (Queen's Guards), Charles Klausmeyer (Thomas), Shabaka/Barry Henley (MamaBigBig), Barbara Sohmers (Elisabeth I), Tony Travis (Egerton), Ron Jenkins (Interpreter)

KING LEAR by William Shakespeare; Director, Stein Winge; Music, Ketil Hvoslef. CAST: J. Edmundo Araiza (King of France/Gentleman), Ron Campbell (Oswald), Francois Chau (Duke of Burgundy/Curan), Vito D'Ambrosio (Duke of Albany), Evelina Fernandez (Goneril), Meg Foster (Regan), Stefan Gierasch (Earl of Gloucester), Ann Hearn (Cordelia/Fool), Dom Magwili (Old Man/Doctor/Messenger), Barry Michlin (Duke of Cornwall), John Nesci (Earl of Kent), Robert O'Reilly (Edmund), Espen Skjonberg (King Lear), Robert Rightman (Edgar)

WHAT THE BUTLER SAW by Joe Orton; Director, Charles Marowitz; Set, Martyn Bookwalter; Lighting, Douglas D. Smith; Costumes, Christine Lewis Hover. CAST: Peter Bromilow (Sgt. March), Jane Carr (Mrs. Prentice), Dakin Matthews (Dr. Rance), John Cameron Mitchell (Nicholas Beckett), Christopher Neame (Dr. Prentice), Jane Windsor (Geraldine Barclay)

ETTA JENKS by Marlane Meyer *(World Premiere);* Director, Robert Levitow; Set, Rosario Provenza; Lighting, Robert Wierzel; Costumes, Ray Naylor. CAST: Jonelle Allen (Sheri), Scott Burkholde (Dwight/Alec/Director's Voice), Abdul Salaam El Razzac (Clyde/Spencer), Evelina Fernandez (Dolly/Woman at Audition), Deirdre O'Connell (Etta), John Pappas (James), J. C. Quinn (Ben), Ebbe Roe Smith (Burt/Sherman/Max), Dendrie Taylor (Kitty/Shelly/Woman at Audition)

THE HOUSE OF CORRECTION by Norman Lock; Director, Bradford O'Neil; Set/Lighting, Douglas D. Smith; Costumes, Sherry Linnell. CAST: Ron Campbell (Carl), Katie King (Marion), Christopher McDonald (Steve)

THE PROMISE by Jose Rivea *(World Premiere);* Director, Jose Luis Valenzuela; Music, Francisco Gonzalez; Set, Rosario Provenza; Lighting, Robert Wierzel; Costumes, Tina Cantu Navarro. CAST: Shawn Elliott (Guzman), Julio Medina (Alegria/Priest), Maruca Medina (Malinche/Woman in Shroud), Ray Oriel (Carmello/Hiberto), Diane Rodriguez (Lolin), Lucy Rodriguez (Lilia), Nestor Serrano (Milton)

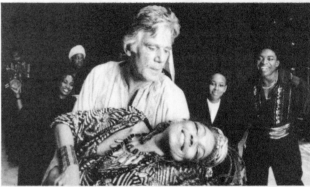

Timian Alsaker, Chris Golker, R. Kaufman

Top: (L) Deirdre O'Connell, Jonelle Allen in "Etta Jenks" (R) Ann Weldon in "Ma Rainey's Black Bottom" Below: Mitchell Ryan, Rosalind Cash in "Antony and Cleopatra"

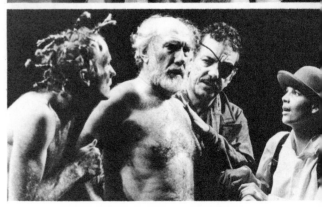

Robert Wightman, Espen Skjonberg, John Nesci, Ann Hearn in "King Lear" Above: Ron Campbell, Christopher McDonald, Katie King in "House of Correction"

MARRIOTT'S LINCOLNSHIRE THEATRE

Lincolnshire, Illinois

Producer, Kary M. Walker; Artistic Director, Dyanne K. Earley; Marketing, Peter R. Grigsby; Musical Director, Kevin Stites; Costumes, Nancy Missimi; Stage Manager, Michael Hendricks; Sound, Randy Allen Johns; Lighting, Diane Ferry Williams; Props, Kathy Klaisner, Robert Weiss; Sets, Thomas M. Ryan

PRODUCTIONS & CASTS

GROVER'S CORNERS with Book & Lyrics by Tom Jones; Music, Harvey Schmidt; *(WORLD PREMIERE)*; Based on the play *Our Town* by Thornton Wilder; Director/Choreographer, Dominic Missimi; Set/Lighting, Diane & John Williams; CAST: Harvey Schmidt (Pianist), Tom Jones (Stage Manager), Deanna Wells (Emily Webb), Richard Henzel (Mr. Webb), Linda Stephens (Mrs. Webb), Todd Schmarak (Wally Webb), Michael Bartsch (George Gibbs), Lex Hinderyckx (Dr. Gibbs), Sharon Carlson, Jr.), Ron Keaton (Howie Newsome), James Harms (Simon Stimson), Renee Matthews (Miss Soames), Kathy Santen (Lois Hershey), Jeanne Croft (Martha Cartwright), Phil Courington (Amos McCarthy), Marilyn Bogetich (Mrs. Corcoran)

MY FAIR LADY; Director, Dyanne K. Earley; Choreographer, Rudy Hogenmiller. CAST: Shannon Cochran (Eliza), Terry James (Freddy), James Harms (Pickering), Ray Frewen (Higgins), Don Forston (Doolittle), Darren Matthias (Jamie), Marilynn Bogetich (Mrs. Pearce), Roslyn Alexander (Mrs. Higgins), James Braet (Lord Boxington), Ann Arvia (Lady Boxington), Dale Morgan (Karpathy), Robert Heitzinger, Rudy Hogenmiller, Catherine Lord, Susan McGhee, Karen Rahn

EVITA; Director, Dominic Missimi; Choreographer, Mark Hoebee. CAST: Paula Scrofano/Linda Balgord (Eva Duarte-Peron), Kurt Johns (Che), Dale Morgan (Juan Peron), Terry James (Magaldi), Robyn Peterman (Mistress), Craig Bennett, Karin Berutti, Randal Boger, James Braet, Deidre Dolan, Jeanne Croft, Patti Davidson, Annette Delatorre, Tina Deleone, Lynn Carol Dunn, Jennifer Fishman, Seth Hoff, Andrew Lupp, Kim Mallery, Darren Matthias, Stephen Reed, Marc Robin, Gordon Schmidt, David Studwell, Alton White

DO BLACK PATENT LEATHER SHOES REALLY REFLECT UP?; Director, Joe Leonardo; Choreographer, Ronna Kaye. CAST: John Ruess (Eddie Ryan), Patti Davidson Gorbea (Secretary/Sister Monica Marie), Susan McGhee (Becky Bakowski), Peggy Roeder (Sister Lee), Thomas Joyce (Father O'Reilly), Kathy Santen (Virginia Lear), James Kall (Felix Lindor), Kathryn Jaeck (Nancy Ralansky), Amy Marie Dolan (Mary Kenny), Don Forston (Louis Shlang), Susan Shuler (Sister Helen)

McCARTER THEATRE

Princeton, New Jersey

Artistic Director, Nagle Jackson; Acting Managing Director, John Herochik; Associate Artistic Director, Robert Lanchester; Business Manager, Robert Gillman; Development Sales, Pamela Vevers Sherin; Communications, Joanne Gere; Administrative Director, Laurence Capo; Assistant to the Directors, Melissa A. Schramm; Production Manager, David York; Stage Managers, Jeanne Anich Stives, Frank X. Kuhn, Peter C. Cook, C. Townsend Olcott II, Megan Miller-Shields, Sarah E. Donnelly, Gwen E. Kramer; Technical Director, Chuck Taylor; Press, Daniel Y. Bauer

PRODUCTIONS & CASTS

THE MIDDLE AGES by A. R. Gurney, Jr.; Director, Nagle Jackson; Set, John Jensen; Costumes, Marie Miller; Lighting, F. Mitchell Dana. CAST: Stephen Stout, Elizabeth Dennehy, Pirie MacDonald, Penelope Reed

CORIOLANUS by William Shakespeare; Director/Set, Liviu Ciulei; Costumes, Smaranda Branescu; Lighting, Beverly Emmons; Sound, Rob Gorton; Movement/Fight Director, David S. Leong; Music, Robert Sprayberry. CAST: Peter Francis James, Keith Langsdale, David O'Brien, Jeff Weiss, Larry Golden, John MacKay, Dan Nutu, Jay Doyle, A. D. Cover, Kevin McCarty, Joseph Hulser, Bruce Gooch, Jonathan Earl Peck, Matt Penn, Michael Cumpsty, John Rensenhouse, David Adamson, Terrence Caza, Alexander Ciprian, Kate Reid, Lizbeth, MacKay, Marceline Hugot, Bruce Abas, David Barbee, F. Reed Brown, Eugene Buica, Jim Burton, Jay Cavadi, Murray Changar, Kevin Confoy, Bill Crouch, Michael Currie, Stephen Day, Dennis Delaney, Jams Galvin, John Hite, Nicholas Hunt, Jens Krummel, Andrew Marvel, Len Matheo, John Nicholson, Greg Petroff, Claywood Sempliner, John Speredakos, Jack Tolbert, Zenon Zelenich

A CHRISTMAS CAROL by Charles Dickens; Adaptation/Director, Nagle Jackson; Set, Brian Martin; Costumes, Elizabeth Covey; Lighting, Richard Moore; Sound, Rob Gorton; Music, Larry Delinger; Choreography, Nancy Thiel. CAST: Robert Lanchester, Randy Lilly, Stephen Stout, Dion Graham, Greg Thornton, Henson Keys, Ann M. Tsuji, Daniel Tamm, Jay Doyle, Kevin McCarthy, Deborah Jeanne Culpin, Kelly Baker, Herbert Mark Parker, Cynthia Martells, Kimberly King, Rebecca Rhodes, Brian Lanchester, Joshua Ballard, Kari Lefkowitz, Nicole Blaine, Miriam A. Levitin; Brian Patrick Hedden; Jennifer Housell; True Star Nager-Urian

THREE WAYS HOME by Casey Kurtti; Director, Chris Silva; Lighting, Anne Militello; Costumes, April Cutis; Set, David York. CAST: Kathlene Flatland, S. Epatha Merkerson, Monte Russell

STEPPING OUT by Richard Harris; Director, Nagle Jackson; Set, Patricia Woodbridge; Lighting, F. Mitchell Dana; Costumes, Elizabeth Covey; Choreography, Nancy Thiel. CAST: Susan Elizabeth Scott, Roo Brown, Tracey Ellis, Heather MacDonald, Patricia Kilgarriff, Deborah Jeanne Culpin, Lenny Wolpe, Jeanette Landis, Cynthia Martells, Marilyn Caskey

THE DARK SONNETS OF THE LADY by Don Nigro *(World Premiere)*; Director, Robert Lanchester; Set, John Jensen; Costumes, Gregg Barnes; Lighting, Victor En Yu Tan; Choreography, Nancy Thiel. CAST: Kate Fuglei, Peggy Cowles, Ian Stuart, Mark Brown, Leslie Brett Daniels, Richard Leighton, Elizabeth Hess, Richard Council

MASTER HAROLD and the boys by Athol Fugard; Director, Jamie Brown; Set, Jeff Modereger; Lighting, Phil Monat; Costumes, Suzanne Elder. CAST: Charles Dumas, Todd Anthony-Jackson, Benjamin White

Clem Fiovi, Randall Hagadorn Photos

**Monte Russell, Kathlene Flatland, S. Epatha Merkerson
in "3 Ways Home" Above: Pirie MacDonald, Stephen Stout,
Elizabeth Dennehy in "The Middle Ages"**

**Top: Lizbeth Mackay, Peter Francis
James in "Coriolanus"**

159

**Jonathan Peck, Robert Colston
in "Sizwe Bansi Is Dead"**

**Allan Murley, Robin
Poley in "Angel Street"**

MERRIMACK REPERTORY THEATRE

Lowell, Massachusetts

Administrative Director, Helene Desjarlais; Marketing, William Connell, Jr.; Development, Veronica Baker-Worth; Business Manager, Anne M. Tocci; Company Manager, Phyllis Leach; Literary Manager, David G. Kent; Production Manager, Stage Manager, C. Elizabeth Murphy; Assistant to Production Manager, Jennifer Brown; Production Assistant, Julie Ann Logiudice; Costumes, Jane Alois Stein; Wardrobe, Kevin R. Pothier; Lighting, John Ambrosone; Sound/Electrician, Erica French; Props, Margaret J. Funk.

PRODUCTIONS & CASTS
THE DIARY OF ANNE FRANK by Frances Goodrich & Albert Hackett; Director, Daniel L. Schay; Set, Alison Ford; Costumes, Jane Alois Stein; Casting, Jay Binder. CAST: George Axler, Derek Campbell, Stephanie Clayman, Joseph Costa, Julia Flood, Derek Hoton, Emily Loesser, Jack R. Marks, Ingrid Sonnichsen, Olga Talyn
A CHRISTMAS CAROL by Charles Dickens; Adaptation, Larry Carpenter; Director, Daniel L. Schay; Set, Leslie Taylor; Costumes, Amanda Aldridge; Original Lighting, David "Sparky" Lockner; Lighting Adaptation, John Ambrosone. CAST: Robin Chadwick, William Charlton, Julie Flood, Tim Howard, Richard McElvain, Tammy Richards, Daniel L. Schary, Alice White, Laura Bowden, Joseph Butkiewicz, Jared Copley, Joshua Glasheen, Radames Gonzals, Daniel Graham, Bonnie Hoisington, Renee Jeffers, Kristina Moore, Eric Nickola
SIZWE BANSI IS DEAD by Athol Fugard, John Kani & Winston Ntshona; Director Tom Markus; Set, Joseph A. Varga; Costumes, Jane Alois Stein; Lighting, Sid Bennett; Casting, Jay Binder. CAST: Robert Colston, Jonathan Peck
MRS. CALIFORNIA by Doris Baizley; Director, Peter H. Clough; Set, Robert Thayer; Costumes, Lynda L. Salsbury; Casting, Stuart Howard Associates. CAST: Dorothy Cantwell, Frank J. Cobb, Pat Dougan, Maureen Garrett, Mark Hofmaier, Kate Kelly, Pamela Nyberg
ANGEL STREET by Patrick Hamilton; Director, Richard Rose; Set, Gary English; Costumes, Amanda Aldridge; Lighting, Kendall Smith; Sound, John Bowen; Stage Manager, Jennifer Lynn-Brown; Casting, Jay Binder. CAST: Ron Johnston, Allan Murley, Patricia Pellows, Robin Poley, Jean Marie Williams
BERTHA, THE SEWING MACHINE GIRL with Book & Lyrics by Robert Emmett; Music, Gordon Connell; *(World Premiere);* Based on the 1872 play by Charles Foster; Director, Maggie L. Harrer; Musical Director, Paulette Haupt; Choreography, David Storey; Set, Jane Clark; Costumes, Debra Stein; Orchestrator, Bob Thompson; Additional Arrangements, Bob Goldstone; Casting, Myers/Teschner. CAST: Abra Bigham, Alan Brasington, Jack Drummond, Teri Gibson, John Hickok, Caryn Kaplan, Lisa McMillan, Patti Perkins, George Riddle, Casper Roos, Gordon Stanley, Glenn Trickel, Beth Trompeter, K. C. Wilson

Kevin Harkins Photos

**Linda Gehringer, Paul DeBoy in "Cat on a
Hot Tin Roof" Above: Eric Brooks, Wil Love,
Joseph Reed in "Guys and Dolls"**

MEADOW BROOK THEATRE

Rochester, Michigan

Artistic & General Director, Terence Kilburn; Assistant to General Director/Tour Director, James Spittle; Stage Directors, Terence Kilburn, Charles Nolte, David Regal, Carl Schurr; Sets, Peter W. Hicks, Barry Griffith; Lighting, Reid Johnson, Daniel Jaffe; Stage Managers, Terry W. Carpenter, Robert Nolte; Technical Director, Daniel Jaffe; Scenic Artists, Shaun Lawrence, Elaine Sutherland; Sound, Paul Fox; Costume Coordinator, Mary Lynn Bonnell; Assistant Costumers, Renee DiFilippo, Christa Gievers-Yntema, Barbara Jenks, Reiko Kubo; Wardrobe, Paula Kalevas; Props, Mary Chmelko-Jaffe, Kathleen Holland, William Ward; Set Technicians, Scot Cleaveland, Neil Patterson

PRODUCTIONS & CASTS
GUYS AND DOLLS with Heidi White (Sarah Brown), Wil Love (Nathan Detroit), Eric Brooks, John Bruning, Roy K. Dennison, Judy Dery, Becky Garrett, Paul Hopper, Paul Jackel, Michael Kelly, Anne Kulakowski, Michael Lackey, Denise LaDonne, Phillip Locker, Rande Rae Norman, Joseph Reed, Brian Schulz, James Lee Stanley, Kathy Tobey, Cheryl Williams, David Young, Linda Barsamian, Susan Diebolt, Tom Emmott, Jean Lyle, George Reizian II, Tom Suda
DEAR LIAR with Juliet Randall, Donald Symington, Susan Diebolt
A CHRISTMAS CAROL with Mary Bremer, Bethany Carpenter, Booth Colman, Tom Haneline, Paul Hopper, Phillip Locker, Thomas Machard, Wayne David Parker, Glen Allen Pruett, Joseph Reed, Mary Riehl, Brian Schulz, Melanie Carpenter, Kaspar Lane, Wade Simpson, Gregory Wilson, Candace Washburn, Susan Diebolt, Sandi Litt, Nora McGowan, D. A. Parker, Rebekka Parker, Robert Rabb, Mary Rychlewski, Steve Sell, Jeffrey Woolley
EDUCATING RITA with Cynthia Darlow, David Regal
CAT ON A HOT TIN ROOF with Paul DeBoy (Brick), Wil Love, Jeanne Arnold, Arthur Beer, Linda Gehriner, Phillip Locker, Peggy Thorp, Jude Angelini, Tom Emmott, Sean Jonaitis, Jennifer Jones, Mindy Martin, James Sephers, Alexis Radogost-Givens
ABSENT FRIENDS with Richert Easley, Jayne Houdyshell, Jane Lowry, Carl Schurr, Sherry Skinker, Wil Love, Peggy Thorp
DEATHTRAP with James Anthony, Jeanne Arnold, Geoffrey Beauchamp, Bethany Carpenter, George Gitto
HARVEY with Roy K. Dennison, Judy Dery, Jayne Houdyshell, Phillip Locker, Wil Love, Judi Mann, Joseph Reed, Tom Suda, Cheryl Williams

Richard Hunt Photos

NATIONAL THEATRE OF THE DEAF

Chester, Connecticut
Twentieth Season

Artistic Director, David Hays; Tour Director, Roddy O'Connor; General Manager, David Relyea; Development, Grace Harvey; Press, Laine Dyer; Company Manager, Betty Beekman; Assistant Director of Development, Lisa Reed; Development Consultant, Leonora Hays; Assistant to Tour/Press Directors, Laurie Beth Roberts; School Director, Andrew Vasnick; Assistant to School Director, Dee Block; Bookkeeper, Deb Coulombe; Stage Managers, Scott Hammar, Fred Noel; Technical Director, Deborah Henderson; Wardrobe, Terry Battisti; Company Interpreter, Nikki Kilpatrick; Scenic Artist, Chuck Baird
COMPANY: Chuck Baird, Sandi Inches, Adrian Blue, Edward Porter, Elena Blue, Mike Lamitola, Chaz Struppmann, Perry Lee Conley, Camille L. Jeter, Andy Vasnick, John Eisner, Cathleen Riddley, Lewis Merkin
PRODUCTIONS: *The Dybbuk: Between Two Worlds* by S. Ansky; Translation, Joseph C. Landis; Director, Will Rhys; Costumes, Fred Voelpel. *A Child's Christmas in Wales* by Dylan Thomas

Edward Porter, Sandi Inches in "The Dybbuk:
Between Two Worlds"
Top Right: Kenneth Albers, Rose Pickering
in "The Matchmaker" Below: Marie Mathay,
Albert Farrar in "Heathen Valley"

MILWAUKEE REPERTORY THEATER

Milwaukee, Wisconsin
Twenty-fourth Season

Artistic Director, John Dillon; Managing Director, Sara O'Connor; Associate Artistic Director, Kenneth Albers; Assistant Director, Imani; Associate Artist, Amlin Gray; Dramatuug, Tanda Dykes; Resident Playwright, John Leicht; Music, John Tanner; Sets, Hugh Landwehr; Costumes, Sappa Fleming, Michael Glich; Lighting, Dan Kotlowitz; Production Supervisor, Richard Rogers; Stage Manager, Cynthia E. Poulson; Sound, Glenn Dasson; Scenic Artist, John Story; Wardrobe, Therese A. Donarski
RESIDENT COMPANY: Kenneth Albers, Tom Blair, Catherine Lynn Davis, Albert Farrar, Gabriella Farra, Peter Jay Fernandez, Steven J. Gefroh, Tamu Gray, David Hurst, Larry G. Malvern, Marie Mathay, Norman Moses, James Pickering, Rose Pickering
GUEST ARTISTS: Richard Halverson, Linda Stephens, Lex Monson, Tom Hewitt, Laurence Ballard, Corey Hansen, Charles Tuthill, Ruth Schudson, Joaquin Romaguera, Eric Hill, Matthew A. Loney, James DeVita, David Asher, Mark Corkins, Jeffrey Bihr, Emil Herrera, Richard Gustin, Daniel Mooney, Kathy Santen, Carol Schultz, Julie Walder, Charles Michael Wright
PRODUCTIONS: Mainstage: *The Matchmaker* by Thornton Wilder, *The Diary of Anne Frank* by Francis Goodrich & Albert Hackett, *Three Sisters* by Anton Chekhov, *The Tale of King Lear* by William Shakespeare, Adaptation, Tadashi Suzuki (WORLD PREMIERE), *The Miracle* by Felipe Santander Translation, Amil Gray (AMERICAN PREMIERE), *The Miser* by Moliere, Translation Sara O'Connor; Stiemke Theater; *Heathen Valley* by Romulus Lunney (WORLD PREMIERE), *Junebug Jabbo Jones II* by and with John O'Neal, *Loot* by Joe Orton, *The Puppetmaster of Lodz* by Gilles Segal, Translation, Sara O'Connor (AMERICAN PREMIERE)

Tom Bamberger, Dennis Corey Photos

Steven J. Gefroh, Albert Farrar
in "Loot"

NEW PLAYWRIGHTS' THEATRE

Washington, D.C.

Artistic Director, Peter Frisch; Managing Director, Catherine M. Wilson; Business Manager, Mary Resing; Production Coordinator, Diane Boothby; Assistant to Artistic Director, Naomi Jacobson; Press/Marketing, Paige Gold; Lighting, Daniel MacLean Wagner; Production Stage Manager, John Lescault

PRODUCTIONS & CASTS

YOU'RE GONNA LOVE TOMORROW: A STEPHEN SONDHEIM EVENING with Music & Lyrics by Stephen Sondheim; Continuity, Paul Lazarus; Director, Peter Frisch; Musical Director/Arrangements, Roy Barbe; Set, Russell Metheny; Costumes, Jeffrey Ullman, Jane Phelan. CAST: Wayne Anderson, Felicia Colvin, Brian Davis, Ann Johnson, Elizabeth van den Berg

OUT! by Lawrence Kelly; Director, Peter Frisch; Set, Thomas F. Donahue; Costumes, Rosemary Pardee-Holz; Assistant Director, Peter Cameron. CAST: John Elko ("Shoeless Joe" Jackson), T. J. Edwards (Oscar "Happy" Felsch), Steven John Evans (Claude "Lefty" Williams), Bill Whitaker (Geroge "Buck" Weaver), Paul Christie (Arnold "Chick" Gandil), Arnie Mazer (Charles "Swede" Risberg), Austin Porter (Eddie Cicotte), Mitchell Patrick (Fred McMullin)

IDIOGLOSSIA by Mark Handley (World Premiere); Director, Susan Einhorn; Set, Thomas F. Donahue; Costumes, Jane Schloss Phelan; Technical Director, Paul Falcon; Assistant Director, Richard Schooch. CAST: Karin Abromaitis (Nell), Mitchell Patrick (Jake), Mary Ellen Nester (TC), Lynn Schrichte (Claud)

THE NIGHT HANK WILLIAMS DIED by Larry L. King (World Premiere); Director, Peter Frisch; Set, Clifton R. Welch; Costumes, Jeffrey Ullman; Music & Lyrics, Larry L. King; Production Coordinator, Diane H. Boothby; Technical Director, Paul Falcon; Assistant Director, Manos M. Clements; Costume Design Associates, Rosemary Pardee-Holz, Patricia Sanftner; Props, Rosemarie Seymour; Wardrobe, Jessica Mendelson. CAST: Mark W. Johnson (Thurmond Stottle), Larry L. King (Gus Gilbert), Elizabeth DuVall (Nellie Bess Powers Clark), Grady Smith (Moon Chilers), Gregory Procaccino (Sheriff Royce Landon, Jr.), Janis Benson (Mrs. Vida Powers)

SPEAKING IN TONGUES by John Logan (World Premiere); Director, Peter Frisch; Set, Michael Franklin-White; Costumes, Jeffrey Ullman, Penny Van Meir; Fight Direction, Bob Giglio; Production Coordinator, Brook Richards; Technical Director, Christopher O'Toole; Props, Elizabeth Kitsos; Sound, Ric Cooper; Film Consultant, Polly Krieger; Assistant Stage Manager, Diane H. Boothby; Assistant Director, Quint Daulton. CAST: Joel Swetow (Pier Paolo Pasolini), John Elko (Lecturer), Sam Brent Riegel (Boy), Kyle Prue (Hustler), Louis Schaefer (Sub-Minister), Barbara Klein (Film Student), Bill Whitaker (Nino), Steven LeBlanc (Vito), Mary R. Woods (Agent), John C. Reed (Priest), Louise Reynolds (Mother), Kathryn Chase Bryer (Technician/Reporter/Carlotta), Lou Dickey (Camerman/Reporter/Giovanni), Allison Green (Lorenz)

Doc Dougherty Photos

Elizabeth Duvall, Larry King, Mark Johnson in "The Night Hank Williams Died" Top: Mitchell Patrick, Karin Abromaitis in "Idioglossia"

Bonnie Sue Arp, Oksana Fedunszyn, Norrice Raymaker "Three Postcards"

NORTHLIGHT THEATRE

Evanston, Illinois

Artistic Director, Russell Vandenbroucke; Managing Director, Susan Medak; Marketing/Development, Michael Godnick; Production Manager, Gregory Murphy; Stage Manager, Anthony Berg

PRODUCTIONS & CASTS

DEALING by June Shellene & Richard Fire (World Premiere); Director, Michael Maggio; Supervised by B. J. Jones; Set, Linda Buchanan; Costumes, Kaye Nottbusch; Lighting, Robert Shook; Music, Rick Snyder. CAST: Ron Dean, Kevin Dunn, Don Franklin, Tim Haligan, Gary Houston, B. J. Jones, Barbara E. Robertson, Jeanette Schwaba

TWO by Ron Elisha (American Premiere); Director, Barbara Damashek; Set, Linda Buchanan; Costumes, Renee Liepins; Lighting, Ria Pietraszek; Sound, Gregory Murphy. CAST: Mike Nussbaum, Barbara E. Robertson

THREE POSTCARDS by Craig Lucas & Craig Carnelia; Director, David Petrarca; Musical Director, Raymond R. Ruggeri; Set, Gary Baugh; Costumes, Jordan Ross; Lighting, Robert Christen; Choreography, Jim Corti; CAST: D. C. Anderson, Bonnie Sue Arp, Oksana Fedunyszyn, Norrice Raymaker, Raymond R. Ruggeri

THE MARRIAGE OF FIGARO by Beaumarchais; Adaptation, Richard Nelson; Director, Robert Berlinger; Music/Sound, Nathan Wang; Set, Jeff Bauer; Costumes, Jessica Hahn; Lighting, Michael S. Philippi; Choreography, Lynda Martha. CAST: Lisa Allenick, Peter Aylward, Carolyn Blackinton, Saralynne Crittenden, William Dick, Terri Enders, Benny P. Goodman, Tom Gossett, Kevin Gudahl, Jean Juarez, James Marsters, Larry McCauley, Holli Resnik, Tria Smith, Peter Van Wagner

THE WHITE PLAGUE by Karel Capek (World Premiere); Translation, Michael Henry Heim; Director, Gwen Arner; Set, Michael S. Philippi; Costumes, Jessica Hahn; Lighting, Michael S. Philippi. CAST: Derek Rhys-Evans, John Gegenhuber, Tom Gossett, Tracy Maria Grant, Jack McLaughlin-Gray, Brent Hendon, Gary Houston, Durwald McDonald, James Marsters, Robert Stormont, Alma Washington, Bruce Young

FEIFFER'S AMERICA by Russell Vandenbroucke, adapted from the works of Jules Feiffer (World Premiere); Director, Russell Vandenbroucke; Set, Jeff Bauer; Costumes, Anne Jaros; Lighting, Rita Pietraszek; Choreography, Lynda Martha. CAST: T. C. Carson, Elizabeth DeBruler, Richard Henzel, Fredric Stone, Victoria Zielinski

Mark Avery, Photos

ODYSSEY THEATRE ENSEMBLE

Los Angeles, California

Artistic Director, Ron Sossi; Associate Artistic Director, Frank Condon; Literary Manager/Development, Jan Lewis; Production Manager, Lucy Pollak; Technical Director, Duncan Mahoney; Business Manager, Garrett Keller; Press, Joyce Crawford

PRODUCTIONS & CASTS

THE ISLAND created by Debbie Devine and the Glorious Players; Director, Debbie Devine; Music, Richard Allen; Accompaniest, Deborah Chew; Stage Manager, Felicia Isaacs; Movement, Tony Hodek; with Cheryl Crabtree, Ginny Clarkson, Kathy Martens, Jay McAdams

MENSCH MEIER by Franz Xavier Kroetz; Translation, Roger Downey; Director, Victor Brandt; Set/Lighting, Gina Gambill; Costumes, Susan Braukis; Sound, John Chamberlin, John Hammers; Stage Manager, Jody Roman; with Diana Bellamy (Martha), David J. Partington (Otto), Peter Jacobs (Ludwig), Pia Romans (Cashier)

BOYS AND GIRLS/MEN AND WOMEN written and directed by Gina Wendkos *(World Premiere);* Set, Eric H. Warren, Richard Ostroff; Lighting, Dawn Hollingsworth; Costumes, Lisa Lovaas; Sound, Steven Barr; Stage Manager, Kip Roach; with Dana Anderson (Tracy), Peter Berg (Brian), Ron Cogan (Scott), James DiStefano (Eddie/Vinnie), Darren M. Modder (David), Yeardley Smith (Ester), Alan Abelew (Matty), Janet Borrus (Stella), Sydney Coberly (Patty), Kathy Bell Denton (Gloria), Frank DiPalermo (Alex), Kurt Fuller (Jerry), Jan Lewis (Anna)

PERSONALITY conceived by Gina Wendkos; Created by Gina Wendkos, Ellen Ratner, Richard Press; with Ellen Ratner

HUNGER AND THIRST by Eugene Ionesco; Director Maurice Attias; Set, Ajax Daniels, Stephen Glassman; Lighting, Dawn Hollingsworth, Suzanne-Michele Northman; Costumes, Joyce Aysta; Makeup, Pamela Malloy; Stage Manager, Sindy Slater; with Sandie Church (Marthe, Museum Keeper), T. Lee Griffin (Brother Accountant), Jack Hatcheson (Jean), Corinne Lorain (Aunt Adelaid), Theresa Karanik (Clown Brechtoll), Gordon Metcalfe (Brother Psychologist), Cameron Milzer (Clown Tripp), Louis R. Plante (Brother Tarabas), Jack Reule (Brother Cook), Eva Wilder (Marie Madeleine)

THE CAGE written & directed by Rick Cluchey; Set, Brandy ALexander; Stage Manager, Stephen Gaines; In association with San Quentin Drama Workshop; with Randal Johnson (Guard Captain), Stefan Kalinka (Jive), Leslie Henderson (Guard/Dream Girl), Rick Cluchey (Hatchet), William Hayes (Al), Douglas Van Leuven (Doc)

THE SHOEMAKERS by S. I. Witkiewicz; Adapted & Directed by Kazimierz Braun; Translation, C. S. Durer, Daniel Gerouls; Music, Darryl Archibald, Zbigniew Karnecki; Musical Director, Darryl Archibald; Set, Susan Lane; Lighting, Ann M. Archbold; Costumes, Anna Ungar Herman; Assistant Director, Juliette Carrillo; Stage Manager, Terri Thomas; with Wayne Grace (Sajetan), Steven Barr (Joe), Peter Schreiner (Andy), Louis R. Plante (Scurvy), Katherine Anne, Catherine Theobald (Secretaries), Marilyn Fox (Duchess), Bill Butts (Fidg'ons), Christopher Janczar (Joseph), Pieter Clements, Tom Miller, Daniel Radell, Lawrence R. Ring, Jeffrey Troyer (Revolutionaries), Daniel Radell (Hyperworkoid), Brian Dunne (Comrade X), Larry Vigus (Comrade Abramowski), Darryl Archibald (Accompanist), Beata Pozniak, Tom Miller, Jeff Wright (Alternates)

THREE TOP HATS by Miguel Mihura; Translation, Marcia Coburn Wellworth; Director, Ron Sossi; Set, Don Llewellyn; Model Town Design/Construction, Susan Lane; Lighting, Dawn Hollingsworth, Suzanne-Michele Northman; Costumes, Anne Reghi; Choreography, Michael Rooney; Stage Manager, Jody Roman; with C. Thomas Cunliffe (Don Rosario), Alan Abelew (Don Dionisio), Ana Helena Berenguer (Paula), Geno Silva (Buby), Beth Hogan (Anny), Stephanie Cushna (Fanny), Patricia Desmond (Carmela), Denise Blasor (Sagra), Marina Palmier (Trudy), William Marquez (Odious Man), Myriam Tubert (Mme. Olga), William Pedraza (Handsome Man), Joseph J. Walsh (Clever Hunter), Walt Beaver (Old General), Daniel Addes (Don Sacramento)

SHAKERS by John Godber & Jane Thornton *(American Premiere);* Director, Ron Link; Set, Fred M. Duer; Lighting, Ann M. Archbold; Costumes, Silvia Jahnsons; Music/Sound, Nathan Wang; Stage Manager, Henry De La Rosa; with Kristin Lowman (Carol), Cameron Milzer (Adele), Leslie Sachs (Nicki), Yeardley Smith (Mel), Susan Alice Clark, Kimberly Johnson (Alternates)

Thomas N. Werner, Dan Raabe Photos

Lower Right Center: Steven Barr, Wayne Grace, Peter Schreiner in "The Shoemakers" Above: Diana Bellamy, Peter Jacobs, David J. Partington in "Mensch Meier" Top: Janet Borrus, Kurt Fuller, Alan Abelew, Jan Lewis in "Boys and Girls/Men and Women"

Corinne Lorain, Jack Hatcheson in "Hunger and Thirst"

OLD GLOBE THEATRE

San Diego, California

Artistic Director, Jack O'Brien; Executive Director, Craig Noel; Managing Director, Thomas Hall

PRODUCTIONS & CASTS

MARRY ME A LITTLE with Songs by Stephen Sondheim; Conceived & Developed by Craig Lucas & Norman Rene; Director, Tom Gardner; Musical Director, Bruce K. Sevy; Choreographer, Wesley Fate; Set, Alan K. Okazaki; Costumes, Lewis Brown; Lighting, Wendy Heffner; Sound, Corey L. Fayman; Stage Managers, Maria Carrera, Diedre Fudge. CAST: Deborah May, George Deloy

THE NIGHT OF THE IGUANA by Tennessee Williams; Director, Craig Noel; Set, Richard Seger; Costumes, Robert Blackman; Lighting, Kent Dorsey; Sound, Mark Sherman; Music, Larry Delinger; Stage Manager, Diane F. DiVita, Robert Drake. CAST: Hugo Sanchez (Pancho) Debra Mooney/Karen Kondazian (Maxine Fault), John Padilla (Pedro), Byron Jennings (Rev. T. Lawrence Shannon), David Wright (Wolfgang), Diane Robinson (Hilda), Mitchell Edmonds (Herr Fahrenkopf), Mary Boersma (Frau Fahrenkopf), Matthew Phillip Davis (Hank), Sandy Kelly Hoffman (Miss Judith Fellowes), Kandis Chappell (Hannah Jelkes), Cynthia Blaise (Charlotte Goodall), Archie Smith (Nonno Jonathan Coffin), Eric Grischkat (Jake Latta)

ANTHONY AND CLEOPATRA by William Shakespeare; Director, Jack O'Brien; Set, Richard Seger; Costumes, Lewis Brown; Lighting, David F. Segal; Sound, Michael Holten; Music, Conrad Susa; Dramaturge, Diana Maddox; Stage Managers, Douglas Pagliotti, D. Adams. CAST: Robert Foxworth, John Bolger, Ray Chambers, Jonathan McMurtry, Julian Gamble, Roderick Horn, Gary Armagnac, Scott Allegrucci, John Walcutt, Rene Moreno, Vyto Ruginis, Stephen Godwin, William Anton, Henry J. Jordan, Mark Hofflund, David R. Conner, David Hall, Hubert Baron Kelly, Joseph Palmas, James R. Winker, Jonathan McMurtry, JoBeth Williams, Marissa Chibas, Sally Smythe, Pippa Pearthree, Kate Frank, Michael D. Edwards, Mark Guin, Randy Reinholz, David R. Conner, Andrew Dolan, Victoria Oritsematosan Edremoda, Marc Raia

BENEFACTOR by Michael Frayn; Director, Thomas Bullard; Set, Fred M. Duer; Costumes, Christina Haatainen; Lighting, Wendy Heffner; Sound, Corey L. Fayman; Stage Managers, Diane F. DiVita, Deidre Fudge. CAST: James R. Winker (David), Sally Smythe (Jane), Vyto Ruginis (Colin), Pippa Pearthree/Victoria Oritsematosan Edremoda (Sheila)

THERE'S ONE IN EVERY MARRIAGE by Georges Feydeau; Translation/Adaptation, Suzanne Grossmann & Paxton Whitehead; Director, Stan Wojewodski, Jr.; Set, Douglas W. Schmidt; Costumes, Lewis Brown; Lighting, David F. Segal; Sound, Michael Holten; Music, Larry Delinger; Stage Managers, Maria Carrera, D. Adams. CAST: Deborah May (Lucienne), William Anton (Pontagnac), Byron Jennings/Stephen Godwin (Vatelin), James R. Whittle (Jean), George Deloy (Roubillon), Lynne Griffin (Clothilde), Carolyn McCormick (Ulla), Roderick Horn (Soldignac), Kandis Chappell (Armandine), John Walcutt (Victor), Henry J. Jordan (Manager), Kate Frank (Clara), Jonathan McMurtry (Princhard), Janice Fuller (Mme. Pinchard), Stephen Godwin/Wric Grischkat Matthew Phillip Davis, Mark Guin, Andrew Dolan (Commissioners), Archie Smith/James R. Whittle (Gerome), Michael D. Edwards (Bellboy), Dana Case, Andrew Dolan, Victoria Ortisematosan Edremoda, Matthew Phillip Davis

THE COMEDY OF ERRORS by William Shakespeare; Director, David McClendon; Set, Douglas W. Schmidt; Costumes, Robert Blackman; Lighting, Kent Dorsey; Sound, Corey L. Fayman; Music, Conrad Susa; Choreographer, Denise Gabriel; Dramaturge, Dakin Matthews; Stage Managers, Douglas Pagliotti, Robert Drake. CAST: Julian Gamble, Mitchell Edmonds, Sandy Kelly Hoffman, John Bolger, Mark Moses, Joseph Palmas, Rene Moreno, Melody Ryane, Marissa Chibas, Alicia Sedwitz, Hubert Baron Kelly, Gary Armagnac, Davis Hall, Andres Monreal, Eric Grischkat, David R. Conner, David Wright, Cynthia Blaise, Victoria Ortisematosan Edremonda, Diane Robinson, Scott Allegrucci, John Padilla, Randy Reinholz, Ray Chambers, Marc Raia, Randy Reinholz

HOLIDAY by Philip Barry; Director, Jack O'Brien; Set, William Bloodgood; Costumes, Robert Wojewodski; Lighting, Robert Peterson; Sound, Corey L. Fayman; Stage Managers, Douglas Pagliotti, Deidre Fudge. CAST: Lise Hilboldt (Linda Seton), William Bumiller (Johnny Case), Ann Gillespie (Julia Seton), Chuck LaFont (Ned Seton), Kandis Chappell (Susan Potter), James R. Winker (Nick Potter), Norman Welsh (Edward Seton), Mimi Smith (Laura Cram), Jonathan McMurtry (Seton Cram), Henry J. Jordan (Henry), Randy Reinholz (Charles), Victoria Ortisematosan Edremoda (Delia)

THE BOILER ROOM by Reuben Gonzalez *(World Premiere);* Director, Craig Noel; Set/Lighting, Kent Dorsey; Costumes, Frank O. Bowers; Sound, Lucy Peckham; Stage Manager, Robert Drake. CAST: Karmin Murcelo (Olga), Juan Del Castillo Jr. (Anthony), Allegra Swift (Olivia), Tim Donoghue (Doug)

JOE TURNER'S COME AND GONE by August Wilson; Director, Lloyd Richards; Set, Scott Bradley; Costumes, Pamela Peterson; Lighting, Michael Giannitti; Musical Director, Dwight D. Andrews; Stage Managers, Karen L. Carpenter, Deidre Fudge. CAST: Mel Winkler (Seth Holly), L. Scott Caldwell (Bertha Holly), Ed Hall (Bynum Walker), Raynor Scheine (Rutherford Selig), Bo Rucker (Jeremy Furlow), Delroy Lindo (Herald Loomis), Shawnda Jacquett/Kimme Stephanson (Zonia Loomis), Kimberleigh Aarn (Mattie Campbell), Tre' Doxley/Donald Robinson (Reuben Mercert), Kimberly Scott (Molly Cunningham), Angela Bassett (Matha Pentecost)

Byron Jennings, Kandis Chappell in "Night of the Iguana" Below: Sally Smythe, JoBeth Williams, Robert Foxworth in "Antony and Cleopatra"

THE VOICE OF THE PRAIRIE by John Olive *(West Coast Premiere);* Director, Thomas Bullard; Set/Costumes, Karen Gerson; Lighting, Wendy Heffner; Sound, Lucy Peckham; Stage Manager, Robert Drake. CAST: William Utay (David/Poppy), Sean Gregory Sullivan (Davey/Leon/James), Lynne Griffin (Frankie/Frances)

SUDS: THE ROCKING 60's MUSICAL SOAP OPERA by Melinda Gilb, Steve Gunderson & Bryan Scott; Arrangements, Steve Gunderson; Director, Will Roberson; Choreography, Javier Velasco; Musical Director, William Doyle; Set, Alan K. Okazaki; Costumes, Gregg Barnes; Lighting, Daniel J. Corson; Sound, Adam Wartnik; Lighting Consultant, Kent Dorsey; Sound Consultant, Michael Holten; Stage Managers, Diane F. DiVita, Robert Drake. CAST: Christine Sevec (Cindy), Melinda Gilb (Marge), Susan Mosher (Dee Dee), Steve Gunderson (Everyone Else)

TEA by Velina Hasu Houston; Director, Julianne Boyd; Set, Cliff Faulkner; Costumes, C. L. Hundley; Lighting, Peter Maradudin; Sound, Bruce Ellman; Stage Managers, Douglas Pagliotti, Deidre Fudge. CAST: Gerrielani Miyazaki (Himiko Hamilton), Shuko Akune (Atsuko Yamamoto), Lily Mariye (Teruko Machelli), Takayo Fischer (Setsuko Banks), Diana Tanaka (Chizuye Juarez)

Will Gullette Photos

Above: William Bumiller, Ann Gillespie in "Holiday"

PAPER MILL PLAYHOUSE

Millburn, New Jersey
Fifty-eighth Year

Executive Producer, Angelo Del Rossi; Artistic Director, Robert Johanson; Sets, Michael Anania; Costumes, Alice S. Hughes; Hair, Paul Germano; Sound; David R. Paterson; Press, Albertina Reilly.

PRODUCTIONS & CASTS

SAYONARA with Book by William Luce; Music, George Fischoff; Lyrics, Hy Gilbert *(World Premiere);* Adapted from the novel by James A. Michener; Director, Robert Johanson; Choreography, Susan Stroman; Musical Director/Dance Arrangements; Lighting, Brian MacDevitt; Costumes, David Toser, Eiko Yamaguchi; Orchestrations, Joe Gianono, Ron Roullier; Hair, Paul Germano; Stage Manager, Jeffry George; Sound, David R. Patterson. CAST: Richard White (Maj. Lloyd Gruver (Ace)), June Angela (Hana-ogi), Kevin Sweeney (Pvt. Joe Kelly), Miho (Katsumi), Colleen Fitzpatrick (Eileen Webster), Mark Zimmerman (Capt. Mike Bailey), Ako (Fumiko), Christopher Wynkoop (Gen. Mark Webster), Eda Seasongood (Miriam Webster), Tony Gilbert (Col. Calhoun Craford), Jeffery Brocklin (Consul), Miho (Katsumi), Zoie Lam, Valerie Lau-Kee (Makino Girls), Brent Black, Robert Hoshour (APs), Yung Yung Tsuai (Takarazuka Teacher), Suzen Murakoshi (Flower Vendor), Lyd-Lyd Gaston, Deborah Harada, Robert Hoshour, Norman Wendall Kauahi, Mia Korf, Setsuko Maruhashi, Yoshiko Matsui, Matthew McClanahan, Suzen Murakoshi, Hiroko Nagatsu, Kuminko Nakajima, Joanna Pang, Christine Toy, Yung Yung Tsuai, Kevin B. Weldon, Chris Wheeler, Sylvia Yamada
MY ONE AND ONLY with Music by George Gershwin; Lyrics, Ira Gershwin; Book, Peter Stone, Timothy S. Mayer; Director, Richard Casper; Choreographer, Patti D'Beck; Musical Director, Mark Goodman; Sets, Adrianne Lobel, Tony Walton; Lighting, Marc B. Weiss; Costumes, Guy Geoly; Orchestrations, Joe Gianono, Ron Foullier; Lighting, Marc B. Weiss; Costumes, Guy Geoly; Stage Manager, Jeffry George. CAST: George Dvorsky (Capt. Billy Buck Chandler), Donna Kane (Edith Herbert), Gibby Brand (Prince Nicolai/Achmed), Peggy O'Connell (Mickey), Roumel Reaux (Rev. J. D. Montgomery Alan Weeks (Mr. Magix), Jeffery C. Ferguson, Garry Q. Lewis, David A. White, Dawn Marie Church, Deanna Dys, Mitzi Hamilton, Dana Leigh Jackson, Jennifer Henson, Conny Lee Sasfai, Keith Bernardo, Frank Cava, Michael Gruber, Darrell Hankey, Kenny Ingram, Dexter Jones
BILOXI BLUES by Neil Simon; Director, John Going; Set, David Mitchell; Lighting, Phil Monat; Stage Manager, Jeffrey George. CAST: Marc Riffon (Eugene Morris Jerome), Barry Cullison (Sgt. Merwin J. Toomey), Jack Stehlin/John Younger (Roy Selridge), Chad Tyler (Joseph Wykowski), Chad Tyler (Joseph Wykowski), Greg Paton (Don Carney), Robert Cicchini (Arnold Epstein), Geoffrey Sharp (James Hennesey), Kathy Danzer (Rowena), Paige Alenius

TWO INTO ONE written & directed by Ray Cooney *(U.S. Premiere);* Set, Michael Anania; Lighting, Jeff Davis; Stage Manager, Jeffry George. CAST: Tony Randall (George Pigden), Millicent Martin (Pamela Willey), Paxton Whitehead (Rt. Hon. Richard Willey M.P.), Paddy Croft (Receptionist), Burt Edwards (Manager), Toshio Sato (Waiter), Beulah Garrick (Lily Chatterton M.P.), Karen Shallo (Maria), Pamela Dillman (Jennifer Bristow), Davis Gaines (Edward), Donald Brooks Ford, Robert Hock, Alexandra O'Karma (Hotel Guests)
JESUS CHRIST SUPERSTAR with Music by Andrew Lloyd Webber; Lyrics, Tim Rice; Directors, Robert Johanson, Charles Blaisdell; Choreography, Susan Stroman; Set, Michael Anania; Musical Director/Conductor, Andrew Carl Wilk. Costumes, Cecilia A. Friederichs; Lighting, Jeff Davis. Stage Manager, Peggy Imbrie CAST: Robert Johanson/Stephen Lehew (Jesus), James Rocco (Judas), Kim Criswell (Mary Magdalene), Raymond Bazemore/Ron Taylor (Caiaphas), Bob Cuccioli (Pontius Pilate), Pi Douglas (Annas), George Dvorsky, Judith McCauley (Mary), John Sloman (King Herod), Mark Maneet, Ryan Perry, Michael Craig Chapiro, Brian Jefferey Jurst, Bob Wrenn, Brent Black, James Hindman, Stanley Douglas Brazell, Norman Wendall Kauahi, Jessica Sheridan, Sue Delano, Gay Willis, Mia Malm, Dorie Herndon, Jane Ferrar, Tracy Lynn Neff, Craig Oldfather, Gregory Butler, Vincent D'Elia, Dan Costa, Malaika Barnes, LaKenya M. Cromwell, Lauren Anne Gaffney, Jeffrey Nelson, Sharon K. Northrup, Buddy Smith, Jessica Smith, Justin Urich

MACK AND MABEL with Book by Michael Stewart; Music, Jerry Herman *(World Premiere* of Revised Version); Director, Robert Johanson; Choreographer, Scott Salmon; Set, Michael Anania; Lighting, Jeff Davis; Costumes, Guy Geoly; Music Director/Additional Orchestrations, Larry Blank; Assistant Director, Philip Wm. McKinley; Assistant Choreographer, Linda Haberman; Additional Dance Arrangements, Richard Riskin; Stage Manager, Robert Vandergriff; Artistic Supervisor, Jerry Herman; Costume Supervisor, Theoni V. Aldredge. CAST: Lee Horsley (Mack Sennett), Janet Metz (Mabel Normand), Dorothy Stanley (Lottie Ames), Scott Ellis (Frank Wyman), Nancy Evers (Ella), Ric Stoneback (Fatty Arbuckle), Ruth Williamson (Iris), Marvin Einhorn (Mr. Fox), Stan Rubin (Mr. Kleiman), Ed Evanko (William Desmond Taylor), Frank Di Pasquale (Freddie), Robert Jensen (Andy), Kevin Ligon (Amos), David Miles (Doe/Barber), Doug Friedman (Moe), Richard Maxon (Harry the Writer), Michael Ricardo (Eddie), James Darrah (Gentleman), Carolyn DeLany (Secretary), David Askler (D. W. Griffih), Ellyn Arons, Joan Donnelly, Lynn Faro, Inga Frederic, Bill Hastings, Denise LeDonne, Stacey Logan, A. Michael McKee, Ken Nagy, Lori Oaks, Gail Pennington, Mimi Quillin

Jerry Dalia, Gerry Goodstein Photos

Top Right: "Sayonara" **Below:** George Dvorsky,
Donna Kane in "My One and Only"

**Lee Horsley in "Mack and Mabel" Above: Robert
Johanson (center) in "Jesus Christ Superstar"**

PENNSYLVANIA STAGE COMPANY

Allentown, Pennsylvania
Fifth Season

Producing Director, Greg Hurst; Managing Director, Dan Fallon; Associate Director/ Literary Manager, Wendy Liscow; Marketing/Press, Lisa Higgins; Development, Mary Ann Confar; Production Manager, Peter Wrenn-Meleck; Stage Managers, Elli Agosto, Thomas M. Kauffman; Technical Director, Glenn Gerchman; Sets, Linda Sechrist; Costumer, Marianne Faust.

PRODUCTIONS & CASTS

BILOXI BLUES by Neil Simon; Director, Martin Herzer; Set, John Falabella; Costumes, Barbara Forbes; Lighting, Stuart Duke. CAST: Jim Burke, Mark Dold, Michael Gerald, Laura MacDermott, Spartan McClure, William Perry, Allyson Rice, Michael Unger, Mitchell Whitfield

JACQUES BREL IS ALIVE AND WELL AND LIVING IN PARIS with Music by Jacques Brel; Conception/English Lyrics/Additiona Material, Eric Blau, Mort Shuman; Director, Greg Hurst; Musical Director, Marty Jones; Set, Atkin Pace; Lighting, David Noling; Costumes, Marianne Faust. CAST: Meghan Duffy, Colleen Fitzpatrick, Louis Padilla, Larry Raiken

HOW THE OTHER HALF LOVES by Alan Ayckbourn; Director, Allen R. Belknap; Costumes, Kathleen Egan; Lighting, Donald Holder; Sound, Chester Bell. CAST: Charles Antalosky, Charlotte Booker, Ellen Dolan, Ann Ducati, Stephen Temperley, Time Winters

STRANGE SNOW by Stephen Metcalfe; Director, Wendy Liscow; Lighting/ Sound, Chester Bell; Costumes, Kathleen Egan. CAST: Ryan Cutrona, Cara Duff-MacCormick, Larry Golden

A DOLL'S HOUSE by Henrik Ibsen; Translation, Larry T. Smith; Director, Wendy Liscow; Costumes, Barbara Forbes; Lighting, Curtis Dretsch; Sound, Chester Bell. CAST: Jean Barker, Ellen Fiske, Susan Gabriel, Andre Khalil, Eve Laurel, Allison Layman, Terry Layman, Jeremy Miller, Joel Rooks, Tom Teti

I'M NOT RAPPAPORT by Herb Gardner; Director, Maureen Heffernan; Set, Atkin Pace; Costumes, Patricia Adshead; Lighting, Donald Holder; Sound, Dirk Kuyck. CAST: Susan Gordon, David S. Howard, Mark L. Mikesell, Christopher Mixon, Will Osborne, Jill Wagner, Samuel E. Wright

TAKING CARE OF BUSINESS by Gil Schwartz *(World Premiere)*; Director, Greg Hurst; Set, Atkin Pace; Costumes, Barbara Forbes; Lighting, Donald Holder; Fight Arrangement, Drew Fracher. CAST: Joel Anderson, James Judy, Anne Lange, John Ramsey

Gregory M. Fota Photos

Louis Padilla, Colleen Fitzpatrick in
"Jacques Brel. . . ."
Above: Susan Gabriel, Terry Layman in
"A Doll's House"

Eevin Hartsough, Jan Leslie Harding
in "Miracle Worker"

Julie Hagerty, David Schramm
in "Born Yesterday"

PHILADELPHIA DRAMA GUILD

Philadelphia, Pennsylvania

Producing Director, Gregory Poggi; Stage Directors, Edmund J. Cambridge, Walter Dalas, Charles Karchmer, Michael Murray, Art Wolff; Costume Supervisor, Nancy Atkinson; Stage Managers, Ralph Batman, Donna E. Curci; Wardrobe, Michael DiNenno; Production Manager, Edward Johnson; Props, Christine Marti Sysko, Maryanne F. Surla: Press, Marilyn Buns; Business Manager, Kathleen Kund Nolan; Executive Assistant/Company Manager, Barbara J. Silzle; Marketing, Roy Wilbur

PRODUCTIONS & CASTS

HOME by Samm-Art Williams; Director, Walter Dalas; Set, Daniel P. Boylen; Costumes, Frankie Fehr; Lighting, Sylvester Weaver. CAST: Tommy Hicks, Elain Graham, Iris Little Roberts

DIVISION STREET by Steve Tesich; Director, Charles Karchmer; Set, R. Michael Miller; Costumes, Gail Brassard; Lighting, Jeff Davis. CAST: Rick Casorla, Jeff Brooks, Christine Farrell, Martin Shakar, Yvette Hawkins, Lela Ivey

BORN YESTERDAY by Garson Kanin; Director, Art Wolff; Set, John Jensen, Costumes, David Murin, Lighting, Dennis Parichy. CAST: Julie Hagerty (Billie Dawn), Mark Moses (Paul Verrall), David Schramm (Harry Brock), Page Johnson (Sen. Norval Hedges), Susan Terry (Helen), John Carpenter (Ed Devery), Bette Henritze (Mrs. Hedges), Rik Collitti (Eddie Brock), David Westerfer (Bellhop), Charles Conwell (Asst. Manager), Margie Hanssens (Manicurist), Peter Pryor (Bellhop/Waiter), Erik Smith (Bootblack)

THE MIRACLE WORKER by William Gibson; Director, Edmund J. Cambridge; Set, Roger Mooney; Costumes, Frankie Fehr; Lighting, William H. Grant, III. CAST: Jan Leslie Harding (Annie Sullivan), James Congdon (Capt. Keller), Lizbeth Mackay (Kate), Eevin Hartsough (Helen Keller), Jeffrey Marcus (James), Raine D'Jonson (Viney), Rene Goodwin (Aunt Ev), Don Auspitz (Anagnos), Quiana Smith (Martha), James Fitts (Percy)

JULIUS CAESAR by William Shakespeare; Director, Michael Murray; Set, Karl Eigstri; Costumes, Karen Roston; Lighting, Neil Peter Jampolis; Sound, Jeff Chestek; Fight Director, Charles Conwell; Music Consultant, Ricardo Martin. CAST: Louis Lippa (Caesar), Mario Arrambide (Cassius), Mark Zeisler (Antony), Chuck Cooper (Brutus), Reno Roop, Kathryn Gay Wilson, Raine D'Jonson, Don Auspitz, Johnnie Hobbs, Jr., Mets Suber, Elain Graham, Michael Genet, David Westerfet, Matthew Styles, Karen Evans-Kandel, Veit Schaeffer, Nicholas Macauley, Mel Donaldson, Ivette Santiago, H. German Wilson

Kenneth Kauffman Photos

PHILADELPHIA FESTIVAL THEATRE

Philadelphia, Pennsylvania

Artistic & Producing Director, Dr. Carol Rocamora; Administrative Director, Grace E. Grillet; Literary Manager, Richard Wolcott; Development/Press, David Warner; Casting, Hilary Missan; Administrative Assistant, Laurie Washburn; Technical Directors, M. R. Daniels, Scott M. Roper; Props, Maryanne Surla; Wardrobe, Ramona Broomer; Sets, Eric Schaeffer; Costumes, Vickie Esposito; Lighting, Curt Senie; Stage Managers, Scott Lesher, Linda Harris

PRODUCTIONS & CASTS
ESTABLISHED PRICE by Dennis McIntyre *(World Premiere)*; Director, Allen R. Belknap; Set, Hugh Landwehr/Eric Schaeffer; Sound, Jeff Chestek; CAST: Kenneth McMillan (Frank Daniels), Timothy Landfield (William Walker), Tony Campisi (Russell Morgan), Richard Seff (Thomas Bailey)
NO STRANGER by Jule Selbo *(World Premiere)*; Director, Gloria Muzio; CAST: Melissa Hurst (Faye Kelly), Michael French (Mark Kelly), Chris Manning (Wally), Jane Moore (Dr. Ann), Mark Kenneth Smaltz (Leon), Donna Davis (Kathy Deeter), Nora Chester (Alicia)
MAGDA & CALLAS by Albert Innaurato *(World Premiere)*; Director, Thomas Gruenewald; Set, Hugh Landwehr; Lighting, Ann G. Wrightson; Costumes, Barbara Forbes; Sound, Adam Wernick; Stage Manager, Linda Harris; Dramaturg, Richard Wolcott. CAST: Dolores Wilson (Nella La Selva), Joan Stanley (Sister Cecilia), Irma St. Paule (Yola), Anne Pitoniak (Rosalie), Gabriel Bologna (Vito De Marco), June Gable (Magda La Selva), Robyn Hatcher (Calas La Selva), Joseph Ragno (Bey De Marco), David Toney (Luther)
SOULFUL SCREAM OF A CHOSEN SON by Ned Eisenberg *(World Premiere)*; Director, Michael Bloom; Sound, Jeff Chestek; Stage Manager, Linda Harris. CAST: Rob Morrow (Max), Marchand Odette (Bernadette), Annie Korzen (Sylvia), Jack R. Marks (Harry), William Christian (Willie), Ralph Remington (Neville), Walter Allen Bennett, Jr. (Sanford), Damon Pressley Saleem (Reggie), Gina Digrazio (Michelle), Robin Green (Sarah)
MIRROR DEMONS by Bruce Graham *(World Premiere)*; Director, James Christy; CAST: Stephen Mailer (Kenny Simmonds), Larry Joshua (Vince DelGatto), Karen Mac Donald (Carmella DelGatto), Allen Fitzpatrick (O'Brien), Theresa Donahue (Mrs. Simmonds), Daniel Richards (Mr. Simmonds), Thomas G. Waites (Deke Winters), Mia Dillon (Diane Sikorski)
DOUBLE FEATURE: *Election '84* by Ellen Byron *(World Premiere)*; Director, Jan Silverman; with Caroline Aaron (Rachel Warberg), Jan Leslie Harding (Wendy Burns), Nick Bakay (Waiter/Announcer). *Paco Latto and the Anchorwoman* by David Kranes *(World Premiere)*; Director, Gloria Muzio; with Nick Bakay (Bellman), Harriet Harris (McLellen McRea), Doug Hutchison (Paco Latto)

Susanne Richelle Photos

Anne Pitoniak in "Magda & Callas"

PIONEER THEATRE COMPANY

Salt Lake City, Utah

Artistic Director, Charles Morey; Managing Director, Jack A. Mark; Development, Josephine Bowman; Business Manager, Helen Royle; Company Manager, Shirley Kilgore; Development, Andrea L. H. Barnes; Costumes, Elizabeth Novak; Lighting, Peter L. Willardson; Sets, George Maxwell; Musical Director, James Prigmore; Production Stage Manager, D. Dale Dean; Stage Manager, John W. Caywood, Jr.; Technical Director, David Deike; Casting, David Tochterman
RESIDENT COMPANY: Joyce Cohen, Marsha Miller, Richard Mathews, Max Robinson, Patrick Page, Robert Peterson, Anne Stewart Mark, Michael Ruud
MY ONE AND ONLY with Music by George Gershwin; Lyrics, Ira Gershwin; Book, Peter Stone, Timothy S. Mayer; Director/Choreographer, Patti D'Beck; Assistant Director/Choreographer, Jerry Yoder; Lighting, Peter L. Willtardson, Ariel Ballif. CAST: Mark Martino (Billy Buck Chandler), Deborah Carlson (Edythe Herbert), Keith Robert Bennett, Omar W. Hester, Garry Q. Lewis, Max Robinson, Jennifer Adams, Kriss Dias, Christie Hale, Keri Lee, Hannah Meadows, Betsy Nagel, Karen B. Alston, Jan Mickens, Bruce Gunersen, Jay H. Gunersen, Kirk Gunersen, Wade Lindstrom, Mark C. Reis, Josef Reiter, D. Brian Wrightman
HAMLET by William Shakespeare; Director, Charles Morey; Music, James Prigmore; Set, Ariel Ballif; Fight Director, David Boushey. CAST: Richard Bekins (Hamlet), Anthony Auer, Bonnie Black, Tracy Griswold, Richard Mathews, Richard Nelson, Patrick Page, Robert Peterson, Max Robinson, Michael Ruud, Doug Stender, Maxine Taylor-Morris
THE DINING ROOM by A. R. Gurney, Jr.; Director, Munson Hicks; Costumes, K. L. Alberts; Lighting, Karl E. Haas. CAST: Joyce Cohen, Jay Devlin, Terry Layman, Monica Merryman, Max Robinson, Dorothy Stinnette
YOU CAN'T TAKE IT WITH YOU by Moss Hart & George S. Kaufman; Director, Thomas Gruenewald; Costumes, Ariel Ballif; Lighting, Kiyono Oshiro. CAST: Maureen Brennan, Joyce Cohen, Richard Cottrell, Margaret Crowell, Mary Ethel Gregory, Bette Henritze, Richard Mathews, Marsha Miller, Victor A. Morris, Alan Nash, Patrick Page, Robert Peterson, Max Robinson, Brenda Thomas
A FLEA IN HER EAR by Georges Feydeau; Translation, John Mortimer; Director, Charles Morey; Set, Peter Harrison. CAST: Joyce Cohen, John Guerrasio, Jim Jansen, Philip LeStrange, Anne Stewart Mark, Richard Mathews, Marsha Miller, D. B. Novak, Patrick Page, Max Robinson, Michael Ruud
DEATH OF A SALESMAN by Arthur Miller; Director, Charles Morey; Music, James Prigmore; Lighting, Karl E. Haas. CAST: John Abajian, Barbara Andres, Brian Drillinger, William Gavin Lawrence, Jayne Luke, Anne Stewart Mark, Richard Mathews, Gerald Richards, Michael Ruud
SINGIN' IN THE RAIN with Book by Betty Comden & Adolph Green; Songs, Nacio Herb Brown, Arthur Freed; Director/Choreographer, Darwin Knight; Assistant Choreographer, Jayne Luke. CAST: Deborah Carlson, Joey Farr, Anne Stewart Mark, Richard Mathews, Marsha Miller, Martin Moran, Robert Peterson, Max Robinson, Todd Taylor, Sally Woodson, Timothy Albrecht, Joey Farr, Andrew W. Foster, Christie Hale, Rebecca Holt, Nanette B. Horman, Scott Huber, Wayne Kennedy, Keri Lee, Anne Stewart Mark, Mearle Marsh, Hannah Meadows, Betsy Nagel, Patti M. Olsen, Mark C. Reis, Kathleen Seymour, J. Kurt Stamm, Sam Stith, S. Kip White, Mary Davis Wilson

Robert Clayton Photos

"A Flea in Her Ear" Above:
Robert Peterson, Richard Bekins
in "Hamlet"

PLAYMAKERS REPERTORY COMPANY

Chapel Hill, North Carolina

Executive Producer, Milly S. Barranger; Artistic Director, David Hammond; Managing Director, Margaret Hahn; Production Manager, Tom Neville; Resident Director, Christian Angermann; Stage Combat/Movement Coach, Craig Turner; Voice Coach, Carol Pendergrast; Sets/Costumes, McKay Coble; Costumes, Bobbi Owen; Lighting, Robert Wierzel; Business Manager, Peter Kernan; Development, Justin Grimes; Press/Marketing, Jon Curtis; Assistant to Managing Director, Mary Robin Wells; Stage Managers, Joseph Millett, Robert Welch
RESIDENT COMPANY Bernard Addison, Patricia Barnett, Constance Conover, Dede Corvinus, John Feltch, Matt Fitzsimmons, Derek Gagnier, Thomas Garvey, Joseph Haj, Deborah Hecht, Candice Milan, Demetrios Pappageorge, Melissa Proctor, Susanna Rinehart, David Whalen, Eben Young
GUEST ARTISTS Simon Brooking, Maury Cooper, Tandy Cronyn, Patrick Egan, Betsy Friday, James Harbour, Leslie Hicks, James Lawson, Kyle MacLachlan, Therese McElwee, James Pritchett, Isa Thomas, Cal Winn
PRODUCTIONS: *Romeo and Juliet* by William Shakespeare; Director, David Hammond; Set/Costumes, Sam Kirkpatrick. *Orphans* by Lyle Kessler; Director, Maureen Heffernan; Set/Lighting, Dale Jordan. *A Child's Christmas in Wales* by Jeremy Brooks & Adrian Mitchell; Director, Christian Angermann. *Mourning Becomes Electra* by Eugene O'Neill; Director, David Hammond; Set/Costumes, Bill Clarke. *On the Verge or The Geography of Yearning* by Eric Overmyer; Director, Christian Angermann; Sets, Phillip Baldwin; Lighting, Marcus Dilliard; Music, Douglas Wagner. *The Beggar's Opera* by John Gay; Adaptation/Director, David Hammond; Costumes, Marianne Custer; Music Arrangements, Doug Wagner

Kevin Keister, Jim Stratakos Photos

Left: Leslie Hicks, Simon Brooking in "Beggar's Opera" Top: Tandy Cronyn, Maury Cooper, Isa Thomas in "Mourning Becomes Electra"

PITTSBURGH PUBLIC THEATER

Pittsburgh, Pennsylvania
Thirteenth Season

Producing Director, William T. Gardner; General Manager, Dan Fallon; Development, Daniel S. Shephard; Press, Curt Powell; Marketing, Rosalind Ruch; Technical Director, A. D. Carson.

PRODUCTIONS & CASTS

THE HAIRY APE by Eugene O'Neil; Director, George Ferencz; Music, Max Roach; Set, Bill Stabile; Costumes, Sally Lesser; Lighting, Blu; Stage Manager, Jane Rothman. CAST: Lamont Arnold, Jim Abele, L. Peter Callender, Michael Galardi, Debra Godson, Doris Hackney, Bruce Kirkpatrick, Peter McCabe, Dermot McNamara, Penny Sandstrom, Eric Stuart, Raymond Antony Thomas, Laura Wenneker
DAMES AT SEA with Book & Lyrics by George Haimsohn & Robin Miller; Music, Jim Wise; Director/Choreographer, Neal Kenyon; Musical Director, Lawrence Goldberg; Assistant Choreographer, Dorothy Stanley; Original Tap Sequences, Dirk Lumbard; Sets, Anne Mundell; Costumes, Mary Mease Warren; Lighting, Kirk Bookman; Stage Manager, Michael John Egan. CAST: Ron Bohmer, Jeff Calhoun, Karen Prunczik, Karyn Quackenbush, Dorothy Stanley, Allan Stevens
EDITH STEIN by Arthur Giron; Director, Lee Sankowich; Set, Ursula Belden; Costumes, Laura Crow; Lighting, Kirk Brookman; Sound, James Capenos; Dramaturg, Mary G. Guaraldi; Stage Manager, J. Barry Lewis. CAST: Jim Abele, Lynne Charney, Kate English, Wynn Harmon, Jens Krummel, Anthony Mainionis, Maura Minteer, Nann Mogg, Susan Riskin, Helena Ruoti, David Yezzi
THE MYSTERY OF IRMA VEP by Charles Ludlan; Director, Bruce Bouchard; Music, Peter Golub; Set, Rick Dennis; Costumes, Martha Hally; Lighting, Jackie Manassee; Special Make-up, Bruce Spaulding Fuller; Stage Manager, Michael John Egan. CAST: Michael J. Hume, James Goodwin Rice
THE NORMAL HEART by Larry Kramer; Director, Lee Sankowich; Set, Anne Mundell; Costumes, Craig A. Humphrey; Lighting, Ann G. Wrightson; Stage Manager, Jane Rothman. CAST: Jim Abele, Lamont Arnold, Allan Byrne, Rosemary DeAngelis, Wynn Harmon, Lance Lewman, John Ottavino, Edwin Owens, William Rhys, William Salzmann
MY HEART BELONGS TO DADDY written and performed by Laury Marker & Nelsie Spencer *(World Premiere);* Director, David Warren; Set, John Arnone; Costumes, David Wollard; Lighting, Kirk Bookman; Stage Manager, Michael John Egan

Ric Evans, Mark Portland, Rich Wilson Photos

Allan Stevens, Karen Prunczik, Karyn Quackenbush, Jeff Calhoun, Ron Bohmer in "Dames at Sea" Above: "The Hairy Ape"

PLAYHOUSE IN THE PARK

Cincinnati, Ohio

Artistic Director, Worth Gardner; Managing Director, Katherine Mohylsky; Associate Director, D. Lynn Meyers; Production Manager, Phil Rundle; Stage Managers, Tom Lawson, Bruce E. Coyle, Stacey A. Milam; Marketing, Richard J. Diehl; Press, Peter M. Robinson; Development Associate, Norma Niinemets; Lighting, Kirk Bookman

PRODUCTIONS & CASTS

FRANKENSTEIN: THE MODERN PROMETHEUS by David Richmond & Bob Hall; Director, Barbara Carlisle; Set, Paul Shortt; Costumes, D. Bartlett Blair; CAST: Jay E. Raphael (Henry Clerval), K. C. Wilson (Mordecai Kneble), Henry Dardenne (Victor Frankenstein), Matthew Lewis (Prof. Krempe), Kathryn Meisle (Justine Moritz), Maura Swanson (Elizabeth Lavenza), Paul Ukena, Jr. (Creature)
MAX AND MAXIE by James McLure; Director, D. Lynn Meyers; Set/Costumes, Eduardo Sicangco; Music, Worth Gardner. CAST: Robin Haynes (Boy), John Newton (Max Love), Sandy Roveta (Maxie L'Amour)
THE FLYING KARAMOZOV BROTHERS IN JUGGLE AND HYDE, A PLAY WITH WORDS; Stage Manager, Peter Dansky; Production Coordinator, Tom Lawson. CAST: Timothy Daniel Furst (Fyodor), Paul David Magid (Dmitri), Randy Nelson (Alyosha), Howard Jay Patterson (Ivan), Sam Williams (Smerdyakov)
CLEAR LIQUOR AND COAL BLACK NIGHTS by Thomas M. Atkinson; Director, Sam Blackwell; Set, Joseph P. Tilford; Costumes, D. Bartlett Blair; Music, Edward P. Cunningham. CAST: Edward P. Cunningham (Singer/Guitar Player), Bob Elkins (Rev. Lloyd Parker/Rev. Elijah), Paul C. Thomas (Skeet Jensen), Paul Ukena, Jr. (Orval Pack), Steve Rankin (Garnett Hinton McComas), Geoffrey Wade (Denvil Cox), Henry Dardenne (Ray Lee Parker), Steven Griffith (Clayton Jensen/Billo Jensen), Sheriden Thomas (Ma McComas), Amelia White (Aunt Maydell/Ma Parker), Jesse Vincent (Boy Garnett/Cecil), Dale Doerman (Jess Coleman/Tony/Bartender), Patricia Ryan (Almina Coleman), Jeff Hasler (Les), Barbara Wilder (Precious Apostolon), Hannah Moreland-Reck (Decretia Pack)
BURKIE by Bruce Graham; Director, Richard Harden; Set, Charles Cosler; Costumes, Rebecca Senske. CAST: Barry Mulholland (Jon Burke), John MacKay (Ed Burke), Thomas Dorff (Dom), Cecelia Riddett (Jess)
MA RAINEY'S BLACK BOTTOM by August Wilson; Director, Israel Hicks; Set/Costumes, Lawrence Casey. CAST: Jack Stubblefield Johnson (Sturdyvant), Geoffrey Wade (Irvin), Lawrence James (Cutler), Roger Robinson (Toledo), Norman Matlock (Slow Drag), Kevin Ramsey (Levee), Ellia English (Ma Rainey), Robert Stocker (Policeman), Sheyvonne Wright (Dussie Mae), Vincent J. Godfrey (Sylvester)
AMERICAN BUFFALO by David Mamet; Director, Sam Blackwell; Set, Jay Depenbrock; Costumes, Rebecca Senske. CAST: Dennis Predovic (Donny Dubrow), Henry Dardenne (Bobby), Paul Ukena, Jr. (Walter Cole-"Teach")
ON THE VERGE OF THE GEOGRAPHY OF YEARNING by Eric Overmyer; Director, Worth Gardner; Set/Costumes, Eduardo Sicangco. CAST: Sheriden Thomas (Mary), Glynis Bell (Fanny), Amelia White (Alex), Geoffrey Wade (Grover/Alphonse/Gorge Troll/Yeti/Gus/Mme. Nhu/Mr. Coffee/Nicky Paradise)
THE BLOOD KNOT by Athol Fugard; Director, Alex Dmitriev; Set, Scott Chambliss; Costumes, Rebecca Senske. CAST: Alan Nebelthau (Morris), Cortez Nance, Jr. (Zachariah)
STEPPING OUT by Richard Harris; Director, Paul Moser; Set, Jay Depenbrock; Costumes, Rebecca Senske; Choreography, Joan Walton. CAST: Diane Armistead, Glynis Bell, Mary A. Dierson, Wanda-Gayle Logan, Cecelia Riddett, Sandy Roveta, Sheriden Thomas, Geoffrey Wade, Linda Wasserman, Amelia White
TAPESTRY with the Music of Carole King; Musical Directors/Arrangements, John Kroner, Scot Woolley; Director, Worth Gardner; Set, Paul Shortt; Costumes, D. Bartlett Blair. CAST: Laurence Clayton, Pattye Darcy, Mary Gutzi, John Hickok, Natalie Oliver, Michael Visconti

Sandy Underwood Photos

Henry Dardenne, Paul Ukena, Jr. in "American Buffalo" Left: Ellia English in "Ma Rainey. . . ."

John Mackay, Cecelia Riddett in "Burkie"
Above: Glynis Bell, Sheriden Thomas
in "On the Verge. . . ."

169

PORTLAND STAGE COMPANY

Portland, Maine

Artistic Director, Barbara Rosoff; Acting Artistic Director, Richard Hamburger; Managing Director, Mark Somers; Development, Jeff Toorish; Marketing, Monica Whitaker; Stage Managers, Rheatha Forster, Maura J. Murphy.

PRODUCTIONS & CASTS

SEASCAPE by Edward Albee; Director, Tom Prewitt; Set/Costumes, G. W. Mercier; Lighting, Jackie Manassee. CAST: Phyllis Somerville (Nancy), Charles Antalosky (Charlie), Richard McMillan (Leslie), Deborah Allison (Sarah)
TARTUFFE by Moliere; Translation, Donald M. Frame; Director, Michael Engler; Set, Christopher Barecca; Costumes, Candice Donnelly; Lighting, Don Holder. CAST: Cherry Jones (Dorine), Victoria Boothby (Mme. Pernelle), Susan Monagan (Flipote), Priscilla Shanks (Elmire), Diane Kinerk (Mariane), John Wendes Taylor (Damis), Joseph Daly (Cleante), Charles Antalosky (Orgon), Leland Orser (Valere), Patrick Kerr (Tartuffe), David Sennett (M. Loyal), Donald Marston (Secretary)
ORPHANS by Lyle Kessler; Director, Phil Killian; Set, Michael Smith; Costumes, Catherine Zuber; Lighting, Stephen Strawbridge. CAST: Lou Milione (Treat), Christopher Cull (Phillip), Larry Golden (Harold)
CHARLES DICKENS' HARD TIMES adapted by Stephen Jeffreys; Director, Richard Hamburger; Set, Christopher Barecca; Costumes, Martha Hally; Lighting, Stephen Strawbridge; Music, Thomas Cabaniss; Dialect Coach, Melissa Cooper. CAST: Leslie Geraci (Louisa/Mrs. Blackpool/Mrs. Pegler), Matthew Kimbrough (Bitzer/Mr. Sleary/Josiah Bounderby Slackridge/James Harthouse), Polly Pen (Sissy Jupe/Mrs. Sparsit/Rachael/Mary Stokes), Derek Smith (Thomas Gradgrind/Young Tom/Stephen Blackpool)
PAINTING CHURCHES by Tina Howe; Director, Evan Yionoulis; Set, Charles McCarry; Costumes, Ellen McCartny; Lighting, Don Holder. CAST: Avril Gentles (Fanny), John Straub (Gardner), Becky London (Margaret)
SHARON AND BILLY by Alan Bowne; Director, Richard Hamburger; Set, Derek McLane; Costumes, Catherine Zuber; Lighting, Robert Wierzel. CAST: Margery Murray (Mom), Stephen Mendillo (Dad), Kathryn Marcopulos (Sharon), Leif Tilden (Billy)

Jenny Tuemmler Photos

Derek Smith, Leslie Geraci, Matthew Kimbrough, Polly Pen in "Hard Times" Above: Priscilla Shanks, Diane Kinerk, Cherry Jones, Joseph Daly in "Tartuffe"

Kelly Walters, Peter Carlton Brown in "Don Juan"

PROJECT THEATRE

Ann Arbor, Michigan

Artistic Director, John Russell Brown; Managing Director, Jeffrey Kuras; Stage Manager, Brett Finley; Production Manager, Mark Sullivan

PRODUCTIONS & CASTS

DON JUAN by Moliere; Translation, John Fowles; Director, John Russell Brown; Set/Costumes, G. W. Mercier; Lighting, Robert Heller; Music/Musical Director, Frank Tichelli; Choreographer, Jessica Fogel; Pianist, Robert Conway; Stage Manager, Brett Finley; Voice Consultant, Patricia Boyette.
CAST: Kelly Walters (Sganarelle), Jonathan Fried (Gusman/La Ramee/Pauper/Don Alonso/Monsieur Dimanche/Don Louis), Peter Carlton Brown (Don Juan), Carol Halstead (Donna Elvira/Mattie/La Violette), Shannon Rye (Charlotte/Ragotin), Daniel Pardo (Peter/Don Carlos/Commande's Statue)
EVERY GOOD BOY DESERVES FAVOUR by Tom Stoppard & Andre Previn; Director, John Russell Brown; Set, Peter Beudert; Costumes, Laura Crow; Lighting, Robert Heller; Stage Manager, Amanda Mengden; Conductor, Gustav Meier; Assistant Conductor, Yves Cohen. CAST: Leigh Woods (Alexander), Yusef Bulos (Ivanov), Richard Klautsch (Doctor), Cynthia Crumlish (Teacher), Matthew Toronto/Matthew Holloran (Sacha), Barry Goldman (Colonel)
WOLF by Nicholas Delbanco with Music by David Gregory *(World Premiere);* Director, John Russell Brown; Music Performed by David Gregory; Set, Peter Beudert; Costumes, Laura Crow; Lighting, Robert Heller; Stage Manager, Amanda Mengden. CAST: Leigh Woods (Edward), Andrea Delbanco (Diana), Cynthia Crumlish (Gloria), Richard Klautsch (Frank), Andrew Benjamin (Boy)

David Smith, Bob Chase Photos

170

REPERTORY THEATRE OF ST. LOUIS

St. Louis, Missouri

Artistic Director, Steven Woolf; Managing Director, Mark D. Bernstein; Technical Director, Max De Volder; Props, John R. Roslevich, Jr.; Costume Manager, Holly Poe Dubin; Tour Director, Kim Bozark; Company Manager, Joyce Ruebel; Artistic Supervisor, Wayne Salomon; Development, Nancy S. Forsyth; Press, Judy Andrews; Stage Managers, Glenn Dunn, Patrick Siler, T. R. Martin

PRODUCTIONS & CASTS

COMPANY with Music & Lyrics by Stephen Sondheim; Book, George Furth; Director, Steven Woolf; Choreographer, J. Randall Hugill; Musical Director, Byron Grant; Sets/Costumes, Carolyn L. Ross; Lighting, Peter E. Sargent; Karate Instructor, Robert Goodwin; Stage Managers, Glenn Dunn, Patrick Siler. CAST: Kurt Peterson (Robert), Kathy Morath (Sarah), Lee Lobenhofer (Harry), Judi Mann (Susan), Todd Thurston (Peter), SuEllen Estey (Jenny), James Hindman (David), Judith Blazer (Amy), Merwin Foard (Paul), K. K. Preece (Joanne), Peter Shawn (Larry), Tina Johnson (Marta), Peggy Taphorn (Kathy), Maggy Gorrill (April)
THE LITTLE FOXES by Lillian Hellman; Director, Timothy Near; Set, John Ezell; Costumes, Jim Buff; Lighting, Max De Volder.
CAST: Esther Scott (Addie), Ron Himes (Cal), Catherine Babcock (Birdie), Jery Mayer (Oscar), David Holt (Leo), Judith Roberts (Regina), Joneal Joplin (William), Philip Pleasants (Benjamin), Tina Sigel (Alexandra), Alan Mixon (Horace)
DAMES AT SEA with Book & Lyrics by George Haimsohn & Robin Miller; Music, Jim Wise; Director/Choreographer, Pamela Hunt; Musical Director, Diane Ceccarini; Set, John Roslevich Jr.; Costumes, Dorothy L. Marshall; Lighting, Peter E. Sargent. CAST: Teri Gibson (Mona Kent), Carol Dilley (Joan), Wayne Bryan (Hennesey/Captain), Peggy Taphorn (Ruby), Jack Doyle (Dick), Gib Jones (Lucky)
THE IMMIGRANT: A HAMILTON COUNTY ALBUM by Mark Harelik; Concept, Mark Harelik, Randal Myler; Director, Susan Gregg; Set/Costumes, John Carver Sullivan; Lighting, Dale F. Jordan. CAST: Andrew Hill Newman (Haskell Harelik), Glynis Bell (Ima Perry), Tony Hoty (Milton Perry), Devora Millman (Leah Harelik)
JULIUS CEASAR by William Shakespeare; Director, Edward Amor; Set, John Ezell; Costumes, Dorothy L. Marshall; Lighting, Max De Volder.
CAST: James Paul (Caesar), Dan Abdon, Jay Albright, Ross Bickell, Alan Clarey, John Contini, Jim Danek, Paul Devine, Al Fialka, Bruce Longworth, John McCabe, Robert McCabe, John Michalski, Larry Michelson; Patrick Morgan; Joe Palmieri, James Paul, Philip Pleasants, John Rensenhouse, John Ruprecht, Jeff Sams, Tim Snay, Joan Ulmer, Lesley Vogel, Trish Adair, Tim Barker, Mary Chaisson, Randy Donaldson
HOW THE OTHER HALF LOVES by Alan Ayckbourn; Director, Edward Stern; Set/Costumes, Arthur Ridley; Lighting, Glenn Dunn; Fight Choreographer, Robert Goodwin. CAST: Darcy Pulliam (Fiona Foster), Lynn Chausow (Terry Phillips), Charles Antalosky (Frank Foster), Seth Jones (Bob Philips), Adam Redfield (William Featherstone), Adele Ahronheim (Mary Featherstone)
A QUIET END by Robin Swados (American Premiere); Director, Sam Blackwell; Set, Mel Dickerson; Costumes, Jim Buff; Lighting, Mark Wilson; Stage Manager, Champe Leary. CAST: Jack Kenny (Max), Tony Hoylen (Tony), Bruce Wieland (Billy), Joe Proctor (Doctor), Jack Koenig (Jason)
DAY SIX by Martin Halpern; Director, Louis D. Pietig; Set, Larry Biedenstein; Costumes, Holly Poe Durbin; Lighting, Peggy Thierheimer; Stage Manager, Champe Leary. CAST: John Michalski (David Porter), Caroline McGee (Eleanor Manning)
AMAZING GRACE by Sandra Deer; Director, William Woodman; Set, Richard Tollkuhn; Costumes, Teri McConnell; Lighting, Max De Volder; Stage Manager, Champe Leary. CAST: Billie Lou Watt (Grace Tanner), Chuck Patterson (Josh Shepard), Pat Nesbit (Maggie Ames), David Holt (Troy)

Judy Andrews Photos

Peter Bradbury, Robert Darnell, David P. Whitehead in "Orphans"

Adele Ahronheim, Adam Redfield, Charles Antalosky in "How the Other Half Loves"
Top: K. K. Preece, Kathy Morath, Judith Blazer, Merwin Foard, Kurt Peterson, SuEllen Estey, Judi Mann in "Company"

SAN JOSE REPERTORY COMPANY

San Jose, California
November 12, 1987–July 17, 1988

Artistic Director, Timothy Near; Managing Director, Shannon Yevak-Leskin; Founder, James P. Reber; Press, Bobby Tyler; Production Manager, T. Jane Bishop; Technical Director, Thomas J. O'Neill; Assistant Set Designer/Scenic Artist, Walter Saunder; Costumes Manager, Casandra Carpenter; Wardrobe, Paul Nelson; Props, Kristine L. Haglund, Cathy Moser; Sound, Gary Jones; Stage Managers, Ken Barton, Jane Chavis, Peggy L. Hess; Assistant General Manager, Edwin Jones; Business Manager, Emma Lou Huckabay; Assistant to Atistic Director/General Manager, Chris Grant; Company Manager, Doeri Welch; Marketing, William "Butch" Coyne; Development, Judy Cosgrove, Jennifer Welling

PRODUCTIONS & CASTS

THE RAINMAKER by N. Richard Nash; Director, Timothy Near; Set/Costumes, Jeff Sturckman; Lighting, Peter Maradudin. CAST: Warren Frost (H. C. Curry), David Dunard (Noah), John McCluggage (Jimmy), Jacqueline Knapp (Lizzie), Brian Connors (File), David Hayes (Sheriff Thomas)
RELATIVELY SPEAKING by Alan Ayckbourn; Director, Skip Foster; Set, Richard R. Goodwin; Lighting, Derek Duarte; Costumes, Beaver Bauer. CAST: Christop Grove (Greg), Brenda Daly (Ginny), Charles Lanyer (Philip), Joyce Harris (Sheila)
ORPHANS by Lyle Kesslerl; Director, Skip Foster; Set, Vicki Smith; Lighting, Peter Maradudin; Costumes, Cassandra Carpenter. CAST: Peter Bradbury (Treat), David P. Whitehead (Phillip), Robert Darnell (Harold)
THE UNEXPECTED GUEST by Agatha Christie; Director, Timothy Near; Assistant Director, John McCluggage; Set/Costumes, Jeffrey Struckman; Lighting, Kurt Landisman; Dialect Coach, Will Leskin. CAST: David Nathan Schwartz (Richard Warwick/Sgt. Cadwallader), Donna Snow (Laura Warwick), Peter Webster (Michael Starkwedder), Adele Proom (Miss Bennett), Sean O'Brien (Jan Warwick), Megan Cole (Mrs. Warwick), Ester Scott (Angell), Skip Foster (Insp. Thomas), James Carpenter (Julian Farrar)
SIZWE BANSI IS DEAD devised by Athol Fugard, John Kani & Winston Ntshona; Director, Claude Purdy; Set/Costumes, Michael Olich; Lighting, Joe Ragey. CAST: Kenny Leon (Styles/Buntu), Ron Canada (Sizwe Bansi)

Dennis Gaxiola Photos

171

SOUTH COAST REPERTORY

Costa Mesa, California
Twenty-third Season

Producing Artistic Director, David Emmes; Artistic Director, Martin Benson; Dramaturg, Jerry Patch; Literary Manager, John Glore; Literary Associate, Jose Cruz Gonzalez; Sets, Cliff Faulkner; Music, Diane King; Casting, Martha McFarland; Artistic Coordinator, Donna Ruzika; Business Director, Paula Tomei; Development, Bonnie Brittain Hall; Marketing, John Mouledoux; Assistant Marketing Director, Laura Newton; Press, Christopher Gross, Madeline Porter; Production Director, Paul Hammond; Production Manager, Ted Carlsson; Lighting, Rom Ruzika; Sound, Serge Ossorguine; Stage Managers, Julie Haber, Bonnie Lorenger, Andy Tighe, Kenneth Paige Jensen, Paul Lockwood, Mary Reardon; Props, Michael Mora, Heather McLarty, S. Huse; Technical Director, Jon Lagerquist; Scenic Artists, Abby Selman-Pait, Mary Zerbst; Costume Manager, Kim Holly; Wigs, Rick Geyer; Stage Directors, Jules Aaron, Steven D. Albrezzi, Martin Benson, David Chambers, David Emmes, John-David Keller, Paul Marcus, Marshall W. Mason, Jody McAuliffe, Norman Rene; Designers, Loy Arcenas, D. Martyn Bookwalter, Michael Devine, Cliff Faulkner, Ralph Funicello, Brian Gale, Susan Denison Geller, Cameron Harvey, Walker Hicklin, Paulie Jenkins, Peter Maradudin, Dwight Richard Odle, Donna Ruzika, Tom Ruzika, Charles Tomlinson, Shigeru Yaji
COMPANY: Robert Almodovar, Mark Arnott, Ron Boussom, Carlease Burke, Michael Canavan, Mark Capri, Richard Doyle, John Ellington, Roberta Farkas, Lynnda Ferguson, Jennifer Flackett, Marilyn Fox, Patricia Fraser, Julie Fulton, I. M. Hobson, Ben Halley Jr., Frank Hamilton, Thomas Harrison, David Haskell, Richard Hoyt-Miller, Jane A. Johnston, Tyrone Granderson Jones, John-David Keller, Sally Kemp, Daniel Kern, Art Koustik, Hal Landon Jr., Charles Lanyer, Darrell Larson, Anni Long, Paul Lovely, Martha McFarland, Mary Anne McGarry, J. Steven Markus, Nan Martin, Ron Michaelson, Armando Molina, Adriene Morgan, Marnie Mosiman, Peter Motson, Mark Murphey, Caitlin O'Heaney, Jennifer Parsons, Angela Paton, Joel Polis, Ford Rainey, Teri Ralston, Bryan Rasmussen, Ray Reinhardt, Dennis Robertson, Howard Shangraw, Joe Spano, Joan Stuart-Morris, Harold Surratt, Sarah Tattersall, Don Took, K. T. Vogt, Laurie Walters, Eva Wilder, Howard Witt, Robert Yacko, Lisa Zane
PRODUCTIONS: *Misalliance* by George Bernard Shaw, *Glengarry Glen Ross* by David Mamet, *A Christmas Carol* by Charles Dickens/Adapted by Jerry Patch, *Aunt Dan and Lemon* by Wallace Shawn, *The School for Scandal* by Richard Brinsley Sheridan, *Benefactors* by Michael Frayn, *Marry Me a Little* with Music by Stephen Sondheim/Concept and developed by Craig Lucas & Norman Rene. Young Conservatory Players: *Tom Sawyer*, *Folk Tales From Far Away Places*, *Charlotte's Web*
PREMIERES: *Prelude to a Kiss* by Craig Lucas (World Premiere), *Golden Girls* by Louise Page (American Premiere), *Haut Gout* by Allan Havis (West Coast Premiere), *V & V Only* by Jim Leonard Jr. (World Premiere), *Dog Logic* by Thomas Strelich (World Premiere)

Ron Stone Photos

**Dick Boccelli, Brian Tarantina, Allan Arbus
in "V & V Only"**

**Top Left: Darrell Larson, Joel Polis, Julie
Fulton, Angela Paton in "Dog Logic"**

ROUND HOUSE THEATRE

Silver Spring, Maryland
Tenth Season

Managing Director, Linda Yost; Artistic Director, Jerry Whiddon; Technical Director/Designer, Jane William Flank; Assistant Technical Director/Designer, Joseph B. Musumeci, Jr.; Costumes, Rosemary Pardee Holz, Marsha M. LeBoeuf; Props, Kathleen Wolfrey; Production Stage Manager, Jana Llynn; Marketing Director, Geri Olson; Sound, Neil McFadden, Lyle Yaeger; Tour Director, Tony Elliott
RESIDENT COMPANY: Christopher Hurt, Steven LeBlanc, Jerry Whiddon, Kathy Yarman, Mary Jo AbiNader, Kathryn Chase Bryer, Brian Davis, Tony Elliot, Michael Frith, Jeffrey Wright
GUESTS ARTISTS: Directors, Gillian Drake, Susann Brinkley, Jeffrey B. Davis, Max Mayer; Sets, Richard H. Young; Lighting, Daniel MacLean Wagner; Sound, Ric Cooper; Actors, Janet Bryant, Debra Cole, Mark Diekmann, Jane Beard, John Michael Higgins, David Ingram, Ernie Meier, Nick Olcott, Mitchell Patrick, Gregory Procaccino, Gerald Payne, Carolyn Swift, Lawrence Redmond, Harry A. Winter, Jason Adams, Jorger Luis Abreu, Jorge Oliver, Ralph Marrero, Jane Ridley, Petrina Huston
PRODUCTIONS: *Rum and Coke* by Keith Reddin, *The Fairy Garden* and *Self Torture & Strenuous Exercise* by Harry Kondoleon, *Zastrozzi* by George F. Walker, *A Hatful of Rain* by Michael V. Gazzo, *On the Verge* by Eric Overmyer

Geri Olson Photos

**John Michael Higgins, Debra Cole
in "Self Torture and Strenuous Exercise"**

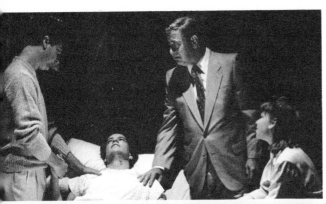

STUDIO ARENA THEATRE

Buffalo, New York
Twenty-third Season

Artistic Director, David Frank; Managing Director, Raymond Bonnard; Associate Director/Dramaturg, Kathryn Long; Development, Anne E. Hayes; Marketing, Dave Mancuso; Press, Blossom Cohan; Production Manager, Randy Engels; Assistant Production Manager, Christine Michael; Costumiere, Mary Ann Powell; Associate Costumiere, Anne E. Gorman; Wardrobe, Anne Langdon; Sound, Rick Menke; Props, Patricia D. Haines, J. Roo Huigen; Technical Director, Colin Stewart; Scenic Artist, Elizabeth L. Linn; Production Stage Managers, Glenn Bruner, Barbara Ann O'Leary

PRODUCTIONS & CASTS

THE NORMAL HEART by Larry Kramer; Director, Donald Driver; Sets, Philipp Jung; Costumes, Mary Ann Powell; Lighting, Heather Carson. CAST: Jeffrey Bingham, David Bottrell, Robertson Dean, Rosemary De Angelis, John Morgan Evans, Frank Hankey, Guy Stroman, Basil Wallace, Neil Zevnik.
TWELFTH NIGHT by William Shakespeare; Director, David Frank; Sets, Joseph A. Varga; Costumes, Robert Morgan; Lighting, Curt Osterman. CAST: Lino Ayala, Brian Coatsworth, David Cromwell, Robert Curtis-Brown, David Fendrick, James K. Fulater, Sean Haberle, Thomas Ikeda, John Kiouses, Barry MacGregor, Dana Mills, Nell Mohn, Joyce O'Conner, William Rauch, Stephanie Roth, John Seidman, Pamela Tucker-White.
STEPPING OUT by Richard Harris; Director, Carl Schurr; Choreographer, Pamela Sousa; Arrangements, Peter Howard; Sets, Michael Miller; Costumes, Maria Mannero; Lighting, Rachel Budin. CAST: Fran Barnes (Mrs. Fraser), Jan Buttram (Mavis), Susan Duvall (Sylvia), Venida Evans (Rose), Jayne Houdyshell (Maxine), Bill Kux (Geoffrey), Susanne Marley (Vera), Leslie Nipkow (Lynne), Mary Ed Porter (Dorothy), Donna Snow (Andy).
BENEFACTORS by Michael Frayn; Director, Kathryn Long; Sets, Loy Arcenas; Costumes, Bill Walker; Lighting, Pat Collins. CAST: Laura Esterman, Dan Hamilton, John Hutton, Cynthia Mace.
TINTYPES by Mary Kyte, Mel Marvin & Gary Pearle; Director/Choreographer, Michael Shawn; Music Director, Donald Rebic; Set/Lighting, Tom Hennes; Costumes, Mary Ann Powell. CAST: Jonathan Brody, Audrey Lavine, T. J. Meyers, Tonia Rowe, Cynthia Sophiea.
ISN'T IT ROMANTIC by Wendy Wasserstein; Director, Kathryn Long; Sets, Victor Becker; Costumes, Marcy Grace Froehlich; Lighting, Nancy Schertler. CAST: Judith Granite, Cynthia Lammel, Darrie Lawrence, Jeremy Lawrence, Bruce Moore, Stan Rubin, Bill Tatum, Melissa Weil.
HEDDA GABLER by Henrik Ibsen; Director, Rosemary Hay; Sets, Robert Morgan; Costumes, Mary Ann Powell; Lighting, Dennis Parichy. CAST: Christine Baranski, John Camera, Arlene Clement, Matthew Cowles, Virginia Doning, Jim Mezon, Juliet Pritner.

Jim Bush, K. C. Kratt Photos

Christine Baranski, John Camera, Jim Mezon
in "Hedda Gabler" Top: Robertson Dean, Frank
Hankey, Jeffrey Bingham, Rosemary DeAngeles
in "The Normal Heart"

STAGEWEST

Springfield, Massachusetts
Twenty-first Season

Artistic Director, Gregory Boyd; Managing Director, Marvin E. Weaver; Artistic Associate, Benita Hofstetter; Production Manager, Jeff Hill; Literary Manager, Catherine Mandel; Business Manager, Val Pori; Development, Pat Ford; Stage Managers, Craig Weindling, Sue Ruocco, Vera Williams, Bruce Resnik; Marketing, Catherine Oliver; Press, Cynthia Fuhrman, Deborah Woodin; Stage Directors, Eric Hill, Marcia Milgrom Dodge, Tadashi Suzuki; Sets, Peter David Gould, Rick Dennis, Sharon Perlmutter, Michael Banner; Costumes, Frances Blau, V. Jane Suttell; Lighting, Robert Jared, Arden Fingerhut, Clifford E. Berek; Sound, David A. Strang; Music Directors, Uel Wade, Michael O. Flaherty; Choreography, Laurie Odell
RESIDENT COMPANY: David Asher, Laurence Ballard, Jeffrey Bihr, Peter Birkenhead, Tom Blair, Mark Corkins, Anthony Dodge, Jossie deGuzman, Jim DeVita, Corey Hansen, Tom Hewitt, Eric Hill, Paul Kandel, Ellen Lauren, Matthew A. Loney, Larry G. Malvern, Nancy Meyer, Nita Moore, Thomas Nahrwold, Anne Newhall, Michael O'Flaherty, Michael Pace, John Pielmeier, Ben Scranton, Noble Shropshire, Charles Tachovsky, Charles Tuthill, Shelly Williams, John Garson Gilbert, Joseph S. Gullitti, Jim Nutter, Dee Pelletier, Naama Potok, Kristin Wold
PRODUCTIONS: *Dracula: A Musical Nightmare* by Douglas Johnson & John Aschenbrenner *The Odd Couple* by Neil Simon, *Billy Bishop Goes to War* by John Gray & Eric Peterson, *Sister Mary Ignatius Explains It All For You & The Actor's Nightmare* by Christopher Durang, *The Real Thing* by Tom Stoppard, *The Tale of Lear* adapted by Tadashi Suzuki, *Visions of an Ancient Dreamer* adapted from Euripides' *"Helen & Iphigenia in Tauris"*
PREMIERES: *The Tale of Lear* adapted by Tadashi Suzuki

Richard Feldman & Mark Avery Photos

Tom Blair, David Asher, Tom Hewitt, Jeffrey
Bihr, Charles Tuthill in "The Tale of Lear"

SYRACUSE STAGE

Syracuse, New York
Fifteenth Season

Producing Artistic Director, Arthur Storch; Managing Director, James A. Clark; Business Manager, Diana Coles; Development, Shirley Lockwood; Marketing, Barbara Beckos; Press, Lynn Z. Schaible; Production Manager, Kerro Knox; Assistant Production Manager, Terri Hudson; Stage Managers, Don Buschmann, Barbara Beeching; Technical Director, William S. Tiesi; Assistant Technical Director, Tom Flattery; Company Manager, Peter Sandwell

PRODUCTIONS & CASTS

STEPPING OUT by Richard Harris; Director, Carl Schurr; Choreographer, Pamela Sousa; Set, Michael Miller; Costumes, Maria Marrero; Lighting, Rachel Budin; Arrangements, Peter Howard. CAST: Jan Buttram (Mavis), Fran Barnes (Mrs. Fraser), Leslie Nipkow (Lynne), Mary Ed Porter (Dorothy), Jayne Houdyshell (Maxine), Donna Snow (Andy), Bill Kux (Geoffrey), Susan Duvall (Sylvia), Venida Evans (Rose), Susanne Marley (Vera)
FUGUE by Leonora Thuna; Director, Arthur Storch; Set, David Potts; Costumes, Maria Marrero; Lighting, Marc B. Weiss; Music/Sound, Scott David Sanders. CAST: Barbara Barrie (Mary), Annie Murray (Zelda), George Murdock (Dr. John Oleander), Tony Plana (Dr. Danny Lucchesi), Tresa Hughes (Mother), Alan Pottinger (Noel), Donna Haley (Liz Kruger), Nicole Caubisens (Tammy)
THE MISER by Moliere; Adaptation, Miles Malleson; Director, John Going; Set/Costumes, William Schroder; Lighting, F. Mitchell Dana; Sound, Steven Rydberg; Movement, Anne Rhodes. CAST: Kathleen Baum/Whitney Webster (Tapestries), Kymberly Kalil (L'Avrice), Alan Brasington (Harpagon), Sal Mistretta (LaFleche), Lisbeth Bartlett (Elise), Peter Webster (Valere), Jason Graae (Cleante), Gerard E. Moses (Maitre Simon), Patricia Gage (Frosine), Peter Bartlett (Maitre Jacques), Daphne Platt (Dame Claude), Eric Radford Weiss (La Merlouche), Peter Rofe (Brindavoine/Old Pedro), Mary-Louise Parker (Mariane), James Hilbrandt (Le Commissaire), Stephen Spinella (Clerk), Derek Murcott (Seigneur Anselme)
7 BY BECKETT; Director, Arthur Storch; Set, Victor A. Becker; Costumes, Nanzi Adzima; Lighting, Natasha Katz; Music, Chris Binaxas, Scott David Sanders; Sound, Scott David Sanders. CAST: Stephen Spinella, Myra Carter, Peter Bartlett, Chris Binaxas
FRANKIE AND JOHNNY IN THE CLAIR DE LUNE by Terrence McNally; Director, Charles Karchmer; Set, James Noone; Costumes, Joseph R. McFate; Lighting, Sandra Schilling; Sound, Scott David Sanders. CAST: Jacqueline Knapp (Frankie), John Spence (Johnny)

Lawrence Mason, Jr. Photos

Jacqueline Knapp, John Spencer in "Frankie and Johnny...." Top: Donna Haley, Barbara Barrie, Tony Plana in "Fugue"

TACOMA ACTORS GUILD

Tacoma, Washington

Artistic Director, William Becvar; Managing Director, Kate Haas; Guest Directors, Robert Robinson, Rick Tutor, Bruce K. Sevy, BJ Douglas; Director, William Becvar; Stage Managers, Hal Meng, Betty Jean Williamson; Sets, Jerry Hooker, Peggy McDonald, Rob Murphy, Judith Cullen; Costumes, Anne Thaxter Watson, Frances Kenny, Wendela K. Jones; Lighting, Richard Devin, James Verdery, Rob Murphy, J. Patrick Elmer; Sound, Chuck Hatcher; Technical Director, Rob Murphy; Assistant Technical Director/Props, Judith Cullen; Costume Supervisor, Wendela K. Jones; Marketing/Press, Connie Lehmen; Administrative Director, Nancy Hoadly; Operations, T. Sue Boyczuk

PRODUCTIONS & CASTS

AMADEUS by Peter Shaffer; with Jim Dean, Tom Hammond, David H. MacIntyre, Robert Martin, McKenna Michals, Tony Pasqualini, Rod Pilloud, Kelly J. Ray, Daniel Renner, Juris Skujins, Kamella Tate, Rocco Dal Vera, Marlene Walker, Keith Wilber
THE BELLE OF AMHERST by William Luce; with Priscilla Hake Lauris
COLE with Words & Music by Cole Porter; Devised by Benny Green, Alan Strachan; Musical Director, Rose This; Choreographer, Raymond Houle; with Mark Anders, Karen Kay Cody, Richard Farrell, Joanne Klein, Priscilla Hake Lauris, Jan Maxwell, Steven Zediker
TRUE WEST by Sam Shepard; with Mark Drusch, Anne Ludlum, Ray Mikesh, David Pichette
HEDDA GABLER by Henrik Ibsen; with Pamela Abas-Ross, Frank Corrado, Mark Drusch, Gregg Loughridge, Anne Ludlum, Rikki Ricard, Cheri Sorenson
SAME TIME, NEXT YEAR by Bernard Slade; with Kim Bennett, Sheree Galpert

Fred Andrews Photos

Cheri Sorenson, Mark Drusch
in "Hedda Gabler"

TENNESSEE REPERTORY THEATRE

Nashville, Tennessee

Executive Director, Mac Pirkle; Managing Director, Brian Laczko; Marketing/Press, Arch Bishop; Production Manager, Jennifer Orth; Technical Director, Sam Craig

PRODUCTIONS & CASTS

HAMLET with Hudson B. Burroughs (Ghost/Player King/Osric), Timothy Casey (Lord/1st Player/1st Clown), Fred Fehrmann (Marcellus/Player Queen/Messenger), Denice E. Hicks (Ophelia), Cliff Jewell (Laertes/Player), Don Jones (Hamlet), Jonathan A. Lutz (Claudius), Tim A. Powell (Francisco/Rosencrantz/Priest), Hugh Sinclair (Bernardo/Guildenstern/2nd Clown), Andrew R. Stahl (Horatio), Ruth K. Sweet (Gertrude), Ken Dale Thompson (Polonius)
CAMELOT with Robert Green Benson (Tom), Jim Busby (Bliant), Kevin Coffey (Hunter/Guilliam), Jim Conrad (Castor/Farmer), Tommy Cresswell (Clarius/Courier), Vickie Wonders Foltz (Eldwyn), Rita Frizzell (Polly/Lady Teazle), Katherine Golter (Maid/Lady), Nan Gurley (Morgan Le Fey/Druid), Lisa Hayes (Lady/Page), Timoth E. Holder (Touphue), Marcia Holt Eubanks (Nurse), Gayle Humphrey (Lady Sybil), W. Dennis Hunt (Merlyn/Pellinore), Andrea Liebert (Elizabeth/Lady Elaine), Jeff Kidwell (Sir Sagramore), Joseph R. Mahowald (Lancelot), Elizabeth Moses (Lady Anne), Myke Mueller (Arthur), Shelean Newman (Nimue/Lady Catherine), Richard Patier (Squire Dap), Brian Russell (Mordred), Ricky Russell (Sir Dinadan), Kelly Sanderbeck (Guenevere), Barry Scott (Sir Lionel)
TO KILL A MOCKINGBIRD with Demetria Bailey (Helen Robinson), Jim Conrad (Nathan Radley), Patrick W. Day (Jem), Debi Derryberry (Scout), Michael Edwards (Heck Tate), Mary Jane Harvill (Jean Louise Finch), Timothy E. Holder (Arthur "Boo" Radley), W. Dennis Hunt (Atticus), Jezrael Jeffries (Mayella Ewell), Barbara E. Jones (Stephanie Crawford), Jane Jones (Maudie Atkinson), Jon Lutz (Judge Taylor), Joseph R. Mahowald (Mr. Gilmer), Myke R. Mueller (Bob Ewell), Barry Scott (Tom Robinson), Ken Dale Thompson (Walter Cunningham), Michael Torrey (Rev. Sikes), Peter Turner (Dill), Jackie Welch (Calpurnia), Sally Welch (Mrs. Dubose)
JESUS CHRIST SUPERSTAR with Bruce Arntson (Herod), Richard Terry Harmon (Annas), Brian K. Hull, Danny Jennings (Priests), Myke R. Mueller (Pilate), Louis Padilla (Jesus), Eric Russell (Simon), Barry Scott (Caiaphas), Pam Tillis (Mary Magdalene), Jackie Welch (Priest/Judith), Ned Wimmer (Peter), Jim Busby (Bartholomew), Kevin Coffey (Andrew), Jim Conrad (Philip), Katherine Cox (Suzanna), Marcia Holt Eubanks (Elizabeth), Vickie Wonders Foltz (Salome), Rita Frizzell (Ruth), Darwin Guenther (Thaddeus), Lisa Hayes (Tabbatha), Denice Hicks (Soul Girl/Leah), Timothy E. Holder (John), Andrea Liebert (Anna), Cindi McCabe (Soul Girl/Rebecca), Shelean Newman (Soul Girl/Rachel), Richard Patier (Thomas), Ken "Scat" Springs (James the Lesser), Michael Torrey (James), Peter Turner (Matthew)

Louis Padilla (top), Pam Tillis
in "Jesus Christ Superstar"

THEATRE VIRGINIA

Richmond, Virginia

Producing Director, Terry Burgler; Head of Design, Charles Caldwell; Stage Manager, Doug Flinchum; Stage Manager/Dramaturg, Bo Wilson; Lighting, Terry Cermak; Designers, David Crank, Ron Keller, Jo Varga, Scott Pickney; Guest Directors, Bill Gregg, Woody King; Musical Directors, Manford Abrahamson, Steve Liebman

PRODUCTIONS & CASTS

NOISES OFF! with Anne Sheldon (Dotty Otley), David Snizek (Lloyd Dallas), John Curless (Garry Lejeune), Katherine Romaine (Brooke Ashton), Carol Hanpeter (Poppy Norton-Taylor), Michael Connolly (Frederick Fellowes), Kate Preston (Belinda Blair), Bobby Smith (Tim Allgood), John Milligan (Selsdon Mowbray), Rick Brandt (Rick's Understudy)
TERRA NOVA with Neil Hunt (Scott), Lennard DeCarl (Amundsen), Jordan Baker (Kathleen), Adrian Williams (Bowers), Edward James Hyland (Oates), Ray Collins (Wilson), John Hickok (Evans)
MY FAIR LADY with Allison Briner (Eliza Doolittle), Barry Boys (Henry Higgins), Richard Buck (Col. Pickering), Bobby Smith (Freddy Eynsford-Hill), Ed Sala (Alfred P. Doolittle), Marjorie Carroll (Mrs. Pearce), Joyce Worsley (Mrs. Higgins), Fiona Hale (Mrs. Eynsford-Hill), Andy Umberger (Harry), Bev Appleton (Jamie), Peggy Bayer, Jan Guarinho, Robert C. Joyce, Fernando Rivandeneira, Adrian Williams, Carl LeMon, Pete Herber, Carl Lemon, Peggy Bayer, Emily Skinner, Robert Throckmorton, Jan Guarino, Amy Perdue, Bev Appleton, Pete Heber, Bobby Smith, K. Strong, Dawn A. Westbrooke
BEYOND THE FRINGE with Terry Burgler, John Curless, David Hall, Steve Liebman
'NIGHT MOTHER with Sally Drayer, Anne Sheldon; Nadyne Cassandra, Marie Goodman Hunter
PUMP BOYS AND DINETTES (no cast list provided)
THE ROBBER BRIDEGROOM with Jason Edwards (Jamie Lockhart), Calvin Remsberg (Clemment Musgrove), Diane Pennington (Salome), Karyn Quackenbush (Rosamund), Trip Plymale (Little Harp), Daryl Clark Phillips (Big Harp), Ford Flannagan (Goat), Jan Guarino (Airie), K Strong (Raven), Kim Story, Rook Strong, Bo Wilson

Bo Wilson, Jan Guarino, Jason Edwards, Karyn
Quackenbush, Ford Flannagan, K Strong, Trip
Plymale in "The Robber Bridegroom"

Top: Nadyne Cassandra, Marie
Goodman-Hunter in " 'night, Mother"

175

Thurman Moss, Ben Roberts, Connie Coit
in "Safety" *(Suzanne O'Brien Photo)*

THEATRE THREE

Dallas, Texas
Twenty-sixth Season

Founding/Artistic Director, Norma Young; Executive Producer-Director, Jac Alder; Associate Producer, Charles Howard; Associate Director, Laurence O'Dwyer; Press, Gary Yawn; Assistant to Producer, Janice Weiss; Literary Manager, Sharon Bunn; Development Associate, Colleen R. Jennett; Administrative Assistant, Barbara Purdy; Lighting, Robert McVay; Production Manager, Cheryl Denson; Stage Manager, Terry Tittle Holman; Technical Director/Sound, Tristan Wilson; Costumier, Christopher Kovarik; Musical Director, Terry Dobson; Scenic Artist, Barbara Murrell; Marketing, Anne Groben-Taylor.

PRODUCTIONS & CASTS

A LUV MUSICAL based on the play by Murray Schisgal; Book, Jeffrey Sweet; Music, Howard Marren; Lyrics, Susan Birkenhead; Director, Laurence O'Dwyer; Musical Directors, Terry Dobson, Gary Mead; Set, Charles Howard; Costumes, Cheryl Denson; Assistant Director, Scott Bradford. CAST: Lynn Mathis, Connie Nelson, Jack Willis.
SAFETY by Patricia Griffith *(World Premiere)*; Director, Jac Alder; Set, Cheryl Denson; Costumes, Christopher Kovarik. CAST: Sharon Bunn, Connie Coit, Dorothy Deavers, Cheryl Denson, Mark Fickert, Thurman Moss, Ben Roberts.
BENEFACTORS by Michael Frayn; Director, Norma Young; Staging/Set, Charles Howard; Assistant Set Designer, Ken Wrobel; Costumes, Georgia Ford. CAST: Hugh Feagin, Jim McQueen, Connie Nelson, Victoria Wright.
LIGHT UP THE SKY by Moss Hart; Director, Laurence O'Dwyer; Set, Cheryl Denson; Lighting, Lee Dulaney; Costumes, Patty Greer McGarity; Wigs/Hair, Robert H. Weaber; Assistant to Director, Tim Burt. CAST: Jac Adler, Esther Benson, John Beaird, Sharon Bunn, Tim Burt, Charles Carroll, Georgia Clinton, David DeMattia, Bob Downs, Cynthia Hestand, Hugh Feagin, David Napper.
THE WALTZ OF THE TOREADORS by Jean Anouilh; Translation, Lucienne Hill; Director, Charles Howard; Set, Charles Howard; Costumes, Giulia de Tetris McDonald; Assistant Set Designer, Barbara Murrell; Music, Gary Mead; Wigs/Hair, Robert H. Weaber; Assistant to Director, Daniel Tamez. CAST: Laurence O'Dwyer, Norma Young, John Beaird, Sharon Bunn, Georgia Clinton, Edmund Coulter, Barbara Munter, Casandra Neckar, Ray Keith Pond, Jennifer Taylor, Cheryl Weaver.
PERSONALS with Book & Lyrics by David Crane, Seth Friedman, Marta Kauffman; Music, William K. Dreskin, Joel Phillip Friedman, Seth Friedman, Alan Menken, Stephen Schwartz, Michael Skloff; Director/Choreographer, Bruce R. Coleman; Musical Director, Gary Mead; Set, Jac Alder; Costumes, Christopher Kovarik; Lighting, Robert J. Kruger. CAST: Bruce Allen, Peggy Billo, Scott Bradford, Amy Mills, Sara Patricia Rankin, Jeffrey Ricketts.
VOICES UNSILENCED, A Festival of Minority Playwrights and Performers; Moderator, Charles Gordone: *Birds* by Lisa Loomer, *The Fishermen* by Dianne Houston, *The Boiler Room* by Reuben Gonzales, *Brown Wilk and Magenta Sunsets* by P. J. Gibson; Directors, Janice Weiss, Charles Howard, Patrick Kelly, Katherine Owens; Festival Coordinator, Janice Weiss; Staff, Laurence O'Dwyer, Sharon Bunn, Edmund Coulter, Dwain Fail, Cecilia Flores, Leslie Evans Leach, Thurman Moss, Susan Steadmann. CASTS: Rhonda Boutte, Cora Cardona, Chris Carlos, Tony de la Cruz, Dolores Godinez, Rebecca Gross, Kevin Hayes, Natalie King, Daniel Saldana, Lisa Lee Schmidt, Octavio Solis, Michael Cal Stewart, Daniel Tamez, Tony Vinto, Cheryle Washington, Tou Uvonna Whittington.
CLAP YO' HANDS: HOMAGE TO GEORGE AND IRA GERSHWIN devised by Jac Alder; Arrangements, Jac Alder, Terry Dobson; Gowns, Victor Costa; Set, Cheryl Denson. CAST: Jac Alder, Connie Coit, Terry Dobson, Dick Dufour, Richard Hobson, Shirley McFatter, Connie Nelson.
THE GRIMM MAIAN PLAYERS: *Hansel and Gretel* written & directed by Laurence O'Dwyer; Lighting, Jimmy Mullen; Set/Props, Rik Tankersley; Costumes, Bryce Jenson; Sound, Kyle McClaran; with Kerrie Peterson, James Palmer, Russ Johnson, Debra Crohn, Kathy Hiller, Daniel Tamez, Bryce Jenson, Jimmy Mullen. *Snow White and Rose Red* adapted by Laurence O'Dwyer; Director, Thurman Moss; Assistant to Director, Daniel Tamez; with Regis Allison, Dianne Brown, Deborah Crohn, Dolores Godinez, R. Allan Gorton, Terry Londeree, Cindee Mayfield, Dusty O'Donnell, Jeffrey Ricketts, Beth Shorey, Daniel Tamez. *Rapunzel and the Witch* adapted & directed by Laurence O'Dwyer; Costumes/Props, Rik Tankersley; Lighting, Jimmy Mullen; Set, Jac Alder; Stage Managers, Andrew Boyer, Daniel Tamez; with Judy French Mahon, Lisa Schmidt, Tim Burt, Laura Wells, Andrew Boyer, Grace McDonald, Susan Myers, Dianne Brown, Daniel Tamez.

Susan Kandell Photos

Top Left: Hugh Feagin, Jim McQueen, Victoria
Wright, Connie Nelson in "Benefactors" Below:
Sharon Bunn, Connie Coit in "Safety"

TRINITY REPERTORY COMPANY

Providence, Rhode Island
July 24, 1987–June 5, 1988
Twenty-fourth Season

Artistic Director, Adrian Hall; Managing Director, E. Timothy Langan; Assistant to Artistic Director, Marion Simon; Musical Director, Richard Cumming; Sets, Eugene Lee, Robert Soule; Lighting, John F. Custer; Costumes, William Lane; Stage Directors, Edward Payson Call, Peter Gerety, Tony Giordano, Richard Jenkins, Philip Minor, William Partlan, David Wheeler; Stage Managers, Christopher Brougham, Wendy Cox, Matthew T. Mundinger.

COMPANY: Katherine Argo, Akin Babatunde, Barbara Blossom, Alan Brown, Vince Ceglie, William Christian, Michael Cobb, Timothy Crowe, William Damkoehler, Margot Dionne, Sheryl Dodd, Janice Duclos, Richard Ferrone, Michael Genet, Peter Gerety, Mary Francina Golden, Ann Hamilton, Ed Hall, Pitt Harding, Lawrence James, Keith Jochim, David C. Jones, Richard Kavanaugh, David Kennet, Richard Kneeland, Geraldine Librandi, Becca Lish, Howard London, Brian McEleney, Patricia McGuire, Derek Meader, Barbara Meek, Andrew Mutnick, Barbara Orson, Ricardo Pitts-Wiley, Anne Scurria, Ed Shea, David PB Stephens, Cynthia Strickland, Frederick Sullivan Jr., Jennifer Van Dyck, Daniel Von Bargen, Rose Weaver, Laura Ann Worthen.

PRODUCTIONS: *The Lady from Maxim's* by Georges Feydeau, translation by John Mortimer; *Mourning Becomes Electra* by Eugene O'Neill; *The House of Blue Leaves* by John Guare; *A Christmas Carol* by Adrian Hall & Richard Cumming, from the story by Charles Dickens; *Ma Rainey's Black Bottom* by August Wilson; *The Man Who Came to Dinner* by Moss Hart & George S. Kaufman; *Aunt Dan and Lemon* by Wallace Shawn; *Camino Real* by Tennessee Williams; *Mensch Meier* by Franz Xaver Kroetz, translation by Roger Downey; *Sherlock's Last Case* by Charles Marowitz.

Mark Morelli Photos

Left: Richard Kneeland, Peter Gerety, Richard Ferrone in "The Man Who Came to Dinner" Above: Peter Gerety as Kilroy in "Camino Real"

Timothy Crowe, Peter Gerety in "Sherlock's Last Case"

Geraldine Librandi, Patricia McGuire, Barbara Orson in "Aunt Dan and Lemon"

VIRGINIA STAGE COMPANY

Norfolk, Virginia
Ninth Season

Artistic Director, Charles Towers; Managing Director, Dan J. Martin; Associate Artistic Director, Christopher Hanna; General Manager, Caroline F. Turner; Development, Lexi Caswell; Marketing, Claudia Keenan; Company Manager, Marge Prendergast; Production Manager, Dan Sedgwick; Stage Manager, Candace LoFrumento; Technical Director, Christopher Fretts; Props, Freda Grim; Costumes, Candice Cain

PRODUCTIONS & CASTS

AH, WILDERNESS! by Eugene O'Neill; Director, Christopher Hanna; Sets, John Doepp; Lighting, Spencer Mosse; Costumes, Candice Cain; Sound, Dirk Kuyk; with Helen-Jean Arthur, David Bridgewater, Stephen Lawrence Brown, Edward Bryce, Christopher Cull, Laura Ruth Davis, Richard Elmore, W. Randolph Galvin, Kurt M. Halow, Dorrie Joiner, Jason McCall, Sharon Round, Karen Sellon, Jennifer Sternberg, T. A. Taylor

GLENGARRY GLEN ROSS by David Mamet; Director, Charles Towers; Sets, Michael Miller; Lighting, Jim Sale; with Carl Don, Richard Elmore, Bill Geisslinger, Geoff Pierson, Roger Serbagi, T. A. Taylor, Mitchell Thomas

SALT-WATER MOON by David French; Director, Charles Towers; Sets, George Hillow; Lighting, Spencer Mosse; Sound, June Cooper; with Dante Di Loreto, Rebecca Ellens

JACQUES BREL IS ALIVE & WELL & LIVING IN PARIS conceived by Mort Shuman & Eric Blau; Music, Jacques Brel; Director, Greogry S. Hurst; Sets, Atkin Pace; Lighting, David Noling; Costumes, Marianne Faust; Musical Director, Mark Goodman; with Robert Alton, Meghan Duffy, Heidi Stallings, Russ Thacker

PLAY YOURSELF by Harry Kondoleon *(World Premiere)*; Director, Christopher Hanna; Lighting, Don Holder; with Alan Brooks, Jane Cecil, Marjorie Lovett, Rose Stockton

MA RAINEY'S BLACK BOTTOM by August Wilson; Director, Israel Hicks; Sets/Costumes, Lawrence Casey; Lighting, Kirk Bookman; Musical Director, Dwight Andrews; with Ellia English, Vincent J. Godfrey, George L. Hasenstab, Lawrence James, Jack Stubblefield Johnson, David Kennett, Norman Matlock, Kevin Ramsey, Roger Robinson, Sheyvonne Wright

Mark Atkinson Photos

Top: Geoff Pierson, Roger Serbagi
in "Glengarry Glen Ross"

Marjorie Lovett, Rose Stockton (and above
with Jane Cecil) in "Play Yourself"

WALNUT STREET THEATRE

Philadelphia, Pennsylvania

Executive Director, Bernard Havard; Associate Director, Charlie Hensley; General Manager, Mary Bensel; Production Manager, Al Franklin; Marketing, Robin Wray; Press, Elizabeth Sanchez-Franklin, David Eric Rosenberg; Development, Donald U. Smith; Technical Director, Anthony Cywinski; Scenic Artist, Melinda B. Oblinger; Costume Manager, Cyndi Orr; Props, Judi K. Guaralnick; Stage Managers, Frank Anzalone, Adrienne Neye, Kathryn Bauer, Mary Ellen Ford, Leora Marion, Carla Friedman

NOISES OFF by Michael Frayn; Director, Donald Ewer; Set, Richard Gould; Lighting, Marcia Madeira. CAST: Mark Capri, Donald Ewer, Celine Havard, Charlie Hensley, Gwendolyn Lewis, Millicent Martin, Erika Peterson, Dudley Swetland, Douglas Wing

FUNNY GIRL with Music by Jule Styne; Lyrics, Bob Merrill; Book, Isobel Lennart; Director, Sue Lawless; Musical Director, Elman Anderson; Choreographer, Sam Viverito; Set, Daniel Ettinger; Costumes, Barbara Forbes; Lighting, Marcia Madeira. CAST: Lynn Albright, Mary Ellen Ashley, Jack Brenton, Hank deLuca, Andy Eddins, Allen Fitzpatrick, Doug Friedman, Steve Goodwillie, Andrea Green, Fanni Green, Anne Gunderson, Rosalind Harris, James Horvath, Reed Jones, Joe Joyce, Diana L. Losk, Julie Ostling, Patrick Rogers, Dan Schiff, Freyda Thomas, Karen Tomzak, Fiddle Viracola, Brian Worley, Teressa Wylie

CAT ON A HOT TIN ROOF by Tennessee Williams; Director, Fred Chappell; Set Gerry Leahy; Costumes, Linda Sarver; Lighting, Marcia Madeira. CAST: Humbert Allen Astredo, Jonathan Banta, Elizabeth Flax, Edward Gavin, Evan Greenstein, Al Hamacher, Jona Harvey, Jana Robbins, Candice Maria Samero, Christi Anne Samero, Mary Nell Santacroce, John Wesley Shipp, Doublas Wing

DUSKY SALLY by Granville Burgess; Director, Sheldon Epps; Set, James Leonard Joy; Costumes, Lee J. Austin III; Lighting, Marcia Madeira. CAST: L. Peter Callender, Allen Fitzpatrick, Leilani Jones, Marilyn McIntyre, Joel Swetow, Tom Tammi

MIKE with Book by Thomas Meehan; Music, Mitch Leigh; Lyrics, Lee Adams: *(World Premiere);* Director, Sue Lawless; Set, Kenneth Foy; Costumes, Waldo Angelo; Lighting, Ken Billington; Production Supervisor, Martin Charnin. CAST: Michael Lembeck, Loni Ackerman, Leslie Easterbrook, Robert Morse, Bob Amaral, William Barker, Nora Cherfy, Colleen Dunn, David Engel, Terry Eno, Alice Evans, Robert Fitch, Tom Flagg, Richard Frisch, Ellen Grace, Patrick Hamilton, Bill Hastings, K. Craig Innes, Eddie Korbich, Alex Kramarevsky, Greg Miles, Sal Mistretta, Polly O'Malley, K. K. Preece, Mimi Quillin, John Russell, Sam Stoneburner, Dan Strickler, Susan Trainor

COTTON PATCH GOSPEL with Music & Lyrics by Harry Chapin; Book, Tom Key, Russell Treyz; Director, Andrew Lichtenberg; Set/Lighting, Anthony Cywinski; Costumes, Robert Bevenger. CAST: John S. Lionarons, Gordon Paddison, Peter Taney, Scott Wakefield, Gregory Linus Weiss

SINS OF THE FATHER by Lezley Steele; Director, Charlie Hensley; Costumes, Cyndi Orr; Lighting, Nina Chwast. CAST: Dana Bate, David McCann, Paul Mulder

AND WHERE SHE STOPS NOBODY KNOWS by Oliver Hailey; Director, Stuart Ross; Set, Alex Polner; Costumes, Kate Corbley; Lighting, Craig R. Ferraro. CAST: Marcia Mahon, Dan Strickler

A CUP OF CHANGE by Robert Perring; Director, Charlie Hensley; Set, Judi Gurainick; Costumes, Michael DiNenno; Lighting, Nina Chwast. CAST: Kathleen Claypool, Elizabeth Flax, Basia McCoy

T BONE 'N' WEASEL by Jon Klein; Director, Deborah Baer Quinn; Set, J. R. Gardner; Costumes, Cyndi Orr; Lighting, De Vida Jenkins. CAST: Steven McCloskey, Ronal Stepney, Douglas Wing

Gerry Goodstein, Kenneth Kaufman, Mimi Sullivan Photos

**Top Right: Dudley Swetland, Erika Petersen,
Mark Capri, Millicent Martin in "Noises Off"
Below: Tom Tammi, Leilani Jones in "Dusky Sally"**

**Robert Morse, Leslie Easterbrook, Michael Lembeck
in "Mike"**

Olympia Dukakis, Antony Ponzini
in "The Rose Tattoo"

Apollo Dukakis in "School for Wives"
Top Left: Ellen Foley, Karen Allen, Maria Cellario,
Amy Van Nostrand, Mia Dillon in "Beautiful Bodies"
Below: Sean Michael Rice, Haskell Anderson III,
Nathan Holland, Anthony Chisholm
in "Tracers"

THE WHOLE THEATRE

Montclair, New Jersey
Fifteenth Season

Producing Artistic Director, Olympia Dukakis; Associate Artistic Director, Apollo Dukakis; Associate Producing Director, David Edelman; Marketing/Press, Bonnie Kraman; Communications, Leigh Zona; Education, Remi Barclay Bosseau, Gerald Fierst; Stage Managers, Kathleen Cuneen, Tom Spital, Anne Marie Hobson, Kathy White; Casting, Dennis Bush

PRODUCTIONS & CASTS

BEAUTIFUL BODIES by Laura Cunningham *(World Premiere);* Director, Vivian Matalon; Set, Michael Miller; Costumes, Sam Fleming; Lighting, Richard Nelson. CAST: Karen Allen, Caroline Aaron, Maria Cellario, Mia Dillon, Ellen Foley, Amy Van Nostrand

AUTOBAHN by Adaptors Movement Theatre; Directors, Tony Brown, Kari Margolis. CAST: Ed Alletto, Erica Babod, Louisa Curtis, Stephan Geros, Jeannie Kranich, Beth Margolis, Joan Merwyn, Bob Modoff, Ben Wildrick

SCHOOL FOR WIVES by Moliere; Adaptation, Richard Wilbur; Director, Margaret Bard; Set, Lewis Folden; Costumes, Sam Fleming; Lighting, Rachel Budin. CAST: Andrew Clark, Apollo Dukakis, Jeff Dunston, Katherine Hiler, Jodie Lynne McClintock, Stefan Peters, Steven Weber, Howard Wesson, Alex Wipf

TRACERS conceived & directed by John DiFusco; Set, John Falabella; Costumes, David Navarro Velasquez; Lighting, Terry Wuthrich. CAST: David Adamson, Haskel V. Anderson III, Anthony Chisholm, John DiFusco, Nathan Holland, Sean Michael Rice, Ray Robertson, Jim Tracy

THE ROSE TATTOO by Tennessee Williams; Director, Apollo Dukakis; Set, Jack Chandler; Costumes, Donna Marie Larsen; Lighting, Phil Monat. CAST: Maggie Abeckerly, Yolanda Childress, Olga Druce, Olympia Dukakis, Venida Evans, James G. Macdonald, Alexi Mylonas, Lola Pashalinski, Anthony Ponzini, Christina Zorich

Barry Morgenstein, Michael Tighe Photos

YALE REPERTORY THEATRE

New Haven, Connecticut

Artistic Director, Lloyd Richards; Managing Director, Benjamin Mordecai; General Manager, Patricia Egan; Dramaturgs, Gitta Honegger, Barbara Davenport, Joel Schechter; Press/Marketing, Robert Wildman; Production Supervisor, Bronislaw J. Sammler; Stage Managers, Maureen F. Gibson, Adair Quinn, Jay Adler, Karen L. Carpenter, Mitchell Erickson, Alan Fox, Gwendolyn M. Gilliam, Anne Marie Hobson, John Handy, Robin Rumpf; Set Design Advisor, Ming Cho Lee; Costume Design Advisor, Jane Greenwood; Lighting Design Advisor, Jennifer Tipton; Speech Advisor, Barbara Somerville; Movement, Wesley Fata; Sets, Michael H. Yeargan; Costumes, Dunya Ramicova; Lighting, William B. Warfel; Scenic Artist Advisor, Kathy Dilkes; Musical Coordinator, Daniel Egan

SARCOPHAGUS by Vladimir Gubaryev *(American Premiere)*; Translation, Michael Glenny; Director, David Chambers; Set, Craig Clipper; Costumes, Teresa Snider-Stein. CAST: Bruce Altman, Sharon Brady, David Brisbin, Pearce Bunting, Yusef Bulos, Christopher Centrella, Gail Dartez, Ray Dooley, Clement Fowler, James Hurdle, David Little, Benjamin Lloyd, Jane Macfie, Tom McGowan, Stephen Mendillo, Betty Miller, Petty Pelzer, Frank Savino, April Shawhan, John Shepard, Steven Skybell

MELONS by Bernard Pomerance *(American Premiere)*; Director, Gitta Honegger; Set, Russell Scott Parkman; Lighting, Stephen Strawbridge. CAST: Madison Arnold, Jo Henderson, Earl Hindman, Kirk Jackson, Ken Jenkins, Tino Juarez, Joel Leffert, Peter Drew Marshall, Victoria Racimo, Gil E. Silverbird

THE PIANO LESSON by August Wilson *(World Premiere)*; Director, Lloyd Richards; Set, E. David Cosier, Jr.; Costumes, Constanza Romero; Lighting, Christopher Akerlind; Music/Musical Director, Dwight Andrews; Sound, J. Scott Servheen. CAST: Rocky Carroll, Starletta DuPois, Carl Gordon, Tommy Hollis, Samuel L. Jackson, Chenee Johnson, Lou Myers, Ylonda Powell, Sharon Washington

WINTERFEST 8: FOUR NEW PLAYS IN REPERTORY; *The My House Play* by Wendy MacLeod *(World Premiere)*; Director, Evan Yionoulis; Set/Costumes, George Denes Suhayda; Lighting, Tim Fricker; Sound, John C. Huntington III; with Doug Hutchinson, Mary Mara, Anne O'Sullivan, Cameron Smith, Phyllis Somerville, William Wise. *Chute Roosters* by Craig Volk *(World Premiere)*; Director, Donato J. D'Albis; Set/Costumes, Tamara Turchetta; Lighting, Ashley York Kennedy; Sound, Victoria Peterson; with Dan Butler, James R. Carroll, Mike Genovese, Earl Hindman, Kirk Jackson, Sharon Schlarth. *Neddy* by Jeffrey Hatcher *(World Premiere)*; Director, Dennis Scott; Set, James A. Schuette; Costumes, Russell Scott Parkman; Lighting, Sarah Lambert; with Ray Dooley, James Glossman, Walker Jones, Bruce Katzman, Kristine Nielsen, J. Smith-Cameron. *The Wall of Water* by Sherry Kramer *(World Premiere)*; Director, Margaret Booker; Set, David Birn; Costumes, Craig Clipper; Lighting, Scott Zielinski; with Terrence Caza, David Chandler, Laurie Kennedy, Caroline Lagerfelt, Tom McGowan, Aleta Mitchell, Debra Jo Rupp, John C. Vennema

THE MISER by Moliere; Translation, Miles Malleson; Director, Andrei Belgrader; Set, Anita C. Stewart; Costumes, Marina Draghici; Lighting, Mark London; Music, William Uttley. CAST: Pearce Bunting, Anne DeSalvo, Colette Kilroy, Benjamin Lloyd, Tom McGowan, Oliver Platt, Donald Plumley, Howard Samuelsohn, Richard Spore, Lewis J. Stadlen, Holley Stewart

LONG DAY'S JOURNEY INTO NIGHT by Eugene O'Neill; Director, Jose Quintero; Set, Ben Edwards; Costumes, Jane Greenwood; Lighting, Jennifer Tipton; Sound, David Budries. CAST: Colleen Dewhurst, Jane Macfie, Jason Robards, Campbell Scott, Jamey Sheridan

AH, WILDERNESS! by Eugene O'Neill; Director, Arvin Brown; Set, Michael H. Yeargan; Costumes, Jane Greenwood; Lighting, Jennifer Tipton; Sound, David Budries. CAST: William Cain, Colleen Dewhurst, Jennifer Dundas, Annie Golden, George Hearn, Jane Macfie, Jason Robards, Raphael Sbarge, Campbell Scott, Kyra Sedgwick, Jamey Sheridan, Steven Skybell, Nicholas Tamarkin, Elizabeth Wilson, William Wise

Gerry Goodstein Photos

Right lower center: Debra Jo Rupp, Caroline Lagerfelt, Laurie Kennedy in "The Wall of Water" Above: Benjamin Lloyd, Lewis J. Stadlen, Colette Kilroy in "The Miser" Top: Rocky Carroll, Starletta DuPois in "The Piano Lesson"

Colleen Dewhurst, Jason Robards in "Long Day's Journey into Night"

ANNUAL SHAKESPEARE FESTIVALS

Montgomery, Alabama
Third Season at Wynfield

Artistic Director, Martin L. Platt; Managing Director, Jim Volz; Artistic Associates, Lori Grifo, Edmond Williams; Artistic Sevices Assistant, Terry Lake; Dramaturg, Susan Willis; Directors, Diana Baffa-Brill, Stephen Hollis, William Partlan, Richard Russell Ramos, Edward Stern; Sets/Costumes David M. Crank; Sets/Lighting, Michael Stauffer; Costumes, Alan Armstrong, James B. Greco, Kristine Kearney; Lighting, Paul Ackerman, Judy Rasmuson, Karen S. Spahn; Sound, Daryl Bornstein; Composer/Director of Music Programs, James Conely; Composers, Philip Rosenberg, Dennis West; Music Director, Randy Foster; Fight Choreographer, David Harum; Choreographer, Don Steffy; Voice, Speech & Dialect Coach, Linda Gates; Casting, Jay Binder, Jack Bowdan; General Manager, Doug Perry; Marketing, Carol Ogus; Development, Barbara W. Larson; Special Projects, Joseph Cowperthwaite; Director, PAT/MFA, Wil York; Production Manager, Bill Gregg; Assistant Production Manager, Chuck Still; Stage Managers, Sara Lee Howell, Julie A. Richardson, Claire McGough; Assistant Stage Manager, Jane Mahler; Production Assistants, Adam Bates, Mark D. Leslie; Media Liaison, Kathy Dell

RESIDENT COMPANY: Elizabeth Aiello, Jack Aranson, Wendy Barrie-Wilson, Susan J. Blommaert, Kermit Brown, Robert Browning, James Carruthers, Evelyn Carol Case, Christopher Clavelli, J. Barrett Cooper, A. D. Cover, Jane Cronin, Kitty Crooks, T. Scott Cunningham, Arlette Dean, Dalton Russell Dearborn, Ray Dooley, Mark Douglas-Jones, Earle Edgerton, Patricia Fraser, Eddie L. Furs, Linda Gates, Cynthia Goodale, Michael Guido, David Harum, Todd Heughens, David B. Heuvelman II, Tad Ingram, Peggy Irons, Maria Jurjevich, Alan Kass, Greta Lambert, Betty Leighton, Ingrid Mac artney, Steven David Martin, Jodie Lynne McClintock, John Milligan, Alex Peabody, Matt Penn, David O. Petersen, John G. Preston, Anne Sperry, Guy Strobel, Greg Thornton, John Tillotson, Tamera Tweedy, Vicky Vee, Jack Waddell, Eric Ware, Terry Weber, Russ Wendt, Michael Wetmore, Arline Williams, Will York, Terence Zeeman

PRODUCTIONS: *Misalliance* by Bernard Shaw, *The Taming of the Shrew* by William Shakespeare, *The Royal Family* by George S. Kaufman and Edna Ferber, *The Tempest* by William Shakespeare, *Othello, The Moor of Venice* by William Shakespeare, *Hedda Gabler* by Henrik Ibsen, *Zelda* by William Luce, *Hayfever* by Sir Noel Coward, *Long Day' Journey Into Night* by Eugene O'Neill, *Little Shop of Horrors* by Howard Ashman and Alan Menken, *Wild Honey* by Anton Chekhov, *Painting Churches* by Tina Howe, *As You Like It* by William Shakespeare, *You Never Can Tell* by George Bernard Shaw, *Hamlet, Prince of Denmark* by William Shakespeare

Left: Ray Dooley as "Hamlet" Right: Jodie Lynn McClintock, Steven David Martin in "As You Like It"

FOLGER SHAKESPEARE THEATRE

Washington, D.C.
Eighteenth Season

Artistic Director, Michael Kahn; Managing Director, Mary Ann de Barbieri; Business Manager, Elizabeth Hamilon; Development, Juli Duke; Press/Marketing, Paula Rothenberg; Press, Chris Westberg; Educational Program Director, Stephen Welch; Production Manager, James Irwin; Costume Manager, Elizabeth Brilkowski; Technical Director, Robert A. Auchter; Props, Kimberley Lynne

PRODUCTIONS & CASTS

THE WITCH OF EDMONTON by Thomas Dekker, John Ford & William Rowley; Director, Barry Kyle; Set, Joel Fontaine; Costumes, Judith Dolan; Lighting, Nancy Schertler; Musical Directors, Scott Reiss, Tina Chancey; Fight Director, David Leong; Vocal Consultant, Barney Hammond; Choreographer, Roberta Gasbarre; Stage Manager, Catherine Carney Hart. CAST: Meredith Beck, Laura Brutsman, Edward Conery, Melissa Galagher, Leslie Geraci, Edward Gero, Philip Goodwin, Ralston Hill, Frank Lowe, Steve Mattila, Joel Miller, Wendell Pierce, Anthony Powell, Brian Reddy, George Riddle, Mary Lou Rosato, Derek D. Smith, Kim Staunton, Carolyn Surrick, James M. Zidar

ALL'S WELL THAT ENDS WELL by William Shakespeare; Director, Michael Kahn; Set, Russell Metheny; Lighting, James Irwin; Costumes, Martin Pakledinaz; Musical Consultant, Bruce Adolphe; Choreographer, Roberta Gasbarre; Vocal Consultant, Elizabeth Smith; Stage Manager, Richard Lundy. CAST: Emery Battis, Marlene Bryan, Lynn Chausow, Michael Donahue, Franchelle Stewart Dorn, T. J. Edwards, Rafael Ferrer, Edward Gero, Bill Grimmette, Francis Hodgins, Floyd King, Leah Maddrie, Brian Reddy, Matt Bradford Sullivan, Richard C. Thompson, Ted Van Griethuyson, Jeffrey Wright, Teresa Wright

MACBETH by William Shakespeare; Director, Michael Kahn; Set, Michael Yeargan; Costumes, Smaranda Branescu; Lighting, Stephen Strawbridge; Music, Robert Parris; Fight Director, David Leong; Movement, Roberta Gasbarre; Vocal Consultant, Elizabeth Smith; Stage Manager, Pat Cochran. CAST: Emery Battis, David Bridgewater, James C. Byrnes, Roberto Conte, Richad Dix, Michael Donahue, Franchelle Stewart Dorn, T. J. Edwards, Phebe Finn, Catherine Flye, Edward Gero, Philip Goodwin, Bill Grimmette, Francis Hodgins, Robert Jason, Floyd King, Rosemary Knower, Geoffrey Lower, Leah Maddrie, K. Lype O'Dell, Andrew Land Prosky, Jeffries Thaiss, Richard C. Thompson, James M. Zidar

THE MERCHANT OF VENICE by William Shakespeare; Director, Michael Langham; Set, Douglas Stein; Costumes, Susan Hirschfeld; Lighting, Nancy Schertler; Music, Stephen Douglas Burton; Vocal Consultant, Elizabeth Smith; Stage Manager, Richard Lundy. CAST: Brigitte Barnett, Emery Battis, Brian Bedford, Kevin Black, Lucy Brightman, Stan Brown, Bob Burns, Marcia Cross, Karen Eterovich, Michele Farr, Edward Gero, Philip Goodwin, Sally Groth, Francis Hodgins, J. C. Hoyt, Robert Jason, Sarah Kimball, Geoffrey Lower, Tim MacDonald, Kelly McGillis, Pedro Porro, Andrew Land Prosky, Jack Ryland, John Seidman, Michael M. Thompson, Richard C. Thompson, Susan Velasquez, Suzanne Wrench

Joan Marcus Photos

Philip Goodwin, Franchelle Stewart Dorn in "Macbeth"
Above: Teresa Wright, Lynn Chausow in "All's Well
That Ends Well"

HOUSTON SHAKESPEARE FESTIVAL

Houston, Texas
July 29–August 13, 1987

Producing Director; Director, Kate Pogue; Sets, Keith Belli; Costumes, Barbara Medlicott

PRODUCTIONS & CASTS

JULIUS CAESAR with Jim Bernhard (Cesar), James Black (Marcus Brutus), James Gale (Cassius), Rutherford Cravens (Brutus), Luisa Amaral-Smith (Portia), Malinda Bailey
THE TAMING OF THE SHREW with Jeff Bennett (Lucentio), Luisa Amaral-Smith (Katherina), Malinda Bailey (Bianca), Timothy Arrington (Gremio), James Gale (Hortensio), James Black (Petruchio), Rutherford Cravens (Grumio), Jim Bernhard (Baptista)

Jim Caldwell Photos

"The Taming of the Shrew" Top: "Julius Caesar"

NEW JERSEY SHAKESPEARE FESTIVAL

Madison, New Jersey

Artistic Director, Paul Barry; Producing Director, Ellen Barry; Production Stage Managers, Dale Kaufman, John Pietrowski; Stage Managers/Lighting, Terry Kaye, C. Renee Alexander; Sets, James A. Bazewicz, Mark Evancho, David Stern; Costumes, Mitchell Bloom, Kathleen P. Brown, Julie Abels Chevan, Heidi Hollmann, Nanalee Raphael-Schirmer; Musical Director, Deborah Martin; Choreographer, Raye Lankford; Master-at-Arms, John Pietrowsi; Production Assistant, Robin Davis; Scenic Design Assistant, Drew Martorella; Props, Robert Conte; Costume Assistants, Michel M. Disco, Vanessa R. Thorpe; General Manager, Laura Aden; Marketing, Elizabet K. Eichler; Assistant to Producing Director, Joanna Bache; Company Manager, George Ryan
ACTING COMPANY: Wendy Barrie-Wilson, Ellen Barry, Paul Barry, Mark Battle, Timothy Boisvert, Andrew Boyer, Madylon Brans, Brendan Burke, David Cecsarini, Joseph Culliton, Tamara Daniel, Emilio Del Pozo, Dru Dempsey, Judith Drake, Clement Fowler, Richard Graham, Suzanne Heitmann, Kevin Hogan, Vivien Landau, Raye Lankford, Miller Lide, Ronald Martell, Maureen McGinnis, Dermot McNamara, Mary McTigue, Lorraine Morgan, Robert Murch, Frank Nastasi, Herman Petras, John Pietrowski, Stephanie Shine, Barbara Sinclair, Thomas Sminkey, Geddeth Smith, Jonathan Smoots, Kevin Thomsen, Eric Tull, George Tynan, Zeke Zaccaro, Debbie Aaron, Alana Albert, Ruthie Ammari, Gregg Baldinger, Paul Battiato, George Bishop, Elizabeth Buchsbaum, James Casey, Tommy Cheng, Keith Cobb, Eleni Constantelos, Jeff Davis, Jeanne DePasquale, Richard Dunn, Dwight Eastwood, Anne Ashby Gilbert, Jeffrey Gitelle, Kumar Goonewardene, Erik M. Greenbert, Dorothy W. Hopton, Kevin Jenkins, Mary B. Kababik, Karen Kornwall, Chester Lee, Rodney Leonard, Kristin Lovelace, Greg MacKenzie, Alecia Michaels, Vinessa Milando, Helen Mutsch, Sue Norris, Kenneth Nova, Susan Orlick, Gemma Pagliei, Chuck Parsons, David Pendergraft, Doug Pendergrass, Tim Pfeiffer, Madeline Jane Pollak, Rus Rainear, Kimberly Rapp, Christopher A. Russell, Matthew Salisbury, Ruth Schneck, Deanna Leigh Schreiber, Kayla Serotte, Andrea Squires, Catherine Tanner, William Thomer, Steve Tobin, Chrissie Viles, Mary L. Walker, Nancy Wilkening, Kathleen Willis
PRODUCTIONS: *The Taming of the Shrew* by William Shakespeare, directed by Paul Barry; *Coriolanus* by William Shakespeare, directed by Paul Barry; *The Winter's Tale* by William Shakespeare, directed by Paul Barry; *Present Laughter* by Noel Coward, directed by Samuel Maupin; *A Streetcar Named Desire* by Tennessee Williams, directed by Davey Marlin; *Translations* by Brian Friel, directed by Paul Barry; *The Diary of Anne Frank* by Frances Goodrich & Albert Hackett, directed by Ken Costigan; *A Christmas Carol* by Paul Barry (WORLD PREMIERE)

Jim DelGiudice Photos

Paul Barry, Kevin Hogan in "Terra Nova"
Above: Robin Leary, Jack Ryland in "Antony and Cleopatra"

Top Left: Jack Ryland, David S. Howard in "Julius Caesar"

183

NORTH CAROLINA SHAKESPEARE FESTIVAL

High Point, N.C.
Eleventh Season

Managing Director, Pedro M. Silva; Artistic Director, Malcolm Morrison; Development, Debra A. Skeen; Marketing/Press, Paul Siceloff; Production Manager, William (Bill) Savage; Directors, Malcolm Morrison, David Pursley, Henson Keys, Kent Thompson; Sets, Mark Pirolo, Sylvie Gagnon, Bland M. Wade, Jr.; Costumes, Christine Turbitt, Henry R. Grillo; Lighting, Paul B. Marsland, Patrick Byers; Sound, John Rankin; Fight Choreographer, Jack Cirillo; Stage Managers, Lydia Goble, Michele McCoy, Elizabeth Edmondo; Technical Director, Jonathan Christman; Scenic Artists, Chip Holton, Stratton McCrady; Props, Bland M. Wade, Jr.; Costume Shop, Christine Turbitt; Wardrobe, Patrick DeHart; Wigs, Keith Lewis; Sound, Abbey Donahower
RESIDENT COMPANY: Don Barbour, Evan Bivins, Mary Lucy Bivins, Matthew Bivins, Steve Boles, Jack Cirillo, John Courtney, Anton Dudley, Roger Forbes, Rhoda Griffis, Chris Harcum, Lucius Houghton, Max Jacobs, Michael LaGue, Valeri Lantz, Dan LaRocque, Bill McCallum, Stephen Rouffy, Suzan Samet, Lilli Shacklett, Scott Sowers, Cynthia Strickland, Jeffrey Turner, Christiann Whitehead, Tracy Wigent, John Woodson, T. Gregory Wright, Eric Zwemer
PRODUCTIONS: *Richard II, A Midsummer Night's Dream, Romeo and Juliet* by William Shakespeare; *Our Town* by Thornton Wilder

William (Bill) Savage, Michael Clapp Photos

Dan LaRocque, Jack Cirillo, John Courtney,
Eric Zwemer, John Woodson in "Richard II"
Above: Michael LaGue, Rhoda Griffis, Dan LaRocque,
John Courtney in "Midsummer Night's Dream"

OREGON SHAKESPEAREAN FESTIVAL

Ashland, Oregon

Artistic Director, Jerry Turner; Associate Director, Pat Patton; Stage Directors, Michael Kevin, Pat Patton, Walter Schoen, Andrew Traister, Jerry Turner, Henry Woronicz; Costumes, Michael Chapman, Jeannie Davidson, Frances Kenny, Michael Olich, Deborah Trout; Lighting, Robert Peterson, James Sale; Music/Sound, Todd Barton, Douglas K. Faerber; Sets, William Bloodgood, Richard L. Hay, Vicki M. Smith; Choreography, Mary Beth Cavanaugh, JoAnn Johnson, Tom Scales; Dramaturg, Cynthia White; Voice Coach, Ursula Meyer; Assistant Musical Director/Gaelic Coach, Pat O'Scannell; Production Manager, Tom Knapp; Costume Manager, Elaine Nicholson; Hair/Wigs, Ranny Beyer, Laurie Theodorou; Wardrobe, Lynn Ramey; Props, Paul-James Martin, Jonathan Pierce; Sound, Douglas K. Faerber; Stage Managers, Kirk Boyd, Kimberley Jean Barry, James L. Burke, Joanne L. Fantozzi; Executive Director, William W. Patton; General Manager, Paul Nicholson; Development, James L. Cox, Robert A. Scholl; Press, Margaret Rubin
RESIDENT COMPANY: Linda Alper, Chiron Alston, Robert A. Barnett, MaryBeth Cavanaugh, Ray Chapman, Philip Davidson, Dante DiLoreto, Francia DiMase, Robert Frank, Buzz Fraser, Bill Geisslinger, Caren Graham, Torrey Hanson, Richard Howard, Michael Kevin, Dan Kremer, Anthony Lee, Marie Livingston, Douglas Markkanen, Steven Matt, William McKereghan, Terri McMahon, Joseph McNally, Penny Metropulos, Ursula Meyer, Ivars Mikelson, Brad Moniz, Michelle Morain, Paul Vincent O'Connor, Kimberly Patton, J. P. Phillips, Demetra Pittman, John Pribyl, Rex Rabold, Bill Richie, Robert Sicular, John Stadelman, Matth Wisterman
PRODUCTIONS: *Richard II* by William Shakespeare, *She Stoops to Conquer* by Oliver Goldsmith, *Curse of the Starving Class* by Sam Shepard, *The Hostage* by Brendan Behan, *The Member of the Wedding* by Carson McCullers, *A Midsummer Night's Dream* by William Shakespeare, *The Shoemakers' Holiday* by Thomas Dekker, *Macbeth* by William Shakespeare, *Taking Steps* by Alan Ayckbourn, *Master Harold . . . and the boys* by Athol Fugard

Christopher Briscoe Photos

Francia DiMase, Michelle Morain
in "She Stoops to Conquer"

Top Left: Rex Rabold, Paul Vincent O'Connor
in "Richard II" **Below:** Dante DiLoreto, Ursula
Meyer in "Curse of the Starving Class"

STRATFORD FESTIVAL

Stratford, Ontario, Canada
Twenty-fifth Season

Artistic Director, John Neville; General Manager, Gary Thomas; Producer, Richard C. Dennison; Director of Music, Berthold Carriere; Communications, Ellen T. Cole; Development, Jeffrey R. Murtagh; Associate Directors, Douglas Campbell, Martha Henry, Brian Macdonald, Tanya Moiseiwitsch, Richard Ouzounian, Robin Phillips, Guy Sprung, John Wood; Resident Director, Robert Beard; Director of Production, Colleen Blake; Production Manager, Peter Lamb; Literary Advisor, Elliott Hayes; Technical Coordinators, Paul Bates, Milton Arnold; Technical Director, Allan De Luca; Assistant to Artistic Director, Margaret Ryerson; Sets, Phillip Silver; Lighting, Michael J. Whitfield; Lighting Assistants, Craig Blackley, Hugh Conacher, Robert Hamilton, Brenda Powell; Assistant Designers, Charlotte Dean, Jacinthe Demers, Andrea Grainger, Kerry Hackett, Lesley Jones, Elis Lam, Andrew Murray, William Schmuck, David Westlake; Music Administrator, Arthur Lang; Music Director, Laura Burton; Sound, Wendy York; Press, Robert Allen; Marketing, Christopher Blake, Leah Hood; Assistant Director of Development, Mary Joyal; Company Manager, Ron Nichol; Stage Managers, Nora Polley, Michael Benoit, Hilary Graham, Peter McGuire, Catherine Russell, Margaret Palmer, J. P. Elins, Marylu Moyer, Catherine Russell, Heather Kitchen, Lauren Snell, Victoria Klein, Ann Stuart, Maribeth Daley, Susan Konynenburg, Dave Gillard, Janet Sellery; Costume Manager, Anne Elsbury, Gayle Larson; Wardrobe, Gail Homersham-Robertson, Sharon Parker, Helen Basson; Wigs, Clayton Shields, Gerald Altenburg, Lena Festoso, Colene Morrison, Dave Kerr, Sherri Neeb; Props, Frank Holte, Roy Brown, Joy Allan; Resident Playwright, Michael Cook; Designers, Susan Benson, Patrick Clark, Ann Curtis, Michael Eagan, Debra Hanson, Astrid Janson, Sue LePage, Andrew Murray, Christina Poddubiuk, Ultz; Composers, Lucio Agostini, Louis Applebaum, Laura Burton, Berthold Carriere, Andre Gagnon, Gary Kulesha, Alan Laing, Allan Rae; Lighting, Harry Frehner, Louise Guinand, John Munro, Michael J. Whitfield; Choreographer, John Broome; Stage Directors, John Neville, Robert Beard, Brian Macdonald, Peter Moss, Robin Phillips, Brian Rintoul, David William, John Wood

RESIDENT COMPANY: Wendy Abbott, Donald Adams, Marion Adler, Edward Atienza, Mervyn Blake, James Blendick, John Bourgeois, Derek Boyes, David Brown, Daniel Buccos, Douglas Campbell, Brent Carver, Eric Coates, Peggy Coffey, Faye Cohen, Susan Cox, Susan Coyne, Patric A. Creelman, Tandy Cronyn, Richard Curnock, Henry Czerny, Hazel Desbarats, Keith Dinicol, Peter Donaldson, Jerry Etienne, David Evans, Colm Feore, Jean-Pierre Fournier, Denise Fergusson, Eli Gabay, Pat Galloway, Maurice Good, Darcy Gordon, John Graham, Allan Gray, Kevin Gudahl, Nigel Hamer, Michael Hanrahan, Ron Hastings, Sharon Heldt, Max Helpmann, Susan Henley, Jennifer Higgin, Kim Horsman, Eric House, William Hutt, John Innes, Nolan Jennings, Andrew Jackson, Lorne Kennedy, Calla Krause, Lee MacDougall, Larry Mannell, Richard March, Sheila MacCarthy, Eric McCormack, Weston McMillan, Dale Mieske, Melanie Miller, Richard Monette, William Needles, John Ormerod, Nancy Palk, Lucy Peacock, Nicholas Pennell, Jeffrey Prentice, Tanya Rich, Anna Louise Richardson, Howard Rollins, Bradley C. Rudy, Stephen Russell, Albert Schultz, Derek Scott, Goldie Semple, Joe-Norman Shaw, Wenna Shaw, Gerard Theoret, Keith Thomas, Brian Tree, William Webster, John Weisgerber, Scott Wentworth, Anne Wright, Susan Wright, Stephanie Young, Joseph Ziegler

PRODUCTIONS: *Cabaret* with Book by Joe Masteroff, Music, John Kander, Lyrics, Fred Ebb; *Mother Courage* by Bertolt Brecht, Translation, Ralph Manheim; *The School for Scandal* by Richard Brinsley Sheridan; *Othello* by William Shakespeare; *Much Ado About Nothing* by William Shakespeare; *Nora* by Ingmar Bergman; *Troilus and Cressida* by William Shakespeare; *The Cherry Orchard* by Anton Chekhov; *Not About Heroes* by Stephen MacDonald; *Intimate Admiration* by Richard Epp; *As You Like It* by William Shakespeare; *Romeo and Juliet* by William Shakespeare; *Journey's End* by R. C. Sherriff; Workshop: *Not Wanted on the Voyage* by Timothy Findley

Michael Cooper Photos

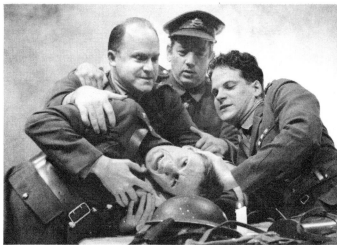

John Ormerod (front), William Webster, Peter Donaldson, Albert Schultz in "Journey's End" Top: Faye Cohen, Susan Henley, Sheila McCarthy, William Hutt, Calla Krause, Gerard Theoret in "School for Scandal"

**Michael Duncan as Falstaff
in "Merry Wives of Windsor"**

WISCONSIN SHAKESPEARE FESTIVAL

Platteville, Wisconsin
July 2–August 6, 1987

Artistic Director, Thomas Collins; Technical Director, Thomas S. Galtry; Costumes, Wendy W. Collins; Lighting, James Latzel; Music, William Penn; Props, David Krebs; Press, Margot King; Stage Manager, P. J. Rockwell

RESIDENT COMPANY: Laurie Birmingham, Garrison Brown, Julian Brown, Julie M. Boyd, Mark Cherniack, Barry Childs, Todd Covert, Sandra Docwra-Jones, Michael Duncan, Joseph Gargiulo, Bert Glanz, Laura Gordon, David P. Hirvela, Brian Holmes, Robert Hoyt, Patti Huber, Arliss Jeffries, Kathleen M. Kohlstedt, Raymond Lynch, Joseph J. Menino, Eric Mogensen, Robert Olsen, Alissa Schilling, Shaun Tandon, Carrie Van Deest, David Van Pelt, Mike Willis, Mic Woicek

GUEST ARTISTS: David P. Hirvela, Michael Duncan (Actors/Directors)

PRODUCTIONS: *Much Ado About Nothing, The Merry Wives of Windsor, The Winter's Tale* by William Shakespeare

Gary Tuescher Photos

185

PREVIOUS THEATRE WORLD
AWARD WINNERS

1944-45: Betty Comden, Richard Davis, Richard Hart, Judy Holliday, Charles Lang, Bambi Linn, John Lund, Donald Murphy, Nancy Noland, Margaret Phillips, John Raitt

1945-46: Barbara Bel Geddes, Marlon Brando, Bill Callahan, Wendell Corey, Paul Douglas, Mary James, Burt Lancaster, Patricia Marshall, Beatrice Pearson

1946-47: Keith Andes, Marion Bell, Peter Cookson, Ann Crowley, Ellen Hanley, John Jordan, George Keane, Dorothea MacFarland, James Mitchell, Patricia Neal, David Wayne

1947-48: Valerie Bettis, Edward Bryce, Whitfield Connor, Mark Dawson, June Lockhart, Estelle Loring, Peggy Maley, Ralph Meeker, Meg Mundy, Douglass Watson, James Whitmore, Patrice Wymore

1948-49: Tod Andrews, Doe Avedon, Jean Carson, Carol Channing, Richard Derr, Julie Harris, Mary McCarty, Allyn Ann McLerie, Cameron Mitchell, Gene Nelson, Byron Palmer, Bob Scheerer

1949-50: Nancy Andrews, Phil Arthur, Barbara Brady, Lydia Clarke, Priscilla Gillette, Don Hanmer, Marcia Henderson, Charlton Heston, Rick Jason, Grace Kelly, Charles Nolte, Roger Price

1950-51: Barbara Ashley, Isabel Bigley, Martin Brooks, Richard Burton, Pat Crowley, James Daly, Cloris Leachman, Russell Nype, Jack Palance, William Smothers, Maureen Stapleton, Marcia Van Dyke, Eli Wallach

1951-52: Tony Bavaar, Patricia Benoit, Peter Conlow, Virginia de Luce, Ronny Graham, Audrey Hepburn, Diana Herbert, Conrad Janis, Dick Kallman, Charles Proctor, Eric Sinclair, Kim Stanley, Marian Winters, Helen Wood

1952-53: Edie Adams, Rosemary Harris, Eileen Heckart, Peter Kelley, John Kerr, Richard Kiley, Gloria Marlowe, Penelope Munday, Paul Newman, Sheree North, Geraldine Page, John Stewart, Ray Stricklyn, Gwen Verdon

1953-54: Orson Bean, Harry Belafonte, James Dean, Joan Diener, Ben Gazzara, Carol Haney, Jonathan Lucas, Kay Medford, Scott Merrill, Elizabeth Montgomery, Leo Penn, Eva Marie Saint

1954-55: Julie Andrews, Jacqueline Brookes, Shirl Conway, Barbara Cook, David Daniels, Mary Fickett, Page Johnson, Loretta Leversee, Jack Lord, Dennis Patrick, Anthony Perkins, Christopher Plummer

1955-56: Diane Cilento, Dick Davalos, Anthony Franciosa, Andy Griffith, Laurence Harvey, David Hedison, Earle Hyman, Susan Johnson, John Michael King, Jayne Mansfield, Sara Marshall, Gaby Rodgers, Susan Strasberg, Fritz Weaver

1956-57: Peggy Cass, Sydney Chaplin, Sylvia Daneel, Bradford Dillman, Peter Donat, George Grizzard, Carol Lynley, Peter Palmer, Jason Robards, Cliff Robertson, Pippa Scott, Inga Swenson

1957-58: Anne Bancroft, Warren Berlinger, Colleen Dewhurst, Richard Easton, Tim Everett, Eddie Hodges, Joan Hovis, Carol Lawrence, Jacqueline McKeever, Wynne Miller, Robert Morse, George C. Scott

1958-59: Lou Antonio, Ina Balin, Richard Cross, Tammy Grimes, Larry Hagman, Dolores Hart, Roger Mollien, France Nuyen, Susan Oliver, Ben Piazza, Paul Roebling, William Shatner, Pat Suzuki, Rip Torn

1959-60: Warren Beatty, Eileen Brennan, Carol Burnett, Patty Duke, Jane Fonda, Anita Gillette, Elisa Loti, Donald Madden, George Maharis, John McMartin, Lauri Peters, Dick Van Dyke

1960-61: Joyce Bulifant, Dennis Cooney, Sandy Dennis, Nancy Dussault, Robert Goulet, Joan Hackett, June Harding, Ron Husmann, James MacArthur, Bruce Yarnell

1961-62: Elizabeth Ashley, Keith Baxter, Peter Fonda, Don Galloway, Sean Garrison, Barbara Harris, James Earl Jones, Janet Margolin, Karen Morrow, Robert Redford, John Stride, Brenda Vaccaro

1962-63: Alan Arkin, Stuart Damon, Melinda Dillon, Robert Drivas, Bob Gentry, Dorothy Loudon, Brandon Maggart, Julienne Marie, Liza Minnelli, Estelle Parsons, Diana Sands, Swen Swenson

1963-64: Alan Alda, Gloria Bleezarde, Imelda De Martin, Claude Giraud, Ketty Lester, Barbara Loden, Lawrence Pressman, Gilbert Price, Philip Proctor, John Tracy, Jennifer West

1964-65: Carolyn Coates, Joyce Jillson, Linda Lavin, Luba Lisa, Michael O'Sullivan, Joanna Pettet, Beah Richards, Jaime Sanchez, Victor Spinetti, Nicolas Surovy, Robert Walker, Clarence Williams III

1965-66: Zoe Caldwell, David Carradine, John Cullum, John Davidson, Faye Dunaway, Gloria Foster, Robert Hooks, Jerry Lanning, Richard Mulligan, April Shawhan, Sandra Smith, Leslie Ann Warren

1966-67: Bonnie Bedelia, Richard Benjamin, Dustin Hoffman, Terry Kiser, Reva Rose, Robert Salvio, Sheila Smith, Connie Stevens, Pamela Tiffin, Leslie Uggams, Jon Voight, Christopher Walken

1967-68: David Birney, Pamela Burrell, Jordan Christopher, Jack Crowder (Thalmus Rasulala), Sandy Duncan, Julie Gregg, Stephen Joyce, Bernadette Peters, Alice Playten, Michael Rupert, Brenda Smiley, Russ Thacker

1968-69: Jane Alexander, David Cryer, Blythe Danner, Ed Evanko, Ken Howard, Lauren Jones, Ron Leibman, Marian Mercer, Jill O'Hara, Ron O'Neal, Al Pacino, Marlene Warfield

1969-70: Susan Browning, Donny Burks, Catherine Burns, Len Cariou, Bonnie Franklin, David Holliday, Katharine Houghton, Melba Moore, David Rounds, Lewis J. Stadlen, Kristoffer Tabori, Fredricka Weber

1970-71: Clifton Davis, Michael Douglas, Julie Garfield, Martha Henry, James Naughton, Tricia O'Neil, Kipp Osborne, Roger Rathburn, Ayn Ruymen, Jennifer Salt, Joan Van Ark, Walter Willison

1971-72: Jonelle Allen, Maureen Anderman, William Atherton, Richard Backus, Adrienne Barbeau, Cara Duff-MacCormick, Robert Foxworth, Elaine Joyce, Jess Richards, Ben Vereen, Beatrice Winde, James Woods

1972-73: D'Jamin Bartlett, Patricia Elliott, James Farentino, Brian Farrell, Victor Garber, Kelly Garrett, Mari Gorman, Laurence Guittard, Trish Hawkins, Monte Markham, John Rubinstein, Jennifer Warren, Alexander H. Cohen (Special Award)

1973-74: Mark Baker, Maureen Brennan, Ralph Carter, Thom Christopher, John Driver, Conchata Ferrell, Ernestine Jackson, Michael Moriarty, Joe Morton, Ann Reinking, Janie Sell, Mary Woronov, Sammy Cahn (Special Award)

1974-75: Peter Burnell, Zan Charisse, Lola Falana, Peter Firth, Dorian Harewood, Joel Higgins, Marcia McClain, Linda Miller, Marti Rolph, John Sheridan, Scott Stevensen, Donna Theodore, Equity Library Theatre (Special Award)

1975-76: Danny Aiello, Christine Andreas, Dixie Carter, Tovah Feldshuh, Chip Garnett, Richard Kelton, Vivian Reed, Charles Repole, Virginia Seidel, Daniel Seltzer, John V. Shea, Meryl Streep, A Chorus Line (Special Award)

1976-77: Trazana Beverley, Michael Cristofer, Joe Fields, Joanna Gleason, Cecilia Hart, John Heard, Gloria Hodes, Juliette Koka, Andrea McArdle, Ken Page, Jonathan Pryce, Chick Vennera, Eva LeGallienne (Special Award)

1977-78: Vasili Bogazianos, Nell Carter, Carlin Glynn, Christopher Goutman, William Hurt, Judy Kaye, Florence Lacy, Armelia McQueen, Gordana Rashovich, Bo Rucker, Richard Seer, Colin Stinton, Joseph Papp (Special Award)

1978-79: Philip Anglim, Lucie Arnaz, Gregory Hines, Ken Jennings, Michael Jeter, Laurie Kennedy, Susan Kingsley, Christine Lahti, Edward James Olmos, Kathleen Quinlan, Sarah Rice, Max Wright, Marshall W. Mason (Special Award)

1979-80: Maxwell Caulfield, Leslie Denniston, Boyd Gaines, Richard Gere, Harry Groener, Stephen James, Susan Kellermann, Dinah Manoff, Lonny Price, Marianne Tatum, Anne Twomey, Dianne Wiest, Mickey Rooney (Special Award)

1980-81: Brian Backer, Lisa Banes, Meg Bussert, Michael Allen Davis, Giancarlo Esposito, Daniel Gerroll, Phyllis Hyman, Cynthia Nixon, Amanda Plummer, Adam Redfield, Wanda Richert, Rex Smith, Elizabeth Taylor (Special Award)

1981-82: Karen Akers, Laurie Beechman, Danny Glover, David Alan Grier, Jennifer Holliday, Anthony Heald, Lizbeth Mackay, Peter MacNicol, Elizabeth McGovern, Ann Morrison, Michael O'Keefe, James Widdoes, Manhattan Theatre Club (Special Award)

1982-83: Karen Allen, Suzanne Bertish, Matthew Broderick, Kate Burton, Joanne Camp, Harvey Fierstein, Peter Gallagher, John Malkovich, Anne Pitoniak, James Russo, Brian Tarantina, Linda Thorson, Natalia Makarova (Special)

1983-84: Martine Allard, Joan Allen, Kathy Whitton Baker, Mark Capri, Laura Dean, Stephen Geoffreys, Todd Graff, Glenne Headly, J. J. Johnston, Bonnie Koloc, Calvin Levels, Robert Westenberg, Ron Moody (Special)

1984-85: Kevin Anderson, Richard Chaves, Patti Cohenour, Charles S. Dutton, Nancy Giles, Whoopi Goldberg, Leilani Jones, John Mahoney, Laurie Metcalf, Barry Miller, John Turturro, Amelia White, Lucille Lortel (Special)

1985-86: Suzy Amis, Alec Baldwin, Aled Davies, Faye Grant, Julie Hagerty, Ed Harris, Mark Jacoby, Donna Kane, Cleo Laine, Howard McGillin, Marisa Tomei, Joe Urla, Ensemble Studio Theatre (Special)

1986-87: Annette Bening, Timothy Daly, Lindsay Duncan, Frank Ferrante, Robert Lindsay, Amy Madigan, Michael Maguire, Demi Moore, Molly Ringwald, Frances Ruffelle, Courtney B. Vance, Colm Wilkinson, Robert DeNiro (Special)

**Nell
Carter**

**Robert
DeNiro**

**Jane
Fonda**

**Dustin
Hoffman**

**Meryl
Streep**

**James
Woods**

1988 THEATRE WORLD AWARD RECIPIENTS
(Outstanding New Talent)

YVONNE BRYCELAND
of "The Road to Mecca"

PHILIP CASNOFF
of "Chess"

BRIAN KERWIN
of "Emily"

DANIELLE FERLAND
of "Into the Woods"

MELISSA GILBERT
of "A Shayna Maidel"

BRIAN MITCHELL
of "Mail"

AIDAN QUINN
of "A Streetcar Named Desire"

LINDA HART
of "Anything Goes"

LINZI HATELEY
of "Carrie"

ERIC ROBERTS
of "Burn This"

B. D. WONG
of "M. Butterfly"

MARY MURFITT
of "Oil City Symphony"

THEATRE WORLD AWARDS presentations, Thursday, May 26, 1988 at the St. Regis Roof. Presented as part of the First New York International Festival of the Arts (Martin E. Segal, Chairman). Top: (L) on platform: Karen Akers, Michael Maguire, Jane Alexander, Yvonne Bryceland, Dorothy Loudon, Christopher Walken, Elizabeth McGovern, (R) Colleen Dewhurst, Judy Kaye and Walter Willison singing, Elizabeth McGovern, Ken Page, Carol Lynley, Harvey Fierstein Below: Yvonne Bryceland, John Rubinstein; Aidan Quinn, Elizabeth McGovern; Colleen Dewhurst, B. D. Wong; Danielle Ferland, Joanna Gleason; Bottom: John Rubinstein, Colleen Dewhurst, Martin Segal (R); Ken Page for Melissa Gilbert; Alexander H. Cohen, Dorothy Loudon, Chistopher Walken, Elizabeth McGovern; Above: Carol Lynley, Philip Casnoff; Eric Roberts, Dorothy Loudon; Tisa Chang, George Wojtasik; Paul Gyngell for Linzi Hateley, Karen Akers

Michael Viade, Van Williams Photos

Top: Jane Alexander, Brian Mitchell; Linda Hart; Mary Murfitt, Christopher Walken; Below: Aidan Quinn, Elizabeth McGovern, Eric Roberts; Brian Kerwin, Harvey Fierstein; Philip Casnoff, Roxanne Hart, Anthony Heald. Bottom: Jerry Greenberg, pianist; Patti Cohenour, Judy Kaye; Linda Hart with brother, mother and grandmother; B. D. Wong; Peggy Cass, Lee Roy Reams, Carol Lynley; Above: Ken Page, Alec Baldwin, Chip Garnett; Lucille Lortel, Juliette Koka; Joanna Gleason, Michael Maguire; Jane Alexander, John Rubinstein, Colleen Dewhurst

Michael Viade, Van Williams Photos

PULITZER PRIZE PRODUCTIONS

1918-Why Marry? **1919**-No award, **1920**-Beyond the Horizon, **1921**-Miss Lulu Bett, **1922**-Anna Christie, **1923**-Icebound, **1924**-Hell-Bent fer Heaven, **1925**-They Knew What They Wanted, **1926**-Craig's Wife, **1927**-In Abraham's Bosom, **1928**-Strange Interlude, **1929**-Street Scene, **1930**-The Green Pastures, **1931**-Alison's House, **1932**-Of Thee I Sing, **1933**-Both Your Houses, **1934**-Men in White, **1935**-The Old Maid, **1936**-Idiot's Delight, **1937**-You Can't Take It with You, **1938**-Our Town, **1939**-Abe Lincoln in Illinois, **1940**-The Time of Your Life, **1941**-There Shall Be No Night, **1942**-No award, **1943**-The Skin of Our Teeth, **1944**-No award, **1945**-Harvey, **1946**-State of the Union, **1947**-No award, **1948**-A Streetcar Named Desire, **1949**-Death of a Salesman, **1950**-South Pacific, **1951**-No award, **1952**-The Shrike, **1953**-Picnic, **1954**-The Teahouse of the August Moon, **1955**-Cat on a Hot Tin Roof, **1956**-The Diary of Anne Frank, **1957**-Long Day's Journey into Night, **1958**-Look Homeward, Angel, **1959**-J. B., **1960**-Fiorello!, **1961**-All the Way Home, **1962**-How to Succeed in Business without Really Trying, **1963**-No award, **1964**-No award, **1965**-The Subject Was Roses, **1966**-No award, **1967**-A Delicate Balance, **1968**-No award, **1969**-The Great White Hope, **1970**-No Place to Be Somebody, **1971**-The Effect of Gamma Rays on Man-in-the-Moon Marigolds, **1972**-No award, **1973**-That Championship Season, **1974**-No award, **1975**-Seascape, **1976**-A Chorus Line, **1977**-The Shadow Box, **1978**-The Gin Game, **1979**-Buried Child, **1980**-Talley's Folly, **1981**-Crimes of the Heart, **1982**-A Soldier's Play, **1983**-'night, Mother, **1984**-Glengarry Glen Ross, **1985**-Sunday in the Park with George, **1986**-No award, **1987**-Fences, **1988**-Driving Miss Daisy

NEW YORK DRAMA CRITICS CIRCLE AWARDS

1936-Winterset, **1937**-High Tor, **1938**-Of Mice and Men, Shadow and Substance, **1939**-The White Steed, **1940**-The Time of Your Life, **1941**-Watch on the Rhine, The Corn is Green, **1942**-Blithe Spirit, **1943**-The Patriots, **1944**-Jacobowsky and the Colonel, **1945**-The Glass Menagerie, **1946**-Carousel, **1947**-All My Sons, No Exit, Brigadoon, **1948**-A Streetcar Named Desire, The Winslow Boy, **1949**-Death of a Salesman, The Madwoman of Chaillot, South Pacific, **1950**-The Member of the Wedding, The Cocktail Party, The Consul, **1951**-Darkness at Noon, The Lady's Not for Burning, Guys and Dolls, **1952**-I Am a Camera, Venus Observed, Pal Joey, **1953**- Picnic, The Love of Four Colonels, Wonderful Town, **1954**-Teahouse of the August Moon, Ondine, The Golden Apple, **1955**-Cat on a Hot Tin Roof, Witness for the Prosecution, The Saint of Bleecker Street, **1956**-The Diary of Anne Frank, Tiger at the Gates, My Fair Lady, **1957**-Long Day's Journey into Night, The Waltz of the Toreadors, The Most Happy Fella, **1958**-Look Homeward Angel, Look Back in Anger, The Music Man, **1959**-A Raisin in the Sun, The Visit, La Plume de Ma Tante, **1960**-Toys in the Attic, Five Finger Exercise, Fiorello! **1961**-All the Way Home, A Taste of Honey, Carnival, **1962**-Night of the Iguana, A Man for All Seasons, How to Succeed in Business without Really Trying, **1963**-Who's Afraid of Virginia Woolf?, **1964**-Luther, Hello Dolly!, **1965**-The Subject Was Roses, Fiddler on the Roof, **1966**-The Persecution and Assassination of Marat as Performed by the Inmates of the Asylum of Charenton under the Direction of the Marquis de Sade, Man of La Mancha, **1967**-The Homecoming, Cabaret, **1968**-Rosencrantz and Guildenstern Are Dead, Your Own Thing, **1969**-The Great White Hope, 1776, **1970**-The Effect of Gamma Rays on Man-in-the-Moon Marigolds, Borstal Boy, Company, **1971**-Home, Follies, The House of Blue Leaves, **1972**-That Championship Season, Two Gentlemen of Verona, **1973**-The Hot l Baltimore, The Changing Room, A Little Night Music, **1974**-The Contractor, Short Eyes, Candide, **1975**-Equus, The Taking of Miss Janie, A Chorus Line, **1976**-Travesties, Streamers, Pacific Overtures, **1977**-Otherwise Engaged, American Buffalo, Annie, **1978**-Da, Ain't Misbehavin', **1979**-The Elephant Man, Sweeney Todd, **1980**-Talley's Folly, Evita, Betrayal, **1981**-Crimes of the Heart, A Lesson from Aloes, Special Citation to Lena Horne, "The Pirates of Penzance, **1982**-The Life and Adventures of Nicholas Nickleby, A Soldier's Play, (no musical honored), **1983**-Brighton Beach Memoirs, Plenty, Little Shop of Horrors, **1984**-The Real Thing, Glengarry Glen Ross, Sunday in the Park with George, **1985**-Ma Rainey's Black Bottom, (no musical), **1986**-A Lie of the Mind, Benefactors, no musical, Special to Lily Tomlin and Jane Wagner, **1987**-Fences, Les Liaisons Dangereuses, Les Miserables, **1988**-Joe Turner's Come and Gone, The Road to Mecca, Into the Woods.

AMERICAN THEATRE WING ANTOINETTE PERRY (TONY) AWARD PRODUCTIONS

1948-Mister Roberts, **1949**-Death of a Salesman, Kiss Me, Kate, **1950**-The Cocktail Party, South Pacific, **1951**-The Rose Tattoo, Guys and Dolls, **1952**-The Fourposter, The King and I, **1953**-The Crucible, Wonderful Town, **1954**-The Teahouse of the August Moon, Kismet, **1955**-The Desperate Hours, The Pajama Game, **1956**-The Diary of Anne Frank, Damn Yankees, **1957**-Long Day's Journey into Night, My Fair Lady, **1958**-Sunrise at Campobello, The Music Man, **1959**-J. B., Redhead, **1960**-The Miracle Worker, Fiorello! tied with The Sound of Music, **1961**-Becket, Bye Bye Birdie, **1962**-A Man for All Seasons, How to Succeed in Business without Really Trying, **1963**-Who's Afraid of Virginia Woolf?, A Funny Thing Happened on the Way to the Forum, **1964**-Luther, Hello Dolly!, **1965**-The Subject Was Roses, Fiddler on the Roof, **1966**-The Persecution and Assassination of Marat as Performed by the Inmates of the Asylum of Charenton under the Direction of the Marquis de Sade, Man of La Mancha, **1967**-The Homecoming, Cabaret, **1968**-Rosencrantz and Guildenstern Are Dead, Hallelujah Baby!, **1969**-The Great White Hope, 1776, **1970**-Borstal Boy, Applause, **1971**-Sleuth, Company, **1972**-Sticks and Bones, Two Gentlemen of Verona, **1973**-That Championship Season, A Little Night Music, **1974**-The River Niger, Raisin, **1975**-Equus, The Wiz, **1976**-Travesties, A Chorus Line, **1977**-The Shadow Box, Annie, **1978**-Da, Ain't Misbehavin', Dracula, **1979**-The Elephant Man, Sweeney Todd, **1980**-Children of a Lesser God, Evita, Morning's at Seven, **1981**-Amadeus, 42nd Street, The Pirates of Penzance, **1982**-The Life and Adventures of Nicholas Nickleby, Nine, Othello, **1983**-Torch Song Trilogy, Cats, On Your Toes, **1984**-The Real Thing, La Cage aux Folles, **1985**-Biloxi Blues, Big River, Joe Egg, **1986**-I'm Not Rappaport, The Mystery of Edwin Drood, Sweet Charity, **1987**-Fences, Les Miserables, All My Sons, **1988**-M. Butterfly, The Phantom of the Opera, Anything Goes

BIOGRAPHICAL DATA ON THIS SEASON'S CAST

ABRAHAM, F. MURRAY. Born Oct. 24, 1939 in Pittsburgh, PA. Attended UTx. Debut OB 1967 in "The Fantasticks," followed by "An Opening in the Trees," "14th Dictator," "Young Abe Lincoln," "Tonight in Living Color," "Adaptation," "Survival of St. Joan," "The Dog Ran Away," "Fables," "Richard III," "Little Murders," "Scuba Duba," "Where Has Tommy Flowers Gone?," "Miracle Play," "Blessing," "Sexual Perversity in Chicago," "Landscape of the Body," "The Master and Margarita," "Biting the Apple," "The Seagull," "Caretaker," "Antigone," "Uncle Vanya," "The Golem," "Madwoman of Chaillot," "Twelfth Night," "Frankie and Johnny in the Claire de Lune," "A Midsummer Night's Dream," Bdwy in "Man in the Glass Booth"(1968), "6 Rms Riv Vu," "Bad Habits," "The Ritz," "Legend," "Teibele and Her Demon," "Macbeth."

ABRY, JONAS. Born May 12, 1975 in NYC. Debut OB (1986) and Bdwy (1987) in "Coastal Disturbances."

ACKERMAN, SHELLE. Born Oct. 14, 1953 in NYC. Attended CCNY. Debut 1973 OB in "Ms. Nefertiti Regrets," followed by "Lyrics and Lyricists," "Jacques Brel Is Alive and Well . . ."

ADAMS, MASON. Born Feb. 26, 1919 in NYC. UWisc. graduate. Bdwy credits include "Get Away Old Man," "Public Relations," "Career Angel," "Violet," "Shadow of My Enemy," "Tall Story," "Inquest," "Trial of the Catonsville 9," "The Sign in Sidney Brustein's Window," OB in "Meegan's Game," "Shortchanged Review," "Checking Out," "The Soft Touch," "Paradise Lost," "The Time of Your Life," "Danger: Memory!", "The Day Room."

ADAMSON, DAVID. Born May 30, 1940 in Orange, NJ. Graduate Bucknell, Yale. Bdwy debut 1971 in "Unlikely Heroes," followed by "Full Circle," "Hamlet," "Hide and Seek," "Children of a Lesser God," OB in "Isadora Duncan Sleeps with the Russian Navy," "Sister Aimee," "Hamlet," "Happy Birthday Wanda June," "Henry V," "Ice Bridge," "Camp Meeting."

ADLER, BRUCE Born Nov. 27, 1944 in NYC. Attended NYU. Debut 1957 OB in "It's a Funny World," followed by "Hard to Be a Jew," "Big Winner," "The Golden Land," "The Stranger's Return," "The Rise of David Levinsky," "On Second Avenue," Bdwy in "A Teaspoon Every Four Hours" (1971), "Oklahoma" (1979), "Oh, Brother!", "Sunday in the Park with George," "Broadway."

AGUTTER, JENNY. Born Dec. 20, 1952 in Taunton, Eng. Bdwy debut 1987 in "Breaking the Code."

AHEARN, DANIEL. Born Aug. 7, 1948 in Washington, DC. Attended Carnegie-Mellon. Debut OB 1981 in "Woyzek," followed by "Brontosaurus Rex," "Billy Liar," "Second Prize Two Months in Leningrad," "No Time Flat."

A'HEARN, PATRICK. Born Sept. 4, 1957 in Cortland, NY. Graduate Syracuse U. Debut 1985 OB in "Pirates of Penzance," followed by "Forbidden Broadway," followed by Bdwy in "Les Miserables" (1987).

AHLIN, MARGIT. Born Feb. 23, 1960 in Chappaqua, NY. Graduate NYU, AMDA. Debut OB in "Romeo and Juliet" (1982), followed by "Social Event," "Vanities," "Standing on the Cheese Line," "Company," "Onlyman," "In Available Light."

AIDEM, BETSY. Born Oct. 28, 1957 in Eastmeadow, NY. Graduate NYU. Debut 1981 OB in "The Trading Post," followed by "A Different Moon," "Balm in Gilead," "Crossing the Bar," "Our Lady of the Tortilla," "Steel Magnolias," "Road."

AKERS, KAREN. Born Oct. 13, 1945 in NYC. Graduate Hunter College. Bdwy debut 1982 in "Nine" for which she received a Theatre World Award, followed by "Jacques Brel Is Alive and Well and Living in New York."

ALDREDGE, TOM. Born Feb. 28, 1928 in Dayton, Oh. Attended Dayton U., Goodman Theatre. Bdwy debut 1959 in "The Nervous Set," followed by "UTBU," "Slapstick Tragedy," "Everything in the Garden," "Indians," "Engagement Baby," "How the Other Half Loves," "Sticks and Bones," "Where's Charley?," "Leaf People," "Rex," "Vieux Carre," "St. Joan," "Stages," "On Golden Pond," "The Little Foxes," "Into the Woods," OB in "The Tempest," "Between Two Thieves," "Henry V," "The Premise," "Love's Labour's Lost," "Troilus and Cressida," "Butter and Egg Man," "Ergo," "Boys in the Band," "Twelfth Night," "Colette," "Hamlet," "The Orphan," "King Lear," "The Iceman Cometh," "Black Angel," "Getting Along Famously," "Fool for Love," "Neon Psalms," "Richard II."

ALDRICH, JANET. (formerly Aldridge). Born Oct. 16, 1956 in Hinsdale, Il. UMiami graduate. Debut 1979 OB in "A Funny Thing Happened on the Way to the Forum," followed by "American Princess," "The Men's Group," "Wanted Dead or Alive," "Comedy of Errors," Bdwy in "Annie" (1982), "The Three Musketeers," "Broadway."

ALESSANDRINI, GERARD. Born Nov. 27, 1953 in Boston, Ma. Graduate Boston Consv. Debut 1982 OB in "Forbidden Broadway."

ALEXANDER, JASON. Born Sept. 23, 1959 in Irvington, NJ. Attended Boston U. Bdwy bow 1981 in "Merrily We Roll Along," followed by "Broadway Bound, OB in "Forbidden Broadway." "Stop the World . . . ," "D," "Personals."

ALICE, MARY. Born Dec. 3, 1941 in Indianola, Ms. Debut 1967 OB in "Trials of Brother Jero," followed by "The Strong Breed," "Duplex," "Thoughts," "Miss Julie," "House Party," "Terraces," "Heaven and Hell's Agreement," "In the Deepest Part of Sleep," "Cockfight," "Julius Caesar," "Nongogo," "Second Thoughts," "Spell #7," "Zooman and the Sign," "Glasshouse," "The Ditch," "Take Me Along," "Departures," "Marathon 86," Bdwy in "No Place to Be Somebody" (1971), "Fences."

ALLEN, ELIZABETH. Born Jan. 25, 1934 in Jersey City, NJ. Attended Rutgers U. Bdwy debut 1957 in "Romanoff and Juliet," followed by "The Gay Life," "Do I Hear a Waltz?," "Sherry!," "42nd Street."

ALLEN, JOAN. Born Aug. 20, 1956 in Rochelle, IL. Attended E. Ill. U., W. ILL. U. Debut 1983 OB in "And a Nightingale Sang" for which she received a Theatre World Award, followed by "The Marriage of Bette and Boo," "Marathon '86," "Burn This!" Bdwy 1987 in "Burn This."

ALLEN, KEITH. Born Feb. 18, 1964 in Daytona Beach, FL. Bdwy debut 1986 in "La Cage aux Folles."

ALLER, JOHN. Born July 5, 1957 in Cuba. Graduate Hofstra U. Debut 1985 OB in "Pacific Overtures," followed by "Encore," "Miami," Bdwy in "Rags" (1986), "Chess."

ALLINSON, MICHAEL. Born in London, Eng. Attended RADA. Bdwy debut 1960 in "My Fair Lady," followed by "Hostile Witness," "Come Live with Me," "Coco," "Angel Street," "My Fair Lady" (1981), "Oliver†" OB in "The Importance of Being Earnest," "Staircase," "Loud Bang on June 1st," "Good and Faithful Servant."

ALTON, DAVID. Born May 21, 1949 in Philadelphia, Pa. Graduate LaSalle Col. Debut OB in Propaganda"(1987), followed by "The Cabinet of Dr. Caligari."

ALVARADO, TRINI. Born in NYC in 1967. Bdwy debut 1978 in "Runaways," OB in "Yours, Anne," "Maggie Magalita," "Godspell."

ANDERSON, CHRISTINE. Born Aug. 6 in Utica, NY. Graduate UWi. Bdwy debut in "I Love My Wife" (1980), OB in "I Can't Keep Running in Place," "On the Swing Shift," "Red, Hot and Blue," "A Night at Texas Guinan's," "Nunsense."

ANDERSON, FRED. Born July 11, 1964 in Memphis, TN. Attended NCSchool of Arts, Joffrey Ballet School. Debut 1988 OB in "Lost in the Stars."

ANDERSON, JEAN. Born Dec. 12, 1907 in Eastbourne, Eng. Graduate RADA. Bdwy debut 1987 in the Royal Shakespeare Co.'s "Les Liaisons Dangereuses," OB in "A Delicate Heart."

ANDERSON, KEVIN. Born Jan. 13, 1960 in Illinois. Attended Goodman School. Debut 1985 OB in "Orphans" for which he received a Theatre World Award, followed by "Moonchildren."

ANDERSON, PHILIP. Born Aug. 13, 1958 in Philadelphia, PA. Graduate AADA, Manhattan Sch. Music, Columbia. Debut 1986 OB in "La Belle Helene," followed by "Ruddigore," "The Civil Wars," "Kismet."

ANDERSON, SYDNEY. Born Apr. 4 in Tacoma, WA. Graduate UWa. Debut 1978 OB in "Gay Divorce," Bdwy in "A Broadway Musical" (1978), followed by "Charlie and Algernon," "Oklahoma!," "La Cage aux Folles."

ANDRES, BARBARA. Born Feb. 11, 1939 in NYC. Catholic U graduate. Bdwy debut 1969 in "Jimmy," followed by "The Boy Friend," "Rodgers and Hart," "Rex," "On Golden Pond," "Doonesbury," OB in "Threepenny Opera," "Landscape of the Body," "Harold Arlen's Cabaret," "Suzanna Andler," "One Act Festival," "Company," "Marathon 87."

ANDREWS, GEORGE LEE. Born Oct. 13, 1942 in Milwaukee, Wi. Debut OB 1970 in "Jacques Brel Is Alive and Well . . . ," followed by "Starting Here Starting Now," "Vamps and Rideouts," "The Fantasticks," Bdwy in "A Little Night Music" (1973), "On the 20th Century," "Merlin," "The Phantom of the Opera."

ANDREWS, MARNIE. Born Dec. 9, 1951 in Cedartown, CA. Graduate UNC. Debut 1981 OB in "The Latecomer," followed by "It's a Jungle Out There," "Wormwood," "Tuneside," "Mrs. Dally Has a Lover," "Graceland."

ANGELA, JUNE. Born Aug. 18, 1959 in NYC. Bdwy debut 1970 in "Lovely Ladies, Kind Gentlemen," followed by "The King and I"(1977), OB in "Dream of Kitamura," "Aldersgate '88."

ANGLIN, FLORENCE. Born Sept. 21 in Brooklyn, NY. Bdwy debut 1945 in "A Bell for Adano," followed by "Skipper Next to God," "Winged Victory," "Lower North," "Street Scene," "Gideon," "Goodbye Fidel," OB in "Morning Noon and Evening," "Madame de Sade," "A Doll's House," "Major Barbara," "Me Dandido," "The Little Foxes," "The Baker's Wife," "Soho They Call It."

APPEL, PETER. Born Oct. 19, 1959 in NYC. BrandeisU graduate. Debut 1987 OB in "Richard II" followed by "Henry IV Part I," "A Midsummer Night's Dream," "Saved from Obscurity."

AQUINO, AMY. Born Mar. 20, 1957 in Teaneck, NJ. Graduate Radcliffe, Yale. Debut 1988 OB in "Cold Sweat," followed by "Right Behind the Flag."

ARANAS, RAUL. Born Oct. 1, 1947 in Manilla, PI. Graduate Pace U. Debut 1976 OB in "Savages," followed by "Yellow Is My Favorite Color," "49," "Bullet Headed Birds," "Tooth of Crime," "Teahouse," "Shepard Sets," "Cold Air," "La Chunga," "The Man Who Turned into a Stick," "Twelfth Night," "Shogun Macbeth," "Boutique Living & Disposable Icons," Bdwy in "Loose Ends" (1978).

ARANHA, RAY. Born May 1, 1939 in Miami. Fl. Graduate Fl. A&M U., AADA. Bdwy debut 1987 in "Fences." OB in "Zooman and the Sign" (1980).

ARBUS, ALLAN. Born Feb. 15 in NYC. Attended CCNY. Debut 1965 OB in "The Cocktail Party," followed by "Uncle Vanya," "Julius Caesar," "The Tramp," "Golden Door," "V & V Only," Bdwy in "Dreyfus in Rehearsal" (1974).

ARCARO, ROBERT (a.k.a. Bob) Born Aug. 9, 1952 in Brooklyn, NY. Graduate Wesleyan U. Debut 1977 OB in "New York City Street Show," followed by "Working Theatre Festival," "Man with a Raincoat," "Working One-Acts."

ARLT, LEWIS. Born Dec. 5, 1949 in Kingston, NY. Carnegie Tech graduate. Bdwy debut 1975 in "Murder among Friends," followed by "Piaf," OB in "War and Peace," "The Interview," "Applause," "House across the Street," "Real Estate."

ARNOLD, MADISON. Born Feb. 7, 1956 in Allentown, PA. Attended ColumbiaU, ViennaU, UBerlin, OB in "The Lower Depths," "Much Ado about Nothing," "The Gamblers," "The Marriage," "Macbeth," "Basic Training of Pavlo Hummel," "Jungle of Cities," "Ride a Black Horse," "In the Boom Boom Room," "The Good Life," "Dash," "Julius Caesar," Bdwy in "The Man in the Glass Booth" (1968).

ARNOLD, TICHINA. Born June 28, 1969 in NYC. Debut 1987 OB in "Little Shop of Horrors," followed by "The Haggadah," "Topsy Turvy."

ARONS, ELLYN. Born Oct. 29, 1956 in Philadelphia, PA. Graduate TempleU. Debut OB in "Plain and Fancy" (1979), followed by Bdwy in "Camelot" (1980), "Mame," "Jerry's Girls," "Teddy and Alice."

ARTHUR, HELEN-JEAN. Born Nov. 2, 1933 in Chicago, IL. Beloit Col. graduate. Debut 1957 OB in "Othello," followed by "The 12 Pound Look," "Streets of New York," "Vera with Kate," "Declasse," "Teach Me How to Cry," "A Touch of the Poet," "Sister Mary Ignatius," "Shirley Basin," Bdwy in "Send Me No Flowers" (1960), "Moon Beseiged," "Look Back in Anger."

ASBURY, CLEVE. Born Dec. 29, 1958 in Houston, Tx. Attended L.A.Valley Col. Bdwy debut 1979 in "Peter Pan," followed by "West Side Story," "Bring Back Birdie," "Copperfield," "Harrigan 'n' Hart," "Me and My Girl."

ASHFORD, ROBERT. Born Nov. 19, 1959 in Orlando, FL. Attended Washington & Lee U. Bdwy debut 1987 in "Anything Goes."

ASHLEY, ELIZABETH. Born Aug. 30, 1939 in Ocala, FL. Attended Neighborhood Playhouse. Bdwy debut 1959 in "The Highest Tree," followed by "Take Her She's Mine" for which she received a Theatre World Award, "Barefoot in the Park," "Ring Round the Bathtub," "Cat on a Hot Tin Roof," "The Skin of Our Teeth," "Legend," "Caesar and Cleopatra," "Hide and Seek," "Agnes of God," OB in "The Milk Train Doesn't Stop Here Anymore."

ASHLEY, MARY ELLEN. Born June 11, 1938 in Long Island City, NY. Queens Col. graduate. Bdwy debut 1943 in "Innocent Voyage," followed by "By Appointment Only," "Annie Get Your Gun," "Yentl," OB in "Carousel," "Polly," "Panama Hattie," "Soft Touch," "Suddenly the Music Starts," "The Facts of Death," "A Drifter, the Grifter and Heather McBride," "Leave It to Me."

ASQUITH, WARD. Born March 21 in Philadelphia, Pa. Graduate UPa., Columbia U. Debut 1979 OB in "After the Rise," followed by "Kind Lady," "Incident at Vichy," "Happy Birthday Wanda June," "Another Part of the Forest," "The Little Foxes," "Sherlock Holmes & the Hands of Othello."

ATIENZA, EDWARD. Born Jan. 27, 1924 in London, Eng. Attended LAMDA. Bdwy debut 1957 in "Romanoff and Juliet," followed by "Becket," CC Old Vic productions, "Andorra," "The Affair," OB in "Ivanov," "Zero Positive."

AUSTIN, BETH. (aka Elizabeth). Born May 23, 1952 in Philadelphia, PA. Graduate Point Park Col., Pittsburgh Playhouse. Debut 1977 OB in "Wonderful Town," followed by "The Prevalence of Mrs. Seal," "Engaged," "Pastoral," "Head over Heels," "A Kiss Is Just a Kiss," "Tales of Tinseltown," "Olympus on My Mind," "Zero Positive," Bdwy in "Sly Fox" (1977), "Whoopee!," "Onward Victoria!"

AUSTIN, IVY. Born Jan. 19, 1958 in Brooklyn, NY. Graduate Colgate U. Bdwy debut 1986 in "Raggedy Ann," followed by NYCOpera's "Candide," "Sweeney Todd," "The Merry Widow," "South Pacific," "Half a World Away."

AVARI, ERICK. Born Apr. 13, 1952 in Calcutta, IN. Graduate Charleston (SC) Col. Debut 1983 OB in "Bhutan," followed by "Comedy of Errors," "Map of the World," "A Midsummer Night's Dream."

AYLWARD, TONY. Born May 30 in NYC. Attended Hunter Col. Debut 1960 OB in "Gay Divorce," followed by "Babes in Arms," "Class Act," "A Hole in the Wall," "Corkscrews," "Gingerbread Lady."

AYR, MICHAEL. Born Sept. 8, 1953 in Great Falls, MT. Graduate SMU. Debut 1976 OB in "Mrs. Murray's Farm," followed by "The Farm," "Ulysses in Traction," "Lulu" "Cabin 12," "Stargazing," "The Deserter," "Hamlet," "Mary Stuart," "Save Grand Central," "The Beaver Coat," "Richard II," "Great Grandson of Jedediah Kohler," "Domestic Issues," "Time Framed," "The Dining Room," "The Sea Gull," "Love's Labour's Lost," "Rum and Coke," "El Salvador," Bdwy in "Hide and Seek" (1980), "Piaf," "The Musical Comedy Murders of 1940."

BABCOCK, KAREN. Born No. 18, 1958 in Homestead, Fl. Graduate Carnegie-Mellon U. Bdwy debut 1988 in "Chess."

BACKUS, RICHARD. Born Mar. 28, 1945 in Goffstown, NH Harvard graduate. Bdwy debut 1971 in "Butterflies Are Free," followed by "Promenade All," for which he received a Theatre World Award, "Ah, Wilderness!," "Camelot" (1981), OB in "Studs Edsel," "Gimme Shelter," "Sorrows of Stephen," "Missing Persons," "Henry V," "Talley and Son," "Tomorrow's Monday," "Bunker Reveries."

BACON, KEVIN. Born July 8, 1958 in Philadelphia, PA. Debut 1978 OB in "Getting Out," followed by "Glad Tidings," "Album," "Flux," "Poor Little Lambs," "Slab Boys," "Men without Dates," "Loot," "Marathon 87."

BAEZ, RAFAEL. Born Aug. 3, 1963 in NYC. Attended CCNY. Debut 1987 OB in "La Puta Vita," followed by "Enough Is Enough," "Ariano."

BAKER, ROBERT MICHAEL. Born Feb. 28, 1954 in Boston, MA. Graduate AADA. Debut 1987 OB in "Company."

BALABAN, ROBERT/BOB. Born Aug. 16, 1945 in Chicago, IL. Attended Colgate, NYU. Debut 1967 OB in "You're a Good Man, Charlie Brown," followed by "Up Eden," "White House Murder Case," "Basic Training of Pavlo Hummel," "The Children," "Marie and Bruce," "Three Sisters," Bdwy in "Plaza Suite" (1968), "Some of My Best Friends," "Inspector General," "Speed-the-Plow."

BALDWIN, ALEC. Born Apr. 3, 1958 in Massapequa, NY. Attended George Washington U, NYU, Lee Strasberg Inst. Bdwy debut 1986 in "Loot," for which he received a Theatre World Award, followed by "Serious Money."

BALLARD, KAYE. Born Nov. 20, 1926 in Cleveland, OH. Debut 1954 OB in "The Golden Apple," followed by "Cole Porter Revisited," "Hey, Ma, Kaye Ballard," "She Stoops to Conquer," "Working 42nd Street at Last!," Bdwy in "The Beast in Me" (1963), "Royal Flush," "Molly," "Pirates of Penzance."

BALOU, BUDDY. Born in 1953 in Seattle, WA. Joined American Ballet Theatre in 1970, rising to soloist. Joined Dancers in 1977. Bdwy debut 1980 in "A Chorus Line," followed by "Song and Dance."

BANES, LISA. Born July 9, 1955 in Chagrin Falls, OH. Juilliard grad. Debut OB 1980 in "Elizabeth I," followed by "A Call from the East," "Look Back in Anger" for which she received a Theatre World Award, "My Sister in This House," "Antigone," "Three Sisters," "The Cradle Will Rock," "Isn't It Romantic," "Fighting International Fat," "Ten by Tennessee," "On the Verge," "Emily."

BARBOUR, ELEANOR. Born Jan. 23, 1945 in NYC. HofstraU graduate. Debut 1976 OB in "Follies," followed by "Manhattan Breakdown," "Stages."

BARKER, CHRISTINE. Born Nov. 26 in Jacksonville, FL. Attended UCLA. Bdwy debut 1979 in "A Chorus Line."

BARKER, JEAN. Born Dec. 20 in Philadelphia, PA. Attended UPa, AmThWing. Debut 1953 OB in "The Bald Soprano," followed by "Night Shift," "A Month in the Country," "Portrait of Jenny," "Knucklebones," "About Iris Berman," "Goodnight, Grandpa," "Victory Bonds," "Cabbagehead," "Oklahoma Samovar," Bdwy in "The Innkeepers" (1956).

BARKER, MARGARET. Born Oct. 10, 1908 in Baltimore, MD. Attended Bryn Mawr. Bdwy debut 1928 in "Age of Innocence," followed by "The Barretts of Wimpole Street," "The House of Connelly," "Men in White," "Gold Eagle Guy," "Leading Lady," "Member of the Wedding," "Autumn Garden," "See the Jaguar," "Ladies of the Corridor," "The Master Builder," OB in "Wayside Motor Inn," "The Loves of Cass McGuire," "Three Sisters," "Details without a Map," "The Inheritors," "Caligula," "The Mound Builders," "Quiet in the Land," "Uncle Vanya."

BARO, REGINA. Born Sept. 7 in NYC. Attended HB Studio. Debut 1987 OB in "Bodega."

BARON, EVALYN. Born Apr. 21, 1948 in Atlanta, GA. Graduate Northwestern., UMinn. Debut 1979 OB in "Scrambled Feet," followed by "Hijinks," "I Can't Keep Running in Place," "Jerry's Girls," "Harvest of Strangers," "Quilters," Bdwy in "Fearless Frank" (1980), "Big River," "Rags." "Social Security."

BARRETT, LAURINDA. Born in 1931 in NYC. Attended Wellesley Col., RADA. Bdwy debut 1956 in "Too Late the Phalatrope," followed by "The Girls in 509," "The Milk Train Doesn't Stop Here Anymore," "UTBU," "I Never Sang for My Father," "Equus," OB in "The Misanthrope," "Palm Tree in a Rose Garden," "All Is Bright," "The Carpenters," "Ah, Wilderness!," "The Other Side of Newark," "The Boys Next Door."

BARTENIEFF, GEORGE. Born Jan. 24, 1933 in Berlin, Ger. Bdwy debut 1947 in "The Whole World Over," followed by "Venus Is," "All's Well That Ends Well," "Quotations from Chairman Mao Tse-Tung," "The Death of Bessie Smith," "Cop-Out," "Room Service," "Unlikely Heroes," OB in "Walking to Waldheim," "Memorandum," "The Increased Difficulty of Concentration," "Trelawny of the Wells," "Charley Chestnut Rides the IRT," "Radio (Wisdom): Sophia Part I," "Images of the Dead," "Dead End Kids," "The Blonde Leading the Blonde," "The Dispossessed," "Growing Up Gothic," "Rosetti's Apologies," "On the Lam," "Samuel Beckett Trilogy," "Quartet," "Help Wanted," "A Matter of Life and Death," "The Heart That Eats Itself," "American Notes," "Us," "An Evening of British Music Hall."

BARTLETT, D'JAMIN. Born May 21 in NYC. Attended AADA. Bdwy debut 1973 in "A Little Night Music" for which she received a Theatre World Award, OB in "The Glorious Age," "Boccaccio," "2 by 5," "Lulu," "Alex Wilder," "Clues to Life," "D'Jamin Sings Lennon & McCartney," "The Grandma Plays."

BARTLETT, PETER. Born Aug. 28, 1942 in Chicago, IL. Attended LoyolaU, LAMDA. Bdwy debut 1969 in "A Patriot for Me," followed by "Gloria and Esperanza," "OB in "Boom Boom Room," "I Remember the House Where I Was Born," "Crazy Locomotive," "Thurber Carnival," "Hamlet."

BARTLETT, ROBIN. Born Apr. 22, 1951 in NYC. Graduate Boston U. Bdwy debut 1975 in "Yentl," followed by "The World of Sholem Aleichem," OB in "Agamemnon," "Fathers and Sons," "No End of Blame," "Living Quarters," "After the Fall," "Cheapside," "The Early Girl," "Cave Life."

BARTON, FRED. Born Oct. 20, 1958 in Camden, NJ. Graduate Harvard. Debut 1982 OB in "Forbidden Broadway."

BASSETT, ANGELA. Born Aug. 16, 1958 in NYC. Graduate YaleU. Debut 1982 OB in "Colored People's Time," followed by "Antigone," "Black Girl," "Henry IV Part I," Bdwy in "Ma Rainey's Black Bottom," "Joe Turner's Come and Gone."

BATES, DAVID. Born Jan. 12, 1962 in Tampa, FL. Graduate FlStateU, NYU. Debut 1988 OB in "Girl of the Golden West."

BATES, KATHY. Born June 18, 1948 in Memphis, TN, Graduate S. Methodist U. Debut 1976 OB in "Vanities," followed by "The Art of Dining," "Curse of the Starving Class," "Frankie and Johnny in the Claire de Lune," "Frankie & Johnny in the Clair de Lune," "The Road to Mecca," Bdwy in "Goodbye Fidel" (1980), "5th of July," "Come Back to the 5 & Dime, Jimmy Dean," " 'night, Mother."

BATT, BRYAN. Born March 1, 1963 in New Orleans, La. Graduate Tulane U. Debut 1987 OB in "Too Many Girls," Bdwy in "Starlight Express" (1988).

BAZZELL, LARRY. Born Dec. 5, 1950 in Baton Rouge, LA. Graduate LaStateU. Debut 1987 OB in "Prime Time," followed by "The Signal Season of Dummy Hoy."

BEDFORD-LLOYD, JOHN. Born Jan. 2, 1956 in New Haven, CT. Graduate Williams Col., Yale. Debut OB 1983 in "Vieux Carre," followed by "She Stoops to Conquer," "The Incredibly Famous Willy Rivers," "Digby," "Rum and Coke," "Trinity Site," "Richard II."

BEECHMAN, LAURIE. Born Apr. 4, 1954 in Philadelphia, Pa. Attended NYU. Bdwy debut 1977 in "Annie," followed by "Pirates of Penzance," "Joseph and the Amazing Technicolor Dreamcoat" for which she received a Theatre World Award. "Some Enchanted Evening" (OB), "Pal Joey in Concert," "Cats."

BEERS, FRANCINE. Born Nov. 26 in NYC. Attended Hunter, CCNY. Debut 1962 OB in "King of the Whole Damned World," followed by "Kiss Mama," "Monopoly," "Cakes with Wine," "The Grandma Plays," Bdwy in "Cafe Crown," "6 Rms Riv Vu," "The American Clock," "Curse of an Aching Heart."

BELANGER, MICHAEL. Born Nov. 26, 1959 in Manchester, NH. Debut 1980 OB in "Friend of the Family," followed by "Psycho Beach Party."

BELMONTE, VICKI. Born Jan. 20, 1947 in U.S.A. Bdwy debut 1960 in "Bye Bye Birdie," followed by "Subways Are for Sleeping," "All American," "Annie Get Your Gun" (LC), OB in "Nunsense."

BEN-ARI, NEAL. (formerly Neal Klein) Born Mar. 20, 1952 in Brooklyn, NY. Graduate UPa. Bdwy debut in "The First" (1981), followed by "Roza," "Chess," OB in "La Boheme," "1-2-3-4-5."

BENDER, JEFF. Born May 20, 1962 in Oakland, CA. Attended Pacific Consv., NYU. Debut 1985 OB in "Second Hurricane," followed by "Alvrone," "Twelfth Night," "Angel City," "The Odyssey."

BENEDICT, KENTON. Born in Whittier, CA. Graduate CSU/Fullerton, TempleU. Debut 1987 OB in "Joe LaPorte," followed by "Nightshade," "Macbeth."

BENING, ANNETTE. Born May 29, 1958 in Topeka, Ks. Graduate SanFranStateU. Debut OB 1986 and Bdwy 1987 in "Coastal Disturbances" for which she received a Theatre World Award, followed OB by "Spoils of War."

Mary Alice	John Aller	Jean Anderson	Philip Anderson	Barbara Andres	Peter Appel
Raul Aranas	Tichina Arnold	Robert Ashford	Mary Ellen Ashley	Ward Asquith	Ivy Austin
Karen Babcock	Rafael Baez	D'Jamin Bartlett	Peter Bartlett	Robin Bartlett	David R. Bates
Bryan Batt	Laurie Beechman	Michael Belanger	Vicki Belmonte	Neal Ben-Ari	Annette Bening
Cindy Benson	David Berman	Barbara Berque	Jeffrey Bihr	Judith Blazer	Robert Blumenfeld

BENNETT, WALTER ALLEN, JR. Born Sept. 4 in Trenton, NJ. Graduate ShawU., UCLA. Debut 1983 OB in "Ceremonies in Dark Old Men," followed by "American Dreams," "Wasted," "That Serious He-Man Ball."

BENSINGER, MIMI. Born May 5 in Pottsville, PA. Attended PennState, AmThWing. Debut OB in "Electra" (1961), followed by "Hadrian's Wall," "The Doctor in spite of Himself," "The Eye of a Bird," "A Doll's House," "Two Orphans," "Hall of North American Forests."

BENSON, CINDY. Born Oct. 2, 1951 in Attleboro, Ma. Graduate St. Leo Col., UIll. Debut 1981 OB in "Some Like It Cole," followed by Bdwy "Les Miserables"(1987).

BERMAN, DAVID. Born Oct. 26, 1950 in Cleveland, OH. Debut 1976 OB in "Marco Polo," followed by "Auto-Destruct," "Pins and Needles," "Chinchilla," "Getting Out," "Hunting Cockroaches," Bdwy in "Man and Superman" (1978), "The News," "The First," "Speed-the-Plow."

BERNHARD, SANDRA. Born June 6, 1955 in Flint, MI. Debut 1988 OB in "Without You I'm Nothing."

BERQUE, BARBARA. Born Aug. 31, 1953 in St. Louis, MO. Debut 1983 OB in "El Salvador ," followed by "The Wonder Years," "What Does a Blind Leopard See?," "The Enclave," "Measure for Measure," "The Hot 1 Baltimore," "You Never Can Tell."

BERRIDGE, ELIZABETH. Born May 2, 1962 in Westchester, NY. Attended Strasberg Inst. Debut 1984 OB in "The Vampires," followed by "The Incredibly Famous Willy Rivers," "Ground Zero Club," "Outside Waco," "Cruise Control," "Sorrows and Sons," "Crackwalker," "Coyote Ugly."

BEVELANDER, NANNETTE. Born Jan. 19, 1956 in Holland. Graduate Canadian College of Dance. Bdwy debut 1983 in "Oh! Calcutta!"

BIHR, JEFFREY. Born Feb. 27, 1949 in San Francisco, CA. Graduate UCBerkeley. Debut 1987 OB in "Hard Times."

BIRNEY, DAVID. Born Apr. 23, 1939 in Washington, DC. Graduate Dartmouth, UCLA. OB in "Comedy of Errors," "Titus Andronicus," "King John," "MacBird," "Crime of Passion," "Ceremony of Innocence," Lincoln Center's "Summertree" for which he received a Theatre World Award, "The Miser," "Playboy of the Western World," "Good Woman of Setzuan," "An Enemy of the People," and "Antigone," "Man and Superman," Bdwy in "Amadeus" (1983), "Benefactors."

BIRNEY, REED. Born Sept. 11, 1954 in Alexandria, Va. Attended Boston U. Bdwy debut 1977 in "Gemini," OB in "The Master and Margarita," "Bella Figura," "Winterplay," "The Flight of the Earls," "Filthy Rich," "Lady Moonsong, Mr. Monsoon," "The Common Pursuit," "Zero Positive."

BLAIR, PAMELA. Born Dec. 5, 1949 in Arlington, Vt. Attended Ntl. Acad. of Ballet. Bdwy debut 1972 in "Promises Promises," followed by "Sugar," "Seesaw," "Of Mice and Men," "Wild and Wonderful," "A Chorus Line," "The Best Little Whorehouse in Texas," "King of Hearts," "The Nerd," OB in "Ballad of Boris K," "Split," "Real Life Funnies," "Double Feature," "Hit Parade."

BLAISDELL, NESBITT. Born Dec. 6, 1928 in NYC. Graduate Amherst, Columbia. Debut 1978 OB in "Old Man Joseph and His Family," followed by "Moliere in spite of Himself," "Guests of the Nation," "Ballad of Soapy Smith," "Custom of the Country," "A Cup of Coffee."

BLATT, BETH. Born Nov. 27, 1957 in Wilmette, IL. Graduate Dartmouth Col. Debut 1983 OB in "She Loves Me," followed by "One Touch of Venus," "The Last Musical Comedy."

BLAZER, JUDITH. Born Oct. 22, 1956 in Dover, NJ. Graduate Manhattan School of Music. Debut 1979 OB in "Oh, Boy!," followed by "Robertan Concert," "A Little Night Music," "Company."

BLOCK, LARRY. Born Oct. 30, 1942 in NYC. Graduate URI. Bdwy bow 1966 in "Hail Scrawdyke," followed by "La Turista," OB in "Eh?," "Fingernails Blue as Flowers," "Comedy of Errors," "Coming Attractions," "Henry IV Part 2," "Feuhrer Bunker," "Manhattan Love Songs," "Souvenirs," "The Golem," "Responsible Parties," "Hit Parade," "Largo Desolato," "The Square Root of 3," "Young Playwrights Festival," "Hunting Cockroaches," "Two Gentlemen of Verona," "Yellow Dog Contract."

BLOOMFIELD, DON. Born in Cambridge, Ma., in 1964. Attended Drew U. Debut 1986 OB in "Lily Dale."

BLUM, MARK. Born May 14, 1950 in Newark, NJ. Graduate UPa, UMinn. Debut 1976 OB in "The Cherry Orchard," followed by "Green Julia," "Say Goodnight, Gracie," "Table Settings," "Key Exchange," "Loving Reno," "Messiah," "It's Only a Play," "Little Footsteps," "Cave of Life," "Gus & Al."

BLUMENFELD, ROBERT. Born Feb. 26, 1943 in NYC. Graduate Rutgers, Columbia U. Bdwy debut 1970 in "Othello," OB in "The Fall and Redemption of Man," "The Tempest," "The Dybbuk," "Count Dracula," "Nature and Purpose of the Universe," "House Music," "The Keymaker," "Epic Proportions," "Tatterdemalion," "Iolanthe," "Temple."

BOAS, PEGGY. Born Oct. 20, 1957 in Havertown, PA. Debut 1988 OB in "Robin's Band."

BOBBY, ANNE MARIE. Born Dec. 12, 1967 in Paterson, NJ. Attended Oxford U. Debut 1983 OB in "American Passion," followed by "The Human Comedy," "The Real Thing," "Hurlyburly," "Precious Sons," "Smile," "Class 1 Acts," "Godspell."

BODLE, JANE. Born Nov 12 in Lawrence, KS. Attended UUtah. Bdwy debut 1983 in "Cats," followed by "Les Miserables."

BOGARDUS, STEPHEN. Born Mar. 11, 1954 in Norfolk, Va. Princeton graduate. Bdwy debut 1980 in "West Side Story," followed by "Les Miserables," OB in "March of the Falsettos," "Feathertop," "No Way to Treat a Lady."

BOGAZIANOS, VASILI. Born Feb. 1, 1949 in NYC. Graduate San Francisco State Col. Debut 1978 OB in "P.S. Your Cat Is Dead" for which he received a Theatre World Award, followed by "Loney's 66," "Fun."

BOGOSIAN, ERIC. Born Apr. 24, 1953 in Woburn, MA. Graduate Oberlin Col. Debut 1982 OB in "Men Inside/Voices of America," followed by "Funhouse," "Drinking in America," "Talk Radio," "Sex, Drugs, Rock & Roll."

BOOCKVOR, STEVEN. Born Nov. 18 1942 in NYC. Attended Queens Col., Juilliard. Bdwy debut 1966 in "Anya," followed by "A Time for Singing," "Cabaret," "Mardi Gras," "Jimmy," "Billy," "The Rothschilds," "Follies," "Over Here," "The Lieutenant," "Musical Jubilee," "Annie," "Working," "The First," "A Chorus Line."

BOONE, MICHAEL KELLY. Born Mar. 13, 1957 in Abingdon, VA. Graduate UTenn. Bdwy debut 1985 in "Take Me Along," OB in "The Merry Widow," "Gifts of the Magi," "The Bone Ring," "Terry by Terry."

BOOTHBY, VICTORIA. Born in Chicago, Il. Graduate Barnard Col. Debut 1971 OB in "Jungle of Cities," "Man's a Man," "Coarse Acting Show," "Beethoven/Karl," "False Confessions," "Professor George," followed by "Roza," Bdwy in "Beethoven's Tenth,"(1984), "Stepping Out."

BORGES, YAMIL. Born June 8, 1958 in San Lorenzo, PR. Attended HB Studio. Bdwy debut 1980 in "West Side Story," OB in "El Bravo," "The Transposed Heads."

BORRELLI, JIM. Born Apr. 10, 1948 in Lawrence, MA. Graduate Boston Col. Debut 1971 OB in "Subject to Fits," followed by "Beyond Therapy," "Basic Training of Pavlo Hummel," "Bullpen," Bdwy in "Grease," "The Nerd."

BORTS, JOANNE. Born June 12, 1961 in Syosset, NY. Graduate SUNY/Binghamton. Debut 1985 OB in "The Golden Land," followed by "On Second Avenue."

BOSCO, PHILIP. Born Sept. 26, 1930 in Jersey City, NJ. Graduate Catholic U. Credits: "Auntie Mame," "Rape of the Belt," "Ticket of Leave Man," "Donnybrook," "Man for All Seasons," "Mrs. Warren's Profession," with LCRep in "The Alchemist," "East Wind," "Galileo," "St. Joan," "Tiger at the Gate," "Cyrano," "King Lear," "A Great Career," "In the Matter of J. Robert Oppenheimer," "The Miser," "The Time of Your Life," "Camino Real," "Operation Sidewinder," "Amphitryon," "Enemy of the People," "Playboy of the Western World," "Good Woman of Setzuan," "Antigone," "Mary Stuart," "Narrow Road to the Deep North," "The Crucible," "Twelfth Night," "Enemies," "Plough and the Stars," "Merchant of Venice," and "A Streetcar Named Desire," "Henry V," "Threepenny Opera," "Streamers," "Stages," "St. Joan," "The Biko Inquest," "Man and Superman," "Whose Life Is It Anyway," "Major Barbara," "A Month in the Country," "Bacchae," "Hedda Gabler," "Don Juan in Hell," "Inadmissible Evidence," "Eminent Domain," "Misalliance," "Learned Ladies," "Some Men Need Help," "Ah, Wilderness!," "The Caine Mutiny Court Martial," "Heartbreak House," "Come Back, Little Sheba," "Love of Anatole," "Be Happy for Me," "Master Class," "You Never Can Tell," "A Man for All Seasons."

BOURNEUF, STEPHEN. Born Nov. 24, 1957 in St. Louis, MO. Graduate S. Louis U. Bdwy debut 1981 in "Broadway Follies," followed by "Oh, Brother!," "Dreamgirls" (1987).

BOUTSIKARIS, DENNIS. Born Dec. 21, 1952 in Newark, NJ. Graduate Hampshire Col. Debut 1975 OB in "Another Language," followed by "Funeral March for a One-Man Band," "All's Well That Ends Well," "A Day in the Life of the Czar," "Nest of the Wood Grouse," "Cheapside," "Rum and Coke," "The Boys Next Door," Bdwy in "Filumena" (1980), "Bent," "Amadeus."

BOVA, JOSEPH. Born May 25 in Cleveland, OH. Graduate Northwestern U. Debut 1959 OB in "On the Town," followed by "Once Upon a Mattress," "House of Blue Leaves," "Comedy," "The Beauty Part," "Taming of the Shrew," "Richard III," "Comedy of Errors," "Invitation to a Beheading," "Merry Wives of Windsor," "Henry V," "Streamers," Bdwy in "Rape of the Belt," "Irma La Douce," "Hot Spot," "The Chinese," "American Millionaire," "St. Joan," "42nd Street."

BOVE, MARK. Born Jan. 9, 1960 in Pittsburgh, Pa. Bdwy debut 1980 in "West Side Story," followed by "Woman of the Year," "A Chorus Line."

BOWDEN, RICHARD. Born May 21 in Savannah, Ga. Graduate UGa., UBristol/Eng. Bdwy debut 1964 in "Don Carlos" (Schiller Theatre), followed by "Captain Brassbound's Conversion"(1972), OB in "Mlle. Colombe," "Pocahontas," "Freedom Train," "As You Like It," "The Tavern."

BOYD, JULIE. Born Jan. 2 in Kansas City, MO. Graduate UUtah, Yale. Bdwy debut 1985 in "Noises Off," followed by OB in "Only You."

BOYLE, ROBERT OTT. Born Mar. 28, 1950 in Spangler, PA. Graduate Carnegie-Mellon U. Debut 1980 OB in "Merton of the Movies," followed by "King of Hearts," "The Rise of David Levinsky," "Esther: A Vaudeville Megillah," Bdwy in "Alice in Wonderland" (1982), "Doubles."

BRADFORD, Gary. Born Jan. 31, 1954 in Dearborn, MI. Attended UMich, Neighborhood Playhouse. Bdwy debut 1988 in "Macbeth."

BRANDT, MAX: Born Aug. 28, 1925 in Hamburg, Ger. Attended London's Webber-Douglas School. Bdwy debut 1973 in "Full Circle," followed by OB in "Beverly's Yard Sale."

BRASSER, VICTORIA. Born May 13, 1959 in Rochester, NY. Graduate Eastman School of Music. Bdwy debut 1985 in "Sunday in the Park with George," followed by OB's "On the 20th Century," "Mlle. Colombe."

BRAZDA, DAVID. Born Sept. 28, 1954 in Weisbaden, Ger. Attended UVa., Circle in the Square. Debut 1985 OB in "Onlyman," followed by "Two Gentlemen of Verona," "Pericles," "Macbeth," "The Imaginary Invalid," "Electra."

BREEN, J. PATRICK. Born Oct. 26, 1960 in Brooklyn, NY. Graduate NYU. Debut 1982 OB in "Epiphany," followed by "Little Murders," "Blood Sports," "Class 1 Acts," Bdwy in "Brighton Beach Memoirs" (1983).

BRENN, JANNI. Born Feb. 13 in Ft. Wayne, IN. Graduate Stanford, Columbia. Debut 1970 OB in "Mod Donna," followed by "Jungle of Cities," "Subject to Fits," "Kaddish," "On Mt. Chimbrazo," "Big and Little," "The Survivor," "The Master and Margarita," "The Seagull," "Words from the Moon," "Romeo and Juliet."

BRENNAN, MAUREEN. Born Oct. 11, 1952 in Washington, DC. Attended UCin. Bdwy debut 1974 in "Candide" for which she received a Theatre World Award, followed by "Going Up," "Knickerbocker Holiday," "Little Johnny Jones," "Stardust," OB in "Shakespeare's Cabaret," "Candide," "Stardust."

BRENNAN, NORA. Born Dec. 1, 1953 in East Chicago, In. Graduate PurdueU. Bdwy debut 1980 in "Camelot," followed by "Cats."

BRIAR, SUZANNE. Born Feb. 8, 1946 in Washington, DC. Graduate USyracuse. Debut 1985 OB in "Tatterdemalion," followed by "The Princess Pat," "The Red Mill," "Oh, Boy!," "No, No, Nanette," "Can't Help Singing Kern!," Bdwy in "Chess" (1988).

BRILL, FRAN. Born Sept. 30 in PA. Attended Boston U. Bdwy debut 1969 in "Red, White and Maddox," OB in "What Every Woman Knows," "Scribes," "Naked," "Look Back in Anger," "Knuckle," "Skirmishes," "Baby with the Bathwater," "Holding Patterns," "Festival of One Acts," "Taking Steps," "Young Playwrights Festival," "Claptrap."

BRISBIN, DAVID. Born June 26, 1952 in Minneapolis, MN. Graduate Augsburg Col. Debut 1980 OB in "Dead End Kids," followed by "Dark Ride," "Flow My Tears, the Policeman Said," "Help Wanted," "The Balcony," "Minnesota," "Gus and Al."

BROADHURST, KENT. Born Feb. 4, 1940 in St. Louis, Mo. Graduate UNe. Debut 1968 OB in "The Fourth Wall," followed by "Design for Living," "Marching Song," "Heartbreak House," "Dark of the Moon," "Hunchback of Notre Dame," "Cold Sweat," "April Snow," Bdwy in "The Caine Mutiny Court-Martial"(1983).

BRODY, JONATHAN. Born June 16, 1963 in Englewood, NJ. Debut 1982 OB in "Shulamith," followed by "The Desk Set," Bdwy in "Me and My Girl" (1986).

BROOKES, JACQUELINE. Born July 24, 1930 in Montclair, NJ. Graduate UIowa, RADA. Bdwy debut 1955 in "Tiger at the Gates," followed by "Watercolor," "Abelard and Heloise," "A Meeting by the River," OB in "The Cretan Woman" for whoch she received a Theatre World Award, "The Clandestine Marriage," "Measure for Measure," "Duchess of Malfi," "Ivanov," "6 Characters in Search of an Author," "An Evening's Frost," "Come Slowly, Eden," "The Increased Difficulty of Concentration," "The Persians," "Sunday Dinner," "House of Blue Leaves," "Owners," "Hallelujah!," "Dream of a Blacklisted Actor," "Knuckle," "Mama Sang the Blues," "Buried Child," "On Mt. Chimorazo," "Winter Dancers," "Hamlet," "Old Flames," "The Diviners," "Richard II," "Vieux Carre," "Full Hookup," "Home Sweet Home/Crack."

BROOKS, JEFF. Born Apr. 7, 1950 in Vancouver, Can. Attended Portland State U. Debut 1976 OB in "Titanic," followed by "Fat Chances," "Nature and Purpose of the Universe," "Actor's Nightmare," "Sister Mary Ignatius Explains It All," "Marathon 84," "The Foreigner," "Talk Radio," "Washington Height," Bdwy in "A History of the American Film"(1978).

BROWN, ANN. Born Dec. 1, 1960 in Westwood, NJ. Graduate Trinity Col. Debut 1987 OB in "Shylock," followed by "Side by Side by Sondheim," "Stages."

BROWN, CHUCK. Born Oct. 16, 1959 in Cleveland, OH. Attended Baldwin-Wallace Col. Debut 1984 OB in "Pacific Overtures," followed by "The Shop on Main Street," "Vampire Lesbians of Sodom."

BROWN, GEORGIA. Born Oct. 21, 1933 in London, Eng. NYC debut 1957 OB in "Threepenny Opera," followed by "Greek," Bdwy in "Oliver!" (1962), "Side by Side by Sondheim," "Carmelina," "Roza."

BROWN, GRAHAM. Born Oct. 24 in NYC. Graduate Howard U. OB in "Widower's Houses" (1959), "The Emperor's Clothes," "Time of Storm," "Major Barbara," "Land Beyond the River," "The Blacks," "Firebugs," "Gos Is a (Guess Who?)," "An Evening of 1 Acts," "Man Better Man," "Behold! Cometh the Vanderkellans," "Ride a Black Horse," "The Great MacDaddy," "Eden," "Nevis Mountain Dew," "Season Unravel," "The Devil's Tear," "Sons and Fathers of Sons," "Abercrombie Apocalypse," "Ceremonies in Dark Old Men," "Eyes of the American," "Richard II," "The Taming of the Shrew," Bdwy in "Weekend" (1968), "Man in the Glass Booth," "River Niger," "Pericles," "Black Picture Show," "Kings."

BROWN, JEB. Born Aug. 11, 1964 in NYC. Bdwy debut 1974 in "Cat on a Hot Tin Roof," followed by "Bring Back Birdie," OB in "A Walk on the Wild Side."

BROWN, ROBIN LESLIE. Born Jan. 18 in Canandaigua, NY. Graduate L.I.U. Debut 1980 OB in "The Mother of Us All," followed by "Yours Truly," "Two Gentlemen of Verona," "The Taming of the Shrew," "The Mollusc," "The Contrast," "Pericles," "Andromache," "Macbeth," "Electra."

BROWN, SHARON. Born Jan. 11, 1962 in NYC. Bdwy debut 1967 in "Maggie Flynn," followed by "Joseph and the Amazing Technicolor Dream Coat," "Dreamgirls," OB in "Cummings and Goings."

BROWN, WILLIAM SCOTT. Born Mar. 27, 1959 in Seattle, WA. Attended UWash. Debut 1986 OB in "Juba," Bdwy in "Phantom of the Opera" (1988).

BRYANT, ADAM. (formerly Sal Biagini). Born Apr. 13, 1952 in Brooklyn, NY. Graduate USFla. Debut 1984 OB in "Sing Me Sunshine," followed by "On the Brink," "3 One Acts," "Rosemarie," "Back in the Big Time," "Jacques Brel Is Alive and Well . . .," Bdwy in "Big River" (1987).

BRYANT, CRAIG. Born Sept. 13, 1961 in Aurora, IL. Graduate NYU. Debut 1986 OB in "Orchards," followed by "Why to Refuse."

BRYANT, DAVID. Born May 26, 1936 in Nashville, Tn. Attended TnStateU. Bdwy debut 1972 in "Don't Play Us Cheap," followed by "Bubbling Brown Sugar," "Amadeus," "Les Miserables," OB in "Up in Central Park," "Elizabeth and Essex," "Appear and Show Cause."

BRYCELAND, YVONNE. Born Nov. 18 in Cape Town, SAfrica. Attended St. Mary's Convent. NYC debut 1988 in "The Road to Mecca" for which she received a Theatre World Award.

BRYDON, W. B. Born Sept. 20, 1933 in Newcastle, Eng. Debut 1962 OB in "The Long, the Short and the Tall," followed by "Live Like Pigs," "Sjt. Musgrave's Dance," "The Kitchen," "Come Slowly, Eden," "The Unknown Soldier and His Wife," "Moon for the Misbegotten," "The Orphan," "Possession," "Total Abandon," "Madwoman of Chaillot," "The Circle," "Romeo and Juliet," Bdwy in "The Lincoln Mask," "Ulysses in Nightown," "The Father."

BRYGGMAN, LARRY. Born Dec. 21, 1938 in Concord, Ca. Attended CCSF, AmThWing. Debut 1962 OB in "A Pair of Pairs," followed by "Live Like Pigs," "Stop, You're Killing Me," "Mod Donna," "Waiting for Godot," "Ballymurphy," "Marco Polo Sings a Solo," "Brownsville Raid," "Two Small Bodies," "Museum," "Winter Dancers," "The Resurrection of Lady Lester," "Royal Bob," "Modern Ladies of Guanabacoa," "Rum and Coke," "Bodies, Rest and Motion," "Blood Sports," "Class 1 Acts," "Spoils of War," Bdwy in "Ulysses in Nighttown" (1974), "Checking Out," "Basic Training of Pavlo Hummel," "Richard III."

BRYNE, BARBARA. Born Apr. 1, 1929 in London, Eng. Graduate RADA. NY debut 1981 OB in "Entertaining Mr. Sloane," Bdwy in "Sunday in the Park with George" (1984), "Hay Fever," "Into the Woods."

BUCKLEY, BETTY. Born July 3, 1947 in Big Spring, TX. Graduate TCU. Bdwy debut 1969 in "1776," followed by "Pippin," "Cats," "Song and Dance," "Carrie," OB in "Ballad of Johnny Pot," "What's a Nice Country Like You . . . ," "Circle of Sound," "I'm Getting My Act Together . . .," "Juno's Swans," "The Mystery of Edwin Drood" (OB and Bdwy).

BUCKLEY, MELINDA. Born Apr. 17, 1954 in Attleboro, MA. Graduate UMa. Bdwy debut 1983 in "A Chorus Line," followed by "Raggedy Ann," OB in "Damn Yankees," "Pal Joey."

BUELL, BILL. Born Sept. 21, 1952 in Paipai, Taiwan. Attended Portland State U. Debut 1972 OB in "Crazy Now," followed by "Declassee," "Lorenzaccio," "Promenade," "The Common Pursuit," "Coyote Ugly," "Alias Jimmy Valentine," Bdwy in "Once a Catholic"(1979), "The First."

BUFFALOE, KATHERINE. Born Nov. 7, 1953 in Greenville, SC. Graduate NCSchool of Arts. Bdwy debut 1981 in "Copperfield," followed by "Joseph and the Amazing Technicolor Dreamcoat," OB in "Non Pasquale," "Charley's Tale," "Mary S.," "Alias Jimmy Valentine."

BUONO, CARA. Born Mar. 1, 1971 in The Bronx, NYC. Debut 1984 OB in "Spookhouse," followed by "Patience and Sarah," "Once Removed," "Hidden Parts," "Evening Star."

BURCH, SHELLY. Born Mar. 19, 1960 in Tucson, AZ. Attended Carnegie-Mellon U. Bdwy debut 1978 in "Stop the World I Want to Get Off," followed by "Annie," "Nine," OB in "Alias Jimmy Valentine."

BURGHOFF, GARY. Born May 24, 1943 in Bristol, CT. Debut 1967 OB in "You're a Good Man, Charlie Brown," Bdwy in "The Nerd" (1987).

BURK, TERENCE. Born Aug. 11, 1947 in Lebanon, IL. Graduate S.Ill.U. Bdwy debut 1976 in "Equus," OB in "Religion," "The Future," "Sacred and Profane Love," "Crime and Punishment."

BURKE, MAGGIE. Born May 2, 1936 in Bay Shore, NY. Graduate Sarah Lawrence Col. OB in "Today Is Independence Day," "Lovers and Other Strangers," "Jules Feiffer's Cartoons," "Fog," "Home Is the Hero," "King John," "Rusty & Rico & Lena & Louie," "Friends," "Butterfaces," "Old Times," "Man with a Raincoat," "Hall of North American Forests," Bdwy debut 1985 in "Brighton Beach Memoirs."

BURKE, ROBERT. Born July 25, 1948 in Portland, ME. Graduate Boston Col. Debut 1975 OB in "Prof. George," followed by "Shortchanged Review," "The Arbor," "Slab Boys," "Gardenia," Bdwy in "Macbeth" (1988).

BURKHARDT, GERRY. Born June 14, 1946 in Houston, Tx. Attended Lon Morris Col. Bdwy debut 1968 in "Her First Roman," followed by "The Best Little Whorehouse in Texas," OB in "Girl Crazy," "Leave It to Me."

BURNETT, ROBERT. Born Feb. 28, 1960 in Goshen, NY. Attended HB Studio. Bdwy debut 1985 in "Cats."

BURNS, EILEEN. Born in Hartsdale, NY. Has appeared in "Native Son," "Christopher Blake," "Small Hours," "American Way," "The Women" (1936), "Merrily We Roll Along," "Daughters of Atreus," "First Lady," "Mourning Becomes Electra," OB in "Albee Directs Albee," "Declassee," "Grandma, Pray for Me."

BURRELL, FRED. Born Sept. 18, 1936. Graduate UNC, RADA. Bdwy debut 1964 in "Never Too Late," followed by "Illya Darling," OB in "The Memorandum," "Throckmorton," "Texas," "Voices in the Head," "Chili Queen."

BURRELL, TERESA (formerly Terry). Born Feb. 8, 1952 in Trinidad, WI. Attended Pace U. Bdwy debut 1977 in "Eubie!," followed by "Dreamgirls," "Honky Tonk Nights," OB in "That Uptown Feeling," "They Say It's Wonderful," "George White's Scandals," "Just So."

BURROWS, VINIE. Born Nov. 15, 1928 in NYC. Graduate NYU. Bdwy in "The Wisteria Trees," "Green Pastures," "Mrs. Patterson," "The Skin of Our Teeth," "The Ponder Heart," OB in "Walk Together, Children," "Sister! Sister!," "Her Talking Drum."

BUTT, JENNIFER. Born May 17, 1958 in Valparaiso, In. Stephens Col. graduate. Debut 1983 OB in "The Robber Bridegroom," followed by "Into the Closet," Bdwy in "Les Miserables" (1987).

CAHN, LARRY. Born Dec. 19, 1955 in Nassau, NY. Graduate NorthwesternU. Bdwy debut 1980 in "The Music Man," followed by "Anything Goes," OB in "Susan B!," "Jim Thorpe—All American," "Play to Win."

CALABRO, THOMAS. Born Feb. 3, 1959 in NYC. Graduate FordhamU. Debut 1987 OB in "Wild Blue," followed by "One Act Festival."

CALDWELL, L. SCOTT. Born in Chicago; Graduate Loyola U. Bdwy debut 1980 in "Home," followed by "Joe Turner's Come and Gone," OB in "About Heaven and Earth," "Colored People's Time," "Old Phantoms," "A Season to Unravel," "The Imprisonment of Obatala," "Everyman," "Daughters of the Mock."

CALL, ANTHONY. Born Aug. 31, 1940 in Los Angeles, CA. Attended UPa. Debut 1969 OB in "The David Show," followed by "Frequency," "Countess Mitzi," "After Crystal Night," Bdwy in "Crown Matrimonial" (1973), "The Trip Back Down," "Suspenders."

CALLAN, MICHAEL. Born Nov. 22, 1935 in Philadelphia, PA. Bdwy credits include "The Boy Friend," "Catch a Star," "West Side Story," "Pal Joey in Concert," OB in "Song for a Saturday."

CAMACHO, BLANCA. Born Nov. 19, 1956 in NYC. Graduate NYU. Debut 1984 OB in "Sarita," followed by "Maggie Magalita," "Salon," "Studio"

CAMP, JOANNE. Born Apr. 4, 1951 in Atlanta, GA. Graduate FlAtlanticU, Geo WashU. Debut 1981 OB in "The Dry Martini," followed by "Geniuses," for which she received a Theatre World Award, "June Moon," "Painting Churches," "Merchant of Venice," "Lady from the Sea," "The Contrast," "Coastal Disturbances," "The Rivals," "Andromache," "Electra," "Uncle Vanya."

CARHART, TIMOTHY. Born Dec. 24, 1953 in Washington, DC. UIll. graduate. Debut 1984 OB in "The Harvesting," followed by "The Ballad of Soapy Smith," "Hitch-hikers," "Highest Standard of Living," "Festival of One Acts."

CARIOU, LEN. Born Sept. 30, 1939 in Winnipeg, Can. Bdwy debut 1968 in "House of Atreus," followed by "Henry V" and "Applause" for which he received a Theatre World Award, "Night Watch," "A Little Night Music," "Cold Storage," "Sweeney Todd," "Dance a Little Closer," "Teddy and Alice" OB in "A Sorrow Beyond Dreams," "Up from Paradise," "Master Class," "Day Six."

CARLIN, CHET. Born Feb. 23, 1940 in Malverne, NY. Graduate Ithaca Col., Catholic U. Bdwy debut 1972 in "An Evening with Richard Nixon . . .," OB in "Under Gaslight," "Lou Gehrig Did Not Die of Cancer," "Graffiti!," "Crystal and Fox," "Golden Honeymoon," "Arms and the Man," "Arsenic and Old Lace," "The Father," "Comedy of Errors," "Never the Sinner," "The Emperor Charles."

CARMICHAEL, MARNIE. Born Sept. 22, 1956 in Chapel Hill, NC. Graduate UNC/Chapel Hill, FlaStateU. Debut 1988 OB in "Side by Side by Sondheim."

CARPENTER, WILLIE C. Born Aug. 9, 1945 in Eutaw, Al. Graduate OhioStateU. Debut 1985 OB in "Rude Times," followed by "A Cup of Coffee," Bdwy in "The Musical Comedy Murders of 1940"(1987).

CARRIGAN, WILLIAM. Born Apr. 11, 1957 in Brooklyn, NY. Graduate NYU. Debut 1985 OB in "Creeps," followed by "Merry Wives of Windsor," "New Mexican Fishing," "Good and Faithful Servant."

CARROLL, ALISA. Born Sept. 16, 1971 in Connecticut. Debut 1987 OB in "Take Me Along."

CARROLL, DANNY. Born May 30, 1940 in Maspeth, NY. Bdwy bow in 1957 "The Music Man," followed by "Flora the Red Menace," "Funny Girl," "George M!," "Billy," "Ballroom," "42nd Street," OB in "Boys from Syracuse," "Babes in the Woods."

CARROLL, DAVID. (formerly David-James). Born July 30, 1950 in Rockville Centre, NY. Graduate Dartmouth Col. Debut 1975 OB in "A Matter of Time," followed by "Joseph and the Amazing Technicolor Dreamcoat," "New Tunes," "La Boheme," "Company," Bdwy in "Rodgers and Hart" (1975), "Where's Charley?," "Oh, Brother!," "7 Brides for 7 Brothers," "Roberta in Concert," "The Wind in the Willows," "Chess."

CARTER, MYRA. Born Oct. 27, 1930 in Chicago, IL. Attended Glasgow U. Bdwy debut 1957 in "Major Barbara," followed by "Maybe Tuesday," "Present Laughter," OB in "Trials of Oz," "Abingdon Square."

CARTER, RICK. Born Apr. 29, 1960 in Des Moines, IA. Graduate Drake U. Debut 1987 OB in "The Signal Season of Dummy Hoy."

CASNOFF, PHILIP. Born Aug. 3, 1953 in Philadelphia. Graduate Wesleyan U. Debut 1978 OB in "Gimme Shelter," followed by "Chincilla," "King of Schnorrers," "Mary Stuart," "Henry IV," Bdwy in "Grease" (1973), "Chess" for which he received a Theatre World Award.

CASSERLY, KERRY. Born Oct. 26, 1953 in Minneapolis, MN. Attended UMinn. Bdwy debut 1980 in "One Night Stand," followed by "A Chorus Line," "My One and Only."

CASSIDY, TIM. Born March 22, 1952 in Alliance, OH. Attended UCincinnati. Bdwy debut 1974 in "Good News," followed by "A Chorus Line," "Dreamgirls."

CASTANOS, LUZ. Born July 15, 1935 in NYC. Graduate CUNY. Debut 1959 OB in "Last Visit," followed by "Eternal Sabbath," "Finis for Oscar Wilde," "Young and Fair," "La Dama Duende," "A Media Luz Los Tres," "Yerma," "House of Bernarda Alba."

CATLIN, JODY. Born July 6, 1946 in Nebraska. Graduate William & Mary Col. Debut 1977 OB in "Porno Stars at Home," followed by "Colonomos," "The Price of Genius," "A Chaste Maid in Cheapside," "Ivanov."

CAVANAUGH, ROBERT D. Born Oct. 7, 1971 in Sumter, SC. Bdwy debut 1984 in "Oliver!," followed by "Teddy and Alice."

CAVETT, DICK. Born Nov. 19, 1936 in Kearny, NE. Graduate Yale U. Bdwy debut 1977 in "Otherwise Engaged," followed by "Into the Woods."

CAVISE, JOE ANTONY. Born Jan. 7, 1958 in Syracuse, NY. Graduate Clark U. Debut 1981 OB in "Street Scene," followed by Bdwy 1984 in "Cats."

CAZA, TERRENCE. Born Mar. 26, 1958 in Detroit, MI. Graduate UMi, UWash. Debut 1984 OB in "Pieces of Eight," followed by "As You Like It," "A New Way to Pay Old Debts," "Orchards," "Terry by Terry."

CECIL, PAMELA. Born Dec. 20 in Newport, RI. Attended Midland Lutheran Col., IowaStateU. Bdwy debut 1981 in "Can-Can," followed by "42nd Street," "La Cage aux Folles."

CELLARIO, MARIA. Born June 19, 1948 in Buenos Aires, Arg. Graduate Ithaca Col. Bdwy debut 1975 in "The Royal Family," followed by OB in "Fugue in a Nursery," "Declassee," "Equinox," "Flatbush Faithful," "Our Lady of the Tortilla," "Half Deserted Streets."

CERVERIS, MICHAEL. Born Nov. 6, 1960 in Bethesda, MD. Graduate Yale U. Debut 1983 OB in "Moon," followed by "Macbeth," "Life Is a Dream," "Total Eclipse," "Green Fields," "Abingdon Square," "Blood Sports."

CHAIKIN, SHAMI. Born Apr. 21, 1938 in NYC. Debut 1966 OB in "America Hurrah," followed by "Serpent," "Terminal," "Mutation Show," "Viet Rock," "Mystery Play," "Electra," "The Dybbuk," "Endgame," "Bag Lady," "The Haggadah," "Antigone," "Loving Reno," "Early Warnings," "Uncle Vanya," "Mr. Universe."

CHALFANT, KATHLEEN. Born Jan. 14, 1945 in San Francisco, CA. Graduate StanfordU. Bdwy debut 1975 in "Dance with Me," followed by "M. Butterfly," OB in "Jules Feiffer's Hold Me," "Killings on the Last Line," "The Boor," "Blood Relations," "Signs of Life," "Sister Mary Ignatius Explains It All," "Actor's Nightmare," "Faith Healer," "All the Nice People," "Hard Times."

CHAN, DAVID. Born June 23, 1978 in Marlton, NJ. Bdwy debut 1987 in "Roza."

CHANDLER, DAVID. Born Feb. 3, 1950 in Danbury, Ct. Graduate Oberlin Col. Bdwy debut 1980 in "The American Clock," followed by "Death of a Salesman," OB in "Made in Heaven," "Black Sea Follies," "One Act Festival."

CHANNING, STOCKARD. Born Feb. 13, 1944 in NYC. Attended Radcliffe Col. Debut 1970 OB in "Adaptation/Next," followed by "The Lady and the Clarinet," "The Golden Age," "Woman in Mind," Bdwy in "Two Gentlemen of Verona," "They're Playing Our Song," "The Rink," "Joe Egg," "House of Blue Leaves."

CHAPIN, MILES. Born Dec. 6, 1954 in NYC. Attended HB Studio. Debut 1974 OB in "Joan of Lorraine," followed by "Two Rooms," "Poor Little Lambs," "Terry by Terry," Bdwy in "Summer Brave."

CHAPMAN, ROGER. Born Jan. 1, 1947 in Cheverly, Md. Graduate Rollins Col. Debut 1976 OB in "Who Killed Richard Corey?," followed by "My Life," "Hamlet," "Innocent Thoughts," "Harmless Intentions," "Richard II," "The Great Grandson of Jedediah Kohler," "Threads," "Time Framed," "Nuclear Follies," "St. Hugo of Central Park."

CHARLES, WALTER. Born Apr. 4, 1945 in East Stroudsburg, PA. Graduate Boston U Bdwy debut 1973 in "Grease," followed by "1600 Pennsylvania Avenue," "Knickerbocker Holiday," "Sweeney Todd," "Cats," "La Cage aux Folles."

CHARNAY, LYNNE. Born April 1 in NYC. Attended UWis., Columbia, AADA. Debut 1950 OB in "Came the Dawn," followed by "A Ram's Head," "In a Cold Hotel," "Amata," "Yerma," "Ballad of Winter Soldiers," "Intimate Relations," "Play Me Zoltan," "Grand Magic," "The Time of Your Life," "Nymph Errant," "Nude with Violin," "American Power Play," "Salon," "Three Not from the Twilight Zone," .Bdwy in "Julia, Jake and Uncle Joe"(1961), "A Family Affair," "Broadway," "Inspector General," "Grand Tour."

CHARNIN, SASHA. Born July 27, 1964 in NYC. Graduate NYU. Debut 1986 OB in "Buskers," followed by "They Say It's Wonderful," "No Frills Revue."

CHATER, GORDON. Born Apr. 6, 1922 in London, Eng. NYC debut 1979 OB in "The Elocution of Benjamin," followed by "Learned Ladies," "Major Barbara in Concert," "An Enemy of the People," "She Stoops to Conquer," "Dandy Dick," Bdwy in "Whodunit" (1982).

CHEN, TINA. Born Nov. 2 in Chung King China. Graduate Brown U. Debut 1972 OB in "A Maid's Tragedy," followed by "Family Devotions," "A Midsummer Night's Dream," "Empress of China," "The Year of the Dragon," "Tropical Tree," "Madame de Sade," Bdwy in "The King and I," "Rashomon," "The Love Suicide at Schofield Barracks."

CHESTERMAN, MARY. Born Apr. 8, 1955 in Oklahoma City, OK. Graduate UWash. Debut 1987 OB in "1-2-3-4-5."

CHIANESE, DOMINIC. Born Feb. 24, 1932 in NYC. Graduate Brooklyn Col. Debut 1952 OB with American Savoyards, followed by "Winterset," "Jacques Brel Is Alive, . . . ," "Ballad for a Firing Squad," "City Scene," "End of the War," "Passione," "A Midsummer Night's Dream," "Recruiting Officer," "The Wild Duck," "Oedipus the King," "Hunting Scenes," "Operation Midnight Climax," "Rosario and the Gypsies," "Bella Figura," "House Arrest," Bdwy in "Oliver!," "Scratch," "The Water Engine," "Richard III," "Requiem for a Heavyweight."

CHIBAS, MARISSA. Born June 13, 1961 in NYC. Graduate SUNY/Purchase. Debut 1983 OB in "Asian Shade," followed by "Sudden Death," "Total Eclipse," "Another Antigone," Bdwy in "Brighton Beach Memoirs," "Fresh Horses."

CHINN, LORI TAN. Born July 7 in Seattle, Wash. Bdwy debut 1970 in "Lovely Ladies, Kind Gentlemen," followed by "M. Butterfly," OB in "Coffins for Butterflies," "Hough in Blazes," "Peer Gynt," "The King and I," "Children," "The Secret Life of Walter Mitty," "Bayou Legend," "Primary English Class," "G.R. Point," "Peking Man," "Ballad of Soapy Smith."

CHRIS, MARILYN. Born May 19, 1939 in NYC. Bdwy debut 1966 in "The Office," followed by "Birthday Party," "7 Descents of Myrtle," "Lenny," OB in "Nobody Hears a Broken Drum," "Fame," "Juda Applause," "Junebug Graduates Tonight," "Man Is Man," "In the Jungle of Cities," "Good Soldier Schweik," "The Tempest," "Ride a Black Horse," "Screens," "Kaddish," "Lady from the Sea," "Bread," "Leaving Home," "Curtains," "Elephants," "The Upper Depths," "Man Enough," "Loose Connections," "Yard Sale."

CHRISTOPHER, THOM. Born Oct. 5, 1940 in Jackson Heights, NY. Attended Ithaca Col., Neighborhood Playhouse. Debut 1972 OB in "One Flew over the Cuckoo's Nest," followed by "Tamara," Bdwy in "Emperor Henry IV" (1973), "Noel Coward in Two Keys" for which he received a Theatre World Award, "Caesar and Cleopatra."

CHRYST, GARY. Born in 1959 in LaJolla, Ca. Joined Joffrey Ballet in 1968, Bdwy debut in "Dancin' " (1979), followed by "A Chorus Line," OB in "One More Song, One More Dance," "Music Moves Me."

CIESLA, DIANE. Born May 20, 1952 in Chicago, IL. Graduate Clark Col. Debut 1980 OB in "Uncle Money," followed by "Afternoons in Vegas," "The Taming of the Shrew," "Much Ado about Nothing."

CIOFFI, CHARLES. Born Oct. 31, 1935 in NYC. UMinn graduate. OB in "A Cry of Players," "King Lear," "In the Matter of J. Robert Oppenheimer," "Antigone," "Whistle in the Dark," "Hamlet"(LC), "Self Defense," "Real Estate."

CLARK, CHERYL. Born Dec. 7, 1950 in Boston, MA. Attended Ind. U., NYU. Bdwy debut 1972 in "Pippin," followed by "Chicago," "A Chorus Line."

CLARKE, RICHARD. Born Jan. 31, 1933 in England. Graduate UReading. With LCRep in "St. Joan" (1968), "Tiger at the Gates," "Cyrano de Bergerac," Bdwy in "Conduct Unbecoming" (1970), "The Elephant Man," "Breaking the Code," OB in "Old Glory," "Looking-Glass."

CLATER, ROBERT. Born Oct. 13, 1957 in Jefferson City, MO. Graduate Vassar Col., Temple U. Bdwy debut 1987 in "Dreamgirls."

COATES, KIM. Born Feb. 21, 1958 in Saskatoon, Canada. Graduate USaskatchewan. Bdwy debut 1988 in "A Streetcar Named Desire."

COATS, STEVE. Born Oct. 5, 1954 in Berkeley, CA. Graduate SanFranStateU. Debut 1982 OB in "The World of Ben Caldwell," followed by "Touched," "The Last Danceman," "Stella."

COHENOUR, PATTI. Born Oct. 17, 1952 in Albuquerque, NMx. Attended UNMx. Bdwy debut 1982 in "A Doll's Life," followed by "Pirates of Penzance," "Big River," "The Mystery of Edwin Drood." "Phantom of the Opera," OB in "La Boheme" for which she received a Theatre World Award.

COLE, DEBRA. Born Oct. 27, 1962 in Buffalo, NY. Graduate NYU. Debut 1984 OB in "Fables for Friends," followed by "Daughters," "Bunker Reveries," Bdwy in "House of Blue Leaves" (1986).

COLE, KAY. Born Jan. 13, 1948 in Miami, FL. Bdwy debut 1961 in "Bye Bye Birdie," followed by "Stop the World I Want to Get Off," "Roar of the Greasepaint . . . ," "Hair," "Jesus Christ Superstar," "Words and Music," "Chorus Line," OB in "The Cradle Will Rock," "Two If By Sea," "Rainbow," "White Nights," "Sgt. Pepper's Lonely Hearts Club Band," "On the Swing Shift," "Snoopy," "Road to Hollywood," "One-man Band."

COLICCHIO, VICTOR. Born Aug. 13 in NYC. Graduate St. Vincent School. Debut 1986 OB in "The Call," followed by "Half Deserted Streets."

COLKER, JERRY. Born Mar. 16, 1955 in Los Angeles, CA. Attended Harvard U. Debut 1975 OB in "Tenderloin," followed by "Pal Joey," "3 Guys Naked from the Waist Down," Bdwy in "West Side Story," "Pippin," "A Chorus Line."

COLL, IVONNE. Born Nov. 4 in Fajardo, PR. Attended UPR, LACC, HB Studio. Debut 1980 OB in "Spain 1980," followed by "Animals," "Wonderful Ice Cream Suit," "Cold Air," "Fabiola," "Concerto in Hi-Fi," Bdwy in "Goodbye Fidel" (1980). "Shakespeare on Broadway."

COLLETT, CHRISTOPHER. Born Mar. 13, 1968 in NYC. Attended Strasberg Inst. Bdwy debut 1983 in "Torch Song Trilogy," followed by OB's "Coming of Age in SoHo," "Spoils of War."

COLLIS, LARRY K. Born Feb. 21, 1936 in Lohrville, IA. Graduate StateUIa. Bdwy debut 1988 in "Mail."

COLTON, CHEVI. Born Dec. 21 in NYC. Attended Hunter Col. OB in "Time of Storm," "Insect Comedy," "The Adding Machine," "O Marry Me," "Penny Change," "The Mad Show," "Jacques Brel Is Alive . . . ," "Bits and Pieces," "Spelling Bee," "Uncle Money," "Miami," "Come Blow Your Horn," Bdwy in "Cabaret," "Grand Tour," "Torch Song Trilogy."

CONE, MICHAEL. Born Oct. 7, 1952 in Fresno, CA. Graduate UWash. Bdwy 1980 in "Brigadoon," followed by OB's "Bar Mitzvah Boy."

CONNELL, JANE. Born Oct. 27, 1925 in Berkeley, CA. Attended UCal. Bdwy debut in "New Faces of 1956," followed by "Drat! The Cat!," "Mame" (1966/'83), "Dear World," "Lysistrata," "Me and My Girl," OB in "Shoestring Revue," "Threepenny Opera," "Pieces of Eight," "Demi-Dozen," "She Stoops to Conquer," "Drat!," "The Real Inspector Hound," "The Rivals," "The Rise and Rise of Daniel Rocket," "Laughing Stock," "The Singular Dorothy Parker," "No No Nanette in Concert."

CONNELL, KELLY. Born June 9, 1956 in Seneca Falls, NY. Attended Cayuga Com.Col. Debut 1982 OB in "The Butter and Egg Man," followed by "Neon Psalms," "Love's Labour's Lost," "Quiet in the Land," "The Musical Comedy Murders of 1940."

CONNELLY, R. BRUCE. Born Aug. 22, 1949 in Meriden, CT. Graduate SConnStateCol. Debut 1975 OB in "Godspell," followed by "Macbeth."

CONOLLY, PATRICIA. Born Aug. 29, 1933 in Tabora, EAfrica. Attended USydney. With APA in "You Can't Take It with You," "War and Peace," "School for Scandal," "The Wild Duck," "Right You Are," "We Comrades Three," "Pantagleize," "Exit the King," "The Cherry Orchard," "The Misanthrope," "The Cocktail Party," and "Cock-a-Doodle Dandy," followed by "A Streetcar Named Desire," "The Importance of Being Earnest," "Blithe Spirit," "Woman in Mind."

CONROY, FRANCES. Born in 1953 in Monroe, GA. Attended Dickinson Col., Juilliard, Neighborhood Playhouse. Debut 1978 OB with the Acting Co. in "Mother Courage," "King Lear," and "The Other Half," followed by "All's Well That Ends Well," "Othello," "Sorrows of Stephen," "Girls Girls Girls," "Zastrozzi," "Painting Churches," "Uncle Vanya," "Romance Language," "To Gillian on Her 37th Birthday," "Man and Superman," "Zero Positive," Bdwy in "The Lady from Dubuque" (1980).

CONVERSE, FRANK. Born May 22, 1938 in St. Louis, MO. Attended Carnegie-Mellon U. Bdwy debut 1966 in "First One Asleep, Whistle," followed by "The Philadelphia Story"(LC), "Brothers," "Design for Living," "A Streetcar Named Desire," OB in "House of Blue Leaves."

COOK, LINDA. Born June 8 in Lubbock, TX. Attended Auburn U. Debut 1974 OB in "The Wager," followed by "Hole in the Wall," "Shadow of a Gunman," "Be My Father," "Ghosts of the Loyal Oaks," "Different People, Different Rooms," "Saigon Rose," "Romantic Arrangements," "No Time Flat."

COOK, VICTOR. Born Aug. 19, 1967 in NYC. Debut 1976 OB in "Joseph and the Amazing Technicolor Dreamcoat," followed by "The Haggadah," "Moby Dick," "Starmites," Bdwy in "Don't Get God Started" (1988).

COOKSON, GARY. Born July 31, 1950 in Roslyn, NY. Graduate NYU. Debut 1974 OB in "Drums at Yale," followed by "The Healers," "Mad Dogs," "A Place of Springs," "Wayside Motor Inn," Bdwy in "A Streetcar Named Desire" (1988).

COONER, ROBERT. Born Oct. 19, 1956 in Houston, TX. Debut 1985 OB in "Very Warm for May," followed by "Mlle. Colombe."

COOPER, MARILYN. Born Dec. 14, 1936 in NYC. Attended NYU. Appeared in "Mr. Wonderful," "West Side Story," "Brigadoon," "Gypsy," "I Can Get It for You Wholesale," "Hallelujah, Baby!," "Golden Rainbow," "Mame," "A Teaspoon Every 4 Hours," "Two by Two," "On the Town," "Ballroom," "Woman of the Year," "The Odd Couple" (1985), "Broadway Bound," OB in "The Mad Show," "Look Me Up," "The Perfect Party."

CORBALIS, BRENDAN. Born Mar. 19, 1964 in Dublin, Ire. Graduate NYU. Debut 1988 OB in "April Snow."

CORBO, GEORGINA M. Born Sept. 21, 1965 in Havana, Cuba. Attended SUNY/Purchase. Debut 1988 OB in "Ariano."

CORFMAN, CARIS. Born May 18, 1955 in Boston, MA. Graduate FlaStateU., Yale. Debut 1978 OB in "Wings," followed by "Fish Riding Bikes," "Filthy Rich," "Dry Land," "All This and Moonlight," Bdwy in "Amadeus" (1980).

CORREA, MIGUEL, JR. Born Oct. 30, 1974 in NYC. Debut 1987 in "Marathon 87," followed by "La Puta Vida."

CORREA, STEPHANIE. Born Dec. 25, 1958 in Louisville, KY. Graduate Boston U. Debut 1987 OB in "Sherlock Holmes and the Hands of Othello," followed by "The Misanthrope."

CORREIA, DON. Born Aug. 28, 1951 in San Jose, CA. Attended SanJoseStateU. Bdwy debut 1980 in "A Chorus Line," followed by "Perfectly Frank," "Little Me," "Sophisticated Ladies," "5-6-7-8 Dance," "My One and Only," "Singin' in the Rain," "Sally in Concert."

CORSAIR, BILL. Born Sept. 5, 1940 in Providence, RI. Debut 1984 OB in "Ernie and Arnie," followed by "In the Boom Boom Room."

CORSAIR, JANIS. Born June 18, 1948 in Providence, RI. Debut OB 1984 in "The Coarse Acting Show," followed by "In the Boom Boom Room."

COSTA, JOSEPH. Born June 8, 1946 in Ithaca, NY. Graduate Gettysburg Col., Yale U. Debut 1978 OB in "The Show-Off," followed by "The Tempest," "The Changeling," "A Map of the World," "Julius Caesar."

COSTIGAN, KEN. Born Apr. 1, 1934 in NYC. Graduate Fordham, Yale U. Debut 1960 OB in "Borak," followed by "King of the Dark Chamber," "The Hostage," "Next Time I'll Sing to You," "Curley McDimple," "The Runner Stumbles," "Peg O' My Heart," "The Show-Off," "A Midsummer Night's Dream," "Diary of Anne Frank," "Knuckle Sandwich," "Seminary Murder," "Declassee," "Big Apple Messenger," "When We Dead Awaken," "The 12 Pound Look," "The Browning Version," "The Changeling," Bdwy in "Gideon" (1962), "A Streetcar Named Desire" (1988).

COULLET, RHONDA. Born Sept. 23, 1945 in Magnolia, AR. Attended UArk, UDenver. Debut 1973 OB in "National Lampoon Lemmings," followed by "A Walk on the Wild Side," Bdwy in "The Robber Bridegroom" (1976).

COUNCIL, RICHARD. Born Oct. 1, 1947 in Tampa, Fl. Graduate UFl. Debut 1973 OB in "Merchant of Venice," followed by "Ghost Dance," "Look, We've Come Through," "Arms and the Man," "Isadora Duncan Sleeps with the Russian Navy," "Arthur," "The Winter Dancer," "The Prevalence of Mrs. Seal," "Jane Avril," Bdwy in "The Royal Family"(1975), "Philadelphia Story," "I'm Not Rappaport."

COUNTRYMAN, MICHAEL. Born Sept. 15, 1955 in St. Paul, Mn. Graduate Trinity Col., AADA. Debut 1983 OB in "Changing Palettes," followed by "June Moon," "Terra Nova," "Out!," "Claptrap," "The Common Pursuit," "Woman in Mind."

COURIE, JONATHAN. Born Oct. 26, 1963 in Raleigh, NC. Graduate UCincinnati. Debut 1986 OB in "Murder at Rutherford House," followed by "The Apple Tree," "The Elephant Man," "Night Games," "A Frog in His Throat."

COUSINS, BRIAN. Born May 9, 1959 in Portland, Me. Graduate Tulane, UWash. Debut 1987 OB in "Death of a Buick," followed by "The Taming of the Shrew."

COWLES, MATTHEW. Born Sept. 28, 1944 in NYC. Attended Neighborhood Playhouse. Bdwy debut 1966 in "Malcolm," followed by "Sweet Bird of Youth," OB in "King John," "The Indian Wants the Bronx," "Triple Play," "Stop, You're Killing Me!," "The Time of Your Life," "Foursome," "Kid Champion," "End of the War," "Tennessee," "Bathroom Plays," "Touch Black," "Paradise Lost," "The Hasty Heart," "Ghosts," "House Arrest."

CRABTREE, DON. Born Aug. 21, 1928 in Borger, TX. Attended Actors Studio. Bdwy bow 1959 in "Destry Rides Again," followed by "Happiest Girl in the World," "Family Affair," "Unsinkable Molly Brown," "Sophie," "110 In the Shade," "Golden Boy," "Pousse Cafe," "Mahagonny" (OB), "The Best Little Whorehouse in Texas," "42nd Street."

CRAIG, BETSY. Born Jan. 5, 1952 in Hopewell, VA. Attended Berry Col. Bdwy debut 1972 in "Ambassador," followed by "Smith," "Brigadoon," "La Cage aux Folles."

CRAIG, NOEL. Born Jan. 4 in St. Louis, MO. Attended Northwestern U., Goodman Theatre, London Guildhall. Bdwy debut 1967 in "Rosencrantz and Guildenstern Are Dead," followed by "A Patriot for Me," "Conduct Unbecoming," "Vivat! Vivat Regina!," "Going Up," "Dance a Little Closer," "A Chorus Line," OB in "Pygmalion," "Promenade," "Family House," "Inn at Lydda," "A Bouquet for Mr. Ziegfeld."

CRAMPTON, GLORY. Born Mar. 30, 1964 in Rockville Cenrer, NY. Graduate NYU. Debut 1988 OB in "The Fantasticks."

CRANDALL, SHELLEY. Born June 30, 1954 in Ann Arbor, MI. Graduate Carnegie-Mellon U. Debut 1986 OB in "Octoberfest," followed by "Amphytrion '38," "Search for Extraterrestrial Intelligence," "Cafe Toulouse."

CRAWFORD, MICHAEL. Born Jan. 19, 1942 in Salisbury, Wiltshire, Eng. Bdwy debut 1967 in "Black Comedy," followed by "Phantom of the Opera" (1988).

CRIVELLO, ANTHONY. Born Aug. 2, 1955 in Milwaukee, Wi. Bdwy debut 1982 in "Evita," followed by "The News," "Les Miserables," OB in "The Juniper Tree."

CRONYN, TANDY. Born Nov. 27, 1945 in Los Angeles, CA. Attended London's Central School. Bdwy debut 1969 in "Cabaret," followed by LC's "Playboy of the Western World," "Good Woman of Setzuan," "An Enemy of the People," and "Antigone," OB in "An Evening with the Poet-Senator," "Winners," "The Killing of Sister George," "Memories of an Immortal Spirit," "A Shayna Maidel."

CROSBY, KIM. Born July 11, 1960 in Fort Smith, Ar. Attended SMU, ManSchMusic. Bdwy debut 1985 in "Jerry's Girls," followed by "Into the Woods."

CRYER, DAVID. Born Mar. 8, 1936 in Evanston, IL. Attended DePauwU. OB in "The Fantasticks," "Streets of New York," "Now Is the Time for All Good Men," "Whispers on the Wind," "The Making of Americans," "Portfolio Revue," "Paradise Lost," "The Inheritors," "Rain," "Ghosts," "Madwoman of Chaillot," "Clarence," "Mlle. Colombe," "A Little Night Music," Bdwy in "110 in the Shade," "Come Summer" for which he received a Theatre World Award, "1776," "Ari," "Leonard Bernstein's Mass," "The Desert Song," "Evita," "Chess."

CUERVO, ALMA. Born Aug. 13 1951 in Tampa, FL. Graduate Tulane U, Yale U. Debut 1977 in "Uncommon Women and Others," followed by "A Foot in the Door," "Put Them All Together," "Isn't It Romantic," "Miss Julie," "Quilters," Bdwy in "Once in a Lifetime," "Bedroom Farce," "Censored Scenes from King Kong," "Is There Life after High School?," "The Sneaker Factor," "Songs on a Shipwrecked Sofa," "Uncle Vanya," "The Grandma Plays."

CUK, ANDREW. Born Jan. 11 in NYC. Graduate Sarah Lawrence Col. Bdwy debut 1987 in "South Pacific"(LC), followed by "The Desert Song," OB in "Kismet."

CUKA, FRANCES. Born in London; graduate Guildhall School. Bdwy debut 1961 in "A Taste of Honey," followed by "Travesties," "Oliver!," "The Life and Adventures of Nicholas Nickleby," OB in "The Entertainer," "It's Only a Play," "Quartermaine's Terms," "Not Waving," "The Vingar Tree."

CULKIN, MACAULAY. Born Aug. 26 1981 in New York City. Debut 1985 OB in "Bach Babies," followed by "After School Special," "Buster B. and Olivia."

CULLITON, JOSEPH. Born Jan. 25, 1948 in Boston, MA. Attended CalStateU. Debut 1982 OB in "Francis," followed by "Flirtations," "South Pacific"(LC), "Julis Caesar," Bdwy 1987 in "Broadway."

CULLIVER, KAREN. Born Dec. 30, 1959 in Florida. Attended Stetson U. Bdwy debut 1983 in "Show Boat," followed by "The Mystery of Edwin Drood," OB in "The Fantasticks."

CULLUM, JOHN DAVID. Born Mar. 1, 1966 in NYC. Bdwy debut 1977 in "Kings," followed by "Shenandoah," OB in "Romance Language," "Losing It," "Madwoman of Chaillot," "Clarence," "Abingdon Square," "Woman in Mind."

CUNNINGHAM, JOHN. Born June 22, 1932 in Auburn, NY. Graduate Yale, Datmouth. OB in "Love Me a Little," "Pimpernel," "The Fantasticks," "Love and Let Love," "The Bone Room," "Dancing in the Dark," "Father's Day," "Snapshot," "Head over Heels," "Quartermaine's Terms," "Wednesday," "On Approval," "Miami," "A Perfect Party," "Birds of Paradise," Bdwy in "Hot Spot" (1963), "Zorba," "Company," "1776," "Rose."

CURTIS, KEENE. Born Feb. 15, 1925 in Salt Lake City, UT. Graduate UUtah. Bdwy bow 1949 in "Shop at Sly Corner," with APA in "School for Scandal," "The Tavern," "Anatole," "Scapin," "Right You Are," "Importance of Being Earnest," "Twelfth Night," "King Lear," "Seagull," "Lower Depths," "Man and Superman," "Judith," "War and Peace," "You Can't Take It With You," "Pantagleize," "Cherry Orchard," "Misanthrope," "Cocktail Party," "Cock-a-Doodle Dandy," and "Hamlet," "A Patriot for Me," "The Rothschilds," "Night Watch," "Via Galactica," "Annie," "Division Street," "La Cage aux Folles," OB in "Colette," "Ride Across Lake Constance."

CYPKIN, DIANE. Born Sept. 10, 1948 in Munich, Ger. Attended Bklyn Col. Bdwy debut 1966 in "Let's Sing Yiddish," followed by "Papa Get Married," "Light Lively and Yiddish," "The Jewish Gypsy," OB in "Yoshke Musikant," "Stempenyu," "Big Winner," "A Millionaire in Trouble," "Winner Take All," "Riverside Drive."

DABDOUB, JACK. Born Feb. 5 in New Orleans, LA. Graduate Tulane U. OB in "What's Up," "Time for the Gentle People," "The Peddler," "The Dodo Bird," "Annie Get Your Gun," "Lola," Bdwy in "Paint Your Wagon" (1952), "My Darlin' Aida," "Happy Hunting," "Hot Spot," "Camelot," "Baker Street," "Anya," "Her First Roman," "Coco," "Man of LaMancha," "Brigadoon" (1980), "Moose Murders," "One Touch of Venus," "Sally in Concert."

DALE, JIM. Born Aug 15, 1935 in Rothwell, Eng. Debut 1974 OB with Young Vic Co. in "Taming of the Shrew," "Scapino" that moved to Bdwy, followed by "Barnum," "Joe Egg," "Me and My Girl."

DALTON, LEZLIE. Born Aug. 12, 1952 in Boston, Ma. Attended Pasadena Playhouse, UCLA. Debut 1980 OB in "Annie and Arthur," followed by "After Maigret," "Blessed Event," "Times and Appetites of Toulouse-Lautrec," "Good and Faithful Servant."

DALY, JOSEPH. Born Apr. 7, 1944 in Oakland, CA. Debut 1959 OB in "Dance of Death," followed by "Roots," "Sjt. Musgrave's Dance," "Viet Rock," "Dark of the Moon," "Shadow of a Gunman," "Hamlet," "The Ride across Lake Constance," "A Doll's House," "Native Bird," "Yeats Trio," "Mecca," "Marching to Georgia," "Comedians," "A Country for Old Men," "Falsies," "Taming of the Shrew," "Working One Acts."

| Victoria Brasser | J. Patrick Breen | Janni Brenn | Fran Brill | David Brisbin | Kent Broadhurst |

| Charles Brown | Ann Brown | William Brown | Barbara Bryne | Terence Burk | Jennifer Butt |

| L. Scott Caldwell | Timothy Carhart | Myra Carter | Tim Cassidy | Luz Castanos | Bobby Cavanaugh |

| Terrence Caza | Pamela Cecil | David Chan | Lynne Charnay | Gordon Chater | Mary Chesterman |

| Marissa Chibas | Thom Christopher | Debra Cole | David Cryer | Karen Culliver | Keene Curtis |

DALY, R. F. Born Apr. 16, 1955 in Denver, CO. Attended NColU. Bdwy debut 1988 in "Chess."

DALY, TIMOTHY. Born Mar. 1, 1956 in NYC. Graduate Bennington Col. Debut 1984 OB in "Fables for Friends," followed by "Oliver Oliver," Bdwy in "Coastal Disturbances"(1987) for which he received a Theatre World Award.

DANEK, MICHAEL. Born May 5, 1955 in Oxford, Pa. Graduate Columbia Col. Bdwy debut 1978 in "Hello, Dolly!" followed by "A Chorus Line," "Copperfield," "Woman of the Year," OB in "Big Bad Burlesque", "Dreams."

DANIELLE, MARLENE. Born Aug. 16 in NYC. Bdwy debut 1979 in "Sarava," followed by "West Side Story," "Marlowe," "Damn Yankees" (JB), "Cats," OB in "Little Shop of Horrors."

DANIELLE, SUSAN. Born Jan. 30, 1949 in Englewood, NJ. Graduate Wm. Patterson Col. Debut 1979 OB in "Tip-Toes," Bdwy in "A Chorus Line" (1985).

DANIELS, LESLIE. Born May 27, 1957 in Princeton, NJ. Graduate UPa. Debut 1985 OB in "Playboy of the Western World," followed by "Touch."

DANNER, BLYTHE. Born in Philadelphia. Graduate Bard Col. Debut 1966 OB in "The Infantry," followed by "Collision Course," "Summertree," "Up Eden," "Someone's Comin' Hungry," "Cyrano," "The Miser" for which she received a Theatre World Award, "Twelfth Night," "The New York Idea," Bdwy in "Butterflies Are Free," "Betrayal," "The Philadelphia Story," "Blithe Spirit," "A Streetcar Named Desire."

DANNER, BRADEN. Born in 1976 in Indianapolis, In. Bdwy debut 1984 in "Nine," followed by "Oliver!," "Starlight Express," "Les Miserables."

DANSON, RANDY. Born Apr. 30, 1950 in Plainfield, NJ. Graduate Carnegie-Mellon. Debut 1978 OB in "Gimme Shelter," followed by "Big and Little," "The Winter Dancers," "Time Steps," "Casualties," "Red and Blue," "The Resurrection of Lady Lester," "Jazz Poets at the Grotto," "Plenty," "Macbeth," "Blue Window," "Cave Life," "Romeo and Juliet."

DANTUONO, MICHAEL. Born July 30, 1942 in Providence, RI. Debut 1974 OB in "How To Get Rid of It," followed by "Maggie Flynn," "Charlotte Sweet," "Berlin to Broadway," Bdwy in "Caesar and Cleopatra," "Can-Can" (1981), "Zorba" (1984), "The Three Musketeers," "42nd Street."

DARLOW, CYNTHIA. Born June 13, 1949 in Detroit, MI. Attended NCSch of Arts, PaStateU. Debut 1974 OB in "This Property Is Condemned," followed by "Portrait of a Madonna," "Clytemnestra," "Unexpurgated Memoirs of Bernard Morgandigler," "Actors Nightmare," "Sister Mary Ignatius Explains It All," "Fables for Friends," "That's It Folks!," "Baby with the Bathwater," "Dandy Dick," Bdwy in "Grease" (1976).

DAVENPORT, COLLEEN. Born Sept. 2, 1958 in Beloit, KS. Graduate LaStateU. Debut 1983 OB in "The Seagull," followed by "New Works '87."

DAVIS, ANDREW. Born Aug. 9, 1950 in San Antonio, TX. Graduate UNewOrleans, Yale. Bdwy debut 1978 in "Crucifer of Blood," OB in "Word of Mouth," "Says I Says He," "Dreck/Vile," "Justice," "Mercenaries," "The American Clock," "American Notes."

DAVIS, BRUCE ANTHONY. Born Mar. 4, 1959 in Dayton, Oh. Attended Juilliard. Bdwy debut 1979 in "Dancin'," followed by "Big Deal," "A Chorus Line."

DAVIS, MARY BOND. Born June 3, 1958 in Los Angeles, Ca. Attended CalStateU/Northridge, LACC. Debut 1985 OB in "In Trousers," Bdwy in "Mail" (1988).

DAVIS, OSSIE. Born Dec. 18, 1917 in Cogdell, Ga. Attended Howard U. Bdwy debut 1946 in "Jeb," followed by "Anna Lucasta," "Leading Lady," "Smile of the World," "The Wisteria Trees," "The Royal Family"(CC), "Green Pastures," "Remains to Be Seen," "Touchstone," "No Time for Sergeants," "Jamaica," "Raisin in theSun," "Purlie Victorious," "The Zulu and the Zayda," "Ain't Supposed to Die a Natural Death," "I'm Not Rappaport," OB in "Ballad of Bimshire," "Take It from the Top."

DAWSON, SUZANNE. Born Jan. 19, 1951 in Montreal, Can. Attended Boston Consv. Debut 1980 OB in "Chase a Rainbow," followed by "New Faces of 1952," "The Last Musical Comedy," "The Great American Backstage Musical."

DAY, CONNIE. Born Dec. 26, 1940 in NYC. Debut 1971 OB in "Look Me Up," followed by "Antigone," "Walking Papers," Bdwy in "Molly"(1973), "The Magic Show," "42nd Street."

DeACUTIS, WILLIAM. Born Sept. 17, 1957 in Bridgeport, CT. Juilliard graduate. Debut 1979 OB in "Spring Awakening," followed by "The Normal Heart," "Talk Radio."

DEAN, LAURA. Born May 27, 1963 in Smithtown, NY. Debut 1973 OB in "The Secret Life of Walter Mitty," followed by "A Village Romeo and Juliet," "Carousel," "Hey Rube," "Landscape of the Body," "American Passion," "Feathertop," "Personals," "Godspell," Bdwy in "Doonesbury" (1983) for which she received a Theatre World Award.

DEARBORN, DALTON. Born Oct. 1, 1930 in Nantucket, MA. Debut 1957 OB in "Mary Stuart," followed by "The Makropoulos Secret," "Undercover Man," "MacBird," "The 12 Pound Look," "The Browning Version," "Lost in the Stars," Bdwy in "Benus Is" (1966).

DeBOUTER, BONNIE J. Born Dec. 2, 1959 in Hackensack, NJ. Graduate RutgersU. Debut 1988 OB in "Monsieur Amilcar."

DECAREAU, DICK. Born Jan. 19, 1950 in Lynn, MA. Graduate SalemStateCol. Bdwy debut 1986 in "Raggedy Ann" followed by OB's "Mlle. Colombe," "Dragons," "Music Man," "Alias Jimmy Valentine."

DEERING, SALLY. Born Nov. 7, 1952 in Jersey City, NJ. Attended AADA. Debut 1983 OB in "Balzaminov's Wedding," followed by "Alternatives."

DeLAURENTIS, SEMINA. Born Jan. 21 in Waterbury, Ct. Graduate Southern Ct. State Col. Debut 1985 OB in "Nunsense," followed by "Have I Got a Girl for You."

DELLA PIAZZA, DIANE. Born Sept. 3, 1962 in Pittsburgh, Pa. Graduate Cincinnati Consv. Bdwy debut 1987 in "Les Miserables."

DeMAIO, PETER. Born in Hartford, CT. Attended New School, Juilliard. Debut 1961 in "Threepenny Opera," followed by "The Secret Life of Walter Mitty," "Dark of the Moon," "Welcome to Black River," "Last Breeze of Summer," "After the Rise," "Anchorman," Bdwy in "Billy," "Indians," "The Changing Room."

DeMATTIS, RAY. Born June 1, 1945 in New Haven, CT. Catholic U. graduate. Bdwy debut 1974 in "Grease," followed by OB's "El Bravo!," "Talk Radio," "Flora the Red Menace."

DEMPSEY, JEROME. Born Mar. 1, 1929 in St. Paul, Mn. Graduate Toledo U. Bdwy debut 1959 in "West Side Story," followed by "The Deputy," "Spofford," "Room Service," "Love Suicide at Schofield Barracks," "Dracula," "Whodunit," "You Can't Take It with You," "The Mystery of Edwin Drood," "The Front Page" (LC), OB in "Cry of Players," "The Year Boston Won the Pennant," "The Crucible," "Justice Box," "Trelawny of the Wells," "Old Glory," "Six Characters in Search of an Author," "Threepenny Opera," "Johnny on the Spot," "The Barbarians," "he and she," "A Midsummer Night's Dream," "The Recruiting Officer," "Oedipus the King," "The Wild Duck," "The Fuehrer Bunker," "Entertaining Mr. Sloane," "The Clownmaker," "Two Gentlemen of Verona," "The Marry Month of May."

DENNEHY, BRIAN. Born in 1938 in Bridgeport, CT. Debut 1988 OB in "The Cherry Orchard."

DENNIS, RONALD. Born Oct. 2, 1944 in Dayton, Oh. Debut 1966 OB in "Show Boat," followed by "Of Thee I Sing," "Moon Walk," "Please Don't Cry," Bdwy in "A Chorus Line"(1975), "My One and Only," "La Cage aux Folles."

DERN, LAURA. Born in California in 1966. Debut 1988 OB in "Palace of Amateurs."

DeSHIELDS, ANDRE. Born Jan. 12, 1946 in Baltimore, MD. Graduate UWi. Bdwy debut 1973 in "Warp," followed by "Rachel Lily Rosenbloom," "The Wiz," "Ain't Misbehavin'," (1978/1988) "Haarlem Nocturne," "Just So," "Stardust," OB in "2008½," "Jazzbo Brown," "The Soldier's Tale," "The Little Prince," "Haarlem Nocturne," "Sovereign State of Boogedy Boogedy."

DESMOND, DAN. Born July 4, 1944 in Racine, Wi. Graduate UWi, Yale. Bdwy debut 1981 in "Morning's at Seven," followed by "Othello," "All My Sons," OB in "A Perfect Diamond," "The Bear," "Vienna Notes," "On Mt. Chimborazo," "Table Settings," "Moonchildren."

DEUTSCH, KURT. Born July 26, 1966 in St. Louis, MO. Attended Syracuse U. Bdwy debut 1988 in "Broadway Bound."

DEVINE, LORETTA. Born Aug. 21 in Houston, TX. Graduate UHouston, Brandeis U. Bdwy debut 1977 in "Hair," followed by "A Broadway Musical," "Dreamgirls," "Big Deal," OB in "Godsong," "Lion and the Jewel," "Karma," "The Blacks," "Mahalia," "Long Time Since Yesterday," "The Colored Museum."

DeVRIES, JON. Born Mar. 26, 1947 in NYC. Graduate Bennington Col., Pasadena Playhouse. Debut 1977 OB in "The Cherry Orchard," followed by "Agamemnon," "The Ballad of Soapy Smith," "The Dreamer examines his pillow," "The Last Musical Comedy," Bdwy in "The Inspector General," "Devour the Snow," "Major Barbara," "Execution of Justice," "the dreamer examines his pillow."

DEWAR, JOHN. Born Jan. 24, 1953 in Evanston, Il. Graduate UMinn. Bdwy debut 1987 in "Les Miserables."

DEWHURST, COLLEEN. Born June 3, 1926 in Montreal, Can. Attended Downer Col., AADA. Bdwy debut 1952 in "Desire under the Elms," followed by "Tamburlaine the Great," "The Country Wife," "Caligula," "All the Way Home," "Great Day in the Morning," "Ballad of the Sad Cafe," "More Stately Mansions," "All Over," "Mourning Becomes Electra," "Moon for the Misbegotten," "Who's Afraid of Virginia Woolf?," "An Almost Perfect Person," "The Queen and the Rebels," "You Can't Take It with You," "Ah, Wilderness ," "Long Day's Journey into Night" (1988) OB in "The Taming of the Shrew," "The Eagle Has Two Heads," "Camille," "Macbeth," "Children of Darkness" for which she received a 1958 Theatre World Award, "Antony and Cleopatra," "Hello and Goodbye," "Good Woman of Setzuan," "Hamlet," "Are You Now or Have You Ever . . .?, "Taken in Marriage," "My Gene."

DIAMOND, KATHERINE. Born in NYC. Graduate AADA. Debut 1978 OB and Bdwy in "Runaways," followed by OB's "The Death of Hamlet," "Poets from the Inside," "The Golden Fleece," "Event of the Year," "The Signal Season of Dummy Hoy."

DIEKMANN, MARK. Born Aug. 10, 1953 in Springfield, Ma. Attended Clark U., HB Studio. Debut 1987 OB in "Misalliance," followed by "Thick Dick."

DILLEHAY, KAYLYN. Born Dec. 1, 1954 in Oklahoma City, OK. Attended TxCU, OkCityU. Debut 1976 OB in "Follies," followed by "Carnival," "Beowulf," Bdwy in "Canterbury Tales" (1980), "Sugar Babies," "Teddy and Alice."

DiPASQUALE, FRANK J. Born July 15, 1955 in Whitestone, NY. Graduate USC. Bdwy debut 1983 in "La Cage aux Folles."

DIXON, ED. Born Sept. 2, 1948 in Oklahoma. Attended OkU. Bdwy in "The Student Prince," followed by "No, No, Nanette," "Rosalie in Concert," "The Three Musketeers," OB in "By Bernstein," "King of the Schnorrers," "Rabboni," "Moby Dick," "Shylock," "Johnny Pye and the Foolkiller."

DOLAN, MICHAEL. Born June 21, 1965 in Oklahoma City, OK. Debut 1984 OB in "Coming of Age in SoHo," Bdwy in "Breaking the Code" (1987).

DONNELLY, DONAL. Born July 6, 1931 in Bradford, Eng. Bdwy debut 1966 in "Philadelphia, Here I Come," followed by "A Day in the Death of Joe Egg," "Sleuth," "The Faith Healer," "The Elephant Man," "Execution of Justice," "Sherlock's Last Case," OB in "My Astonishing Self" (solo performance), "The Chalk Garden," "Big Maggie."

DONOHOE, ROB. Born Dec. 25, 1950 in Bossier City, LA. Graduate ENewMxU, AmThArts. Debut 1987 OB in "The LongBoat," followed by "The Last Resort."

DORAN, JESSE. Born June 23; attended AMDA. Bdwy debut 1976 in "The Runner Stumbles," OB in "Goose and Tom Tom," "Fool for Love," "Spookhouse," "Snowman," "My Papa's Wine," "The God Muggers."

DORFMAN, ROBERT. Born Oct. 8, 1950 in Brooklyn, NY. Attended CUNY, HB Studio. Debut 1979 OB in "Say Goodnight, Gracie," followed by "America Kicks," "Winterplay," "The Normal Heart," "Waving Goodbye," "Richard II," Bdwy in "Social Security" (1987).

DOUGHERTY, J. P. Born July 25, 1953 in Lincoln, Ill. Attended S.Ill.U. Debut 1982 OB in "The Frances Farmer Story," followed by "The Little Prince," "The Sound of Music," "The Trojan Women," "Tropical Fever in Key West," "Have I Got a Girl For You," "Conrack," Bdwy in "The Three Musketeers"(1984).

DOUGLASS, PI. Born in Sharon, CT. Attended Boston Consv. Bdwy debut 1969 in "Fig Leaves Are Falling," followed by "Hello, Dolly!," "Georgy," "Purlie," "Ari," "Jesus Christ Superstar," "Selling of the President," "The Wiz," "La Cage aux Folles," OB in "Of Thee I Sing," "Under Fire," "The Ritz," "Blackberries," "Dementos."

DOVEY, MARK. Born Jan. 13, 1954 in Vancouver, Can. Attended UBritishColumbia. Bdwy debut 1980 in "A Chorus Line," followed by "The Little Prince and the Aviator," "Cabaret" (1987).

DOWNEY, ROMA. Born in Derry, N. Ireland. Graduate Brighton Polytechnic. Debut 1987 OB in "Tamara."

DOWNING, VIRGINIA. Born March 7 in Washington, DC. Attended Bryn Mawr. Bdwy debut 1937 in "Father Malachy's Miracle," followed by "Forward the Heart," "The Cradle Will Rock," "A Gift of Time," "We Have Always Lived in a Castle," "Arsenic and Old Lace" (1987), OB in "Juno and the Paycock," "Man with the Golden Arm," "Palm Tree in a Rose Garden," "Play with a Tiger," "The Wives," "The Idiot," "Medea," "Mrs. Warren's Profession," "Mercy Street," "Thunder Rock," "Pygmalion," "First Week in Bogota," "Rimers of Eldritch," "Les Blancs," "Shadow of a Gunman," "All the Way Home," "A Winter's Tale," "Billy Liar," "Shadow and Substance," "Silent Catastrophe," "Ernest in Love," "Night Games," "A Frog in His Throat."

DOYLE, LEAH. Born Jan. 18, 1961 in NYC. Graduate Vassar, Neighborhood Playhouse. Debut 1988 OB in "Washington Heights."

DRAKE, DONNA. Born May 21, 1953 in Columbia, SC. Attended USC, Columbia. Bdwy debut 1975 in "A Chorus Line," followed by "It's So Nice to Be Civilized," "1940's Radio Hour," "Woman of the Year," "Sophisticated Ladies," "Wind in the Willows," OB in "Memories of Riding with Joe Cool."

DuCLOS, DEANNA. Born Apr. 18, 1979 in NYC. Debut 1987 OB in "1984."

DUDLEY, CRAIG. Born Jan. 22, 1945 in Sheepshead Bay, NY. Graduate AADA, AmThWing. Debut 1970 OB in "Macbeth," followed by "Zou," "I Have Always Believed in Ghosts," "Othello," "War and Peace," "Dial 'M' for Murder," "Misalliance."

DUKES, DAVID. Born June 6, 1945 in San Francisco, CA. Attended Mann Col. Bdwy debut 1971 in "School for Wives," followed by "Don Juan," "The Play's the Thing," "The Visit," "Chemin de Fer," "Holiday," "Rules of the Game," "Love for Love," "Travesties," "Dracula," "Bent," "Amadeus," "M. Butterfly," OB in "Rebel Women."

DUNN, SALLY. Born Dec. 23, 1950 in Detroit, MI. Stephens Col. graduate. Debut 1982 OB in "The Holly and the Ivy," followed by "How He Lied to Her Husband," "Winners," "As You Like It," "Romeo and Juliet," "Stopping the Desert."

DUQUETTE, JOE. Born Mar. 9, 1949 in Fall River, MA. Graduate SEMaU. Debut 1980 OB in "The Meehans," followed by "Counter Service."

DURANG, CHRISTOPHER. Born Jan. 2, 1949 in Montclair, NJ. Graduate Harvard, Yale. Debut 1976 OB in "Das Lusitania Songspiel," followed by "The Hotel Play," "Sister Mary Ignatius Explains It All," "The Birthday Present," "The Marriage of Betty and Boo," "Laughing Wild."

DUTTON, CHARLES S. Born Jan. 30, 1951 in Baltimore, MD. Graduate Yale U. Debut 1983 OB in "Richard III," followed by "Pantomime," "Fried Chicken and Invisibility," "Splendid Mummer," Bdwy in "Ma Rainey's Black Bottom" (1984) for which he received a Theatre World Award.

EARL-EDWARDS, STEVEN. Born Dec. 15, 1946 in Glendale, CA. Graduate TexWesleyan, UArk. Debut 1976 OB in "Hadrian's Hill," followed by "Night over Tiber," "A Circle on the Cross."

ECKHOUSE, JAMES. Born Feb. 14, 1955 in Chicago, IL. Juilliard graduate. Bdwy debut 1982 in "Beyond Therapy," OB in "The Rise and Rise of Daniel Rocker," "Geniuses," "In the Country," "Sister Mary Ignatius Explains It All," "Dubliners," "The Ballad of Soapy Smith," "Emma," "Emily."

eda-YOUNG, BARBARA. Born Jan. 30, 1945 in Detroit, MI. Bdwy debut 1968 in "Lovers and Other Strangers," followed by LC's "The Time of Your Life," "Camino Real," "Operation Sidewinder," "Kool Aid," and "A Streetcar Named Desire," OB in "The Hawk," "The Gathering," "The Terrorists," "Drinks before Dinner," "Shout across the River," "After Stardrive," "Birdbath," "Crossing the Crab Nebula," "Maiden Stakes," "Come Dog Come Night," "Two Character Play," "Mensch Meier," "Glory in the Flower," "Goodbye Freddy," "A Rosen by Any Other Name," "After Crystal Night."

EDDLEMAN, JACK. Born Sept. 7, 1933 in Millsap, TX. Attended UTulsa, UMKC. Bdwy debut 1957 in "Shinbone Alley," followed by "Carousel" (CC), "Oh, Captain!," "Camelot," "Hot Spot," "The Girl Who Came to Supper," "Oh What a Lovely War," "My Fair Lady" (CC), OB in "Diversions," "Lend an Ear," "Great Scott!," "Jacques Brel is Alive . . . ," "Swan Song," "A Perfectly Weill Evening."

EDDY, MELISSA. Born Nov. 4 in Kansas City, MO. Attended SanFranStateU, AADA. Debut 1982 OB in "Phedre," followed by "Shrunken Heads," "Bad Girls," "The World of Wallowitch."

EDELHART, YVETTE. Born Mar. 26, 1928 in Oak Park, IL. Attended Wright Col. Debut 1984 OB in "Office Mishegoss," followed by "Home Movies," "Night Must Fall," "The Miser," "Heart of a Dog."

EDELMAN, GREGG. Born Sept. 12, 1958 in Chicago, Il. Graduate Northwestern U. Bdwy debut 1982 in "Evita," followed by "Oliver!," "Cats," "Cabaret," OB in "Weekend," "Shop on Main Street," "Forbidden Broadway."

EDENFIELD, DENNIS. Born July 23, 1946 in New Orleans, LA. Debut 1970 OB in "The Evil That Men Do," followed by "I Have Always Believed in Ghosts," "Nevertheless They Laugh," "Cowboy," Bdwy in "Irene" ('73), "A Chorus Line."

EDMEAD, WENDY. Born July 6, 1956 in NYC. Graduate NYCU. Bdwy debut 1974 in "The Wiz," followed by "Stop the World . . . ," "America," "Dancin'," "Encore," "Cats."

EDWARDS, BRANDT. Born Mar. 22, 1947 in Holly Springs, MS. Graduate UMiss. NY debut off and on Bdwy 1975 in "A Chorus Line," followed by "42nd Street."

EDWARDS, DAVID. Born Dec. 13, 1957 in NYC. Graduate NYU. Bdwy debut 1972 in "The Rothschilds," followed by "The Best Little Whorehouse in Texas," "42nd Street," "A Chorus Line," OB in "Wish You Were Here," "Bittersuite," "Bittersuite, One More Time."

EINHORN, MARVIN. Born Aug. 30, 1920 in Philadelphia, PA. Graduate Carnegie Tech. Debut 1976 OB in "Othello," followed by "Th Time of Your Life," "Inherit the Wind," "Free Fall," "Second Man," "Wedding of the Siamese Twins."

ELICH, MICHAEL. Born Nov. 27, 1954 in Richamond, CA. Graduate UCalRiverzide, Juilliard. Debut 1984 OB in "Romance Language," followed by "Company."

ELKINS, FLORA MAE. Born July 28 in NYC. Attended Neighborhood Playhouse. Bdwy debut 1961 in "Rhinoceros," followed by OB's "Ardele," "The Geranium Hat," "Othello," "Troilus and Cressida," "Baal," "Stephen D," "Candle in the Wind," "A Touch of the Poet," "Ruffles First Lay."

ELLIOTT, ALICE. Born Aug. 22, 1950 in Durham, NC. Graduate Carnegie-Mellon, Goodman Theatre. Debut 1972 OB in "In the Time of Harry Harass," followed by "American Gothic," "Bus Stop," "As You Like It," "My Early Years," "The Color of the Evening Sky."

ELLIOTT, PATRICIA. Born July 21, in Gunnison, Co. Graduate UCo., London Academy. Debut 1968 with LCRep in "King Lear" and "A Cry of Players," followed by OB's "Henry V," "The Persians," "A Doll's House," "Hedda Gabler," "In Case of Accident," "Water Hen," "Polly," "But Not for Me," "By Bernstein," "Prince of Homburg," "Artichokes," "Wine Untouched," "Misalliance," "Virginia," "Sung and Unsung Sondheim," "Voice of the Turtle," "Lillian Wald," "Bunker Reveries," "Bunker Reveries," "Phaedra," Bdwy debut 1973 in "A Little Night Music" for which she received a Theatre World Award, followed by "The Shadow Box," "Tartuffe," "13 Rue d L'Amour," "The Elephant Man," "A Month of Sundays."

ELLIS, ANTONIA. Born Apr. 30, 1944 in Newport, Isle of Wight. Bdwy debut 1975 in "Pippin," followed by "Mail."

ELLIS, FRASER. Born May 1, 1957 in Boulder, CO. Graduate UCo. Bdwy debut 1982 in "A Chorus Line."

ELMORE, STEVE. Born July 12, 1936 in Niangua, MO. Debut 1961 in "Madame Aphrodite," followed by "Golden Apple," "Enclave," Bdwy in "Camelot," "Jenny," "Fade in Fade Out," "Kelly," "Company," "Nash at 9," "Chicago," "42nd St."

EMERY, LISA. Born Jan. 29 in Pittsburgh, PA. Graduate Hollins Col. Debut 1981 OB in "In Connecticut," followed by "Talley & Son," Bdwy in "Passion" (1983), "Burn This."

ENG, RICHARD. Born July 29, 1943 in Spokane, WA. Graduate WashStateU. Debut 1988 OB in "Loose Ends."

ENGEL, DAVID. Born Oct. 19, 1959 in Orange, CA. Attended UCal/Irvine. Bdwy debut 1983 in "La Cage aux Folles."

ENGLISH, DONNA. Born Jan. 13, 1962 in Norman, OK. Graduate NorthwesternU. Bdwy debut 1987 in "Broadway," followed by OB's "Company," "The Last Musical Comedy."

ERDE, SARA. Born Mar. 18, 1970 in NYC. Debut 1987 OB in "Roosters," followed by "Dancing Feet," "A Midsummer Night's Dream."

ERWIN, BARBARA. Born June 30, 1937 in Boston, MA. Debut 1973 OB in "The Secret Life of Walter Mitty," followed by "Broadway," "One Way to Ulan Bator," Bdwy in "Annie," "Ballroom," "Animals."

ESPOSITO, GIANCARLO. Born Apr. 26, 1958 in Copenhage, Den. Bdwy debut 1968 in "Maggie Flynn," followed by "The Me Nobody Knows," "Lost in the Stars," "Seesaw," "Merrily We Roll Along," "Don't Get God Started," OB in "Zooman and the Sign" for which he received a Theatre World Award, "Keyboard," "Who Loves the Dancer," "House of Ramon Iglesias," "Do Lord Remember Me," "Balm in Gilead," "Anchorman."

ESTERMAN, LAURA. Born April 12 in NYC. Attended Radcliffe, LAMDA. Debut 1969 OB in "The Time of Your Life," followed by "Pig Pen," "Carpenters," "Ghosts," "Macbeth," "The Seagull," "Rubbers," "Yankees 3 Detroit O," "Golden Boy," "Out of Our Father's House," "The Master and Margarita," "Chinchilla," "Dusa, Fish, Stas and Vi," "A Midsummer Night's Dream," "The Recruiting Officer," "Oedipus the King," "Two Fish in the Sky," "Mary Barnes," "Tamara," Bdwy in "Waltz of the Toreadors" (1973), "God's Favorite," "Teibele and Her Demon," "The Suicide."

ESTEY, SUELLEN. Born Nov. 21 in Mason City, IA. Graduate Stephens Col., Northwestern U. Debut 1 1970 OB in "Some Other Time," followed by "June Moon," "Buy Bonds Buster," "Smile, Smile, Smile," "Carousel," "Lullaby of Broadway," "I Can't Keep Running," "The Guys in the Truck," "Stop the World," "Bittersuite-One More Time," Bdwy in "The Selling of the President" (1972), "Barnum," "Sweethearts in Concert."

EVANS, HARVEY. Born Jan. 7, 1941 in Cincinnati, OH. Bdwy debut 1957 in "New Girl in Town," followed by "West Side Story," "Redhead," "Gypsy," "Anyone Can Whistle," "Hello, Dolly!," "George M!," "Our Town," "The Boy Friend," "Follies," "Barnum," "La Cage aux Folles," OB in "Sextet."

EVERHART, REX. Born June 13, 1920 in Watseka, IL. Graduate UMo, NYU. Bdwy debut 1955 in "No Time for Sergeants," followed by "Tall Story," "Moonbirds," "Tenderloin," "A Matter of Position," "A Rainy Day in Newark," "Skyscraper," "How Now Dow Jones," "1776," "The Iceman Cometh," "Chicago," "Working," "Woman of the Year," "Anything Goes," OB in "Playboy of the Western World."

EVERS, BRIAN. Born Feb. 14, 1942 in Miami, FL. Graduate Capital U, UMiami. Debut 1979 OB in "How's the House?," followed by "Details of the 16th Frame," "Divine Fire," "Silent Night, Lonely Night," "Uncommon Holidays," "The Tamer Tamed," "Death of a Buick," "The Racket," Bdwy in "House of Blue Leaves" (1986).

FABER, RON. Born Feb. 16, 1933 in Milwaukee, WI. Graduate Marquette U. Debut 1959 OB in "An Enemy of the People," followed by "The Exception and the Rule," "America Hurrah," "They Put Handcuffs on Flowers," "Dr. Selavy's Magic Theatre," "Troilus and Cressida," "The Beauty Part," "Woyzeck," "St. Joan of the Stockyards," "Jungle of Cities," "Scenes from Everyday Life," "Mary Stuart," "3 by Pirandello," "Times and Appetites of Toulouse-Lautrec," "Hamlet," "Johnstown Vindicator," Bdwy in "Medea" (1973), "First Monday in October."

FALAT, STEPHEN. Born Nov. 9, 1956 in Concord, NH. Graduate Adelphi U. Debut 1987 OB in "Fire in the Basement," followed by "Transformational Country Dances."

FARINA, MARILYN J. Born Apr. 9, 1947 in NYC. Graduate Sacred Heart Col. Debut 1985 OB in "Nunsense."

FARO, LYNN. Born June 30, 1951 in Los Angeles, Ca. Graduate UCal/Irvine. Bdwy debut 1985 in "La Cage aux Folles."

FARWICK, RICK. Born Sept. 13, 1954 in Cincinnati, OH. Graduate Northwestern U. Debut 1988 OB in "Leave It to Me."

FASS, ROBERT. Born Aug. 15, 1958 in Wantagh, NY. Graduate MacAlester Col. Debu 1984 OB in "The Desk Set," followed by "Poland/1931."

FEAGAN, LESLIE. Born Jan. 9, 1951 in Hinckley, OH. Graduate OhioU. Debut 1978 OB in "Can-Can," followed by "Merton of the Movies," "Promises Promises," "Mowgli," Bdwy in "Anything Goes" (1987).

FEINSTEIN, MICHAEL. Born in 1957 in Columbus, OH. Bdwy debut 1988 in "Michael Feinstein in Concert."

FELDSHUH, TOVAH. Born Dec. 27, 1953 in NYC. Graduate Sarah Lawrence Col., UMn. Bdwy debut 1973 in "Cyrano," followed by "Dreyfus in Rehearsal," "Rodgers and Hart," "Yentl" for which she received a Theatre World Award, "Sarava," OB in "Yentl the Yeshiva Boy," "Straws in the Wind," "Three Sisters," "She Stoops to Conquer," "Springtime for Henry," "The Time of Your Life," "Children of the Sun," "The Last of the Red Hot Lovers."

FELICIANO, NICKIE. Born May 16, 1974 in Paterson, NJ. Debut 1986 OB in "The Time of the Cuckoo," followed by "Henhouse."

FERLAND, DANIELLE. Born Jan. 31, 1971 in Derby, CT. Debut 1983 OB in "Sunday in the Park with George," followed by "Paradise," Bdwy in "Sunday in the Park with George" (1984), "Into the Woods" for which she received a Theatre World Award.

FIEDLER, JOHN. Born Feb. 3, 1925 in Plateville, Wi. Attended Neighborhood Playhouse. OB in "The Seagull," "Sing Me No Lullaby," "The Terrible Swift Sword," "The Raspberry Picker," "The Frog Prince," "Raisin in the Sun," "Marathon '88," Bdwy in "One Eye Closed" (1954), "Howie," "Raisin in the Sun," "Harold," "The Odd Couple," "Our Town."

FIELD, CRYSTAL. Born Dec. 10, 1942 in NYC. Attended Juilliard, Graduate Hunter Col. Debut OB in "A Country Scandal (1960)," and most recent appearance was in "A Matter of Life and Death," followed by "The Heart That Eats Itself," "Ruzzante Returns from the Wars," "An Evening of British Music Hall," "The Ride That Never Was," "House Arrest," "Us," "Beverly's Yard Sale."

FISCHER, TAKAYO. Born Nov. 25 in Hardwick, CA. Attended Rollins Col. Bdwy debut 1958 in "The World of Suzie Wong," followed by OB's "The Happy Bar," "Tea."

FISKE, ELLEN. Born May 1 in Paterson, NY. Graduate Wilmington Col., OhioU. Debut 1974 OB in "Arms and the Man," followed by "La Ronde," "The Art of Coarse Acting," "Under the Skin," Bdwy in "The Royal Family" (1976).

FITZ-GERALD, JASON. Born May 23 in Guyana, SAm. Attended AADA. Debut 1983 OB in "Poppie Nongena," followed by "Painting a Wall," "Stopping the Desert."

FITZGERALD, FERN. Born Jan. 7, 1947 in Valley Stream, NY. Bdwy debut 1976 in "Chicago," followed by "A Chorus Line."

FITZPATRICK, JIM. Born Nov. 26, 1950 in Omaha, NE. Attended UNeb. Debut 1977 OB in "Arsenic and Old Lace," followed by "Merton of the Movies," "Oh, Boy!," "Time and the Conways," "Street Scene," "The Duchess of Malfi," "Comedy of Errors," "Much Ado about Nothing."

FLANAGAN, KIT. Born July 6 in Pittsburgh, PA. Graduate Northwestern U. Debut 1979 OB in "The Diary of Anne Frank," followed by "An Evening with Dorothy Parker," "Still Life," "Cloud 9," "Alto Part," "A Step Out of Line," "Goodbye Freddy," "The Wonder Years," Bdwy in "All My Sons" (1987).

FLANAGAN, WALTER. Born Oct. 4, 1928 in Ponta, TX. Graduate Houston U. Bdwy in "Once for the Asking," "A Texas Trilogy," "A Touch of the Poet," "The Iceman Cometh," OB in "Bedtime Story," "Coffee and Windows," "Opening of a Window," "The Moon Is Blue," "Laughwind," "The Dodo Bird," "Julius Caesar."

FLANINGAM, LOUISA. Born May 5, 1945 in Chester, SC. Graduate UMd. Debut 1971 OB in "The Shrinking Bridge," followed by "Pigeons on the Walk," "Etiquette," "The Knife," "The Wonder Years," Bdwy in "Magic Show," "Most Happy Fella" (1979), "Play Me a Country Song," "Sally in Concert."

FLEISS, JANE. Born Jan. 28 in NYC. Graduate NYU. Debut 1979 OB in "Say Goodnight, Gracie," followed by "Grace," "The Beaver Coat," "The Harvesting," "D.," "Second Man," "Of Mice and Men," Bdwy in "5th of July" (1981), "Crimes of the Heart," "I'm Not Rappaport."

FLOREK, DAVE. Born May 19, 1953 in Dearborn, MI. Graduate Eastern MiU. Debut 1976 OB in "The Collection," followed by "Richard III," "Much Ado About Nothing," "Young Bucks," "Big Apple Messenger," "Death of a Miner," "Marvelous Gray," "Journey to Gdansk," "The Last of Hitler," "Thin Ice," "The Incredibly Famous Willy Rivers," "Responsible Parties," "For Sale," "The Foreigner," "Copperhead," "Moonchildren," "Emily," Bdwy 1980 in "Nuts."

FOERSTER, RAND. Born Jan. 25, 1951 in Saginaw, MI. Graduate Central MiU, Yale. Debut 1980 OB in "Our Father," followed by "Truck Stops Here," "Mojave," "The Hooded Eye."

FOGARTY, MARY. Born in Manchester, NH. Debut 1959 OB in "The Well of Saints," followed by "Shadow and Substance," "Nathan the Wise," "Bonjour La Bonjour," "Family Comedy," "Steel Magnolias," Bdwy in "The National Health," "Watch on the Rhine" (1980), "Of the Fields Lately."

FORD, SPENCE. Born Feb. 25, 1954 in Richmond, VA. Attended UVa. Debut 1976 OB in "Follies," followed by "Pal Joey," Bdwy in "King of Hearts," "Carmelina," "Peter Pan," "Copperfield," "Dancin'," "Merlin," "La Cage aux Folles."

FOWLER, BETH. Born Nov. 1, 1940 in New Jersey. Graduate Caldwell Col. Bdwy debut 1970 in "Gantry," followed by "A Little Night Music," "Over Here," "1600 Pennsylvania Avenue," "Peter Pan," "Baby," "Teddy and Alice," OB in "Preppies."

FOX, COLIN. Born Nov. 20, 1938 in Aldershot, Can. Attended UWestern Ontario. Bdwy debut 1968 in "Soldiers," followed by "Pack of Lies," OB in "The Importance of Being Earnest," "Declassee," "Love's Labour's Lost," "Anteroom," "Resistance."

FRANCINE, ANNE. Born Aug. 8, 1917 in Philadelphia, PA. Bdwy debut in "Marriage Is for Single People" (1945), followed by "By the Beautiful Sea," "The Great Sebastians," "Tenderloin," "Mame," "A Broadway Musical," "Snow White," "Mame," "Anything Goes," OB in "Guitar," "Valmouth," "Asylum," "Are You Now or Have You Ever Been."

FRANCIS-JAMES, PETER. Born Sept. 16, 1956 in Chicago, IL. Graduate RADA. Debut 1979 OB in "Julius Caesar," followed by "Long Day's Journey into Night," "Antigone," "Richard III," "Romeo and Juliet."

FRANKS, LAURIE. Born Aug. 14, 1929 in Lucasville, OR. Bdwy debut 1956 in "Bells Are Ringing," followed by "Copper and Brass," "Pleasures and Palaces," "Something More," "Anya," "Mame," "The Utter Glory of Morrissey Hall," "The Human Comedy," "Cabaret" (1987), OB in "Leave It to Jane," "Jimmy and Billy," "Around the World in 80 Days."

FRANZ, ELIZABETH. Born June 18, 1941 in Akron, OH. Attended AADA. Debut 1965 OB in "In White America," followed by "One Night Stands of a Noisy Passenger," "The Real Inspector Hound," "Augusta," "Yesterday Is Over," "Actor's Nightmare," "Sister Mary Ignatius Explains It All," "The Time of Your Life," "Children of the Sun," Bdwy in "Rosencrantz and Guildenstern Are Dead," "The Cherry Orchard," "Brighton Beach Memoirs," "The Octette Bridge Club," "Broadway Bound."

FRANZ, JOY. Born in 1944 in Modesto, Ca. Graduate UMo. Debut 1969 OB in "Of Thee I Sing," followed by "Jacques Brel Is Alive . . .," "Out of This World," "Curtains," "I Can't Keep Running in Place," "Tomfoolery," "Penelope," "Bittersuite," Bdwy in "Sweet Charity," "Lysistrata," "A Little Night Music," "Pippin," "Musical Chairs," "Into the Woods."

FRASER, ALISON. Born July 8, 1955 in Natick, Ma. Attended Carnegie-Mellon U., Boston Conservatory. Debut 1979 OB in "In Trousers," followed by "March of the Falsettos," "Beehive," "Four One-Act Musicals," "Tales of Tinseltown," "Next Please!," Bdwy in "The Mystery of Edwin Drood" (1986), "Romance Romance "

FRATANTONI, DIANE. Born Mar. 29, 1956 in Wilmington, DE. Bdwy debut 1979 in "A Chorus Line," followed by "Cats."

FRECHETTE, PETER. Born Oct. 3, 1956 in Warwick, RI. Graduate URI. Debut 1979 OB in "The Hornbeam Maze," followed by "Scooter Thomas Makes It to the Top of the World," "Harry Ruby's Songs My Mother Never Sang," "We're Home," "Flora the Red Menace."

FREDERICKS, CONNIE. Born Aug. 30, 1948 in Springfield, Ma. Attended Fashion Inst. Debut 1984 OB in "Oh, Baby!," followed by "Forever, My Darlin'," "Abyssinia," "A Walk on the Wild Side," "Lost in the Stars."

FREEMAN, AL, JR. Born Mar. 21, 1934 in San Antonio, TX. Attended CCLA. Bdwy in "The Long Dream" (1960), "Tiger, Tiger Burning Bright," "Living Premise," "Blues for Mr. Charlie," "Dozens," "Look to the Lilies," OB in "Slave," "Dutchman," "Trumpets of the Lord," "Medea," "The Great McDaddy," "One Crack Out," "Long Day's Journey into Night," "Trinity," "Anchorman."

FREEMAN, MORGAN. Born June 1, 1937 in Memphis, Tn. Attended LACC. Bdwy debut 1967 in "Hello, Dolly!," followed by "The Mighty Gents," "OB in "Ostrich Feathers," "Niggerlovers," "Exhibition," "Black Visions," "Cockfight," "White Pelicans," "Julius Caesar," "Coriolanus," "Mother Courage," "The Connection," "The World of Ben Caldwell," "Buck," "The Gospel at Colonus," "Medea and the Doll," "Driving Miss Daisy."

FREEMAN, TOM. Born Jan. 3, 1964 in Seattle, WA. Debut 1987 OB in "Kismet."

FRENCH, ARTHUR. Born in NYC. Attended Bklyn Col. Debut 1962 OB in "Raisin' Hell in the Sun," followed by "Ballad of Bimshire," "Day of Absence," "Happy Ending," "Jonah," "Ceremonies in Dark Old Men," "An Evening of 1 Acts," "Man Better Man," "Brotherhood," "Perry's Mission," "Rosalee Pritchett," "Moonlight Arms," "Dark Tower," "Brownsville Raid," "Nevis Mt. Dew," "Julius Caesar," "Friends," "Court of Miracles," "The Beautiful LaSalles," "Blues for a Gospel Queen," "Black Girl," "Driving Miss Daisy," Bdwy in "Ain't Supposed to Die a Natural Death," "The Iceman Cometh," "All God's Chillun Got Wings," "The Resurrection of Lady Lester," "You Can't Take It With You," "Design for Living," "Ma Rainey's Black Bottom."

FRIAR, RALPH E. Born Oct. 9, 1924 in Buffalo, NY. Graduate UBuffalo, Hunter Col. Debut 1957 in "Tartuffe," followed by "Guadeloupe."

FRID, JONATHAN. Born Dec. 1924 in Hamilton, Ont., Can. Graduate McMaster U., Yale, RADA. Debut 1959 OB in "The Golem," followed by "Henry IV, Parts I & II," "The Moon in the Yellow River," "The Burning," "Murder in the Cathedral," Bdwy in "Roar Like a Dove" (1964), "Arsenic and Old Lace" (1986).

FRISCH, RICHARD. Born May 9, 1933 in NYC. Graduate Juilliard. Bdwy debut 1964 in "The Passion of Josef D," followed by "Fade Out-Fade In," "Rags," "Roza," OB in "Jonah," "Antigone," "The Mother of Us All," "Up from Paradise," "Pere Goriot," "Pearls."

FUGARD, ATHOL. Born June 11, 1932 in Middleburg, SAf. Attended UCape Town. Bdwy debut (as an actor) 1985 in "The Blood Knot," and OB in "The Road to Mecca" (1988), both written by him.

GAIL, TIM. Born in Tokyo, Japan, and attended AADA. Debut 1985 OB in "Getting Married," followed by "Murder on Broadway," "The Business of America," "Charlie Dante," "Private Wars," "The Man of Destiny," "Dirty Hands," "Thighs like Tina Turner," "2 More by Myers," "A Circle."

GALLAGHER, HELEN. Born in 1926 in Brooklyn, NY. Bdwy debut 1947 in "Seven Lively Arts," followed by "Mr. Strauss Goes to Boston," "Billion Dollar Baby," "Brigadoon," "High Button Shoes," "Touch and Go," "Make a Wish," "Pal Joey," "Guys and Dolls," "Finian's Rainbow," "Oklahoma!," "Pajama Game," "Bus Stop," "Portofino," "Sweet Charity," "Mame," "Cry for Us All," "No, No, Nanette," "A Broadway Musical," "Sugar Babies," OB in "Hothouse," "Tickles by Tucholsky," "The Misanthrope," "I Can't Keep Running in Place," "Red Rover," "Tallulah," "The Flower Palace," "Tallulah Tonight "

GAM, RITA. Born Apr. 2, 1928 in Pittsburgh, PA. Attended Columbia, Actors Studio. Bdwy debut 1946 in "A Flag Is Born," followed by "Temporary Island," "Insect Comedy"(CC), "The Young and the Fair," "Montserrat," "There's a Girl in My Soup," OB in "Hamlet."

GAMACHE, LAURIE. Born Sept. 25, 1959 in Mayville, ND. Graduate Stephens Col. Bdwy debut 1982 in "A Chorus Line."

GARBER, VICTOR. Born Mar. 16, 1949 in London, Can. Debut 1973 OB in "Ghosts" for which he received a Theatre World Award, followed by "Joe's Opera," "Cracks," "Wenceslas Square," Bdwy in "Tartuffe," "Deathtrap," "Sweeney Todd," "They're Playing Our Song," "Little Me," "Noises Off," "You Never Can Tell."

GARFIELD, DAVID. Born Feb. 6, 1941 in Brooklyn, NY. Graduate Columbia, Cornell U. Debut 1964 OB in "Hang Down Your Head and Die," followed by "Government Inspector," "Old Ones," "Family Business," "Ralph Roister Doister," "Actors Deli," "Traps," Bdwy in "Fiddler on the Roof," "The Rothschilds."

GARSIDE, BRAD. Born June 2, 1958 in Boston, MA. Graduate NorthTexState U. Debut 1983 OB in "Forbidden Broadway."

GARZA, TROY. Born Aug. 20, 1954 in Hollywood, Ca. Attended RADA. Bdwy debut 1977 in "A Chorus Line," followed by "Got Tu Go Disco," OB in "Fourtune," "Paris Lights."

GAVON, IGORS. Born Nov. 14, 1937 in Latvia. Bdwy bow 1961 in "Carnival," followed by "Hello, Dolly!" "Marat/deSade," "Billy," "Sugar," "Mack and Mabel," "Musical Jubilee," "Strider," "42 St," OB in "Your Own Thing," "Promenade," "Exchange," "Nevertheless They Laugh," "Polly," "The Boss," "Biography: A Game," "Murder in the Cathedral."

GEE, KEVIN JOHN. Born Mar. 19, 1962 in San Francisco, Ca. Attended Chabot Col. Debut 1977 OB in "Helen," followed by "Boticelli," "Tropical Tree," "Prime Time," "The Wedding of the Siamese Twins."

GEFFNER, DEBORAH. Born Aug. 26, 1952 in Pittsburgh, PA. Attended Juilliard, HB Studio. Debut 1978 OB in "Tenderloin," Bdwy in "Pal Joey," "A Chorus Line."

GEHMAN, MARTHA. Born May 15, 1955 in NYC. Graduate Sarah Lawrence Col. Debut 1984 OB in "Cinders," followed by "Day Room."

GEIER, PAUL. Born Aug. 7, 1944 in NYC. Graduate Pratt Inst. Debut 1980 OB in "Family Business," followed by "Women in Shoes," "Johnstown Vindicator," "No Time Flat," Bdwy in "Lunch Hour" (1981).

GELFER, STEVEN. Born Feb. 21, 1949 in Brooklyn, NY. Graduate NYU, IndU. Debut 1968 OB and Bdwy in "The Best Little Whorehouse in Texas," followed by "Cats."

GELKE, BECKY. Born Feb. 17, 1953 in Ft. Knox, KY. Graduate WKyU. Debut 1978 OB/Bdwy in "The Best Little Whorehouse in Texas," followed by "A Streetcar Named Desire" (1988), OB in "Altitude Sickness," "John Brown's Body," "Chamber Music," "To Whom It May Concern," "Two Gentlemen of Verona."

GENEST, EDMOND. Born Oct. 27, 1943 in Boston, Ma. Attended Suffolk U. Debut 1972 OB in "The Real Inspector Hound," followed by "Second Prize: Two Months in Leningrad," "Maneuvers," "Pantomime," "Scooncat," Bdwy in "Dirty Linen/New Found Land" (1977), "Whose Life Is It Anyway?"

GENEVIERE, DEBORAH. Born Oct. 15, 1961 in Tokyo, Japan. Graduate SUNY/Stonybrook. Bdwy debut 1988 in "Chess."

GERACI, FRANK. Born Sept. 8, 1939 in Brooklyn, NY. Attended Yale. Debut 1961 OB in "Color of Darkness," followed by "Mr. Grossman," "Balm in Gilead," "The Fantasticks," "Tom Paine," "End of All Things Natural," "Union Street," "Uncle Vanya," "Success Story," "Hughie," "Merchant of Venice," "The Three Zeks," "Taming of the Shrew," "The Lady from the Sea," "Rivals," "Deep Swimmer," "The Imaginary Invalid," "Candida," "Uncle Vanya," Bdwy in "The Love Suicide at Schofield Barracks" (1972).

GERAGHTY, MARITA. Born Mar. 26, 1965 in Chicago, IL. Graduate UIll. Bdwy debut 1987 in "Coastal Disturbances," followed by "The Night of the Iguana."

GERARD, DANNY. Born May 29, 1977 in NYC. Bdwy debut 1986 in "Into the Light," followed by "Les Miserables," OB in "Today I Am a Fountain Pen," "Second Hurricane."

GERDES, GEORGE. Born Feb. 23, 1948 in NYC. Graduate Carnegie Tech. Debut 1979 OB in "Modigliani," followed by "The Idolmakers," "The Doctor and the Devils," "The Hit Parade," "A Country for Old Men," "Fool for Love," "To Whom It May Concern," "New Works '87."

GERRINGER, ROBERT. Born May 12, 1926 in NYC. Graduate Fordham U., Pasadena Playhouse. Debut 1955 OB in "Thieves Carnival," followed by "Home," "The Birthday Party," Bdwy in "Pictures in the Hallway," "A Flea in Her Ear," "Andersonville Trial," "Waltz of the Toreadors," "After the Fall," "A Doll's House," "Hedda Gabler," "Hide and Seek."

GERRITY, DAN. Born Dec. 21, 1957 in Red Bank, NJ. Attended SUNY/Albany, Neighborhood Playhouse. Debut 1987 OB in "Bouncers."

GERROLL, DANIEL. Born Oct. 16, 1951 in London, Eng. Attended Central Sch. of Speech. Debut 1980 OB in "The Slab Boys," followed by "Knuckle" and "Translations" for which he received a Theatre World Award," "The Caretaker," "Scenes from La Vie de Boheme," "The Knack," "Terra Nova," "Dr. Faustus," "Second Man," "Cheapside," "Bloody Poetry," "The Common Pursuit." "Woman in Mind," "Poets' Corner," Bdwy in "Plenty" (1982).

GIANNINI, CHERYL. Born June 15 in Monessen, PA. Bdwy debut 1980 in "The Suicide," followed by "Grownups," "I'm Not Rappaport," OB in "Elm Circle," "Spoils of War."

GIANOPOULOS, DAVID. Born Aug. 9, 1959 in Stoneybrook, NY. Graduate Pacific Conservatory. Debut 1987 OB in "Richard II," followed by "Henry IV Part I."

GIBSON, JULIA. Born June 8, 1962 in Norman, OK. Graduate UIowa, NYU. Debut 1987 OB in "A Midsummer Night's Dream."

GIBSON, THOMAS. Born July 3, 1962 in Charleston, SC. Graduate Juilliard. Debut 1985 OB in "Map of the World," followed by "Twelfth Night," "Bloody Poetry," "Marathon 87," "Two Gentlemen of Verona." "Class 1 Acts," Bdwy in "Hay Fever (1985)."

GIFFIN, NORMA JEAN. Born Oct. 31, 1956 in Haverhill, Ma. Graduate Barat Col., AADA. Debut 1980 OB in "Last Stop Blue Jay Lane" followed by "On Extended Wings," "Shirley Basin."

GILBERT, MELISSA. Born May 8, 1964 in Los Angeles, CA. Debut 1987 OB in "A Shayna Maidel" for which she received a Theatre World Award.

GILES, LEE ROY. Born Dec. 3, 1936 in Witchita, Ks. Attended Fordham, Adelphi, L.I.U. Bdwy debut 1971 in "No Place to Be Somebody," OB in "Deep Swimmer," "Big City Breakdown," "Dash"

GILES, NANCY. Born July 17, 1960 in Queens, NYC. Graduate Oberlin Col. Debut 1985 OB in "Mayor" for which she received a Theatre World Award, followed by "The Sneaker Factor," "Young Playwrights," "One Act Festival," "Urban Blight."

GILL, RAY. Born Aug. 1, 1950 in Bayonne, NJ. Attended Rider Col. Bdwy debut 1978 in "On the 20th Century" followed by "Pirates of Penzance," "The First," "They're Playing Our Song," "Sunday in the Park with George," OB in "A Bundle of Nerves," "Driving Miss Daisy."

GILLETTE, ANITA. Born Aug. 16, 1938 in Baltimore, MD. Debut 1960 OB in "Russell Patterson's Sketchbook" for which she received a Theatre World Award, followed by "Rich and Famous," "Dead Wrong," "Road Show," "Class 1 Acts," Bdwy in "Carnival," "All American," "Mr. President," "Guys and Dolls," "Don't Drink the Water," "Cabaret," "Jimmy," "Chapter Two," "They're Playing Our Song," "Brighton Beach Memoirs."

GLEASON, JAMES. Born Sept. 30, 1952 in NYC. Graduate Santa Fe Col. Debut 1982 OB in "Guys in the Truck," followed by "Corkscrews!," "Patrick Pearse Motel," "Taboo in Revue," "Curse of the Starving Class," "Curse of the Starving Class," "Signal Season," Bdwy in "Guys in the Truck" (1983).

GLEASON, JOANNA. Born June 2, 1950 in Toronto, CAN. Graduate UCLA. Bdwy debut 1977 in "I Love My Wife" for which she received a Theatre World Award, followed by "The Real Thing," "Social Security," "Into the Woods," OB in "A Hell of a Town," "Joe Egg," "It's Only a Play."

GLEASON, LAURENCE. Born Nov. 15, 1956 in Utica, NY. Graduate Utica Col. Debut 1984 OB in "Romance Language," followed by "Agamemnon," "A Country Doctor," "The Misanthrope," "The Sleepless City," "Electra."

GLUSHAK, JOANNA. Born May 27, 1958 in NYC. Attended NYU. Debut 1983 OB in "Lenny and the Heartbreakers," followed by "Lies and Legends," "Miami," Bdwy in "Sunday in the Park with George" (1984), "Rags" "Les Miserables."

GOLER, LAUREN. Born Nov. 10, 1961 in Washington, DC. Bdwy debut 1980 in "Happy New Year," followed by "Onward Victorial!," "Smile," "Late Night Comic," OB in "Joseph."

GOMEZ, MIKE. Born May 18, 1951 in Dallas, TX. Bdwy debut 1979 in "Zoot Suit."

GONZALEZ, CORDELIA. Born Aug. 11, 1958 in San Juan, PR. Graduate UPR, Yale. Debut 1985 OB in "Impact," followed by "The Love of Don Perlimplin," Bdwy in "Serious Money" (1988).

GONZALEZ, JOSE CRUZ. Born May 17, 1957 in NYC. Debut 1970 OB in "Monkey, Monkey," followed by "The Imaginary Invalid," "Pancho Diablo," "First Class."

GOODMAN, LISA. Born in Detroit, MI. Attended UMi. Debut 1982 OB in "Taling With," followed by "The First Warning," "The Show-Off," "Escape from Riverdale," "Jesse's Land," "State of the Union," "The Wonder Years," "Girl of the Golden West."

GOODWIN, JAMES M. Born July 24, 1961 in Biloxi, MS. Graduate OkStateU, SMU. Debut 1987 OB in "Two Gentlemen of Verona."

GORDON-CLARK, SUSAN. Born Dec. 31, 1947 in Jackson, Ms. Graduate Purdue U. Debut 1984 OB in "The Nunsense Story," followed by "Chip Shot," "Nunsense."

GORNEY, KAREN LYNN. Born Jan. 28, 1945 in Los Angeles, CA. Graduate Carnegie Tech, Brandeis U. Debut 1972 OB in "Dylan," followed by "Life on the Third Rail."

GOSSETT, ROBERT. Born Mar. 3, 1954 in The Bronx, NY. Attended AADA. Debut 1973 OB in "One Flew over the Cuckoo's Nest," followed by "The Amen Corner," "Weep Not for Me," "Colored People's Time," "A Soldier's Play," "Sons and Fathers of Sons," "Manhattan Made Me," "A Visitor to the Veldt," Bdwy in "Fences" (1987).

GOTLIEB, BEN. Born June 27, 1954 in Kfar Saba, Israel. Attended RADA, CUNY, Bklyn Col. Bdwy debut 1979 in "Dogg's Hamlet and Cahoot's Macbeth," OB in "Kohlhass," "Relatively Speaking," "The Underlings," "A Match Made in Heaven," "Oklahoma Samovar."

GOTTLEIB, MATTHEW. Born Apr. 6, 1951 in Ann Arbor, MI. Graduate CalnstArts. Debut 1980 OB in "Friend of the Family," followed by "Henry IV Part 2," "The Racket."

GOTTSCHALL, RUTH. Born Apr. 14, 1957 in Wilmington, DE. Bdwy debut 1981 in "The Best Little Whorehouse in Texas," followed by "Cabaret" (1987).

GOUGH, MICHAEL. Born Nov. 23, 1917 in Malaya. Attended Old Vic School. Bdwy debut 1937 in "Love of Women," followed by "The Fighting Cock," "Bedroom Farce," "Breaking the Code."

GOZ, HARRY. Born June 23, 1932 in St. Louis, MO. Attended St. Louis Inst. Debut 1957 followed by "Bajour," "Fiddler on the Roof," "Two by Two," "Prisoner of Second Avenue," "Chess," OB in "To Bury a Cousin," "Ferocious Kisses."

GRACIE, SALLY. Born in Little Rock, AR. Attended Neighborhood Playhouse. Bdwy debut 1942 in "Vickie," followed by "At War with the Army," "Dinosaur Wharf," "Goodbye Again," "Major Barbara," "Fair Game," "But Seriously," "Born Yesterday," "Venus at Large," "Picnic," "Third Best Sport," "Arms and the Man," OB in "Naomi Court," "Dream Come True," "A Lie of the Mind," "Words from the Moon."

GRAFF, RANDY. Born May 23, 1955 in Brooklyn, NY. Graduate Wagner Col. Debut 1978 OB in "Pins and Needles," followed by "Station Joy," "A . . . My Name Is Alice," "Once on aSummer's Day," Bdwy in "Sarava," "Grease," "Les Miserables."

GRAFF, TODD. Born Oct. 22, 1959 in NYC. Attended SUNY/Purchase. Debut 1983 OB in "American Passion," followed by "Birds of Paradise," Bdwy in "Baby" (1983) for which he received a Theatre World Award.

GRAHAM, DEBORAH. Born Jan. 20, 1959 in Speedway, IN. Graduate UCinn. Debut 1982 OB in "Snoopy," followed by "Romance! Romance," Bdwy in "Romance/Romance" (1988).

GRANT, LISA ANN. Born June 7, 1965 in NYC. Bdwy debut 1980 in "Camelot," followed by "Dreamgirls," "Leader of the Pack," "Les Miserables," "A New York Summer," "The Magnificent Christmas Spectacular," OB in "American Passion," "Prescribed Affairs."

GRANT, MICKI. Born June 30 in Chicago, IL. Attended UIll. Bdwy debut 1963 in "Tambourines to Glory," followed by "Don't Bother Me, I Can't Cope," OB in "Fly Blackbird," "The Blacks," "Brecht on Brecht," "Jerico-Jim Crow," "The Cradle Will Rock," "Leonard Bernstein's Theatre Songs," "To Be Young, Gifted and Black," "Anchorman."

GRANT, SCHUYLER. Born Apr. 29, 1970 in San Jose, CA. Attended Yale Drama School. Debue 1987 OB in "The Hooded Eye."

GRANT, VINCENT. Born May 11, 1961 in Denver, CO. Graduate Richland Col. Debut 1984 OB in "A Step Out of Line," followed by "Johnstown Vindicator."

GRAY, KATHLEEN. Born May 5th in NYC. Attended Briarcliff, Yale. Debut 1968 OB in "The American Pig," followed by "The American Sunrise," "Can-Can," "The Big Apple," "El Manifesto," "The Party," "The Importance of Being Earnest," "New Girl in Town," Bdwy in "Teddy and Alice" (1987).

GRAY, KEVIN. Born Feb. 25, 1958 in Westport, Ct. Graduate Duke U. Debut 1982 OB in "Lola," followed by "Pacific Overtures," "Family Snapshots," "The Baker's Wife," "The Knife," "Magdalena in Concert."

GREEN, DAVID. Born June 16, 1942 in Cleveland, OH. Attended KanStateU. Bdwy debut 1980 in "Annie," followed by "Evita," "Teddy and Alice," OB in "Once on a Summer's Day," "Miami," "On the 20th Century."

GREENE, LYN. Born May 21, 1955 in Boston, MA. Graduate NYU, Juilliard. Debut 1984 OB in "Kid Purple," followed by "Flora the Red Menace."

GREENHOUSE, MARTHA. Born June 14 in Omaha, NE. Attended Hunter Col., AmThWing. Bdwy debut 1942 in "Sons and Soldiers," followed by "Dear Me, the Sky Is Falling," "Family Way," "Woman Is My Idea," "Summer Brave," OB in "Clerambord," "Our Town," "3 by Ferlinghetti," "No Strings," "Cackle," "Philistines," "Ivanov," "Returnings," "Love Games," "Dancing to Dover," "Pushing the D Train Back to Brooklyn," "Washington Heights."

GREGG, CLARK. Born Apr. 2, 1962 in Boston, MA. Graduate NYU. Debut 1987 OB in "Fun," followed by "The Detective," "Boy's Life."

GREGORIO, ROSE. Born in Chicago, Ill. Graduate Northwestern, Yale. Debut 1962 OB in "The Days and Nights of Beebee Fenstermaker," followed by "Kiss Mama," "The Balcony," "Bivouac at Lucca," "Journey to the Day," "Diary of Anne Frank," "Weekends Like Other People," "Curse of the Starving Class," "Dream of a Blacklisted Actor," Bdwy in "The Owl and the Pussycat," "Daphne in Cottage D," "Jimmy Shine," "The Cuban Thing," "The Shadow Box," "A View from the Bridge," "M. Butterfly."

GREGORY, MICHAEL ALAN. Born Feb. 1, 1955 in Coral Gables, FL. Graduate Wheaton Col., UWash. Debut 1985 OB in "Season's Greetings," followed by "Dracula," "Kiss Me, Kate," Bdwy in "Macbeth" (1988).

GREGORY, MICHAEL SCOTT. Born Mar. 13, 1962 in Ft. Lauderdale, Fl. Attended Atlantic Foundation. Bdwy debut 1981 in "Sophisticated Ladies," followed by "Starlight Express."

GREY, JOEL. Born Apr. 11, 1932 in Cleveland, Oh. Attended Cleveland Play House. Bdwy debut 1951 in "Borscht Capades," followed by "Come Blow Your Horn," "Stop the World—I Want to Get Off," "Half a Sixpence," "Cabaret," (1966/1987) "George M!," "Goodtime Charley," "Grand Tour," OB in "The Littlest Revue," "Harry Noon and Night," "Marco Polo Sings a Solo," "The Normal Heart."

Katherine Diamond	Rob Donohoe	Roma Downey	Craig Dudley	Melissa Eddy	Steven Earl-Edwards
Yvette Edelhart	Brandt Edwards	Alice Elliott	Fraser Ellis	Donna English	Brian Evers
Stephen Falat	Lynn Faro	Robert Fass	Takayo Fischer	Walter Flanagan	Mary Fogarty
Beth Fowler	Tom Freeman	Rita Gam	Paul Geier	Deborah Geneviere	Danny Gerard
Cheryl Giannini	David Gianopoulos	Nancy Giles	Laurence Gleason	Karen Lynn Gorney	David Green

205

GRIFFITH, EDWARD D. Born Jan. 8, 1949 in Osaka, Japan. Graduate Georgetown U. Debut 1980 OB in "Fugue in a Nursery," followed by "Death Takes a Holiday," "Behind a Mask," "Twelfth Night."

GRIFFITH, KRISTIN. Born Sept. 7, 1953 in Odessa, Tx. Juilliard Graduate. Bdwy debut 1976 in "A Texas Trilogy," OB in "Rib Cage," "Character Lines," "3 Friends/2 Rooms," "A Month in the Country," "Fables for Friends," "The Trading Post," "Marching to Georgia," "American Garage," "A Midsummer Night's Dream," "Marathon 87," "Bunker Reveries."

GRIFFITH, LISA. Born June 18 in Honolulu, Hi. Graduate Brandeis U, Trinity U. Debut 1977 OB in "The Homesickness of Capt. Rappaport," followed by "The Kennedy Play," "Chalkdust," "Murder at the Vicarage," "Ah, Wilderness!," "Stud Silo," "The Miser," "Twelfth Night."

GRIMES, TAMMY. Born Jan. 30, 1934 in Lynn, MA. Attended Stephens Col., Neighborhood Playhouse. Debut 1956 OB in "The Littlest Revue," followed by "Clerambard," "Molly Trick," "Are You Now or Have You Ever Been," "Father's Day," "A Month in the Country," "Sunset," "Waltz of the Toreadors," "Mlle. Colombe," "Tammy Grimes in Concert," Bdwy in "Look after Lulu" (1959) for which she received a Theatre World Award, "The Unsinkable Molly Brown," "Private Lives," "High Spirits," "Rattle of a Simple Man," "The Only Game in Town," "Musical Jubilee," "California Suite," "Tartuffe," "Pal Joey in Concert," "42nd Street."

GRIZZARD, GEORGE. Born Apr. 1, 1928 in Roanoke Rapids, VA. Graduate UNC. Bdwy debut 1954 in "All Summer Long," followed by "The Desperate Hours," "The Happiest Millionaire" for which he received a Theatre World Award, "The Disenchanted," "Big Fish, Little Fish," with APA 1961–62, "Who's Afraid of Virginia Woolf?," "The Glass Menagerie," "You Know I Can't Hear You When the Water's Running," "Noel Coward's Sweet Potato," "The Gingham Dog," "The Inquest," "Country Girl," "Creation of the World and Other Business," "Crown Matrimonial," "The Royal Family," "California Suite," "Man and Superman," OB in "The Beach House," "Another Antigone."

GROENENDAAL, CRIS. Born Feb. 17, 1948 in Erie, PA. Attended Allegheny Col, Exeter U, HB Studio. Bdwy debut 1979 in "Sweeney Todd," followed by "Sunday in the Park with George," "Brigadoon" (LC), "Desert Song" (LC), "Phantom of the Opera," OB in "Francis," "Sweethearts in Concert," "Oh, Boy " "No No Nanette in Concert," LC's "South Pacific" and "Sweeney Tood."

GRUSIN, RICHARD. Born Nov. 2, 1946 in Chicago, IL. Graduate Goodman School, Yale. Debut 1978 OB in "Wings," followed by "Sganerelle," "Heat of Re-Entry," "For Sale," "The Time of Your Life," "Perfect Crime," "Terry by Terry," "Marathon '88."

GUAN, JAMIE H. J. Born June 19, 1950 in Beijing, China. Attended Beijing InstPerforming-Arts. Bdwy debut 1988 in "M. Butterfly."

GUERRASIO, JOHN. Born Feb. 18, 1950 in Brooklyn, NY. Attended Bklyn Col., Boston U. Debut 1971 OB in "Hamlet," followed by "And They Put Handcuffs on Flowers," "Eros and Psyche," "The Marriage Proposal," "Macbeth," "K.," "Sunday Promenade," "Family Business," "Knuckle Sandwich," "Imperialists at the Club Cave Canum."

GUIDO, MICHAEL. Born Jan. 13, 1950 in Woodside, NY. Graduate USFla, Brandeis U. Debut 1982 OB in "The Workroom," followed by "Strictly Dishonorable," "Flatbush Faithful," "Largo Desolato," "A Map of the World," "Talk Radio," "Isolate."

GUNCLER, SAM. Born Oct. 17, 1955 in Bethlehem, PA. Graduate LeHighU. Debut 1983 OB in "Her Honor, the Mayor," followed by "The Racket," "Sail Away."

GUNN, MOSES. Born Oct. 2, 1929 in St. Louis, MO. Graduate UTn, AIU, UKan. OB in "Measure for Measure," "Bohikee Creek," "Day of Absence," "Happy Ending," "Baal," "Hard Travelin'," "Lonesome Train," "In White America," "The Blacks," "Titus Andronicus," "Song of the Lusitanian-Bogey," "Summer of the 17th Doll," "Kongi's Harvest," "Daddy Goodness," "Cities in Bezique," "Perfect Party," "To Be young, Gifted and Black," "Sty of the Blind Pig," "Twelfth Night," "American Gothis," "Tapman," Bdwy in "A Hand Is on the Gate," "Othello," "First Breeze of Summer," "The Poison Tree," "I Have a Dream."

GUNN, NICHOLAS. Born Aug. 28, 1947 in Brooklyn, NY. Appeared with Paul Taylor Dance Co. before Bdwy debut in "The Mystery of Edwin Drood" (1985), followed OB by "Tango Apasionado."

GUNTON, BOB. Born Nov. 15, 1945 in Santa Monica, CA. Attended UCal. Debut 1971 OB in "Who Am I?," followed by "The Kid," "Desperate Hours," "Tip-Toes," "How I Got That Story," "Hamlet," "Death of Von Richthofen," "The Man Who Could See Through Time," "The Music Man" (LC), Bdwy in "Happy End" (1977), "Working," "King of Hearts," "Evita," "Passion," "Big River," "Roza."

GURNEY, RACHEL. Born March 5 in England. NY debut 1977 OB in "You Never Can Tell," followed by "Heartbreak House," Bdwy in "Major Barbara" (1980), "The Dresser," "Breaking the Code."

GUTTMAN, RONALD. Born Aug. 12, 1952 in Brussels, Belg. Graduate Brussels U. Debut OB (1986) and Bdwy (1987) in "Coastal Disturbances."

GWILLIM, JACK. Born Dec. 15, 1915 in Canterbury, Eng. Attended Central School. Bdwy debut 1956 in "Macbeth," followed by "Romeo and Juliet," "Richard II," "Troilus and Cressida," "Laurette," "Ari," "Lost in the Stars," "The Iceman Cometh," "The Constant Wife," "Romeo and Juliet" (1977), "My Fair Lady" (1981), "Macbeth" (1988), OB in "The Farm."

GWILLIM, SARAH-JANE. Born March 4 in Plymouth, Eng. Attended London Central School of Speech. NY debut 1977 OB in "You Never Can Tell," Bdwy in "St. Joan" (1977), "Macbeth" (1988).

GYNGELL, PAUL. Born Jan. 26, 1963 in Church Village, South Wales. Attended Italia Conti Stage School. Bdwy debut 1988 in "Carrie."

HACK, STEVEN. Born Apr. 20, 1958 in St. Louis, MO. Attended CalArts, AADA, Debut 1978 OB in "The Coolest Cat in Town," followed by Bdwy in "Cats" (1982).

HACKETT, JEAN. Born Aug. 28, 1956 in York, PA. Graduate NYU, RADA. Debut 1983-OB in "Ah, Wilderness!," followed by "The Education of One Miss February," Bdwy in "A Streetcar Named Desire" (1988).

HADARY, JONATHAN. Born Oct. 11, 1948 in Chicago, IL. Attended Tufts U. Debut 1974 OB in "White Nights," followed by "El Grande de Coca-Cola," "Songs from Pins and Needles," "God Bless You, Mr. Rosewater," "Pushing 30," "Scrambled Feet," "Coming Attractions," "Tom-foolery," "Charley Bacon and Family," "Road Show," "1-2-3-4-5," "Wenceslas Square," Bdwy in "Gemini," (1977/also OB), "Torch Song Trilogy, "As Is."

HADDAD, AVA. Born in New York City. Debut 1986 OB in "Passover," followed by "The Milk Train Doesn't Stop Here Anymore," "A Shayna Maidel."

HAFNER, JULIE J. Born June 4, 1952 in Dover, Oh. Graduate KentStateU. Debut 1976 OB in "The Club," followed by "Nunsense," Bdwy in "Nine."

HALL, CHARLES EDWARD. Born Nov. 12, 1951 in Frankfort, KY. Graduate Murray-State U. Debut 1977 OB in "Molly's Dream," followed by "Sheridan Square," "The Doctor in spite of Himself," "Loudspeaker," "Action," "The Tavern," Bdwy in Radio City's "Snow White" (1979), and the "Christmas Spectacular" (1987).

HALL, ED. Born Jan. 11, 1931 in Roxbury, MA. Attended Harvard. Bdwy credits include "The Climate of Eden," "No Time for Sergeants," "A Raisin in the Sun," "Wilson in the Promise Land," "The Zulu and the Zayda," "Joe Turner's Come and Gone," OB in "The Death of Bessie Smith," "Trumpets of the Lord."

HALL, GEORGE. Born Nov. 19, 1916 in Toronto, Can. Attended Neighborhood Playhouse. Bdwy bow 1946 in "Call Me Mister," followed by "Lend an Ear," "Touch and Go," "Live Wire," "The Boy Friend," "There's a Girl in My Soup," "An Evening with Richard Nixon ..," "We Interrupt This Program," "Man and Superman," "Bent," "Noises Off," "Wild Honey," OB in "The Balcony," "Ernest in Love," "A Round with Rings," "Family Pieces," "Carousel," "The Case Against Roberta Guardino," "Marry Me!" "Arms and the Man," "The Old Glory," "Dancing for the Kaiser," "Casualties," "The Seagull," "A Stitch in Time," "Mary Stuart," "No End of Blame," "Hamlet," "Colette Collage," "The Homecoming," "And a Nightingale Sang," "The Bone Ring," "Much Ado about Nothing."

HALL, STEVEN. Born June 4, 1958 in Washington, DC. Attended NCSchArts. Bdwy debut 1981 in "Marlowe," followed by OB's "T.N.T.," "Collette Collage," "Conrack."

HALLEY, BEN, JR. Born Aug. 6, 1951 in Harlen, NY. Graduate CCNY, Yale. Bdwy debut 1978 in "A History of the American Film," OB in "A Day in the Life of the Czar," "A Midsummer Night's Dream," "The Recruiting Officer," "The Wild Duck," "Oedipus the King," "Death and the King's Horseman" (LC), "Zangezi."

HALLIDAY, ANDY. Born Mar. 31, 1953 in Orange, Ct. Attended USIU/San Diego. Debut OB 1985 in "Vampire Lesbians of Sodom," followed by "Times Square Angel," "Psycho Beach Party."

HAMILTON, LAWRENCE. Born Sept. 14, 1954 in Ashdown, AR. Graduate Henderson State U. Debut 1981 OB in "Purlie," Bdwy in "Sophisticated Ladies" (1982), "Porgy and Bess," "The Wiz," "Uptown It's Hot," "The River."

HANAN, STEPHEN. Born Jan 7, 1947 in Washington, DC. Graduate Harvard, LAMDA. Debut 1978 OB in "All's Well That Ends Well," followed by "Taming of the Shrew," "Rabboni," Bdwy in "Pirates of Penzance" (1978),"Cats."

HANDLER, EVAN. Born Jan. 10, 1961 in NYC. Attended Juilliard. Debut 1979 OB in "Biography: A Game," followed by "Strider," "Final Orders," "Marathon 84," "Found a Peanut," "What's Wrong with This Picture?" "Bloodletters," "Young Playwrights Festival," Bdwy in "Solomon's Child" (1982), "Biloxi Blues," "Brighton Beach Memoirs," "Broadway Bound."

HANKET, ARTHUR. Born June 23, 1934 in Virginia. Graduate UVa., FlaStateU. Debut 1979 OB in "Cuchculain Cycle," followed by "The Boys Next Door," "In Perpetuity throughout the Universe."

HANLEY, ELLEN. Born May 15, 1926 in Lorain, OH. Attended Juilliard. Bdwy debut 1946 in "Annie Get Your Gun," followed by "Barefoot Boy with Cheek" for which she received a Theatre World Award, "High Button Shoes," "Lend an Ear," "Two's Company," "First Impressions," "Fiorello!," "The Boys from Syracuse" (OB), "The Rose Tattoo," "1776," "Anything Goes."

HANSEN, PEDER. Born Sept. 23, 1947 in NYC. Graduate SUNY/Cortland, Geo.Wash.U., Catholic U. Debut 1986 OB in "Girl Crazy," followed by "Give My Regards to Broadway."

HARDING, JAN LESLIE. Born in 1956 in Cambridge, MA. Graduate Boston U. Debut 1980 OB in "Album," followed by "Sunday Picnic," "Buddies," "The Lunch Girls," "Marathon '86," "Traps."

HARDWICK, MARK. Born Apr. 18, 1954 in Carthage, TX. Graduate SMU. Bdwy debut 1982 in "Pump Boys and Dinettes," followed by OB's "Oil City Symphony."

HARDY, STEPHANI. Born June 13, 1957 in Dallas, TX. Graduate Baylor U. Debut 1986 OB in "What's a Nice Country like You Doing in a State like This?," followed by "The No Frills Revue."

HARE, WILL. Born Mar. 30, 1919 in Elkins, WVa. Attended AmActorsTh. Bdwy credits include "The Eternal Road," "The Moon Is Down," "Suds in Your Eye," "Only the Heart," "The Visitor," "The Trip to Bountiful," "Witness for the Prosecution," "Marathon '33," OB in "The Viewing," "Winter Journey," "Dylan," "Older People," "Crystal and Fox," "Long Day's Journey into Night," "Boom Boom Room," "Old Times," "Dream of a Blacklisted Actor," "Philistines."

HARGROVE, BRIAN. Born Apr. 2, 1956 in Edgecombe County, NC. Graduate UNC, Juilliard. Debut 1981 OB in "How It All Began," followed by "Henry IV Part I," "Boiling Point," "Never Say Die," "The Three Sisters," "Vieux Carre," "About Face."

HARMAN, PAUL. Born July 29, 1952 in Mineola, NY. Graduate Tufts U. Bdwy debut 1980 in "It's So Nice to Be Civilized," followed by "Les Miserables," "Chess," OB in "City Suite."

HARMON, JENNIFER. Born Dec. 3, 1943 in Pasadena, CA. Attended UMs. With APA in "Right You Are," "You Can't Take It with You," "War and Peace," "Wild Duck," "School for Scandal, OB in "The Effect of Gamma Rays on Man-in-the-Moon Marigolds," "The Hot l Baltimore," "Learned Ladies," "The Holly and the Ivy," "In Perpetuity throughout the Universe."

HARPER, JAMES. Born Oct. 8, 1948 in Bell, Ca. Attended Marin Col., Juilliard. Bdwy debut 1973 in "King Lear," followed by "The Robber Bridegroom," "The Time of Your Life," "Mother Courage," "Edward II," OB in "A Midsummer Night's Dream," "Recruiting Officer," "The Wild Duck," "The Jungle of Cities," "The Cradle Will Rock," "All the Nice People," "Cruelties of Mrs. Schnayd," "Territorial Rites," "Johnstown Vindicator," "Guadeloupe."

HARRAN, JACOB. Born July 23, 1955 in NYC. Graduate Hofstra U. Debut 1984 OB in "Balm in Gilead," followed by "Awake and Sing," "Crossing Delancey," "Romeo and Juliet," "Cabbagehead," "Oklahoma Samovar."

HART, LINDA. Born Aug. 1, 1950 in Dallas, TX. Attended LACC. Debut 1982 OB in "Livin' Dolls," followed by "Sunday Serenade," "Gospel Rocks the Ballroom," Bdwy in "Bette Midler's Divine Madness" (1979), "Anything Goes" (1987) for which she received a Theatre World Award.

HART, PAUL E. Born July 20, 1939 in Lawrence, Ma. Graduate Merrimack Col. Debut 1977 OB in "Turandot," followed by "Darkness at Noon," "Light Shines in the Darkness," "Pictures at an Exhibition," "Blessed Event," "Cork," "Sail Away," Bdwy in "Fiddler on the Roof" (1981).

HARUM, EIVIND. Born May 24, 1944 in Stavanger, Norway. Attended Utah State U. Credits include "Sophie," "Foxy," "Baker Street," "West Side Story" ('68),"A Chorus Line," "Woman of the Year."

HARVEY, JOAN. Born Mar. 26, 1935 in NYC. Attended UCLA, Neighborhood Playhouse. Bdwy credits include "Middle of the Night," "Make a Million," OB in "Tevya's Daughters," "All the King's Men," "Courtyard," "Cry of the Raindrop," "Agent Zero Zero."

HATCHER, ROBYN. Born Sept. 8, 1956 in Philadelphia, Pa. Graduate Adelphi U. Debut 1983 OB in "Macbeth," followed by "Edward II," "Deep Sleep," "Flatbush Faithful," "Pardon/Permission."

HATELEY, LINZI. Born Oct. 23, 1970 in Birmingham, Eng. Attended Italia Conti Acad. of Theatre. Bdwy debut 1988 in "Carrie" for which she received a Theatre World Award.

HAWKES, TERRI. Born Dec. 26 in Montreal, Can. Graduate UCalgary. Debut 1986 OB in "Sorrows and Sons," followed by "The Taming of the Shrew," "The Greenhouse Keeper Died," "Tamara."

HAWTHORNE, MAGGIE. Born Nov. 11 in Waco, TX. Graduate Baylor U. Debut 1978 OB in "The Passion of Dracula," followed by "The Misanthrope," "Playboy of the Western World," "The Winter's Tale."

HAYDEN, SOPHIE. Born Feb. 23 in Miami, FL. Graduate Northwestern U. Bdwy debut 1979 in "Whoopee!," followed by "Barnum," "Comedy of Errors," OB in "She Loves Me," "Jessie's Land," "Passover," "Lies My Father Told Me," "Torpedo Bra," "Fun."

HAYES, LOREY. Born Oct. 12, 1956 in Wallace, NC. Graduate UNC Arts, UWisc. Debut 1975 OB in "For Colored Girls," followed by "The Michigan," "Forty-Deuce," "Like Them That Dream," Bdwy in "Home" (1980), "Inacent Black."

HEALD, ANTHONY. Born Aug. 25, 1944 in New Rochelle, NY. Graduate MiStateU. Debut 1980 OB in "The Glass Menagerie," followed by "Misalliance" for which he received a Theatre World Award, "The Caretaker," "The Fox," "Quartermaine's Terms," "The Philanthropist," "Henry V," "Digby," "Principia Scriptoriae," Bdwy in "The Wake of Jamey Foster" (1982), "Marriage of Figaro," "Anything Goes."

HEARD, CORDIS. Born July 27, 1944 in Washington, DC. Graduate Chatham Col. Bdwy debut 1973 in "Warp," followed by "The Elephant Man," "Macbeth," OB in "Vanities," "City Junket," "Details without a Map," "Inside Out."

HEATH, D. MICHAEL. Born Sept. 22, 1953 in Cincinnati, Oh. Graduate UCin. Bdwy debut 1979 in "The Most Happy Fella," followed by "Starlight Express," OB in "Chanticler," "Street Scene."

HECHT, PAUL. Born Aug. 16, 1941 in London, Eng. Attended McGill U. OB in "Sjt. Musgrave's Dance," "MacBird," "Phaedra," Bdwy in "Rosencrantz and Guildenstern Are Dead," "1776," "The Rothschilds," "The Ride across Lake Constance," "The Great God Brown," "Don Juan," "Emperor Henry IV," "Herzl," "Caesar and Cleopatra," "Night and Day," "Noises Off."

HEINS, BARRY. (aka Barrett) Born Dec. 5, 1956 in El Paso, TX. Graduate UTx/Austin, Juilliard. Bdwy debut 1982 in "Good," followed by "Les Liaisons Dangereuses," OB in "Spring Awakening" (1978), "Twelfth Night," "The Country Wife," "An Enemy of the People," "Ten by Tennessee," "On the Verge."

HEINSOHN, ELISA. Born Oct. 11, 1962 in Butler, PA. Debut 1984 OB in "Oy, Mama, Am I in Love," followed by "Scandal," Bdwy in "42nd Street" (1985), "Smile," "Phantom of the Opera."

HEMPLEMAN, TERRY. Born Dec. 6, 1960 in Asheville, NC. Graduate UNC. Debut 1986 OB in "Out!" followed by "After Sarah," "Odd Jobbers."

HENDERSON, JO. Born in Buffalo, NY. Attended WMiU. OB in "Camille," "Little Foxes," "An Evening with Merlin Finch," "20th Century Tar," "A Scent of Flowers," "Revival," "Dandelion Wine," "My Life," "Ladyhouse Blues," "Fallen Angels," "Waiting for the Parade," "Threads," "Bella Figura," "Details without a Map," "The Middle Ages," "Time Framed," "Isn't It Romantic," "Little Footsteps," "Cave Life," Bdwy in "Rose" (1981), "84 Charing Cross Road," "Play Memory."

HENSLEY, DALE. Born Apr. 9, 1954 in Nevada, MO. Graduate SouthwestMoStateU. Debut 1980 OB in "Annie Get Your Gun," Bdwy in "Anything Goes" (1987).

HERRMANN, EDWARD. Born July 21, 1943 in Washington, DC. Graduate BucknellU, LAMDA. Debut 1970 OB in "The Basic Training of Pavlo Hummel," followed by "A Midsummer Night's Dream," "Tom and Viv," "Not about Heroes," "Julius Caesar," Bdwy in "Moonchildren" (1971), "Mrs. Warren's Profession," "The Philadelphia Story."

HESS, ELIZABETH. Born July 17, 1953 in Ontario, Can. Graduate York U. Debut 1982 OB in "The Frances Farmer Story," followed by "Nothing But Bukowski."

HIBBERT, EDWARD. Born Sept. 9, 1955 in NYC. Attended Hurstpierpont Col., RADA. Bdwy debut 1982 in "Alice in Wonderland," followed by "Me and My Girl," OB in "Candida in Concert," "Dandy Dick."

HIKEN, GERALD. Born May 23, 1927 in Milwaukee, WI. Attended UWisc. Bdwy in "Lovers" (1968), followed by "Cave Dwellers," "Nervous Set," "Fighting Cock," "49th Cousin," "Gideon," "Foxy," "Three Sisters," "Golda," "Strider," "Fools," OB in "The Cherry Orchard," "The Seagull," "Good Woman of Setzuan," "The Misanthrope," "The Iceman Cometh," "The New Theatre," "Strider," "The Chosen."

HILER, KATHERINE. Born June 24, 1961 in Carson City, NV. Graduate Mt. Holyoke Col. Bdwy debut 1985 in "Hurlyburly," followed by OB's "Liebelei" (1987), "The Year of the Duck," "A Shayna Maidel."

HILLIARD, KEN. Born June 9, 1946 in Pittsburgh, PA. Graduate IndU. Bdwy debut 1978 in "On the 20th Century," followed by "Evita," "Zorba," "Into the Light," "Teddy and Alice," OB in "Passionate Extremes."

HILLNER, NANCY. Born June 7, 1949 in Wakefield, RI. Graduate ULowell. Bdwy debut 1975 in "Dance with Me," followed by OB in "Nite Club Confidential," "Trading Places," "Nunsense."

HIPKINS, BILLY. Born May 18, 1961 in Verona, NJ. Attended AADA. Debut 1988 OB in "Alias Jimmy Valentine."

HIRSCH, JUDD. Born Mar. 15, 1935 in NYC. Attended AADA. Bdwy debut 1966 in "Barefoot in the Park," followed by "Chapter Two," "Talley's Folly," OB in "On the Necessity of Being Polygamous," "Scuba Duba," "Mystery Play," "Hot l Baltimore," "Prodigal," "Knock Knock," "Life and/or Death," "Talley's Folly," "The Sea Gull," "I'm Not Rappaport."

HIRSCH, VICKI. Born Feb. 22, 1951 in Wilmington, DE. Graduate UDel, VillanovaU. Debut 1985 OB in "Back County Crimes," followed by "Casualties," "Mr. Universe."

HIRSCHFIELD, MARK. Born Mar. 8, 1956 in Los Angeles, CA. Graduate UCLA, FlaState/AsoloConsv. Debut 1988 OB in "Much Ado about Nothing."

HITT, ROBERT. Born Sept. 11, 1942 in Washington, DC. Graduate ULouisville, Yale. Debut 1975 OB in "The Zykovs," followed by "Washington Heights."

HOCHSCHILD, ROSEMARY. Born Oct. 7, 1953 in Cape Town, SAfr. Graduate Cape Town Col. Debut 1987 OB in "Isle of Swans."

HODES, GLORIA. Born Aug. 20 in Norwich, Ct. Bdwy debut in "Gantry" (1969), followed by "Me and My Girl," OB in "The Club" for which she received a Theatre World Award, "Cycles of Fancy," "The Heroine," "Pearls," "Songs of Pyre."

HODGES, PATRICIA. Born in Puyallup, Wa. Graduate UWa. Debut 1985 OB in "The Normal Heart," followed by "On the Verge," "Hard Times."

HOFFMAN, JANE. Born July 24 in Seattle, Wa. Graduate UCal. Bdwy debut 1940 in "Tis of Thee," followed by "Crazy with the Heat," "Something for the Boys," "One Touch of Venus," "Calico Wedding," "Mermaids Singing," "Temporary Island," "Story for Strangers," "Two Blind Mice," "The Rose Tattoo," "The Crucible," "Witness for the Prosecution," "Third Best Sport," "Rhinoceros," "Mother Courage and Her Children," Fair Game for Lovers," "A Murderer among Us," "Murder among Friends," OB in "American Dream," "Sandbox," "Picnic on the Battlefield," "Theatre of the Absurd," "Child Buyer," "A Corner of the Bed," "Slow Memories," "Last Analysis," "Dear Oscar," "Hocus Pocus," "Lessons," "The Art of Dining," "Second Avenue Rag," "One Tiger to a Hill," "Isn't It Romantic?," "Alto Part," "Marathon 84," "The Frog Prince," "Alterations," "The Grandama Plays."

HOFFMAN, PHILIP. Born May 12, 1954 in Chicago, IL. Graduate UIll. Bdwy debut 1981 in "The Moony Shapiro Songbook," followed by "Is There Life after High School?," "Baby," "Into the Woods," OB in "The Fabulous '50's," "Isn't It Romantic."

HOFMAIER, MARK. Born July 4, 1950 in Philadelphia, Pa. Graduate UAz. Debut 1978 OB in "A Midsummer Night's Dream," followed by "Marvelous Gray," "Modern Romance," "Relative Values," "The Racket."

HOFVENDAHL, STEVE. Born Sept. 1, 1956 in San Jose, Ca. Graduate USantaClara, Brandeis U. Debut 1986 OB in "A Lie of the Mind," followed by "Ragged Trousered Philanthropists," "The Miser," "A Midsummer Night's Dream."

HOGAN, JONATHAN. Born June 13, 1951 in Chicago, Il. Graduate Goodman Theatre. Debut 1972 OB in "The Hot l Baltimore," followed by "The Mound Builders," "Harry Outside," "Cabin 12," "5th of July," "Glorious Morning," "Innocent Thoughts, Harmless Intentions," "Sunday Runners," "Threads," "Time Framed," "Balm in Gilead," "Burn This!," Bdwy in "Comedians" (1976), "Otherwise Engaged," "5th of July," "The Caine Mutiny Court-Martial," "As Is," "Burn This."

HOGAN, TESSIE. Born Aug. 23, 1957 in Chicago, Ill. Graduate UIll, Yale. Debut 1985 OB in "Faulkner's Bicycle," followed by "Terry by Terry."

HOLBROOK, ANNA. Born April 18 in Fairbanks, AL. Attended TrinityU, UAz. Debut 1988 OB in "St. Hugo of Central Park," followed by "The Great Nebula in Orion."

HOLBROOK, RUBY. Born Aug. 28, 1930 in St. John's, Nfd. Attended Denison U. Debut 1963 OB in "Abe Lincoln in Illinois," followed by "Hamlet," "James Joyce's Dubliners," "Measure for Measure," "The Farm," "Do You Still Believe the Rumor?," "The Killing of Sister George," "An Enemy of the People," Bdwy in "Da" (1979), "5th of July," "Musical Comedy Murders of 1940."

HOLGATE, RONALD. Born May 26, 1937 in Aberdeen, SD. Attended Northwestern U., NewEngConserv. Debut 1961 OB in "Hobo," followed by "Hooray, It's a Glorious Day," "Blue Plate Special," Bdwy in "A Funny Thing Happened on the Way. . .," "Milk and Honey," "1776," "Saturday Sunday Monday," "The Grand Tour," "Musical Chairs," "42nd Street."

HOMBERG, TERRI. Born Jan. 5, 1959 in Jacksonville, Fl. Attended SanJoseStateU, Neighborhood Playhouse. Bdwy debut 1982 in "Joseph and the Amazing Technicolor Dreamcoat," followed by "Jerry's Girls," "Into the Light," "Starlight Express."

HONDA, CAROL A. Born Nov. 20 in Kealakekua, HI. Graduate UHi. Debut 1983 OB in "Yellow Fever," followed by "Empress of China," "Manoa Valley," "Once Is Never Enough," "Life of the Land," "Rosie's Cafe."

HORAN, BONNIE. Born Aug. 20, 1928 in Dayton, TX. Graduate UHouston, UParis, Geo.Wash.U. Debut 1980 OB in "The Devil's Disciple," followed by "The Meehans," "Arms and the Man," "Her Great Match," "Uncle Vanya."

HORGAN, PATRICK. Born May 26, 1929 in Nottingham, Eng. Attended Stoneyhurst Col. Bdwy debut 1958 in "Redhead," followed by "Heartbreak House," "The Devil's Advocate," "Beyond the Fringe," "Baker Street," "Crown Matrimonial," "Sherlock Holmes," "My Fair Lady," "Deathtrap," "Noises Off," OB in "The Importance of Being Earnest," "Tamara."

HORVATH, JAN. Born Jan. 31, 1958 in Lake Forrest, IL. Graduate CinConsv. Bdwy debut 1983 in "Oliver!," followed by "Sweet Charity," "Phantom of the Opera," OB in "Sing Me Sunshine," "Jacques Brel Is Alive and Well."

HOUGHTON, KATHARINE. Born Mar 10, 1945 in Hartford, CT. Graduate Sarah Lawrence Col. Bdwy debut 1965 in "A Very Rich Woman," followed by "The Front Page" (1969), OB in "A Scent of Flowers" for which she received a Theatre World Award, "To Heaven in a Swing," "Madwoman of Chaillot," "Vivat! Vivat Regina!" "The Time of Your Life," "Children of the Sun," "Buddha," "On the Shady Side," "The Right Number," "The Hooded Eye."

HOXIE, RICHMOND. Born July 21, 1946 in NYC. Graduate Dartmouth Col., LAMDA. Debut 1975 OB in "Shaw for an Evening," followed by "The Family," "Justice," "Landscape with Waitress," "3 from the Marathon," "The Slab Boys," "Vivien," "Operation Midnight Climax," "The Dining Room," "Daddies," "To Gillian on Her 37th Birthday," "Dennis," "Traps."

HOYT, LON. Born Apr. 6, 1958 in Roslyn, NY. Graduate Cornell U. Bdwy debut 1982 in "Rock 'n' Roll," followed by "Baby," "Leader of the Pack," "Starlight Express."

HUBER, KATHLEEN. Born Mar. 3, 1947 in NYC. Graduate UCal. Debut 1969 OB in "A Scent of Flowers," followed by "The Virgin and the Unicorn," "The Constant Wife," "Milestones," "Tamara."

HUDSON, RODNEY. Born Oct. 14, 1948 in St. Louis, MO. Graduate USEMo, USDak, UMich. Debut 1977 OB in "Agamemnon," followed by "Indulgencies," "Runaways," "Dispatches," "Alice in Concert," "American Notes."

HUDSON, TRAVIS. Born Feb. 2 in Amarillo, Tx. UTx graduate. Bdwy debut in "New Faces of 1962," followed by "Pousse Cafe," "Very Good Eddie," "The Grand Tour," OB in "Triad," "Tattooed Countess," "Young Abe Lincoln," "Get Thee to Canterbury," "The Golden Apple," "Annie Get Your Gun," "Nunsense."

HUFFMAN, FELICITY: Born Dec. 9, 1962 in Westchester, NY. Graduate NYU, AADA, RADA. Debut 1988 OB in "Boys' Life," followed by "Been Taken," Bdwy in "Spped-the-Plow" (1988).

HUGHES, NANCY. Born Apr. 15, 1959 in Clarksville, IN. Graduate Butler U., AMDA. Debut 1987 OB in "Kismet."

HUGHES, TRESA. Born Sept. 17, 1929 in Washington, DC. Attended Wayne U. OB in "Electra," "The Crucible," "Hogan's Goat," "Party on Greenwich Avenue," "Fragments," "Passing Through from Exotic Places," "Beggar on Horseback," "Early Morning," "The Old Ones," "Holy Places," "Awake and Sing," "Standing on My Knees," "Modern Ladies of Guanabacoa," "After the Fall," "Claptrap," Bdwy in "The Miracle Worker," "The Devil's Advocate," "Dear Me, the Sky Is Falling," "The Last Analysis," "Spofford," "Man in the Glass Booth," "Prisoner of Second Avenue," "Tribute," "A View from the Bridge," "V & V Only."

HULCE, THOMAS. Born Dec. 6, 1953 in Plymouth, MI. Graduate NCSchArts. Bdwy debut 1975 in "Equus," followed by OB's "A Memory of Two Mondays," "Julius Caesar," "Twelve Dreams," "The Rise and Rise of Daniel Rocket," "Haddock's Eyes."

HULL, BRYAN. Born Sept. 12, 1937 in Amarillo, TX. Attended UNMx, Wayne State U. Bdwy debut 1976 in "Somethin's Afoot," followed by "War and Peace," OB in "The Fantasticks," "Two Gentlemen of Verona,""Here Be Dragons."

HUNT, ANNETTE. Born Jan. 31, 1938 in Hampton, VA. Graduate VaIntermontCol. Debut 1957 OB in "Nine by Six," followed by "The Taming of the Shrew," "Medea," "Anatomist," "The Misanthrope," "The Cherry Orchard," "Electra," "Last Resort," "The Seducers," "A Sound of Silence," "Charades," "Dona Rosita," "Rhinestones," "Where's Charley?," "The White Rose of Memphis," "M. Amilcar," "The Seagull," Bdwy in "All the Girls Came Out to Play" (1972).

HUNT, LINDA. Born Apr. 2, 1945 in Morristown, NJ. Attended Goodman Sch. Debut 1975 OB in "Down by the River," followed by "The Tennis Game," "Metamorphosis in Miniature," "Little Victories," "Top Girls," "Aunt Dan and Lemon," "The Cherry Orchard," Bdwy in "Ah, Wilderness" (1975), "End of the World."

HUNT, W. DENNIS. Born Mar. 1, 1944 in Los Angeles, CA. Attended USCal. Debut 1971 OB in "James Joyce Memorial Liquid Theatre," followed by "Holy Ghosts."

HUNTER, KIM. Born Nov. 12, 1922 in Detroit, MI. Attended Actors Studio. Bdwy Debut 1947 in "A Streetcar Named Desire," followed by "Darkness at Noon," "The Chase," "The Children's Hour," "The Tender Trap," "Write Me a Murder," "Weekend," "Penny Wars," "The Women," "To Grandmother's House We Go," OB in "Come Slowly, Eden," "All Is Bright," "The Cherry Orchard," "When We Dead Awaken," "Territorial Rites," "Faulkner's Bicycle," "Man and Superman."

HUNTER, PATRICIA. Born Sept. 14, 1954 in Kileen, TX. Graduate PortlandStateU. OB credits: "Merry Wives of Windsor," "Victory Bonds," "Phaedra," "Red Peppers," "Asylum," "The Tavern."

HURLEY, JOHN PATRICK. Born May 7, 1949 in Salt Lake City, UT. Graduate UUtah. Debut 1982 OB in "Inserts," followed by "Sharing," "Why Hanna's Skirt Won't Stay Down," "Celebration Off River Street," "House Arrest," Bdwy in "Aren't We All?" (1985).

HURT, MARY BETH. Born Sept. 26, 1948 in Marshalltown, IA. Attended UIowa, NYU. Debut 1972 OB in "More Than You Deserve," followed by "As You Like It," "Trelawny of the Wells," "The Cherry Orchard," "Love for Love," "A Member of the Wedding," "Boy Meets Girl," "Secret Service," "Father's Day," "Nest of the Wood Grouse," "The Day Room," Bdwy in "Crimes of the Heart" (1981), "The Misanthrope," "Benefactors."

HYMAN, EARLE. Born Oct. 11, 1926 in Rocky Mount, NC. Attended New School, AmThWing. Bdwy debut 1943 in "Run Little Chillun," followed by "Anna Lucasta," "Climate of Eden," "Merchant of Venice," "Othello," "Julius Caesar," "The Tempest," "No Time for Sergeants," "Mr. Johnson" for which he received a Theatre World Award, "St. Joan," "Hamlet," "Waiting for Godot," "The Duchess of Malfi," "Les Blancs," "The Lady from Dubuque," "Execution of Justice," "Death of the King's Horseman," OB in "The White Rose and the Red," "Worlds of Shakespeare," "Jonah," "Life and Times of J. Walter Smintheus," "Orrin," "The Cherry Orchard," "House Party," "Carnival Dreams," "Agamemnon," "Othello," "Julius Caesar," "Coriolanus," "Remembrance," "Long Day's Journey into Night," "Sleep Beauty," "Driving Miss Daisy."

INGE, MATTHEW. Born May 29, 1950 in Fitchburg, MA. Attended Boston U., Harvard. Bdwy debut 1976 in "Fiddler on the Roof," followed by "A Chorus Line."

INNES, LAURA. Born Aug. 16, 1957 in Pontiac, MI. Graduate Northwestern U. Debut 1982 OB in "Edmond," followed by "My Uncle Sam," "Life Is a Dream," "Alice and Fred," "A Country Doctor," "Vienna Lusthaus," "Stella," "Prison-Made Tuxedos," "American Notes," "In Perpetuity throughout the Universe."

IRVING, AMY. Born Sept. 10, 1953 in Palo Alto, CA. Attended LAMDA. Debut 1970 OB in "And Chocolate on Her Chin," followed by "The Road to Mecca," Bdwy in "Amadeus" (1983), "Heartbreak House."

IRVING, GEORGE S. Born Nov. 1, 1922 in Springfield, Ma. Attended Leland Powers Sch. Bdwy debut 1943 in "Oklahoma!," followed by "Call Me Mister," "Along 5th Avenue," "Two's Company," "Me and Juliet," "Can-Can," "Shinbone Alley," "Bells Are Ringing," "The Good Soup," "Tovarich," "A Murderer Among Us," "Alfie," "Anya," "Galileo," "4 on a Garden," "An Evening with Richard Nixon . . .," "Irene," "Whos Who in Hell," "All Over Town," "So Long 174th Street," "Once in a Lifetime," "I Remember Mama," "Copperfield," "Pirates of Penzance," "On Your Toes," "Rosalie in Concert," "Pal Joey in Concert," "Me and My Girl."

IRWIN, BILL. Born Apr. 11, 1950 in California. Attended UCLA, Oberlin, Clown Col. Debut 1982 OB in "The Regard of Flight," followed by "The Courtroom," Bdwy in "5–6–7–8 Dance" (1983), "Accidental Death of an Anarchist," "The Regard of Flight" (LC), "Largely" New York."

ISHEE, SUZANNE. Born Oct. 15 in High Point, NC. Graduate UNC, Manhattan Sch. of Music. Bdwy debut 1983 in "Show Boat," followed by "Mame," "La Cage aux Folles."

IVANEK, ZELJKO. Born Aug. 15, 1957 in Lujubljana, Yugo. Graduate Yale, LAMDA. Bdwy debut 1981 in "The Survivor," followed by "Brighton Beach Memoirs," "Loot," OB in "Cloud 9," "A Map of the World," "The Cherry Orchard."

IVES, JANE. Born Nov. 6, 1949 in NYC. Attended ConnCol. Debut 1981 OB in "Murder in the Cathedral," followed by "Street Scene," "Night Games," "A Frog in His Throat."

IVEY, DANA. Born Aug. 12, in Atlanta, GA. Graduate Rollins Col. LAMDA. Bdwy debut 1981 in "Macbeth" (LC), followed by "Present Laughter," "Heartbreak House," "Sunday in the Park with George," "Pack of Lies," "Marriage of Figaro," OB in "A Call from the East," "Vivien," "Candida in Concert," "Major Barbara in Concert," "Quartermaine's Terms," "Baby with the Bathwater," "Driving Miss Daisy," "Wenceslas Square."

IVEY, JUDITH. Born Sept. 4, 1951 in El Paso, Tx. Bdwy debut 1979 in "Bedroom Farce," followed by "Steaming," "Hurlyburly," "Blithe Spirit," OB in "Dulsa, Fish, Stas and Vi," "Sunday Runners," "Second Lady," "Hurlyburly," "Mrs. Dally Has a Lover."

JABLONS, KAREN. Born July 19, 1951 in Trenton, NJ. Juilliard graduate. Debut 1969 OB in "The Student Prince," followed by "Sound of Music," "Funny Girl," "Boys from Syracuse," "Sterling Silver," "People in Show Business Make Long Goodbyes," "In Trousers," Bdwy in "Ari," "Two Gentlemen of Verona," "Lorelei," "Where's Charley?," "A Chorus Line."

JACKEL, PAUL. Born June 30, 1952 in Winchester, MA. Graduate Harvard U. Debut 1983 OB in "The Robber Bridegroom," followed by "Side by Side by Sondheim."

JACKS, SUSAN J. Born Nov. 5, 1953 in Brooklyn, NY. Graduate SUNY. Debut 1983 OB in "Forbidden Broadway," followed by "Stages."

JACKSON, DAVID. Born Dec. 4, 1948 in Philadelphia, Pa. Bdwy debut 1980 in "Eubie!," followed by "My One and Only," "La Cage aux Folles."

JACKSON, ERNESTINE. Born Sept. 18 in Corpus Christi, TX. Graduate Del Mar Col., Juilliard. Debut 1966 in "Show Boat" (LC), followed by "Finian's Rainbow," "Hello Dolly!," "Applause," "Jesus Christ Superstar," "Tricks," "Raisin" for which she received a Theatre World Award, "Guys and Dolls," "Bacchae," OB in "Louis," "Some Enchanted Evening," "Money Notes," "Jack and Jill," "Black Girl," "Brownstone," "Sophie."

JACKSON, GLENDA. Born May 9, 1936 in Hoylake, Cheshire, Eng. Attended RADA. Bdwy debut 1965 in "Marat/Sade," followed by "Rose" (1981), "Strange Interlude" (1985), "Macbeth" (1988)."

JACOBI, DEREK. Born Oct. 22, 1938 in Leytonstone, Eng. Graduate St. John's Col., Cambridge U. Bdwy debut 1980 in "The Suicide," followed by "Cyrano de Bergerac," "Much Ado about Nothing," "Breaking the Code."

JAMES, ELMORE. Born May 3, 1954 in NYC. Graduate SUNY/Purchase. Debut 1970 OB in "Moon on a Rainbow Shawl," followed by "The Ups and Downs of Theopholus Maitland," "Carnival," "Until the Real Thing Comes Along," "A Midsummer Night's Dream," "The Tempest," "Jacques Brel Is Alive and Well . . ." Bdwy in "But Never Jam Today" (1979), "Your Arms Too Short to Box with God," "Big River."

JAMES, KELLI. Born Mar. 18, 1959 in Council Bluffs, Iowa. Bdwy debut 1987 in "Les Miserables."

JAMROG, JOSEPH. Born Dec. 21, 1932 in Flushing, NY. Graduate CCNY. Debut 1970 OB in "Nobody Hears a Broken Drum," followed by "Tango," "And Whose Little Boy Are You?," "When You Comin' Back, Red Ryder?," "Drums at Yale," "The Boy Friend," "Love, Death Plays," "Too Much Johnson," "A Stitch in Time," "Pantagleize," "Final Hours," "Returnings," "Brass Birds Don't Sing," "And Things That Go Bump in the Night," "Fun."

JAY, MARY. Born Dec. 23, 1939 in Brooklyn, NY Graduate UMe, AmThWing. Debut 1962 OB in "Little Mary Sunshine," followed by "Toys in the Attic," "Telecast," "Sananda Sez," "Soul of the White Ant," "The Quilling of Prue," "Summit Conference," Bdwy in "The Student Gypsy," "Candida" (1981), "Beethoven's Tenth," "Teddy and Alice."

JAY, WILLIAM. Born May 15, 1935 in Baxter Springs, KS. Attended OmahaU. Debut 1963 OB in "Utopia," followed by "The Blacks," "Loop the Loop," "Happy Ending," "Day of Absence," "Hamlet," "Othello," "Song of the Lusitanian Bogey," "Ceremonies in Dark Old Men," "Man Better Man," "The Harangues," "Brotherhood," "Perry's Mission," "Rosalee Pritchett," "Sister Sadie," "Coriolanus," "Getting Out," "Henrietta," "The Boys Next Door."

JBARA, GREGORY. Born Sept. 28, 1961 in Wayne, Mi. Graduate UMi, Juilliard. Debut 1986 OB in "Have I Got a Girl for You!", "Serious Money."

JEROME, TIMOTHY. Born Dec. 29, 1943 in Los Angeles, CA. Graduate Ithaca Col. Bdwy debut 1969 in "Man of La Mancha," followed by "The Rothschilds," "Creation of the World . . . ," "Moony Shapiro Songbook," "Cats," "Me and My Girl," OB in "Beggar's Opera," "Pretzels," "Civilization and Its Discontents," "The Little Prince," "Colette Collage," "Room Service."

JETER, MICHAEL. Born Aug. 26, 1952 in Lawrenceburg, TN. Graduate Memphis State U. Bdwy debut 1978 in "Once in a Lifetime," OB in "The Master and Margarita," "G. R. Point" for which he received a Theatre World Award, "Alice in Concert," "El Bravo," "Cloud 9," "Greater Tuna," "The Boys Next Door."

JILER, JOHN. Born Apr. 4, 1946 in NYC. Graduate UHartford. Debut 1982 OB in "The Frances Farmer Story," followed by "Trouble/Idle Hands," "One Room with Bath," "Emerald City," "Beverly's Yard Sale."

JOHANSON, DON. Born Oct. 19, 1952 in Rock Hill, SC. Graduate USC. Bdwy debut 1976 in "Rex," followed by "Cats," OB in "The American Dance Machine."

JOHNS, KURT T. Born Feb. 28, 1954 in Cincinnati, OH. Graduate Cincinnati ColConsv. Bdwy debut 1988 in "Chase."

JOHNSON, DANIEL TIMOTHY. Born Aug. 13, 1947 in Cass County, MI. Graduate WMiU, UOre. Debut 1980 OB in "Romeo and Juliet," followed by "The Scarecrow," "Meetings with Ben Franklin," "Edward II," "Two Wills," "Julius Caesar," "Porter's Brandy," "Leave It to Me."

JOHNSON, ONNI. Born Mar. 16, 1949 in NYC. Graduate Brandeis U. Debut 1964 in "Unfinished Business," followed by "She Stoops to Conquer," "22 Years," "The Master and Margarita," "Haggedah," "Fragments of a Greek Trilogy," Bdwy in "Oh, Calcutta!"

JOHNSON, PAGE. Born Aug. 25, 1930 in Welch, WV. Graduate Ithaca Col. Bdwy bow 1951 in "Romeo and Juliet," followed by "Electra," "Oedipus," "Camino Real," "In April Once," for which he received a Theatre World Award, "Red Roses for Me," "The Lovers," "Equus," "You Can't Take It With You," OB in "The Enchanted," "Guitar," "4 in 1," "Journey of the Fifth Horse," APA's "School for Scandal," "The Tavern," and "The Seagull," "Odd Couple," "Boys In The Band," "Medea," "Deathtrap," "Best Little Whorehouse in Texas," "Fool for Love."

JOHNSON, TIM. Born Apr. 6, 1956 in Cleveland, OH. Graduate Baldwin-Wallace Col. Debut 1987 OB in "The Death of Bessie Smith," followed by "Porgy and Bess," "Lost in the Stars."

JOHNSTON, J. J. Born Oct. 24, 1933 in Chicago, IL. Debut 1981 OB in "American Buffalo," and Bdwy 1983 in "American Buffalo" for which he received a Theatre World Award, followed by "Glengarry Glen Ross," "Arsenic and Old Lace."

JOHNSTON, JUSTINE. Born June 13 in Evanston, Il. Debut 1959 OB in "Little Mary Sunshine," followed by "The Time of Your Life" (CC), "The Dubliners," "The New York Idea," Bdwy in "Pajama Game," "Milk and Honey," "Follies," "Irene," "Molly," "Angel," "Me and My Girl."

JONES, CHERRY. Born Nov. 21, 1956 in Paris, Tn. Graduate Carnegie-Mellon U. Debut 1983 OB in "The Philanthropist," followed by "He and She," "The Ballad of Soapy Smith," "The Importance of Being Earnest," "I Am a Camera," "Claptrap," Bdwy in "Stepping Out" (1987), "Macbeth (1988).

JONES, EDDIE. Born in Washington, PA. Debut 1960 OB in "Dead End," followed by "Curse of the Starving Class," "The Ruffian on the Stairs," "An Act of Kindness," "Big Apple Messenger," "The Skirmishers," "Maiden Stakes," "The Freak," "Knights Errant," "Slacks and Tops," "Burkie," "Curse of the Starving Class" (1985), "Sorrows and Sons," "Bigfoot Stole My Wife," "April Snow," Bdwy in "That Championship Season" (1974), "Devour the Snow."

JONES, FRANZ. Born Nov. 11, 1951 in Washington, DC. Graduate TxChristianU. Debut 1974 OB in "Holocaust," followed by "Trade-Offs," "Brainwashed," "Pepperwine," "Things of the Heart," "Yevi/The Singing Tortoise," Bdwy in "Big River" (1985).

JONES, JAMES EARL. Born Jan. 17, 1931 in Arktabula, Ms. Graduate UMi. OB debut 1957 in "Wedding in Japan," followed by "The Pretender," "The Blacks," "Clandestine on the Morning Line," "The Apple," "A Midsummer Night's Dream," "Moon on a Rainbow Shawl" for which he received a Theatre World Award, "Henry V," "Measure for Measure," "Richard II," "The Tempest," "Merchant of Venice," "Macbeth," "P.S. 193," "The Last Minstrel," "Love Nest," "Bloodknot," "Othello," "Baal," "Danton's Death," "Boesman and Lena," "Hamlet," "The Cherry Orchard," Bdwy in "The Egghead" (1957), "Sunrise at Campobello," "The Cool World," "Infidel Caesar," "Next Time I'll Sing to You," "Coriolanus," "Troilus and Cressida," "A Hand Is on the Gate," "The Great White Hope," "Les Blancs," "King Lear," "The Iceman Cometh," "Of Mice and Men," "Paul Robeson," "A Lesson from Aloes," "Othello," "Master Harold..and the boys," "Fences."

JONES, JAY AUBREY. Born Mar. 30, 1954 in Atlantic City, NJ. Graduate Syracuse U. Debut 1981 OB in "Sea Dream," followed by "Divine Hysteria," "Inacent Black and the Brothers," "La Belle Helene," Bdwy in "Cats" (1986).

JONES, JEN. Born Mar. 23, 1927 in Salt Lake City, Ut. Attended UUt. Debut 1960 OB in "Drums under the Window," followed by "The Long Voyage Home," "Diff'rent," "Creditors," "Look at Any Man," "I Knock at the Door," "Pictures in the Hallway," "Grab Bag," "Bo Bo," "Oh, Dad, Poor Dad..," "Henhouse," "Uncle Vanya," Bdwy in "Dr. Cook's Garden," "But Seriously," "Ecentricities of a Nightingale," "The Music Man" (1980), "The Octette Bridge Club."

JONES, REED. Born June 30, 1953 in Portland, OR. Graduate USIU. Bdwy debut 1979 in "Peter Pan," followed by "West Side Story," "America," "Play Me a Country Song," "Cats," "Loves of Anatole," OB in "Music Moves Me," "Jubilee in Concert."

JONES, SHANNON LEE. Born Dec. 9, 1960 in Louisville, Ky. Attended Kennasaw Col. Debut 1983 OB in "Skyline," Bdwy in "La Cage aux Folles" (1986).

JONES, SIMON. Born July 27, 1950 in Wiltshire, Eng. Attended Trinity Hall. Debut 1984 OB in "Terra Nova," followed by "Magdalena in Concert," "Woman in Mind," Bdwy in "The Real Thing" (1984), "Benefactors."

JORDAN, BOB. Born May 2, 1926 in Boston, MA. Graduate MoU, NorthwesternU. OB in "The American Cantata," "Lippe," "The Warm Heart," "Murder among Friends," "Changing Roles," "To Feed Their Hopes," "A Delicate Heart."

JOY, ROBERT. Born Aug. 17, 1951 in Montreal, Can. Graduate Nfd. Memorial U. Oxford U. Debut 1978 OB in "The Diary of Anne Frank," followed by "Fables for Friends," "Lydie Breeze," "Sister Mary Ignatius Explains It All," "Actor's Nightmare," "What I Did Last Summer," "The Death of Von Richthofen," "Lenny and the Heartbreakers," "Found a Peanut," "Field Day," "Life and Limb," Bdwy in "Hay Fever" (1985), "The Nerd."

JUDD, REBECCA. Born in Fresno, CA. Graduate UNev. Debut 1988 OB in "Dutchman" followed by "Lost in the Stars."

KALEMBER, PATRICIA. Born Dec. 30, 1956 in Schenectady, NY. Graduate IndU. Debut 1981 OB in "The Butler Did It," followed by "Sheepskin," "Playboy of the Western World," "Poets' Corner," Bdwy in "The Nerd" (1987).

KAMMER, NANCY-ELIZABETH. Born Mar. 27, 1953 in Valdosta, GA. Attended NYU. Debut 1977 OB in "Carnival," followed by "Turnbuckle," "My Own Stranger," "The Taming of the Shrew."

KANDEL, PAUL. Born Feb. 15, 1951 in Queens, NYC. Graduate Harpur Col. Debut 1977 OB in "Nightclub Cantata," followed by "Two Grown Men," "Scrambled Feet," "The Taming of the Shrew," "Lucky Stiff."

KANE, CAROL. Born June 18, 1952 in Cleveland, OH. Bdwy credits include "The Prime of Miss Jean Brodie," "The Tempest" and "Macbeth" (LC), "The Effect of Gamma Rays on Man-in-the-Moon Marigolds" (1978), OB in "The Lucky Spot," "The Debutante Ball."

KANE, DONNA. Born Aug. 12, 1962 in Beacon, NY. Graduate Mt. Holyoke Col. Debut 1985 OB in "Dames at Sea" for which she received a Theatre World Award, followed by "The Vinegar Tree," "Johnny Pye and the Foolkiller."

KANSAS, JERI. Born Mar. 10, 1955 in Jersey City, NJ. Debut 1978 OB in "Gay Divorce," Bdwy 1979 in "Sugar Babies," followed by "42nd Street."

KANTOR, KENNETH. Born Apr. 6, 1949 in The Bronx, NY. Graduate SUNY, Boston U. Debut 1974 OB in "Zorba," followed by "Kiss Me, Kate," "A Little Night Music," "Buried Treasure," "Sounds of Rodgers and Hammerstein," "Shop on Main Street," "Kismet," Bdwy in "The Grand Tour" (1979), "Brigadoon" (1980), "Mame" (1983).

KARIBALIS, CURT. Born Feb. 24, 1947 in Superior, WI. Graduate UWis. Debut 1971 OB in "Woyzeck," followed by "The Taming of the Shrew," Bdwy in "The Great God Brown" (1972), "Don Juan," "The Visit," "Chemin de Fer," "Holiday," "Goodbye Fidel."

KATARINA, ANNA. Born Feb. 25, 1956 in Bern, Switz. Attended Bern Consv. Debut 1987 OB in "Tamara."

KAYE, JUDY. Born Oct. 11, 1948 in Phoenix, AZ. Attended UCLA, Ariz. State U. Bdwy debut 1977 in "Grease," followed by "On the 20th Century" for which she received a Theatre World Award, "Moony Shapiro Songbook," "Oh, Brother!," "Phantom of the Opera," OB in "Eileen in Concert," "Can't Help Singing," "Four to Make Two," "Sweethearts in Concert," "Love," "No No Nanette in Concert," "Magdalena in Concert."

KEARNEY, JEFFREY. Born June 30, 1963 in Lexington, KY. Attended ULondon, AADA. Debut 1988 OB in "Cave Life."

KEATING, CHARLES. Born Oct. 22, 1941 in London, Eng. Bdwy debut 1969 in "Arturo Ui," followed by "The House of Atreus," "Loot," OB in "An Ounce of Prevention," "A Man For All Seasons," "There Is a Dream Dreaming Us."

KEITH, LAWRENCE/LARRY. Born Mar. 4, 1931 in Brooklyn, NY. Graduate Bklyn Col, IndU. Bdwy debut 1960 in "My Fair Lady," followed by "High Spirits," "I Had a Ball," "Best Laid Plans," "Mother Lover," OB in "The Homecoming," "Conflict of Interest," "The Brownsville Raid," "M. Amilcar," "The Rise of David Levinsky," "Miami," "Song for a Saturday."

KELLER, JEFF. Born Sept. 8, 1947 in Brooklyn, NY. Graduate Monmouth Col. Bdwy debut 1974 in "Candide," followed by "Fiddler on the Roof," "On the 20th Century," "The 1940's Radio Show," "Dance a Little Closer," "Phantom of the Opera," OB in "Bird of Paradise," "Charlotte Sweet," "Roberta in Concert," "Personals."

KELLETT, ROBERT. Born Aug. 29, 1955 in Minneapolis, MN. Attended UIll, Goodman Theatre. Debut 1981 OB in "Oh, Johnny!," followed by "Sex Acts," Bdwy in "Anything Goes" (1987).

KELLY, CRAIG. Born Feb. 2, 1964 in Witchita Falls, TX. Graduate NYU. Debut 1988 OB in "Anchorman."

KEMLER, ESTELLE. Born March 8 in NYC. Attended Carnegie-Mellon U. Debut 1981 OB in "Amidst the Gladiolas," followed by "Goodnight, Grandpa," "Made in Heaven," "My Three Angels," "Night Watch," "The Women in the Family."

KENNEDY, LAURIE. Born Feb. 14, 1948 in Hollywood, Ca. Graduate Sarah Lawrence Col. Debut 1974 OB in "End of Summer," followed by "A Day in the Death of Joe Egg," "Ladyhouse Blues," "He and She," "The Recruiting Officer," "Isn't It Romantic?," "After the Fall," "The Miracle Worker," "Resistance," Bdwy in "Man and Superman" (1978) for which she received a Theatre World Award, "Major Barbara."

KENNY, JACK. Born Mar. 9, 1958 in Chicago, Il. Attended Juilliard. Debut 1983 OB in "Pericles," followed by "Tartuffe," "Play and Other Plays," "A Normal Heart," "The Rise of David Levinsky," "Rum & Coke," "Philistines," "Taming of the Shrew," "Emily."

KENT-DUNCAN, DARYN. Born May 17 in Newburyport, MA. Attended LIU. Debut 1962 OB in "Medea," followed by "The Disposal," "Three in Time."

KEPROS, NICHOLAS. Born Nov. 8, 1932 in Salt Lake City, UT. Graduate UUtah, RADA. Debut 1958 OB in "The Golden Six," followed by "Wars of Roses," "Julius Caesar," "Hamlet," "Henry IV," "She Stoops to Conquer," "Peer Gynt," "Octaroon," "Endicott and the Red Cross," "The Judas Applause," "Irish Hebrew Lesson," "Judgment at Havana," "The Millionairess," "Androcles and the Lion," "The Redemptor," "Othello," "The Times and Appetites of Toulouse-Lautrec," "Two Fridays," Bdwy in "St. Joan" (1968), "Amadeus," "Execution of Justice."

KERNS, LINDA. Born June 2, 1953 in Columbus, Oh. Attended Temple U, AADA. Debut 1981 OB in "Crisp," "Henry the 8th at the Grand Ole Opry," Bdwy in "Nine" (1982), "Big River."

KERR, E. KATHERINE. (formerly Elaine) Born Apr. 20, 1940 in Indianapolis, IN. Graduate IndU, Neighborhood Playhouse. Debut 1963 OB in "Trojan Women," followed by "The Contrast," "Cloud 9," "Laughing Wild," "Urban Blight," Bdwy in "No Place to Be Somebody" (1969), "Nightwatch," "Passion."

KERR, PHILIP. Born Apr. 9, 1940 in NYC. Attended Harvard, LAMDA. Bdwy debut 1969 in "Tiny Alice," followed by "A Flea in Her Ear," "Three Sisters," "Jockey Club Stakes," "Macbeth" (1988), OB in "Hamlet," "The Rehearsal," "Cuchlain."

KERSEY, BILLYE. Born Oct. 15, 1955 in Norfolk, VA. Bdwy debut 1981 in "42nd Street."

KERSHAW, WHITNEY. Born Apr. 10, 1962 in Orlando, FL. Attended Harkness/Joffrey Ballet Schools. Debut 1981 OB in "Francis," Bdwy in "Cats."

KERWIN, BRIAN. Born Oct. 25, 1949 in Chicago, ILL. Graduate USCal. Debut 1988 OB in "Emily" for which he received a Theatre World Award.

KEYS, HENSON. Born Oct. 7, 1949 in Lincoln, ILL. Graduate UOk., FlaStateU. Debut 1975 OB in "Hamlet," followed by "Night Games," "A Frog in His Throat."

KING, GINNY. Born May 12, 1957 in Atlanta, GA. Attended NCSch of Arts. Bdwy debut 1980 in "42nd Street."

KING, ROBERT. Born June 15, 1936 in NYC. Juilliard graduate. Bdwy debut 1972 in "An Evening with Richard Nixon . . .," followed by OB's "Under the Skin."

KING, W. McGREGOR. Born Apr. 1, 1952 in Fitchburg, Ma. Graduate Bryant & Stratton Col. Debut 1976 OB in "Lysistrata," followed by "The Lower Depths," "Maid to Marry," "Times Square," "The Ugly Truckling," "The Lunch Girls," "Creeps," "Cork," "Timbuktu," "Perfect Crime."

KINGSLEY-WEIHE, GRETCHEN. Born Oct. 6, 1961 in Washington, DC. Attended Tulane U. Debut 1985 OB in "Mowgli," followed by "This Could Be the Start," Bdwy in "Les Miserables" (1987).

KINGSTON, KAYE. Born Sept. 5, 1924 in Youngstown, OH. Graduate UChicago. Bdwy debut 1955 in "Catch a Star," followed by "A Midsummer Night's Dream," "As You Like It," "Call It Virtue," "Tiger at the Gates," "The Trial," "The Mating Dance," "Victims," "Gemini," OB in "An Absence of Light," "Philistines."

KIRBY-NUNES, MIZAN. Born Oct. 8 in Port-of-Spain, Trinidad. Graduate UChicago. Debut 1987 OB in "Sherlock Holmes and the Hands of Othello," followed by "The Trial of Adam Clayton Powell," "La Mulata," "In the Beginning . . ."

KIRSCH, CAROLYN. Born May 24, 1942 in Shreveport, LA. Bdwy debut 1963 in "How to Succeed . . . ," followed by "Follies Bergere," "La Grosse Valise," "Skyscraper," "Breakfast at Tiffany's," "Sweet Charity," "Hallelujah, Baby!," "Dear World," "Promises, Promises," "Coco," "Ulysses in Nighttown," "A Chorus Line," OB in "Silk Stockings," "Telecast."

KIRSTEIN, DALE. Born May 18 in Washington, DC. Graduate Ithaca Col. Bdwy debut 1981 in "Camelot," followed by "Show Boat," Radio City Music Hall Specials, "Phantom of the Opera."

KLATT, DAVID. Born July 15, 1958 in Martins Ferry, OH. Attended West Liberty State Col. Bdwy debut 1984 in "La Cage aux Folles."

KLEIN, ROBERT. Born Feb. 8, 1942 in NYC. Graduate Alfred U., Yale. OB in "Six Characters in Search of an Author," "Second City Returns," "Upstairs at the Downstairs," Bdwy in "The Apple Tree," "New Faces of 1968," "Morning Noon and Night," "They're Playing Our Song," "The Robert Klein Show," "Robert Klein on Broadway."

KLEMPERER, WERNER. Born in Germany; graduate Pasadena Playhouse. Bdwy debut 1947 in "Heads or Tails," followed by "Galileo," "The Insect Comedy," "20th Century," "Dear Charles," "Night of the Tribades," "Cabaret," and OB in "Master Class."

Jennifer Harmon	James Harper	Jona Harvey	Paul Hecht	Elisa Heinsohn	Gerald Hiken

Billy Hipkins	Gloria Hodes	Philip Hoffman	Felicity Huffman	Bryan Hull	Patricia Hunter

Matthew Inge	Laura Innes	Zeljko Ivanek	Jane Ives	Susan Jacks	Elmore James

Gregory Jbara	Justine Johnston	Page Johnson	Cherry Jones	Franz Jones	Jen Jones

Donna Kane	Jeff Kearney	Whitney Kershaw	Henson Keys	Juliette Kurth	Jordan Lage

KLIBAN, KEN. Born July 26, 1943 in Norwalk, CT. Graduate UMiami, NYU. Bdwy debut 1967 in "War and Peace," followed by "As Is," OB in "Puppy Dog Tails," "Istanbul," "Persians," "Home," "Elizabeth the Queen," "Judith," "Man and Superman," "Boom Boom Room," "Ulysses in Traction," "Lulu," "The Beaver Coat," "Troilus and Cressida," "Richard II," "The Great Grandson of Jedediah Kohler," "It's Only a Play," "Time Framed," "Love's Labour's Lost," "Wild Blue."

KLUNIS, TOM. Born in San Francisco, CA. Bdwy debut 1961 in "Gideon," followed by "The Devils," "Henry V," "Romeo and Juliet," "St. Joan," "Hide and Seek," "Bacchae," "Plenty," "M. Butterfly," OB in "The Immoralist," "Hamlet," "Arms and the Man," "The Potting Shed," "Measure for Measure," "Romeo and Juliet," "The Balcony," "Our Town," "The Man Who Never Died," "God Is My Ram," "Rise Marlow," "Iphigenia in Aulis," "Still Life," "The Master and Margarita," "As You Like It," "The Winter Dancers," "When We Dead Awaken," "Vieux Carre," "The Master Builder," "Richard III," "A Map of the World."

KOKA, JULIETTE. Born Apr. 4, 1930 in Finland. Attended Helsinki School of Dramatic Arts. Debut 1977 OB in "Piaf . . . A Remembrance" for which she received a Theatre World Award, followed by "Ladies and Gentlemen Jerome Kern," "Salon."

KOLINSKI, JOSEPH. Born June 26, 1953 in Detroit, Mi. Attended UDetroit. Bdwy debut 1980 in "Brigadoon," followed by "Dance a Little Closer," "The Three Musketeers," "Les Miserables," OB in "Hijinks!," "The Human Comedy" (also Bdwy).

KOPACHE, THOMAS. Born Oct. 17, 1945 in Manchester, NH. Graduate SanDiegoStateU, CalInstArts. Debut 1976 OB in "The Architect and the Emperor of Assyria," followed by "Brontosaurus Rex," "Estravagant Triumph," "Caligula," "The Tempest," "Macbeth," "Measure for Measure," "Hunting Scenes from Lower Bavaria," "The Danube," "Friends Too Numerous to Mention," "Twelfth Night," "A Winter's Tale," "Working 1 Acts."

KORBICH, EDDIE. Born Nov. 6, 1960 in Washington, DC. Graduate Boston Consv. Debut 1985 OB in "A Little Night Music," followed by "Flora the Red Menace," "No Frills Revue," "The Last Musical Comedy," "Godspell," Bdwy in "Singin' in the Rain" (1986).

KOREY, ALEXANDRA. Born May 14 in Brooklyn, NY. Graduate Columbia U. Debut 1976 OB in "Fiorello!," followed by "Annie Get Your Gun," "Jerry's Girls," "Rosalie in Concert," "America Kicks Up Its Heels," "Gallery," "Feathertop," "Bittersuite," Bdwy in "Hello, Dolly!" (1978), "Show Boat" (1983).

KORF, MIA. Born Nov. 1, 1965 in Ithaca, NY. Attended Cornell U., Ithaca Col. Debut 1987 OB in "Two Gentlemen of Verona," followed by "The Seagull," "Godspell."

KORNBERG, DAI. Born Apr. 6, 1957 in NYC. Graduate NYU. Debut 1987 OB in "This Wooden O," followed by "Firing Squad," "The Elephant Man."

KORTHAZE, RICHARD. Born Feb. 11 in Chicago, IL. Graduate Chicago Musical Col. Bdwy debut 1953 in "Pal Joey," followed by "Wonderful Town," "Happy Hunting," "Conquering Hero," "How to Succeed in Business . . .," "Skyscraper," "Walking Happy," "Promises, Promises," "Pippin," "Chicago," "Dancin'," "Take Me Along" (1985), "Anything Goes," OB in "Phoenix '55" (1955).

KRAG, JAMES. Born July 23, 1962 in Chicago, IL. Graduate DePaul U. Bdwy debut 1988 in "Burn This."

KRAKOWSKI, JANE. Born Oct. 11, 1968 in New Jersey. Debut 1984 OB in "American Passion," followed by "Miami," "A Little Night Music," Bdwy in "Starlight Express" (1987).

KRAMAREVSKY, ALEX. Born Jan. 5, 1959 in Moscow, Russia. Attended Moscow School of Arts, AmBallet School. Bdwy debut 1987 in "Teddy and Alice."

KRATKY, BOB. Born May 10, 1955 in East St. Louis, IL. Graduate SIllU, FlaStateU. Debut 1985 OB in "Cherokee County," followed by "The Two Mrs. Trumps."

KRESS, DONNA. Born Dec. 29, 1959 in Pittsburgh, PA. Graduate Boston U. Debut 1982 OB in "Twelfth Night," followed by "The Country Wife," "Pericles," "Tartuffe," "Camille/Ivanov."

KUHN, BRUCE. Born Dec. 7, 1955 in Davenport, IA. Graduate UWVa, UWash. Bdwy debut 1987 in "Les Miserables."

KUHN, JUDY. Born May 20, 1958 in NYC. Graduate Oberlin Col. Debut 1985 OB in "Pearls," followed by "The Mystery of Edwin Drood (OB & Bdwy)," "Rags," "Les Miserables," "Chess."

KUROWSKI, RON. Born Mar. 14, 1953 in Philadelphia, Pa. Attended Temple U., RADA. Bdwy debut 1977 in "A Chorus Line."

KURTH, JULIETTE E. Born July 22, 1960 in Madison, Wi. Graduate SUNY/Purchase. Debut 1984 OB in "The Miser," followed by Bdwy in "La Cage aux Folles" (1986).

KURTZ, MARCIA JEAN. Born in The Bronx, NY. Juilliard graduate. Debut 1966 OB in "Jonah," followed by "America Hurrah," "Red Cross," "Muzeeka," "The Effects of Gamma Rays . . .," "The Year Boston Won the Pennant," "The Mirror," "The Orphan," "Action," "The Dybbuk," "Ivanov," "What's Wrong with This Picture?" "Today I Am a Fountain Pen," "The Chopin Playoffs," "The Last of the Red Hot Lovers," Bdwy in "The Chinese and Dr. Fish," "Thieves," "Execution of Justice."

KURTZ, SWOOSIE. Born Sept. 6 in Omaha, Ne. Attended USCal, LAMDA. Debut 1968 OB in "The Firebugs," followed by "The Effect of Gamma Rays . . .," "Enter a Free Man," "Children," "Museum," "Uncommon Women and Others," "Wine Untouched," "Summer," "The Beach House," Bdwy in "Ah, Wilderness!" (1975), "Tartuffe," "A History of the American Film," "5th of July," " House of Blue Leaves."

LAGE, JORDAN. Born Feb. 17, 1963 in Pao Alto, CA. Graduate NYU. Debut 1988 OB in "Boy's Life."

LALLY, JAMES. Born Oct. 2, 1956 in Cleveland, Oh. Attended Sarah Lawrence Col. Debut 1977 OB in "The Mandrake," followed by "The Taming of the Shrew," "All's Well That Ends Well," "As You Like It," "Murder in the Mummy's Tomb," "Two Gentlemen of Verona," "Guadeloupe."

LAMB, MARY ANN. Born July 4, 1959 in Seattle, Wa. Attended Neighborhood Playhouse. Bdwy debut 1985 in "Song and Dance," followed by "Starlight Express."

LAMBERT, KEN. Born June 6, 1951 in Roanoke, VA. Graduate UVa. Debut 1988 OB in "Much Ado about Nothing."

LANE, EDDIE. Born May 25, 1933 in McKees Rocks, PA. Attended UPittsburgh, Pittsburgh Playhouse. Debut 1988 OB in "The Good and Faithful Servant."

LANE, LAURA. Born Oct. 13 in Pittsburgh, PA. Graduate UMi. Debut 1988 OB in "The Good and Faithful Servant."

LANE, NANCY. Born June 16, 1951 in Passaic, NJ. Attended Va. CommonwealthU., AADA. Debut 1975 OB and Broadway in "A Chorus Line."

LANE, NATHAN. Born Feb. 3, 1956 in Jersey City, NJ. Debut 1978 OB in "A Midsummer Night's Dream," followed by "Love," "Measure for Measure," Bdwy in "Present Laughter" (1982), "Merlin," "Wind in the Willows," "Claptrap," "The Common Pursuit."

LANGELLA, FRANK. Born Jan. 1, 1940 in Bayonne, NJ. Graduate Syracuse U. Debut 1963 OB in "The Immoralist," followed by "The Old Glory," "Good Day," "The White Devil," "Yerma," "Iphigenia in Aulis," "A Cry of Players," "Prince of Homburg," "After the Fall," Bdwy in "Seascape" (1975), "Dracula," "Amadeus," "Passion," "Design for Living," "Hurlyburly," "Sherlock's Last Case."

LANGMUIR, MOLLY. Born Nov. 4, 1979 in Port Jefferson, NY. Debut 1987 OB in "Words from the Moon."

LANSING, ROBERT. Born June 5, 1929 in San Diego, CA. Bdwy debut 1951 in "Stalag 17," followed by "Cyrano de Bergerac," "Richard III," "Charley's Aunt," "The Lovers," "Cue for Passion," "Great God Brown," "Cut of the Axe," "Finishing Touches," OB in "The Father," "The Cost of Living," "The Line," "Phaedra."

LARSEN, LIZ. Born Jan. 16, 1959 in Philadelphia, PA. Attended Hofstra U, SUNY/Purchase. Bdwy debut 1981 in "Fiddler on the Roof," OB in "Kuni Leml," "Hamlin," "Personals," "Starmites," "Company," "After These Messages."

LARSON, JILL. Born Oct. 7, 1947 in Minneapolis, Mn. Graduate Hunter Col. Debut 1980 OB in "These Men," followed by "Peep," "Serious Bizness," "It's Only a Play," "Red Rover," "Enter a Freeman," "Scooncat," Bdwy in "Romantic Comedy" (1980), "Death and the King's Horseman" (LC).

LASKY, ZANE. Born Apr. 23, 1953 in NYC. Attended Manhattan Col. HB Studio. Debut 1973 OB in "The Hot l Baltimore," followed by "The Prodigal," "Innocent Thoughts, Harmless Intentions," "Time Framed," "Balm in Gilead," "Shlemiel the First," "Caligula," "The Mound Builders," "Quiet in the Land," "El Salvador," Bdwy in "All Over Town" (1974).

LAUB, SANDRA. Born Dec. 15, 1956 in Bryn Mawr, Pa. Graduate Northwestern U. Debut 1983 OB in "Richard III," followed by "Young Playwrights Festival," "Domestic Issues," "Say Goodnight Gracie," "Les Mouches," "Three Sisters," "Edward II," "Intricate Acquantances."

LAUREANO, PAUL. Born Dec. 26 in Hartford, CT. Graduate Hartt School of Music. Bdwy debut 1988 in "Chess."

LAURENSON, DIANA. Born Sept. 25, 1957 in Elmont, NY. Graduate UMa/Amherst. Debut 1981 OB in "Manhattan Rhythm," followed by "No, No, Nanette," Bdwy in "The Little Prince and the Aviator" (1981), "Big Deal."

LAVIN, LINDA. Born Oct. 15, 1939 in Portland, Me. Graduate William & Mary Col. Bdwy debut 1962 in "A Family Affair," followed by "Riot Act," "The Game Is Up," "Hotel Passionato," "It's a Bird . . . It's Superman!," "On a Clear Day You Can See Forever," "Something Different," "Cop-Out," "Last of the Red Hot Lovers," "Story Theatre," "The Enemy Is Dead," "Broadway Bound," OB in "Wet Paint" for which she received a Theatre World Award, "Comedy of Errors."

LAWLESS, RICK. Born Dec. 31, 1960 in Bridgeport, Ct. Graduate Fairfield U. Debut 1985 OB in "Dr. Faustus," followed by "The Foreigner," "Camp Meeting," "Lady Moonsong, Mr. Monsoon," "Fun."

LAWRENCE, HOWARD. Born Dec. 20 in Brooklyn, NY. Graduate SUNY/Oneonta. Debut 1981 OB in "The Fantasticks."

LAWRENCE, SHARON. Born June 29, 1961 in Charlotte, NC. Attended UNC/Chapel Hill. Debut 1984 OB in "Panache," followed by "Berlin in Light," Bdwy in "Cabaret" (1987).

LaZEBNIK, KENNETH. Born Nov. 11, 1954 in Levitown, PA. Graduate MacAlester Col, RADA. Debut 1985 OB in "The Taming of the Shrew," followed by "Camille/Ivanov."

LAZORE, MARK. Born Sept. 1, 1956 in Chicago, IL. Attended UIll. Debut 1987 OB in "Surviving in New York," Bdwy in "Teddy and Alice" (1987).

LEE, JENNIFER. Born July 19, 1967 in Chicago, Il. Attended UTx. Debut 1985 OB in "The Fantasticks."

LEE-ARANAS, MARY. Born Sept. 23, 1959 in Taipei, Taiwan. Graduate UOttawa. Debut 1984 OB in "Empress of China," followed by "A State without Grace," "Return of the Phoenix," "Yellow Is My Favorite Color," "The Man Who Turned into a Stick," "The Impostor," "Rosie's Cafe."

LEEDS, JORDAN. Born Nov. 29, 1961 in Queens, NYC. Graduate SUNY/Binghamton. Bdwy debut 1987 in "Les Miserables."

LeFEVRE, ADAM. Born Aug. 11, 1950 in Albany, NY. Graduate Williams Col, UIowa. Debut 1981 OB in "Turnbuckle," followed by "Badgers," "Goose and Tomtom," "In the Country," "Submariners," "Boys Next Door."

LEHMAN, JEANNE. Born Sept. 14 in Woodland, CA. Graduate UC/San Francisco. Debut 1972 OB in "The Drunkard," followed by "Leave It to Jane," "Oh, Lady, Lady!," "Zip Goes a Million," "Oh, Boy!," "No, No, Nanette," "Company," Bdwy in "Irene" (1973), "Rodgers and Hart," "Going Up," "A Musical Jubilee," "Jerome Kern Goes to Hollywood."

LEIGH-SMITH, ANDREA. Born Dec. 21, 1962 in Louisville, Ky. Attended SUNY/Purchase. Bdwy debut 1986 in "Smile," followed by "Radio City Christmas Spectacular."

LeMASSENA, WILLIAM. Born May 23, 1916 in Glen Ridge, NJ. Attended NYU. Bdwy debut 1940 in "Taming of the Shrew," followed by "There Shall Be No Night," "The Pirate," "Hamlet," "Call Me Mister," "Inside U.S.A.," "I Know My Love," "Dream Girl," "Nina," "Ondine," "Fallen Angels," "Redhead," "Conquering Hero," "Beauty Part," "Come Summer," "Grin and Bare It," "All Over Town," "A Texas Trilogy," "Deathtrap," "Blithe Spirit," OB in "The Coop," "Brigadoon," "Life with Father," "F. Jasmine Addams," "The Dodge Boys," "Ivanov."

LEMMON, SHIRLEY. Born May 15, 1948 in Salt Lake City, UT. Graduate UtStateU. Bdwy debut 1971 in "Company," followed by "Smith," "Words and Music," "Nine," OB in "2 by 5," "Life Is a Dream," "Bittersuite."

LENOX, ADRIANE. Born Sept. 11, 1956 in Memphis, TN. Graduate Lambuth Col. Bdwy debut 1979 in "Ain't Misbehavin'," followed by "Dreamgirls," OB in "Beehive."

LEONARD, ROBERT SEAN. Born Feb. 28, 1969 in "Westwood, NJ. Debut 1985 OB in "Sally's Gone, She Left Her Name," followed by "Coming of Age in SoHo," "The Beach House," Bdwy in "Brighton Beach Memoirs," "Breaking the Code."

LEONE, NICHOLAS (aka Nick). Born Mar. 31, 1955 in Camden, NJ. Graduate Catholic U. Debut 1988 OB in "No, No, Nanette."

LETTIERE, JEFF. Born June 28, 1961 in San Luis Obispo, CA. Graduate San Jose State U. Debut 1987 OB in "Kismet."

LEVINE, ANNA. Born Sept. 18, in NYC. Debut 1975 OB in "Kid Champion," followed by "Uncommon Women and Others," "City Sugar," "A Winter's Tale," "Johnny-on-the-Spot," "The

Wedding," "American Days," "The Singular Life of Albert Nobbs," "Cinders," "Rose Cottages," "School of Giorgione," "The Maderati," "Abingdon Square," "Poets' Corner."

LEWIS, GILBERT. Born Apr. 6, 1941 in Philadelphia, PA. Attended Morgan State Col. Bdwy debut 1969 in "The Great White Hope," followed by "Fences," OB in "Who's Got His Own," "Transfers," "Ballet behind the Bridge," "Coriolanus," "Appear and Show Cause," "In Splendid Error," "Julius Caesar," "In the Well of the House," "The River Niger," "The Brownsville Raid," "Top Hat."

LEWIS, LOUISE. Born Jan. 31, 1961 in New Orleans, LA. Attended NCSchoolArts. Debut 1987 OB in "Serious Money."

LEWIS, MARCIA. Born Aug. 18, 1938 in Melrose, Ma. Attended UCin. OB in "The Impudent Wolf," "Who's Who, Baby," "God Bless Coney," "Let Yourself Go," "Romance Language," Bdwy in "The Time of Your Life," "Hello, Dolly!," "Annie," "Rags," "Roza."

LEWIS, VICKI. Born Mar. 17, 1960 in Cincinnati, Oh. Graduate CinConsv. Bdwy debut 1982 in "Do Black Patent Leather Shoes Really Reflect Up?," followed by "Wind in the Willows," OB in "Snoopy," "A Bundle of Nerves," "Angry Housewives," "1-2-3-4-5," "One Act Festival," "The Love Talker."

LEYDEN, LEO. Born Jan. 28, 1929 in Dublin, Ire. Attended Abbey ThSch. Bdwy debut 1960 in "Love and Libel," followed by "Darling of the Day," "Mundy Scheme," "The Rothschilds," "Capt. Brassbound's Conversion," "The Plough and the Stars" (LC), "Habeas Corpus," "Me and My Girl."

LIBERATORE, LOU. Born Aug. 4, 1959 in Jersey City, NJ. Graduate Fordham U. Debut 1982 OB in "The Great Grandson of Jedediah Kohler," followed by "Threads," "Black Angel," "Richard II," "Thymus Vulgaris," "As Is," "Burn This!," Bdwy "As Is" (1985), "Burn This" (1987).

LICATO, FRANK. Born Apr. 20, 1952 in Brooklyn, NY. Attended Emerson Col. Debut 1974 OB in "Deathwatch," followed by "Fever," "American Music," "Angel City," "Killer's Head," "Haunted Lives," "The Taming of the Shrew."

LIDE, MILLER. Born Aug. 10, 1935 in Columbia, SC. Graduate USC, AmThWing. Debut 1961 OB in "3 Modern Japanese Plays," followed by "The Trial at Rouen," "Street Scene," "Joan of Arc at the Stake," "The Heiress," "The Doctor's Dilemma," Bdwy in "Ivanov," "Halfway Up the Tree," "Who's Who in Hell," "We Interrupt This Program," "The Royal Family," "84 Charing Cross Road."

LIGHTSTONE, MARILYN. Born June 28, 1940 in Montreal, Can. Graduate McGill U. Bdwy debut 1968 in "King Lear," followed by OB's "Tamara."

LINARES, CARLOS. Born July 26, 1954 in El Salvador, C.A. Attended Lehman Col. Debut 1988 OB in "Senora Carrar's Rifles."

LINDO, DELROY. Born Nov. 18, 1952 in London, Eng. NYC Debut 1979 OB in "Spell #7," followed by "Les Blancs," Bdwy in "Master Harold . . . and the boys" (1983), "Joe Turner's Come and Gone."

LINDSAY, ROBERT. Born Dec. 13, 1951 in Ilkeston, Derbyshire, Eng. Attended RADA. Bdwy debut 1986 in "Me and My Girl" for which he received a Theatre World Award.

LITHGOW, JOHN. Born Oct. 19, 1945 in Rochester, NY. Graduate HarvardU. Bdwy debut 1973 in "The Changing Room," followed by "My Fat Friend," "Comedians," "Anna Christie," "Once in a Lifetime," "Spokesong," "Bedroom Farce," "Division Street," "Beyond Therapy," "Requiem for a Heavyweight," "The Front Page" (LC), "M. Butterfly," OB in "Hamlet," "Trelawny of the Wells," "A Memory of Two Mondays," "Secret Service," "Boy Meets Girl," "Salt Lake City Skyline," "Kaufman at Large."

LOAR, ROSEMARY. Born in NYC. Attended UOhio, UOre. Bdwy debut 1984 in "You Can't Take It with You," followed by "Sally in Concert," "Chess."

LOBENHOFER, LEE. Born June 25, 1955 in Chicago, IL. Graduate UIll. Debut 1986 OB in "Rainbow," followed by "I-Married an Angel in Concert," "Hans Christian Andersen," "Bittersweet," "Robin Hood," "Lost in the Stars."

LOCKE, KEITH. Born Sept. 19, 1958 in North Carolina. Graduate UNC/Greensboro, UCin. Bdwy debut 1982 in "Encore," followed by "Teddy and Alice."

LOCKWOOD, LISA. Born Feb. 13, 1958 in San Francisco, CA. Bdwy debut 1988 in "Phantom of the Opera."

LOCRICCHIO, MATTHEW. Born June 3, 1947 in Detroit, MI. Attended EMiU. Debut 1983 OB in "Fool for Love," followed by "Largo Desolato," "Of Mice and Men."

LONDON, BECKY. Born Feb. 11, 1958 in Philadelphia, Pa. Graduate Yale U. Debut 1985 OB in "Isn't It Romantic," followed by "Vampire Lesbians of Sodom," "Psycho Beach Party," "Last of the Red Hot Lovers."

LONDON, CHET. Born Apr. 8, 1931 in Boston, Ma. Attended St. Alselm's Col. Bdwy debut 1961 in "First Love," followed by "Calculated Risk," OB in "The Shoemaker and the Peddler," "Romeo and Juliet," "A Midsummer Night's Dream," "Hamlet," "The Deadly Game," "Macbeth," "Women Beware Women," "Like Them That Dream."

LONG, JODI. Born in NYC; graduate SUNY/Purchase. Bdwy debut 1963 in "Nowhere to Go but Up," followed by "Loose Ends," "Bacchae," OB in "Fathers and Sons," "Family Devotions," "Rohwer," "Tooth of Crime," "Dream of Kitamura," "A Midsummer Night's Dream," "Madame de Sade."

LOR, DENISE. Born May 3, 1929 in Los Angeles, Ca. Debut 1968 OB in "To Be or Not to Be," followed by "Alias Jimmy Valentine," Bdwy in "42nd Street" (1987).

LOUDON, DOROTHY. Born Sept. 17, 1933 in Boston, MA. Attended Emerson Col., Syracuse U. Debut 1961 in "World of Jules Feiffer," Bdwy 1963 in "Nowhere to Go but Up" for which she received a Theatre World Award followed by "Noel Coward's Sweet Potato," "Fig Leaves Are Falling," "Three Men on a Horse," "The Women," "Annie," "Ballroom," "West Side Waltz," "Noises Off," "Jerry's Girls."

LOVE, PETER. Born Feb. 20, 1963 in Aberdeen MD. Attended UWis/LaCrosse. Debut 1987 OB in "Holy Heist."

LOVETT, MARJORIE. Born Oct. 4, 1932 in Long Branch, NJ. Debut 1975 OB in "Another Language," followed by "The Last Resort," Bdwy in "Einstein and the Polar Bear" (1981).

LOWE, STANJA. Born Sept. 5, 1929 in Cleveland, OH. Attended Bennington Col, Cleveland Play House. Bdwy debut 1944 in "Dear Ruth," followed by "King Lear," "Songs at Twilight," "Coastal Disturbances."

LUCAS, J. FRANK. Born in Houston, TX. Graduate TCU. Debut 1943 OB in "A Man's House," followed by "Coriolanus," "Edward II," "The Trip to Bountiful," "Orpheus Descending," "Guitar," "Marcus in the High Grass," "Chocolates," "To Bury a Cousin," "One World at a Time," "The Vinegar Tree," Bdwy in "Bad Habits," "The Best Little Whorehouse in Texas."

LUCAS, ROXIE. Born Aug. 25, 1951 in Memphis, TN. Attended UHouston. Bdwy debut 1981 in "The Best Little Whorehouse in Texas," followed by "Harrigan 'n Hart," OB in "Forbidden Broadway," "The Best of Forbidden Broadway."

LUDWIG, KAREN. Born Oct. 9 in San Francisco, CA. Bdwy debut 1964 in "The Deputy," followed by "The Devils," "Bacchae," "Broadway Bound," OB in "The Trojan Women," "Red Cross," "Muzeeka," "Huui, Huui," "Our Last Night," "The Seagull," "Museum," "Nasty Rumors," "Daisy," "Gethsemane/Springs," "After the Revolution," "Before She Is Even Born," "Exiles," "Messiah," "Love As We Know It," "The Chopin Playoffs."

LuPONE, PATTI. Born Apr. 21, 1949 in Northport, NY. Juilliard graduate. Debut 1972 OB in "School for Scandal," followed by "Women Beware Women," "Next Time I'll Sing to You," "Beggar's Opera," "Scapin," "The Robber Bridegroom," "Edward II," "The Woods," "Edmond," "America Kicks Up Its Heels," "The Cradle Will Rock," Bdwy in "The Water Engine" (1978), "Working," "Evita," "Oliver!," "The Accidental Death of an Anarchist," "Anything Goes."

LuPONE, ROBERT. Born July 29, 1956 in Brooklyn, NY. Juilliard graduate. Bdwy debut 1970 in "Minnie's Boys," followed by "Jesus Christ Superstar," "The Rothschilds," "Magic Show," "A Chorus Line," "St. Joan," "Late Night Comic," OB in "Charlie Was Here," "Twelfth Night," "In Connecticut," "Snow Orchid," "Lennon," "Black Angel," "The Quilling of Prue," "Time Framed," "Class 1 Acts."brance," "Children of Darkness," "Kill."

LUTSKY, MARC. Born Apr. 15 in NYC. Attended Lehman Col. OB in "The Misanthrope," "The Investigation," "Twelfth Night," "And Baby Makes Four," "The Lunch Girls," "Between Time and Timbuktu," "Perfect Crime."

LYLES, LESLIE. Born in Plainfield, NJ. Graduate Monmouth Col, Rutgers U. Debut 1981 OB in "Sea Marks," followed by "Highest Standard of Living," "Vanishing Act," "I Am Who I Am," "The Arbor," "Terry by Terry," "Marathon '88," Bdwy in "The Real Thing" (1985).

LYND, BETTY. Born In Los Angeles, CA. Debut 1968 OB in "Rondelay," followed by "Love Me, Love My Children," Bdwy in "The Skin of Our Teeth" (1975), "A Chorus Line."

LYNDECK, EDMUND. Born Oct. 4, 1925 in Baton Rouge, La. Graduate Montclair State Col., Fordham U. Bdwy debut 1969 in "1776," followed by "Sweeney Todd," "A Doll's Life," "Merlin," "Into the Woods," OB in "The King and I" (JB), "Mandragola," "A Safe Place," "Amoureuse," "Piaf, A Remembrance," "Children of Darkness," "Kill."

LYNG, NORA MAE. Born Jan. 27, 1951 in Jersey City, NJ. Debut 1981 OB in "Anything Goes," followed by "Forbidden Broadway," "Road to Hollywood," "Tales of Tinseltown," Bdwy in "Wind in the Willows" (1985), "Cabaret" (1987).

MacLACHLAN, KYLE. Born Feb. 22, 1959 in Yakima, WA. Graduate UWash. Debut 1988 OB in "The Palace of Amateurs."

MacPHERSON, LORI. Born July 23 in Albany, NY. Attended Skidmore Col. Bdwy debut 1988 in "The Phantom of the Opera."

MacRAE, SHEILA. Born Sept. 24, 1929 in London, Eng. Bdwy debut 1973 in "Absurd Person Singular," and OB in "Guys and Dolls" (1965CC), followed by "Bunker Reveries."

MADONNA. Born Aug. 16, 1958 in Bay City, MI. Bdwy debut 1988 in "Speed-the-Plow."

MAGLIONE, CHRISTINE. Born Aug. 24, 1964 in Orange, NJ. Graduate Cornell U. Debut 1987 OB in "Kismet."

MAIS, MICHELE. Born July 30, 1954 in NYC. Graduate CCNY. Debut 1975 OB in "Godspell," followed by "Othello," "Superspy," "Yesterday Continued," "We'll Be Right Back," "Que Ubo?," "El Bravo!," "Opening Night," "Surrender/a flirtation," "Catch of the Day," Bdwy in "Zoot Suit" (1979), "Roza."

MANDAN, ROBERT. Born Feb. 2, 1932 in Clever, MO. Attended Pomona Col. Bdwy debut 1956 in "Debut," followed by "Speaking of Murder," "Maggie Flynn," "But Seriously," "Applause," "Mail," OB in "No Exit."

MANOFF, DINAH. Born Jan. 25, 1958 in NYC. Attended CalArtsU. Bdwy debut 1980 in "I Ought to Be in Pictures" for which she received a Theatre World Award, followed by "Leader of the Pack," OB in "Gifted Children," "The Value of Names."

MANSELL, LILENE. Born Aug. 4, 1944 in Beaver Falls, PA. Graduate Carnegie Tech. Debut 1983 OB in "Ivanov," followed by "Walk the Dog, Willie," "Tied by the Leg," "Late One Night in Okabeena," "Approaching Zero," "When I Was Your Age," "Like Them That Dream."

MANSON, ALAN. Born in NYC. Bdwy debut 1940 in "Journey to Jerusalem," followed by "This Is the Army," "Call Me Mister," "Southern Exposure," "Angels Kiss Me," "Ponder Heart," "Maybe Tuesday," "Tenth Man," "Gideon," "Nobody Loves an Albatross," "Funny Girl," "A Place for Polly," "40 Carats," "No Hard Feelings," "Broadway Bound," OB in "Dr. Jekyll and Mr. Hyde," "A Midsummer Night's Dream," "Oh Say Can You See L. A.?," "The Other Man."

MARCHAND, NANCY. Born June 19, 1928 in Buffalo, NY. Graduate Carnegie Tech. Debut 1951 in CC's "Taming of the Shrew," followed by "The Merchant of Venice," "Much Ado about Nothing," "Three Bags Full," "After the Rain," "The Alchemist," "Yerma," "Cyrano de Bergerac," "Mary Stuart," "Enemies," "The Plough and the Stars," "40 Carats," "And Miss Reardon Drinks a Little," "Veronica's Room," "Awake and Sing," "Morning's at 7," "The Octette Bridge Club," OB in "The Balcony," "Children," "Taken in Marriage," "Sister Mary Ignatius Explains It All," "Elektra."

MARCUS, JEFFREY. Born Feb. 21, 1960 in Harrisburg, PA. Attended Carnegie-MellonU. Bdwy debut 1982 in "Almost an Eagle," OB in "Short Change," followed by "Snow White Falling."

MARIYE, LILY. Born in Las Vegas, NV. Graduate UCLA. Debut 1987 OB in "Tea."

MARTELLS, CYNTHIA. Born Sept. 8, 1960 in London, Eng. Attended Rutgers U. Debut 1983 OB in "Under Heaven's Eye," followed by "Lightning," "Rules of Love," "Thornwood," "No, No, Nanette."

MARTIN, LEILA. Born Aug. 22, 1932 in NYC. Bdwy debut 1944 in "Peepshow," followed by "Two on the Aisle," "Wish You Were Here," "Guys and Dolls," "Best House in Naples," "Henry, Sweet Henry," "The Wall," "Visit to a Small Planet," "The Rothschilds," "42nd Street," "The Phantom of the Opera," OB in "Ernest in Love," "Beggar's Opera," "King of the U.S.," "Philemon," "Jerry's Girls."

MARTIN, ROBERT LEE. Born July 30, 1960 in NYC. Graduate Wagner Col. Debut 1987 OB in "The Tavern."

MASON, JACKIE. Born June 9, 1934 in Sheboygan, WI. Bdwy debut 1969 in "A Teaspoon Every Four Hours," followed by "The World according to Me."

MASTRONE, FRANK. Born Nov. 1, 1960 in Bridgeport, CT. Graduate CentralStStateU. Bdwy debut 1988 in "The Phantom of the Opera."

MATESKY, JARED. Born May 30, 1947 in Washington, DC. Graduate UMd, CatholicU. Debut 1977 OB in "Twelfth Night," followed by "Hot Coffee."

MAURER, LISA. Born Jan. 20 in NYC. Debut 1978 OB in "The Hallway," followed by "The House of Ramon Iglesia," "The Dolphin Position," "Festival of 1 Acts."

MAXWELL, ROBERTA. Born in Canada. Debut 1968 OB in "Two Gentlemen of Verona," followed by "A Whistle in the Dark," "Slag," "The Plough and the Stars," "Merchant of Venice," "Ashes," "Mary Stuart," "Lydie Breeze," "Before the Dawn," "Real Estate," Bdwy in "The Prime of Miss Jean Brodie," "Henry V," "House of Atreus," "The Resistible Rise of Arturo Ui," "Othello," "Hay Fever," "There's One in Every Marriage," "Equus," "The Merchant."

MAY, DONALD. Born Feb. 22, 1929 in Chicago, IL. Graduate UOk, Yale. Debut 1988 OB in "Emily."

MAYER, JERRY. Born May 12, 1941 in NYC. Graduate NYU. Debut 1968 OB in "Alice in Wonderland," followed by "L'Ete," "Marouf," "Trelawny of the Wells," "King of the Schnorrers," "Mother Courage," "You Know Al," "Goose and Tomtom," "The Rivals," "For Sale," "Two Gentlemen of Verona," "Julius Caesar," Bdwy in "Much Ado about Nothing" (1972), "Play Memory."

McCARTY, CONAN. Born Sept. 16, 1955 in Lubbock, TX. Attended USCal, AADA/West. Debut 1980 OB in "Star Treatment," followed by "Beyond Therapy," "Henry IV Part I," Bdwy in "Macbeth" (1988).

McCLINTOCK, JODIE LYNNE. Born Apr. 7, 1955 in Pittsburgh, PA. Graduate Westminster Col. Debut 1983 OB in "As You Like It," followed by "1984," Bdwy in "Long Day's Journey into Night" (1986).

McCONNELL, TY. Born Jan. 13, 1940 in Coldwater, MI. Graduate UMi. Debut 1962 OB in "The Fantasticks," followed by "Promenade," "Contrast," "Fashion," "Dubliners," "Lovesong," "Superspy," "Hamlet," Bdwy in "The Lion in Winter," "Dear World."

McCORMICK, MICHAEL. Born July 24, 1951 in Gary, IN. Graduate NorthwesternU. Bdwy debut 1964 in "Oliver!," followed by OB's "Coming Attractions," "Tomfoolery," "The Regard of Flight," "Charlotte Sweet," "Half a World Away."

McCRANE, PAUL. Born Jan. 19, 1961 in Philadelphia, PA. Debut 1977 OB in "Landscape of the Body," followed by "Dispatches," "Split," "Hunting Scenes," "Crossing Niagara," "Hooters," "Fables for Friends," "Moonchildren," "Right Behind the Flag," Bdwy in "Runaways" (1978), "Curse of an Aching Heart," "The Iceman Cometh" (1985).

McCUTCHEON, BILL. Born in 1924 in Russell, KY. Attended OhioU. Bdwy credits: "New Faces of 1956," "Dandelion Wine," "Out West of Eighth," "My Daughter, Your Son," "Over Here," "West Side Story," "The Front Page," "The Man Who Came to Dinner," "You Can't Take It with You," "Anything Goes," OB in "How to Steal an Election," "Wet Paint," "One's a Crowd," "Shoestring Revue," "Upstairs at the Downstairs," "The Little Revue," "The Marriage of Bette and Boo."

McDERMOTT, DYLAN. Born Oct. 26, 1961 in Waterbury, CT. Graduate FordhamU, Neighborhood Playhouse. Bdwy debut 1985 in "Biloxi Blues," OB in "Scooncat" (1987).

McDONALD, TANNY. Born Feb. 13 in Princeton, NJ. Graduate Vassar Col. Debut 1961 OB with "American Savoyards," followed by "All in Love," "To Broadway with Love," "Carricknabauna," "The Beggar's Opera," "Brand," "Goodbye Dan Bailey," "Total Eclipse," "Gorky," "Don Juan Come Back from the War," "Vera with Kate," "Francis," "On Approval," "A Definite Maybe," Bdwy in "Fiddler on the Roof," "Come Summer," "The Lincoln Mask," "Clothes for a Summer Hotel," "Macbeth" (1988).

McDONNELL, MARY. Born in 1952 in Ithaca, NY. Graduate SUNY/Fredomia. Debut 1978 OB in "Buried Child," followed by "Letters Home," "Still Life," "Death of a Miner," "Black Angel," "A Weekend Near Madison," "All Night Long," "Savage in Limbo," "Three Ways Home," Bdwy in "Execution of Justice" (1986).

McDORMAND, FRANCES. Born in 1958 in the South. Yale graduate. Debut 1983 OB in "Painting Churches," followed by "On the Verge," Bdwy in "Awake and Sing" (1984), "A Streetcar Named Desire" (1988).

McELDOWNEY, HARRISON. Born May 6, 1962 in Dallas, TX. Debut 1987 OB in "Too Many Girls."

McELHINEY, BILL. Born Oct. 17, 1955 in Berlin, Ger. Graduate Hobart Col., Neighborhood Playhouse. Debut 1985 OB in "America Kicks Up Its Heels," followed by "The Elephant Man."

McGINLEY, JOHN C. Born Aug. 3, 1959 in NYC. Graduate NYU. Debut 1984 OB in "Danny and the Deep Blue Sea," followed by "The Ballad of Soapy Smith," "Jesse and the Games," "Love as We Know It," "Talk Radio."

McGUIRE, KEVIN. Born Dec. 31, 1958 in Bennington, VT. Attended RADA. Debut 1981 OB in "A Midsummer Night's Dream," followed by "Forbidden Broadway," "Big Maggie," "Waiting for Godot," "Hamlet."

McGUIRE, MITCHELL. Born Dec. 26, 1936 in Chicago, IL. Attended Goodman Theatre, Santa Monica City Col. OB in "The Rapists," "Go, Go, God Is Dead!," "Waiting for Lefty," "The Bond," "Guns of Carrar," "Oh! Calcutta!," "New York! New York!," "What a Life!," "Butter and Egg Man," "Almost in Vegas," "Festival pf 1 Acts," "Prime Time Punch Line," "The Racket."

McINTYRE, GERRY. Born may 31, 1962 in Grenada, West Indies. Graduate MontclairStateCol. Debut 1985 OB in "Joan of Arc at the Stake," followed by "Homeseekers," Bdwy in "Anything Goes" (1987)

McINTYRE, MARILYN. Born May 23, 1949 in Erie, PA. Graduate PaStateCol, NCSchArts. Debut 1977 OB in "The Perfect Mollusc," followed by "Measure for Measure," "The Promise," "Action," "Blithe Spirit," "All the Nice People," "Stopping the Desert," Bdwy in "Gemini" (1980), "Scenes and Revelations."

McKINLEY, PHILIP WILLIAM. Born June 22, 1952 in Avon, IL. Debut 1982 OB in "Applause," followed by "Babes in Toyland," "Letters to Ben," "Homeseekers," "New Faces of 1952," "Desert Song."

McMANUS, DON R. Born in 1960 in Sylacauga, AL. Graduate Yale U. Debut 1987 OB in "Holy Ghosts."

McMARTIN, JOHN. Born in Warsaw, IN. Attended ColumbiaU. Debut 1959 OB in "Little Mary Sunshine" for which he received a Theatre World Award, followed by "Too Much Johnson," "The Misanthrope," "Sung and Unsung Sondheim," "Julius Caesar," Bdwy in "Conquering Hero"

(1961), "Blood, Sweat and Stanley Poole," "Children from Their Games," "A Rainy Day in Newark," "Sweet Charity," "Follies," "The Great God Brown," "Don Juan," "The Visit," "Chem de Fer," "Love for Love," "Rules of the Game," "Happy New Year," "Solomon's Child," "A Little Family Business."

McNABB, BARRY. Born Aug. 26, 1960 in Toronto, CAN. Graduate UOre. Bdwy debut 1986 in "Me and My Girl," followed by "The Phantom of the Opera."

McNAMARA, PAT. Born July 22, 1938 in Astoria, NY. Attended ColumbiaU., AADA. Debut 1961 OB in "Red Roses for Me," followed by "Crystal and Fox," "Nobody Hears a Broken Drum," "The Passing Game," "Killings on the Last Line," Bdwy in "The Poison Tree" (1976), "Brothers," "The Iceman Cometh" (1985), "Sherlock's Last Case."

MEADE, MICHELLE. Born May 6, 1961 in NY. Attended Parsons Sch., EmpireStateCol. Debut 1988 OB in "Leave It to Me."

MEISLE, KATHRYN. Born June 7 in Appleton, WI. Graduate Smith Col., UNC/Chapel Hill. Debut 1988 OB in "Dandy Dick."

MERRILL, TODD. Born July 21, 1963 in Cottage Grove, MN. Graduate NCSchArts. Debut 1987 OB in "Young Playwrights Festival," followed by "Present Tense," "Sparks in the Park."

METZO, WILLIAM. Born June 21, 1937 in Wilkes-Barre, PA. Graduate King's Col. Debut 1963 OB in "The Bald Soprano," followed by "Papers," "A Moon for the Misbegotten," "Arsenic and Old Lace," "Super Spy," "Hamlet," Bdwy in "Cyrano" (1973).

MICHELE, LINDA (aka Linda Lee Agee). Born June 2 in Oakland, CA. Graduate UPacific. Bdwy debut 1979 in "The Most Happy Fella," followed by "The Desert Song" (LC).

MICKEY, LEILANI. Born Jan. 18, 1955 in Honolulu, HI. Juilliard graduate. Debut 1981 OB in "Everybody's Gettin' into the Act," followed by "Kismet."

MIDDLETON, ROGER. Born Dec. 14, 1940 in Detroit, MI. Graduate ColStateU. Debut 1969 OB in "Getting Married," followed by "The Ragdoll," "Hard Times," "Side by Side by Sondheim."

MILLER, PENELOPE ANN. Born Jan. 13, 1964 in Santa Monica, CA. Attended Menlo Col. Bdwy debut 1985 in "Biloxi Blues," followed by OB's "Moonchildren."

MILLER, REBECCA. Born in 1962 in Roxbury, CT. Attended Yale U. Debut 1988 OB in "The Cherry Orchard."

MINER, JAN. Born Oct. 15, 1917 in Boston, MA. Debut 1958 OB in "Obligato," followed by "Decameron," "Dumbbell People," "Autograph Hound," "A Lovely Sunday for Creve Coeur," "The Music Keeper," "Gertrude Stein and Companion," "Dandy Dick," Bdwy in "Viva Madison Avenue" (1960), "Lady of the Camelias," "The Freaking Out of Stephanie Blake," "Othello," "The Milk Train Doesn't Stop Here Anymore," "Butterflies Are Free," "The Women," "Pajama Game," "Saturday Sunday Monday," "The Heiress," "Romeo and Juliet," "Watch on the Rhine," "Heartbreak House."

MITCHELL, BRIAN. Born Oct. 31, 1957 in Seattle, WA. Bdwy debut 1988 in "Mail" for which he received a Theatre World Award.

MITCHELL, GREGORY. Born Dec. 9, 1951 in Brooklyn, NY. Juilliard graduate. Principal with Eliot Feld Ballet before Bdwy debut 1983 in "Merlin," followed by "Song and Dance," "Phantom of the Opera," OB in "One More Song, One More Dance," "Tango Apasionado."

MOFFAT, DONALD. Born Dec. 26, 1930 in Plymouth, Eng. Attended RADA. Bdwy debut 1957 in "Under Milk Wood," followed by "Much Ado about Nothing," "The Tumbler," "Duel of Angels," "Passage to India," "The Affair," "Father's Day," "Play Memory," "The Wild Duck," "Right You Are," "You Can't Take It with You," "War and Peace," "The Cherry Orchard," "Cock-a-Doodle Dandy," "Hamlet," "The Iceman Cometh," OB in "The Bald Soprano," "Jack," "The Caretaker," "Misalliance," "Painting Churches," "Henry IV Part I."

MOGENTALE, DAVID. Born Dec. 28, 1959 in Pittsburgh, PA. Graduate Auburn U. Debut 1987 OB in "The Signal Season of Dummy Hoy."

MOHRMANN, AL. Born July 7, 1949 in Hoboken, NJ. Graduate Montclair State, UMich. Debut 1988 OB in "Circle on the Cross."

MONK, ISABELL. Born Oct. 4, 1952 in Washington, DC. Graduate TowsonStateU, Yale. Debut 1981 OB in "The Tempest," followed by "The Gospel at Colonus," "Elektra," Bdwy in "Execution of Justice" (1986).

MONTEZ, PAUL-FELIX. Born Nov. 18, 1950 in NYC. Attended Cooper Union. Debut 1968 OB in "Gloria and Esperanza," followed by "Standard Safety," "The Kitchen," "Caucasian Chalk Circle," "Full Moon," "Juba," "Slow Poison," "Brothers and Sisters," "Cowboy Mouth," "Clowns," "Faust," "Missionary Ridge," "Birds of Prey," "The White Ice Cream Suit," "The Blackman," "Iced," "Kid Twist," "First Class," Bdwy in "Gloria and Esperanza" (1968).

MONTGOMERY, ANDRE. Born May 17, 1959 in Toledo, OH. Graduate UToledo. Debut 1987 OB in "The No Frills Revue."

MOONEY, DEBRA. Born in Aberdeen SD. Graduate Auburn, UMn. Debut 1975 OB in "Battle of Angels," followed by "The Farm," "Summer and Smoke," "Stargazing," "Childe Byron," "Wonderland," "A Think Piece," "What I Did Last Summer," "The Dining Room," "The Perfect Party," "Another Antigone," Bdwy in "Chapter 2" (1978), "Talley's Folly," "The Odd Couple" (1985).

MOONEY, WILLIAM. Born in Bernie, MO. Attended UCol. Bdwy debut 1961 in "A Man for All Seasons," followed by "A Place for Polly," "Lolita," OB in "Half Horse, Half Alligator" (1966), "Strike Heaven on the Face," "Conflict of Interest," "Overnight," "The Brownsville Raid," "The Truth," "The Upper Depths," "Damn Everything But the Circus," "Manhattan Punch Line 1 Acts."

MORIN-TORRE, LORRAINE. Born in Houston, TX. Debut 1987 OB in "El Salvador."

MORRA, GENE A. Born July 16, 1935 in Rochester, NY. Graduate CCNY. Debut 1972 OB in "The Prime of Miss Jean Brodie," followed by "Men in White," "Songs from the Piano Bar," "Unemployment Line," "Blessed Event," "The Good and Faithful Servant."

MORRIS, GARY. Born Dec. 7 in Ft. Worth, TX. Debut 1984 OB in "La Boheme," followed by Bdwy in "Les Miserables" (1987).

MORRIS, KENNY. Born Nov. 4, 1954 in Brooklyn, NY. Graduate UNC/Chapel Hill. Debut 1981 OB in "Francis," followed by "She Loves Me," "Half a World Away," "Jacques Brel Is Alive and Well," Bdwy in "Joseph and the Amazing Technicolor Dreamcoat" (1983).

MORSE, PETER G. Born Oct. 9, 1958 in Hanover, NH. Graduate Dartmouth Col, UCal/San Diego. Debut 1983 OB in "That's It, Folks!," followed by "The Weekend," "The Merchant of Venice," "The Racket."

MORSE, ROBIN. Born July 8, 1963 in NYC. Bdwy debut 1981 in "Bring Back Birdie," followed by "Brighton Beach Memoirs," OB in "Green Fields," "Dec. 7th," "Class 1 Acts."

MOSTEL, JOSHUA. Born Dec. 21, 1946 in NYC. Graduate Brandeis U. Debut 1971 OB in "The Proposition," followed by "More Than You Deserve," "The Misanthrope," "Rocky Road," "The Boys Next Door," Bdwy in "Unlikely Heroes" (1971), "American Millionaire," "Texas Trilogy."

MUELLER, JULIA A. Born Apr. 16, 1961 in Ft. Dix, NJ. Graduate Dartmouth Col. Debut 1987 OB in "Come Blow Your Horn."

MUENZ, RICHARD. Born in 1948 in Hartford, CT. Attended Eastern Baptist Col. Bdwy debut 1976 in "1600 Pennsylvania Avenue," followed by "The Most Happy Fella," "Camelot," "Rosalie in Concert," "Chess."

MULLINS, MELINDA. Born Apr. 20, 1958 in Clanton, AL. Graduate Mt. Holyoke Col, Juilliard. Bdwy debut 1987 in "Sherlock's Last Case," followed by "Serious Money."

MUNDY, MEG. Born in London, Eng. Attended Inst. Musical Art. Bdwy debut 1936 in "Ten Million Ghosts," followed by "Hoorah for What," "The Fabulous Invalid," "Three to Make Ready," "How I Wonder," "The Respectful Prostitute" for which she received a Theatre World Award, "Detective Story," "Love's Labour's Lost," "Love Me a Little," "Philadelphia Story," "You Can't Take It with You," OB in "Lysistrata," "Rivers Return," "The Last Resort."

MUNGER, MARY. Born Oct. 31, 1955 in Topeka, KS. Graduate UNC/Chapel Hill. Debut 1986 OB in "Angry Housewives," followed by "Internal Combustion," "Plainsong," Bdwy in "Cabaret" (1987).

MURAKOSHI, SUZEN. Born May 20, 1958 in Honolulu, HI. Graduate UHi. Debut 1980 OB in "Shining House," followed by "Primary English Class," "Much Ado about Nothing," Bdwy in "The King and I" (1984).

MURAOKA, ALAN. Born Aug. 10, 1962 in Los Angeles, CA. Graduate UCLA. Bdwy debut 1988 in "Mail."

MURCH, ROBERT. Born Apr. 17, 1935 in Jefferson Barracks, MO. Graduate Wash.U. Bdwy debut 1966 in "Hostile Witness," followed by "The Harangues," "Conduct Unbecoming," "The Changing Room," OB in "Charles Abbot & Son," "She Stoops to Conquer," "Transcendental Love," "Julius Caesar."

MURFITT, MARY. Born Mar. 29, 1954 in Kansas City, MO. Graduate Marymount Col. Debut 1987 OB in "Oil City Symphony" for which she received a Theatre World Award.

MURRAY, BARBARA. Born Apr. 30 in Brooklyn, NY. Graduate HofstraU, DenverU. Debut 1987 OB in "Holy Ghosts."

MURRAY, LELAND. Born Nov. 13, 1929 in NYC. Attended CCNY. Debut 1988 OB in "Tamara."

MURRAY, PEG. Born in Denver, CO. Attended Western Reserve U. OB in "Children of Darkness" (1958), "A Midsummer Night's Dream," "Oh, Dad, Poor, Dad. . . .," "Small Craft Warnings," "Enclave," "Landscape of the Body," "A Lovely Sunday for Creve Couer," "Isn't It Romantic," Bdwy in "The Great Sebastians" (1956), "Gypsy," "Blood, Sweat and Stanley Poole," "She Loves Me," "Anyone Can Whistle," "The Subject Was Roses," "Something More," "Cabaret," (1966/1967) "Fiddler on the Roof," "Royal Family."

NACKMAN, DAVID. Born June 20, 1962 in NYC. Attended CornellU. Bdwy debut 1988 in "Broadway Bound."

NAHRWOLD, THOMAS. Born June 25, 1954 in Ft. Wayne, In. Attended U.S.Intl.U., AmConsTh. Bdwy debut 1982 in "84 Charing Cross Road," followed by OB "A Midsummer Night's Dream," "Bigfoot Stole My Wife," "Resistance."

NAIMO, JENNIFER. Born Oct. 2, 1962 in Oaklawn, IL. Graduate NYU. Debut 1985 OB in "Jack and Jill," followed by "Bachelor's Wife," "And the Beat Goes On," "To Whom It May Concern," "Our Lady of the Tortilla."

NASTASI, FRANK. Born Jan. 7, 1923 in Detroit, MI. Graduate WayneU, NYU. Bdwy debut 1963 in "Lorenzo," followed by "Avanti," OB in "Bonds of Interest," "One Day More," "Nathan the Wise," "The Chief Things," "Cindy," "Escurial," "The Shrinking Bride," "Macbird," "Cakes with the Wine," "Metropolitan Madness," "Rockaway Boulevard," "Scenes from La Vie de Boheme," "Agamemnon," "Happy Sunset Inc.", "3 Last Plays of O'Neill," "Taking Steam," "Lulu," "Body! Body?"

NEASE, BYRON. Born Oct. 22, 1953 in Los Angeles, CA. Attended CalStateU/Northridge. Debut 1979 OB in "Annie Get Your Gun," followed by "Lola," "Bittersuite," Bdwy in "Mame" (1983).

NEIDEN, DANIEL. Born July 9, 1958 in Lincoln, NE. Graduate DrakeU. Debut 1980 OB in "City of Life," followed by "Ratman and Wilbur," "Nuclear Follies," "Pearls," "Sophie."

NEIL, ROGER. Born Nov. 19, 1948 in Galesburg, IL. Graduate Northwestern U. Debut 1974 OB in "The Boy Friend," followed by "Scrambled Feet," "The Fantasticks," "Bittersuite-One More Time."

NELLIGAN, KATE. Born Mar. 16, 1951 in London, Can. Attended YorkU., Central School of Speech. Debut 1982 OB in "Plenty," followed by "Virginia," "Spoils of War," Bdwy in "Plenty" (1983), "Moon for the Misbegotten" (1984), "Serious Money."

NELSON, MARK. Born Sept. 26, 1955 in Hackensack, NJ. Graduate Princeton U. Debut 1977 OB in "The Dybbuk," followed by "Green Fields," "The Keymaker," "The Common Pursuit," Bdwy in "Amadeus" (1981), "Brighton Beach Memoirs," "Biloxi Blues," "Broadway Bound."

NELSON, P. J. Born Nov. 17, 1952 in NYC. Attended Manhattan School of Music. Bdwy debut 1978 in "Hello, Dolly!," followed by "The Music Man," OB in "Something for the Boys," "New Girl in Town," "Company."

NEUBERGER, JAN. Born Jan. 21, 1953 in Amityville, NY. Attended NYU. Bdwy debut 1975 in "Gypsy," OB in "Silk Stockings," "Chase a Rainbow," "Anything Goes," "A Little Madness," "Forbidden Broadway," "After These Messages."

NEWMAN, ANDREW HILL. Born Oct. 23, 1959 in Scarsdale, NY. Graduate UVt., Brandeis U. Bdwy debut 1982 in "Merlin," followed by "Big River," OB in "Little Shop of Horrors," "Bird of Paradise."

NEWTON, JOHN. Born Nov. 2, 1925 in Grand Junction, CO. Graduate UWash. Debut 1951 OB in "Othello," followed by "As You Like It," "Candida," "Candaules Commissioner," "Sextet," LCRep's "The Crucible" and "A Streetcar Named Desire," "The Rivals," "The Subject Was Roses," "The Brass Ring," "Hadrian VII," "The Best Little Whorehouse in Texas," "A Midsummer Night's Dream," "Night Games," "A Frog in His Throat," Bdwy in "Weekend," "First Monday in October," "Present Laughter."

NICOLAISEN, KARI. Born Feb. 16, 1961 in San Francisco, Ca. Debut 1987 OB in "Wish You Were Here," followed by "Something for the Boys," Bdwy in "A Chorus Line" (1987).

NIKKO, MATT. Born July 8, 1959 in Elmer, NJ. Graduate WestchesterU. Debut 1983 OB in "Teahouse," followed by "Bentley's War," "Tender Offer," "Zero," "Sparts and His Desire," "Broadcast News," "Wedding of the Siamese Twins."

NIVEN, KIP. Born May 27, 1945 in Kansas City, MO. Graduate KanU. Debut 1987 OB in "Company," followed by Bdwy in "Chess" (1988).

NIXON, CYNTHIA. Born Apr. 9, 1966 in NYC. Debut 1980 in "The Philadelphia Story"(LC) for which she received a Theatre World Award, OB in "Lydie Breeze," "Hurlyburly," "Sally's Gone, She Left Her Name," "Lemon Sky," "Cleveland and Half-Way Back," "Alterations." "Young Playwrights," "Moonchildren," "Romeo and Juliet." Bdwy in "The Real Thing" (1983), "Hurlyburly."

NOONAN, TOM. Born Apr. 12, 1951 in Greenwich, CT. Graduate Yale U. Debut 1978 OB in "Buried Child," followed by "The Invitational," "Farmyard," "The Breakers," "Five of Us," "Spookhouse," "Marathon '88."

NORCIA, PATRIZIA. Born Apr. 6, 1954 in Rome, Italy. Graduate Hofstra U., Yale. Debut 1978 OB in "Sganarelle," followed by "The Master and Margarita," "The Loves of Cass McGuire," "Fanshen," "The Price of Genius," "The Taming of the Shrew," "Epic Proportions," "Oklahoma Samivar."

NORMAN, DARA. Born Aug. 8 in NYC. Attended UCin., UMiami. Bdwy debut 1975 in "The Magic Show," followed by "Oh! Calcutta!," OB in "Dr. Selavy's Magic Theatre," "Beggar's Opera," "The Boys in the Live Country Band," "Talking Dirty," "Between Time and Timbuktu."

NORMAN, JOHN. Born May 13, 1961 in Detroit, Mi. Graduate Cincinnati Conservatory. Bdwy debut 1987 in "Les Miserables."

NORRIS, BRUCE. Born May 16, 1960 in Houston, TX. Graduate NorthwesternU. Bdwy debut 1985 in "Biloxi Blues," followed by OB's "A Midsummer Night's Dream," "Wenceslas Square," "The Debutante Ball."

NOTO, LORE. Born June 9, 1923 in NYC. Attended AADA. Debut 1940 OB in "The Master Builder," followed by "Chee Chee," "Time Predicted," "Bomb Shelter," "Armor of Light," "Truce of the Bear," "Shake Hands with the Devil," "The Italian Straw Hat," "The Failures," "The Fantasticks" (continuously since 1972).

NOZICK, BRUCE. Born Jan. 29, 1960 in Winchester, MA. Graduate NYU. Debut 1982 OB in "Romeo and Juliet," followed by "And That's How the Rent Gets Paid," "Too Ugly for L.A.," "Sundance," "A Shayna Maidel."

NUGENT, JAMES. Born June 22, 1940 in The Bronx, NY. Graduate UFla. Debut 1984 OB in "Air Rights," followed by "The Merchant of Venice," "Arms and the Man," "Mme. Colombe," "Two Gentlemen of Verona," "Days to Come," "The Good Doctor," "Pericles," "The Rivals," "Lady from the Sea," "Deep Swimmer," "Macbeth," "The Imaginary Invalid," "Uncle Vanya."

NURIDDIN, MUNIR. Born July 28, 1957 in Brooklyn, NY. Attended NYCC. Debut 1987 in "Death and the King's Horseman" (LC), followed by OB's "Kismet."

NUSSBAUM, MIKE. Born Dec. 29, 1923 in Chicago, Il. Attended UWisc. Bdwy debut 1984 in "Glengarry Glen Ross," followed by "House of Blue Leaves," OB in "The Shawl," "Principia Scriptoriae," "Marathon '86," "Little Murders," "The Cherry Orchard."

NUTE, DON. Born Mar. 13, in Connellsville, PA. Attended Denver U. Debut OB 1965 in "The Trojan Women" followed by "Boys in the Band," "Mad Theatre for Madmen," "The Eleventh Dynasty," "About Time," "The Urban Crisis," "Christmas Rappings," "The Life of a Man," "A Look at the Fifties," "Aunt Millie."

O'BRIEN, DALE. Born Oct. 7, 1957 in Omaha, NB. Graduate Kearney State Col, UArk. Debut 1986 in "Rainbow," followed by "Mixed Doubles," "The Fantasticks."

O'HARE, TIM. Born Dec. 2, 1956 in Montclair, NJ. Graduate UMd. Debut 1981 OB in "Couples," followed by "Shadow of a Gunman," "Moonie's Kid Don't Cry," "Cain," "Troilus and Cressida," "Richard III," "Macbeth."

O'KEEFE, MICHAEL. Born Apr. 24, 1955 in Westchester, NY. Attended NYU. Debut 1974 OB in "The Killdeer," followed by "Christmas on Mars," "Short Eyes," "Uncle Vanya," "Phaedra," Bdwy in "5th of July," "Mass Appeal" for which he received a Theatre World Award.

O'KELLY, AIDEEN. Born in Dalkey, Ire. Member of Dublin's Abbey Theatre. Bdwy debut 1980 in "A Life," followed by "Othello," OB in "The Killing of Sister George" (1983), "Man Enough," "Resistance."

O'REILLY, CIARAN. Born Mar. 13, 1959 in Ireland. Attended Carmelite Col., Juilliard. Debut 1978 OB in "Playboy of the Western World," followed by "Summer," "Freedom of the City," "Fannie," "The Interrogation of Ambrose Fogarty," "King Lear," "Shadow of a Gunman," "The Marry Month of May," Bdwy in "The Corn Is Green" (1983).

O'ROURKE, KEVIN. Born Jan. 25, 1956 in Portland, OR. Graduate Williams Col. Debut 1981 OB in "Declassee," followed by "Sister Mary Ignatius . . .," "Submariners," "A Midsummer Night's Dream," "Visions of Kerouac," "Self Defense," "Spoils of War," Bdwy in "Alone Together" (1984).

O'SHEA, MILO. Born June 2, 1926 in Dublin, Ire. Bdwy debut 1968 in "Staircase," followed by "Dear World," "Mrs. Warren's Profession," "Comedians," "A Touch of the Poet," "Mass Appeal," "Corpse," OB in "Waiting for Godot," "Mass Appeal," "The Return of Herbert Bracewell," "Educating Rita," "Romeo and Juliet."

O'STEEN, MICHELLE. Born May 7, 1964 in Pittsburgh, PA. Bdwy debut 1986 in "Sweet Charity."

O'SULLIVAN, BRIAN. Born Dec. 11, 1958 in Jackson, MI. Graduate MiState,UMi. Debut 1987 OB in "Mud," followed by "All's Well That Ends Well," "The Tempest," "The Elephant Man."

OAKES, ALICE ANNE. Born Aug. 30, 1956 in Edison, NJ. Graduate Butler U. Bdwy debut 1981 in "Broadway Follies," followed by "Anything Goes."

OAKES, CINDY. Born Mar. 25, 1959 in Homestead, Pa. Graduate UPittsburgh. Bdwy debut 1986 in "Me and My Girl," followed by "Smile."

ODO, CHRIS: Born Feb. 7, 1954 in Kansas City, MO. Attended SWMoStateU. Debut 1984 OB in "A Midsummer Night's Dream," followed by "Oedipus," "Sleepless City," "Summer Face Woman," Bdwy in "M. Butterfly" 1988).

ORBACH, RON. Born Mar. 23, 1952 in Newark, NJ. Graduate Rider Col. Debut 1985 OB in "Lies and Legends," followed by "Philistines," "The Skin of Our Teeth," "Mrs. Dally Has a Lover."

ORMAN, ROSCOE. Born June 11, 1944 in NYC. Debut 1962 OB in "If We Grow Up," followed

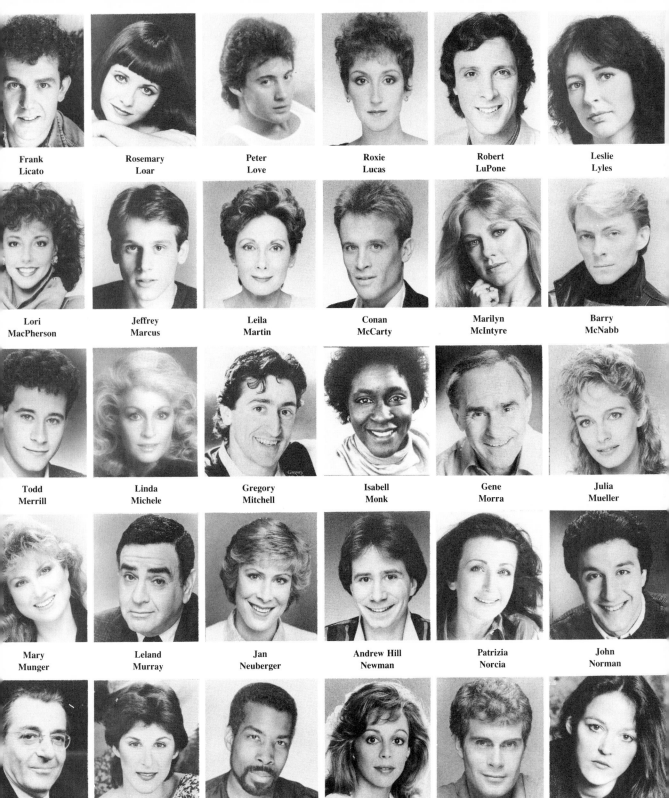

Frank Licato	Rosemary Loar	Peter Love	Roxie Lucas	Robert LuPone	Leslie Lyles
Lori MacPherson	Jeffrey Marcus	Leila Martin	Conan McCarty	Marilyn McIntyre	Barry McNabb
Todd Merrill	Linda Michele	Gregory Mitchell	Isabell Monk	Gene Morra	Julia Mueller
Mary Munger	Leland Murray	Jan Neuberger	Andrew Hill Newman	Patrizia Norcia	John Norman
Lore Noto	Dara Norman	Munir Nuriddin	Alice Anne Oakes	Don Nute	Park Overall

215

by "Electronic Nigger," "The Great McDaddy," "The Sirens," "Every Night When the Sun Goes Down," "The Last Street Play," "Julius Caesar," "Coriolanus," "The 16th Round," "20 Year Friends," Bdwy in "Fences" (1988).

OSBURN, ALAN. Born Nov. 18, 1956 in Tulsa, OK. Graduate Grand Canyon Col, UHouston. Debut 1988 OB in "Side by Side by Sondheim," followed by "The Wonder Years."

OVERALL, PARK. Born Mar. 15, 1957 in Nashville, TN. Graduate Tusculum Col. Bdwy debut 1986 in "Biloxi Blues," followed by OB's "The Skin of Our Teeth," "Wild Blue," "Only You," "Loose Ends," "Marathon '88."

OVERMIRE, LAURENCE. Born Aug. 17, 1957 in Rochester, NY. Graduate Muskingum Col., UMn. Debut 1982 OB in "Don Juan," followed by "Summit Conference," "Psycho Beach Party," Bdwy in "Amadeus."

OVERTON, ZACHARIAH. Born July 12, 1976 in West Islip, NY. Bdwy debut 1987 in "The Nerd," followed by OB's "Responsible for Dates," "Washington Heights."

OWENS, ELIZABETH. Born Feb. 26, 1938 in NYC. Attended New School, Neighborhood Playhouse. Debut 1955 OB in "Dr. Faustus Lights the Lights," followed by "Chit Chat on a Rat," "The Miser," "The Father", "The Importance of Being Earnest," "Candida," "Trumpets and Drums," "Oedipus," "Macbeth," "Uncle Vanya," "Misalliance," "The Play's the Thing," "The Rivals," "Death Story," "The Rehearsal," "Dance on a Country Grave," "Othello," "Little Eyolf," "The Winslow Boy," "Playing with Fire," "The Chalk Garden," "The Entertainer," "The Killing of Sister George," "Waltz of the Toreadors," "The Miracle Worker," "Johnstown Vindicator," Bdwy in "The Lovers," "Not Now Darling," "The Play's the Thing."

OWENS, GEOFFREY. Born Mar. 18, 1961 in Brooklyn, NY. Yale graduate. Debut 1985 OB in "The Man Who Killed the Buddha," followed by "A Midsummer Night's Dream," "Richard II."

PACINO, AL. Born Apr. 25, 1940 in NYC. Attended Actors Studio. Bdwy debut 1969 in "Does a Tiger Wear a Necktie?" for which he received a Theatre World Award, followed by "The Basic Training of Pavlo Hummel," "Richard III," "American Buffalo," OB in "Why Is a Crooked Letter," "Peace Creeps," "The Indian Wants the Bronx," "Local Stigmatic," "Camino Real," "Jungle of Cities," "American Buffalo," "Julius Caesar."

PADDISON, GORDON. Born Jan. 26, 1955 in Washington, DC. Debut 1984 OB in "Blue Plate Special," followed by "Ballad of Conrad and Loretta," "Sout Up a Mornin'," "Beautiful Lady," "Cotton Patch Gospel," "Twelfth Night," "Bent," "Loos Ends," "Bosoms and Neglect," "Rocky Horror Show," "A Midsummer Night's Dream," Bdwy in "Macbeth" (1988).

PAGAN, PETER. Born July 24, 1921 in Sydney, Australia. Attended Scots Col. Bdwy debut 1953 in "Escapade," followed by "Portrait of a Lady," "The Dark Is Light Enough," "Child of Fortune," "Hostile Witness," "Aren't We All?," OB in "Busybody," "M. Amilcar."

PAIS, JOSH. Born June 21, 1958 in Princeton, NJ. Graduate Syracuse U., LAMDA. Debut 1985 OB in "Short Change," followed by "I'm Not Rappaport," "The Lower Depths," "The Survivor," "Untitled Play," Bdwy in "I'm Not Rapport" (1987).

PAISNER, DINA. Born in Brooklyn, NY. OB in "The Cretan Woman," "Pullman Car Hiawatha," "Lysistrata," "If 5 Years Pass," "Troubled Waters," "Sap of Life," "Cave at Machpelah," "Threepenny Opera," "Montserrat," "Gandhi," "Blood Wedding," "The Trial of Dr. Beck," "Amidst the Gladiolas," "The Long Valley," "A Slight Ache," "Veronica's Room," "Ivanov," Bdwy in "Andorra" (1963), "Medea" (1973).

PALANCE, BROOKE. Born Feb. 7, 1954 in NYC. Attended CalInst of Arts. Debut 1986 OB in "The Fox," followed by "Bedroom Farce," "Between Daylight and Booneville."

PARKER, ELLEN. Born Sept. 30, 1949 in Paris, Fr. Graduate BardCol. Debut 1971 OB in "James Joyce Liquid Theatre," followed by "Uncommon Women and Others," "Dusa, Fish, Stas and Vi," "A Day in the Life of the Czar," "Fen," "Isn't It Romantic," "The Winter's Tale," "Aunt Dan and Lemon," "Cold Sweat," Bdwy in "Equus," "Strangers," "Plenty."

PARKER, HERBERT MARK. Born Dec. 2, 1954 in Louisville, KY. Graduate Stephens Col, OhioU. Debut 1984 OB in "Bells Are Ringing," followed by "Much Ado about Nothing."

PARLATO, DENNIS. Born Mar. 30, 1947 in Los Angeles, Ca. Graduate Loyola U. Bdwy debut 1979 in "A Chorus Line," followed by "The First," "Chess," OB in "Beckett," "Elizabeth and Essex," "The Fantasticks," "Moby Dick," "The Knife," "Shylock," "Have I Got A Girl for You," "Romance! Romance!

PARRY, NATASHA. Born Dec. 2, 1930 in London, Eng. Attended Arts Educational School. Bdwy debut 1959 in "The Fighting Cock," followed by OB appearances in "Conference of Birds," "The Cherry Orchard" (1988).

PATTERSON, JAY. Born Aug. 22 in Cincinnati, OH. Attended OhioU. Bdwy debut 1983 in "K-2," followed by OB's "Caligula," "The Mound Builders," "Quiet in the Land," "Of Mice and Men," "Domino."

PATTISON, LIANN. Born Apr. 12, 1957 in Chico, CA. Attended CalStateU/Chico, UWash. Debut 1985 OB in "I'm Not Rappaport, followed by Bdwy in "Serious Money" (1988).

PATTON, LUCILLE. Born in NYC; attended Neighborhood Playhouse. Bdwy debut 1946 in "A Winter's Tale," followed by "Topaze," "Arms and the Man," "Joy to the World," "All You Need Is One Good Break," "Fifth Season," "Heavenly Twins," "Rhinoceros," "Marathon 33," "The Last Analysis," "Dinner at 8," "La Strada," "Unlikely Heroes," "Love Suicide at Schofield Barracks," OB in "Ulysses in Nighttown," "Failures," "Three Sisters," "Yes Yes No No," "Tango," "Mme. de Sade," "Apple Pie," "Follies," "Yesterday Is Over," "My Prince, My King," "I Am Who I Am," "Double Game," "Love in a Village," "1984," "A Little Night Music."

PAUL, ADRIAN. Born May 29, 1959 in London, Eng. Attended Bromley Theatrical Playhouse. NYC debut 1987 OB in "Bouncers."

PAWK, MICHELE. Born Nov. 16, 1961 in Pittsburgh, PA. Graduate CincinnatiConsv. Bdwy debut 1988 in "Mail."

PAYNTER, LYNN. Born May 8, 1962 in Jeffersonville, IN. Graduate Stephens Col. Debut 1987 OB in "No Frills Revue."

PAYTON-WRIGHT, PAMELA. Born Nov. 1, 1941 in Pittsburgh, PA. Graduate Birmingham Southern Col, RADA. Bdwy debut 1967 in "The Show-Off," followed by "Exit the King," "The Cherry Orchard," "Jimmy Shine," "Mourning Becomes Electra," "The Glass Menagerie," "Romeo and Juliet," "Night of the Iguana," OB in "The Effect of Marigolds on. . . .," "The Crucible," "The Seagull," "Don Juan," "In the Garden."

PEACOCK, CHIARA. Born Sept. 19, 1962 in Ann Arbor, Mi. Graduate Sarah Lawrence Col. Debut 1985 OB in "Yours, Anne," followed by "Maggie Magalita," "One Step at a Time," "Octoberfest '87," "A Shayna Maidel."

PEARLMAN, STEPHEN. Born Feb. 26, 1935 in NYC. Graduate Dartmouth Col. Bdwy bow 1964 in "Barefoot in the Park," followed by "La Strada," OB in "Threepenny Opera," "Time of the Key," "Pimpernel," "In White America," "Viet Rock," "Chocolates," "Bloomers," "Richie," "Isn't It Romantic," "Bloodletters," "Light Up the Sky," "The Perfect Party," "Come Blow Your Horn," "A Shayna Maidel."

PEARSON, SCOTT. Born Dec. 13, 1941 in Milwaukee, WI. Attended Valparaiso U, UWisc. Bdwy debut 1966 in "A Joyful Noise," followed by "Promises, Promises," "A Chorus Line."

PENDLETON, AUSTIN. Born Mar. 27, 1940 in Warren, Oh. Attended Yale U. Debut 1962 OB in "Oh, Dad, Poor Dad . . .," followed by "The Last Sweet Days of Isaac," "The Three Sisters," "Say Goodnight, Gracie," "The Office Murders," "Up from Paradise," "The Overcoat," "Two Character Play," "Master Class," "Educating Rita," "Uncle Vanya," Bdwy in "Fiddler on the Roof," "Hail Scrawdyke," "The Little Foxes," "American Millionaire," "The Runner Stumbles," "Doubles."

PENDLETON, WYMAN. Born Apr. 18, 1916 in Providence, RI. Graduate Brown U. Bdwy debut in "Tiny Alice" (1964), followed by "Malcolm," "Quotations from Chairman Mao Tse-Tung," "Happy Days," "Henry V," "Othello," "There's One in Every Marriage," "Cat on a Hot Tin Roof," "Scenes and Revelations," OB in "Gallows Humor," "American Dream," "Zoo Story," "Corruption in the Palace of Justice," "Giant's Dance," "Child Buyer," "Happy Days," "Butter and Egg Man," "Othello," "Albee Directs Albee," "Dance for Me, Simeon," "Mary Stuart," "The Collyer Brothers," "Period Piece," "A Bold Stroke for a Wife," "Hitch-Hikers," "Waltz of the Toreadors," "Time of the Cuckoo," "Stopping the Desert."

PENNINGTON, GAIL. Born Oct. 2, 1957 in Kansas City, MO. Graduate SMU. Bdwy debut 1980 in "The Music Man," followed by "Can-Can," "America," "Little Me" (1982), "42nd Street," OB in "The Baker's Wife."

PERCASSI, DON. Born Jan. 11 in Amsterdam, NY. Bdwy debut 1964 in "High Spirits," followed by "Walking Happy," "Coco," "Sugar," "Molly," "Mack and Mabel," "A Chorus Line," "42nd Street."

PEREZ, LUIS. Born July 28, 1959 in Atlanta, Ga. With Joffrey Ballet before 1986 debut in "Brigadoon" (LC), followed by "Phantom of the Opera," OB in "The Wonderful Ice Cream Suit," "Tango Apasionada."

PEREZ, MERCEDES. Born Oct. 25, 1961 in Arlington, Va. Debut 1983 OB in "Skyline," followed by Bdwy in "Take Me Along" (1985), "A Chorus Line."

PERKINS, RON. Born Dec. 11, 1949 in Jeffersonville, IN. Graduate IndU, Neighborhood Playhouse. Debut 1978 OB in "The Devil's Disciple," followed by "Bruce Lee Is Dead and I'm Not Feeling Too Good Either," "Of Mice and Men."

PERRI, PAUL. Born Nov. 6, 1953 in New Haven, CT. Attended Elmira Col, UMe, Juilliard. Debut 1979 OB in "Say Goodnight, Gracie," followed by "Henry VI," "Agamemnon," "Julius Caesar," "Waiting for Godot," "Home," "Aunt Dan and Lemon," Bdwy in "Bacchae," "Macbeth," "A View from the Bridge," "Burn This."

PESATURO, GEORGE. Born July 29, 1949 in Winthrop, MA. Graduate Manhattan Col. Bdwy debut 1976 in "A Chorus Line," OB in "The Music Man" (JB).

PETERS, BERNADETTE. Born Feb. 28, 1948 in Jamaica, NY. Bdwy debut in "Girl in the Freudian Slip," followed by "Johnny No-Trump," "George M!" for which she received a Theatre World Award, "La Strada," "On the Town," "Mack and Mabel," "Sunday in the Park with George," "Song and Dance," "Into the Woods," OB in "Curley McDimple," "Penny Friend," "Most Happy Fella," "Dames at Sea," "Nevertheless They Laugh," "Sally and Marsha."

PETERS, MARK. Born Nov. 20, 1952 in Council Bluffs, IA. Yale graduate. Debut 1977 OB in "The Crazy Locomotive," followed by "The Legend of Sleepy Hollow," "Kismet."

PETERSON, KURT. Born Feb. 12, 1948 in Stevens Point, Wi. Attended AMDA. Bdwy debut 1969 in "Dear World," followed by "Follies," "Knickerbocker Holiday," OB in "An Ordinary Miracle," "West Side Story" (LC), "Dames at Sea," "By Bernstein," "I Married an Angel in Concert," "Alias Jimmy Valentine."

PETERSON, PATRICIA BEN. Born Sept. 11 in Portland, OR. Graduate Pacific Lutheran U. Debut 1985 OB in "Kuni Leml," followed by "The Chosen," "The Grand Tour."

PETTIT, DODIE. Born Dec. 29 in Princeton, NJ. Attended Westminster Choir Col. Bdwy debut 1984 in "Cats," followed by "The Phantom of the Opera."

PHELPS, GREG. Born Apr. 13, 1959 in Owensboro, KY. Graduate WKyU, CincinnatiConsv. Debut 1988 OB in "No, No, Nanette."

PHELPS, TRACEY. Born Mar. 10, 1935 in Brooklyn, NY. Attended NYU. Debut 1961 OB in "Shadow of Heroes," followed by "Funny Girl," "Tomorrow's Broadway," "Counter Service."

PHILIPSON, ADAM. Born Oct. 10, 1966. Attended NYU. Debut 1987 OB in "Show Me a Hero," followed by "Holy Heist," "Buskers," "Final Passages," Bdwy in "Broadway Bound" (1987).

PHILLIPS, ETHAN. Born Feb. 8, 1950 in Rockville Center, NY. Graduate BostonU, CornellU. Debut 1979 OB in Modigliani," followed by Eccentricities of a Nightingale," "Nature and Purpose of the Universe," "The Beasts," "The Dumb Waiter," "The Indian Wants the Bronx," "The Last of the Red Hot Lovers."

PHILLIPS, LACY DARRYL. Born Feb. 24, 1963 in NYC. Attended Lehman Col. Debut 1981 OB in "Raisin," followed by "The Late Great Ladies," Bdwy in "Anything Goes" (1987).

PICARD, NICOLE. Born Oct. 19, 1960 in Rhode Island. Graduate Sarah Lawrence Col. Debut 1984 OB in "A View from the Bridge," followed by "Cry of Angels," Bdwy in "Starlight Express" (1987).

PICCIANO, ANTHONY. Born Aug. 13, 1946 in NYC. Attended Hunter Col. Debut 1978 OB in "Hamlet," followed by "Macbeth," "King Lear," "Henry IV," "Dylan," "Show Boat," "Damn Yankees," "Boom Boom Room," "Sweet Bird of Youth," "Woycezk," "Richard II," "Spoils of War."

PIERCE, DAVID. Born Apr. 3, 1959 in Albany, NY. Graduate Yale U. Debut 1982 on Bdwy in "Beyond Therapy," followed by OB in "Summer," "That's It, Folks!," "The Three Zeks," "Donuts," "Hamlet," "The Maderati," "Marathon 87," "The Cherry Orchard," "Zero Positive."

PIERCE, VERNA. Born in New Jersey. Attended UKan, AADA. Bdwy debut 1974 in "A Little Night Music," followed by "Pippin," OB in "Fiorello!," "The Elephant Man."

PIETROPINTO, ANGELA. Born Feb. 5, in NYC. Graduate NYU. OB credits include "Henry IV," "Alice in Wonderland," "Endgame," "Our Late Night," "The Sea Gull," "Jinx Bridge," "The Mandrake," "Marie and Bruce," "Green Card Blues," "3 by Pirandello," "The Broken Pitcher," "A

Midsummer Night's Dream," "The Rivals," "Cap and Bells," "Thrombo," "Lies My Father Told Me," "Twelfth Night," "Romeo and Juliet," Bdwy in "The Suicide" (1980).

PINCUS, WARREN. Born Apr. 13, 1938 in Brooklyn, NY Attended CCNY. OB in "Miss Nefertiti Regrets," "Circus," "Magician," "Boxcars," "Demented World," "In the Time of Harry Harrass," "Yoshe Kolb," "After Crystal Night," Bdwy in "Zalmen, or the Madness of God," "Gemini," "The Inspector General."

PIRKL, KATHLEEN. Born Nov. 6, 1961 in Racine, WI. Graduate NCSchArts. Debut 1986 OB in "Please Wait for the Beep," "The Age of Pie," "The Elephant Man."

PITONIAK, ANNE. Born Mar. 30, 1922 in Westfield, MA. Attended UNC Women's Col. Debut 1982 OB in "Talking With," followed by "Young Playwrights Festival," "Phaedra," "Steel Magnolias," Bdwy in "'night, Mother" (1983) for which she received a Theatre World Award, "The Octette Bridge Club."

PLANK, SCOTT. Born Nov. 11, 1958 in Washington, DC. Attended NCSch of Arts. Bdwy debut 1981 in "Dreamgirls," followed by "A Chorus Line," OB in "Death of a Buick."

PLAYTEN, ALICE. Born Aug. 28, 1947 in NYC. Attended NYU. Bdwy debut 1960 in "Gypsy" followed by "Oliver," "Hello, Dolly!," "Henry Sweet Henry," for which she received a Theatre World Award, "George M!," OB in "Promenade," "The Last Sweet Days of Isaac," "National Lampoon's Lemmings," "Valentine's Day," "Pirates of Penzance," "Up from Paradise," "A Visit," "Sister Mary Ignatius Explains It All," "An Actor's Nightmare," "That's It, Folks," "1-2-3-4-5," "Spoils of War."

PLUMMER, AMANDA. Born Mar. 23, 1957 in NYC. Attended Middlebury Col., Neighborhood Playhouse. Debut 1978 OB in "Artichoke," followed by "A Month in the Country," "A Taste of Honey" for which she received a Theatre World Award, "Alice in Concert," "A Stitch in Time," "Life under Water," "A Lie of the Mind," "The Milk Train Doesn't Stop Here Anymore," Bdwy in "A Taste of Honey," "Agnes of God," "The Glass Menagerie," "You Never Can Tell," "Pygmalion" (1987).

PLUMMER, CHRISTOPHER. Born Dec. 13, 1929 in Toronto, Can. Bdwy debut 1954 in "Starcross Story," followed by "Home Is the Hero," "The Dark Is Light Enough" for which he received a Theatre World Award, "Medea," "The Lark," "Night of the Auk," "J. B.," "Arturo Ui," "Royal Hunt of the Sun," "Cyrano," "The Good Doctor," "Othello," "Macbeth" (1988), OB in "Drinks before Dinner" (1978).

PLUNKETT, MARYANN. Born In 1953 in Lowell, Ma. Attended UNH. Bdwy debut 1983 in "Agnes of God," followed by "Sunday in the Park with George," "Me and My Girl."

POE, RICHARD. Born Jan. 25, 1946 In Portola, Ca. Graduate USanFrancisco, UCal/Davis. Debut 1971 OB in "Hamlet," followed by "Seasons Greetings," "Twelfth Night," Bdwy in "Broadway" (1987), "M. Butterfly."

POLETICK, ROBERT. Born Feb. 28 in Brooklyn, NY. Debut 1988 OB in "Brotherhood," followed by "Beyond the Horizon," "Hamlet," "Holding Out."

PORTER, ADINA. Born Feb. 18, 1963 in NYC. Attended SUNY/Purchase. Debut 1988 OB in "The Debutante Ball," followed by "Inside Out," "Tiny Mommie," "Footsteps in the Rain."

POTTER, DON. Born Aug. 15, 1932 in Philadelphia, Pa. Debut 1961 OB in "What a Killing," followed by "Sunset," "You're a Good Man, Charlie Brown," "One Cent Plain," "The Ritz," Bdwy in "Gypsy" (1974), "Snow White," "Moose Murders," "42nd Street."

PRESTON, LAWRENCE. Born Jan. 24, 1963 in North Miami, FL. Graduate NYU. Debut 1986 OB in "The Private Ear."

PRESTON, WILLIAM. Born Aug. 26, 1921 in Columbia, PA. Graduate PaStateU. Debut 1972 OB in "We Bombed in New Haven," followed by "Hedda Gabler," "Whisper into My Good Ear," "A Nestless Bird," "Friends of Mine," "Iphigenia in Aulis," "Midsummer," "The Fantasticks," "Frozen Assets," "The Golem," "The Taming of the Shrew."

PRICE, LONNY. Born Mar. 9, 1959 in NYC. Attended Juilliard. Debut 1979 OB in "Class Enemy" for which he received a Theatre World Award, followed by "Up from Paradise," "Rommel's Garden," "Times and Appetites of Toulouse-Lautrec," "Room Service," "Come Blow Your Horn," Bdwy 1980 in "The Survivor," followed by "Merrily We Roll Along," "Master Harold and the boys," "The Time of Your Life," "Children of the Sun," "Rags," "Broadway," "Burn This."

PRUD'HOMME, JUNE. Born June 8 in San Francisco, CA. Attended SFJrCol, AADA. Bdwy debut 1953 in "Richard II," followed by "Halfway Up the Tree," "Henry V," OB in "Blood Wedding," "Church Street," "Bruno and Sidney," "Sugar and Spice," "Scarcrow Richard," "The Potting Shed," "Philistines."

PSAKI, JENNY. Born June 2, 1964 in Philadelphia, PA. Graduate NYU. Debut 1987 OB in "1984."

PUGH, RICHARD WARREN. Born Oct. 20, 1950 in NYC. Graduate Tarkio Col. Bdwy debut 1979 in "Sweeney Todd," followed by "The Music Man," "The Five O'Clock Girl," "Copperfield," "Zorba" (1983), "Phantom of the Opera," OB in "Chase a Rainbow."

PURSLEY, DAVID. Born July 13, 1938 in Lewisburg, PA. Graduate HarvardU, BaylorU. Debut 1969 OB in "Peace," followed by "The Faggott," "Wings," "The Three Musketeers," Bdwy in "Happy End" (1977), "Snow White," "Anything Goes."

QUINN, AIDAN. Born Mar. 8, 1959 in Chicago, IL. Debut 1984 OB in "Fool for Love," followed by "A Lie of the Mind," Bdwy in "A Streetcar Named Desire" (1988) for which he received a Theatre World Award.

QUINN, BRIAN. Born Aug. 12, 1955 in Chicago, IL. Graduate PurdueU. Bdwy debut 1981 in "Copperfield," followed by "Little Me," "Peg," OB in "Give My Regards to Broadway" (1987).

RAEBECK, LOIS. Born in West Chicago, Il. Graduate Columbia U. Debut 1986 OB in "Rule of Three," followed by "Cork," "Between Time and Timbuktu," "The Women in the Family."

RAIDER-WEXLER, VICTOR. Born Dec. 31, 1943 in Toledo, Oh. Attended UToledo. Debut 1976 OB in "The Prince of Homburg," followed by "The Passion of Dracula," "Ivanov," "Brandy before Breakfast," "The Country Girl," "Dream of a Blacklisted Actor," "One Act Festival," "Loveplay," "Our Own Family," "The Boys Next Door," Bdwy in "Best Friend" (1976), "Ma Rainey's Black Bottom."

RAINES, RON. Born Dec. 2, 1949 in Texas City, TX. Graduate OkCityU, Juilliard. Bdwy debut 1983 in "Show Boat," followed by "Teddy and Alice," OB in "Olympus on My Mind" (1986), "A Little Night Music" (1988).

RAINEY, DAVID. Born Jan. 30, 1960 in Tucson, AZ. Graduate ENMexU, Juilliard. Debut 1987 OB in "Richard II," followed by "Henry IV Part I," "Julius Caesar."

RAITT, JOHN. Born Jan. 29, 1917 in Santa Ana, CA. Graduate RedlandsU. Bdwy debut 1945 in "Carousel" for which he received a Theatre World Award, followed by "Magdalena," "Three Wishes for Jamie," "Pajama Game," "A Joyful Noise," "On a Clear Day You Can See Forever," "Musical Jubilee," OB in "Magdalena in Concert" (1987).

RAMSAY, REMAK. Born Feb. 2, 1937 in Baltimore, MD. Graduate Princeton U. Debut 1964 OB in "Hang Down Your Head and Die," followed by "The Real Inspector Hound," "Landscape of the Body," "All's Well That Ends Well," "Rear Column," "The Winslow Boy," "The Dining Room," "Pygmalion in Concert," "Save Grand Central," "Quartermaine's Terms," "Woman in Mind," Bdwy in "Half a Sixpence," "Sheep on the Runway," "Lovely Ladies, Kind Gentlemen," "On the Town," "Jumpers," "Private Lives," "Dirty Linen," "Every Good Boy Deserves Favor."

RANDEL, MELISSA. Born June 16, 1955 in Portland, ME. Graduate UCal/Irvine. Bdwy debut 1980 in "A Chorus Line."

RANDELL, RON. Born Oct. 8, 1920 in Sydney, Aust. Attended St. Mary's Col. Bdwy debut 1949 in "The Browning Version," followed by "Harlequinade," "Candida," "World of Suzie Wong," "Sherlock Holmes," "Mrs. Warren's Profession," "Measure for Measure," "Bent," "The Troll Palace," OB in "Holy Places," "After You've Gone," "Patrick Pearse Motel," "Maneuvers," "Swan Song," "A Man for All Season," "Rosencrantz and Guildenstern Are Dead," "M. Amilcar."

RANDOLPH, JOHN. Born June 1, 1915 in The Bronx, NY. Attended CCNY, Actors Studio. Bdwy debut 1937 in "Revolt of the Beavers," followed by "The Emperor's New Clothes," "Capt. Jinks," "No More Peace," "Coriolanus," "Medicine Show," "Hold on to Your Hats," "Native Son," "Command Decision," "Come Back, Little Sheba," "Golden State," "Peer Gynt," "Paint Your Wagon," "Seagulls over Sorrento," "Grey-Eyed People," "Room Service," "All Summer Long," "House of Flowers," "The Visit," "Mother Courage," "Sound of Music," "Case of Libel," "Conversation at Midnight," "My Sweet Charlie," "The American Clock," "Broadway Bound," OB in "An Evening's Frost," "The Peddler and the Dodo Bird," "Our Town," "Line," "Baba Goya," "Nourish the Beast," "Back in the Race," "The American Clock."

RASCHE, DAVID Born Aug. 7, 1944 in St. Louis, MO. Graduate Elmhutst Col., UChicago. Debut 1976 OB in "John," followed by "Snow White," "Isadora Duncan Sleeps with the Russian Navy," "End of the War," "A Sermon," "Routed," "Geniuses," "Dolphin Position," "Gillian on Her 37th Birthday," "Custom of the Country," Bdwy in "Shadow Box" (1977), "Loose Ends," "Lunch Hour," "Speed-the-Plow."

RASHOVICH, GORDANA. Born Sept. 18 in Chicago, Il. Graduate Roosevelt U., RADA. Debut 1977 OB in "Fefu and Her Friends" for which she received a Theatre World Award, followed by "Selma," "Couple of the Year," "Mink Sonata."

RATHGEB, LAURA. Born Sept. 5, 1962 in Burlington, VT. Graduate St. Michael's Col. Debut 1987 OB in "deep Swimmer," followed by "The Imaginary Invalid," "Electra."

RAY, STACY Born in Jacksonville, FL. Graduate UNC/Greensboro, ACT. Debut 1988 OB in "Steel Magnolias."

REAMS, LEE ROY. Born Aug. 23, 1942 in Covington, KY. Graduate U. Cinn. Cons. Bdwy debut 1966 in "Sweet Charity," followed by "Oklahoma!" (LC), "Applause," "Lorelei" "Show Boat" (JB), "Hello, Dolly!" (1978), "42nd Street," "La Cage aux Folles," OB in "Sterling Silver," "Potholes," "The Firefly in Concert."

REAUX, ANGELINA. Born Jan. 23, 1954 in Houston, TX. Graduate NorthwesternU. Debut 1979 OB in "King of Schnorrers," followed by "My Heart Is in the East," "La Calisto."

REAVES-PHILLIPS, SANDRA. Born Dec. 23 in Mullins, SC. Bdwy debut 1973 in "Raisin," OB in "Li'l Bit," "Ragtime Blues," "Blues in the Night," "Basin Street," "Karma," "Sparrow in Flight," "Take Care," "American Dreams," "The Late Great Ladies," "Oh! Oh! Obesity!," "The Late Great Ladies of Blues and Jazz."

REBHORN, JAMES. Born Sept. 1, 1948 in Philadelphia, PA. Graduate Wittenberg U, Columbia U. Debut 1972 OB in "Blue Boys," "Are You Now Or Have You Ever Been," "Trouble with Europe," "Othello," "Hunchback of Notre Dame," "Period of Adjustment," "The Freak," "Half a Lifetime," "Touch Black," "To Gillian on Her 37th Birthday," "Rain," "The Hasty Heart," "Husbandry," "Isn't It Romantic," "Blind Date," "Cold Sweat," "Spoils of War," Bdwy in "I'm Not Rappaport."

REDELL, CHARLES. Born Dec. 13, 1973 in NYC. Debut 1988 OB in "Counter Service."

REED, PAMELA. Born Apr. 2, 1949 in Tacoma, WA. Graduate UWa. Bdwy debut 1978 in "November People," followed by OB's "The Curse of the Starving Class," "All's Well That Ends Well," "Seduced," "Getting Out," "The Sorrows of Stephen," "Standing on My Knees," "Criminal Minds," "Fen," "Mrs. Warren's Profession," "Aunt Dan and Lemon," "Elektra."

REGION, DANIEL. Born Nov. 11, 1948 in Sandwich, IL. Debut 1981 OB in "Cowboy Mouth," followed by "Widows and Children First," "A Midsummer Night's Dream," "Beyond Therapy," "Taming of the Shrew," "Her Great Match," "Pericles," "Candida," "Uncle Vanya," Bdwy in "Torch Song Trilogy" (1982).

REID, MICHAEL EARL. Born Aug. 29, 1949 in Belleville, Ont. Can. Graduate Camosun Col. Debut 1977 OB in "Revenge of the Space Pandas," followed by "The Investigation," "Girl of the Golden West."

REINHARDSEN, DAVID. Born Jan. 13, 1949 in NYC. Graduate Westminster Col. Bdwy debut 1976 in "Zalmen or the Madness of God," OB in "Altar Boys," "Extenuating Circumstances," "The Spare Seraphim," "Countess Mitzi," "The Racket."

REISSA, ELEANOR. Born May 11 in Brooklyn, NY. Graduate Brooklyn Col. Debut 1979 OB in "Rebecca the Rabbi's Daughter," followed by "That's Not Funny That's Sick," "The Rise of David Levinsky," "Match Made in Heaven," "Song for a Saturday," "No, No, Nanette."

REMME, JOHN. Born Nov. 21 in Fargo, ND. Attended UMn. Debut 1972 OB in "One for the Money," followed by "Anything Goes," "The Rise of David Levinsky," "Jubilee in Concert," "The Firefly in Concert," "Sweet Adeline in Concert," "George White's Scandals in Concert," Bdwy in "The Ritz" (1975), "The Royal Family," "Can-Can," "Alice in Wonderland," "Teddy and Alice."

RENFROE, REBECCA. Born Nov. 9, 1951 in Alexandria, VA. Graduate UCincinnati. Bdwy debut 1981 in "Bring Back Birdie," followed by OB's "The Gifts of the Magi" (1987).

REPOLE, CHARLES. Born May 24, 1945 in Brooklyn, NY. Graduate Hofstra U. Bdwy debut 1975 in "Very Good Eddie," for which he received a Theatre World Award, followed by "Finian's Rainbow," "Whoopee!," "Doubles," OB in "Make Someone Happy," "George White's Scandals," "Olympus on My Mind," "Magdalena in Concert."

RESNIK, REGINA. Born Aug. 30, 1924 in NYC. Graduate Hunter Col. After a career as an internationally acclaimed operatic singer, she made her debut on Bdwy in "Cabaret" (1987).

REYNOLDS, DIANE. Born Feb. 20, 1951 in Philadelphia, PA. Graduate Temple U. Debut 1978

OB in "Circles," followed by "Journey of the Fifth Horse," "Lion Woman," "Cafe Toulouse."

REYNOLDS, SARAH. Born July 27, 1973 in Rochester, NY. Attended Rochester Acad. Bdwy debut 1985 in "Sunday in the Park with George," followed by "Teddy and Alice."

RICE, REVA. Born in Toledo, Ohio, in 1961. Attended Boston Cons. of Music. Bdwy debut 1987 in "Starlight Express."

RICE, SARAH. Born Mar. 5, 1955 in Okinawa. Attended AzStateU. Debut 1974 OB in "The Fantasticks," followed by "The Enchantress," "The Music Man," "Swan Song," Bdwy 1979 in "Sweeney Todd" for which she received a Theatre World Award.

RICHARDS, CAROL. Born Dec. 26 in Aurora, IL. Graduate Northwestern U, Columbia U. Bdwy debut 1965 in "Half a Sixpence," followed by "Mame," "Last of the Red Hot Lovers," "Company," "Cats."

RICHARDS, LINC. Born Nov. 16, 1964. Graduate Occidental Col. Bdwy debut 1988 in "A Streetcar Named Desire."

RICHERT, WANDA. Born Apr. 18, 1958 in Chicago, IL. Bdwy debut 1980 in "42nd Street" for which she received a Theatre World Award, followed by "Nine," "A Chorus Line."

RIEGERT, PETER. Born Apr. 11, 1947 in NYC. Graduate UBuffalo. Debut 1975 OB in "Dance with Me," followed by "Sexual Perversity in Chicago," "Sunday Runners," "Isn't It Romantic," "La Brea Tarpits," "A Hell of a Town," "Festival of One Acts," "A Rosen by Any Other Name," "The Birthday Party," Bdwy in "The Nerd" (1987).

RIEHLE, RICHARD. Born May 12, 1948 in Menomonee Falls, WI. Graduate UNotreDame, UMn. Bdwy debut 1986 in "Execution of Justice," followed by OB's "A Midsummer Night's Dream," "The Birthday Party," "Right Behind the Flag."

RIFKIN, RON. Born Oct. 31, 1939 in NYC. Graduate NYU. Bdwy debut 1960 in "Come Blow Your Horn," followed by "The Goodbye People," OB in "Rosebloom," "The Art of Dining," "Temple."

RIGNACK, ROGER. Born Sept. 24, 1962 in NYC. Graduate Emerson Col. Debut 1985 OB in "Dead! A Love Story," followed by "Disappearing Acts," "The Red Madonna," "Our Lady of the Tortilla," "In Available Light."

RINEHART, ELAINE. Born Aug. 16, 1958 in San Antonio, TX. Graduate NCSchArts. Debut 1975 OB in "Tenderloin," followed by "Native Son," "Joan of Lorraine," "Dumping Ground," "Fairweather Friends," "The Color of the Evening Sky," "The Best Little Whorehouse in Texas," "The Wedding of the Siamese Twins."

RINGHAM, NANCY. Born Nov. 16, 1954 in Minneapolis, MN. Graduate St. Olaf Col, Oxford U. Bdwy debut 1954 in "My Fair Lady" (1981), followed by OB's "That Jones Boy," "Bugles at Dawn," "Not-So-New Faces of 1982," "Trouble in Tahiti," "Lenny and the Heartbreakers," "Four I-Act Musicals," "Esther, a Vaudeville Megillah."

RITCHIE, ESTELLE. Born in Boston, MA. Attended Boston Teachers Col, UNC. Debut 1959 OB in "The Buffalo Skinner," followed by "Ruffles First Lay."

RIVERS, JOAN. Born June 8, 1933 in Brooklyn, NY. Graduate Barnard Col. Bdwy debut 1971 in "Fun City," followed by "Broadway Bound."

ROBARDS, JASON. Born July 26, 1922 in Chicago, Il. Attended AADA. Bdwy debut 1947 with D'Oyly Carte, followed by "Stalag 17," "The Chase," "Long Day's Journey into Night" for which he received a Theatre World Award, "The Disenchanted," "Toys in the Attic," "Big Fish Little Fish," "A Thousand Clowns," "Hughie," "The Devils," "We Bombed in New Haven," "The Country Girl," "Moon for the Misbegotten," "A Touch of the Poet," "You Can't Take It with You," "The Iceman Cometh," "A Month of Sundays," "Ah, Wilderness!," "Long Days Journey into Night" (1988), OB in "American Gothic," "The Iceman Cometh," "After the Fall," "But For Whom Charlie," "Long Day's Journey into Night."

ROBB, R. D. Born Mar. 31, 1972 in Philadelphia, Pa. Bdwy debut 1980 in "Charlie and Algernon," followed by "Oliver!," "Les Miserables."

ROBBINS, JANA. Born Apr. 18, 1947 in Johnstown, PA. Graduate Stephens Col. Bdwy debut 1974 in "Good News," followed by "I Love My Wife," "Crimes of the Heart," "Romance/Romance," OB in "Tickles by Tucholsky," "Tip-Toes," "All Night Strut," "Colette Collage," "Circus Gothic."

ROBBINS, REX. Born in Pierre, SD. Bdwy debut 1964 in "One Flew over the Cuckoo's Nest," followed by "Scratch," "The Changing Room," "Gypsy," "Comedians," "An Almost Perfect Person," "Richard III," "You Can't Take It with You," "Play Memory," OB in "Servant of Two Masters," "The Alchemist," "Arms and the Man," "Boys in the Band," "A Memory of Two Mondays," "They Knew What They Wanted," "Secret Service," "Boy Meets Girl," "Three Sisters," "The Play's the Thing," "Julius Caesar," "Henry IV Part I," "The Dining Room," "Urban Blight."

ROBERTS, ERIC. Born Apr. 18, 1956 in Biloxi, MS. Attended RADA, AADA. Debut 1976 OB in "Rebel Women," followed by "Mass Appeal," Bdwy in "Burn This" (1988) for which he received a Theatre World Award.

ROBESON, ALEC. Born July 19, 1935 in NYC. Graduate Cornell U. Debut 1960 OB in "A Country Scandal," followed by "Hop, Signor," "Don Carlos," "The Storm," "Picture of Dorian Gray," "The Petition," "Romeo and Juliet," "Kismet."

ROBINSON, MEGHAN. Born Aug. 11, 1955 in Wilton, Ct. Graduate Bennington Col. Debut 1982 OB in' "The Dubliners," followed by "The Habits of Rabbits," "Episode 26," "Macbeth," "King Lear," "Sleeping Beauty or Coma," "Vampire Lesbians of Sodom," "Psycho Beach Party," "Hunger," "3 Pieces for a Warehouse."

ROBINSON, ROGER. Born May 2, 1941 in Seattle, WA. Attended USCal. Bdwy debut 1969 in "Does a Tiger Wear a Necktie?," followed by "Amen Corner," "The Iceman Cometh," OB in "Walk in Darkness," "Jericho-Jim Crow," "Who's Got His Own," "Trials of Brother Jero," "The Miser," "The Interrogation of Havana," "Lady Day," "Do Lord Remember Me," "Of Mice and Men."

ROCCO, JAMIE. Born Sept. 8, 1956 in Astoria, NYC. Debut 1972 OB in "Morality," followed by "Lost in the Stars," "Nite Club Confidential," Bdwy in "Cats," "Wind in the Willows."

RODRIGUEZ, AL. Born May 29, 1960 in NYC. Graduate SyracuseU. Debut 1983 OB in "The Senorita from Tacna," followed by "Savings," "Merchant of Venice," "Death of Garcia Lorca," Bdwy in "Open Admissions" (1984).

ROFFMAN, ROSE. Has appeared OB in "La Madre," "Harold Pinter Plays," "Arthur Miller Double Bill," "Happy Hypocrite," "Under Gaslight," "Beaux Stratagem," "Tea Party," "The Boy Friend," "Marlon Brando Sat Here," "Sing Me Sunshine," "Three Sisters," "The Marry Month of May."

ROGERS, ANNE. Born July 29, 1933 in Liverpool, Eng. Attended St. John's Col. Bdwy debut 1957 in "My Fair Lady," followed by "Zenda," "Half a Sixpence," "42nd Street."

ROGERS, DAVID. Born in NYC. Attended AmThWing. Bdwy debut 1985 in "Doubles," followed by "Broadway."

ROLF, FREDERICK. Born Aug. 14, 1926 in Berlin, Ger. Bdwy debut 1951 in "St Joan," followed by "The Egg," "Time Remembered," OB in "Coriolanus," "The Strong Are Lonely," "The Smokeweaver's Daughter," "Between Two Thieves," "Hedda Gabler," "The Day the Whores Came Out to Play Tennis," "Hogan's Goat," "In the Matter of J. Robert Oppenheimer," "Dark Lady of the Sonnets," "Tamara."

ROMAGUERA, JOAQUIN (aka Fidel Romann). Born Sept. 5, 1932 in Key West, FL. Graduate FlSouthernCol. Debut 1961 OB in "All in Love," followed by "Mlle. Colombe," Bdwy in "Sweeney Todd" (1979).

ROSE, NORMAN. Born June 23, 1917 in Philadelphia, PA. Graduate George Washington U. Bdwy in "Cafe Crown," "St. Joan," "Land of Fame," "Richard III," "Fifth Season," OB in "Career," "Hemingway Hero," "Wicked Cooks," "Empire Builders," "The Old Ones," "The Wait."

ROSENBAUM, DAVID. Born in NYC. Debut OB 1968 in "America Hurrah," followed by "The Cave Dwellers," "Evenings with Chekhov," "Out of the Death Cart," "After Miriam," "The Indian Wants the Bronx," "Allergy," "Family Business," "Beagleman and Brackett," Bdwy in "Oh! Calcutta!"

ROSENBERG, STEPHEN. Born Dec. 31, 1973 in Norwalk, CT. Bdwy debut 1987 in "Roza."

ROSENBLATT, MARCELL. Born July 1 in Baltimore, MD. Graduate UNC, YaleU. Debut 1979 OB in "Vienna Notes," followed by "Sorrows of Stephen," "The Dybbuk," "Twelfth Night," "Second Avenue Rag," "La Boheme," "Word of Mouth," "Twelve Dreams," "Don Juan," "A Midsummer Night's Dream," "Mud," "The Return of Pinocchio," Bdwy in "Stepping Out" (1986), "Macbeth" (1988).

ROSS, ELIZABETH. Born Aug. 28, 1926 in Morristown, NJ. Attended CatholicU. Bdwy debut 1946 in "The Song of Bernadette," followed by "The Story of Mary Surratt," "Minnie and Mr. Williams," "In the Summer House," OB in "The House of Bernarda Alba."

ROSS, JAMIE. Born May 4, 1939 in Markinch, Scot. Attended RADA. Bdwy debut 1962 in "Little Moon of Alban," followed by "Moon Beseiged," "Ari," "Different Times," "Woman of the Year," "La Cage aux Folles," "42nd Street," OB in "Penny Friend," "Oh, Coward!"

ROSS, JUSTIN. Born Dec. 15, 1954 in Brooklyn, NY. Debut 1974 OB in "More Than You Deserve," followed by "Fourtune," "Ready for More?," "Weekend," "Party Mix," "No Frills Revue," Bdwy in "Pippin" (1975), "A Chorus Line," "Got to Go Disco."

ROSSETTER, KATHY. Born July 31 in Abington, Pa. Graduate Gettsburg Col. Debut 1982 OB in "After the Fall," followed by "The Incredibly Famous Willy Rivers," "A Midsummer Night's Dream," "How to Say Goodbye," "Year of the Duck," Bdwy in "Death of a Salesman" (1984).

ROTH, STEPHANIE. Born in 1963 in Boston, MA. Juilliard graduate. Bdwy debut 1987 in "Les Liaisons Dangereuses," followed by OB's "The Cherry Orchard" (BAM 1988).

ROTHMAN, NANCY. Born Oct. 13, 1950 in Boston, Ma. Graduate Emerson Col. Debut 1983 OB in "Small Help," followed by "Action," "Haunted Lives," "American Music," "Goodnight, Texas."

ROUTMAN, STEVE. Born Aug. 28, 1962 in Washington, DC. Graduate NorthwesternU. Bdwy debut 1987 in "Broadway."

ROWE, HANSFORD. Born May 12, 1924 in Richmond, Va. Graduate URichmond. Bdwy debut 1968 in "We Bombed in New Haven," followed by "Porgy and Bess," "Mourning Becomes Electra," "Da," "Nuts," "Singin' in the Rain," OB in "Curley McDimple," "The Fantasticks," "Last Analysis," "God Says There Is No Peter Ott," "Bus Stop," "Secret Service," "Boy Meets Girl," "Getting Out," "The Unicorn," "The Incredibly Famous Willy Rivers," "The Knife," "Bigfoot Stole My Wife," "Saved from Obscurity."

ROWE, STEPHEN. Born June 3, 1948 in Johnstown, PA. Graduate Emerson Col., Yale. Debut 1979 OB in "Jungle Coup," followed by "A Private View," "Cinders," "Coming of Age in SoHo," "The Normal Heart," "Whispers," "Terry by Terry," Bdwy in "Serious Money" (1988).

ROYCE, CHERYL LESLEY. Born Sept. 27, 1947 in Greenwich, CT. Graduate UCt. Debut 1987 OB in "Under the Skin," followed by "Closing," "Talking Dirty."

RUBINSTEIN, JOHN. Born Dec. 8, 1946 in Los Angeles, CA. Attended UCLA. Bdwy debut 1972 in "Pippin" for which he received a Theatre World Award, followed by "Children of a Lesser God," "Fools," "The Soldier's Tale," "The Caine Mutiny Court-Martial," "Hurlyburly," OB in "Rosencrantz and Guildenstern Are Dead," "Urban Blight."

RUCK, PATRICIA. Born Sept. 11, 1963 in Washington, DC. Attended Goucher Col. Bdwy debut 1986 in "Cats."

RUCKER, BO. Born Aug. 17, 1948 in Tampa, FL. Debut 1978 OB in "Native Son" for which he received a Theatre World Award, followed by "Blues for Mr. Charlie," "Streamers," "Forty Deuce," "Dustoff," Bdwy in "Joe Turner's Come and Gone" (1988).

RUFFELLE, FRANCES. Born in 1966 in London, Eng. Bdwy debut 1987 in "Les Miserables" for which she received a Theatre World Award.

RUISINGER, THOMAS. Born May 13, 1930 in Omaha, NE. Graduate SMU, Neighborhood Playhouse. Bdwy debut 1959 in "Warm Peninsula," followed by "The Captain and the Kings," "A Shot in the Dark," "Frank Merriwell," "The Importance of Being Earnest," "Show White," "Manhattan Showboat," "A Stitch in Time," OB in "The Balcony," "Thracian Horses," "Under Milk Wood," "6 Characters in Search of an Author," "Papers," "As to the Meaning of Words," "Damn Yankees," "The Holly and the Ivy," "Alias Jimmy Valentine."

RUIVIVAR, FRANCIS. Born Dec. 21, 1960 in Hong Kong, China. Graduate Loretto Heights Col. Bdwy debut 1988 in "Chess."

RUIZ, ELIZABETH. Born May 21, 1958 in NYC. Graduate Hunter Col. Debut 1986 OB in "The Red Madonna," followed by "Ariano."

RULE, CHARLES. Born Aug. 4, 1928 in Springfield, MO. Bdwy debut 1951 in "Courtin' Time," followed by "Happy Hunting," "Oh, Captain!," "The Conquering Hero," "Donnybrook," "Bye Bye Birdie," "Fiddler on the Roof," "Henry Sweet Henry," "Maggie Flynn," "1776," "Cry for Us All," "Gypsy," "Goodtime Charley," "On the 20th Century," "Phantom of the Opera," OB in "Family Portrait."

RUPERT, MICHAEL. Born Oct. 23, 1951 in Denver, CO. Attended Pasadena Playhouse. Bdwy debut 1968 in "The Happy Time" for which he received a Theatre World Award, followed by

"Pippin," "Sweet Charity" (1986), "Mail," OB in "Festival," "Shakespeare's Cabaret," "March of the Falsettos."

RUSSELL, CATHY. Born Aug. 6, 1955 in New Canaan, CT. Graduate Cornell U. Debut 1980 OB in "City Sugar," followed by "Miss Schuman's Quartet," "A Resounding Tinkle," "Right to Life," "Collective Choices," "The Lunch Girls," "Home on the Range," "Perfect Crime."

RYALL, WILLIAM. Born Sept. 18, 1954 in Binghamton, NY. Graduate AADA. Debut 1979 OB in "Canterbury Tales," followed by "Elizabeth and Essex," "He Who Gets Slapped," "The Seagull," "Tartuffe," Bdwy in "Me and My Girl" (1986).

RYAN, MICHAEL. Born Mar. 19, 1929 in Wichita, KS. Attended St. Benedict's Col. GeorgetownU. Bdwy debut 1960 in "Advise and Consent," followed by "The Complaisant Lover," "Best Friend," OB in "Richard III," "King Lear," "Hedda Gabler," "Barroom Monks," "Portrait of the Artist as a Young Man," "Autumn Garden," "Naomi Court," "Caveat Emptor," "The Devil's Fable," "The Price," "Arms and the Man," "The Cabinet of Dr. Caligari."

RYAN, TIM. Born Mar. 1, 1958 in Staten Island, NY. Attended Rutgers U. Bdwy debut 1987 in "Coastal Disturbances."

RYLAND, JACK. Born July 2, 1935 in Lancaster, Pa. Attended AADA. Bdwy debut 1958 in "The World of Suzie Wong," followed by "A Very Rich Woman," "Henry V," OB in "A Palm Tree in a Rose Garden," "Lysistrata," "The White Rose and the Red," "Old Glory," "Cyrano de Bergerac," "Mourning Becomes Electra," "Beside the Seaside," "Quartermaine's Terms," "The Miracle Worker," "A Midsummer Night's Dream."

SADUSK, MAUREEN. Born Sept. 8, 1948 in Brooklyn, NY. Attended AADA. Debut 1969 OB in "We'd Rather Switch," followed by "O Glorious Tintinnabulation," "New Girl in Town," "McKean Street," "The Making of Americans," "Canterbury Tales," "Wings," "Non Pasquale," Bdwy in "Fiddler on the Roof" (1976), "Canterbury Tales," "Ladies at the Alamo," "Broadway."

SAFFRAN, CHRISTINA. Born Oct. 21, 1958 in Quincy, IL. Attended Webster Col. Bdwy debut 1978 in "A Chorus Line," followed by "A New York Summer," "Sally in Concert," OB in "Music Moves Me."

ST. JOHN, MARCO. Born May 7, 1939 in New Orleans, La. Graduate Fordham U. Bdwy debut 1964 in "Poor Bitos," followed by "And Things That Go Bump in the Night," "The Unknown Soldier and His Wife," "Weekend," "40 Carats," "We Comrades Three," "War and Peace," OB in "Angels of Anadarko," "Man of Destiny," "Timon of Athens," "Richard III," "Awake and Sing," "Desire under the Elms," "Hamlet," "Twelfth Night," "Richard II."

SALATA, GREGORY. Born July 21, 1949 in NYC. Graduate Queens Col. Bdwy debut 1975 in "Dance with Me," followed by "Equus," "Bent," OB in "Piaf: A Rembrance," "Sacraments," "Measure for Measure," "Subject of Childhood."

SANCHEZ, GEORGE EMILIO. Born Aug. 2, 1953 in Los Angeles, CA. Attended Cypress Col, Neighborhood Playhouse. Debut 1988 OB in "Girl of the Golden West," followed by "Senor Discretion."

SANCHEZ, JAIME. Born Dec. 19, 1938 in Rincon, PR. Attended Actors Studio. Bdwy debut 1957 in "West Side Story," followed by "Oh, Dad, Poor Dad . . .," "A Midsummer Night's Dream," "Richard III," OB in "The Toilet"/"Conerico Was Here to Stay" for which he received a Theatre World Award, "The Ox-Cart," "The Tempest," "Merry Wives of Windsor," "Julius Caesar," "Coriolanus," "He Who Gets Slapped," "State without Grace," "The Sun Always Shines for the Cool," "Othello," "Elektra," "Domino."

SANDY, GARY. "Born Dec. 25, 1945 in Dayton, Oh. Attended Wilmington Col., AADA. Debut 1973 OB in "The Children's Mass," followed by "Romeo and Juliet," Bdwy in "Saturday, Sunday, Monday," (1974), "Pirates of Penzance," "Arsenic and Old Lace."

SANTANA, MERLIN. Born Mar. 14, 1976 in NYC. Debut 1988 OB in "Tapman."

SANTARELLI, GENE. Born Feb. 20, 1946 in Kingston, Pa. Graduate Wilkes Col., Bloomsbury State Col. Debut 1983 OB in "George by George by George," followed by "The Taming of the Shrew," "Holy Heist," Bdwy in "Chess" (1988).

SANTELL, MARIE. Born July 8 in Brooklyn, NY. Bdwy debut 1957 in "Music Man," followed by "A Funny Thing Happened on the Way . . .," "Flora, the Red Menace," "Pajama Game," "Mack and Mabel," "La Cage aux Folles," OB in "Hi, Paisano!," "Boys from Syracuse," "Peace," "Promenade," "The Drunkard," "Sensations," "The Castaways," "Fathers and Sons."

SANTIAGO, SOCORRO. Born July 12, 1957 in NYC. Attended Juilliard. Debut 1977 OB in "Crack," followed by "Poets from the Inside," "Unfinished Women," "Family Portrait," "Domino," Bdwy in "The Bacchae" (1980).

SANTORIELLO, ALEX. Born Dec. 30, 1956 in Newark, NJ. Attended Ks. State, Kean State. Debut 1986 OB in "La Belle Helene," followed by "A Romantic Detachment," Bdwy in "Les Miserables" (1987).

SAUNDERS, NICHOLAS. Born June 2, 1914 in Kiev, Russia. Bdwy debut 1942 in "Lady in the Dark," followed by "A New Life," "Highland Fling," "Happily Ever After," "The Magnificent Yankee," "Anastasia," "Take Her, She's Mine," "A Call on Kuprin," "Passion of Josef D," OB in "An Enemy of the People," "End of All Things Natural," "The Unicorn in Captivity," "After the Rise," "All My Sons," "My Great Dead Sister," "The Investigation," "Past Tense," "Scenes and Revelations," "Zeks," "Blood Moon," "Family Comedy," "American Power Play," "Take Me Along," "The Tavern."

SAVAGE, JOHN. Born Aug. 25, 1949 on Long Island, NY. Attended AADA. Debut OB in "The Drunkard," followed by "Sensations," "Of Mice and Men" (1987), Bdwy in "Fiddler on the Roof," "Ari," "American Buffalo."

SAVAGE, KEITH. Born June 9, 1953 in Hampton, VA. Graduate Wm.& Mary Col. Bdwy debut 1982 in "Little Johnny Jones," followed by "Take Me Along," "Teddy and Alice," OB in "Sugar," "A Girl Singer," "Going Hollywood," "Alias Jimmy Valentine."

SAVIN, RON LEE. Born July 20, 1947 in Norfolk, Va. Graduate Wm. & Mary Col. Debut 1981 OB in "Francis," followed by "Greater Tuna," "Road to Hollywood," "Streetheat," "One Act Festival," "The Fantasticks," "Johnny Pye and the Foolkiller."

SAVIOLA, CAMILLE. Born July 16, 1950 in The Bronx, NY. Debut 1970 OB in "Touch," followed by "Rainbow," "Godspell," "Starmites," "Battle of the Giants," "Dementos," "Spookhouse," "A Vaudeville," "Road to Hollywood," "Hollywood Opera," "Secrets of the Lava Lamp," "Angry Housewives," "Tango Apasionado," "South Pacific" (NYC Opera), Bdwy in "Nine" (1982).

SCANLAN, DICK. Born Apr. 14, in Washington, DC. Attended Carnegie-Melon U, LAMDA. Debut 1986 OB in "Pageant," followed by "No, No, Nanette."

SCANLON, BARBARA. Born Jan. 17, 1956 in Detroit, MI. Graduate MiStateU. Debut 1984 OB in "Elizabeth and Essex," followed by "A Little Night Music," "Bittersuite-One More Time."

SCARFE, ALAN. Born June 8, 1946 in London, Eng. Attended UBritColumbia, LAMDA. Debut 1986 OB in "Africanis Instructus," followed by "Black Sea Follies," "As It Is in Heaven," "Henry IV Part I," Bdwy in "Macbeth" (1988).

SCARPONE, JUDITH. Born Nov. 6, 1942 in Jersey City, NJ. Graduate Douglass Col. Debut 1984 OB in "Sacraments," followed by "Postcards," "Rule of Three," "Holy Heist."

SCHAUT, ANN LOUISE. Born Nov. 21, 1956 in Minneapolis, MN. Attended UMn. Bdwy debut 1981 in "A Chorus Line."

SCHEINE, RAYNOR. Born Nov. 10 in Emporia, VA. Graduate VaCommonwealthU. Debut 1978 OB in "Curse of the Starving Class," followed by "Blues for Mr. Charlie," "Salt Lake City Skyline," "Mother Courage," "The Lady or the Tiger," "Bathroom Plays," "Wild Life," "Re-Po," "Almos' a Man," Bdwy in "Joe Turner's Come and Gone" (1988).

SCHLARTH, SHARON. Born Jan. 19 in Buffalo, NY. Graduate SUNY/Fredonia. Debut 1983 OB in "Full Hookup," followed by "Fool for Love," "Love's Labour's Lost," "Caligula," "The Mound Builders," "Quiet in the Land," "The Early Girl," "Borderlines," Bdwy in "Sleight of Hand" (1987).

SCHMITZ, PETER. Born Aug. 20, 1962 in St. Louis, MO. Graduate Yale, NYU. Debut 1987 OB in "Henry IV Part I," followed by "We the People."

SCHODITSCH, PEGGY. Born Aug. 19 in Cleveland, OH. Graduate Ithaca Col. Debut 1979 OB in "Modigliani," followed by "The District Line," "Flight of the Earls," "The Gingerbread Lady."

SCHOEFFLER, PAUL-G. Born Nov. 21, 1958 in Montreal, Can. Graduate UCBerkeley, Carnegie-Mellon, UBrussels. Debut 1988 OB in "Much Ado about Nothing."

SCHRAMM, DAVID. Born Aug. 14, 1946 in Louisville, Ky. Attended Western Ky.U, Juilliard. Debut 1972 OB in "School for Scandal," followed by "Lower Depths," "Women Beware Women," "Mother Courage," "King Lear," "Duck Variations," "The Cradle Will Rock," "Twelfth Night," "Palace of Amateurs," Bdwy in "Three Sisters," "Next Time I'll Sing to You," "Edward II," "Measure for Measure," "The Robber Bridegroom," "Bedroom Farce," "Goodbye, Fidel," "The Misanthrope."

SCOTT, MICHAEL. Born Jan. 24, 1954 in Santa Monica, CA. Attended CalStateU. Debut 1978 OB and Bdwy in "The Best Little Whorehouse in Texas," followed by "Happy New Year," OB in "Leave It To Me."

SCOTT, SERET. Born Sept. 1, 1949 in Washington, DC. Attended NYU. Debut 1969 OB in "Slave Ship," followed by "Ceremonies in Dark Old Men," "Black Terror," "Dream," "One Last Look," "My Sister My Sister," "Weep Not for Me," "Meetings," "The Brothers," "Eyes of the American," "Remembrances/Mojo," "Tapman."

SCOTT, SUSAN ELIZABETH. Born Aug. 9 in Detroit, MI. Graduate UDenver. Debut 1971 OB in "The Drunkard," followed by "Mother," "Company," "Dames at Sea," Bdwy in "Music Is" (1976), "On the 20th Century," "Fearless Frank," "1940's Radio Hour."

SEAMAN, JANE. Born Nov. 18 in Bellevue, OH. Graduate StanfordU, WittenbergU. Debut 1982 OB in "Street Scene," Bdwy in "Anything Goes" (1987)

SEFF, RICHARD. Born Sept. 23, 1927 in NYC. Attended NYU. Bdwy debut 1951 in "Darkness at Noon," followed by "Herzl," "Musical Comedy Murders of 1940," (also OB), OB in "Big Fish, Little Fish," "Modigliani," "Childe Byron," "Richard II," "Time Framed," "The Sea Gull," "Only You."

SELDES, MARIAN. Born Aug. 23, 1928 in NYC. Attended Neighborhood Playhouse. Bdwy debut 1947 in "Medea," followed by "Crime and Punishment," "That Lady," "Tower Beyond Tragedy," "Ondine," "On High Ground," "Come of Age," "The Chalk Garden," "The Milk Train Doesn't Stop Here Anymore," "The Wall," "A Gift of Time," "A Delicate Balance," "Before You Go," "Father's Day," "Equus," "The Merchant," "Deathtrap," OB in "Different," "Ginger Man," "Mercy Street," "Isadora Duncan Sleeps with the Russian Navy," "Painting Churches," "Gertrude Stein and Companion," "Richard II," "The Milk Train Doesn't Stop Here Anymore."

SERABIAN, LORRAINE. Born June 12, 1945 in NYC. Graduate HofstraU. OB in "Sign of Jonah," "Electra," "Othello," "Secret Life of Walter Mitty," "Bugs and Veronica," "Trojan Women," "American Gothics," "Gallows Humor," "Company," Bdwy in "Cabaret," "Zorba."

SERBAGI, ROGER. Born July 26, 1937 in Waltham, MA. Attended AmThWing. Bdwy debut 1969 in "Henry V," followed by "Gemini," OB's "A Certain Young Man," "Awake and Sing," "The Partnership," "Monsters," "The Transfiguration of Benno Blimpie," "Family Snapshots," "Till Jason Comes," "1984."

SERRECCHIA, MICHAEL. Born Mar. 26, 1951 in Brooklyn, NY. Attended Brockport State U. Teachers Col. Bdwy debut 1972 in "The Selling of the President," followed by "Heathen!," "Seesaw," "A Chorus Line," OB in "Lady Audley's Secret."

SESMA, THOM. Born June 1, 1955 in Sasebo, Japan. Graduate UCal. Bdwy debut 1983 in "La Cage aux Folles."

SETRAKIAN, ED. Born Oct. 1, 1928 in Jenkintown, WVa. Graduate Concord Col, NYU. Debut 1966 OB in "Drums in the Night," followed by "Othello," "Coriolanus," "Macbeth," "Hamlet," "Baal," "Old Glory," "Futz," "Hey, Rube," "Seduced," "Shout Across the River," "American Days," "Sheepskin," "Inserts," "Crossing the Bar," "Boys Next Door," Bdwy in "Days in the Trees" (1976), "St. Joan," "The Best Little Whorehouse in Texas."

SEVERS, WILLIAM. Born Jan. 8, 1932 in Britton, OK. Attended Pasadena Playhouse, Columbia Col. Bdwy debut 1960 in "Cut of the Axe," OB in "The Moon Is Blue," "Lulu," "Big Maggie," "Mixed Doubles," "The Rivals," "The Beaver Coat," "Twister," "Midnight Mass," "Gas Station," "Firebugs," "Fellow Travellers."

SEVRA, ROBERT. Born Apr. 15, 1945 in Kansas City, MO. Graduate StanfordU, UMi. Debut 1972 OB in "Servant of Two Masters," followed by "Lovers," "After These Messages," Bdwy in "Charlie and Algernon" (1980), "Torch Song Trilogy."

SHAKAR, MARTIN. Born Jan. 1, 1940 in Detroit, Mi. Attended Wayne State U. Bdwy bow 1969 in "Our Town," OB in "Lorenzaccio," "Macbeth," "The Infantry," "American Pastoral," "No Place to Be Somebody," "World of Mrs. Solomon," "And Whose Little Boy Are You," "Investigation of Havana," "Night Watch," "Owners," "Actors," "Richard III," "Transfiguration of Benno Blimpie," "Jack Gelber's New Play," "Biko Inquest," "Second Story Sunlight," "Secret Thighs of New England Women," "After the Fall," "Faith Healer," "Hunting Cockroaches," "Yellow Dog Contract."

SHALHOUB, TONY. Born Oct. 9, 1953 in Green Bay, Wi. Graduate Yale U. Bdwy debut 1985 in

Chiara
Peacock

Wyman
Pendleton

Mercedes
Perez

Adam
Philipson

Angela
Pietropinto

Richard
Poe

Lawrence
Preston

Jenny
Psaki

Brian
Quinn

Melissa
Randel

David
Rasche

Angelina
Reaux

Eleanor
Reissa

John
Remme

Carol
Richards

Linc
Richards

Jana
Robbins

Al
Rodriguez

Thomas
Ruisinger

Maureen
Sadusk

Keith
Savage

Peggy
Schoditsch

Michael
Scott

Jane
Seaman

Lorraine
Serabian

Mark
Shannon

Claudia
Shell

J. K.
Simmons

Victor
Slezak

Neva
Small

"The Odd Couple," OB in "Richard II," "Henry IV Part I," "One Act Festival," "Zero Positive."
SHANNON, MARK. Born Dec. 13, 1948 in Indianapolis, IN. Attended UCin. Debut 1969 OB in "Fortune and Men's Eyes," followed by Brotherhood," "Nothing to Report."
SHARMAT, MARY. Born Nov. 22, 1936 in Long Beach, CA. Attended UNH, ColumbiaU. Debut 1987 OB in "The Tavern."
SHAW, MARCIE. Born June 19, 1954 in Franklin Square, NY. Attended UIll. Bdwy debut 1980 in "Pirates of Penzance," followed by "Les Miserables," OB in "A Midsummer Night's Dream," "Non Pasquale," "Promenade," "La Boheme."
SHAWHAN, APRIL. Born Apr. 10, 1940 in Chicago, IL. Debut 1964 OB in "Jo," followed by "Hamlet," "Oklahoma!," "Mod Donna," "Journey to Gdansk," "Almost in Vegas," "Bosoms and Neglect," "Stella," "The Vinegar Tree," Bdwy in "Race of Hairy Men," "3 Bags Full" (1966) for which she received a Theatre World Award, "Dinner at *," "Cop-Out," "Much Ado about Nothing," "Over Here," "Rex," "A History of the American Film."
SHEEN, MARTIN. Born Aug. 3, 1940 in Dayton, OH. Bdwy debut 1964 in "Never Live over a Pretzel Factory," followed by "The Subject Was Roses," "Death of a Salesman," OB in "The Connection," "Many Loves," "Jungle of Cities," "Wicked Cooks," "Hamlet," "Romeo and Juliet," "Hello and Goodbye," "Julius Caesar."
SHELL, CLAUDIA. Born Sept. 11, 1959 in Passaic, NJ. Debut 1980 OB in "Jam," Bdwy in "Merlin," followed by "Cats."
SHELLEY, CAROLE. Born Aug. 16, 1939 in London, Eng. Bdwy debut 1965 in "The Odd Couple," followed by "The Astrakhan Coat," "Loot," "Noel Coward's Sweet Potato," "Hay Fever," "Absurd Person Singular," "The Norman Conquests," "The Elephant Man," "The Misanthrope," "Noises Off," "Stepping Out," OB in "Little Murders," "The Devil's Disciple," "The Play's the Thing," "Double Feature," "Twelve Dreams," "Pygmalion in Concert," "A Christmas Carol," "Jubilee in Concert," "Waltz of the Toreadors."
SHELTON, SLOANE. Born Mar. 17, 1934 in Asheville, NC. Attended Bates Col., RADA. Bdwy debut 1967 in "The Imaginary Invalid," followed by "A Touch of the Poet," "Tonight at 8:30," "I Never Sang for My Father," "Sticks and Bones," "The Runner Stumbles," "Shadow Box," "Passione," "Open Admission," OB in "Androcles and the Lion," "The Maids," "Basic Training of Pavlo Hummel," "Play and Other Plays," "Julius Caesar," "Chieftans," "Passione," "The Chinese Viewing Pavilion," "Blood Relations," "The Great Divide," "Highest Standard of Living," "The Flower Palace," "April Snow."
SHENAR, PAUL. Born Feb. 12, 1936 in Milwaukee, WI. Graduate UWi. Bdwy debut 1969 in "Tiny Alice," followed by "Three Sisters," "Macbeth" (1988), OB in "Six Characters in Search of an Author," "Hedda Gabler."
SHEPARD, JOHN. Born Dec. 9, 1952 in Huntington Park, CA. Graduate UCal/Irvine. Debut 1982 OB in "Scenes from La Vie de Boheme," followed by "Crimes of Vautrin," "Dr. Faustus," "Fabiola," "1984," Bdwy in "A View from the Bridge" (1983), "American Buffalo."
SHEPHERD, GWENDOLYN. Born Oct. 20 in East Meadowbrook, NY. Graduate NYU, FordhamU. Bdwy debut 1983 in "Porgy and Bess," followed by OB's "A Midsummer Night's Dream."
SHERRICK, DAVID. Born Nov. 3, 1946 in Detroit, MI. Debut 1985 OB in "The Second Shepherd's Play," followed by "Frankenstein," "Brand," "The Tavern."
SHEW, TIMOTHY. Born Feb. 7, 1959 in Grand Forks, ND. Graduate Millikin U., UMi. Debut 1987 OB in "The Knife," Bdwy in "Les Miserables."
SHIELDS, DALE. Born Nov. 4, 1952 in Cleveland, OH. Graduate OhioU. Debut 1976 OB in "Sing America," followed by "Fashion," "Contributions," "Anyone Can Whistle," "Liberty Call," "Barefoot in the Park."
SHIMIZU, KEENAN. Born Oct. 22, 1956 in NYC. Bdwy debut 1965 in "South Pacific" and "The King and I"(CC), OB in "Rashomon," "The Year of the Dragon," "The Catch," "Peking Man," "Flowers and Household Gods," "Behind Enemy Lines," "Station J," "Rosie's Cafe," "Boutique Living and Disposable Icons."
SHORT, JOHN. Born July 3, 1956 in Christopher, IL. Graduate Hanover Col. Debut 1981 OB in "Unfettered Letters," followed by "Sister Mary Ignatius Explains It All," "And They Danced Real Slow in Jackson," "The Boys Next Door," Bdwy in "Big River" (1985).
SHULMAN, CONSTANCE (a.k.a. Connie). Born Apr. 4, 1958 in Johnson City, Tn. Graduate UTn. Debut 1985 OB in "Walking Through," followed by "Windfall," "Pas de Deux," "Steel Magnolias."
SHULMAN, HEATHER. Born Aug. 25, 1973 in Livings on, NJ Debut 1984 OB in "Papushko" followed by Bdwy in "Sunday in the Park with George" (1984), "Into the Woods."
SICARI, JOSEPH. Born Apr. 29, 1939 in Boston, MA. Graduate CatholicU. Debut 1965 OB in "The Parasite," followed by "The Comedy of Errors," "Henry IV," "Love and Let Love," "Dames at Sea," "Comedy," "Loose Ends."
SIEBERT, RON. Born Feb. 26 in Kenosha, IL. Graduate UWis, Brandeis U. Bdwy debut 1973 in "The Changing Room," followed by "The Iceman Cometh," OB in "A Little Madness," "Wild Blue."
SIEGLER, BEN. Born Apr. 9, 1958 in Queens, NYC. Attended HBStudio. Debut 1980 OB in "Innocent Thoughts, Harmless Intentions," followed by "Threads," "Many Happy Returns," "Snow Orchid," "The Diviners," "What I Did Last Summer," "Time Framed," "Gifted Children," "Levitations," "Elm Circle," "Romance Language," "Raw Youth," "Voices in the Head," "V & V Only," Bdwy in "5th of July" (1981).
SILVER, JOE. Born Sept. 28, 1922 in Chicago, IL. Attended UIll, AmThWing. Bdwy debut 1942 in "Tobacco Road," followed by "Doughgirls," "Heads or Tails," "Nature's Way," "Gypsy," "Heroine," "Zulu and the Zayda," "You Know I Can't Hear You . . . ," "Lenny," "The Roast," "The World of Sholom Aleichem," OB in "Blood Wedding," "Lamp at Midnight," "Joseph and His Brethern," "Victors," "Shrinking Bride," "Family Pieces," "Cakes with Wine," "The Homecoming," "Cold Storage," "Rich Relatives," "Old Business."
SILVER, RON. Born July 2, 1946 in NYC. Graduate SUNY, St. John's U. Debut OB in "El Grande de Coca Cola," followed by "Lotta," "Kaspar," "More Than You Deserve," "Emperor of Late Night Radio," "Friends," "Hunting Cockroaches," Bdwy in "Hurlyburly" (1984), "Social Security," "Speed-the-Plow."
SILVERMAN, JONATHAN. Born Aug. 5, 1966 in Los Angeles, CA. Attended USCal. Bdwy debut 1983 in "Brighton Beach Memoirs," followed by "Broadway Bound."
SILVERMAN, MEL. Born Jan. 26, 1923 in Brooklyn, NY. Graduate Bklyn Col, NYU. Debut 1987 OB in "The Actors" followed by "Sadness of a Faded Dream," "Canadian Gothic," "Legal Tender."
SIMMONS, J. K. (formerly Jonathan). Born Jan. 9, 1955 in Detroit, MI. Graduate UMon. Debut 1987 OB in "Birds of Paradise," followed by "Dandy Dick."
SIMONS, LESLIE A. Born Aug. 8, 1957 in Hatboro, PA. Graduate Beaver Col. Bdwy debut 1983 in "La Cage aux Folles."
SINGER, MARLA. Born Aug. 2, 1957 in Oklahoma City, OK. Graduate OkCityU. Debut 1981 OB in "Seesaw," followed by Bdwy's "42nd Street" (1985).
SINKYS, ALBERT. Born July 10, 1940 in Boston, Ma. Attended Boston U., UCLA. Debut 1981 OB in "In the Matter of J. Robert Oppenheimer," followed by "The Caine Mutiny Court-Martial," "Man in the Glass Booth," "Six Candles," "Fellow Travelers."
SISTI, MICHELAN. Born May 27, 1949 in San Juan, PR. Graduate UBuffalo. Debut 1979 OB in "A Midsummer Night's Dream," followed by "All of the Above," Bdwy in "Fiddler on the Roof" (1981), "Cabaret" (1987).
SLEZAK, VICTOR. Born July 7, 1957 in Youngstown, Oh. Debut 1979 OB in "The Electra Myth," followed by "The Hasty Heart," "Ghosts," "Alice and Fred," "The Widow Claire," "The Miracle Worker," "Talk Radio."
SMALL, LARRY. Born Oct. 6, 1947 in Kansas City, MO. Attended Manhattan School of Music. Bdwy debut 1971 in "1776," followed by "La Strada," "Wild and Wonderful," "A Doll's Life," OB in "Plain and Fancy," "Forbidden Broadway."
SMALL, NEVA. Born Nov. 17, 1952 in NYC. Bdwy debut 1964 in "Something More," followed by "The Impossible Years," "Henry Sweet Henry," "Frank Merriwell," "Something's Afoot," OB in "Ballad for a Firing Squad," "Show Me Where the Good Times Are," "How Much How Much," "F. Jasmine Addams," "Macbeth," "Yentl and the Yeshiva Boy," "Life Is Not a Doris Day Movie," "The Golden Land," "Half a World Away."
SMITH, COTTER. Born May 29, 1949 in Washington, DC. Graduate Trinity Col. Debut 1980 OB in "The Blood Knot," followed by "Death of a Miner," "A Soldier's Play," "El Salvador," "Borderlines."
SMITH, EBBE ROE. Born June 25, 1949 in San Diego, CA. Graduate San FranciscoStateU. Debut 1978 OB in "Curse of the Starving Class," followed by "New Jerusalem," "Shout across the River," "Sunday Runners," "After the Revolution," "Etta Jenks."
SMITH, JENNIFER. Born Mar. 9, 1956 in Lubbock, TX. Graduate TxTechU. Debut 1981 OB in "Seesaw," followed by "Suffragette," "Henry the 8th and the Grand Ole Opry," "No Frills Revue," Bdwy in "La Cage aux Folles" (1983).
SMITH, LOIS. Born Nov. 3, 1930 in Topeka, Ks. Attended UWVa. Bdwy debut 1952 in "Time Out for Ginger," followed by "The Young and the Beautiful," "Wisteria Trees," "The Glass Menagerie," "Orpheus Descending," "Stages," OB in "A Midsummer Night's Dream," "Non Pasquale," "Promenade," "La Boheme," "Bodies, Rest and Motion," "Marathon 87," "Gus and Al."
SMITH, LOUISE. Born Feb. 8, 1955 in NYC. Graduate Antioch Col. Debut 1981 OB in "The Haggadah," followed by "Salt Speaks," "The Tempest," "Betty and the Blenders," "Life Simulated," "Coyote Ugly."
SMITH, REX. Born Sept. 19, 1955 in Jacksonville, Fl. Bdwy debut 1978 in "Grease," followed by "The Pirates of Penzance" for which he received a Theatre World Award, "The Human Comedy," OB in "Brownstone," "Common Pursuit."
SMITH, SHEILA. Born Apr. 3, 1933 in Coneaut, OH. Attended Kent State U., Cleveland Play House. Bdwy debut 1963 in "Hot Spot," followed by "Mame" for which she received a Theatre World Award, "Follies," "Company," "Sugar," "Five O'Clock Girl," "42nd Street," OB in "Taboo Revue," "Anything Goes," "Best Foot Forward," "Sweet Miami," "Florello," "Taking My Turn," "Jack and Jill," "M. Amilcar."
SNYDER, DREW. Born Sept. 25, 1946 in Buffalo, NY. Graduate Carnegie Tech. Bdwy debut 1968 in APA's "Pantagleize," "The Cocktail Party," "Cock-a-Doodle Dandy" and "Hamlet," OB in "Henry VI," "Richard II," "Sticks and Bones," "The Cretan Bull," "Quail Southwest," "Wayside Motor Inn," "Words from the Moon."
SOOK, DENNIS. Born Apr. 29, 1945 in Marshall, MN. Graduate MankatoStateU, SIllU. Debut 1971 OB in "The Debate," followed by "The Fantasticks," "White, Brown, Black," "Stud Silo," "New Mexican Rainbow Fishing."
SOPER, TONY. Born Nov. 20, 1958 in Yakima, WA. Graduate UWash. Debut 1987 OB in "Henry IV Part I."
SOREL, ANITA. Born Oct. 25 in Hollywood, CA. Graduate UUtah, CalState/Long Beach. Debut 1980 OB in "The Time of the Cuckoo," followed by "Bourgeois Gentlemen," "Hedda Gabler," "Merry Wives of Scarsdale," "Counter Service."
SOREL, THEODORE/TED. Born Nov. 14, 1936 in San Francisco, CA. Graduate Col. of Pacific. Bdwy debut 1977 in "Sly Fox," followed by "Horowitz and Mrs. Washington," "A Little Family Business," OB in "Arms and the Man," "Moon Mysteries," "A Call from the East," "Hedda Gabler," "Drinks before Dinner," "Tamara."
SPAISMAN, ZIPORA. Born Jan. 2, 1920 in Lublin, Poland. Debut 1955 OB in "Lonesome Ship," followed by "In My Father's Court," "Thousand and One Nights," "Eleventh Inheritor," "Enchanting Melody," "Fifth Commandment," "Bronx Express," "The Melody Lingers On," "Yoshke Muzikant," "Stempenyu," "Generations of Green Fields," "Shop," "A Play for the Devil," "Broome Street America," "Flowering Peach," "Riverside Drive."
SPECTOR, DANIEL. Born Feb. 24, 1962 in Buffalo, NY. Graduate Eastman School, NYU. Debut 1987 OB in "Two Gentlemen of Verona," followed by "Gus and Al."
SPENCER, REBECCA. Born Apr. 29, 1960 in Levittown, PA. Graduate IthacaCol. Debut 1986 OB in "The Desert Song," followed by
SPENCER, VERNON. Born Dec. 1, 1955 in Brooklyn, NY. Attended QueensCol. Debut 1976 OB in "Panama Hattie," followed by "Happy with the Blues," "Street Jesus," "Amahl and the Night Visitors," "Dreams of the Son," Bdwy in "The Human Comedy" (1984), "Dreamgirls" (1987).
SPIELBERG, ROBIN. Born Nov. 20, 1962 in New Jersey. Attended MiStateU, NYU. Debut 1988 OB in "Boys' Life."
SPIVAK, ALICE. Born Aug. 11, 1935 in Brooklyn, NYC. Debut 1954 OB in "Early Primrose," followed by "Of Mice and Men," "Secret Concubine," "Port Royal," "Time for Bed," "House of Blue Leaves," "Deep Six the Briefcase," "Selma," "Ferry Tales," "Temple."
SQUIBB, JUNE. Born Nov. 6 in Vandalia, IL. Attended Cleveland Play House. Debut 1956 OB in

"Sable Brush," followed by "The Boy Friend," "Lend an Ear," "Another Language," "Castaways," "Funeral March for a One-Man Band," "Gorey Stories," "Blues for Mr. Charlie," "The Workroom," "Family Portrait," "House of Bernarda Alba," Bdwy in " Gypsy"(1960), "The Happy Time," "Gorey Stories."

STADLEN, LEWIS J. Born Mar. 7, 1947 in Brooklyn, NY. Attended Stella Adler Studio. Bdwy debut 1970 in "Minnie's Boys" for which he received a Theatre World Award, followed by "The Sunshine Boys," "Candide," "The Odd Couple," OB in "The Happiness Cage," "Heaven on Earth," "Barb-A-Que," "Don Juan and Non Don Juan," "Olympus on My Mind," "1-2-3-4-5."

STAHL, MARY LEIGH. Born Aug. 29, 1946 in Madison, WI. Graduate JacksonvilleStateU. Debut 1974 OB in "Circus," followed by "Dragons," "Sullivan and Gilbert," "The World of Sholem Aleichem," Bdwy in "The Phantom of the Opera" (1988).

STANLEY, DOROTHY. Born Nov. 18 in Hartford Ct. Graduate Ithaca Col., Carnegie-Mellon U. Debut 1978 OB in "Gay Divorce," followed by "Dames at Sea," Bdwy in "Sugar Babies" (1980), "Annie," "42nd Street," "Broadway."

STANLEY, GORDON. Born Dec. 20, 1951 in Boston, Ma. Graduate Brown U., Temple U. Debut 1977 OB in "Lyrical and Satirical," followed by "Allegro," "Elizabeth and Essex," "Red Hot and Blue," "Two on the Isles," "Moby Dick," "Johnny Pye and the Foolkiller," Bdwy in "Onward Victoria," (1980), "Joseph and the Amazing Technicolor Dreamcoat," "Into the Light," "Teddy and Alice."

STANTON, ROBERT. Born Mar. 8, 1963 in San Antonio, Tx. Graduate George Mason U, NYU. Debut OB 1985 in "Measure for Measure," followed by "Rum and Coke," "Cheapside," "Highest Standard of Living," "One Act Festival," "Emily."

STATTEL, ROBERT. Born Nov. 20, 1937 in Floral Park, NY. Graduate Manhattan Col. Debut 1958 OB in "Heloise," followed by "When I Was a Child," "Man and Superman," "The Storm," "Don Carlos," "Taming of the Shrew," "Titus Andronicus," "Henry IV," "Peer Gynt," "Hamlet," LCRep's "Danton's Death," "The Country Wife," "The Caucasian Chalk Circle," and "King Lear," "Iphigenia in Aulis," "Ergo," "The Persians," "Blue Boys," "The Minister's Black Veil," "Four Friends," "Two Character Play," "The Merchant of Venice," "Cuchulain," "Oedipus Cycle," "Gilles de Rais," "Woyzeck," "King Lear," "The Fuehrer Bunker," "Learned Ladies," "Domestic Issues," "Great Days," "The Tempest," "Brand," "A Man for All Seasons," "Bunker Reveries."

STEHLIN, JACK. Born July 21, 1956 in Allentown, PA. Graduate Juilliard. Debut 1984 OB in "Henry V," followed by "Gravity Shoes," "Julius Caesar," "Romeo and Juliet."

STEIN, JUNE. Born June 13, 1950 in NYC. Debut 1979 OB in "The Runner Stumbles," followed by "Confluence," "Am I Blue," "Balm in Gilead," "Danny and the Deep Blue Sea," "The Miss Firecracker Contest," "As Is," "Acts of Faith."

STEINER, STEVE. Born Nov. 30, 1951 in Chicago, Il. Graduate Webster U. Debut 1986 OB in "Two Blind Mice," followed by "Hot Sake," "Anything Goes" (LC).

STEPHENSON, DON. Born Sept. 10, 1964 in Chattanooga, Tn. Graduate UTn. Debut 1986 OB in "Southern Lights," followed by "Hypothetic," "The Tavern"

STERLING, PHILIP. Born Oct. 9, 1922 in NYC. Graduate UPa. Bdwy debut 1955 in "Silk Stockings," followed by "Interlock," "An Evening with Richard Nixon . . . ," "Broadway Bound," OB in "Victims of Duty," "Opening of a Window," "Trojan Women," "Party for Divorce," "Party on Greenwich Avenue," "Peddler," "Summertree," "Older People."

STERNHAGEN, FRANCES. Born Jan. 13, 1932 in Washington, DC. Graduate Vassar Col. OB in "Admirable Bashful," "Thieves' Carnival," "Country Wife," "Ulysses in Nighttown," "Saintliness of Margery Kemp," "The Room," "A Slight Ache," "Displaced Person," "Playboy of the Western World," "The Prevalence of Mrs. Seal," "Summer," "Laughing Stock," "The Return of Herbert Bracewell," "Little Murders," "Driving Miss Daisy," Bdwy in "Great Day in the Morning," "The Right Honourable Gentleman," with APA in "The Cocktail Party," and "Cock-a-Doodle Dandy," "The Sign in Sidney Brustein's Window," "Enemies" (LC), "The Good Doctor," "Equus," "Angel," "On Golden Pond," "The Father," "Grownups," "You Can't Take It With You."

STILLMAN, ROBERT. Born Dec. 2, 1954 in NYC. Graduate Princeton U. Debut 1981 OB in "The Haggadah," followed by "Street Scene," "Lola," "No Frills Revue."

STITT, DON. Born Jan. 25, 1956 in NYC. Graduate SanFranciscoStateU. Bdwy debut 1982 in "Do Black Patent Leather Shoes Really Reflect Up?," followed by "Late Nite Comic."

STOCKTON, ROSE. Born in Urbano, OH. Graduate Antioch Col. Debut 1983 OB in "Primal Time," followed by "The 3 Zeks," "Arms and the Man," "Antigone," "Two Gentlemen of Verona," "The Rivals," "The Imaginary Invalid," "Candida."

STOCKWELL, RICK. Born Sept. 22, 1951 in Buffalo, NY. Graduate USIU. Debut 1979 OB in "Mary," followed by Bdwy in "Mail" (1988).

STOUT, MARY. Born Apr. 8, 1952 in Huntington, WVa. Graduate MarshallU. Debut 1980 OB in "Plain and Fancy," followed by "Sound of Music," "Crisp," "A Christmas Carol," "Song for a Saturday," Bdwy in "Copperfield" (1981).

STOUT, STEPHEN. Born May 19, 1952 in Berwyn, IL. Graduate SMU. Bdwy debut 1981 in "Kingdoms," followed by OB's "Cloud 9," "A Midsummer Night's Dream," "Loose Ends."

STRAIGHT, BEATRICE. Born Aug. 2, 1916 in Old Westbury, NY. Attended Darlington Hall. Bdwy debut 1934 in "Bitter Oleander," followed by "Twelfth Night," "Land of Fame," "The Wanhope Building," "Eastward in Eden," "Macbeth," "The Heiress," "The Innocents," "The Grand Tour," "The Crucible," "Everything in the Garden," OB in "Sing Me No Lullaby," "River Line," "Ghosts," "All My Sons," "Hamlet," "Phaedra."

STRIANO, DON. Born Mar. 4, 1948 in Brooklyn, NYC. Attended BklynCol, LIU, RichmondCol. Debut 1987 OB in "Nothing to Report."

STRICKLER, JERRY. Born Dec. 4, 1939 in Goose Creek, TX. Attended SouthwesternU, AmThWing. Bdwy debut 1962 in "Mr. President," followed by "Venus Is," "Love and Kisses," OB in "Rate of Exchange," "My Alamo Family."

STROMAN, GUY. Born Sept. 11, 1951 in Terrell, TX. Graduate TxChristianU. Bdwy debut 1979 in "Peter Pan," followed by "Annie," OB in "After the Rain," "Berlin to Broadway," "Jerome Moross Revue," "Close Your Eyes," "Juno and the Paycock," "Glory Hallelujah!," "To Whom It May Concern," "Aldersgate '88."

SULLIVAN, BRAD. Born Nov. 18, 1931 in Chicago, IL. Graduate UMe, AmThWing. Debut 1961 OB in "Red Roses for Me," followed by "South Pacific," "Hot House," "Leavin' Cheyenne," "The Ballad of Soapy Smith," "Cold Sweat," Bdwy in "The Basic Training of Pavlo Hummel" (1977), "Working," "The Wake of Jamie Foster," "The Caine Mutiny Court-Martial."

SUMMERHAYS, JANE. Born Oct. 11, in Salt Lake City, Ut. Graduate UUt., Catholic U. Debut 1980 OB in "Paris Lights," followed by "On Approval," Bdwy in "Sugar Babies" (1980), "A Chorus Line," "Me and My Girl."

SWANSEN, LARRY. Born Nov. 10, 1930 in Roosevelt, OK. Graduate UOk. Bdwy debut 1966 in "Those That Play the Clowns," followed by "The Great White Hope," "The King and I," OB in "Dr. Faustus Lights the Lights," "Thistle in My Bed," "A Darker Flower," "Vincent," "MacBird," "The Unknown Soldier and His Wife," "The Sound of Music," "Conditioning of Charlie One," "Ice Age," "Prince of Homburg," "Who's There," "Heart of a Dog," "Grandma, Pray for Me."

SWARBRICK, CAROL. Born Mar. 20, 1948 in Inglewood CA. Graduate UCLA, NYU. Debut 1971 OB in "Drat!," followed by "The Glorious Age," Bdwy in "Side by Side by Sondheim," "Whoopee!," "42nd Street."

SWETOW, JOEL. Born Dec. 30, 1951 in Kew Gardens, NY. Graduate Hamilton Col. Debut 1982 OB in "Shenandoah," followed by "Songs of the Religious Life," "Tiger at the Gates," "Switching Channels," "Three i-Act Plays," "Macbeth."

SWIFT, ALLEN. Born Jan. 16, 1924 in NYC. Debut 1961 OB in "Portrait of the Artist," followed by "A Month of Sundays," "Where Memories Are Magic," "My Old Friends," "Divine Fire," "Royal Bob," "The New Yorkers," "The Value of Names," Bdwy in "The Student Gypsy" (1961), "Checking Out," "The Iceman Cometh."

SZARABAJKA, KEITH. Born Dec. 2, 1952 in Oak Park, IL. Attended TrinityU, UChicago. Bdwy debut 1973 in "Warp!," followed by "Doonesbury," OB in "Bleacher Bums," "Class Enemy," "Digby," "Rich Relations," "Women of Manhattan," "Class 1 Acts."

SZYMANSKI, WILLIAM. Born May 16, 1949 in Omaha, Ne. Attended UNe. Debut 1979 OB in "Big Bad Burlesque," followed by "Little Shop of Horrors," "The Winter's Tale."

TAFLER, JEAN. Born Nov. 18, 1957 in Schenectady, NY. Graduate HofstraU. Debut 1981 OB in "Mandragola," followed by "Lady Windermere's Fan," "Richard II," "Towards Zero," "The Cotton Web," "A Lady Named Joe," "Guadeloupe."

TALMAN, ANN. Born Sept. 13, 1957 in Welch, WVa. Graduate PaStateU. Debut 1980 OB in "What's So Beautiful about a Sunset over Prairie Avenue?," followed by "Louisiana Summer," "Winterplay," "Prairie Avenue," "Broken Eggs," "Octoberfest," "We're Home," "Yours Anne," "Songs on a Shipwrecked Sofa," "House Arrest," Bdwy in "The Little Foxes" (1981), "House of Blue Leaves."

TALYN, OLGA. Born Dec. 5 in West Germany. Attended SyracuseU, UBuffalo. Debut 1973 OB in "The Proposition," followed by "Corral," "Tales of Tinseltown," "Shop on Main Street," Bdwy in "A Doll's House," "The Phantom of the Opera."

TANKERSLEY, MARK. Born Apr. 23, 1958 in Houston, TX. Attended Houston Baptist U, Juilliard. Debut 1985 OB in "Life Is a Dream," followed by "Macbeth."

TARANTINA, BRIAN. Born Mar. 27, 1959 in NYC. Debut 1980 OB in "Innocent Thoughts and Harmless Intentions," followed by "Time Framed," "Fables for Friends," "Balm in Gilead," "V & V Only," Bdwy in "Angels Fall" (1983) for which he received a Theatre World Award, "Biloxi Blues," "Boys of Winter."

TARTEL, MICHAEL. Born Mar. 21, 1936 in Newark, NJ. Attended Manhattan Col. Debut 1969 OB in "The Fantasticks," followed by "Swan Song," "Mlle. Colombe," Bdwy in "Billy" (1969), followed by "Going Up."

TAYLOR, MYRA. Born July 9, 1960 in Ft. Motte, SC. Graduate Yale U. Debut 1985 OB in "Dennis," followed by "The Tempest," "Black Girl," "Marathon '86," Bdwy in "A Streetcar Named Desire"(1988).

TAYLOR, REGINA. Born Aug. 22, 1960 in Dallas, Tx. Graduate SMU. Debut 1983 OB in "Young Playwrights Festival," followed by "As You Like It," "Macbeth," "Map of the World," "The Box," "Dr. Faustus," Bdwy in "Shakespeare on Broadway" (1987).

TAYLOR, ROBIN. Born May 28 in Tacoma, Wa. Graduate UCLA. Debut 1979 OB in "Festival," followed by "On the 20th Century," Bdwy in "A Chorus Line" (1985).

TAYLOR, SCOTT. Born June 29, 1962 in Milan, Tn. Attended Ms.State U. Bdwy in "Wind in the Willows" (1985), followed by "Cats."

TELLER (no first name): Born in Philadelphia, Pa. in 1948. Graduate Amherst Col. Debut 1985 OB in "Penn & Teller," Bdwy in same (1987).

TESTA, MARY. Born June 4, 1955 in Philadelphia, Pa. Attended URI. Debut 1979 OB in "In Trousers," followed by "Company," "Life Is Not a Doris Day Movie," "Not-So-New Faces of '82," "American Princess," "Mandrake," "4 One-act Musicals," "Next Please!," "Daughters," "One Act Festival," "The Knife," "Young Playwrights," "Lucky Stiff," Bdwy in "Barnum" (1980), "Marilyn," "The Rink."

THIGPEN, LYNNE. Born in 1940 in Joliet, IL. Graduate UIll. Bdwy debut 1975 in "The Night That Made America Famous," followed by "The Magic Show," "Timbuktu!," "Working," "But Never Jam Today," "Tintypes," "A Month of Sundays," "Fences," OB in "Tintypes," "Balm in Gilead."

THOLE, CYNTHIA. Born Sept. 21, 1957 in Silver Spring, Md. Graduate Butler U. Debut 1982 OB in "Nymph Errant," followed by Bdwy in "42nd Street" (1985), "Me and My Girl."

THOMAS, BEN. Born Mar. 8, 1946 in Cairo, GA. DEbut 1987 OB in "The Signal Season of Dummy Hoy."

THOME, DAVID. Born July 24, 1951 in Salt Lake City, UT. Bdwy debut 1971 in "No, No, Nanette," followed by "Different Times," "Good News," "Rodgers and Hart," "A Chorus Line," "Dancin'," "Dreamgirls" (1981/1987).

THOMPSON, EVAN. Born Sept. 3, 1931 in NYC. Graduate UCal. Bdwy debut 1969 in "Jimmy," followed by "1776," OB in "Mahagonny," "Treasure Island," "Knitters in the Sun," "Half-Life," "Fasnacht Dau," "The Importance of Being Earnest," "Under the Gaslight," "Henry V," "The Fantasticks," "Walk the Dog, Willie," "Macbeth," "1984," "Leave It to Me."

THOMPSON, LAUREN. Born in 1950. Attended PaStateU, Pittsburgh Playhouse. Bdwy debut 1979 in "Dracula," followed by "A Life," "Whodunnit," OB in "The Wedding of the Siamese Twins."

THOMPSON, SADA. Born Sept. 27, 1929 in Des Moines, IO. Graduate Carnegie Tech. Debut 1953 OB in "Under Milk Wood," followed by "Clandestine Marriage," "Murder in the Cathedral," "White Devil," "Carefree Tree," "The Misanthrope," "U.S.A.," "River Line," "Ivanov," "The Last Minstrel," "An Evening for Merlin Finch," "The Effect of Gamma Rays. . . ," "Wednesday," "Real Estate," Bdwy in "Festival," "Juno," "Johnny No-Trump," "American Dream," "Happy Days," "Twigs," "Saturday Sunday Monday."

THOMPSON, WEYMAN. Born Dec. 11, 1950 in Detroit, MI. Graduate WayneStateU, UDetroit. Bdwy debut 1980 in "Clothes for a Summer Hotel," followed by "Dreamgirls" (1985/1987), "Shakespeare's Cabaret," OB in "Daddy Goodness."

THORNE, RAYMOND. Born Nov. 27, 1934 in Lackawanna, NY. Graduate UCt. Debut 1966 OB in "Man with a Load of Mischief," followed by "Rose," "Dames at Sea," "Love Course," "Blue Boys," "Jack and Jill," Bdwy in "Annie" (1977), "Teddy and Alice" (1987).

TILLMAN, JUDITH. Born Apr. 25, 1934 in Cleveland, Oh. Graduate Case Western Reserve U. Debut 1963 OB in "The Darker Flower," followed by "Do I Hear a Waltz?," "Ten Little Indians," "Patrick Pearse Motel," "Deathtrap," "Cowboy," "St. Hugo of Central Park."

TIPPIT, WAYNE. Born Dec. 19, 1932 in Lubbock, TX. Graduate UIowa. Bdwy debut 1959 in "Tall Story," followed by "Only in America," "Gantry," "The Nerd," OB in "Dr. Faustus," "Under the Sycamore Tree," "Misalliance," "The Alchemist," "MacBird," "Trainor, Dean Liepolt & Co.," "Young Master Dante," "Boys in the Band," "Wayside Motor Inn," "For Sale," "Lemon Sky," "Alterations."

TOLAN, KATHLEEN. Born Aug. 10, 1950 in Milwaukee, WI. Attended NYU. Debut 1974 OB in "Hothouse," followed by "More Than You Deserve," "Wicked Women Revue," "Museum," "Imperialists at the Club Cave Canum."

TOLAN, MICHAEL. Born Nov. 27, 1925 in Detroit, MI. Graduate WayneU. Bdwy debut 1955 in "Will Success Spoil Rock Hunter?," followed by "A Hatful of Rain," "The Genius and the Goddess," "Romanoff and Juliet," "A Majority of One," "A Far Country," "Unlikely Heroes," OB in "Coriolanus," "Journey of the 5th Horse," "Close Relations," "Faces of Love/Portrait of America," "A Step Out of Line," "Bedroom Farce."

TOM, LAUREN. Born Aug. 4, 1959 in Highland Park, IL. Graduate NYU. Debut 1980 OB in "The Music Lesson," followed by "Family Devotions," "Non Pasquale," "Dream of Kitamura," "American Notes," "Madame de Sade," Bdwy in "A Chorus Line" (1980), "Doonesbury," "Hurlyburly."

TOMEI, MARISA. Born Dec. 4, 1964 in Brooklyn, NY. Attended Boston U., NYU. Debut 1986 OB in "Daughters" for which she received a Theatre World Award, followed by "Class 1 Acts," "Evening Star."

TOMLINSON, ROBERT MICHAEL. Born Aug. 29, 1953 in Brooklyn, NYC. Graduate Temple U. Debut 1984 OB in "Delirious," followed by "Mirandolina," "Hedda Gabler," "Gravity Shoes," "Murder in the Mummy's Tomb," "Stopping the Desert."

TOMPOS, DOUG. Born Jan. 27, 1962 in Columbus, OH. Graduate SyracuseU, LAMDA. Debut 1985 OB in "Very Warm for May," followed by A Midsummer Night's Dream," "Mighty Fine Music," "Muzeeka," "Wish You Were Here."

TONER, THOMAS. Born May 25, 1928 in Homestead, Pa. Graduate UCLA. Bdwy debut 1973 in "Tricks," followed by "The Good Doctor," "All Over Town," "The Elephant Man," "California Suite," "A Texas Trilogy," "The Inspector General," "Me and My Girl," OB in "Pericles," "The Merry Wives of Windsor," "A Midsummer Night's Dream," "Richard III," "My Early Years," "Life and Limb," "Measure for Measure," "Little Footsteps."

TORAN, PETER. Born July 16, 1955 in McLean, VA. Graduate TuftsU. Debut 1980 OB in "Romeo and Juliet," followed by "It's Wilde!," "The Marquis," "Mr. Universe."

TOWEY, JOHN MADDEN. Born Feb. 13, 1940 in Rochester, MN. Graduate St. John's U., Goodman Theatre Sch. Debut 1970 OB in "To Be Young, Gifted and Black," followed by "God Bless You, Mr. Rosewater," "A Dream out of Time," "Fashion," "My Heart Is in the East," "Crossing the Crab Nebula," "Talk Radio," "Julius Caesar."

TRAVIS, NANCY. Born Sept. 21, 1961 in NYC. Graduate NYU. Debut 1983 OB in "It's Hard to Be a Jew," followed by "The Signal Season of Dummy Hoy," Bdwy in "I'm Not Rappaport" (1986).

TRIBBLE, DARRYL. Born Mar. 20, 1960 in Brooklyn, NY. Attended SUNY/Purchase. Bdwy debut 1980 in "West Side Story," followed by "Dreamgirls" (1987).

TROTT, KAREN. Born Mar. 13, 1954 in Lawrence, MA. Graduate UVt. Debut 1979 OB in "Strider," followed by "3 Postcards," Bdwy in "Strider" (1979), "Barnum," "Arsenic and Old Lace."

TROY, LOUISE. Born Nov. 9 in NYC. Attended AADA. Debut 1955 OB in "The Infernal Machine," followed by "Merchant of Venice," "Conversation Piece," "Salad Days," "O, Oysters!," "A Doll's House," "Last Analysis," "Judy and Jane," "Heartbreak House," "Rich Girls," Bdwy in "Pipe Dream" (1955), "A Shot in the Dark," "Tovarich," "High Spirits," "Walking Happy," "Equus," "Woman of the Year," "Design for Living," "42nd St."

TSOUTSOUVAS, SAM. Born Aug. 20, 1948 in Santa Barbara, Ca. Attended UCal, Juilliard. Debut 1969 OB in "Peer Gynt," followed by "Twelfth Night," "Timon of Athens," "Cymbeline," "School for Scandal," "The Hostage," "Women Beware Women," "Lower Depths," "Emigre," "Hello Dali," "The Merchant of Venice," "The Leader," "The Bald Soprano," "The Taming of the Shrew," "Gus & Al," "Tamara," Bdwy in "The Three Sisters," "Measure for Measure," "Beggar's Opera," "Scapin," "Dracula."

TSUJI, ANN M. Born July 3, 1961 in Yokohama, Japan. Graduate URochester,OhioU. Debut 1987 OB in "Rosie's Cafe," followed by "Madame de Sade," "Boutique Living and Disposable Icons."

TUCCI, MARIA. Born June 19, 1941 in Florence, It. Attended Actors Studio. Bdwy debut 1963 in "The Milk Train Doesn't Stop Here Anymore," followed by "The Rose Tattoo," "The Little Foxes," "The Cuban Thing," "The Great White Hope," "School for Wives," "Lesson from Aloes," "Kingdoms," "Requiem for a Heavyweight," "The Night of the Iguana," OB in "Corruption in the Palace of Justice," "Five Evenings," "Trojan Women," "White Devil," "Horseman, Pass By," "Yerma," "Shepherd of Avenue B," "The Gathering," "Man for All Seasons."

TURNER, PATRICK. Born Dec. 2, 1952 in Seattle, WA. Attended UWash., AmConsTheatre. Debut 1984 OB in "The Merchant of Venice," followed by "Double Inconstancy," "The Taming of the Shrew," "Lady from the Sea," "Two Gentlemen of Verona," "The Contrast," "Pericles," "The Rivals," "Rosaline," "Much Ado about Nothing."

TURTURRO, JOHN. Born Feb. 28, 1957 in Brooklyn, NYC. Graduate SUNY/New Paltz, Yale U. Debut 1984 OB in "Danny and the Deep Blue Sea" for which he received a Theatre World Award, followed by "Men without Dates," "Chaos and Hard Times," "Steel on Steel," "Tooth of Crime," "Of Mice and Men," "Jamie's Gang," "Marathon '86," "The Bald Soprano/The Leader," "La Puta Vita Trilogy," "The Bald Soprano," Bdwy in "Death of a Salesman" (1984).

TWAIN, MICHAEL. Born Nov. 1, 1936 in Lawrence, NY. Graduate OhioStateU. Debut 1936 in "Mr. Roberts," followed by OB's "Kill the One-eyed Man," "The Duchess of Malfi," "Recess," "The Empire Builders," "Pictures at an Exhibition," "Holy Heist."

ULISSEY, CATHERINE. Born Aug. 4, 1961 in NYC. Attended Ntl. Acad. of Arts. Bdwy debut 1986 in "Rags," followed by "The Mystery of Edwin Drood," "Phantom of the Opera."

ULLETT, NICK. Born Mar. 5, 1947 in London, Eng. Graduate Cambridge U. Debut 1967 OB in "Love and Let Love," followed by "The Importance of Being Earnest," Bdwy in "Loot" (1986), "Me and My Girl."

UNDERWOOD, ERIC. Born Apr. 27, 1959 in Coral Gables, Fl. Attended UUtah. Bdwy debut 1985 in "La Cage aux Folles."

UNGER, DEBORAH. Born July 2, 1953 in Philadelphia, PA. Graduate UPittsburg, FlaStateU. Debut 1981 OB in "Seesaw," followed by "The Rise of David Levinsky," "Henry the 8th at the Grand Ole Opry."

URICH, TOM. Born Mar. 26 in Toronto, Oh. Attended CinConsvMusic. Bdwy debut 1970 in "Applause," followed by "Musical Chairs," "La Cage aux Folles," OB in "Streets of NY," "The Fantasticks," "Shoemaker's Holiday."

URLA, JOE. Born Dec. 25, 1958 in Pontiac, Mi. Graduate UMi, Yale U. Debut 1985 OB in "Measure for Measure," followed by "Henry V," "Principia Scriptoriae" for which he received a Theatre World Award, " Our Own Family," "Return of Pinocchio," "The Boys Next Door."

VANCE, COURTNEY B. Born Mar. 12, 1960 in Detroit, Mi. Harvard graduate. Bdwy debut 1987 in "Fences" for which he received a Theatre World Award.

VAUGHAN, MELANIE. Born Sept. 18 in Yazoo City, Ms. Graduate LaStateU. Bdwy debut 1976 in "Rex," followed by "Sunday in the Park with George," "On the 20th Century," "Music Is," "Starlight Express," OB in "Canterbury Tales."

VEDDER, WILLIAMSON. Born Aug. 21, 1962 in York, PA. Graduate Ohio Wesleyan U. Debut 1986 OB in "Light Up the Sky."

VENNEMA, JOHN C. Born Aug. 24, 1948 in Houston, TX. Graduate Princeton U, LAMDA. Bdwy debut 1976 in "The Royal Family," followed by "The Elephant Man," "Otherwise Engaged," OB in "Loot" (1973), "Statements after an Arrest," "The Biko Inquest," "No End of Blame," "In Celebration," "Custom of the Country," "The Basement," "A Slight Ache," "Young Playwrights Festival," "Dandy Dick."

VENTRISS, JENNIE. Born Aug. 7, 1935 in Chicago, IL. Graduate DePaulU. Debut 1954 OB in "Ludlow Fair," followed by "I Can't Keep Running in Place," "Lautrec," "The Contest," "Warren G.," "Mirage," "Look after Lulu," "Between Daylight and Boonville," Bdwy in "Luv" (1966), "Prisoner of Second Avenue," "Gemini," "Sherlock's Last Case."

VINCENT, ROBERT. Born Apr. 13, 1950 in Lafayette, IN. Graduate IndU. Bdwy debut 1983 in "Show Boat," OB in "The Fantasticks" (1987), followed by "Pajama Game."

VIPOND, NEIL. Born Dec. 24, 1929 in Toronto, Can. Bdwy debut 1956 in "Tamburlaine the Great," followed by "Macbeth," OB in "Three Friends," "Sunday Runners," "Hamlet," "Routed," "Mr. Joyce Is Leaving Paris," "The Time of Your Life," "Children of the Sun," "Romeo and Juliet."

VIRTA, RAY. Born June 18, 1958 in L'Anse, MI. Debut 1982 OB in "Twelfth Night," followed by "The Country Wife," "Dubliners," "Pericles," "Tartuffe," "The Taming of the Shrew."

VISCARDI, JOHN. Born Aug. 18, 1961 in NYC. Graduate ColumbiaU. Debut 1988 OB in "Cave Life," followed by "Borderlines."

VIVIANO, SAL. Born July 12, 1960 in Detroit, MI. Graduate EIllU. Bdwy debut 1984 in "The Three Musketeers," followed by "Romance/Romance," OB in "Miami" (1986), "Hot Times and Suicide," "Romance/Romance."

VOET, DOUG. Born Mar. 1, 1951 in Los Angeles, CA. Graduate BYU. Bdwy debut in "Joseph and the Amazing Technicolor Dreamcoat" (1982), OB in "Forbidden Broadway."

VOSBURGH, DAVID. Born Mar. 14, 1938 in Coventry, RI. Attended Boston U. Bdwy debut 1968 in "Maggie Flynn," followed by "1776," "A Little Night Music," "Evita," "A Doll's Life," "Cabaret" (1987), OB in "Smith," "The Rise of David Levinsky."

WAARA, SCOTT. Born June 5, 1957 in Chicago, IL. Graduate SMU. Debut 1982 OB in "The Rise of Daniel Rocket," followed by "The Dining Room," "Johnny Pye and the Foolkiller," Bdwy in "The Wind in the Willows" (1985).

WAGNER, CHUCK. Born June 20, 1958 in Nashville, TN. Graduate USCal. Bdwy debut 1985 in "The Three Musketeers," followed by "Into the Woods."

WAITE, JOHN THOMAS. Born Apr. 19, 1948 in Syracuse, NY. Attended SyracuseU. Debut 1976 OB in "The Fantasticks," Bdwy in "Amadeus" (1982).

WALKER, JANET HAYES. Born June 11 in Shanghai, China. Graduate NewEngConsv, Hunter Col. Bdwy debut 1954 in "The Golden Apple," followed by "Anyone Can Whistle," "Camelot," "The Music Man," "Damn Yankees," OB in "Boys from Syracuse," "A Touch of the Poet," "Plain and Fancy," "Candide," "Rain," "The Subject Was Roses," "Relatively Speaking," "Nude with Violin," "The Buck Stops Here," "Night Games," "A Frog in his Throat."

WALKER, RAY. Born Aug. 13, 1963 in St. Johnsbury, VT. Graduate NYU. Debut 1985 OB in "Christmas Spectacular," followed by "Merrily We Roll Along," Bdwy 1988 in "Les Miserables."

WALLER, KENNETH. Born Apr. 12, 1945 in Atlanta, Ga. Graduate Piedmont Col. Debut 1976 OB in "Boys from Syracuse," Bdwy in "Sarava" (1979), "Onward Victoria," "Me and My Girl," "Phantom of the Opera."

WALLOWITCH, JOHN. Born Feb. 11 in Philadelphia, PA. Graduate TempleU, Juilliard. Debut OB in "Big Charlotte," followed by "Cracked Cups," "The World of Wallowitch."

WALSH, BARBARA. Born June 3, 1955 in Washington, DC. Attended Montgomery Col. Bdwy debut 1982 in "Rock 'n' Roll: The First 5000 Years," followed by "Nine," OB in "Forbidden Broadway."

WALSH, ELIZABETH. Born Oct. 12 in PuertoRico. Graduate UWisc, UMa. Debut 1987 OB in "Mademoiselle Colombe."

WALSH, TENNEY. Born Oct. 18, 1963 in New Haven, CT. Attended YaleU. Debut 1981 OB in "The Wild Duck," followed by "A Think Piece," "Joe Egg," "Even in Laughter," "Breaking the Prairie Wolf Code," "Tomorrow's Monday," "A Tapestry of Dreams," "The White Rose of Memphis," Bdwy in "Joe Egg" (1985).

WALTERS, KELLY. Born May 28, 1950 in Amarillo, TX. Graduate UWash. Debut 1973 OB in "Look We've Come Through," followed by "The Tempest," "The Taming of the Shrew," Bdwy in "Candide" (1975), "Canterbury Tales," "Barnum," "Grind."

WALTON, JIM. Born July 31, 1955 in Tachikawa, Japan. Graduate UCincinnati. Debut 1979 OB in "Big Bad Burlesque," followed by "Scrambled Feet," "Stardust," Bdwy in "Perfectly Frank"

(1980), "Merrily We Roll Along," "42nd Street," "Stardust," "42nd Street."

WARD, JANET. Born Feb. 19 in NYC. Attended Actors Studio. Bdwy debut 1945 in "Dream Girl," followed by "Anne of a Thousand Days," "Detective Story," "King of Friday's Men," "Middle of the Night," "Miss Lonelyhearts," "J. B.," "Cheri," "The Egg," "The Impossible Years," "Of Love Remembered," "OB in "Chapparal," "The Typists," "The Tiger," "Summertree," "Dream of a Blacklisted Actor," "Cruising Speed 600MPH," "One Flew over the Cuckoo's Nest," "Love Gotta Come by Saturday Night," "Home Is the Hero," "Love Death Plays," "Olympic Park," "Hillbily Wives," "Q.E.D.," "Yellow Dog Contract."

WARNER, AMY. Born June 29, 1951 in Minneapolis, MN. Graduate Principia Col. Debut 1982 OB in "Faust," followed by "Ghost Sonata," "Wild Oats," "Big Little/Scenes," "Hamlet," "George Dandin," "The Underpants," "As the Wind Rocks the Wagon."

WARNER, MALCOLM JAMAL. Born Aug. 18, 1970 in Jersey City, NJ. Debut 1988 OB in "Three Ways Home."

WARREN, JOSEPH. Born June 5, 1916 in Boston, MA. Graduate UDenver. Bdwy debut 1951 in "Barefoot in Athens," followed by "One Bright Day," "Love of Four Colonels," "Hidden River," "The Advocate," "Philadelphia, Here I Come," "Borstal Boy," "Lincoln Mask," OB in "Brecht on Brecht," "Jonah," "Little Black Sheep," "Black Tuesday," "The Show-Off," "Big Apple Messenger," "The Ballad of Soapy Smith," "Her Great Match," "Measure for Measure," "Hamlet," "The Rivals," "Of Mice and Men," "Uncle Vanya."

WARRILOW, DAVID. Born Dec. 28, 1934 in Stone, Eng. Graduate UReading. Debut 1970 OB in "The Red Horse Animation," followed by "Penguin Touquet," "A Piece of Monologue," "Three Plays by Samuel Beckett," "Messiah," "Golden Windows," "Zangezi."

WATERBURY, MARSHA (formerly Marsha Skaggs). Born Aug. 23, 1949 in Bedford, Oh. Attended Purdue U., AADA. Bdwy debut 1981 in "They're Playing Our Song," followed by "Einstein and the Polar Bear," "Smile," OB in "Little Shop of Horrors."

WATERSTON, SAM. Born Nov. 15, 1940 in Cambridge, MA. Yale Graduate. Bdwy debut 1963 in "Oh, Dad, Poor Dad . . .," followed by "First One Asleep Whistle," "Halfway Up the Tree," "Indians," "Hay Fever," "Much Ado about Nothing," "A Meeting by the River," "Lunch Hour," "Benefactors," "A Walk in the Woods," OB in "As You Like It," "A Thistle in My Bed," "The Knack," "Fitz," "Biscuit," "La Turista," "Posterity for Sale," "Ergo," "Museeka," "Red Cross," "Henry IV," "Spitting Image," "I Met a Man," "Brass Butterfly," "Trial of the Catonsville 9," "Cymbeline," "Hamlet," "The Tempest," "A Doll's House," "Measure for Measure," "Chez Vous," "Waiting for Godot," "Gardenia," "The Three Sisters."

WATSON, DOUGLASS. Born Feb. 24, 1921 in Jackson, GA. Graduate UNC. Bdwy debut 1947 in "The Iceman Cometh," followed by "Antony and Cleopatra" for which he received a Theatre World Award, "Leading Lady," "Richard III," "The Happiest Years," "That Lady," "The Wisteria Trees," "Romeo and Juliet," "Desire under the Elms," "Sunday Breakfast," "Cyrano de Bergerac," "Confidential Clerk," "Portrait of a Lady," "The Miser," "The Young and Beautiful," "Little Glass Clock," "The Country Wife," "A Man for All Seasons," "Chinese Prime Minister," "Marat/Sade," "The Prime of Miss Jean Brodie," "Pirates of Penzance," "Over Here," "The Philadelphia Story," OB in "Much Ado about Nothing," "King Lear," "As You Like It," "Hunger," "Dancing for the Kaiser," "Money," "My Life," "Sightlines," "Glorious Morning," "Hamlet," "Upside Down on the Handlebars."

WEBER, STEVEN. Born Mar. 4, 1961 in NYC. Attended SUNY/Purchase. Debut 1983 OB in "The Inheritors," followed by "Rain," "Paradise Lost," "Ghosts," "Come Back, Little Sheba," "Marathon '88."

WEDGEWORTH, ANN. Born Jan. 21, 1935 in Abilene, TX. Bdwy debut 1958 in "Make a Million," followed by "Blues for Mr. Charlie," "The Last Analysis," "Thieves," "Chapter 2," OB in "Chapparal," "The Crucible," "The Days and Nights of Beebee Fenstermaker," "Ludlow Fair," "Line," "Elba," "A Lie of the Mind," "The Debutante Ball."

WEINER, JOHN. Born Dec. 17, 1954 in Newark, NJ. Graduate Wm. & Mary Col. Bdwy debut 1983 in "La Cage aux Folles."

WEISS, GORDON J. Born June 16, 1949 in Bismarck, ND. Attended Moorhead State Col. Bdwy debut 1974 in "Jumpers," followed by "Goodtime Charley," "King of Hearts," "Raggedy Ann," OB in "A Walk on the Wild Side."

WEISS, JEFF. Born in 1940 in Allentown, Pa. Debut 1986 OB in "Hamlet," followed by "The Front Page" (LC), Bdwy in "Macbeth" (1988).

WELBY, DONNAH. Born May 4, 1952 in Scranton, PA. Graduate Catholic U. Debut 1981 OB in "Between Friends," followed by "Double Inconstancy," "The Taming of the Shrew," "The Contrast," "Macbeth," "Electra."

WELLS, CHRISTOPHER. Born June 18, 1955 in Norwalk, CT. Graduate Amherst Col. Debut 1981 OB in "Big Apple Country," followed by "Broadway Jukebox," "Savage Amusement," "Overruled," "Heart of Darkness," Bdwy in "Harrigan 'n' Hart" (1985), "Broadway," "Teddy and Alice."

WELLS, CRAIG. Born July 2, 1955 in Newark, NJ. Graduate Albion Col. Debut 1985 OB in "Forbidden Broadway," "The Best of Forbidden Broadway," Bdwy in "Chess" (1988).

WELLS, DEANNA. Born Aug. 7, 1962 in Milwaukee, Wi. Graduate Northwestern U. Debut 1985 OB in "On the 20th Century," followed by "After These Messages," "The Fantasticks," Bdwy in "Smile," "South Pacific" (LC).

WEST, MATT. Born Oct. 2, 1958 in Downey, CA. Attended Pfiffer-Smith School. Bdwy debut in "A Chorus Line" (1980).

WEST, RACHEL. Born Jan. 18, 1976 in NYC. Debut 1987 OB in "The Miracle Worker," followed by "Resistance."

WESTENBERG, ROBERT. Born Oct. 26, 1953 in Miami Beach, FL. Graduate UCal/Fresno. Debut 1981 OB in "Henry IV Part I," followed by "Hamlet," "The Death of von Richthofen," Bdwy in "Zorba" (1983) for which he received a Theatre World Award, "Sunday in the Park with George," "Into the Woods."

WESTPHAL, ROBIN. Born Nov. 24, 1953 in Salt Lake City, UT. Graduate UUtah. Debut 1983 OB in "June Moon," followed by "Taming of the Shrew," "Merchant of Venice," "Somewheres Better," "Lady from the Sea," "Her Great Match," "Antigone," "Pericles," "The Rivals," "Murder in the Mummy's Tomb," "Macbeth," "Uncle Vanya."

WETHERALL, JACK. Born Aug. 5, 1950 in Sault Ste. Marie, Can. Graduate Glendon Col. York U. Bdwy debut 1979 in "The Elephant Man," followed by OB's "Tamara." (1987).

WHITE, RICHARD. Born Aug. 4, 1953 in Oak Ridge, Tn. Graduate Oberlin Col. Bdwy debut 1979 in "The Most Happy Fella," followed by "Brigadoon" (LC), OB in "Elizabeth and Essex," "South Pacific" (LC), "The Desert Song" (LC).

WIKES, MICHAEL. Born June 22, 1955 in Brackenridge, Pa. Graduate Boston U. OB in "Talk to Me Like the Rain," "Old Business," "Self Defense."

WILDING, MICHAEL. Born Jan. 6, 1955 in Los Angeles, Ca. Debut 1986 OB in "Dead Wrong," followed by "Dispatches from Hell," "Bedroom Farce," "Perfect Crime."

WILHOITE, KATHLEEN. Born June 29, 1964 in Santa Barbara, Ca. Attended USCa. Debut 1987 OB in "Division Street," followed by "Moonchildren."

WILKINSON, COLM. Born June 5, 1944 in Dublin, Ire. Bdwy debut 1987 in "Les Miserables" for which he received a Theatre World Award.

WILKINSON, KATE. Born Oct. 25 in San Francisco, Ca. Attended San Jose State Col. Bdwy debut 1967 in "Little Murders," followed by "Johnny No Trump," "Watercolor," "Postcards," "Ring Round the Bathtub," "The Last of Mrs. Lincoln," "Man and Superman," "Frankenstein," "The Man Who Came to Dinner," OB in "La Madre," "Ernest in Love," "Story of Mary Surratt," "Bring Me a Warm Body," "Child Buyer," "Rimers of Eldritch," "A Doll's House," "Hedda Gabler," "The Real Inspector Hound," "The Contractor," "When the Old Man Died," "The Overcoat," "Villager," "Good Help Is Hard to Find," "Lumiere," "Rude Times," "Steel Magnolias."

WILLIAMS, BARRY. Born Sept. 30, 1954 in Santa Monica, CA. Attended Pepperdine U. Bdwy debut 1977 in "Pippin," followed by "Romance/Romance."

WILLIAMS, BILLY DEE. Born Apr. 6, 1938 in NYC. Attended NtlAcadFineArts. Bdwy debut 1945 in "Firebrand of Florence," followed by "Cool World," "A Taste of Honey," "Hallelujah, Baby!," "I Have a Dream," "Fences," OB in "Blue Boy in Black," "Firebugs," "Ceremonies in Dark Old Men," "Slow Dance on the Killing Ground."

WILLIAMS, ELLIS. Born June 28, 1951 in Brunswick, GA. Graduate BostonU. Debut 1977 OB in "Intimation," followed by "Spell #7," "Mother Courage," "Ties That Bind," "Kid Purple," "The Boys Next Door," Bdwy in "The Basic Training of Pavlo Hummel," "Pirates of Penzance," "Solomon's Child," "Trio," "Requiem for a Heavyweight."

WILLIAMS, L. B. Born May 7, 1949 in Richmond, VA. Graduate Albion Col. Bdwy debut 1976 in "Equus," OB in "Spa," "Voices," "5 on the Blackhand Side," "Chameleon," "Forbidden Copy," "Song of Solomon," "G. R. Point," "New Works '87."

WILLIAMS, VAN. Born Apr. 10, 1925 in PHARR, TX. Attended UTx, Yale U. Bdwy debut 1951 in "Richard II," followed by "St. Joan," "Dial'M'for Murder," "Little Moon of Alban," "No Time for Sergeants," "The Teahouse of the August Moon."

WILLIS, RICHARD. Born in Dallas, TX. Graduate CornellU, NorthwesternU. Debut 1986 OB in "Three Sisters," followed by "Nothing to Report."

WILLIS, SUSAN. Born in Tiffin, OH. Attended Carnegie Tech, Cleveland Play House. Debut 1953 OB in "The Little Clay Cart," followed by "Love and Let Love," "Glorious Age," "The Guardsman," "Dangerous Corners," "Children of the Sun," "The Wedding of the Siamese Twins," Bdwy in "Take Me Along" (1959), "Gypsy," "Dylan," "Come Live with Me," "Cabaret," "Oliver!"

WILLISON, WALTER. Born June 24, 1947 in Monterey Park, Ca. Bdwy debut 1970 in "Norman, Is That You?," followed by "Two by Two" for which he received a Theatre World Award, "Wild and Wonderful," "A Celebration of Richard Rodgers," "Pippin," "A Tribute to Joshua Logan," "A Tribute to George Abbott," OB in "South Pacific in Concert," "They Say It's Wonderful," "Broadway Scandals of 1928," and "Options," both of which he wrote, "Aldersgate 88."

WILLOUGHBY, RONALD. Born June 3, 1937 in Boss, MS. Graduate Millsaps Col., Northwestern U. Debut 1963 OB in "Walk in Darkness," followed by "Little Eyolf," "Antony and Cleopatra," "Balm in Gilead," "Dracula: Sabbat," "The Faggot," "King of the U.S.," "Twelfth Night," "Black People's Party," "Mrs. Warren's Profession," "Why Marry?" "The Green Bay Tree," "Julius Caesar," "A Man's World," "The Sound of Murder," "Milestones," "Sailor, Beware!", "The Elephant Man."

WILLS, RAY. Born Sept. 14, 1960 in Santa Monica, CA. Graduate WichitaStateU, BrandeisU. Debut 1988 OB in "Side by Side by Sondheim."

WILSON, JULIE. Born in 1925 in Omaha, Neb. Bdwy debut 1946 in "Three to Make Ready," followed by "Kiss Me, Kate," "Kismet," "The Pajama Game," "Jimmy," "Park," OB in "From Weill to Sondheim."

WILSON, K. C. Born Aug. 10, 1945 in Miami, Fl. Attended AADA. Debut 1973 OB in "Little Mahagonny," followed by "The Tempest," "Richard III," "Macbeth," "Threepenny Opera," "The Passion of Dracula," "Francis," "Robin Hood," "Tatterdemalion," "Beef," "The Art of War," "A Walk on the Wild Side," Bdwy in "Smile" (1986).

WILSON, MARY LOUISE. Born Nov. 12, 1936 in New Haven, CT. Graduate Northwestern U. Bdwy debut 1963 in "Hot Spot," followed by "Flora the Red Menace," "Criss-Crossing," "Promises, Promises," "The Women," "The Gypsy," "The Royal Family," "Importance of Being Earnest," "Philadelphia Story," "Fools," "Alice in Wonderland," "The Odd Couple," OB in "Our Town," "Upstairs at the Downstairs," "Threepenny Opera," "A Great Career," "Whispers on the Wind," "Beggar's Opera," "Buried Child," "Sister Mary Ignatius Explains It All," "Actor's Nightmare," "Baby with the Bathwater," "Musical Comedy Murders of 1940."

WILSON, TREY. Born Jan. 21, 1948 in Houston, Tx. Bdwy debut 1979 in "Peter Pan," followed by "Tintypes," "The First," "Foxfire," OB in "Personals," "Custom of the Country," "The Front Page" (LC), "Debutante Ball."

WINDE, BEATRICE. Born Jan. 6 in Chicago, Il. Debut 1966 OB in "In White America," followed by "June Bug Graduates Tonight," "Strike Heaven on the Face," "Divine Comedy," "Crazy Horse," "My Mother My Father and Me," "Steal Away," "The Actress," "Richard II," "1-2-3-4-5." Bdwy in "Ain't Supposed to Die a Natural Death" (1971) for which she received a Theatre World Award.

WINSON, SUZI. Born Feb. 28, 1962 in NYC. Bdwy debut 1980 in "Brigadoon," followed by OB in "Moondance," "Nunsense."

WINSTON, HATTIE. Born Mar. 3, 1945 in Greenville, MS. Attended HowardU. OB in "Prodigal Son," "Say of Absence," "Pins and Needles," "Weary Blues," "Man Better Man," "Billy Noname," "Sambo," "The Great MacDaddy," "A Photo," "Oklahoma!," "The Michigan," "Mother Courage," "God Is a (Guess What?)," "Kongi's Harvest," "Summer of the 17th Doll,"

Carol Swarbrick	Keith Szarabajka	Jean Tafler	Mark Tankersley	Mary Testa	Ben Thomas
Michael Tolan	Marisa Tomei	Darryl Tribble	Ann M. Tsuji	Eric Underwood	Melanie Vaughan
Jennie Ventriss	John Viscardi	Janet Hayes Walker	Ray Walker	Elizabeth Walsh	John Weiner
Gordon Weiss	Donnah Welby	Jack Wetherall	Kate Wilkinson	Richard White	Beatrice Winde
Suzi Winson	Jim Winston	Charlaine Woodard	Ron Yamamoto	Jo Ann Yeoman	Mark Zimmerman

"Song of the Lusitanian Bogey," "Long Time Since Yesterday," "A Walk on the Wild Side," Bdwy in "The Me Nobody Knows," "Two Gentlemen of Verona," "Does a Tiger Wear a Necktie?," "Hair," "Scapino," "I Love My Wife," "The Tap Dance Kid."

WINSTON, JIM. Born June 29 in Lynn, MA. Attended AMDA. Debut 1988 OB in "A Circle on the Cross."

WITHAM, JOHN. Born Apr. 3, 1947 in Plainfield, NJ. Graduate AMDA. Debut 1972 OB in "Two If by Sea," followed by "Comedy," Bdwy in "1600 Pennsylvania Avenue" (1976), "Teddy and Alice."

WOLFE, ELISSA. Born Mar. 17, 1963 in New Rochelle, NY. Attended AADA. Bdwy debut 1979 in "I Remember Mama," followed by OB's "Snapshot," "A Tapestry of Dreams."

WOLFE, JIM. Born July 8, 1954 in Omaha, NE. Bdwy debut 1979 in "Peter Pan," followed by "Cabaret" (1987).

WOLPE, LENNY. Born Mar. 25, 1951 in Newburgh, NY. Graduate Geo. Wash. U, UMn. Debut 1978 OB in "Company," followed by "Brownstone," "Mayor," "The Wonder Years," Bdwy in "Onward Victoria" (1980), "Copperfield," "Mayor," "Into the Light."

WONG, B. D. (aka Bradd). Born Oct. 24, 1962 in San Francisco, CA. Debut 1981 OB in "Androcles and the Lion," followed by "Applause," Bdwy in "M. Butterfly" (1988) for which he received a Theatre World Award.

WOODARD, CHARLAINE. Born Dec. 29 in Albany, NY. Graduate Goodman Theatre, SUNY. Debut 1975 OB in "Don't Bother Me, I Can't Cope," followed by "Dementos," "Under Fire," "A . . . My Name Is Alice," "Twelfth Night," "Hang on to the Good Times," "Paradise," Bdwy in "Hair," "Ain't Misbehavin'" (1978/1988).

WOODS, CAROL. Born Nov. 13, 1943 in Jamaica, NY. Graduate Ithaca Col. Debut 1980 OB in "One Mo' Time," followed by "Stepping Out," Bdwy in "Grind" (1985), "Big River."

WOODS, RICHARD. Born May 9, 1923 in Buffalo, NY. Graduate Ithaca Col. Bdwy in "Beg, Borrow or Steal," "Capt. Brassbound's Conversion," "Sail Away," "Coco," "Last of Mrs. Lincoln," "Gigi," "Sherlock Holmes," "Murder among Friends," "The Royal Family," "Deathtrap," "Man and Superman," "The Man Who Came to Dinner," "The Father," "Present Laughter," "Alice in Wonderland," "You Can't Take It with You," "Design for Living," "Smile," OB in "The Crucible," "Summer and Smoke," "American Gothic," "Four-in-One," "My Heart's in the Highlands," "Eastward in Eden," "The Long Gallery," "The Year Boston Won the Pennant," "In the Matter of J. Robert Oppenheimer," "with APA in "You Can't Take It with You," "War and Peace," "School for Scandal," "Right You Are," "The Wild Duck," "Pantagleize," "Exit the King," "The Cherry Orchard," "Cock-a-Doodle Dandy," and "Hamlet," "Crimes and Dreams," "Marathon 84," "Much Ado about Nothing."

WORKMAN, SHANELLE. Born Aug. 3, 1978 in Fairfax, VA. Bdwy debut 1988 in "Les Miserables."

WRIGHT, AMY. Born Apr. 15, 1950 in Chicago, Il. Graduate Beloit Col. Debut 1977 OB in "The Stronger," followed by "Nightshift," "Hamlet," "Miss Julie," "Slacks and Tops," "Terrible Jim Fitch," "Village Wooing," "The Stronger," "Time Framed," "Trifles," "Words from the Moon," Bdwy in "5th of July" (1980), "Noises Off."

WRIGHT, TOM. Born Nov. 29, 1952 in Englewood, NJ. Attended Westchester State Col. Debut 1981 OB in "A Taste of Honey," followed by "Turnbuckle," "The Box," "Women of Manhattan," "That Serious He-Man Bull," Bdwy in "A Taste of Honey" (1981).

WRIGHT-BEY, MARVIN. Born Feb. 18, 1952 in Cleveland, OH. Attended Coastal Carolina Com.Col., CuyhogaComCol. Debut 1975 OB in "Langston," followed by Bdwy in "Don't Get God Started" (1987).

WYMAN, NICHOLAS. Born May 18, 1950 in Portland, Me. Graduate Harvard U. Bdwy debut 1975 in "Very Good Eddie," followed by "Grease," "The Magic Show," "On the 20th Century," "Whoopee!," "My Fair Lady" (1981), "Doubles," "Musical Comedy Murders of 1940," "Phantom of the Opera," OB in "Paris Lights," "When We Dead Awaken," "Charlotte Sweet," "Kennedy at Colonus," "Once on a Summer's Day," "Angry Housewives."

YAMAMOTO, RONALD. Born Mar. 13, 1953 in Seattle, WA. Graduate Queens Col. Debut 1983 OB in "A Song for a Nisei Fisherman," followed by "Pacific Overtures," "Rosie's Cafe."

YEOMAN, JOANN. Born Mar. 19, 1948 in Phoenix, AZ. Graduate AzStateU, PurdueU. Debut 1974 OB in "The Boy Friend," followed by "Texas Starlight," "Ba Ta Clan," "A Christmas Carol."

YOUNGMAN, CHRISTINA. Born Sept. 14, 1963 in Philadelphia, Pa. Attended Point Park Col. Debut 1983 OB in "Emperor of My Baby's Heart," followed by "Carousele des Folles," Bdwy in "Starlight Express" (1987).

ZACHARIAS, EMILY. Born July 27, 1953 in Memphis, Tn. Graduate Northwestern U. Debut 1980 OB in "March of the Falsettos," followed by "America Kicks Up Its Heels," "Crazy He Calls Me," "Olympus on My Mind," "Dirty Work," "3 Pieces for a Warehouse," Bdwy in "Perfectly Frank" (1980).

ZAGNIT, STUART. Born Mar. 28, in New Brunswick, NJ. Graduate MontclairStateCol. Debut 1978 OB in "The Wager," followed by "Manhattan Transference," "Women in Tune," "Enter Laughing," "Kuni Leml," "Tatterdemalion," "The Golden Land," "Little Shop of Horrors," "Lucky Stiff," "The Grand Tour."

ZALOOM, JOE. Born July 30, 1944 in Utica, NY. Graduate CatholicU. Bdwy debut 1972 in "Capt. Brassbound's Conversion," followed by "Kingdoms," OB in "The Nature and the Purpose of the Universe," "Plot Counter Plot," "A Midsummer Night's Dream," "Madrid, Madrid."

ZALOOM, PAUL. Born Dec. 14, 1951 in Brooklyn, NY. Graduate Goddard Col. Debut 1979 OB in "Fruit of Zaloom," followed by "Zalooming Along," "Zaloominations," "Crazy as Zaloom," "Return of the Creature from the Blue Zaloom," "Theatre of Trash."

ZANG, EDWARD. Born Aug. 19, 1934 in NYC. Graduate BostonU. OB in "The Good Soldier Schweik," "St. Joan," "Boys in the Band," "The Reliquary of Mr. and Mrs. Potterfield," "The Last Analysis," "As You Like It," "More Than You Deserve," "Polly," "Threepenny Opera," "Largo Desolato," "The New York Idea," "The Misanthrope," "Banana Box," "The Penultimate Problem of Sherlock Holmes," "Henry IV Part I," "Richard II," "Palace of Amateurs."

ZARAGOZA, GREGORY. Born Aug. 23, 1954 in San Jose, CA. Graduate San Jose State, UCalBerkeley, NYU. Bdwy debut 1988 in "Macbeth."

ZARISH, JANET. Born Apr. 21, 1954 in Chicago, IL. Juilliard graduate. Debut 1981 OB in "The Villager," followed by "Playing with Fire," "Royal Bob," "An Enemy of the People," "A Midsummer Night's Dream," "Festival of 1 Acts."

ZEISLER, MARK. Born Mar. 23, 1960 in NYC. Graduate SUNY/Purchase. Debut 1984 OB in "Crime and Punishment," followed by "Measure for Measure," "Acts of Faith."

ZIEMBA, KAREN. Born Nov. 12, in St. Joseph, Mi. Graduate UAkron. Debut 1981 OB in "Seesaw," followed by "I Married an Angel in Concert," Bdwy in "A Chorus Line" (1982), "42nd Street," "Teddy and Alice."

ZIEN, CHIP. Born in 1947 in Milwaukee, WI. Attended UPa. OB in "You're a Good Man, Charlie Brown," followed by "Kadish," "How to Succeed . . . ," "Dear Mr. G," "Tuscaloosa's Calling," "Hot 1 Baltimore," "El Grande de Coca Cola," "Split," "Real Life Funnies," "March of the Falsettos," "Isn't It Romantic," "Diamonds," Bdwy in "All Over Town" (1974), "The Suicide," "Into the Woods."

ZIMMERMAN, MARK. Born Apr. 19, 1952 in Harrisburg, PA. Graduate UPa. Debut 1976 OB in "Fiorello!," followed by "Silk Stockings," "On a Clear Day You Can See Forever," "110 in the Shade," "Fellow Travelers," Bdwy in "Brigadoon" (1981).

ZISKIE, DANIEL. Born in Detroit, MI. Debut 1970 OB in "Second City," followed by "The Seagull," "Ballymurphy," "The Rivals," "Listen to the Lions," "Halloween Bandit," "Mamet Plays," "At Home," "The Castaways," Bdwy in "Morning's at 7" (1980), "Breakfast with Les and Bess," "I'm Not Rappaport."

ZISKIE, KURT. Born Apr. 16, 1956 in Oakland, CA. Graduate StanfordU, Neighborhood Playhouse. Debut 1985 OB in "A Flash of Lightning," followed by Bdwy in "Broadway" (1987).

OBITUARIES

VERA ALLEN, 89, New York City-born actress on stage, screen, TV and radio, died of heart failure August 10 in Croton-on-Hudson, New York. She made her debut in 1925 in "The Grand Street Follies" followed by as *The Dybbuk, The Critic,* appeared on Broadway in *The Silver Cord, Susan and God, A Woman's a Fool to be Clever, The Philadelphia Story, Glorious Morning, At Home Abroad, The Philadelphia Story, The Show Is On, The Two Mrs. Carrolls, Strange Fruit, Ladies of the Corridor,* and she was a president of the American Theatre Wing. Survived by a son and two grandchildren.

JEAN ANOUILH, 77, Bordeaux-born, France's foremost and most enduring playwright and screenwriter, his work translated into 27 languages, died Oct 3 of a heart attack in Lausanne, Switzerland. He wrote some 62 plays, including *The Ermine, The Robbers' Ball, Rendevous at Senlis, Traveller Without Luggage, Antigone* (on Broadway with Katharine Cornell in 1945–46), *Ring Around the Moon, Colombe, Legend of Lovers, Cry of the Peacock, The Lark* (Lillian Hellman's adaptation of his *Joan of Arc*), *Becket, Waltz of the Toreadors, Time Remembered, The Fighting Cock,* and *Poor Bitos,* to name just a few. He also adapted three Shakespeare comedies, Wilde's *Importance of Being Ernest* and O'Neill's *Desire Under the Elms* for the French stage, wrote a ballet for Roland Petit, and several TV plays. In 1988 he published *"The Viscontess of Eristal Has Not Received Her Mechanical Carpet Sweeper"*, a book of reminiscences. He is survived by his wife, a son and three daughters, including actress Monelle Anouilh.

FRED ASTAIRE, 88, Omaha-born stage, screen, radio and TV dancer, actor, and choreographer who's incomparable elegance, charismatic personality, and creative genius made him one of our greatest screen legends, died of pneumonia in the arms of his wife, former jockey Robyn Smith, on June 22 in Los Angeles, CA. Before moving on to his great film successes, he appeared in 11 Broadway shows, partnered with his sister Adele in *Over the Top* in 1916, followed by shows including *The Passing Show of 1918, Apple Blossoms, The Love Letter, For Goodness Sake* (a London hit as *Stop Flirting*), *The Bunch and Judy, Lady Be Good, Funny Face* (Adele's last show before retiring to marry Lord Charles Cavendish), and he first appeared solo in *The Gay Divorce.* His many honors include the Special Academy Award in 1949 for "raising the standards of all musicals," two Emmys, the 1978 Kennedy Center Honors, and The American Film Institute Life Achievement Award in 1981. He is survived by his wife, a son, a daughter, and a stepson.

RUTH ATTAWAY, 77, Mississippi-born veteran actress of stage and screen died September 21 at New York Hospital of injuries resulting from an apartment fire. She made her Broadway debut in 1936 in *You Can't Take It With You,* followed by *The Grass Harp, Mrs. Patterson, Mister Johnson, The Egghead, After the Fall,* and *Yerma.* A sister survives.

JAMES BALDWIN, 63, Harlem-born novelists, essayist, and playwright, died of stomach cancer Dec. 1, 1987, at his home in St. Paul de Vence in southern France. His plays include *Blues for Mister Charlie* and *The Amen Corner.* He is survived by his mother, five sisters, and three brothers.

PAULA BAUERSMITH, 78, Pittsburg-born stage, radio and TV actress, died of cancer August 6, 1987 in New York City. She made her Broadway debut in 1931 in *Lean Harvest,* followed by *East of Broadway, The Warrior's Husband, The Anatomist, Three-Cornered Moon, All Good American, Mahogany Hall, Let Freedom Ring, Bury the Dead, 200 Were Chosen, 20th Century, The Lesson, Sail Away,* and with National Repertory Theatre. She is survived by a daughter, actress Jennifer Warren, a son and three grandchildren.

OLGA BELLIN, 54, Wisconsin-born stage, screen and TV actress, died Nov. 8, 1987 of cancer in Manhattan. She made her debut Off-Broadway in 1855 in *The Carefree Tree,* followed by *A Month in the Country, Zelda* (directed by her husband, Paul Roebling, in 1984), and she was on Broadway in *Protective Custody* and *A Man for All Seasons.* She is survived by her husband and her son, Kristian.

MICHAEL BENNETT, 44, Buffalo-born, innovative director-choreographer, producer, actor and dancer of stage, screen, and TV, and the winner of two 1976 Tony Awards (Best Director/Best Choreographer with Bob Avian) for the Pulitzer Prize winning *A Chorus Line* died July 2 at his Tucson, AZ home of AIDS-related lymphoma. One of Broadway's greatest creative geniuses, began his career performing in such shows as *Subways Are For Sleeping, Here's Love,* and *Bajour,* and was unofficial dance assistant on *How Now, Dow Jones, Your Own Thing,* and *By Jupiter,* before garnering Tony nominations for choreographing *A Joyful Noise, Henry Sweet Henry, Promises Promises, Coco,* and *Company.* He produced *Twigs,* directed *God's Favorite,* and earned seven Tony awards for shows including *Follies* (Best Choreography/Best Director with Harold Prince), *Seesaw* (Best Choreography), *Ballroom* (Best Choreography with Bob Avian), and *Dreamgirls* (Best Choreography with Michael Peters). Married briefly to *A Chorus Line* star Donna McKechnie in 1976, he is survived by his mother and a brother.

GENE BLAKELY, 66, stage, film, and TV actor, died of bone cancer Nov. 23 in Creston, Iowa. He made his Broadway debut in 1946 in *Brighten the Corner,* followed by plays including *Red Gloves, Mr. Barry's Etchings, The Male Animal, The Traitor, The Desperate Hours, Teachouse of the August Moon, A Mighty Man Is He, Calculated Risk, Weekend,* and *Tunnel of Love.* There are no immediate survivors.

Vera Allen

Fred Astaire

Paula Bauersmith

Olga Bellin

Michael Bennett

Gene Blakely

DeWITT BODEEN, 79, Fresno-born playwright, screenwriter and author, died March 12 of bronchial pneumonia in Woodland Hills, CA. His work include the plays *Escape to Autumn, Whistling for a Wind, Argosy at 40, Embers at Haworth, A Thing of Beauty, Fallen Angel, Morning Star,* adaptations *Bunner Sisters* and *Emma,* translations of *Camille* and *A Glass of Water,* and his best known screenplays for *Cat People, The Curse of the Cat People,* and *I Remember Mama.* He is survived by a sister and brother.

JOSEPH BOLAND, 83, stage, radio, and TV actor, died of natural causes June 21 in Newington, CT. He appeared on Broadway in *Third Best Sport, Philadelphia, Here I Come,* and *The Rope Dancers.* He is survived by his wife and two daughters.

DeVEREN BOOKWALTER, 47, Pennsylvania-born stage and screen actor and director, died of stomach cancer July 23, 1987 in Manhattan. He made his Broadway debut in 1967 in *The Promise,* and was Off-Broadway in *Philosophy in the Boudoir, Enemy of the People,* and *Sweet Prince.* He is survived by his wife, actress Ruth Kidder, a son, his parents and a sister.

AUSTIN BRIGGS-HALL, 73, actor and, with others, founder of the American Negro Theatre in the 1930's, died of heart failure Jan 13, 1988 in Kings County Hospital. He began his career with the Rose McLendon Players and was a member of Margaret Webster's Shakespeare Company, the first professional interracial Shakespearean touring company in the US. Survived by his wife and two sons.

HAROLD CHAPMAN, 37, England-born founder, first artistic director, and education director of the Young Playwrights Festival in New York City, died Sept. 23, 1987 in Manhattan of undisclosed causes. He was director of the Young People's Theatre and the annual Young Writers' Festival at the Royal Court Theartre in London, when he was invited by then Dramatists Guild President Stephen Sondheim to start the Young Playwrights Festival here, which won a Drama Critics Circle Award in 1963. He also directed plays at Circle Rep., and *Annie Wobbler* Off-Broadway. He is survived by his parents and a brother.

VIRGILIA CHEW, 82, Houston-born stage, screen and TV actress, died in Englewood, NJ July 23, 1987, after a long illness. She made her Broadway debut in *Ethan Frome,* followed by *The Women, Anniversary Waltz, Orpheus Descending, Blue Denim,* and *Cry of Players.* She is survived by her adopted son.

ROBERT CRAWLEY, 70, actor and later stage manager for Emlyn Williams, died of osteoporosis Oct. 19, 1987 in New York. He made his Broadway bow in 1942 in *The Great Big Doorstep,* followed by *The Moon Vine, Harvest of Years, Command Decision, Montserrat, Ondine, Fallen Angels,* and *Elizabeth the Queen.* He is survived by a sister and brother.

CAL CULVER (John Calvin Culver aka Casey Donovan), 43, Canandaigua, New York-born stage and film actor, died Aug. 10 in Inverness, Fla of a pulmonary infection resulting from a respiratory deficiency. He made his Broadway debut in 1972 in *Capt. Brassbound's Conversion,* followed by *Tubstrip, The Ritz* (revival), and *The Merchant of Venice,* Off-Broadway. His last screen appearances were in *Chance of a Lifetime* and *Inevitable Love.* He is survived by his parents and a brother.

VIOLA DANA, 90, Brooklyn-born star of the stage and silent screen, died July 3 of heart failure in Woodland Hills, CA. After early stage appearances as a child with her younger sister, future screen actress Shirley Mason, she starred on Broadway in the smash hit *Poor Little Rich Girl* in 1913, which led to her becoming one of the best known and highest-paid ingenues in silent films. After 15 years and more than 50 films, the coming of sound brought her retirement. Married to director John H. Collins, then screen cowboy Maurice (Lefty) Flynn, she left no immediate survivors.

ROGER DeKOVEN, 81, Chicago-born stage, TV and radio actor, died of cancer Jan. 28, 1988 in New York. He made his Broadway debut in 1926 in *Juarez and Maximilian,* followed by *Once in a Lifetime, Murder in the Cathedral* (Federal Theatre, 1936), *The Eternal Road,* Erwin Piscator's *King Lear* (first U.S. production, at the New School), *The Assassins, Joan of Lorraine, Abie's Irish Rose* (1954), *The Lark, The Hidden River, Compulsion, The Miracle Worker, The Fighting Cock, Tovarich, Arturo Ui, Funny Girl, Strider* and Off-Broadway in 1986 in *Roots.* He is survived by his wife, daughter and son.

DIVINE (Harris Glenn Milstead), 42, character actor of stage and screen, died March 7, 1988 of hypertrophic cardiomyopathy, in his room at the Regency Plaza Hotel in Los Angeles. Best known for his comedic female roles, he appeared Off-Broadway in *Women Behind Bars* and *Neon Women.* Survived by his parents.

JAMES DOBSON, 67, Tennessee-born stage, screen, and TV actor and director, died of a heart attack Dec. 6, 1987 in Hollywood. His Broadway appearances include *Life With Father, The Wind is 90, Firebrand of Florence,* and *Mr. Adam.* He is survived by a brother.

GWYDA DonHOWE, 53, stage, film, and TV actress, was murdered Jan. 15, 1988 by her husband, who then committed suicide, in New York City. She made her Broadway debut in 1957 in *Separate Tables,* followed by such shows as *The Shadow Box, Applause, The Flip Side, Paris is Out, Half a Sixpence, A Broadway Musical,* with APA-Phoenix Repertory Co. in *The Show Off, You Can't Take It With You, War and Peace, Right You Are if You Think You Are,* and Off-Broadway in *Philosophy in the Boudoir, Head Over Heels, How Far Is It To Babylon?, Rich Girls,* and she was the only American in the Czechoslovakian production of *Laterna Magika* at Carnegie Hall. She married Norman Kean in 1958 and is survived by their son, David.

KING DONOVAN, 69, Manhattan-born stage, screen and TV actor, died of cancer June 30 in Branford, CT. The son of vaudevillians, he first acted at the old Butler Davenport Theatre Off-Broadway, toured in rep with the Jitney Players and the Hendrickson Shakespeare Company before making his Broadway debut in 1948 in *The Vigil,* followed by such plays as *The Girls in 509* and *Morning's at Seven.* He is survived by his wife, actress Imogene Coca, two sons and a daughter.

WARDE DONOVAN (Warde Donovan Tatum), 72, stage, screen and TV actor, died April 16, 1988 in LA. He made his Broadway debut in 1946 in *Toplitski of Notre Dame,* followed by *Saratoga, Wonderful Town, Destry Rides Again,* and *By the Beautiful Sea.* Survived by his wife, actress-comedienne Phyllis Diller, and two sons.

ANDREW DUGGAN, 64, Indiana-born stage, film, and TV actor, died of throat cancer May 15, 1988 at his Los Angeles home. He appeared on Broadway in *Dream Girl, The Innocents, The Rose Tatto, Gently Does It, Anniversary Waltz, and Fragile Fox.* He is survived by his wife, a son and two daughters.

GLORIA EDWARDS, 43, stage, screen and TV actress, died of cancer Feb. 12, 1988 in Los Angeles. She appeared on Broadway in *What the Wine Sellers Buy* and *Ain't Supposed to Die a Natural Death,* and Off-Broadway in *Showdown, In New England Winter, One,* and *Black Girl* (recreating her role in the 1972 film). She is survived by her husband, son and daughter.

ROBERT ELSTON, 53, Manhattan-born stage, screen and TV actor, producer, playwright and teacher, died of AIDS-related pulmonary embolism Dec. 10, 1987 in Amsterdam, The Netherlands. He made his Broadway debut in 1958 in *Maybe Tuesday,* followed by *Spoon River Anthology, Tall Story, You Know I Can't Hear You When the Water's Running* and *Vivat!Vivat!Regina.* He formed American Renaissance Theatre in 1975, producing 35 plays, cowrote *Run, Children, Run* and *Murder at the Gaiety,* and penned *After Many a Summer, Portrait of a Man,* and *Notes,* which he co-produced with John Bacher. There are no immediate survivors.

PARKER W. FENNELLY, 96, playwright, character actor of stage, screen, TV and radio, best known as Titus Moody on radio's *Allen's Alley* in the 40's and 50's and then as the spokesman for Pepperidge Farm on radio and TV commercials until 1977, died Jan. 22, 1988 in Peekskill, NY after a brief illness. He made his Broadway debut in 1924 in *Mr. Pitt,* followed by such plays as *Our Town, The Southwest Corner,* and *Carousel* (1966), and his plays include *Fulton of Oak Falls* (coauthored with George M. Cohan) and *Cuckoos on the Hearth.* He is survived by his wife and two daughters.

ROBERT FITZSIMMONS, 73, actor and union leader, died Jan. 31, 1988 of cardiac and pulmonary arrest in New York City. He was on Broadway in *Abe Lincoln in Illinois, Legal Grounds, The Sselling of the President,* and *Time Remembered.* He was an AEA council member from 1975–87 and treasurer '80–82, recently named councilor emeritus and president of the board of Equity Library Theatre for eight years. No reported survivors.

BOB FOSSE, 60, Chicago-born actor, dancer, award-winning director-choreographer on stage, screen and TV, and a genius of the musical theatre, died of a heart attack Sept. 23, 1987 in Washington, DC, after a rehearsal for the revival of his *Sweet Charity.* He was the son of a vaudeville performer, and became a burlesque hoofer before he married Mary Ann Niles and they became a popular dance team. His Bdwy debut was in *Dance Me a Song,* where he met his second wife, dancer-actress Joan McCracken. After featured roles in films, he returned to Bdwy to choreograph *The Pajama Game* (Tony Award), *Damn Yankees* (Tony Award), *Bells Are Ringing* (collaborating with Jerome Robbins), *New Girl in Town,* played the title role in *Pal Joey* (CC), and directed and choreographed *Redhead* (Tony Award), *Sweet Charity, Pippin* (two Tony Awards), *Chicago, Dancin'* (Tony Award), *Big Deal,* and the revival of *Sweet Charity.* He holds the distinction of winning the "triple crown" in 1973: Two Tony Awards *(Pippin),* an Academy Award *(Cabaret),* and an Emmy *(Liza With a Z),* an unprecedented achievement. Surviving is his daughter actress-dancer Nicole Fosse, by his third wife Gwen Verdon, from whom he was divorced.

FLORIDA FRIEBUS, 79, stage and TV actress best remembered as Mrs. Gillis on TV's *The Many Loves of Dobie Gillis,* died May 27, 1988 in Laguna Niguel, CA. She appeared on Broadway in *Triple Crossed, The Ivory Door, The Lady From the Sea,* Civic Rep. Theatre Co. in *Pride and Prejudice, The Primrose Path,* Off-Broadway in *Church Street,* and *The Victors, Come Back, Little Sheba, Collector's Item, Tea and Sympathy,* and *Absence of A Cello.* There are no reported survivors.

PHIL FRIEDMAN, 66, veteran Broadway stage manager, died March 21, 1988 of an apparent heart attack in New York City. He was production manager for over 85 Broadway shows, including *Kismet, How to Succeed in Business Without Really Trying, Little Me, The Act, The Boy Friend,* and 11 shows associated with Bob Fosse, including *Pippin, Chicago, Dancin', Sweet Charity* (revival), and *Big Deal,* and he played the stage manager in Mr. Fosse's film *All That Jazz.* He received the first Del Hughes Award for Lifetime Achievement in Stage Management in 1985. Two sisters survive.

ADRIENNE GESSNER, 90, Austrian-born actress and a preeminent figure of the Viennese theatre, died June 23, 1987 in Vienna. She appeared on Broadway in such shows as *I Remember Mama, Another Sun, Claudia, Thank You, Svoboda,* and *I Remember Mama* before returning to Vienna Burgtheater, and also in the 1968 season of repertory at City Center.

JACKIE GLEASON, 71, Brooklyn-born actor known as "the great one" and forever immortalized by his portrayal of Ralph Kramden in *The Honeymooners* on TV, died June 24 of cancer of the colon and liver at his home in Fort Lauderdale, FL. He was on Broadway in *Hellzappoin'* (1938), *Keep Off the Grass, Artists & Models, Follow the Girls, Along Fifth Avenue,* and *Take Me Along,* for which he received the 1959 Tony Award. His survivors include his third wife and two daughters.

LEE GOODMAN, 64, stage, screen and TV actor and nightclub comedian, died Feb. 6, 1988 at his Manhattan home. He made his Broadway debut at age 8 in *Conversation Piece* and was also in *Dead End, A Funny Thing . . ., On the Twentieth Century, So Long 174th Street.* He is survived by a sister.

CHRISTOPHER GORE, 42, playwright, lyricists and screenwriter who was nominated for an Oscar for his *Fame* screenplay, died May 8, 1988 of cancer in Santa Monica, CA. For Broadway he wrote *Via Galactica* and *Nefertiti.* Survived by his mother and three brothers.

Gwyda
DonHowe

King
Donovan

Robert
Elston

Robert
Fitzsimmons

Bob
Fosse

Florida
Friebus

Jackie
Gleason

Lee
Goodman

Lorne
Greene

Ken
Harper

Elizabeth
Hartman

John
Huston

Norman
Kean

Harold J.
Kennedy

Madge
Kennedy

Edward
Kleban

June
Knight

Joseph E.
Levine

Frederick
Loewe

Clare Booth
Luce

Charles
Ludlam

Kevin
Marcum

Leona
Maricle

Steve
Mills

Mary Ann
Niles

Mairin
O'Sullivan

Geraldine
Page

Ray
Parker

Natalie
Priest

Lester
Rawlins

John **Reardon**	**Betty** **Rhodes**	**Kurt** **Richards**	**Hayden** **Rorke**	**George** **Rose**	**Dean** **Santoro**

LORNE GREENE, 72, Canadian-born actor of stage, screen and TV, remembered as patriarch Ben Cartwright on TV's *Bonanza*, died of adult respiratory distress syndrome Sept. 11 in Santa Monica, CA. He made his Broadway debut in 1953 in *The Prescott Proposals* starring Katharine Cornell, followed by *Speaking of Murder* and *Edwin Booth*. He is survived by his second wife, a son and two daughters.

LEE GUBER, 67, Philadelphia-born legit producer and co-owner of the Westbury and Valley Forge Music Fairs, died of a brain tumor March 27, 1988 in New York. His Broadway productions include *The King and I* (1977), *Lorelei, Catch Me, If You Can, Sherry, Inquest, The World of Sholom Aleichem, Rags,* and revivals of *Fiddler on the Roof, Mame, Hello, Dolly!,* and *Camelot*. He is survived by his wife, writer Lois Wyse, son Zev, general manager at Westbury, daughter Carol, marketing director at the theater, an adopted daughter (with former wife Barbara Walters), a stepson and stepdaughter.

DOROTHY HAMMERSTEIN (Dorothy Blanchard), 87, Australian-born former New York interior designer and widow of Oscar Hammerstein 2nd, died August 3, 1987 at her Manhattan home. She appeared on Broadway in *Charlot's Revue*, touring the US and Canada as Beatrice Lillie's understudy. She married Hammerstein in 1929 and the marriage lasted until his death in 1960. She is survived by a sister, two sons, a daughter and two stepchildren.

KEN HARPER, 48, Tony Award winning producer of *The Wiz*, died of respiratory failure after a long illness on Jan. 20, 1988 in his Manhattan apartment. He is survived by his adoptive parents.

ELIZABETH HARTMAN, 45, Ohio-born stage, screen and TV actress who received an Oscar nomination in 1966 for *A Patch of Blue*, leapt to her death from her fifth-floor apartment in Pittsburg on June 10, 1987. She made her Broadway debut in 1969 in *Our Town*, also appeared in *Everybody Out, The Castle Is Sinking*, and won the L.A. Critics Award for her role in the national company of *Morning's at Seven*. She is survived by her mother, sister and brother.

STARK HESSELTINE, 58, Massachusetts-born theatrical agent credited with the discovery of such stars as Robert Redford and Christopher Reeve, among others, died of AIDS-related illness Nov. 4, 1987 in New York City. He began as casting director for the Phoenix Theatre in the early 50's, co-produced *Phoenix 55*, was an agent with MCA, his own HBS Ltd, Vice president of CMA's legit department in 1969, and in 1975 he joined Robert Baker to form Hesseltine, Baker Associates Ltd., from which he retired in 1984. He also represented such stars as Elizabeth Ashley, Linda Lavin, Hume Cronyn and Jessica Tandy. There are no immediate survivors.

MARTHA HODGE (AMORY), 76, former legit actress, died May 27, 1987 in Pittsburgh. The daughter of actor-playwright-director William Hodge, her Broadway appearances include *Remember the Day, Small Miracle, On to Fortune,* and *Spring Dance*. A daughter survives.

FRITZ HOLT (George W. Holt 3rd), San Francisco-born legit producer and director, died July 14, 1987 of complications from pneumonia in Montclair, NJ. He was stage manager for the Broadway productions of *Indians*, and production stage manager for *Company* and *Follies*, before joining with partner Barry Brown to produce *Gypsy* (revival), *The Royal Family, Clams on the Half Shell,* and *Perfectly Frank*. He was executive producer of *La Cage aux Folles*, and directed the AFA salute to George Abbott's 100th birthday at the Palace theatre the month before he died. He is survived by his parents and a sister.

JOHN HUSTON, 81, Nevada,Mo-born actor, director, playwright, screenwriter, and screen legend, died in his sleep of complications from emphysema Aug. 28, 1987 in Middletown, R.I. The two time Oscar winner and 14 time nominee made his New York acting debut in 1924 in *The Triumph of the Egg*, followed by *Ruint*, with the Provincetown Players, directed *A Passenger to Bali* on Broadway (1940), and *No Exit* (1946), and wrote *In Time to Come*. His many honors include the 11th American Film Institutes's Life Achievment Award, and his autobiography "*An Open Book*" was published in 1980. Surviving are three natural children, Tony, Anjelica and Danny, and two adopted children, Pablo and Allegra.

NORMAN KEAN, 53, Colorado-born legit producer, died Jan. 15, 1988 after murdering his wife, actress Gwyda DonHowe, when he jumped to his death from the roof of their apartment building in Manhattan. He was general manager for *Oh! Calcutta!* Off-Broadway in 1969 and took over from Hillard Elkins as producer of the Broadway production in 1976. He also produced shows including *Max Morath at the Turn of the Century* (OB), *Sizwe Bansi is Dead* and *The Island, Boccaccio, Me and Bessie, By Strouse* (OB), and *A Broadway Musical*. He is survived by his mother and son.

HAROLD J. KENNEDY, 73, Massachusetts-born actor, director, producer and playwright, who had been in declining health for some time, died Jan. 10, 1988 in New York City. After an early career as an actor with the Mercury Theater, he wrote plays including *A Goose for the Gander* (Gloria Swanson's Broadway debut), and *Reprise*, and directed plays including *The Front Page* (1969 revival), and *Candida* Off-Broadway. He wrote a book of reminiscences entitled "*No Pickle, No Performance*." There are no reported survivors.

JOHN KENNEDY, 90, New York City-born director and producer, died May 13, 1988 in Vancouver, British Columbia, after a brief illness. His Broadway productions include *The First Million* (1943 debut), *Artists Models, Mexican Hayride, Up in Central Park, The Would-Be Gentleman, Sweethearts, Angel in the Wings,* and *The Ziegfeld Follies*, and his productions of musicals for the St. Louis Municipal Opera numbered in the hundreds. Survived by a daughter, a stepson and stepdaughter.

MADGE KENNEDY, 96, Chicago-born star of stage and silent screen who made a comeback as a film character actress, died of respiratory failure June 9, 1987 in Woodland Hills, CA. She made her Broadway debut in 1912 in *Little Miss Brown*, followed by *Twin Beds, Fair and Warmer, Poppy* (costarring with W. C. Fields in her most popular success), *Badges, Beware of Widows, Love in a Mist, The Springboard, Paris Bound, Vaudeville at the Palace, Private Lives* (succeeding Gertrude Lawrence), *Bridal Wise,* and *A Very Rich Woman* in 1965. Her second husband, actor William Hanley, died in 1959 and she leaves no survivors.

EDWARD KLEBAN, 48, New York City-born Tony Award-winning lyricist of *A Chorus Line*, and teacher with the BMI Musical Theatre Workshop died of cancer Dec. 28, 1987 in Manhattan. He also wrote *Gallery*, an unstaged 1981 Public Theatre production, and wrote two new songs, with composer-collaborator Marvin Hamlisch, for the film version of *A Chorus Line*. He is survived by his father and a sister.

JUNE KNIGHT, 74, Hollywood-born stage and screen dancer and actress, died June 16, 1987 of complications from a stroke in Los Angeles. Beginning her career as a child performer, she made her Broadway debut in 1929 in *Fifty Million Frenchmen*, followed by *Girl Crazy, The Nine O' Clock Revue, Hot Cha!, Take a Chance, Jubilee, The Overtons, The Would-Be Gentleman,* and *Sweethearts*. She retired in 1949 and is survived by her second husband, Jack Buhler.

RICHARD W. KRAKEUR, 87, theatrical producer, died March 23, 1988 in Los Angeles. In partnership with Horace Schmidlapp and Vinton Freedly, he produced such Broadway shows as *Affairs of State, Cabin in the Sky,* and *Strike Up the Band*. Survived by a daughter and two grandchildren.

JEAN Le POULAIN, 63, Marseilles-born, one of France's most respected actors and administrative director of the Comedie-Francaise, died of a heart attack March 1, 1988 at his home in Paris. After achieving great success in works by Offenbach, Brecht, Corneille, and as Shakespeare's Falstaff, he formed his own theatre company in 1952, directing and acting in over 100 plays, including several by Jean Cocteau, and becoming one of Paris's biggest stars in the 50's. He wrote his memoirs, entitled "*I Will Have the Last Laugh*." Survivors were not reported.

JOSEPH E. LEVINE, 81, New England-born entrepreneur of theatre and films who became the leading independent producer and showman of the 60's, died July 31, 1988 after a brief illness in Greenwich, CT. Nicknamed the "Boston Barnum." He is survived by his wife, a son, producer Richard Levine, and a daughter, Tricia.

JERRY LIVINGSTON, 78, Denver-born composer for stage, screen, and TV, and a three time Oscar nominee (for "Bibbidy Bobbidy Boo" from *Cinderalla*, and his scores for *Cat Ballou* and *The Hanging Tree*) died of a heart condition July 1, 1987 at his Beverly Hills home. He wrote Broadway revues including *Hollywood Revels* and *Bright Lights of '44*, and the musical *Molly*. A president of the Songwriters Guild of America, he was inducted into the National Academy of Popular Music's Songwriters Hall of Fame in 1981. He is survived by his wife and a son.

FREDERICK LOEWE, 86, Berlin-born composer who formed, with Alan Jay Lerner, one of the legendary partnerships of the musical theatre, died Feb. 14, 1988 of cardiac arrest in Palm Springs, CA. After an inauspicious debut in 1942 with *Life of the Party*, followed by *What's Up* (1942) and *Day Before Spring* (1945), the team achieved success with the landmark musicals *Brigadoon* (1947), *Paint Your Wagon* (1951), *My Fair Lady* (1956), *Camelot* (1960), and *Gigi* (stage adaptation of their film success, 1973). Their last collaboration was the 1974 film *Little Prince*. There are no survivors.

LENORE LONERGAN, 59, Ohio-born stage and film actress of the 30's and 40's, died of cancer Aug. 31, 1987 at her home in Stuart, FLA. She made her debut at age 6 in *Mother Lode*, followed by plays including *The Philadelphia Story, Junior Miss, Dear Ruth, Crime Marches On, Of Thee I Sing* and *Fields Beyond*. She is survived by her husband and son.

CLAIRE BOOTH LUCE, 84, New York City-born playwright, novelist, war correspondent, editor of Vanity Fair magazine, and diplomat who used her husband's wealth and power and her own brains and beauty to become one of the century's most influential women, died of cancer Oct. 9, 1987 at her Washington home. After an initial flop on Broadway with *Abide with Me* in 1935, she went on to great success with *The Women* (1936), *Kiss the Boys Goodbye*, and *Margin for Error*. She married Henry R. Luce, publisher of Time, Fortune and Life, in 1935, a marriage that lasted until his death in 1967, and is survived by two stepsons.

CHARLES LUDLAM, 44, Long Island-born actor, playwright, director, producer, and one of the most extrordinary avant-garde artists in the theatre, died of pneumonia resulting from AIDS May 28, 1987 in New York City. In 1967 he established The Ridiculous Theatrical Company Off-Broadway, where he was star, director, and producer of such plays as *Conquest of the Universe, When Queens Collide, Eunuchs of the Forbidden City, The Ventriloquist's Wife, The Enchanted Pig, Camille, Der Ring Gott Farblonjet, Le Bourgeois Avant-Garde, Reverse Psychology, Galas, How to Write a Play, Salammbo*, and his most popular works, *The Mystery of Irma Vep* and *The Artificial Jungle*. He appeared as *Hedda Gabler* in the American Theatre production in Pittsburgh, staged the American premiere of *The English Cat* for Sante Fe Opera, and made his screen debut in *The Big Easy*. He is survived by his mother and two brothers.

ROUBEN MAMOULIAN, 90, Russian-born innovative and distinctive director of Rodgers & Hammerstein's landmark musicals *Oklahoma!* and *Carousel*, Gershwin's *Porgy & Bess*, and more than a dozen films, died of natural causes Dec. 4, 1987 in Woodland Hills, CA. After being told he was "not the type to direct an American play" by the Theatre Guild in 1926, he went on to great success on Broadway with such as *Clarence, Enter Madame, He Who Gets Slapped, Porgy, Marco Millions, Congai, A Month in the Country* (which he also adapted), *These Modern Women, Wings Over Europe, R.U.R., Solid South, A Farewell to Arms, Sadie Thompson* (also coauthor), *St. Louis Woman, Leaf and Bough, Lost in the Stars, Arms and the Girl*, he wrote *The Devil's Hornpipe* with Maxwell Anderson, and also directed *Die Glucklich Hand (The Hand of Fate)* at the Met. He is survived by his wife.

KEVIN MARCUM, 31, Illinois-born stage actor, died of a cocaine overdose July 20, 1987 in his Upper West Side apartment in Manhattan. He made his Broadway debut in 1976 in *My Fair Lady*, followed by *I Remember Mama, Cats, Sunday in the Park with George*, and he was to have taken over the lead role of Jean Valjean in *Les Miserables* in October '87. His survivors were not reported.

LEONA MARICLE, 81, stage and screen actress, died of an apparent heart attack March 25, 1988 in her Manhattan apartment. She made her Broadway debut in 1927 in *The Trial of Mary Dugan*, followed by such shows as *The Sex Fable, The Music Man*, and *Never Too Late* (1962). There are no immediate survivors.

DELORES MARTIN, 72, Georgia-born stage actress and singer, best remembered for introducing the song "Necessity" in *Finian's Rainbow*, died July 17, 1987 in Manhattan. She also appeared on Broadway in *Shuffle Along, Kiss Me Kate, Raisin in the Sun*, and *Showboat*, among others. Survived by a sister and three brothers.

TIMOTHY S. MAYER, 44, playwright, director and lyricist who won a Tony Award nomination for the book for *My One and Only*, died April 9, 1988 of lung cancer in Linlithgo, NY. As associate director of the Boston Shakespeare Company under Peter Sellars, he directed the acclaimed 1984 revival of *Mother Courage*, then moved to the American National Theatre in Washington, and in 1986 he and Donna Cusimano established the Hudson Valley Theater in Hyde Park, NY. Survived by his father.

MAXIM MAZUMDAR, 36, Canadian-born actor, playwright, and director, died April 28, 1988 in Halifax, Novia Scotia after a brief illness. He wrote and starred in his one man show *Oscar Remembered*, Off-Broadway, 1981 and also wrote *Invitation to the Dance, Dance for Gods*, and *Gilgamesh*. He was artistic director of the Stephenville Festival in Newfoundland and directed extensively in Canada. He is survived by his wife and brother.

ELIZABETH MEARS (JAMESON), 88, former actress and casting director, died April 19, 1988 in Danbury, CT, having been in failing health for some months. Daughter of Broadway producer John Henry Mears, she made her Broadway debut in 1920 in *My Golden Girl*, followed by *Judy, Queen at Home*, and *Singapore*. There are no survivors.

STEVE MILLS, 92, Boston-born actor and vaudeville comedian, died March 9, 1988 at his Warwick, R.I. home. His Broadway appearances include *Whiz Bang Babies* (1924), *Miss Tabasco, Three Little Girls, No,No,Nannette!, Prince of Pilsen, 70 Girls 70*, and *This Was Burlesque*. He is survived by his wife, a daughter and four grandchildren.

MARY ANN NILES, 64, New York City-born actress, singer, dancer, comedienne and choreographer of stage, screen and TV frequently called "the queen of the Broadway gypsies," died of cancer Oct. 4, 1987 in her Manhattan apartment. She appeared in nightclubs as a dance team partner with then husband Bob Fosse, before making her Broadway debut in 1945 in *Girl from Nantucket*, followed by *Dance Me a Song, Call Me Mister, Make Mine Manhattan, La Plum de Ma Tante, Carnival, Flora the Red Menace, Sweet Charity, George M, No No Nannette, Irene, Ballroom*, Off-Broadway in *The Boys from Syracuse*, CC's *Wonderful Town* and *Carnival*. She often was dance captain and uncredited assistant choreographer on her later Broadway shows. A half-sister and half-brother survive.

PAUL OSBORN, 86, Indiana-born playwright and screenwriter whose 1939 play *Morning's at Seven* won the 1980 Tony Award for best revival, died May 13, 1988 in New York City. His other plays include *Hotbed* (1928), *The Vinegar Tree* (1930), *Oliver Oliver* (1934), *Tomorrow's Monday* (1936), *On Borrowed Time* (1938), *The Innocent Voyage* (1943), *A Bell for Adano* (1944), *Point of No Return* (1951), and *The World of Suzie Wong* (1958). He is survived by his wife and a daughter.

MAIRIN D. O'SULLIVAN, 68, Irish-born stage, radio and TV actress, died of unreported causes Oct. 27, 1987 in Dublin. She established herself as a character actreess with the Abbey Theater in the 40's, and subsequently won a 1986 Tony Award nomination for *Philadelphia, Here I Come*, also appearing on Broadway in *Lovers* and *Borstal Boy*. She is survived by two sons and a daughter.

GERALDINE PAGE, 62, Kirksville, Mo-born stage, screen and TV actress who first rose to prominence Off-Broadway in 1952 in *Summer and Smoke* and who won the 1985 Best Actress Oscar for *A Trip to Bountiful*, died of a heart attack, after being treated for kidney disease, June 13, 1987 at her Manhattan home. She made her Broadway bow in 1953 in *Midsummer* for which she received a Theatre World Award, followed by *The Immortalist, The Rainmaker, Innkeepers, Separate Tables, Sweet Bird of Youth, Strange Interlude, Three Sisters, P.S. I Love You, The Great Indoors, White Lies, Black Comedy, The Little Foxes, Angela, Absurd Person Singular, Clothes for a Summer Hotel, Agnes of God*, and she appeared Off-Broadway in *Seven Mirrors* (debut), *Yerma, Macbeth, Look Away, The Stranger, The Human Office, The Inheritors, Paradise Lost, Ghosts, Madwoman of Chaillot, Clarence, Vivat!Vivat, Regina!, A Lie of the Mind*, and *The Circle*. At the time of her death she was starring in the Broadway revival of *Blithe Spirit*. She won two Emmy awards, for *A Christmas Memory* and *The Thanksgiving Visitor*, seven Oscar nominations and was twice nominated for Tony Awards. Surviving is her husband, actor Rip Torn, a brother, two sons and a daughter.

RAY PARKER, age unreported, stage actor, died of cancer Oct. 19, 1987 in Harrison, NY. His Broadway appearances include *Children of the Wind, The World of Carl Sandburg, Sabrina Fair*, and *Star Wagon*. Survived by his wife.

KEVIN PATTERSON, 32, playwright and press representative for the New York Shakespeare Festival and many Broadway and Off-Broadway shows, died of complications from AIDS March, 18, 1988 at his New York home. His produced plays include *A Most Secret War, A Safe Harbor*, and *Fascination Cha-Cha*. Survived by his mother, a sister and brother.

MATHILDE PINCUS, 71, Philadelphia-born music preparation supervisor who worked on the orchestrations for over 150 Broadway shows, Off-Broadway, Films and TV, and received a special 1976 Tony Award in recognition of her work, died March 6, 1988 after a brief illness in Dania, FLA. There are no immediate survivors.

NATALIE PRIEST, 68, New York-born actress died of cancer July 7, 1987 in New York. Her New York appearances include *God Bless You Harold Fineberg, Yentl, The Respectful Prostitute, Venus Is*, and Off-Broadway in *Looking Forward*. She is survived by a son and daughter.

JOHN QUALEN, 87, Canada-born, veteran character actor of stage, screen and TV, died of heart failure Sept. 12, 1987 in Torrance, CA. He made his Broadway debut in 1929 in *Street Scene*, followed by *Counselor-At-Law*, acting in the screen versions of both plays, and subsequently made more than 120 films. He is survived by his wife and three daughters.

LESTER RAWLINS, 63, Pennsylvania-born stage and TV actor who won a 1978 Tony Award as Best Actor for *Da*, died of cardiac arrest March 22, 1988 at his Manhattan home. He won Obie Awards for *The Quare Fellow, Hedda Gabler*, and *Benito Cereno*, and also appeared in such plays as Orson Welles' 1956 *King Lear, Romeo and Juliet, Richard III, Othello, Macbeth*, several productions of *Hamlet, Endgame*, and *Nightride*. He is survived by his mother and two sisters.

JOHN REARDON, 58, New York City-born actor and singer, noted for his works at the New York City Opera, the Metropolitan Opera, and on TV's *Mister Rodgers' Neighbor* as "The Opera Maker Reardon," as well as on Broadway, died of pneumonia April 16, 1988 at his home in Santa Fe, NM. His career began on Broadway in 1954 in *The Saint of Blecker Street*, followed by *New Faces of 1916, Song of Norway, Do Re Mi*, and *New Moon in Concert*. He is survived by a sister.

T. MICHAEL REED, 42, Broadway dancer, dance supervisor of *Cats* and *A Chorus Line*, and an assistant to Michael Bennett on *Ballroom*, died of complications from AIDS Sept. 16, 1987 at his Manhattan home. His other Broadway appearances include *Seesaw* and *The Magic Show*. Survived by his mother, a sister and a brother.

BETTY RHODES, 52, Washington-born stage actress and singer best known for her appearances in the original 1968 production of *Jacques Brel is Alive and Well* . . . and the '81 and '83 revivals, died of cancer Dec. 30, 1987 in New York. She also appeared frequently in New York and around the country in cabarets and in concert at Carnagie Hall, and recently released her last album, *No Regrets*. She is survived by her daughter and five grandchildren.

KURT RICHARDS/JONATHAN KIDD, 73, character actor of stage, screen and TV, died after surgery for an aortal aneurism Dec. 15, 1987 in LA. Under his given name he appeared in 16 Broadway shows, including *Anastasia, Come Back, Little Sheba, King Lear, A Streetcar Named Desire*, and *Hamlet*, before performing on stage and screen in Hollywood as "Jonathan Kidd." There are no immediate survivors.

HAYDEN RORKE, 76, Brooklyn-born stage, screen and TV actor, died of cancer Aug. 19, 1987 in Toluca Lake, CA. The last surviving member of Walter Hampton's repertory company, best known to TV audiences as Dr. Bellows in 140 episodes of *I Dream of Jeannie*, his 70 appearances on Broadway include *Three Men On a Horse, The Country Wife, The Philadelphia Story, Personal Appearance, The Iceman Cometh, A Moon for the Misbegotten*, and *Dream Girl*, and he made more than 50 films and more than 400 TV shows. He is survived by his two brothers.

| James
Secrest | Tom
Spratley | Clinton
Sundberg | Lee
Theodore | Jeff
Veazey | Emlyn
Williams |

GEORGE ROSE, 68, English-born, veteran character actor of stage and screen, best remembered for his endearing Tony Award winning performances in *My Fair Lady* (1979) and *The Mystery of Edwin Drood* (1985), was brutally murdered on May 5, 1988 near his vacation home in the Dominican Republic. He made his Broadway bow with the Old Vic in 1946 in *Henry IV,* followed by *Much Ado About Nothing, A Man for All Seasons, Hamlet, Royal Hunt of the Sun, Walking Happy, Loot, My Fat Friend* (1974 Drama Desk Award, Tony nomination), *She Loves Me, Peter Pan,* BAM's *The Play's the Thing, The Devil's Disciple, Julius Caesar, The Kingfisher* (1970 Drama Desk Award), *Pirates of Penzance* (Tony nomination), *Dance a Little Closer, You Can't Take It with You, Beethoven's Tenth,* and *Aren't We All?* There were no survivors.

DEAN SANTORO, 49, Pennsylvania-born stage and TV actor, third national v.p. of SAG and AFTRA board member, died of undisclosed causes June 10, 1987 in Sherman Oaks, CA. His Broadway credits include *Hadrian VII* and *Borstal Boy,* and he appeared in more than 50 regional theatre productions. He is survived by his mother and several brothers and sisters.

TIMOTHY SCOTT (Timothy Scott Schnell), 32, who created the role of Mr. Mistoffolees in *Cats,* died of complications from AIDS Feb. 24, 1988 at his Los Angeles home. He also appeared on Broadway in *King of Hearts* and *Dancin',* and was featured in the film *A Chorus Line.* He is survived by his parents.

JAMES SECREST, 51, North Carolina-born stage, radio and TV actor, died of lymphoma of the brain Nov. 18, 1987 in New York. He appeared Off-Broadway in *The Trial of the Catonsville Nine, John Brown's Body,* and *The Private Ear.* Survived by his parents and sister.

WILLIAM SHUTTLEWORTH, 25, legit pressagent who represented Broadway and Off-Broadway shows died of AIDS June 1, 1988 in Glen Cove, NY. In 1987, at age 23, he became the youngest person admitted to the Assn. of Theatrical Press Agents and Managers. His parents survive.

GEORGE SKLAR, 79, playwright, screenwriter, and novelist, who helped to organize the Theater Union and was on the board of the Federal Theater Project, died of cardiac arrest May 15, 1988 in New York. His plays include *Merry-Go-Round* (with Albert Maltz), *Peace on Earth* (with Paul Peters), *Parade, Stevedore, Laura* (with Vera Caspary), *And People All Around,* and *Brown Pelican.* He is survived by a daughter, two sons, a brother and two grandchildren.

CHARLIE SMALLS, 43, Long Island City-born composer-lyricist who won two Tony Awards, a Drama Desk award and a Grammy for his score for *The Wiz,* died Sept. 4, 1987 of cardiac arrest during emergency surgery in Bruges, Belgium. He was also represented on Broadway in *Lena Horne: The Lady and Her Music.* Survived by his son.

THOMAS REAY SPRATLEY, 74, stage, screen and TV actor and singer, died June 10, 1987 after a short illness following heart surgery in Encino, CA. His Broadway credits include *South Pacific, How to Succeed in Business . . . ,* and *Plaza Suite.* He is survived by two sons and a brother.

MICHAEL STEWART, 63, Manhattan-born playwright and lyricist, and winner of Tony Awards for *Bye Bye Birdie* in 1961 and *Hello, Dolly* in 1964, died of pneumonia, following surgery for a perforated colon Sept. 20, 1987 in New York. He began writing for the theatre in 1951 with sketches and lyrics for *Razzle Dazzle,* followed by *The Shoestring Revue, The Littlest Revue,* and *Shoestring '57* Off-Broadway, before moving on to his greatest successes *Carnival* (1961 Drama Critics Circle Award), *George M, Mack and Mabel, I Love My Wife* (also lyrics), and from 1974 in collaboration with Mark Bramble, *The Grand Tour, Barnum* (lyrics), *Harrigan 'n Hart, Bring Back Birdie, Elizabeth and Essex* (OB), and *42nd Street.* He is survived by his mother, a brother and sister.

CLINTON SUNDBERG, 81, South Dakota-born character actor of stage and screen, died of heart failure Dec. 14, 1987 in Santa Monica, CA. His Broadway credits include *Michael and Mary, Boy Meets Girl, Room Service, Arsenic and Old Lace, The Rugged Path, The Diary of Anne Frank,* and he appeared in dozens of films. Survivors were not reported.

HOWARD M. TEICHMANN, 71, Chicago-born playwright, biographer and raconteur, died of amyotrophic lateral sclerosis July 7, 1987 in New York. His plays include *The Solid Gold Cadillac* (with George S. Kaufman), *The Girls in 509, A Rainy Day in Newark, Miss Lonelyhearts,* and the stage version of his biography *"Smart Alec: The Wit, World and Life of Alexander Woollcott."* He also penned biographies of George S. Kaufman, Alice Roosevelt Longworth and Henry Fonda. He is survived by his wife, a daughter and two grandchildren.

LEE THEODORE (Lee Becker), 54, Newark, New Jersey-born actress, dancer and choreographer, and founder of the American Dance Machine in 1962, died Sept. 3, 1987 in the Bronx, after a long illness. She was the original Anybodys in *West Side Story* (1957), also appeared in *Gentlemen Prefer Blondes, The King and I, Damn Yankees,* and *Tenderloin,* choreographed *Baker Street, The Apple Tree* (Tony nomination), and *Flora, the Red Menace,* and was chosen by Jerome Robbins to make her directorial debut with a 1968 revival of *West Side Story.* She is survived by her husband, Paris Theodore, and two sons.

ELEANOR TREIBER, 60, stage, screen and TV ballet dancer and choreographer died Feb. 4, 1988 in New York City. She appeared on Broadway in *The Boy Friend, Half a Sixpence, Mame, High Button Shoes, Kelly, Anyone Can Whistle, Tovarich,* and *The Music Man.* Her parents, son and brother survive.

SEYMOUR VALL, 62, Queens-born theatrical producer and playwright, and founder of the First Theater Investing Service, died of cancer Oct. 30, 1987 in Manhattan. He produced such Broadway shows as *A Funny Thing Happened on the Way to the Forum* and *Blood Red Roses,* wrote plays including *How to be a Jewish Mother* and *The Really Portable Hamlet Company,* and helped finance some 60 productions. He is survived by his wife, two sons and his sister.

GLADYS VAUGHAN (Gladys Eileen Regier), 64, Iowa-born stage director, and in 1961 the first woman to direct a New York Shakespeare Festival production, died Dec. 30, 1987 of a sudden illness in her Manhattan home. Plays she directed for NYSF include *Richard II* (1961), *Macbeth, King Lear* and *The Merchant of Venice* (codirected with Joseph Papp, 1962), *The Winter's Tale* ('63), *Othello* ('64), *Coriolanus* ('65), *Measure for Measure* and *Richard III* ('66). Survived by her brother.

JEFF VEAZEY, 33, New Orleans-born dancer and choreographer, died of AIDS April 3, 1988 at his Manhattan home. He made his Broadway bow in 1975 in *Dr. Jazz,* followed by *The Grand Tour, Sugar Babies, Sophisticated Ladies,* was Off-Broadway in *Speakeasy, Trading Places, Nightclub Confidential,* and *Funny Girl,* and he choreographed shows including *Vampire Lesbians of Sodom, Psycho Beach Party,* and the *Broadway Tonight* revues. He is survived by his mother, three brothers and a sister.

HUGH WHEELER, 75, British-born playwright, librettist, screenwriter and novelist, who won three Tony Awards, for his books for *A Little Night Music* (1972), *Candide* (1973) and *Sweeney Todd* (1978), died of lung and heart failure July 27, 1987 in Pittsfield, Mass. His other plays include *Big Fish Little Fish, Look: We've Come Through, We Have Always Lived in the Castle,* and the libretto for the musicals *Softly, Irene, Pacific Overtures,* Mozart's *Impresario, Bodo, Truckloads, Silverlake,* and he was writing a stage adaptation of *Meet Me in St. Louis* at the time of his death. He left no immediate survivors.

EMLYN WILLIAMS, 81, Welsh-born playwright, actor and director, best known for his 1938 autobiographical play *The Corn is Green,* died Sept. 25, 1987 following recent cancer surgery in London. He made his Broadway debut in 1927 in *And So To Bed,* and also acted in *The Deputy, A Man for All Seasons, The Winslow Boy, Daughter of Silence, Criminal at Large, The Case of the Frightened Lady,* and his own plays *Night Must Fall, He Was Born Gay,* and his one-man shows *Emlyn Williams; Charles Dickens* and *Emlyn Williams: Dylan Thomas.* His other 20 plays include *Port Said, A Murder Has Been Arranged, The Light of Heart,* and *Beyond Belief.* He wrote two volumes of autobiography, *"George"* and *"Emlyn,"* and the novel *"Headlong."* His 1935 marriage to Irish actress Molly O'Shann lasted until her death in 1970. They had two sons.

234

236

238

243

244

253